P9-COP-939

By Myself

and Then Some

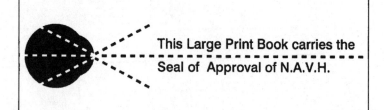

This Large Print Book carries the
Seal of Approval of N.A.V.H.

Lauren Bacall

By Myself

and Then Some

Thorndike Press • Waterville, Maine

Published in 2005 by arrangement with William Morrow, an imprint of HarperCollins Publishers Inc.

Thorndike Press® Large Print Biography.

The tree indicium is a trademark of Thorndike Press.

The text of this Large Print edition is unabridged. Other aspects of the book may vary from the original edition.

Set in 16 pt. Plantin by Elena Picard.

Printed in the United States on permanent paper.

Library of Congress Cataloging-in-Publication Data

Bacall, Lauren, 1924–
    By myself and then some / by Lauren Bacall.
        p. cm. — (Thorndike Press large print biography)
    ISBN 0-7862-7556-1 (lg. print : hc : alk. paper)
    1. Bacall, Lauren, 1924– 2. Motion picture actors and actresses — United States — Biography. 3. Large type books. I. Bacall, Lauren, 1924– Lauren Bacall by myself. II. Title. III. Thorndike Press large print biography series.
PN2287.B115A35 2005a
    791.4302'8'092—dc22   2005002430

By Myself

For my children Stephen, Leslie, Sam

and in memory of my mother

All I had known of films was Bette Davis and Leslie Howard. (I was in love with him — alas, was never to meet him.) She was my fifteen-year-old idea of perfection — fine actress, dramatic bravery, doomed tragedy, sardonic wit — all an actress should be, and when I cut school I would sit all day in a movie house sobbing through *Dark Victory* or *Jezebel* or *The Old Maid*, smoking in the balcony (I paid for a whole package, so I had to finish it). Forbidden at home, of course — getting sick on tobacco, and Sen-Sen to get the stench out of my mouth so as to go undetected by Mother and Uncle Charlie. One morning my uncle came in to kiss me goodbye before leaving for work and said, 'Have you been smoking?' Shaking, I replied, 'Of course not.' Whereupon he went into the next room to tell my mother he was certain I *was* smoking — whereupon they both faced me, trembling in my bed. 'We know you have been, we can smell it on your breath.' What had happened to Sen-Sen? — it had failed me for the first time. In a flood of tears I confessed — I had, but I would never do it again! 'Please forgive me — I promise.' Mother: 'You'd better not, a girl your age — disgusting — what kind of a girl do you want to become — nice girls of fifteen don't smoke!' Oh God — would I survive this humiliation!

Tail between the legs for days afterward — Charlie and Mother sniffing daily, trying to detect the evil weed. My first confrontation with the Sam Spade syndrome. Wouldn't I ever grow up — be on my own, free to do what I wished? Wouldn't I ever live alone? The purity of Jewish upbringing — the restrictions that one carries through life being a 'nice Jewish girl' — what a burden. But if you were — and I was — you had it drummed into your head from childhood by your mother, grandmother, uncles, that nice Jewish girls didn't smoke — weren't fast — nice Jewish girls had character. 'Don't chase a boy, ever — if he wants to see you, he'll call; if not, forget him.' But what were you to do if your head was filled with dreams of beauty, glamour, romance, accomplishment, and if you were stuck with being tall, ungainly (I didn't know I was 'colt-like' until a critic said I was), with big feet, flat chested — too young to have finished high school at fifteen, too inexperienced, shy, frightened to know what to do with a boy when I did have a date? If my dream would only come true, then I would know how to behave,

8

then things would fall into place — wouldn't they?

I wouldn't always be a wallflower. Already there was one boy who had a fantastic crush on me. I went out with him because there was no one else, and I tried to make him part of my romantic dream. He'd kiss me goodnight. He was sweet to me, he was boring, but he did call — I'd better be nice to him. It was soon Christmas, then New Year's, and I didn't want to be alone New Year's Eve — not when my friends had dates — so I went to a party with him on New Year's Eve — just sixteen, sweet sixteen — and we danced to 'Deep Purple' while I pretended he was Leslie Howard. Pretending started early. What a fantasy world — so much better than the real one. We sat on a sofa in the darkened room, he had his arm around me — he kissed me, I guess — all the kids were doing the same thing — 'Happy New Year!' Why wasn't he Leslie Howard just for that moment I looked at him? It wasn't good enough, I thought, to have someone crazy about you if you felt nothing. No — it would not do. I couldn't stand him, couldn't bear to let him touch me. I should have known right then that it would always be the same — I had to be madly in love or utterly revolted. No happy mediums for me! So I started that year —

1941 — deciding not to see him again. I always made out a list of New Year's resolutions and that was one of them. I didn't keep the others, but I did keep that one. No compromises in life for me — I wouldn't settle — I'd rather not go out, just live with my dreams.

Each time I was in love — this was it. The hunger to belong. Imagination is the highest kite that can fly. When you have nothing but dreams, that's all you think about, all that matters, all that takes you away from humdrummery — the fact that your mother was working too hard and didn't have enough in her own life, that your grandmother, loving though she was, wanted you to get a decent job to help your mother, that you didn't have enough money to do anything you wanted to do, even buy a lousy coat for $17.95. Dreams were better — that was where my hope lay — I'd hang on to them, never let go. They were my own.

It wasn't that I was deprived — we just had to live on a strict budget. No, it was that everything I fantasized about had nothing to do with everything I lived. Not a thing! Yet Mother gave me everything — everything she could — more. She was a decent, proud, honorable woman who despite her struggles never lost her sense of humor. She just wanted me to be perfect.

She wanted me to have it all, but to know and to learn while the search was on; to realize that there were other things not to lose sight of. She wasn't proud of having to count the pennies — not resentful — just very private about that and everything else to do with family. Some things are never told to anyone — one protects the family, all skeletons are left in the closet. She had the strongest family feeling of any of her brothers or sisters. She wanted everyone together. She felt that the family finally would never let each other down — outsiders might. She could accept the live-and-let-live theory from any and all but relations.

She was not demonstrative, but I never doubted her love and her total dedication to me. We had happy times — my grandmother cooking, singing me German songs, reading constantly in French, German, Rumanian, Russian, and English. She and Mother spoke Rumanian or German when they didn't want me to understand. Not too often, but family problems were to be kept from me. Nothing came easy — everything was worked for — but with it all there was laughter. Charlie and Mother led the field in that area. Charlie was rhyme-happy. At any important or semi-important occasion he would write a pertinent rhyme. Everyone in the family had humor. Everyone was educated, they all had professions: two lawyers, one executive secretary, one businessman, one housewife (self-employed). My father was Polish with I think some French. But what I learned, I learned from my mother's side.

Mother left Rumania by ship — aged somewhere between one and two — with her mother, father, older sister, baby brother. Her father had been in the wheat business, had been wiped out, and had turned over whatever silver and jewelry there was left to a sister for money enough to transport his family to the promised land — the new young world, America. They arrived on Ellis Island and gave their name — Weinstein-Bacal (meaning wineglass in German and Russian). The man must have written down just the first half of the name — too many people from too many countries, too many foreign names — so it was Max and Sophie Weinstein, daughters Renee and Natalie, son Albert. Grandfather Max borrowed enough money from United Hebrew Charities to go to a place in downtown New York, live in a ghastly apartment, set up a pushcart with all sorts of household goods for sale. 'Never tell anyone about that, Betty.' One family fact that Mother always hated — the pushcart. A whispered word. (I found it wonderful — dramatic.) Not like the wheat business. He wanted something better for his family — there were cousins who lived in a place called the Bronx that would be better. The family moved there, bought a candy store, found a small apartment. Grandpa Max did the best he could. Two more children — Charlie and Jack — were born in America. Grandma worked in the candy store, Renee, the eldest, helped after school; Natalie — my mother — was still too young. Grandpa had suffered with a goiter for years and was given much medication for it — heart-weakening medication. One afternoon he went to a movie, came home, lay down for a while, and died. He was fifty-five.

With the small insurance left by him, Grandma made improvements in the candy store and moved to a better apartment. Strong woman. All the children went to work at early ages, with Charlie and Jack going to night school at City College to get their law degrees. My mother worked as a secretary. She met my father, William Perske, who fell madly in love with her and showered her with attention. She was in her early twenties — nice girls were married by then, said Grandma. So, out of a combination of fear of not doing the right thing and fear of him, she consented. He was in medical supplies. After a while she became pregnant. As the nine months came to a close, Mother went to a movie one hot September evening, started to feel the anxious creature within her make her first moves to push her way out, left the movie house, and at about two o'clock in the morning at the Grand Concourse Sanitarium I was born.

From the start, Mother knew the marriage was a mistake — they didn't get along, her heart never leapt with excitement at the thought, sight, or touch of him. In truth, she didn't really like him, she was afraid of him, he was insanely jealous, so no more children — she'd do the best she could with what she had. She always did the best she could. She was determined that she would give her daughter all she had never had in the way of opportunity. Her brothers always backed her, helped her. She had strength of character. She would make it somehow — if only to make certain her daughter did. So she sacrificed her personal life. But I was not to be deprived. And I wasn't.

Since she worked, she used to send me to a warm, jolly cousin of Renee's husband Bill who had a home in Chichester, New York. There was a swimming hole — she had two daughters there my age — and it got me into the country air. One summer day when I was six years old my mother came to visit. I shall never forget her kneeling beside me with her arms around me, tears rolling down her face, as she told me that she had left my father. There would be a divorce — I would live with her, but of course I would see him regularly. The tears were for me — never for herself. It is one of the few clear pictures I have of my early childhood.

She never tried to turn me against my father. She was too busy going about the business of making a living, paying the rent, feeding and clothing me. But she never thought or behaved like a martyr — not her scene at all. She took me to visit my cousins in Brooklyn, my cousins in Connecticut. I spent a lot of time with Jack's beautiful Russian wife, Vera, and their babies. The family must remain close, stay together. 'Your family never lets you down — remember that. When all else is lost, you can always depend on the family.'

She lost track of my father — he stopped his Sunday visits when I was eight. Of course I loved him — I guess I loved him, I was a little girl. I looked forward to those visits. He was my father. He gave me a watch once — not a very good watch. I wore it for a while, then gave it to Mother for safekeeping. The next time I saw him, he asked me where the watch was. 'I gave it to Mother to keep for me.' 'Get it,' he said. I did — he took it — end of watch.

When they were divorced, my mother decided to take the second half of her name for her use and mine. Her brother Jack had done the same. So when I was eight, she became Natalie Bacal and I was Betty Bacal.

Mother had her own dreams. She had several beaux — I can remember her getting dressed up for an evening out. But that was not the heart of her life. She had women friends — they'd play bridge once a week — close friends, bright women, all hard workers, and at least two of them with unfulfilled lives. They had mothers to support — there were no men in their lives, they never expected there would be. Mother did — only she would never settle. No compromise in love a second time. He would be her knight in shining armor or there would be no one. But she didn't talk about it — she felt it.

She always taught me character. That was the most important thing in life. There was right and wrong. You did not lie — you did not steal — you did not cheat. You worked for a living and you worked hard. Accomplishment. Being the best you could be was something to be proud of. You learned the value of a dollar — money was not to be squandered, it was too hard to come by, and you never knew when you might need it. Save for a rainy day (a lesson still unlearned). She had great humor — it was always possible for her to see the funny side. I guess that's how she got through the tough times.

She had curiosity and enthusiasm for anything new. And she stood behind me all the way. If I wanted to be a dancer, an actress — that was what I would be if there was anything she could do about it. She would help me, encourage me, while the rest of the family thought she was mad. Who had ever heard of an actress in the family? Grandma was horrified at the thought — a nice Jewish girl, why didn't I make an honest living doing something she could understand? Why was my mother doing without to send me to dancing schools, dramatic schools? No good would come of it.

Mother would have none of it. I was her daughter. I was special. I had talent. Her eyes shone when she looked at me. She always made me feel that I could do anything once I made up my mind. She started me in dancing school when I was three. Yet she was not pushy — anything but a stage mother. How could she be a stage mother? — she wouldn't have known where to begin. She did take me to John Robert Powers' modeling agency when I was twelve to see if he could use me. I was so beautiful in her eyes, how could he refuse? She took me to a photographer he recommended to have pictures taken to send out to various agencies. She didn't see that I was tall for my age, underdeveloped for my age, and had feet much too big for the rest of me. Through her belief in me and her abounding love for me, she convinced me that I could conquer the world — any part of it or all of it. Whatever I wanted.

In the worst of times I never heard her complain. Whatever resentment she might have felt — whatever sadness for what she didn't have — she kept it all inside. She was basically a shy woman. But she was a realist — she accepted her own fate in life while I was growing up. But nothing on earth could make her accept that fate for me. She put the bit in my teeth and I ran with it. There was many a clash. I was selfish — spoiled by her — I wanted what I wanted. And when she thought I was wrong — boy, did she tell me! There were no doubts. 'You've gone too far, my girl. Pull up. Remember who you are — what you owe yourself.' I respected her and I loved her. If she but held my hand, I felt safe.

My childhood is a confusion. I spent the

first five years living in Brooklyn on Ocean Parkway. My baby record reveals nothing except that my mother was too busy caring for me to keep it in any detail. I was exceptional to no one but her.

I recall having recurring nightmares at one period in early childhood when I would awake in tears in the middle of the night: having heard footsteps down the hall, I would open my eyes and see a white towel flailing in the air. It all stemmed from arguments between my parents. I remember my father punishing me once with a strap on my rear — hitting my mother — he was a man who invented jealousies. I remember being threatened with a cat-o'-nine-tails, but do not recall his using it. In all fairness, how does a child of three or four or five know what goes on between a man and a woman? I make no judgments. But I also have no recollections of any great display of affection for me, not much in the hugging-and-kissing department, no memories of cozy reading of bedtime stories. I don't say it never happened — I only say it's not remembered. When Mother came to tell me she was leaving my father, I don't remember reacting in any way at all. I can only assume that my attachment was always to her, not to him.

Mother and I moved to Manhattan after the divorce, and I recall little of any special home between the ages of six and ten. My last recollection of my father was when he came to collect me one Sunday. He took me to his parents, who are shadows in my mind. I recall coming home at the end of the day with him — and watching him as his car took him out of my life forever. My Uncle Jack tried to find my father so that he might contribute to my support, but was totally unsuccessful. He had flown the coop. Rejection Number One!

Mother started to work and hired a maid to come in so I wouldn't be alone when I returned from school. The girl she hired turned out to be slightly mad — she locked me in a closet one afternoon. That experience convinced Mother that the solution was for me to go to boarding school. There I would be safe from crazy maids — I'd be with girls my own age, not too far from home. Ideal. But it was expensive. Uncle Jack offered to lend her the money. So it was decided I would attend the Highland Manor school for girls in Tarrytown, New York. It was an hour or so by train from New York. The campus was beautiful — we lived in houses — I shared a room with a girl named Gloria who became my best friend. She too studied dancing. Each year a show was put on where all who could performed. We each danced, had our moment.

Mother used to visit every Sunday, take me out to lunch to a pretty local restaurant where I would unfailingly have my favorite ice-cream sundae: chocolate ice cream with chocolate syrup, marshmallow sauce, and chocolate sprinkles. I couldn't wait for those visits. After all, I was only eight years old — pretty young for boarding school. There were all ages, all types, and I was always interested in what the older girls were doing. They had boyfriends, while all I did was go to classes, dream of being a dancer and actress, and miss my mother. For some reason I skipped a grade — had a good scholastic year somewhere in the middle and was able to graduate from grade school at the age of eleven.

Highland Manor also had a summer camp. Named Highland Nature, it was situated on Lake Sebago near Portland, Maine. We went there by overnight train. How I loved lying in my berth, watching the lights flicker in all the small towns as we passed en route. It seemed so romantic and adventurous. There has always been mystery to me about trains moving through towns and villages — through the night. What happens behind those lighted windows — what kind of lives are being lived?

I loved sports — played volleyball, basketball, baseball, and I loved to swim. There was a rule that in order to swim from the dock out to the raft one had to pass a test. I can see the test morning now. A group of small girls waiting their turns. I didn't know how I was going to do it, but after two years of swimming near the dock I was ready to move on. The girl before me was taking her test. She had a lovely stroke and there was no question that she would pass. I watched her very carefully to see when she breathed — how she turned her head — kicked her feet. I was next. I went down the ladder and proceeded to do exactly what she had done. Miraculously, it worked — I had won and it was the raft from then on. One step away from childhood. And there were weekly dramatic programs — sometimes plays, sometimes musical recitals, dances. I clearly remember doing a scarf dance my last year at Highland Nature. I felt as though I were really performing — I was so grown-up. Had the stage all to myself. I really felt good — the music was romantic, and I loved to dance. And I was in plays — in one I pulled my long hair back in a bun to look like Ann Harding. There were campfires — roasting marshmallows — overnight canoe trips — sleeping under the stars — skinny-dips before breakfast in the cold, clean lake. I suppose those years were as close to carefree as I had known or ever would again.

It was decided after my graduation from

Highland Manor that I would go to high school in New York. Mother and I would live with my grandmother and Uncle Charlie and share the rent. I would go to Julia Richman High School on 67th Street and Second Avenue. They found an apartment on 84th Street and West End Avenue. My uncle had a room, Mother and Grandma shared one, and next to them, separated by glass doors, was a tiny room for me. All to myself, the first time I would have a room to myself. Mother bought me a canary and I named him Petie. He was my first pet. I would talk to him — he would tweet to me. I'd close the windows and let him fly around the room. It was hell catching him, but I felt he was entitled to some freedom. One ghastly day when I suppose I thought he was well trained enough, and attached to me enough, I must have been a bit careless about a window, because he got out. He flew away — I never saw him again. I cried so. Mother tried replacing him with another canary, but it was never the same.

I remember those years of living with my grandmother. She was a marvelous cook. I was her pet grandchild and she made the most delicious cookies I've ever tasted and stuffed cabbage and kreplach (pieces of dough, pinched at the corners, stuffed with cheese). I've never tasted those dishes anywhere in the world to match hers. When I was little she would bounce me on her leg, hobby-horse style, and sing an old German nursery rhyme:

Bettelein ging allein	Little Betty went alone
In die weite Welt hinein	Into the wide world
Stock und Hut	Walking stick and hat
Steht ihr gut	Suits her well
Ist ganz wohl gemut	She's well satisfied (well off)
Aber Mutter weinet sehr	But Mother cries a lot
Hat ja nun kein Betty mehr	She has no Betty anymore
Wünsch' ihr Glück	Wish her luck
Sagt ihr Blick	Say her eyes
Kehr nur bald zurück	Come back soon

Grandmother sang those words exactly as written above, except that sometimes she seemed to be singing, 'But Betty cries a lot — she has no mother anymore.' Was it real or did I imagine the change in those two lines?

I remember watching her sit in a chair reading book after book, each in a different language. Her telling me how I must always help my mother — how hard my mother worked. Grandma was quite religious. A candle was lit every Friday night for my grandfather. She would comb her long hair, wind it round into a bun (never looking in a mirror), put on her coat and hat, and go to Temple. Dishes were changed for the proper holidays. She had a fierce temper — not lost too often, but when it was, she was wild. All those years of frustration, hard work, and worry had to come out some way. And we lived so closely with no room for privacy. The day that King Edward renounced his throne for Wallis Simpson I rushed home. There was Grandma sitting in front of an ancient Atwater Kent radio. I sat next to her — the King started to speak — through it all, this young girl and old woman sat and sobbed as so many throughout the world did. It was the most romantic story ever told, wasn't it? To renounce a throne for love! I couldn't get over it — it filled my head and heart for weeks.

And then there was my Uncle Charlie, the man who surely had the most influence in my life through my growing-up years. He was Assistant Corporation Counsel for the city of New York under Mayor La Guardia — an attractive man, fair, blue twinkling eyes, medium height, highly intelligent, and very funny. Funny — witty and funny — silly. He always made me laugh. He told me I must read *The New*

York Times every day, that as I was in high school now, I should learn what was going on in the world. How could I tell him that I only cared about my own world — the me that was going to be? I had so little room for other thoughts. Franklin Delano Roosevelt was my god — my father, my grandfather, my true hero. I grew up with him. One election year Roosevelt appeared in Madison Square Garden — it must have been 1940 — and Charlie got tickets. We were very far from the stage, but I was in the same building with Roosevelt, he was there and I was there! He walked with a cane and the aid of one of his sons, but he was there for me to see and hear, and I would never forget it, the emotion of that experience. Charlie gave me that too.

Charlie was seeing a girl named Rosalie. She was Italian, Catholic, and my grandmother couldn't bear it. Clearly they were very much in love — but they couldn't get married: she was not Jewish. It *couldn't* happen, it had never happened in our family before. There is prejudice of all kinds, everywhere. Rosalie's mother was not crazy about the match either. But they were sure — they had to get married. Charlie had lived with his mother, sister, and niece long enough, he was entitled to his own life. Theirs was the first wedding I attended. She was beautiful, brilliant, and I adored her. I was given a prize seat at the civil ceremony. My grandmother sat on one side of the aisle, Rosalie's mother on the other — neither of them looking to one side or the other — and Charlie and Rosalie were wed. Love conquered all. After the honeymoon Rosalie moved in with us until they found a place. We would have to move as well. Mother couldn't afford an apartment like that. Anyway, the neighborhood was not that safe.

We had moved to 84th Street because the apartment we'd lived in before was not that safe either. Not for little girls. I used to climb fences with boys — tomboyish. Also, the superintendent was very friendly. One afternoon he invited me down to the basement. How exciting, I thought, I'd never been there before. He smoked a cigarette — sat me on his lap — asked me if I wanted to try a puff of the cigarette. Adventure — of course I did. I thought nothing of sitting on his lap — but he put his arm around me and when a hand landed on my leg I was frightened. I couldn't have been more than eight, but I knew that wasn't right. I finally got out of there and told my mother and Charlie. Their fury cannot be imagined. That precipitated the first move. As I always traveled to high school by bus and subway, I was subjected to the same experiences everyone is who travels that way — men exposing themselves behind newspapers, asking if you didn't want an ice-cream cone. The usual. I was well trained on that score, but always terrified. When I took the subway home, I had to walk from Broadway to West End Avenue. When it was dark, you really had to watch out. There were men popping from basement doors, coming out of alleys. One night as I was walking that endless block a man started following me in a car — he crept along next to me, calling softly and suggestively out of his window. I never thought I'd get through my apartment-house door safely. A few experiences like that and there was no question we'd have to move. Mother was worried to death.

She found an apartment on 86th Street, just under the Sixth Avenue El. It was small — one living room, two small bedrooms (one for Mother and me, one for Grandma), a kitchen. But it was friendly, although the noise from the El was indescribable. My mother had a great gift for making the drabbest place cheery. There was no fancy furniture ever, but she would throw pillows on a sofa, put decorative ashtrays and cigarette boxes on the tables, personal photographs, anything she could add that cost little — anything to make things less dreary. I spent my last two years of high school in that apartment.

I had two very close friends in high school. One was Sylvia Berne, whose Russian grandmother served hot tea in a glass, Russian style, every time I was there. Sylvia and I spent all our spare time together, like sisters. Once we went shopping together — to Macy's. Mother said I could buy one skirt and one sweater if the price was right. I felt very grown-up. Sylvia and I took the subway, talking all the way as sophisticatedly as we could. We wanted to be sure that when we got to Macy's we would sound like experienced women of the world. Not easy to do when you're fourteen. However, all went well — into the shopping crush we charged and found just what we wanted. As we wished to be sisters, and pretended that we were, we would dress alike. We bought the same pleated skirt — hers in plum, mine in olive green — and the same Shetland crewnecked sweater — hers in pale blue, mine in yellow. Those outfits were a smashing success, worn until they could be worn no more, and mostly at the same time, so that we almost believed our own invention.

Then there was Betty Kalb, who had a big family including two older brothers. They had more money than we did — their apartment was bigger, her clothes were better — but we shared the same dream: to become actresses. She wanted to be in films, I wanted to be on the stage. We were both mad about Bette Davis — we'd see her films, imitate her, play scenes word for word, look for look, step for step.

I didn't ever have a true boyfriend. There wasn't much opportunity to meet boys going to a school of five thousand girls, then home to do homework. If I met anyone ever, it was always through a friend. There were one or two blind dates — they never ended well. I never seemed to know what to say, nor did the young men. In addition, I was younger than my friends by two years or more — too young for the boys.

I spent my last year in school filled with restlessness and frustration. If the sun was shining, I wanted to be outside. If it rained, I wanted to be watching a Bette Davis film. I was a good student — not *summa cum laude,* mind you, but able to get through well without too much effort. What mattered was that Saturday mornings I took classes at the New York School of the Theatre. Mother agreed that I could go and that was what I got through the week for. There I had my first taste of improvisation, of memorizing scenes, playing parts of all ages. Oh, it was fun — but it was so short, only a few hours each week.

And I was continuing my dancing lessons. My last year at school I studied ballet with a great old Russian dancer, Mikhail Mordkin, who had been Pavlova's partner on many of her tours. We would all get into our leotards and stand at the barre in our toe shoes opposite a mirror, and he would conduct class. He was somewhat eccentric. During class one day when we were doing our steps he picked up a wooden chair with a loose leg, pulled out the leg, sat down in the three-legged chair, and proceeded to play an invisible violin, using the leg as the bow, humming — completely overwhelmed by his music. Yet he was very strict. I used to stuff as much lamb's wool in my toe shoes as would fit — my toes were so long that every time I was on point I found myself standing on the first joint of my second toe instead of the ends of all five. It was agony. And I could never spot-turn, with the result that I was always dizzy at the end of a series of pirouettes. It sounds like a disaster — and must have looked like one! One day toward the end of the year's study Mother came to pick me up at class, and to see what Mr Mordkin felt about my ability. He told her, 'Mrs Bacal, Betty's feet always hurt — they are built wrong for ballet. She will never be exceptional. Forget it.' I had known for some time that I was put together wrong for ballet, but it's terrible to hear someone say it out loud. So that was that. I *couldn't* do everything — that dream was not to be dreamed again. Henceforth I would have to content myself with almost nightly dreams of dancing in marble palaces with Fred Astaire. I was always in flowing chiffon, there were great pillared halls, and Fred Astaire was doing the most intricate, romantic dance with me, throwing me in the air — a never ending whirl to the best Gershwin music ever written.

I continued venting my energy on acting. At the end of the year, students of the New York School of the Theatre performed for parents. I had learned the potion scene from *Romeo and Juliet*. For weeks I studied it — during class, in school, on the street (why I wasn't hit by a truck I'll never know), at home. The day came and my moment with it. And the shaking started. I got through it, with Mother, Grandma, Charlie and Rosalie, Vera and Jack in attendance. It must have been awful — but what mattered was that I had done it, and that meant I would continue. No stopping me now.

My restlessness with regular school was due to the fact that I wanted to get on with real life — or away from real and on to pretend. I cut classes three times one week — once to go to the zoo, the other times for Bette Davis — and wrote a note saying I'd been ill and signed my mother's name. I always got to the morning mail first, but one morning I didn't. There was a letter from the principal's office saying I'd been out and they'd like to speak with Mother. What a scene! My tears — 'Oh, Mother, forgive me, I'll never do it again.' Mother asking how I'd got away with it. My confession to signing her name to a note. She: 'Don't you know that's against the law? That you can go to jail for that?' What was it in me — why and how was I able to do such things? For a girl who was dedicated to truth, it was most strange. Was it just mischief? Or was it a streak of my father — perish the thought! It reminded me of a time when I was about eleven. My friends and I used to walk through the five-and-ten-cent store. That's what it really was then, you could buy almost everything for five or ten cents. As I had no money, I used to look at all the appetizing items on the counters and imagine which I would buy. On one counter were pencil cases — cheap little pencil cases, but I'd never had one and I wanted one so badly. So badly that I took it. I suppose most kids have done something like that once in their lives — there's so much to see, to buy. And when you don't have the money, so much that is beyond your reach — even a silly pencil case. I went home as usual and Mother noticed the case. She took me by both arms, looked at me, and said, 'When did you get this pencil case?'

'I found it.' Eyes slightly off center.

'Where did you find it?'

'On the street, Mother.'

'You're lying, Betty. It's brand new. Now tell me where you got it.'

My chin trembled — I couldn't help it — I was caught, and frightened of what I had done. 'I took it from the five-and-ten,' in the smallest voice — a voice only birds could hear.

'Well, you are going right back there and return it. And when you return it you are to give it to the woman behind the counter, tell her that you took it, and apologize.'

'How can I ever do that? I'll be punished! Can't I just put it back on the counter and leave?'

'No — you do as I say. Let this be a lesson to you. Taking what isn't yours is stealing — it's against the law. If you return it now, they will do nothing to you.'

She walked with me to the store, went in with me, and quietly stood to one side while I made my confession. The woman took it back, and it was an experience I never forgot — nor was it ever followed by another like it. Facing a situation head on was the only way to deal with anything. I learned the lesson early. My mother gave me a solid foundation. Any little quirks along the way were my own. It was hard growing up. (It's still hard.)

I studied journalism at Julia Richman to fulfill a momentary dream of becoming a reporter. It must have been the result of a comic strip — that and seeing *His Girl Friday*. Years before when I saw a rerun of Loretta Young in *The White Parade*, saw how beautiful she was, how brave, how dedicated, I knew I would be a nurse. That is until my first sight of blood and the wave of nausea that accompanied it. The nursing dream became a thing of the past.

All this came from wanting so desperately to be someone — something; to have my own identity, my own place in life. The best thing about dreams is that youth holds on to them. I was always sure mine would come true — one of them, anyway. Clearly my fantasies resulted from my identification with movies and certain stars. Like the time I had seen Margaret Sullavan in a movie. She was a wonderful actress and I loved her looks. I wanted to look like that. My hair was long — it had been for years. Time for a change. But my mother and grandmother would be furious, so I pondered for days. Finally I decided I'd pondered enough. Time for action. I was to have my hair trimmed. Mother gave me the money. I took off for the shop. I was so excited — I'd leave 86th Street looking like me, I'd return looking like Margaret Sullavan. Thrilling. I sat in the barber chair and told the man what I wanted — I had a small photograph of Margaret Sullavan with me. He looked at me and said, 'Are you sure that's what you want?' 'I'm sure. Cut it *all* off.' He picked up his scissors and began. One side went and I looked cockeyed. It was awful, but it would be lovely when both sides were done. They finally were. I looked in the mirror. The hair was Margaret Sullavan, all right — very short, just below the ears, bangs — but the face was still mine. The two definitely did not go together. But it was too late now, there was nothing for it but to go home and face the music. I walked in the door and when my grandmother saw me she gave a horrified scream, as did my mother. 'Are you crazy — cutting that beautiful hair? Whatever got into you?' 'All I wanted to do was look like Margaret Sullavan. I love it — I've had my long hair long enough. I'm not a baby anymore.' But it *was* awful — I looked hideous and I hated it. But it would grow back — I hoped. Fortunately, it did before I had finished high school. I was an awkward mess anyway, the hair just added to the picture.

Movies were accessible to me, of course — they were the cheapest entertainment form that I knew — twenty-five cents for entry. My exposure to the theatre was almost non-existent, as I could simply not afford it. I was given a very special treat in 1939 — seeing John Gielgud as Hamlet. The combination of John Gielgud, Shakespeare, and a Broadway theatre was almost too much for me. The feeling of walking into a legitimate theatre — the shape of it, the boxes, balconies, upholstered seats, and the curtain with the magical stage behind it. What seemed like thousands of people crowded inside. So this was what a real theatre was like! It lived up to every vision I had ever conjured up in my mind. I reached my seat, program clutched in hand. The house lights dimmed — the chatter ceased — the entire audience was focused on the stage — the hush — the feeling of awe — and the power actors have to affect people's lives while they sit in a theatre. At the rise of the curtain one could feel the expectation, the concentration of everyone in that house. What followed depended on what was given by the actors — they could do almost anything, they could lead an audience anywhere, make them feel anything. The power of it — it was unforgettable. That day I was transported for two and a half hours from my perch high in the balcony. Even the wave of applause that came at the end of each act did not shake me back to reality. Would I ever come close? Was there any way for me to be anywhere near that good? Gielgud's performance was so affecting that, despite my youth and my inability to understand Shakespeare's language totally, I left the theatre in a complete daze, bumping into people, being stepped on, unaware of where I was. Since then, of course, I have realized that Gielgud's Hamlet was one of the great performances of all time. And I can still see the beauty of that head and his total immersion in his role. It took some time for me to return to my reality. Leslie Howard was also playing Hamlet at a nearby theatre. Curious that I missed that — except rumor had it that he was not so good in the role. Perhaps I didn't want to face less than perfection in my hero.

Graduation at last — the end of school and the beginning of the pursuit of my destiny. We were photographed for the yearbook, called *Spotlight*, and alongside each photo was a two-line phrase meant to be the key to our personalities. Mine said, 'Popular ways that win. May your dreams of being an actress overflow the brim.' I briefly thought of going to college — another fantasy — campus life (all romance, no work) — but there was no real point in pretending, I was not meant for football games and sorority life. It all had nothing to do with my goal, so I gave it up very quickly and painlessly.

Mother agreed that I could go to the American Academy of Dramatic Arts. It would be a struggle, but with the help of Jack and Charlie once more, it could be accomplished. I had to make up my mind that I could have little allowance — no extras — essentials only. But I would be a full-time student and at last could devote all day, every day, to learning about the theatre. And I needed to learn. Four years of Saturdays at the New York School of the Theatre had given me a clue, but the Academy program would be quite different. Meanwhile I was forever inflicting my Katharine Hepburn and Bette Davis imitations on anyone who would sit still for them. Needless to say, Charlie and Mother were my best audience.

The spring before high school ended, Betty Kalb and I had read that Bette Davis was coming to New York. She always stayed at the Gotham Hotel. Traveling with her was her friend Robin Byron, who also happened to be a friend of my Uncle Jack. I called and asked him — begged him — to call Robin and try to arrange for me to meet my idol. While waiting for the answer, Betty Kalb and I stalked the Gotham Hotel. One afternoon when we were skulking in the lobby, Bette Davis came in — walked directly to the elevator. We rushed in after her and tremblingly rode to the tenth floor with her. She was wearing a small black hat, her hair was pulled back with a black ribbon — she was smaller than I'd thought she'd be, but that face was there, just as I'd seen it magnified so many times so far away on the screen. We stared at her openly. When the elevator stopped at ten, she got out. We asked the elevator operator to stop at eleven, rushed for the staircase, ran down one flight only to see her back as she walked through the door of her suite. We laughed weakly and waited awhile to compose ourselves before facing the questioning eyes of the elevator operator. But Bette Davis was wonderful — everything we had imagined. We *had* to meet her, we'd die if we didn't.

Finally my darling Uncle Jack called. He'd spoken with Robin, and though Miss Davis had a very busy schedule, Betty and I could come to her hotel on Saturday afternoon at four o'clock. Betty and I were hysterical. We spent hours on the phone — what would we wear — how would we do our hair — what would we say? We did our imitations of her walk, speech — to get *that* out of our systems at least. It was so exciting — the high point of my life, a dream come true!

I was warned by Uncle Jack to make it brief — not to linger and for God's sake to behave. 'Don't make a fool of yourself — this is a big favor Robin is doing, arranging this. Don't let me down, and tell Betty Kalb to keep calm.' Keep calm? Ha! Well, we'd just have to *act*. Oh, I wished I looked more grown-up. Betty's figure was well developed — she was actually built not unlike Bette Davis — while I was this tall, gawky fifteen-year-old.

Saturday came — Mother and Grandma couldn't wait for it all to be over, they'd heard nothing but Bette Davis for days on end. Betty arrived to pick me up. I was trying to look my most sophisticated, but as nothing in my wardrobe suggested sophistication, I was wearing my best suit. My friend looked much better than I did, I thought — less like a stagestruck kid.

We went to the hotel and I asked the receptionist to call Miss Davis' room and announce that Miss Bacal was in the lobby with friend, we had an appointment. How would I keep from shaking — how would Betty keep from fainting? We were told to go right up. This time we looked the elevator operator squarely in the eye and said, 'Ten, please.' By then we were so caught up in thinking how to present ourselves — how to keep from falling apart until after the visit — that we couldn't speak. The elevator arrived at ten too quickly. Out we stepped and proceeded shakily down the long corridor to Suite 1009–10. We grasped each other's hands — took deep breaths — checked our hair — and finally I pressed the doorbell. I was trembling from head to foot. Inside and out. The door opened — it was Robin. She smiled at me — I introduced Betty to her — and she ushered us into a living room. There was a sofa with two chairs facing it. I sat on the edge of one of the chairs, Betty on the other. At last the door to the bedroom opened and out walked Bette Davis with that Bette Davis walk — Queen of Films — the best actress in the world. Oh, God!

We stood up immediately — she shook our hands and moved to the sofa. I sat down again in the same chair — I was terrified to take a step — but Betty plunked herself down next to the Queen. Bette Davis was open, direct, easy, and sympathetic. She asked us about ourselves, said she had been told by Robin that I wanted to be an actress. In a voice barely audible, I said that I did and that I had been going to drama classes on Saturdays until I finished school. Betty was much more talk-ative than I — seemed to have more to say. I suppose I was tongue-tied. I was so nervous, my hands were shaking. She offered us tea, but I didn't dare pick up a cup and saucer for fear it would fall on the floor or spill all over me. She motioned me to come sit on the other side of her on the sofa. I don't know how I got there, but I did. Of course we told her we had seen all of her films many times over. The silences seemed endless, why was my mind so blank? I couldn't think of any words.

Bette Davis was very patient. She said, 'Well, if you want to act, you should probably try to work in summer stock. That's the best way to learn your craft.' 'Oh yes, that's what I want to do — I want to start on the stage and then go into films just as you did.' 'Well, be sure it's really what you want to do with your life. It's hard work and it's lonely.' I remembered she had said in an interview when talking about her life, 'I have two Oscars on my mantelpiece, but they don't keep you warm on cold winter evenings.' More silence. Robin looked at me — I knew it was time to go. I said, 'Thank you so much, Miss Davis, for your time — for seeing us — I am so grateful.' Betty said much the same. Bette Davis shook our hands, wished us luck. Robin opened the door and out we went.

Betty had started down the corridor and

near the end of it she fell in a heap of emotion. I panicked — Bette Davis mustn't hear us, mustn't know this was going on. I helped Betty up — we staggered to the elevator — rushed to the nearest drugstore so we could sit down. What a relief! Ordeal over. We both started talking at once. 'I will never wash my hand again!' 'Nor will I!' 'Wasn't she wonderful — did you notice her walk as she came into the room?' 'What do you think she thought of us?' 'Why didn't I ask her what her favorite film was?' 'Why didn't I ask her what it was really like to work in films — to be a star?' 'Why was I so nervous? She must have thought I was a fool.' 'I want to be just like her.' 'We must write her and thank her.' 'We mustn't let her forget us.' 'Maybe next time she comes to New York she'll invite us to see her again.'

It was truly generous of Bette Davis to have seen us. It meant so much. To be stage-struck and star-struck is an unbeatable, overpowering combination. Such emotion! Only kids who have wanted to be something really badly and have had a specific someone or something to identify with know that feeling. It's more than ambition. It comes at a time when you're still in school and your life work is still very far away, but you feel you're getting closer to the gold ring and maybe someday you'll not only catch the ring but keep it. Everything seems possible, but your life is all frustration because you can't do anything about it yet.

I reported to Jack that I would be forever indebted to him for making this happen. No crown of diamonds placed on the head of a fairy princess by a handsome prince could mean as much. I told Mother and Granny all about it, almost. I left out Betty's collapse — that didn't come out till years later. Then I wrote Bette Davis the fan letter to end all fan letters — I composed it at least twenty times, choosing only the best words from each version — thanking her and saying some things I'd been too nervous or shy to say when I saw her. Betty wrote her too. We sent the letters to Maine, as we knew from the fan magazines that she had a house there where she spent a good deal of time. About a week later the morning mail brought a blue envelope with unfamiliar writing. In it, a letter from Bette Davis thanking me for my flattering words — saying she had enjoyed our visit — wishing me luck — and at the end: 'I hope we meet again sometime.' I couldn't believe it — all in longhand! I treasured that letter — read and reread it hundreds of times. Betty Kalb got one too. Writing us was another generous thing for that busy actress to do.

★ ★ ★

The next play I saw, some years after *Hamlet*, was *The Philadelphia Story*, starring my other favorite, Katharine Hepburn. Again I was nested in the balcony, but the atmosphere in the theatre was totally different from what it had been for Gielgud. There was the excitement of seeing a movie star in the flesh — live — onstage. And because the play was billed as a comedy, the audience entered the theatre with different attitudes.

Katharine Hepburn was mysterious, wonderful — offering her considerable self and her incredible personality that was totally there for you even in the second balcony. She was so beautiful — and so funny and so touching. And the play was so good and funny. The leading men were new names to me — Joseph Cotten, Van Heflin. Shirley Booth played the second female lead. Hepburn's clothes were floating, graceful — her hair was shoulder length and shining — she was glorious — the theatre was filled with laughter. To be able to give such joy!

Would I ever be able to do that? I thought. It was one thing to make people in a room laugh, especially relatives. But to do the same for strangers was quite another. Katharine Hepburn that afternoon made me glad to be alive — and sure that

46

being an actress was the *only* goal in life.

A year later came the appearance of Laurence Olivier and Vivien Leigh on Broadway in *Romeo and Juliet*. Julia Richman had gotten seats for seniors. To see two brilliant actors from England in Shakespeare — I convinced Mother it was an essential part of my training. Even then I could feel the difference between American and English actors in their delivery of Shakespeare. The language seemed so natural as the Oliviers spoke it. And they were so beautiful in addition to everything else — they were blessed. Critically the production was not well received, but the theatre was packed and I felt very lucky to be in the audience.

The fall of 1940 was the beginning of serious training for my life's work. There would be no distractions. School was finally behind me. I was free to start down that long, winding, one-way street with my head free and clear. And with my entry into the American Academy I could turn myself over completely to learning anything and everything I could about acting — eat and breathe it, live it, make it real. This would be the start of my life as an actress. I couldn't fail. There was no doubt, no doubt whatever.

The American Academy of Dramatic Arts was located on 57th Street just next to Carnegie Hall. It had rooms filled with chairs set in a semicircle — one desk in the center — for voice lessons and improvisations. There were large rooms for fencing, body work such as dancing, learning to fall; there were rehearsal rooms with small stages for scenes; a room with counters and small mirrors and lights for learning how to use make-up.

That was a golden year. A friend from summer camp, Marcella Markham, was there — we had lunch together daily, shared classes. Also in some of my classes were Nina Foch and Terese Hayden. I chose all morning classes. That gave me the afternoons to study the parts I was assigned and left me free to attend plays put on by the second-year students (called the Senior Stock Company) at the Empire Theatre on Tuesday afternoons. The Empire Theatre was to me the theatre of John Gielgud and his Hamlet. It was on Broadway at 40th Street, lavish and beautiful in the old and true theatre tradition.

The curriculum of the Academy was very comprehensive and geared totally to the stage. There were rules to be observed — no employment of any kind was allowed without special permission of the Board. They stressed self-discovery — studying life, as that was what acting was all about. Learning technically how to speak — how to breathe. How to use one's body to project emotion. How to analyze plays and characters. It was a marvelous way to start. My year there was very serious and every course taught me something that in one way or another I have been able to apply practically. All through the years I have found myself observing people, animals. The Academy taught me to be aware of humanity in a new way — a vital part of an actor's equipment. In life-study class, at first I would imitate the moves of another student — very elementary at first; as observation grew keener, we would bring things into the classroom and reproduce scenes observed outside. In pantomime I learned to use every part of my body to express emotion. I was taught body control — each section of the body to be separately developed and used. I had never realized all that was involved in becoming an actress, I had only thought in terms of vocal expression — standing on a stage, speaking lines. But there is so much more involved — so many preliminaries to learn before you reach the point of standing on a stage. Really before you have the *right* to stand on a stage. I didn't learn them all, but it was a beginning of awareness of what I would have to know someday.

My days were full and near perfect that year. All of us, boys and girls alike, hungry to learn. Some more frightened than others, but all willing to try our wings. There was self-consciousness to overcome — we all wanted to give the impression of enormous confidence, but most of us were floundering. I loved learning to fence — it was so dramatic to stand with foil and face mask in hand, learning the preliminary moves before 'En garde.' I couldn't figure out where I might ever use that training, but it was fun. Speech classes taught us the beginnings of voice placement, breathing, projection. All of us facing an open window, breathing deeply the then unpolluted air — hands on rib cage — using the diaphragm — making incredible sounds accompanied by even more incredible face-making. It was funny and I remember feeling an incredible fool. I did giggle a lot. But I loved every class.

Playing scenes was the most difficult at first. You had to learn the lines and stand in the middle of the classroom with another actor — the rest of the class sitting and watching. I was very self-conscious, very nervous, but you began to get a sense of yourself and what acting was all about.

Dance class was funny. Our instructor, Mr Riley, was full of innuendo. For the rhumba, for instance, we would be in lines five across and he would move among us saying, 'You can't do the rhumba until you've lived — you know what I mean!' I didn't know quite what he *did* mean and I never asked. In body-movement class for posture, learning how to move around a stage, we practiced sitting in a chair with a book on our heads, then rising and walking all round the room. In the same class I learned how to faint — on stairs or at floor level. Walk a few steps, slow down a bit, a slow weave and then down a bit to the side, knees, then hip, then torso. I haven't used it much, but it was all part of the loosening process. When Ralph Richardson fell three or four times in Harold Pinter's *No Man's Land*, his limbs hit the deck in that same order. Whenever I see an actor faint or fall, I recognize my basic training.

We learned all sorts of character make-ups — old age, tarts, middle age, and straight. That was fun, and there was a reason for it. In the theatre one does one's own make-up. As a result of that training, even in films I have always found it difficult to lie back while a make-up man worked on me. I do it, of course, those are the rules, but I always make up my own eyes and lips.

Improvisation — Mrs Alice Parke's class — stands out most clearly. Of course I had already learned at the New York

School of the Theatre how to wash my hands and face at an imaginary sink. Stand up, walk to the invisible sink, turn on the hot and then the cold water, pick up the invisible bar of soap, wet one's hands, moving the soap around them, put the soap back on the side of the sink, wash one's hands, rinse them, shake them, turn off the faucets, pick up a towel, and dry them. It may seem simple-minded — people make fun of the idea — but there is a point. The point is observation. In Mrs Parke's class she would say, 'Be a teapot.' You have to think very carefully, feeling a complete fool, then *be* one. (Imagine being her, standing at the head of the class looking at twenty teapots. Hysterical!)

We had a poem to recite — 'A wise old owl sat on an oak; the more he saw, the less he spoke; the less he spoke, the more he heard; I want to be like that wise old bird.' As she called on us, we'd walk to a chair in the center of the room — the back of the chair facing the class served as a perch — climb onto the chair as an owl, look around as an owl, *be* an owl, and speak the words. I did it and was given high marks — I was a very good owl. One day we were sitting around the room talking very generally of things we'd seen. She asked us if there were any animals we had ever noticed in particular. I said, 'Oh, yes — I always watch the squirrels in Central Park moving from place to place, finding acorns on the ground, and carrying them up a tree to some secret place of their own.' Mrs Parke said, 'Well, Betty, you sound as though you really have studied them. All right, be one now — be a squirrel.' The next thing I knew, I was squatting on the floor, hopping around the room, nibbling on imaginary acorns. There were a few titters, of course — but I had clearly watched squirrels carefully during those days I had played hookey from school. And you damn well say to yourself, I feel like a fool, I look like a fool, but I have to forget that or I'll never do anything.

During the year Mrs Parke asked us to write two monologues — one dramatic, one comic. They were to be telephone conversations. I racked my brain. Marcella and I talked endlessly about what our subjects would be. I finally arrived at mine — my dramatic conversation was to tell the tale of the loss of my canary. I enlarged on the story, dramatized it, saying that I'd had only this small bird to confide all my hopes and dreams in, and every night when I came home from work I'd talk to him — me, this lonely, sad woman — and that one day when he flew away it was as though my life had ended. The monologue was funny too — but very sad. Mrs Parke liked it. My idea for the second one tickled my funny bone to such an extent I could barely sit still to write it. This time I was a girl with a harelip who, having just graduated from college, was telephoning a friend and explaining that she had decided to become a speech teacher. Can you imagine? A sixteen-year-old mind at work overtime. The idea of having a speech defect — which of course I exaggerated in my delivery — and wanting to be a speech teacher seemed really funny to me. And Marcella was so doubled over with laughter she was out of control. I was sure I'd be the hit of the day. But Mrs Parke was not amused. When I finally finished: 'Miss Bacal, there is no humor in making fun of the physical defects of others. They cannot help it — it is never funny. Now, your first telephone conversation is the one you should have used for comedy. That had humor and warmth. This one is the tragedy.' I was devastated — but I learned something. Making a bad choice in acting is not the end of the world. Each one is bound to be a lesson of some sort. And making a fool of yourself is something all actors have to risk doing. That's part of our business. And that too is not the end of the world, though it can seem so at the time.

One of the best things about the American Academy was attending the weekly plays put on by the senior class. Downstairs in the building there was a theatre called the Carnegie Lyceum where the plays were performed on Friday nights. One of the actors in these plays I thought was marvelous — so attractive and so good. I saw him first in a straight part, then as a fop in a Restoration comedy. One Friday night, at intermission, I was on the landing chatting with friends when I glanced down the stairs and there he was, looking at me — my hero, the marvelous actor. Blond hair, blue eyes, cleft chin. Name — Kirk Douglas. Of course I started to tremble. All my life, at any emotional time, I have trembled. As the atmosphere at these plays was always very informal, it wasn't too difficult to meet, and when I saw him a couple of Fridays after that, we talked. Briefly and casually — and then talked more and more easily. I had a wild crush on Kirk. He finally invited me out — took me to a Chinese restaurant in Greenwich Village. He lived there on Third Street (in the Village, not in the Chinese restaurant). He told me all about himself. He was on a scholarship at the Academy. He had no money at all. Once he spent a night in jail because he had no place to sleep. The drama of that — and the effect it had on one as impressionable as I! Oh, how he has suffered! I thought. He really had struggled.

I was such a child. I had no idea really how to behave with a man. I had never had a romance — certainly never had a love affair. Nice Jewish girls stayed virgins until they were married, they saved themselves for the man they were going to spend their lives with, so necking in dark corners was about my speed and I was terrified to venture into the unknown beyond that. I went out with Kirk as often as he asked me. He came to my house, where my grandmother would cook for him. He adored her — and he made a great impression on her, of course, my old-fashioned grandma. A nice Jewish boy at last — what could be better? He and Mother got on famously. I even introduced him to Charlie. Poor Kirk must have been scared to death. I remember he had only one coat — reversible, very thin, tweed on one side, raincoat on the other. I thought he must be frozen in the winter. I knew that Charlie had an old winter coat that he never wore and I prevailed on him, adorable man that he was, to let me give it to Kirk. Kirk and I made a date one Saturday — I told him I had a surprise for him — Uncle Charlie brought me downtown with the coat and I marched up the stairs to Kirk's flat. He was thrilled and grateful. There was a button loose and I remember sitting in Kirk's flat and sewing on the button. Of course I had domestic visions at the time — Kirk and I together on the stage, off the stage, doing everything for each other. I always fantasized, always magnified things out of proportion — and it was all in my mind, I was always disappointed — it took me over twenty years to figure that out. Anyway, Kirk did not really pursue me. He was friendly and sweet — enjoyed my company — but I was clearly too young for him. I became somewhat friendly with a girl named Diana Dill, who was a senior at the Academy. One night I stayed over at her apartment. As we were reviewing life, Kirk's name came into the conversation. She said, 'Oh, don't ever get mixed up with anyone like him. You'll get hurt. Actors are unreliable. Not really to be trusted. He's all right to have fun with — don't get serious about him.' Thank God I didn't tell her how I felt about Kirk. I realized that they had been going together rather steadily. They had split up and that's when I had made my entry onto the scene. (In retrospect, I realize that from then on, almost every man I have been attracted to has belonged to someone else or wanted to belong to someone else.) Diana and Kirk ended up getting married a few years later.

Kirk was always kind to me. I, being the hopelessly romantic creature I was, used to go home at night, turn classical music on the radio, and write poetry. I loved to write poetry. Always dramatic — often about unrequited love (I didn't know any other kind). One sample:

> *How beautiful it was–*
> *A perfect moment.*
> *But alas! It was a dream.*

When Kirk left the Academy, he joined the Navy. He wrote me from time to time — the letters I wanted to receive. They were written out of loneliness, I knew, but I adored having them. I remember his dream was to bring his family to New York to see him on the stage. He became a busboy at Schrafft's on Broadway at 86th Street, then a waiter. Of course I'd drag a friend in, or my mother, and we'd order one thing, as we couldn't afford much in the way of extras. And he was terrific — a perfect busboy and waiter, playing the parts to perfection until the big break came.

The moment approached for our examination plays at the Academy. I was cast in a dramatic scene from *The Silver Cord*, a comedy scene as a maid in a play I've forgotten, and a character scene in another forgotten play. I remember *The Silver Cord* for two reasons: the scene was highly emotional — I had to break down at the end and I was never very good at that — and at the rise of the curtain I was to pour tea. There was dialogue among four characters onstage, and the noise of teacup hitting saucer in the shaking hands of yours truly interfered from time to time. It was my first time on the stage of the Carnegie Lyceum Theatre. In the audience were senior students, some outsiders, and all the instructors with pad and pencil taking notes. They would decide whether we were good enough to be invited back for a second year — whether we were fit to be in the theatre or not. Rehearsals were fun, as always — the choosing of costumes, makeup — it was my first taste of semi-professional performing. But to be judged like that at sixteen is pretty strong stuff. You learn very early on about pressure and how well you perform under it.

After the examination plays were over, there was nothing to do but wait for the final judgment. Lists were put up on the bulletin board of times for interviews with the head man, Mr Diestel, at which we would be given the final word. When the day came for mine, I was not ready. Having already discussed it with Mother, I knew there was no money for me to return for the second year. I could only hope that if he asked me back, the Academy might consider giving me a scholarship. So in I went. Mr Diestel, a large man sitting imposingly behind his desk, rose, invited me to sit down, and proceeded to read the comments of my various teachers. Some were very good — some not so good, suggesting I had improved but needed work along special lines. But all agreed that I should return — that I had something to offer the theatre. I was thrilled with that, but miserable with what I knew I had to tell him with tear-filled eyes and trembling chin — that I could not return. He stood firm on the 'no scholarships for women' policy and I stood firm on no money to pay for a second year. If I was good enough to be asked back, why couldn't they make an exception and give me a scholarship? But it was no go, we both knew it, and in my heart of hearts I suppose I had always felt it was better to get on with the fight to break into Broadway. I left the office. Marcella and I had a cup of coffee in a drugstore — I was crying, she was crying — we were trying to help each other out. We would make it anyway, but it was an awful way to end a year of hope.

My poor mother was upset for me — even my grandma was, though she was happy that now I would have to get a real job. I knew I would have to get one too.

But what could I do? I went to Harry Conover's model agency — it was the biggest at the time for young, fresh faces. He looked at me, felt I was not much different from the girls he had except that they were already established and I was still flat-chested. Sitting in the outer office waiting for that interview, seeing all those beautiful girls come in with their hatboxes to pick up their assignments for the day, it looked so glamorous. I wanted to be able to do all that too. They seemed so grown-up, so sure of themselves. The answer to me was, 'No, sorry.' The only thing left was the garment center.

In Harry Conover's outer office I asked a couple of other girls how to find work modeling clothes on Seventh Avenue. They said I should look in the telephone book or go down to certain Seventh Avenue buildings — nothing really below 500 Seventh Avenue. The best houses were in 550 or 530 and you could squeeze in 495, but that was it — anything below that was tacky. So I went to 530 and chose a name at random from the directory on the wall. The elevator took me to the proper floor and I proceeded to the name chosen, with shaking knees of course. I asked the girl at the desk if they were looking for new models to show their collections. She called a woman to speak to me. I said I was looking for a job — did she have any openings? She said she didn't, but why didn't I try David Crystal at 498? — he always took on extra models for the season. Down I trudged to 37th Street. Seventh Avenue is unlike any other street anywhere, it is peculiar to itself. Young men pushing racks of clothes of every description up and down the street — loading trucks, or unloading enormous bolts of fabric from other trucks — clothing in all colors, sizes, shapes, some hideous, some not. The streets always flooded with people wildly active from very early morning to day's end at 6:00 p.m. — and inside perhaps eight buildings just about everything to do with clothing in America happens. It's fascinating — noisy, dirty, creative, alive.

I found David Crystal after being pushed and shoved in all directions in the maelstrom of humanity filling the street. Having had one tiny experience half an hour earlier, I walked in with a suggestion of confidence. I was acting the part of a self-assured girl on the go. After waiting awhile I was asked to go through a door into what I later discovered was the showroom — a large gray room with open booths separated by half-walls — a table and two or three straight chairs around them. It was very quiet. A woman came out, looked at me, asked me about my experience — I told her I had been a photographic model for several years (a white lie), that I was an actress, that I knew how to move and would certainly be a very good model. A man wearing glasses came into the show-room and sat in the far booth. From a curtained doorway a girl walked toward him, turned around with hips slung forward, then faced him again and stopped while he mumbled something to her. Clearly she was modeling some item of the present line. I watched her so I'd have a clue about what to do if I were asked to display my wares. The woman went over to the man and they exchanged a few words in low tones — obviously she was saying, 'That girl is looking for a modeling job — do you want to see her?' I tried to seem brimming over with assurance. The woman called me over and introduced me to the man, who turned out to be Phil Crystal. 'My God, it's his place!' I thought. He talked to me for a bit, asked me to walk for him. I kept telling myself, 'It's a part — *play it*. Remember swimming to the raft.' Finally the woman asked me if I would try on one of the model dresses. She led me through those curtains to where a couple of models were sitting, and I put on the dress she chose. It was a bit big and I tried to make it fit better by adjusting collar, belt, etc. David Crystal clothes were sportswear, which was lucky for me — simple sports clothes always suited me. The dress was a simple brown-and-white tweed that buttoned down the front, short sleeves, brown leather belt –I'll never forget it.

I walked through the curtains. Mr Crystal asked me to turn — I did, without falling down or getting dizzy — he examined the fit of the dress carefully, said, 'Okay, you can change into your own clothes now and come talk to me.' I did as I was told. Mr Crystal said, 'We can use you starting in a week — the salary is thirty dollars. Bring your Social Security number with you and leave other information with Miss . . .' whatever her name was — Jones?

Only after it was over did I realize how terrified I had been. But I had a *job!* And thirty dollars a week — a fortune — Mother and Grandma would be thrilled! It was my lucky day — I must remember the day, it was a Wednesday. (All good things and bad, all *big* things in my life would happen on a Tuesday or a Wednesday from then on.) I rushed home feeling as though I had accomplished some great feat. Thirty dollars — no more allowance, asking my mother for money — at last I would be able to give some to her, help her, and possibly save a bit each week. It was the beginning of financial independence for me. A big step.

I spent the next week going through my scant wardrobe to make certain I had enough to wear to work. Then a trip to Loehmann's in Brooklyn. Loehmann's was a large store that stocked clothes from all the Seventh Avenue houses — lower-priced clothes of unknown designers as well as the most expensive from Traina-Norell to Hattie Carnegie. Mother had been shopping there for years and had been taking me from the age of fourteen. There were no dressing rooms in the store. Women learned when new dresses would be coming in — Thursday nights were always good, I remember. Women ran around in their slips, girdles, and bras — all shapes and sizes — grabbing things from saleswomen as they brought them down. A madhouse. Downstairs were the least expensive items, upstairs the better things — and a small room in the rear reserved for special designer clothes. Everything on racks in the open. On the landing between the two floors any poor husband who had been bulldozed into accompanying his wife was made to wait. It was insanity, but it was bargain heaven!

I started my professional modeling career on Seventh Avenue in May of 1941. I was still sixteen years old and very immature. But I was full of bravado, and although I really had nothing in common with the other models, I liked them and I made them laugh. I soon learned the routine. On arrival at Crystal's you undressed and either sat in a slip or put on a cotton smock. There was a long make-up table with a chair for each of us. The two girls I remember were a luscious blonde named Cynthia and the beautiful, tall brunette named Audrey whom I had seen on my first interview. I watched them as they applied their make-up — a base, then full eye make-up. It didn't look heavy, but it was there. I did the best I could do with the face confronting me in the mirror. I used no base — only a little mascara, eyebrow pencil, and lipstick. I had never felt that make-up enhanced my looks very much. Not that there was no room for enhancing — there was plenty — but make-up made me look unreal to myself.

That summer moved along fairly pleasantly. I got along fine with the girls. I was the baby of the group, looking up to the older girls who knew all about life — perhaps I would garner some knowledge from them. Each model was assigned the ten or twelve outfits made on her, and they made a few outfits on me, but not many — I was too thin, too underdeveloped. When I showed a dress and a buyer would ask to see it close to, I'd be motioned forward. The buyer, male or female, would then feel the fabric, discuss it — I'd stand there until I was dismissed. An occasional male buyer would feel the goods a bit more than was necessary and I never knew what to do. I was petrified, though no one ever was really fresh, just suggestive — just enough to make me aware that I'd better keep on my toes, protect myself. I suppose my experience in the garment center helped me to build a small wall around myself, taught me to take care of myself, defend myself. It also started me on the road to saying something funny, acting funny, to promote a laugh instead of a feel. It was all I could think of to do — I wasn't sophisticated enough to sluff things off or make some telling remark. I felt safer with the distraction of laughter. Their reaction, I hoped, would be 'funny kid' as opposed to 'possible bed material.'

The summer was suffocating — in the garment center you're always modeling heavy winter clothes in 100-degree heat and flimsy summer wear in the dead of winter. At the end of the summer Audrey took her two-week holiday — she went to California, which seemed as far away to me as Outer Mongolia. She returned singing its praises, looking great — told of sleeping well, awakening to a large glass of *fresh* orange juice every morning, swimming, sunshine, and meeting Errol Flynn! I hung on her every word. Flynn had a reputation as a great ladies' man and he was beautiful. I never imagined that California life for me — it all sounded a fairyland, which I guess it was in 1941. I still identified only with Broadway — New York. I used to meet Betty Kalb for lunch when I had a full hour to eat. We'd go to Walgreen's Drug Store at 44th Street and Broadway, a well-known hangout for out-of-work actors, and although we didn't know anyone there, the atmosphere was so pungent it carried me through those hours just seven blocks south that seemed to be lived in another country. Enemy territory, for it took me away from the theatre; anything that took me away from the theatre was against me. So I stumbled through those months enjoying my paycheck and little else. Soon it was time to prepare for cruise wear — the designs had been made, the clothes were to be ready for showing in October. They started to make a couple of things on me, but there was something in the air.

As I felt the firm beginning to lose interest in fitting me for cruise wear, the ax was indeed about to fall. Shortly before its descent came the day we all were casually talking about our lives. The other girls seemed fairly uncomplicated to me — they would keep on modeling until Mr Right came along and then they'd get married and be all set. No dreams of names in lights to get in their way. Audrey and I ended up in the ladies' room talking about our families — she talked more than I did, and that's when she said from her stall to me in mine, 'What are you?' That's when — not knowing she meant ancestry, not religion — I said, 'I'm Jewish.' And that's when she said, 'Oh — but you don't look it at all.' I'd like to meet the man who decided that people do or don't *look* Jewish. What the hell does that mean anyway? Is it the American penchant for pinning things down, categorizing, for pigeonholing people? Whatever it is, it's wrong. Audrey's idea, I suppose, was that I didn't have a large nose and I wasn't ugly, the standard Gentile concept of Jewish looks at the time. She wasn't nasty, unpleasant, or even bigoted — just very surprised.

We returned to our dressing room and the conversation went on, bringing in one of the other girls. 'Can you believe Betty is Jewish?' 'My God, you sure don't look it.' I didn't know what to say. I resented the discussion — and I resented being Jewish, being singled out because I was, and being some sort of freak because I didn't look it. Who cares? What is the difference between Jewish and Christian? But the difference is there — I've never really understood it and

I spent the first half of my life worrying about it. More.

A few days later Phil Crystal called me into his office and said something like, 'Betty, you're a good model and I hate to have to do this, but we won't be needing you anymore. It was only a trial, you're a bit too thin for our clothes' — underdeveloped, you mean — flat-chested '— we've enjoyed having you with us and wish you luck.' Oh God, I thought, let me not cry now. Of course I knew modeling wasn't my life's work and I'd never felt really comfortable there — but being fired is *not* pleasant. And it did not feed my frail ego. I was very stiff-upper-lip — went back to the dressing room, didn't talk much, went to the girls' room, cried it out in the loo, then back to the dressing room. The girls must have known it was coming. I braved it through, making jokes about how now the theatre could have me full time, how had it managed this long without me? . . . I finished out my week at David Crystal and took my leave, praying I wouldn't trip as I exited the room for the last time. I didn't.

I had heard models were needed at a place called Sam Friedlander at 495 Seventh. Friedlander made evening gowns. I went to see him and, miracle of miracles, was hired. He was a friendly, nice man who enjoyed my dreams of becoming an actress. Of course I thought he was nice — he liked me.

I was much happier at Friedlander's than at Crystal's. He laughed at all my little jokes, the other models were good girls (there were only two of them), the feeling was much cozier. I still spent most of my lunch hours rushing to Walgreen's to grab *Actor's Cue* and look for a job in the theatre. *Actor's Cue* was published by a man called Leo Shull. It consisted of about four pages of listings of producers' offices, plays being cast, road tours, everything pertaining to the theatre. Leo had a table in the basement of Walgreen's where copies of *Actor's Cue* were piled up and sold for ten cents apiece. I prevailed on him to let me sell some. He finally said okay — to get me off his back, I think. I took them half a block away to Sardi's Restaurant and there I'd stand outside, stopping all and sundry to buy my product. I kept my eyes peeled for sight of a recognizable producer, actor, anyone who might help me get a job. I really was crazy, now that I think of it, and rather fresh, flip, nervy. But it was fun to do — it was heady, being in the vicinity of theatre life, so much so that I threw caution to the winds and blatantly charged up to Max Gordon, one of the most successful and respected producers on Broadway, asking him to please buy an *Actor's Cue* and also when was he casting his next production. I guess he thought I was funny, for he chatted with me whenever I saw him on that lucky street. He was a kind man, forever generous to struggling actors, always approachable. My face also became familiar to John Golden, Brock Pemberton, and other important producers, which all helped, since when I went to their offices when plays were being cast, they at least recognized me when they said no.

In the summer of 1941 there was casting for *Best Foot Forward*, a musical to be directed by George Abbott. I had worked on my singing and had rehearsed a number called 'Take and Take and Take' from an old Rodgers-and-Hart show. I had rehearsed gestures and naturally thought I'd be a wow at the audition. There was an open call, which meant *everyone* was there. I wore a turquoise-blue sharkskin playsuit — my only and my best — and low-heeled shoes. We were to come prepared to demonstrate dance steps at the snap of Mr Abbott's fingers. I arrived fully equipped and found myself in the midst of beautiful, mature girls wearing high-heeled shoes, bathing suits, leotards — *experienced*, grown-up, and stacked. I knew right away I was all wrong — I looked twelve and just would not do. We were lined up on the stage — four or five rows, eight across — told to walk downstage in rotation, told to do the time step. I felt good doing that since I wasn't out there alone. Finally we were called one by one — Mr Abbott was in the darkened orchestra with some other people — a piano was wheeled downstage left and the auditions began in earnest. One terrible light was focused on the stage. It made my hands and feet feel twice as large as they were. I felt completely naked. Awful! Finally my turn came. I gave my name — no experience except American Academy of Dramatic Arts. I gave my sheet music to the accompanist, a faceless young man — I was so terrified I didn't see a thing. Mr Abbott called to me to move out to center stage. First he asked me to do the time step again — which I could do, God knows, but my knees were shaking so badly I even had trouble with that. Then the dreaded song. I wanted to hang on to the piano, but that was out. I sang it, or talked and sang it, or did something with it. I got through it terribly without confidence or voice — at the end I was told to leave my name with the stage manager, thanked for my trouble, and the next name was called. I knew I'd never hear from them. What an experience! It was like going to the chair. Auditions are hell. I honestly don't know how anyone ever gets a job based on them — they show an actor at his worst, in the glare of a naked spotlight, surrounded by strangers, laying his life on the line. My audition was no good — I'd done it all wrong. But at least I'd done it, and I never forgot what it was like. But I never did it again — not for a musical.

After six months of modeling all day and pounding pavements at lunchtime (and not eating of course) I became fairly rundown, although I survived the winter of '41 still modeling for Friedlander. Mother was due for her yearly two-week holiday and she was tired too. So my loving grandma, who had a very small insurance policy, decided to cash it in and give it to Mother and me to go to Florida, where we could rest in the warmth of the sunshine and be rejuvenated by the soothing, healing powers of the sea. It came to something like $1,500, which was a fortune to us. It was a gift of love. I left Sam Friedlander, as it seemed foolish for me to stay — I wasn't getting any closer to the stage in the garment district and knew I'd have to find something else, something that would bring me within smelling distance of a theatre.

Mother and I went to Florida by train. She had made a reservation in what turned out to be a good hotel on the sea, but expensive for us. We looked for rooms in a smaller establishment and found a charming old house with a sign outside advertising rooms to let. Mother told me to go in to inquire, which I did, whereupon the manager asked, 'Religion?' 'Jewish,' was my response. 'Sorry, no rooms,' was his. Mother was furious, and I was too — but we had each other, so the hell with it. We stayed where we were — it cost too much, but at least no apologies had to be made for being what we were.

I had never been in a tropical climate before and I loved it. The balmy air, palm trees, beach beautiful and white, a blue warm sea. We met a couple of people at the hotel — I even met a fairly attractive young man who played in the hotel orchestra and actually went out with him one night, walking romantically, always romantically, on the beach, trying to talk myself into another fantasy at least for the time I was there. It was all harmless and pleasant, and the warm climate did what it was supposed to for Mother and me. We returned to New York ready to face whatever the future would bring — and it brought a lot, including of course, America's presence in the War after Pearl Harbor.

I had decided that I had to devote my days to finding work in the theatre. A couple of girls I knew were theatre ushers at night. The pay was ridiculous — eight dollars a week — but at least I'd have my days free. The eight dollars would only take care of carfare and lunches with a bit left over. It would mean the end of my helping Mother for a while — until my ship came in, please God. I had put aside something from my modeling — maybe $100, which was a great deal to me. I had lunch at Chock Full O'Nuts — cream-cheese sandwiches on date-and-nut bread, ten cents; orange drink or coffee, five cents. Not substantial, but filling, and it got me through the day. I had saved up enough money to buy a skunk coat whole-sale to keep me warm in New York win-ters. The only problem with it, I was to discover, was that when rain or any other moisture hit, people in elevators or offices would begin sniffing curiously and looking around to see where the poor dead animal lay. On me, alas. I broached the subject of ushering to Mother — she of course agreed. She would always give me the chance to prove that I was right to want what I wanted. By then we had moved to Greenwich Village — 75 Bank Street. It was a small apartment, but the neighbor-hood was clean and fun — totally different from the West Eighties. The bus on the corner took me uptown in no time.

I went to the office of the Shuberts, Lee and J.J., who owned most of the theatres on Broadway, to apply for a job as usher. Why they paid eight dollars weekly while independent theatres paid the lavish sum of eleven dollars I don't know, except, as I was to discover later, they were not known for their generosity to employees. At that point I only wanted to be hired — to work in a theatre — to feel part of it. The hell with the salary. Since I had left the Academy, nothing even resembling a break in the theatre had turned up. I had to start concentrating only on that. I had decided I would give myself ten years to make the grade. If it didn't happen by then, it never would. But I had to be around live theatre — if I couldn't learn by actually practicing the craft, then perhaps I could learn by watching others. Professionals! So I was hired by the Shuberts.

Before I was assigned to a theatre permanently I was sent to a few theatres for a week or two of apprenticeship — that meant learning exactly what was expected of me. The rules, etc. Wearing a black skirt and sweater, I reported to the head usher at the Morosco Theatre on 45th Street, where Noel Coward's *Blithe Spirit* was playing. The stars were Clifton Webb, Leonora Corbett, Peggy Wood, and Mildred Natwick. The curtain was to go up at

8:30. I arrived at 7:45 — earlier than necessary, but I couldn't wait. The head usher arrived before eight — she gave me a white collar and a pair of white cuffs to adorn my black sweater. That was the usher's uniform of the day. She showed me how the programs were to be piled neatly at the head of the aisle, and as the theatre doors opened I observed carefully the procedure to be followed. First, 'Tickets, please' to the theatregoers — then directing them to the correct aisle, or leading them to their seats down one's assigned aisle, giving them one program each. Then back up the aisle to stand at your station until the next ticket stubs were presented. I did nothing but watch that first time. Another part for me to play — and in a theatre! The lights went down, the curtain went up, the play began. I was in heaven. I never took my eyes from that stage. It was a marvelous, funny play, beautifully acted, and I made myself believe that because I was an usher, standing in the rear of the theatre, I was a part of it. No longer just a spectator — a participant. But even with my wild fantasizing I could never have dreamed that so many years later I would be acting in that same play — playing Leonora Corbett's part, with Noel Coward himself in Clifton Webb's part, and that Clifton would be my friend.

It was exciting to find myself in the

theatre before and after the play. The mystery of it all was magnified even more. I watched the play carefully for half a week, fascinated by the actors' ability to make the audience laugh at each performance. But, alas, I couldn't stay on. The head usher told me I was to go for the rest of the week to the Imperial Theatre, to usher at *Let's Face It* starring Danny Kaye. A great way to see plays. Cheap, too. *Let's Face It* was a wonderful show — Danny Kaye had made an enormous hit and Eve Arden was in it with him. To be ushering at a musical really lifted me off the ground. I'd had no idea how different it would be; how the atmosphere, from the moment the doors opened and the audience started to arrive, was totally altered by whether it was a drama, comedy, or musical comedy. After the people were seated, the overture started. Music! Fidgety feet! It was all I could do to keep myself from dancing down the aisle. The Shuberts would have loved that — I don't think! Danny Kaye was funny and marvelous. How I'd love to meet him. So what did I do? I went backstage after the show one night, knocked on his dressing-room door, and he opened it. He was washing his make-up off. I nervously told him I was a would-be actress who had been ushering in his theatre — how good I thought he was and would he give me his autograph, please? He asked a few polite questions about my non-existent career and gave me his autograph, for which I thanked him profusely and left. I felt safe going backstage because I knew this was not my permanent ushering assignment.

I still spent my days pounding the pavements, going from office to office, trying to get a foot in the door — any door. Still selling *Actor's Cue* during lunch. I also collected weekly unemployment insurance, being eligible from my time in the garment center. Ushers were non-union then, and no one — not even the government — expected anyone to live on eight bucks a week. Standing in line in those dingy offices to collect money that is yours to begin with is a somewhat humiliating experience. I know that — but then I was damn glad to get it. When the money was taken from my weekly check I hadn't missed it that much, and getting it back was like a gift.

I was sent to the Golden Theatre to usher for several performances of *Angel Street*. I loved it — Vincent Price and Judith Evelyn were so good and so mysterious. I followed my Danny Kaye pattern with Vincent Price, who was also removing his make-up when I went around. He was warm and gentle — 'God, actors are nice people,' I thought. I don't know what *they* thought; nothing, more than likely. After what amounted to a two-week apprenticeship I was set for the St James Theatre, where the Boston Comic Opera Company, performing Gilbert and Sullivan, was to share a season with the Jooss Ballet. I had my own place in my own theatre, and I felt important and very possessive about it.

The Boston Comic Opera Company was great fun to watch. Opening night I was very excited and, as there was an opening night for each Gilbert and Sullivan operetta, I was excited a good deal of the time. I learned to recognize the critics. I'd lower my voice, saying, 'Tickets, please.' During the interval I'd stand in the lobby saying, 'No smoking — please extinguish all cigarettes before entering the theatre — curtain going up,' in my best American Academy voice. Hoping I'd be noticed, of course — discovered. The Jooss dancers were first-class. When I arrived at the theatre they would be doing their warm-ups in the rear aisle. I got to know a few of them well enough to strike up a mild conversation. They were all foreign and didn't speak English too well. They danced *The Green Table* and that was my first exposure to the best of ballet. Hans Zullig was a principal dancer in it and very fine. That ballet, I was to learn later, was a classic and he was admired by balletomanes the world over. I had a tiny crush on him, ready to enlarge it at the slightest provocation (was constantly looking for someone — anyone — to have a crush on), so spoke with him whenever I could. He was very small and shy, very sweet. When he asked me if I'd have dinner with him on a Sunday night, of course I was thrilled. My mother told me to relax — again I was trying to make something out of nothing — looking for a romance — but I had to have *something*. He came down to the Village to pick me up — away from the theatre, in ordinary clothes, he looked smaller than ever. My mother could not believe him — but he was very nice, very soft-spoken. We went to a tiny bistro, talked of our lives — he missed his home, but loved to dance. He came to life then, much as we all do, I guess. The evening ended in friendly fashion, but no romance in my eyes or his. Another fantasy shot to hell.

My days continued to be filled with making the rounds. Broadway was alive with fantastic shows then, and stars — Gertrude Lawrence in *Lady in the Dark*, in which Danny Kaye had first been noticed — Paul Lukas in *Watch on the Rhine* — Dorothy McGuire in *Claudia* — Boris Karloff in *Arsenic and Old Lace*. I still stood outside Sardi's at lunch trying to meet and talk to anyone who might help me. One day Paul Lukas emerged. I brazenly cornered him, of course, knowing what a marvelous actor he was. He asked me if I was an actress — I said yes — he asked me if I'd like to see his play — oh, yes, I would love it, I answered. So he asked me to come around backstage when I could, and he would get me a seat.

One day his play had a matinee and we didn't. I rushed to the Martin Beck Theatre, backstage to Paul Lukas' dressing room — he remembered me, got me a seat, and asked me to come round afterward. He was staying in between shows. Lillian Hellman's *Watch on the Rhine* was another extraordinary experience — a beautiful, strong play, magnificently acted. The audience was in tears at the final curtain and the cheers for Paul Lukas were deafening. Again I was transported, and felt privileged to be allowed into his dressing room. He was friendly and easy — sat me down, asked me about myself, what I had done, what I wanted to do. He was my first important friend in the theatre; though I was still a baby, I went to him for counsel and he treated me seriously. I don't know why he was so good to me, but he was. He allowed me to watch the play whenever I could — listened while I told him which latest producer I had tried to see, my frustrations, all of it. He was sympathetic and tremendously helpful, and of course I respected and admired him.

The Stage Door Canteen was about to open in New York and it needed hostesses. Only theatre folk qualified. I signed up for Monday nights. I was to dance with any soldier, sailor, or marine who asked me — get drinks or coffee for them, listen to their stories. Many of them had girls at home — were homesick — would transfer their affections to one of us out of loneliness and need. Some would come every Monday night to see the same girl. It was really very sweet and sad and fun, a natural set-up for a dreamer. There was always music, and stars would appear each night to entertain or talk to the boys from the small stage. My first night there I couldn't believe it — Alfred Lunt and Lynn Fontanne were washing dishes and serving coffee. Helen Hayes too. Betty Kalb and I had signed up together. Each of us was so busy watching the famous stars coming in that there wasn't time for us to compare notes until the end of the evening. On Monday nights there was fierce jitterbugging. Many a time I found myself in the middle of a circle — everyone clapping to the music — while I was being whirled and twirled by one guy, then passed on to another, nonstop, until I thought I would drop. Judy Garland and Johnny Mercer came in one night and sang some of Mercer's songs — John Carradine came in — and many, many others. It wasn't much to do for the war effort, but it was something. At least the boys had a place to go that was clean and fun and a relaxing change for them.

I overdramatized every situation for myself. A young sailor took a fancy to me — I think I reminded him of his girl. He came in every Monday night for weeks, then one night he told me he was going to sea — didn't know where, of course. He was charming and very homesick. He asked if he could write to me. 'Certainly,' I said, 'I'll let you know what's going on back here.' I didn't know what to say to him — war was a fiction to me, not a reality. I didn't really understand what it meant — how could I?

I continued to pound pavements — make the rounds. They were casting a show called *Johnny 2 x 4* by a man called Rowland Brown. He was producing it himself and it was to be staged by his brother, Anthony Brown. It called for a large cast, I was told, so I headed for the Brown office. I met both brothers — it was a small office filled with actors, and the Browns were accessible. Rowland Brown told me the speaking parts were already cast, but there were to be many walk-ons. The setting was a speakeasy and they wanted atmosphere. Would I leave my name and address and they would call me. That again! I had left my name in so many offices it had become routine. I still hoped and still prayed with the same fervor, but nothing had ever happened. The next Monday, I *was* called and asked if I'd come to the Brown office. I couldn't believe it. I got myself together and marched over to 44th Street. Rowland Brown told me there was an opening for me as a walk-on. The salary was only fifteen dollars per week — I would have to join Equity — it was not a speaking part, but it was on a stage! On Broadway! I was beside myself. In as controlled a voice as possible, I said I would love to be in his play. Mr Brown said he would make the arrangements with Equity, call me when the contracts were ready, and get all the information to me about rehearsals, wardrobe, etc. The play was not going out of town, but would rehearse for three weeks, play a few previews, and open in New York.

I was on a cloud. At last I would be a professional actress — a full-fledged member of that hallowed union, Actors' Equity. It wasn't a real part, but it was a beginning. Perhaps the tide was beginning to turn — my luck beginning to change. I had no idea what I would need in the way of clothing for the show — make-up — what I would actually have to do. How would I be able to wait for that call to sign my name on the piece of paper — how would I wait for that first day of rehearsal? Mother was thrilled because I was thrilled. It was a beginning, a breakthrough. There is no high on earth like the high of realizing even part of one's dream. I was in a daze. Couldn't wait to get to the Canteen that night to tell Betty Kalb. What did I care that the salary was fifteen dollars a week? It was Broadway, and I'd be behind the footlights — other girls would be leading people to their seats, and they'd be coming to see *me* for a change. Did I have a shock coming! Betty was as happy as I was, and I told everyone else who would listen. I was bursting that night. It was my first feeling of complete happiness. At that moment I had everything I wanted.

A few days later I went to the Brown office to sign my contract. By this time I had added another *l* to my last name. There was too much irregularity of pronunciation — 'Backle' some would say, 'Bacahl' others — with the added *l,* that last syllable was clearly to be pronounced one way and one way only — *call* (cawl). It was a standard Equity contract — standard for walkons, that is. The entry fee for Equity was

$50. Rehearsals were to start in a week. I was to provide my own clothes and when we were into rehearsals a bit I'd know what I needed. So one day in February 1942 I went to the stage door of the Longacre Theatre to start my professional acting career. I walked to the wings, where the stage manager was waiting to check us all in. There were so many people — apart from the leads, there were about ten small parts and another ten walk-ons. The whole experience was magical. Chairs were placed onstage — a few tables — an upright piano. I knew no one, but I was still in seventh heaven.

Rehearsals began — those of us who had no parts sat in the back of the theatre. Those of the cast who had musical numbers had already rehearsed them and went through them roughly that first day. I thought it was a marvelous play, I loved everything about it — I had no judgment. Johnny, played by Jack Arthur, owned a speakeasy — Monica Lewis sang there. Barry Sullivan was the hero, Evelyn Wyckoff the heroine. Harry Bellaver had a large part — Jack Lambert was the heavy — there were bodyguards, B-girls, guests (I was one of the latter). In the first act I was onstage with a group of others sitting at a table. As rehearsals progressed I was given more to do. In the second act I made an entrance down the stairs center stage chatting with two men — no audible dialogue, need I say? — and sat at a table downstage with a couple of the B-girls. One of them was a girl named Carolyn Cromwell, who became my friend at once and has remained so all of my life. In the third act I was to be doing the jitterbug as the curtain rose, and when the music ended, my partner and I were to sit at a table stage right. I felt I had been singled out. I wasn't merely a walk-on, I had something special to do in each act — I was an 'outstanding' walk-on (my name for it — no one else's).

The show was full of music, laughter, melodrama — the smoke of a speakeasy — the Yacht Club Boys singing songs onstage and moving through the audience — love — shooting. It had everything. We opened on March 16, 1942. I was as nervous as though I had had a large part — or even a small one. When the curtain went up on the third act my partner and I were dancing and I was shaking from head to toe. To see all those faces out front, what an extraordinary feeling. I was terrified and I didn't even have to open my mouth. But still the incredible excitement backstage — in the dressing rooms — each actor, each walk-on making sure he had what he needed for the performance. The fact that one doesn't speak doesn't make it less of a performance — at least, in my eyes it didn't. I was there for a purpose, I had a specific function to perform — it might not be noticed individually, but it was part of the whole. In my inexperience and fright, I felt that all eyes were on me when I was onstage, but it wasn't ego or conceit, it was anxiety, nerves, and built-in self-consciousness and insecurity. My mother, Charlie, and Rosalie came to the opening night; the rest of my relatives staggered their visits, Jack and Vera bringing Grandma to watch her favorite granddaughter's debut. On opening night I remember standing in the wings watching Barry Sullivan and Evelyn Wyckoff waiting to go on, and I knew at that moment that I was right, that being an actress was the best possible choice in life.

Of course after the reviews appeared, everyone was aware that the play wouldn't run. It was my first theatrical heartbreak — but not my last. One night during the run I stayed overnight with Carolyn Cromwell at the Barbizon, and we stayed up most of the night talking, me again about my hopes and dreams. We sent out to Hamburger Heaven for hamburgers — it made me feel like a character in *Stage Door*. After eight weeks we closed. Arrangements were being made to play the subway circuit — Brooklyn, the Bronx, and Queens — so called because one got there by subway. That meant another three weeks' work, one week in each borough.

I immediately resumed pavement pounding, even before the subway circuit began. I auditioned for *My Sister Eileen*, read once for the part of Eileen, then was asked to see the play that night and come back and read again the following day. Hopes rose — I saw the play, loved the part (I would have loved *any* part), read again, and didn't get the job. John Golden was looking for an actress to play *Claudia* on tour. Dorothy McGuire had made an enormous hit playing in New York. I trapped John Golden outside Sardi's to ask if I could read for it. He said yes I could and would I come to his office the next morning. Hopes rose again. I went to his office. He asked me if I'd seen the play — of course I hadn't, I couldn't afford it. He made arrangements for me to go to a matinee and read afterward. There was a man working for him named Fred Spooner, a warm, friendly man who had been around the theatre for years. He would be in the theatre during that performance and take me backstage for my audition. It was the beginning of another friendship. I made Fred laugh — and my innocence and wild, blind dedication must have appealed to him. For no other reason than that, he helped me — not practically, but emotionally. Claudia was a young married woman who in the course of the play — with her husband, and in dealing with her mother's terminal illness — grew up. A marvelous part. God, I wanted it! I auditioned for it after the matinee in my old friendly theatre, the St James — on the stage this time. They liked me enough to ask me to see another performance and read again. I rushed to tell Paul Lukas. He thought it was great news and gave me a bit of advice — not to get my hopes up too high, to think carefully of the scenes I was asked to read, to be simple. Fred Spooner gave me confidence, telling me other actresses were being considered, but that the management was obviously interested in me, not just being polite. I remember standing in the back of the theatre watching that play, living every moment of it. Inch by inch I was feeling a part of the theatre, less an outsider, with each audition I had, each office I became more familiar with, each producer who came to recognize me. It was a good, warm feeling.

After the performance Fred and I walked up 44th Street and stood outside the theatre looking at the darkened marquee as I verbalized my dream of seeing my name in lights up there. The next day — another audition. The Golden office gave me a script, told me to look at two specific scenes. I did, and read again that afternoon. There was hushed talk in the orchestra and I was thanked and told they would call me. 'Oh, not again,' I thought, 'I'll never hear another word from them, nothing will ever happen to me.' I went home depressed. My mother told me not to worry, something would happen, don't give up too easily. 'They asked you back three times, they must have liked you.' Of course she was right, I thought, trying to convince myself — they must have liked me or they wouldn't have had me read so many times. But lurking in the back of my mind were visions of the unknown actress who had also auditioned — who had more experience than I — who was better. Even then, with all my bravado, and though I did believe in my ability to be good and succeed, I never really thought I was better than anyone else. I'm still not sure. But I would never give up. My ten-year plan still had nine years to go.

A few days later the Golden office called and asked me to come down again. Having prepared myself for the worst, I got on a bus headed for 44th Street. Mr Golden told me he and the others, stage managers, had liked my readings. The part of Claudia was cast for the tour — I trembled a little at that — but the job of understudy was open and they were offering that to me. It would mean being on the road for a year and playing the part if the leading lady was ever sick. I came to life with that offer, thanked him profusely, told him I would have to talk it over with my mother — I was still only seventeen — and would let him know by Monday. That would give me a few days' grace and I'd have a chance to ask Paul Lukas' advice — he knew the theatre better than anyone else I knew, and was clearly the one to talk to.

I had no alternatives to *Claudia* at this point, though I had signed a contract with the Walter Thornton model agency. His was the least of the big three — Powers, Conover — but I was in no position to choose. I had done a small amount of photographic modeling for Montgomery Ward catalogues — nothing exciting, and my future in the modeling area looked far from brilliant. When I went to see Paul Lukas to tell him what had happened, I really was in a quandary. I didn't know what going on tour entailed. Paul told me, 'Look, if you accept this job it will mean (a) that you'll be out of New York for a year, and (b) that the chances of your ever playing the part are slim. During that year you might have an opportunity to act in a new play here. If you're away for a year, that is a year out of your life without being able to really practice your craft and learn. I would say: don't take it.' What he said made sense. If I accepted Golden's offer, I would lose touch with all the people on Broadway who had come to know me a little — at least enough to speak to me or allow me to speak to them about new plays. And touring for a year, while an adventure if you've never done it, would be frustrating if I never got to play the part. I was dejected, but I knew that Paul was right, so I went to Mr Golden's office and told him of my decision. It wasn't easy. But he couldn't have been more agreeable or understanding, this important producer who people said was gruff and unapproachable. He wished me luck and said that he hoped my break would come — perhaps even with him. So that was that! But, having made the decision, what was I going to do next? Please God, let it not be a mistake!

I went to the Stage Door Canteen on Monday nights all through *Johnny 2 x 4*, and after the show closed, being there made me feel I was still an active member of the theatre. Identification with it was all-important. Everyone could understand the high of being in a show and the low of the closing and being thrust onto the pavements again.

I don't know how it happened, but on

May 29, 1942, I was crowned Miss Greenwich Village. It clearly had something to do with my being a Walter Thornton model, as it was he who officiated. I don't think anyone else was seriously competing for that dubious title created to promote Greenwich Village. The contest was free to all entrants and the winner was to be sent to Atlantic City to compete in the Miss America competition, all expenses paid. There were no bathing suits, thank God — that would have been pathetic. I do remember walking onto a raised platform, smiling nervously in my high-heeled shoes and my pretty chintz dress. The newspaper reported three other girls as runners-up, but I was too nervous to notice anyone else. The 'crowning' got my picture into a few very obscure newspapers. I lied about my age, as we had to be eighteen and I wasn't yet. On another occasion I sold kisses for the Smoke Screen Fund — whatever that was (it was sponsored by the local Kiwanis Club). Another promotion signifying nothing, another picture in a newspaper no one ever saw. Needless to say, I never went to Atlantic City, and no advantage was gained by my title or by any modeling I did for the Walter Thornton agency.

Every year George Jean Nathan wrote a page in *Esquire* appraising the past theatre season and listing merits and demerits. On the merit side in the July 1942 issue was the following: 'The prettiest theatre usher — the tall slender blonde in the St James Theatre, right aisle, during the Gilbert & Sullivan engagement — by general rapt agreement among the critics, but the bums are too dignified to admit it.' I really enjoyed that one. Being noticed by someone renowned in theatrical circles — anyone — was *something*. It wouldn't get me a part, but it couldn't hurt and it was better than just disappearing.

In August I actually met the critic George Jean Nathan at a USO drive. Young actresses were stationed at various nightclubs around the city to sit at tables and try prettily to collect money. I was assigned to Café Society Downtown, where a new young entertainer had just exploded on the scene. His name: Zero Mostel. One night Nathan came in with William Saroyan and a lovely blonde girl and a lovely dark girl. The blonde was Saroyan's soon-to-be wife, Carol, and the dark-haired girl was Oona O'Neill. Nathan invited me to sit with them for a while. Another thrill and another first for me — sitting with a famous, highly thought-of playwright like Saroyan. Nathan asked me if I'd like to have lunch with him the next day at a place called the '21' Club on West 52nd Street. I had never heard of it, but said yes, thinking perhaps I'd see or meet someone in the theatre. I dressed up in my best dress. I had never been in such a grand restaurant. It was 1:30 — late for lunch, and the crowd was beginning to thin out. I looked around the room at the well-dressed men and women, all clearly used to being there, totally at ease. A world I knew nothing about. George asked what was happening with my career — I told him everything, including the *Claudia* offer and my decision. He said I probably had done the right thing. He never made the slightest suggestion of a pass — the men I had met in the theatre who had lecherous reputations had never displayed them to me — I guess my inexperience and youth stuck out all over, as opposed to my chest. I looked across the room and saw the familiar face of Burgess Meredith staring at me. He was considered one of the finest actors in the theatre, having starred in *Winterset* and *High Tor*. He was very attractive — had a devilish, witty face. At the end of the lunch I went to the ladies' room and returned to find Meredith talking to George. We were introduced, then he went back to his table. With a wink Nathan said, 'He's a devil with the ladies — look out.' I knew nothing except that he was appealing — a beautiful actor — and I wanted to go out with him.

He sent me a note asking for my phone number. I wrote back, 'I'm in the book under my mother's name, Natalie Bacal.' And that was all. We left and I couldn't know if I would hear from him. I went home starry-eyed, praying the phone would ring — acted out many scenes in my head, all ending with Buzz Meredith being the Prince and me Cinderella. What a child! Several nights later the phone did ring — it was Mr Meredith. He said, 'Hello — there's a big evening at Madison Square Garden Sunday night. A Night of Stars. Would you like to go with me?' I was so unsubtle — didn't have a clue how to play the game. 'Oh, I'd love to,' I said. I was walking on air. My mother was a little horrified. 'You don't even know the man,' she said. 'You practically let him pick you up — he'll have no respect for you.' I laughed it off, saying it was the Night of Stars — every name I'd ever heard of would be there. What would I wear? I had no long dress. Next day we rushed to Loehmann's, where we found a long-sleeved navy-blue chiffon dress with a lace jabot. Very pretty — not very daring — and I was to wear it to any and every event for years to come. The big night came and of course my mother had lectured me to be home by midnight — be careful — who knew what kind of man Burgess Meredith might be (she was unimpressed by his stardom) — I was under age and she'd be waiting up for me. I was headstrong, thought I knew what I was doing and had no intention of coming home until I was ready. Buzz picked me up and off I went on my first evening among the stars with a star. What, oh, what would happen that night? As it turned out, nothing. Buzz was adorable to me. Paulette Goddard was there looking ravishing and exciting. I had known something was going on between them, but I didn't know they were in love and had broken up temporarily for some reason or other. I was hardly a threat.

The year 1942 brought what turned out to be my last time spent in the theatre for seventeen years. Max Gordon was casting a new comedy called *Franklin Street* by Arthur Sheekman and Ruth and Augustus Goetz. It was to be directed by George S. Kaufman and star Sam Jaffe. The period was 1900; place, a boardinghouse in Philadelphia where an ex-actor runs a dramatic school, trying to keep wolves away from the door. As I've said, Max Gordon always gave me access to himself and his office in the Lyceum Theatre, and this time there might actually be a part for me. When I went to see him, he told me I could read and that George Kaufman was probably in the Lyceum lobby at that moment. So, fresh, persistent kid that I was, I ran down to the lobby. (For one as insecure as I was, I sure had no compunction about running up to strangers and brazenly introducing myself. I was damn lucky all my strangers had class!) There were two men standing in a corner. I asked a man in the box office if one of them was George Kaufman and he pointed him out. Once having seen George Kaufman, you could never forget him. He was very tall, very, very thin, with a long face, steel-rimmed glasses, and black hair that seemed to stand straight up. Slouching so as to look smaller, younger, I walked up to him, introduced myself, and told him I had spoken to Mr Gordon and hoped there'd be a part I could read for in his new play. He introduced me to the man standing next to him, who turned out to be one of the authors, Arthur Sheekman. He asked what I had done — I told him (that must have made him chuckle) and said, 'I really am very good, I can act and I know I would add to your play. I can look younger, smaller, anything you want — just let me read for you, please.' It was all said in a rush — the hammerhead approach — and caught him somewhat unaware. He was patient and said, 'Well, there might be something — why don't you come to the reading next week and we'll see what happens.' 'Oh, thank you, Mr Kaufman — I'll be there, you won't be sorry. Thank you, Mr Sheekman.' God knows exactly what I said or how I looked — no different from the hundred other girls who were looking for that same break. Those men must have been inundated with girls like me, singing their own praises, searching, praying for the break, for discovery — for *the answer*.

The following week I reported to the Lyceum Theatre. All I knew was that the play was a comedy with four or five ingenue roles. When I arrived at the stage door, a faceless young man directed me to the stage manager. As usual, he had a small table set up in the wings with many bits of paper on it — all identifying actors, I suppose. Many other girls were hovering in the wings — we were all there for the same reason, and once again there'd be losers and winners. When my turn came, I was handed 'sides' by the stage manager. Sides are pieces of paper about five by seven inches that have only one individual role typed on them, with cues from other roles. Simpler, less complicated for auditions, they take the place of scripts for every Tom, Dick, and Betty who reads for a part. The stage manager gives sides to auditioning actors so they can familiarize themselves with the words, mood, etc., before they are called upon to step center stage.

After I'd studied the part briefly, I

walked out onto the stage. I tried to be calm and behave as though I was in control — a fine professional. I was anything but — yet I felt better this time because I knew Max Gordon would help to get me a part if he possibly could. And I hoped the impression I had made on George Kaufman was positive and appealing rather than negative and un-. But I was terrified again, shaking with nerves — why, dear God, did there have to be auditions? Was all life to be proving yourself over and over? Was all life rejection if you didn't catch the fancy of one higher up? Did everything in life depend on *that* moment? Were there always tests — were you always challenged — was there always that naked light and you alone with nothing to lean on and darkness facing you while it was decided whether you would live or die? And would my damned kidneys give me trouble — why did I always have to pee just as my name was called — how would I ever make it on a stage? Christ, here I go again, at my worst. I stepped center stage, started to read the part. My hands wouldn't stop shaking, my mouth twitched — what was I doing here? Why did no one else's nerves show?

After I read — I can't even remember what I read, I was so petrified — George Kaufman beckoned me forward, smiled, said he was pleased to see me, told me a bit about the character of the girl I was reading, suggested I try it another way, said, 'Take it easy.' He spoke very softly, very kindly. Whereupon I stepped back and started again. I was probably even more nervous — certain I'd read it all wrong to begin with. I'm sure he knew that. How many of these auditions had he held, how many actors in a state of terror, laying their lives on the line, had he witnessed? I got through it and made some kind of joke, trying to be easy, trying to show George S. Kaufman, the most successful, sought-after director of the day, that I was worthy. He called the stage manager over and told him to give me another set of sides; he wanted to hear me read another part. I could look it over while another girl was auditioning.

I walked into the wings, sat down, and tried to concentrate on this next character in the play. Another unknown quantity. If he asked me to read again, he must think I was a possible at least. He must like me, I thought. My head was full of reasons why I would be chosen for one part or another. Hard to think of acting when your head is off on mind-reading expeditions. 'Pay attention, you fool. Get as much out of this part as you can. Think! This may be your golden opportunity. Don't blow it.' The stage manager asked if I was ready to read.

Of course, I said — it didn't occur to me to say as one more experienced might, 'I'd like a few minutes more, please.' I didn't say it and I didn't get the few minutes more. I stood center stage again, with that lovely naked bulb hanging over my head. And I read the part. That character's name was Maud Bainbridge. She was a dreamer — always quoting poetry, always in another world (where I wanted to be at that moment). The scene was over — they were talking quietly to each other out front. George Kaufman said, 'Fine, Betty. Thank you. Can you come back tomorrow to read once more? Take the sides of both parts home with you — read them over and we'll do it again tomorrow.'

What a relief. It wasn't a yes, but it wasn't a no either. I took my sides and rushed out. I had to get a part. I had to. 'Please God, let it happen this time. Don't let me lose this one.' I headed for Walgreen's. Fred Spooner might be there. Since my *Claudia* readings he had been a good friend to me. I could tell him anything — dream my dreams aloud and he wouldn't laugh — he believed in me, always said he'd be on the lookout for plays for me. He was there. We ordered coffee — a nickel a cup and great coffee. I told him all, every detail — how George Kaufman had looked, what he'd said, how he'd reacted to my readings, what I thought he'd thought. I showed Fred the sides of the two parts. We talked about them. Fred said: 'I'll bet you get it. This could be the break you've been looking for. It's not the leading role, that will come, but it's a speaking part on Broadway under the best auspices in the business. Go home, really become familiar with those characters, get in there tomorrow and knock 'em dead. You can do it, we know that. Let me know what happens tomorrow. I'll be around the office all day.' He walked me to the bus stop on Eighth Avenue, watched me get on, waved and smiled.

Clutching the sides, I headed for home. I couldn't read in the bus, it's always made me dizzy and queasy. I'd have to content myself with thinking about the audition, going over it again. Who else had been there? I hadn't even thought of the other girls — there were only five ingenue parts, after all, and more than three dozen were trying out. But Kaufman had asked me to read more than once, he had seemed to like me. Oh, it just had to work out! I got home, hugged my beloved cocker spaniel Droopy, told him all about it. He was very sympathetic. I could and did always say everything to him, everything outrageous, sublime. I could fantasize totally with him, go to any extreme and he was all love, all compassion. What must dogs think! As an only child of a working mother, I was happy to have him to unload to, he was a comfort and a friend and he didn't talk back!

I studied my two characters, garnering what understanding of the play was possible from sides. Mother came home and I happily went through it all again. She always was excited for me, lived through all my emotions with me, cared desperately, but remained the voice of reason, always telling me to do my best, to try my hardest, while still urging me not to build my hopes up too high. Of course she didn't know anything about the theatre, but I didn't know a hell of a lot more.

I got through dinner, walked Droopy, went to bed — that three-quarter box spring and mattress shared with Mother — and of course could not sleep. 'Please God, let me get one of the parts. Let Kaufman really like me, let it be the beginning, please, please.' Finally sleep, but not for long.

At ten o'clock the next morning I was at the Lyceum stage door. The same stage doorman, the same stage manager, smiles of the same girls. There were fewer of us this day, but still more girls than parts. But there were familiar faces and that felt good.

A girl called Jacqueline Gately read Maud Bainbridge and Adele Stanley. Joyce Gates read another part. The same group were out front — we'd read, they'd whisper, we'd stand onstage trying not to faint or cry. At one point, about seven of us were asked to stand onstage together. It was not like a chorus call, but to see what the physical mix was, how we complemented one another. And when were we going to find out if we'd gotten a part? A lunch break, then would we come back — *would* I? None of us auditioning could bear lunch together, we weren't sure where we stood, we didn't know one another and it was too tricky emotionally. We were too apprehensive to share. I got back to an almost empty theatre. The stage manager and his assistant were having sandwiches at their table and going over something. Kaufman, Sheekman, Gordon, etc., had not returned. The other girls had not returned. So I sat backstage and looked at the sides again, trying to discover something new in the characters to try at the next reading. Gradually I sensed the arrival of others. Joyce and Jackie came back, asked if anything had happened. No, I said, though I thought it would be any moment now as there seemed to be sounds emanating from out front. So we sat, smelling the theatre. The glamour, the mystery were all in my head, they certainly didn't exist backstage at that moment. The stage was bare, the wings dark and musty. If I could just be a part of it, really a part of it! Finally the stage manager walked out on stage and Sam Jaffe, the star of the show, joined us from the orchestra. A wonderful actor, a kindly face, but I could only see Gunga Din, his great movie role, as I looked at him. We were introduced one by one, and one by one asked to read a scene with him. Kaufman asked Jackie to read Maud, me Adele, and Joyce Agatha. It was my first reading with a professional actor — all the others had been with the stage manager. Jaffe read with authority and grace, and with accompanying gestures. I was mesmerized and much too tense to judge which of us auditioners was good or why, I only sensed something special was going on. Kaufman asked us to line up alone, then with Sam Jaffe. Wouldn't someone say something definitely, please! My nerves could take no more. We three girls retired to the wings once again while another conference took place. We didn't exchange a word — we were all so tense, we each wanted a part so badly. There was nothing to do, nothing — life in the theatre is one enormous wait. At last a signal to Jackie Gately to go onstage. Joyce and I were left to wait. Finally Jackie came off talking to the stage manager, looking happy. She must have gotten something. Next Joyce was summoned. It was really beyond bearing for me. I was quivering, I felt sick. Another interminable wait. Then Joyce emerged the same way Jackie had, but she did give me a glance, was smiling, *she* must have gotten something. Well, it wouldn't be long now, at least I would know. But why had I been kept for last? There loomed in the back of my mind the possibility of being told I wasn't quite right for the part, but in the nicest way, the Messrs Gordon and Kaufman being the kind of gentlemen they were. At last the stage manager asked me to walk onstage. I tried to bluff myself into positive thinking. I was asked to step downstage, the better to see the faces who were to determine my future. George Kaufman looked up at me with a smile, saying, 'Congratulations, you've got the part,' and Max Gordon, coming down to the apron, 'See, I told you I'd find something in one of my plays for you.' I couldn't believe it, was it really true, would no one change his mind? Oh God, let me out of there before they did. My first speaking part in a Broadway show, produced by Max Gordon, directed by George S. Kaufman. It wasn't so bad to be a little Jewish girl, now was it? As a matter of fact, it was the best possible thing to be. Oh, was I happy!

I stopped at the stage manager's desk after thanking them all profusely and telling them I'd never let them down. He took my address and phone number again, said he'd get in touch with me about rehearsals, wardrobe, etc., and did I have an agent? An agent — what was that? I knew nothing about actors' agents then — they were not considered as important for beginners as they are now.

I guess I walked out of the stage door, I really don't remember. I immediately felt I had an identity, this was my theatre, we would probably rehearse here. I knew absolutely nothing about rehearsal pay, out-of-town salary — I signed on at minimum, which was then fifty dollars a week.

It had to be Walgreen's before I took the Eighth Avenue bus and headed for home. Just to see if anyone was there, Fred maybe. No one was. Wait till I told Mother and Grandma. They would be thrilled. Well, Mother would be. Grandma would be happy I had a job so I could help Mother with expenses, but she didn't put much store in acting as a profession. Questionable people, actors — unreliable, immoral, all the obvious feelings and reactions to a world she had never been exposed to and didn't understand. But Mother never faltered in her encourage-

ment of me and belief that I could succeed.

As soon as I got home, I rushed to the
phone to call Betty Kalb. I told her every
detail, every nuance in Kaufman's dialogue, Max Gordon's. I would tell it many
times over, never tiring of the moment, the
magic moment, when they said, 'You've
got the part.' Life could be good, couldn't
it! The elation that coursed through my entire body made me understand what being
five feet off the ground truly felt like. Was
there anything that could match the joy of
that day?

At last Mother came home from work. I
threw my arms around her, sat her down,
and told her every syllable that had passed
anybody's lips that day. Mother was not
one to jump up and down — she was sane,
and years of disappointments and hard
work had taught her to close in rather than
open out. But she was happy for me, she
wanted me to have it all and knew that I
could and would. That I could fulfill that
promise for her meant everything to me,
that her faith and support and self-depriva-
tion should not have been in vain. She had
had little pleasure in her life except me.

I called Grandma at Charlie and
Rosalie's, where she was staying. Even she
was happy, and, as I had guessed, what
pleased her most about it was the steady

job, the weekly income. What she didn't know, of course, was that rehearsal pay was less than salary — but she didn't have to know that.

I went to sleep that night knowing I was an actress, that I knew something and felt something no one else knew or felt. I had it all figured out, of course, how during rehearsals Kaufman and Gordon would see how talented I was, how when we opened I would make a special impression, be singled out, get a leading role in another play, and have my name in lights in no time. Having one's name in lights was so very important, part of acceptance. Part of 'Cinderella' and every other fairy tale we've ever read. Also part of having an identity — proof positive of making it. My need for favor, esteem, approbation was inordinate.

The next day I went to Max Gordon's office in the Lyceum Theatre, smiling happily as I walked from Eighth Avenue and 44th Street, past Sardi's — no more selling of *Actor's Cue*, I thought — past Walgreen's to Seventh Avenue with my secret. I suppose I wore an air of confidence unfamiliar in me. Confidence born of approval, of course — that hasn't changed. The Gordon office was alive with the coming production. I asked if

I might have a script. I thanked Gordon again and hugged him in gratitude. He said the contracts would be ready the following week and rehearsals would begin in about two weeks' time, that I would hear from the stage manager about measurements for costumes, etc.

Of course I had to tell Paul Lukas. 'See,' he said, 'I was right to tell you not to go on the road with *Claudia*. If you had, this wouldn't have happened. Now you have an opportunity to work with a great director and producer and really learn something.'

For the next two weeks I spent my time reading and rereading the play, reading my lines to a mirror from all angles and dreaming the hours away as Adele Stanley. I continued my Monday-night hostess job at the Stage Door Canteen, had my coffee in Walgreen's basement — with Fred Spooner, with Betty Kalb — but my attitude had changed. It was no longer 'When will I get a part, what will I do if I don't find something soon, who's casting what?' Rather it was 'I've got a part, in a play being produced by Max Gordon, directed by George S. Kaufman.' Everyone was congratulating me, my actor and usher friends. Buzz Meredith had called me and I told him about it — he was coming to town in a couple of weeks. I wrote Kirk about it. Leo Shull and I agreed that selling *Actor's Cue* outside Sardi's hadn't been such a dumb thing to do. I didn't think the time would ever pass until rehearsals began, but it did. Time always does.

I got the call to come to Max Gordon's office for the signing of the contracts the week of August 8. Rehearsals were to start August 15. My contract was basic Equity minimum, written in language I did not understand then and do not understand now. I trusted Max Gordon and I was right. He was one of the few producers I have ever known who told the truth and who cared about quality. I gave my copy of the contract to my Uncle Jack, who kept it in his files for me. It promised me whatever the going rate for rehearsal was at the time, fifty dollars per week when we went out of town, and minimum daily living expenses on the road. We were to open in Wilmington, Delaware, on September 18, play one preview and four performances; then the Colonial Theater in Washington, D.C., for two weeks and the Wilbur in Boston for two, then the Big Street — Broadway.

On the first day of rehearsal I was a wreck. Christ, I had the part, why was I so damn nervous? But I felt terrific at the start of the day. At the stage door of the Lyceum Theatre, the familiar face of the stage manager. New scripts were passed out, as there had been some changes. I saw Joyce Gates and Jacqueline Gately; we were all introduced to Dorothy Peterson, who played Mrs Ladd, the professor's wife; to Sam Jaffe, the star. George Kaufman was onstage, Arthur Sheekman and the other authors, Ruth and Augustus Goetz, were onstage, Max Gordon was onstage. Chairs were placed along three sides of two long tables, where we were all told to sit. Kaufman welcomed us, told us we would just read through the play today, become familiar with one another and the parts we were playing, and tomorrow we'd start moving around. So the reading began. I kept taking deep breaths, telling myself to be calm, face buried in my script, thinking of everything but the character I was playing, trying not to shake or at least not to show that I was and praying that my voice would not quiver when the time came. The pros seemed very much in control, started to mark their scripts. Even at this reading there was a suggestion of what their characters would be like. My first cue came and a sound came out, not a true vocal sound, a totally forgettable sound. The other girls didn't sound like that. I was shaking so, I felt sick. I kept my head down, didn't dare look in the direction of Kaufman, the authors, or even the other actors. Well, it had to get better, God knows I couldn't sound worse. We got through the first act, took a ten-minute break, the beginning of coffee in paper cups. I started then as I've continued all through my life — telling everyone how nervous I was, hoping that talking about it would make it go away. It doesn't. It makes it worse. Later you discover that everyone is nervous. All actors are terrified — they just learn how to control it.

The second read-through was easier, but not by much for me. At day's end George thanked us all, told us he'd see us tomorrow. I apologized for my nerves — he said, 'Don't worry, we have three weeks of rehearsal, no one expects perfection the first day, there's time. Take it easy.' Of course I had also learned that the first five days of rehearsal are a trial period for an actor — or can be. Any time during that period the producer or director can decide to replace you with no obligation on their part. So I'd gotten the job, but until four more days had passed, disaster could strike. I went home, exhausted by my apprehensions and anxieties, started marking my script and studying my lines. The next day I'd have to stand up — walk around — without the protection of a table in front of me and people close on either side. On day number two I was there before ten. The stage manager was onstage putting tape on the floor to mark off the room — where the walls would be — and placing chairs opposite each other to signify a door, other chairs for a sofa, a window, etc. Immediately we had to begin to imagine where everything would be — what it might look like. Make-believe was beginning.

So the rehearsals went smoothly for the next three days. I began to make a bit more sense with my part. I'd sneak looks at Kaufman, Sheekman, the Goetzes to see if they disapproved. Every time they whispered or glanced in my direction I thought the end was near. George would pace up and down the center aisle with his arms bent and his hands under his armpits, wearing a terrible squinting expression that made him look as though he hated everything. He would always speak softly and individually to the actors when giving direction. If there was something in particular he wanted to say, he'd come onstage, put his arm around the actor's shoulder, walk him off to one side and tell him what he wanted. It is the most graceful way of directing I have ever seen. No wonder he had been so successful and highly thought of — he did not embarrass or humiliate the actors, he instilled trust, and they gave their best to him. And he'd make a joke every now and then. One day he walked down the center aisle, to the edge of the stage and whispered, 'There's a Japanese spy in the house.' All who understood laughed. He meant that Lee Shubert — one of the famed theatre owners — was in the back of the house. Shubert wore an inscrutable expression and sneaked around a lot. Clearly he was not a popular fellow. Just as clearly Kaufman was — the actors warmed to him, though Sam Jaffe seemed to be having some difficulty. Not acting difficulty, but something was not quite right. Each of us ingenues had to curtsy to him in the play — a formality observed as we started our day's lessons. I remember how Sam Jaffe took my hand and pulled me down to a low curtsy and kept me there until he pulled me up. I did as he wanted — too scared not to.

On the fifth day of rehearsal we all streamed back after the lunch break. George Kaufman, in the orchestra, beckoned to me to come over to him. 'Oh God,' I thought, 'this is it. He doesn't like me in the part. I won't do. Oh, I'll die right here and now!' I nervously (what else?) walked downstage. He motioned me to squat down so he could talk to me. 'Betty — we've been thinking . . .' It never occurred to him I would be in such a panic, so unsure of myself that I would be telling myself, 'Oh, this is it. I'm going to

be fired! Don't cry now, whatever you do.'
'We've talked it over — Arthur, Ruth and Gus, and myself — and we'd like you to try reading Maud instead of Adele. You and Jackie switch parts for the rest of the day.'

'Was I doing something wrong, Mr Kaufman?'

He must have sensed my panic. 'For heaven's sake, no. We just think the other part is better for you — better for the play.'

'Of course,' I said. I felt some relief, didn't totally fall apart, managed to stand up and prepare myself for the switch. He must have been right about my playing Maud, for I remember things about her and nothing about Adele. At the end of the day George came up to me and said, 'You stick with Maud, it's much better this way.' And I did and it was.

So the rehearsals continued into the second week and so did I. They went smoothly. I was very happy playing Maud, but Sam Jaffe and Kaufman did not seem to be getting along. We supporting players were not privy to the facts, but we sensed it. A few days before we were to leave for Wilmington it happened. We arrived for rehearsal one morning and Kaufman announced that by mutual agreement Sam Jaffe had withdrawn. After much thought as to whether they should recast, they had decided to let the understudy, Reynolds Evans, play the part for the day and then make a final decision. What a burden for poor Reynolds Evans! All I cared about was that the play must continue. My first speaking part — I had to be heard on Broadway, otherwise how would I get those fabulous notices I had planned in my fantasies?

We got through the morning. The authors, producer, and director had a lengthy luncheon meeting, of course — then we continued through the afternoon. George worked with Reynolds Evans, kindly and helpfully as always. It was a relief to take the focus off oneself and concentrate on someone else. At the end of the second day with Reynolds we were asked to gather onstage. George then made the announcement: they were going all the way with Evans and felt sure that he would do the job well and that the play would be a success. That led to a round of applause for Reynolds, who was all smiles. So it would go on, and we were all pulling for him, the play, Kaufman, and our jobs. The unity that exists in the theatre is what makes it the most special place on earth. Not in any other branch of the entertainment world does one get the sense of everyone pulling for the success of the whole. It's a coopera-

tive effort, an exchange between people —
that's what's important, that's what we all
love about it. . . . At least that's what the
pros love about it.

Finally came the dress rehearsal and a
chance to put on make-up. To put to practical use some of those hours spent at the
American Academy. It was so exciting —
the smell of the greasepaint. Corny but
true. Greasepaint was still being used, and
I bought all the necessary paraphernalia. It
was great to be in make-up and costume
and see everyone else that way — to work
with props. We were not going to rehearse
on the actual set until Wilmington, but we
all were realizing what we would have to
do then, and I thought it was the best play
in the world. I'd forgotten I had thought
Johnny 2 x 4 was the best play in the world
too — it was, I guess, until it opened.

Travel day was the following day — we
were all to meet at Penn Station. Oh, glorious excitement! We all said, 'See you in
Wilmington . . . see you at the station . . .
see you!' I met Fred Spooner for a cup of
coffee before heading home to pack, and of
course Betty Kalb was there as well —
Walgreen's being 'there.' I was off on my
first real adventure in the theatre, the first
rung on the ladder — it was actually happening. Fred and Betty kissed me goodbye,
wished me luck.

Of course I had no luggage of my own, so used a suitcase of Mother's. I didn't have much to take, but I packed what I had — one good dress, slacks, sweaters, skirt. I had never been anywhere without her but summer camp or school. Here I was going off on my own a few days before my eighteenth birthday on September 16, still a minor. Oh, it was a lot to absorb. Also, Buzz Meredith had called me. He was still in the Army and hadn't got to New York during the rehearsal period, but he wanted to wish me luck — asked what theatre I was opening in, what day, and where in Washington. Said I must see the Lincoln Memorial by moonlight, and if he was there while I was, he'd take me. It was all too much to hope for.

Mother, of course, was worried that her baby might fall prey to theatrical wolves. 'Remember — never give anything away. No man really wants that. Every man wants his wife to be a virgin when he marries her.' My 'nice Jewish girl' upbringing pounded into my head constantly. 'Keep your distance — darling.'

I slept and dreamed all the right dreams. Up at dawn the next day. I said goodbye to Grandma, Charlie and Rosalie, Jack and Vera, Renee and Bill by phone. Mother and I were a little weepy — after all, it was my first step toward leaving the nest. Not final, but it was the beginning and we both knew it. Yet the truth is that, though I saw myself living alone or sharing an apartment like a big girl, a serious life without my mother had not really occurred to me.

At the station the assistant stage manager was waiting at the appointed gate and the company had begun to gather. There was anticipation in the air — everyone was in high spirits, laughing, joking — even the most experienced performers could only feel optimistic at a new beginning. Anything was possible, and with that happy attitude we boarded the train. A family of actors all going to make it or not, together. Interdependent. No one could do it alone.

We arrived at Wilmington and went to the hotel next door to the Playhouse Theatre. We were to report to the theatre that evening, but I went right over — I didn't want to miss a minute. They had begun to hang the set. There's nothing like a theatre as all the pieces of a play are being assembled. There are lights on the stage, the set designer and lighting designer and their assistants are at work, all sorts of technical directions are being given. It is the labor preceding childbirth. The cast was told to go to the lounge downstairs, where we would just run the play for lines. We wouldn't get on the stage until the next day, when the technical rehearsal would begin. Pictures of the company were to go up the next day — we'd been photographed in costume and make-up at the dress rehearsal in New York. So much was happening and going to happen, how could one sleep? The next day, September 15, was the day before my eighteenth birthday. What was I going to do to celebrate? Nothing, obviously — what better celebration than being in Wilmington, Delaware, doing what I was doing?

The technical went on all day and night. Every time a new character walked onstage he had to be lit — new scene, move from stage left to right, downstage to up. It's a slow process. When I wasn't in a scene I sat in the orchestra watching. I loved being there. Of course I wanted to be around George Kaufman as much as possible. I worshipped him. Finally we were dismissed. George and Sheekman wished me happy dreams on my last night as a seventeen-year-old. I blushed, smiled, and said something funny and fresh, I suppose. I always seemed to be more knowing than I was. I actually knew nothing of life and of relationships — men and women together were a mystery to me. I had never been much exposed to such relationships in my childhood, so what I thought I knew was all imagination.

The next morning I was eighteen years

old! I looked in the mirror — same face, same flat chest. But I knew it was a milestone day — I could legally be served a drink in some places at eighteen, I could do almost everything but vote. I hopped out of bed. Usually I slept so soundly not even a fire would wake me, and for the first hour was always grumpy and very slow in coming to. But that day I did hop. Dressed, rushed downstairs for breakfast — there were telegrams from Mother and Grandma, Charlie and Rosalie, Jack and Vera, wishing me happy birthday. Everyone in the company wished me a happy birthday. Dorothy and Florence Sundstrom (semi-leading lady and funny) told me Arthur had been kidding George, saying, 'She's no longer jail bait — should we invite her out for a drink?' I was never invited, thank God — I didn't drink, and in no way would I have lived up to anyone's expectations.

And then, the next evening, the first preview with an audience. We were in our dressing rooms at 7:30 to start getting ready. Sitting at the make-up table, checking make-up. The voice comes over the loud-speaker: 'Half-hour, please — half-hour.' My heart skipped twelve beats — the first call from the stage manager, announcing that we had half an hour until curtain time. Then 'Fifteen minutes — fifteen minutes, please.' I was dressed and well on my way to my first set of shakes. 'Five minutes — five minutes.' I made sure I had everything, ran to the john at least five times in that half-hour, started toward the wings, stage left, for my props — I was to make my entrance carrying a few books. 'Places, please — places, please.' Total silence now — the curtain is raised — the play begins. The sound of dialogue emanating from the stage — audience reactions being heard for the first time — applause for Dorothy Peterson, familiar from films more than from theatre. I peeked through the curtain to see faceless forms in the audience — one always started out with a full house, especially out of town, I was told. My cue coming up. Maud appeared onstage as a daydreamer, reciting poetry — I think my opening line was 'The robbed who smiles steals something from the thief.' I took a deep, deep breath, held tightly to the books, and started to move. Knees knocking, I walked onstage and said my line. The audience began to laugh. I almost died — had I done something wrong? Was my slip showing? Oh God, what was Kaufman thinking? It was a comedy, they were supposed to laugh, but not when I made my entrance, as far as I knew.

I pressed on with the scene. I had to, of

course. Everything went fairly smoothly through the first act — introduction of characters, plot. At the interval I was given no answers. Everyone was so busy with costume changes — running to the ladies' — repairing make-up — general nerves — that there would be no discussion until after the performance. I did tell Florence I was nervous about that laugh — why had they reacted that way? She said not to worry, George would explain it when we all gathered for notes after the performance. 'Places, please.' So the second act began — which was more fun and was fraught with the problems of the main characters. All of us young girls got our instructions from the professor in that act, and at one moment when he was demonstrating how to enter a room and curtsy, Maud (me) said, 'Oh, isn't he the very personification of grace!' (Sigh.) The audience laughed at that too — not a belly laugh, mind you, but a laugh nonetheless. That should give a notion of my role. The play went on to the end, we took our calls — and I was just as nervous through those as at any other time. What a relief as we ripped off our costumes and threw on our street clothes to rush onstage for notes. Now I would have the answer to my opening laugh. George was sweet and kind as always — told us we'd done well — gave us the changes he wanted for the next night's opening — and did we have any questions? I was too shy to ask about my laugh in front of the entire company and decided to wait until the end. But the principals stayed on with George, so there was no opportunity for me. He hadn't said anything about it, so I assumed it was not disastrous, but I still wanted to know.

The next morning — 'Tonight will be my first real opening night' — the combination of nerves, excitement, apprehension, dreams. How wonderful to be an actress. There was nothing about it I didn't love, now that I had a job.

I went to the theatre — the only place I wanted to be — found George Kaufman and approached him. 'Mr Kaufman, could I ask you something, please? I was wondering why the audience laughed when I made my entrance last night.' He smiled and said, 'Well, as you know, Maud is a dreamer and you walk onstage, very tall and looking off into space, and say your line and this pleases the audience. It's a good warm laugh. Don't worry about it.' 'Of course,' I thought, 'that makes sense — most people moving around as in a dream can look funny.' I didn't know until much later that just the sight of me — this tall, gawky girl with her skirt to above the ankles, high button shoes, long blond hair and flat pancake hat — was funny. So they laughed.

Kaufman, Sheekman, and the Goetzes were almost always together, talking about something to do with the play. I can guess now what it was, but I certainly couldn't guess then. We got through the day by rehearsing — no time to sit and stew. There was so much to think about that even the shaking didn't begin until I started my make-up. I checked the mailbox on entering the theatre and found a few telegrams. From the family, of course, and one very unexpected one which read:

> You may as well start being a star in Wilmington as anywhere. So be good tonight.
>
> Buzz Meredith

Oh, I was ecstatic about that!

I went through the same panic as the night before with one difference: there were critics out front tonight. Which meant there'd be reviews tomorrow. There were — and they were mixed. The experienced actors all had known that some things would be changed as we went along, that's what tryouts are for. But they all believed in the play. Yet it was clear even to innocent me that there were problems. Of course they would be solved, but something was not quite right. Kaufman seemed preoccupied, and was always meeting with the authors and producers. Some changes were made each day — a new scene, some new dialogue, restaging — but nothing major until Washington, when we would have a day or two without performances while the set was being hung and lit.

Washington was another new world. First of all, it was a large, beautiful city — many hotels, so we wouldn't all be together. And it had the White House, in which a man I worshipped, Franklin Roosevelt, resided. As we weren't due for rehearsal until the following morning, we had a few hours to ourselves. Of course I wouldn't allow the day to end without at least seeing the Colonial Theatre — the stage, the backstage, the dressing rooms — but I told Joyce and Florence I'd be back in about an hour and then go with them to the theatre. I walked a bit and found a taxi and told the driver I wanted to go to the White House! I'll always remember seeing it for the first time. It sits far back from the street and isn't really beautiful, but *he* was in it and it was a hallowed place. I walked toward the gate gazing at the building as if I were in a church, scrutinizing the grounds, thinking, hoping, that maybe I'd see Mrs Roosevelt if not the President. Or maybe even Fala, his Scottie. Each time an automobile drove in or out of the gates my heart skipped a beat, but it was never F.D.R. or Eleanor or anyone recognizable to me. Still, I was thrilled to be walking around as much as I was allowed to — there were guards at every gate and you weren't supposed to linger for too long. I saw the Capitol dome and the Washington Monument in the distance, but I was saving the Lincoln Memorial for Buzz.

The days passed. I was still happy at being in a play and out of town, but I felt somewhat lost. Monday came as it always does and I felt better. We'd all be together again, working, creating — the nerves would start again and I'd feel alive again. I quickly ate my tiny breakfast and dashed over to the theatre. It was filled with life. The hum of preparation, expectation. Actors were going in and out of their dressing rooms, paper cups were filled with coffee — it was wonderful. George Kaufman arrived — our director, our leader, our security blanket. I felt good when he was there, certain that everything would be all right. We were given new scenes. George told us we would read them through, then work on them roughly, then onstage, then technical. A full rehearsal day. Scenes were passed around to the principals and the principal supporting actors. They sounded better than the old scenes, and as we started to stage them, they seemed funnier. This was what all those meetings had been about. New scenes always, or almost always, make actors feel more solid psychologically. For me at that time it seemed that change was improvement, and that improvement must lead to success. It wasn't that I'd expected disaster, but things hadn't seemed quite right. Anyway, the changes were thoroughly rehearsed, and another opening night was got through. The Washington reaction was not the same as Wilmington's. A different kind of audience, more sophisticated. They laughed, but in different places and not often enough. But there was still a laugh when I walked onstage. I guess I would have looked funny to anyone who saw the play anywhere.

We went for something to eat and waited for the reviews. Just some of the actors — not George, not Max Gordon or the authors. It was always very nervous-making, waiting for Judgment. Would they like it? Would they mention me? Most of us thinking the same worried thoughts. At long last the important Washington review. This one really mattered, it would affect the New York reception. It was a very mild reaction. The critic was pleased by some of it, but it didn't measure up to expectations; some good characters in it, and all the students were good, with special mention to 'Jackie Gately and Betty Bacall.' My name in a newspaper! Something to cut out and take home to Mother. The other papers didn't mention me and were far from crazy about the play. It wasn't terrible, they said — it just wasn't anything definite enough, didn't succeed enough in its concept. But with Kaufman's knowledge and talent it could be fixed.

The next night at the theatre I received a call from Buzz. Had I seen the Lincoln Memorial yet? No. Okay, I'll take you tonight after the show. I hung up, jumped up and down like a child with a great new toy. Buzz was there! He must just like me a little bit.

No one else was jumping for joy at the theatre. Nothing specific was said, but the more experienced actors were all aware of something. I couldn't imagine what it might be — perhaps a cast change? No one would tell me anything. The general drift was that the play was in trouble.

Buzz picked me up after the performance, and when we emerged from the theatre, what was waiting but a horse and buggy! What a way to go to the Lincoln Memorial! I laughed, and loved it. Could anything in life be better than the combination of Lincoln, Buzz Meredith, and a horse and buggy? Not for me on that night. We approached the Washington Monument, passed the pool in front of it, and stopped at the foot of the Lincoln Memorial. It was a clear, moonlit night. We started to climb the steps, and as we approached the top, there were shafts of light coming from the inside. There were white marble pillars — it is all white — and what I saw when I reached the top made me gasp. There, sitting in a chair, was Abraham Lincoln, looking as though he were about to rise. It was awesome — an extraordinary emotional experience. And reassuring. One felt such tremendous pride in America — that everything was possible. Nothing I've seen since has affected me the way that monument did. And still does.

The next night at the theatre there was no George Kaufman around. We hadn't had a rehearsal and I still didn't know what was going on. There were meetings that night. What did they talk about at all those meetings? The next day Florence told me. She and Dorothy had seen George and he had said we were going to close after our Washington run. I burst into tears. It had never occurred to me that this might happen. I'd never dreamed that we would not open in New York. That was my second heartbreak in the theatre. I cried and cried, and when I cry I am a sight to see. Swollen red eyes, a mess! Florence and Dorothy tried to comfort me, telling me not to say anything until an official announcement was made. I knew that if I met anyone else in the cast, they'd know in a minute just by looking at me. So I went back to the Lincoln Memorial.

It was a crisp, clear day. When I got to the Memorial quite a few people were there, but everyone was whispering. It was too overwhelming to do anything else. Lincoln was still in his chair, still looking at me, eyes following me as I moved. I went over to one side to see if he might turn his head. He didn't. I read the speeches inscribed there — the Gettysburg Address on one side, the Second Inaugural Address on the other — and was transported again, my own sorrow pushed to the back of my mind for the moment. I stayed for almost an hour, but as I walked down the steps and away from him, my own pain came to the fore again.

Would I see George that evening? When would everybody be told? I'd have to call Mother and give her the bad news. All dreams shattered once more. When I got to the theatre, I found a letter in my box at the stage door. It was addressed to 'Peggy Bacall,' on Hotel Carlton stationery. It said,

Dear Peggy,
I suppose you know the play is closing

until it gets fixed. I hope there will be
another, or maybe this one all over again.

George

He didn't know my name, but it was kind
of him and thoughtful to write me a note.
No one else got one. I would treasure it,
right name or wrong name.

The cast was gathering onstage. The
stage manager stood there and grimly announced that the closing notice would be
put up tonight. There was going to be a rewrite of the play. Messrs Kaufman,
Gordon, Sheekman, and the Goetzes were
very sorry, thanked us all, and hoped we
would all be together soon again. That
softened the blow a bit — for a novice like
me. There was at least hope, hope that it
would all happen again and soon. The pros
were not surprised, they said sure it might
reopen, but who knew when? Better not
count on it. Could it all fall apart so
quickly, all that work, the sets, costumes,
lighting, actors? All those people out of
work so quickly? Yes, it could.

The drama of performing the play — a
comedy in particular — knowing it was
going to close. We had ten more shows.
That's what they meant when they said the
show must go on. How valiant the actors
were, I thought. The audience would never
guess. The company was working just as

hard, caring just as much. I realized then what a noble profession the acting profession is, what terrific people professionals are. What a dramatic situation for an imagination like mine! Smiling through tears, drama within drama within drama. Made to order for the likes of me.

Was it all over? I had taken so long, I thought, to get this part. Would it be another year before I got another?

We all went for a snack after the show, building each other up, rehashing what all those past meetings had meant, trying to be hopeful about the play being done again. It was still only the beginning of October, maybe there would be plays casting for January openings. Anything could happen! We said good night sadly, we all felt closer to each other. Nothing like disaster to bring people together.

In my room I went over and over what had happened. I read and reread George's note, clinging to the hope of a new play or this one again. I would savor every day onstage for the next eight days and try not to feel totally defeated at the end of that time.

I called Mother, told her we were closing for a while, they thought it was wiser to rewrite the play and then call us all back, it probably wouldn't take more than a few weeks. Being totally unknowledgeable about the theatre, she believed me, and I was so convincing, I did too. 'Anyway, I'll be home soon and I miss you.' She was wonderful as always. She knew how disappointed I was, said, 'Keep your chin up, you'll be back at work in no time.' So we buoyed each other up on mutual love and no reality.

The ten performances came and went. We packed up Saturday night — make-up, personal effects back at the hotel — but not heading for Boston, our next stop on the road to success. Instead, back home to our failure. Some of us promised to keep in touch, we'd see each other soon, after the rewrite, meantime good luck. Goodbye Washington, goodbye Roosevelt, goodbye Lincoln . . . goodbye hope. Hello despair.

At least I had been mentioned in a review. At least George had written me a personal note — that might help the next time around. Eighteen can be knocked down, but eighteen doesn't stay down for long.

I arrived home, showed Mother my clipping, my note from Kaufman. I called Charlie and Grandma, they were loving and sweet. My family made me feel safe. Charlie was full of encouragement and his usual rhymes: 'Don't be disheartened, you've only just started, I can see from afar, you will be a star.' I adored him.

The next day I went to Max Gordon's

139

office. He was warm, apologized for the way things had turned out, and said the play might come to pass again. He told me I had looked very good in the play and that everyone involved had liked me. But if a job came up, take it; *Franklin Street* would not be done again quickly. Keep in touch with him and his office, and let him know how I was faring. That was the end of that chapter.

Back to Walgreen's, back to the casting lists in *Actor's Cue.* Of course I told Betty Kalb and other friends that the play was going to be done again. I made it all sound more hopeful than it was, made my meeting with Buzz more dramatic, my conversations with Kaufman the same. I was the only one who had ever been on the road, after all — I knew things they didn't know. That made me feel better. My fantasy world was a marvel. It allowed me to laugh and joke, to feel hope again.

Back to pounding pavements. I could not think in terms of going back to the garment center or ushering, though I surely would need the money soon. I had saved something from the tour — there hadn't been much to save, but maybe it would get me through until the next job.

It was not easy being on the outside once

more. Funny how you get the feeling that once you have a part in a play the work will never stop. Was that ever a wrong feeling — as I would spend the next thirty years discovering! At least I had one more credit — and a good one — when I went into producers' offices, but that mattered not at all if there were no parts.

George Kaufman was casting a new play — Well, there must be something for me in it! I went charging up to Max Gordon's office, asking where I could find George. Couldn't I read the play, couldn't I at least see him? He was never around when I was, so I had to content myself with leaving messages with everyone in sight. And hounding the office, making a general pest of myself.

One day I received a letter in the mail. The heading in red, center of the page:

George S. Kaufman
410 Park Avenue
New York City

Wednesday October 28

Dear Betty Bacall —
I'm not so hard to reach as all that — the Lyceum Theatre or a note here (above). There's nothing near your age in the play, so there's nothing I can do

about that. But there ought to be another play sometime and I'll always try hard.

The best of wishes, and cheer up. It can happen any minute.

George Kaufman

That gave me such a lift, though it didn't mean a job or even an audition; it did mean that he thought enough of me to write, and something might come along one day and he'd always give me a chance!

One Saturday morning in 1942, Mother and Rosalie took me to the Capitol Theatre to see a movie called *Casablanca*. We all loved it, and Rosalie was mad about Humphrey Bogart. I thought he was good in it, but mad about him? Not at all. She thought he was sexy. I thought she was crazy. Mother liked him, though not as much as she liked Chester Morris, who she thought was *really* sexy — or Ricardo Cortez, her second favorite. I couldn't understand Rosalie's thinking at all. Bogart didn't vaguely resemble Leslie Howard. Not in any way. So much for my judgment at that time.

Sometime in November of that year I met an English writer named Timothy Brooke. He was very tall, very thin, very charming and funny — a good deal older than I, but we got along well. There was no attraction on my part, I just enjoyed his company tremendously, I'd never met anyone like him. He'd lived in America for many years, knew all sorts of people like Evalyn Walsh McLean, who owned the Hope Diamond, Mabel Mercer, Nicolas de Gunzburg, who was an editor of *Harper's Bazaar*. That fact and his growing attachment to me started the chain of circumstances that would reshape my life. Timothy didn't have much money, but enough to take me to Tony's, a little club in the east Fifties where Mabel Mercer sang. It was a very popular club, and she was adored by Europeans, Americans, anyone who knew Paris, anyone romantic, all musicians. She would sit on a wooden stool with a piano behind her, a light on her, and bouquets and tables all around. That was my first taste of nostalgia.

One night at Tony's, Timothy said he had told Nicky de Gunzburg about me. Perhaps I could be used in photographic modeling. Tim thought Nicky might be there that evening, so I should be prepared. Wouldn't that be wonderful? I thought. Not a nine-to-five job, but I'd make enough money and still be free to pound those theatrical pavements. As promised, Nicky de Gunzburg did turn up — a dapper, friendly, charming man —

a baron! Another first for me.

He came over to the table and Tim introduced me — 'This is the girl I've been talking to you about.' Nicky (he wasn't Nicky to me for a long time) said, 'If you will come to my office tomorrow, I'll send you over to one of our fashion editors to see if she can use you.' I thanked him fervently (I did everything fervently) and said I'd see him the following day.

The following day I was just as nervous as if I were trying out for a play. Nicky told me the fashion editor's name was Diana Vreeland — he'd mentioned me to her and we would go over to her office. A secretary said we could go in to where an extraordinary-looking woman sat at a desk covered with papers, photographs, boxes with bits and pieces of jewelry, scarves. She was very thin. Black hair combed straight back, turned under and held in place by a black net snood with a flat band on top. She was wearing a black skirt, a black sweater, and black ankle boots. She had white skin, brown eyes, red mouth, long nose, pink cheeks, lovely teeth, long fingernails painted dark red. Definitely an original. Very direct in manner and speech. She stood up, shook my hand, looked at my face — with her hand under my chin, turned it to the right and to the left. She saw I was awkward, not made up, far from

144

the perfect model. She asked me what I'd done before, I told her — it was practically nothing and some time back. She said, 'I'd like Louise Dahl-Wolfe to see you. We're having a sitting tomorrow — could you come to the studio? It won't take long.' I said, 'Of course I could.' I was scared to death. The efficiency and matter-of-factness of the whole magazine operation and particularly of Mrs Vreeland were intimidating. I'd never been in the offices of so grand and powerful a fashion magazine as *Harper's Bazaar*. I hadn't a clue what Mrs Vreeland's reaction to me had been. I knew I felt like a gawk — never thought I was a beauty, so I never really expected too much. I just hoped.

The next day I went to the appointed studio at the appointed time. There was a sort of dressing room, rather like the theatre — make-up lights around mirrors, canvas chairs, clothes on hangers, and boxes of accessories, all of which, I was to learn, were permanent fixtures at fashion sittings. The studio was a large room with lights, backings — and Dahl-Wolfe and her cameras. She was a rather short, stocky woman whose sandy hair was pulled up tight in a bun or braid on the top of her head. A friendly, open woman who was number one in her profession. Diana Vreeland was there and brought me in to meet her. Dahl-Wolfe said, 'Let's take a few shots first.' She wanted to see what her camera could catch. I had no makeup on, but she said this wasn't a serious sitting, it was just for her, really. She had me stand in the middle of the studio floor. I was a basket case of nerves. She had her Rolleiflex camera around her neck — that was her favorite camera — and another one on a tripod. She put the lights where she wanted them and through my twitching said, 'Look left . . . look right . . . turn to the right and look over your shoulder . . . left profile.' She asked me about myself, snapping away very quickly as she talked. There was no real posing, she just caught me as I fell and as she wanted it. It was much less painful than any other modeling I had done. I was still shaking — I couldn't seem to find a way out of that. The only thing that ever helped was for me to talk — to make jokes — and to not stand still for too long. I didn't dare go too far, as I was a stranger in those parts and wasn't sure what their reaction would be. But it was my nature to try to make people laugh or at least smile, and it eased my twitching mouth, made me feel more an actress, less a model.

After about half an hour Mrs Vreeland thanked me and asked me to leave my phone number. Did I work through an agency? Not anymore. 'We'll call you as soon as we go over our layouts.' I made some stunning remark like 'I hope the camera will still work after it's looked at me.' Knocking myself out of the box before anyone else did. I didn't much like the idea of modeling, though it might be fun for a while, but I did like the two women — even though they'd frightened me a little.

A couple of days later Diana Vreeland called and asked if I could come in the next Tuesday to pose. I had the weekend ahead of me — to rest up and talk about this until I drove everyone mad. My mother always said, 'The trouble with you is you have a one-track mind. When you make up your mind about one thing, you erase everything else.' But Tuesday came at last and off I went. Mrs Wolfe was there — and Mrs Vreeland. She put a suit on me, told me which make-up to use — but very little. 'Betty, I don't want to change your look.' (Whatever *that* was.) When all was done she put a scarf round my neck — knew just how to tie it, a little off-center — and I was ready for my first sitting for *Harper's Bazaar*. From that day on, my life would take a different course.

It was fun working with those two ladies. Diana would be there through the sitting, making sure the clothes were on straight, that the hair was the way she wanted it. Louise would snap away. They worked perfectly together.

I'd say almost anything that came into my head — about acting, the theatre, my being an usher. A lot of it made them laugh — though all through it, Dahl-Wolfe never looked up from the camera, never really took her mind off what she was doing. A total professional. I asked what issue the pictures might be in — they thought probably January. Almost two months ahead — that was the way those magazines worked.

The pictures were okay, I was told. Good enough to use. Then things began to move. I posed in glorious apartments — one was Helena Rubinstein's; on a bathtub in a one-piece jersey undergarment looking over my shoulder; on a sofa in a jumpsuit (a jumpsuit in 1942!); sewing; standing by a window in a slip; wearing hats in an antique shop; in a printer's shop. I loved being with Louise and Diana — felt comfortable — and I was getting paid ten dollars an hour.

Once I was sent to Hoyningen-Huené, one of the great fashion photographers of the day. His work methods could not have been more different from Dahl-Wolfe's. I was standing in a tailored suit; he posed me like a statue. 'Put your left foot forward a bit — turn the toe out — shoulders straight and out front — head down, a little to the right. Hold very still.' Agony, every part of my body was going in a different direction. Whenever he said, 'Hold still,' I started to shake. I was a disaster. He was not pleased. *I* was not pleased. Not pleased? I was suffering. I hated him. The tenser I became, the more strained my facial expression. 'I'll never work again — I couldn't be a model, not this kind of model.' I was not a mannequin. Somehow the sitting came to a close. I doubted that Huené had got even one picture he could use. Certainly I'd never work for him again — wait till Diana Vreeland heard from him! I wanted to tell her first, but didn't feel secure enough with her; I'd just have to wait and see what happened. Years later I met Georges Huené again at George Cukor's house and reminded him of that day. He turned out to be a very pleasant man, and we laughed about my fright and my inability to cope. We could then — it was over for both of us.

Diana asked me if I could go to St Augustine, Florida, for two weeks of pictures for the May issue. She'd take another girl along — Eileen McLory, a nice girl and good model whom I knew a little — and Dahl-Wolfe. Would I ask my mother? Diana would be happy to explain it all to her.

I was excited — I'd never been to St Augustine, the oldest, and one of the quaintest cities in America. I rushed to tell Mother, who, of course, was pleased for me but who, of course, wanted to be assured by Mrs Vreeland that I would be well looked after. There was a war on, St Augustine was on the sea, and there'd be a lot of servicemen around. Still so protected at eighteen. My old-fashioned mother. She spoke with Mrs Vreeland and, having had her fears and apprehensions put to rest, agreed that I could go.

So I packed for my first location work — it was the first week in December and we'd be returning to New York by the 20th or 21st. We boarded the train — Diana Vreeland, Louise Dahl-Wolfe, and her husband, Mike, Eileen McLory and myself, plus boxes of film, reflectors, Louise's cameras. Everything very compactly put together for travel. All pictures were to be shot outside in natural light, so we'd have to start early in the morning.

In Florida the air was balmy, palm trees everywhere, tropical in feeling, so different from New York. We arrived at the recommended hotel, which turned out to be the ninth-best hotel in St Augustine. It and all the others were being taken over by the Seabees. Eileen and I shared one room. Diana had hers — the Wolfes theirs. The town was charming — horses and carriages, great, burly, friendly black men with top hats driving them. The place had not been spoiled by what is laughingly known as progress — all the old torn down to make way for the new, the shiny, the ugly.

I remember going into Diana Vreeland's room one evening as she was sitting in her one-piece undergarment — not a girdle, it was all easy, like thin knitted cotton or wool. She was rolling her hair with eau de cologne — she found it dried quickly, worked well. We talked of how the work was going. I talked more of my ambitions, my dreams. We talked of the hotel. More Seabees were moving in — she said to pay no attention to the young freckled-faced porter who seemed drunk on sherry. Eileen and I were not to wander around on our own, especially as the evening approached.

The work was finally done and we were to leave the next evening on the night train for New York. Diana told me I was to pretend to be her pregnant daughter — that was the only way we'd got our tickets, because servicemen had priority. I didn't know until years later that she'd been sitting in the hotel bar near the president of the railroad and overheard his name. And the next day she'd walked two and a half miles in the rain to the train station and told her sad story to someone there — her little girl was going to have a baby; the railroad president, a good friend, had told her to mention his name when necessary, and of course she realized the Armed Forces had priority — there was a war on — there were five of us — it was *so* important for her little girl. Talk of acting — what a character! She got the tickets. They must have bumped someone. All Diana knew was that she'd told my mother she'd get me back and that's what she aimed to do. That's why she flourished. Talent — her gift of creativity — is not enough — determination, perseverance, resolution, that's what makes the difference.

It was a very funny scene. The train jammed with servicemen heading home for Christmas, not too many civilians in sight. Our group boarding the train — me leaning on Diana for benefit of porters, conductors, God knows who — playing the death scene from *Camille* — trying to be brave — feeling a bit faint — where did I ever get that idea of pregnancy? Diana saying, 'There, there, dear. Take it easy now, you have to rest.' Not the best acting I'd ever seen — we were both overdoing it. Finally got into a seat — berths were going to be made up before dinner or during. Dinner was a mess. As the train was so jammed, we didn't dare leave all the seats untended, so I sat in my 'weakened' condition while Diana and Eileen scrounged for food. Diana could certainly function. She did what had to be done. No wonder she had so much clout in the fashion-magazine world. They came up with something finally — enough — and word was passing through the train that Martha Raye was in the club car entertaining the servicemen. She had been traveling overseas to do that. I was dying to see her — anybody connected with show business gave me a boost. I was determined to get to that club car. Diana was determined that I shouldn't — 'Remember you are not very well, Betty — you must think of the baby.' We might be put off the train at any stop if we were discovered. 'I need to get my mind off myself for a while, Mother.' I got to that club car. Martha Raye was sitting with a drink in her hand, talking to everyone in the car, cracking jokes, singing songs. I huddled in a corner and never took my eyes off her until finally, not to press my luck, I consented to go back to the berth with Diana. It must have been about two in the morning when I got to bed, being carefully and noisily, for the porters' benefit, tucked in by my 'mother.'

The January issue of *Harper's Bazaar* was on the stands at the end of December and many copies were sold to the Bacalls and Weinsteins of the world. Only one picture, but it was my first in a national magazine and everyone cared about that. There would be more in the February issue. Diana had told me I'd be very happy with those. I had posed in white blouses. It was to be a double-page spread — the other models were Martha Scott, who'd had a great success in *Our Town*, and Margaret Hayes, a promising young actress.

In January I posed in a blue suit with an off-the-face hat, standing before a window with 'American Red Cross Blood Donor Service' lettered on it. It was a color picture and would be a full page.

Mid-January Diana showed me the February issue of *Bazaar*. There on the double-page spread of the two actresses and me in blouses, alongside one of my pictures was printed: 'Worn by the young actress, Betty Becall' (my name misspelled, but who cared?).

I almost fainted, I was so happy. I hugged Diana — hugged everyone in sight. You'd have thought my name was up in lights — it *was* my name, in print, even spelled wrong, and that would do for the time being.

About mid-February Diana called my mother to tell her there were stacks of letters on her desk asking who I was and where I could be reached. She said, 'Listen, Mrs Bacall, I think Betty's too young to make these decisions, so I'm sending it all on to you.' Diana was always terrific to me and about me. She was so smart, had such wisdom. Also it turned out that the Blood Donor picture was going to be on the March cover. The cover! I couldn't believe it when I heard; there'd be no living with me now.

Mother showed all the letters she thought might be important to my Uncle Jack. He did represent *Look* magazine — he was the wisest lawyer in the family for business and the entertainment world. Charlie was involved in city-government law.

There was an inquiry from David O. Selznick's office. Someone who worked for him had told him there was this girl who looked something like K. T. Stevens, whom he had discovered — he ought to take a look at her, possibly test her. They asked for more photographs of me. Then Howard Hughes had made an inquiry. Jack felt we should move very carefully on all this. Obviously there'd be other inquiries as a result of the *Bazaar* cover, let's work slowly, wait awhile. He talked to Mother first before I heard anything, wanting to make sure she understood it all. He also knew I'd be so hysterical that I might accept the first offer made, not knowing anything about the movie world.

An appointment was made with Selznick — not with him personally, since he was in California, but with his number-one man. I went to the man's office, talked with him for a while, gave him what little history there was of my no accomplishments. The interview didn't last long — about half an hour. Mr Selznick would be given all this information together with photographs and I'd hear from them.

Columbia Pictures was making a movie starring Rita Hayworth — title, *Cover Girl*. An inquiry came from Columbia Pictures — there were going to be eight or ten actual cover girls in the film. Would I be the *Harper's Bazaar* cover girl? The catch was — isn't there always a catch? — Columbia insisted on my signing a year's contract with options in case they wanted to use me in something else.

At the same time there was another inquiry. Howard Hawks wanted to know about me. One day in the *Look* office Jack and I sat down and talked it all out. I had never heard of Howard Hawks. Jack had, and listed his movies. He had directed some really outstanding films, including *Twentieth Century*, *Only Angels Have Wings*, *Air Force*, *Bringing Up Baby*. Charles K. Feldman, his agent and partner, wanted to know if I would come to California to make a screen test — it would mean

156

staying in California for six to eight weeks. If they liked the test, Hawks would sign me to a personal contract.

All of these offers were from unknown people — unknown to me — who lived in an unknown place. This was the first design in a pattern of work that was to continue all my life. Either everything at once or nothing — feast or famine. One had to say 'yes' to one, 'no' to all the others. I had no way of knowing, nor did Jack really, and certainly Mother didn't, how to make the right choice.

Diana Vreeland and Carmel Snow were more than happy about the Columbia offer. They wanted me to be the *Harper's Bazaar* cover girl. I told Diana of the Hawks offer. She said, 'Of course you must do what is best for you. We would adore it if you'd represent us in the movie biz, but if you must accept his offer, you must.'

Charles Feldman, representing Hawks, had called Jack several times. They would pay me fifty dollars a week until the test was made. If they liked me, they would draw up a contract and pay me more. But I had to decide about coming to California. Jack told him there were other offers to be considered and a great deal of interest in me. Feldman was very articulate about Hawks and very persuasive.

After we had talked it over again, Jack

said, 'Look, if you accept the Columbia offer, you will be in a movie. There will be lots of other girls in that movie. And if Columbia decides to, they can pick up your option and keep you for at least a year or even seven years. That's the standard Hollywood contract length. If you accept the Feldman-Hawks offer, you will make a screen test which Hawks will direct. If he likes you, he will sign you to a personal contract. It seems to me that with Hawks' record and reputation you'd be better off going with him. He'd give you personal care and you'd know very quickly whether he liked you enough to keep you out there or not.' I thought about that — remembered *Bringing Up Baby* and *Only Angels Have Wings* and how good they were — and agreed with Jack. Better to have care taken by one director than to be one of ten cover girls with maybe one or two lines to speak. I'd never be noticed in a movie with Rita Hayworth and those other really beautiful, professional models. Not with *my* face.

Jack discussed it fully with Mother, explaining in as much detail as he could. We all agreed — take the chance with Hawks. It would mean going off alone, three thousand miles away, to a place where I knew no one. But it wouldn't be for long and I'd be working.

Jack told Charles Feldman I would accept Hawks' offer. Feldman would send me a round-trip ticket to Los Angeles, put me up in a small hotel. The test would be made, seen, and decided upon within four to six weeks. He was certain I had made the right decision. Jack said, 'I entrust Betty to your care. She's only eighteen and doesn't know anyone in California. If her mother accompanied her, she'd have to leave her job — which she can't afford to do. Especially in view of the fact that Betty might soon be back here for good.' Feldman understood and said my mother was not to worry, he and his wife would look after me.

So the die was cast. Charles Feldman was sure I'd made the right decision. He'd send an agreement to Jack in writing, and how soon could I come out there? He'd check with Hawks about when approximately the test would be made. It would be soon.

Columbia had to be called — their offer was refused. There had been no further word from Howard Hughes, and Selznick had felt I was *too much* like K. T. Stevens. So it was two out of four. A lot better than anything I'd had before. I called Diana and told her of my choice. She was sorry for *Bazaar*, but glad for me. The May issue of the magazine would have the St Augustine pictures, and there was still some modeling

I could do between now and the time I was to leave.

Suddenly there was no more time. I had to see Betty Kalb, Fred Spooner, had to sort out my clothes, and, of course, be with Mother a lot, and the family, plus take the time to fantasize my first meeting with Feldman and Hawks and plan the entire rest of my life. I was excited at the prospect of California, excited beyond belief. I had never thought of myself in film terms, it was always agreed that Betty Kalb would be the movie star and I the stage star. But some agreements must be broken — by fate, luck, coincidence, whatever you want to call it.

The plan was that I would leave New York by train on April 3, and it was getting closer. The Bacall menage was alive with activity — phones ringing — the cleaner, the laundry, packing — the goodbyes.

Charles Feldman had sent a typewritten agreement to Jack. He had signed it on behalf of Howard Hawks and himself. It stated that they would have the option to sign me to a contract if they so wished after the test was made.

Having made the investment of money and time, they were entitled to that.

I signed one copy, which Jack returned to Feldman, and Jack kept the other.

The deed was irrevocable. No turning back.

My family gave me a farewell dinner. Four or five years back Mother had spent a holiday on a ranch in upstate New York and had met there a very nice and attractive man named Lee Goldberg. Lee was an auctioneer and an Assistant Marshal of the City of New York. His father had been a Marshal (Democratic) for years — they lived in Brooklyn — it was family tradition. He and Mother liked each other a lot. I can remember his coming to collect her for a special evening out — white tie and tails, top hat, and he always brought Mother flowers — she looked beautiful and radiant as all women in love do. She'd say, 'Isn't he stunning?' She never confided her hopes and dreams to me, but she was happier than I had ever seen her after she met him.

Lee came to my farewell dinner along with Grandma and the uncles and aunts. It was one of the few times I remember all the brothers, sisters, and in-laws being together with Grandma — a happy night and an emotional one. Toasts were made, by Charlie mostly, of course — his silly, funny rhymes about my going to Hollywood, knocking Howard Hawks on his ear — everyone would love me and I'd be a star. All the family laughed. The dinner was happy and a bit sad — Mother was both glowing with pride in her daughter and emotional at the thought of the separation, at my moving further out of the nest. Grandma was very happy for her favorite grandchild, though I believe she never felt there was a life for me in California — she knew nothing of the land of sunshine, but was convinced it was filled with wicked people.

I closed my suitcase on April 3. Mother's boss had allowed her to take the day off so she could put me on the train — a rare exception, as she was never given time off. Rosalie and Charlie came to collect us. I had a long talk with Droopy, explaining that I could not take him with me, but I would miss him and write to him. It was a reality. I was really leaving. I would not see home for a while at least. Not Mother, not Grandma, not my dog. I was frightened — excited but frightened. Grandma had stayed overnight with us to be with me and help her daughter — she knew how Mother would miss her little girl.

We were going to Lindy's for lunch, a restaurant on Broadway with among other things Jewish delicatessen food and famous for its cheesecake. Jack and Vera would meet us there. No one was working that afternoon.

We had a gay, jokey lunch. Charlie promised to take care of Mother. Grandma told me to take care of me. Jack advised me to just be myself — to remember that Howard Hawks was very important in the movie world, that Charles Feldman was a very important agent, that I was getting a very lucky break and must work hard. They all had faith in me. They all loved me. They brought me a corsage of gardenias, my favorite flower. They were sending me on my way with jokes, joy, confidence, and a few tears. It was an ending of sorts. I loved them all very, very much. We all went together to Grand Central Station. I had my ticket in my hand, a very impressive ticket — I was in Bedroom A. A bedroom, not just a berth! Unbelievable.

Finally the moment of parting came. I hugged and kissed everyone many times. I felt very grown-up, but when I came to Grandma I could feel the tears start, and when I turned to Mother they welled up even more. She was trying to hold hers back — I was doing the same. I said, 'Don't worry, Mother darling, I'll be fine. It's all going to come true. We'll be together very soon — I love you.' She said, 'Take care of yourself,' put her hand under my chin, squeezed me as she always did when she was bursting with love, and said, 'That's a sweetheart — that's the best.' We never bared our feelings completely with one another. I guess we both knew that if one of us did, the other would fall apart completely. Some constraint was always in order. But the bond was so strong, we knew what we felt without much display.

They all left the train. I rushed to my bedroom, looked at them through the windows, waved, blew kisses, smiled, cried — and the train started to move away. I sat back in my large seat, looked at myself in the small mirror opposite me, and said, 'Well, Betty Bacall, this is it. This train is taking you on a new adventure, totally different from anything you've ever known. Take a deep breath.'

It was not so much an ending after all. It was a beginning.

The train moved slowly out of New York. I sat looking out the window, my mind gradually leaving my family and starting to look ahead. As the dinner hour approached, I would have to devise something — I couldn't bear walking into a restaurant anywhere — having a meal alone with strange eyes watching me — couldn't then — can't now. The porter had told me he would bring me anything I liked once the train was out of the station. I didn't drink, so I couldn't ask for a cocktail. On rare occasions I had drunk an Orange Blossom — gin and orange juice — to make me feel grown-up, but I didn't really like it. But I pushed the porter button anyway and when he arrived I ordered a ginger ale.

I sat back on the long sofa-like seat and started acting to the mirror. Ridiculous but very comforting. In about ten minutes the buzzer rang. I opened the door and the porter was standing there with a glass filled with ice, a small bottle of ginger ale, a mixer, and a napkin on a small round tray. He raised the table and set the tray down. I felt very luxurious. He said the call for dinner would be around seven o'clock — if I wished a table I should go to the dining car early, and after tonight I could reserve a table for each day. I asked about breakfast and he told me he would gladly bring my breakfast on a tray whenever I wished it. What service! Only Mother had ever served breakfast to me, and never on a tray. When I was alone once more, I sat again, held my glass of ginger ale as though it were a drink, and started to play a scene with Charles Feldman.

What did he look like? I imagined a dark-haired, faceless man of no particular age and carried on what I thought was a simple first conversation with him. 'How do you do, Mr Feldman?' with a slight smile. 'Yes, the trip out was lovely. . . . Oh, do you really think so? . . . Well, thank you. I'm very much looking forward to meeting Mr Hawks and going to work. I've never been to California before, but

I'm sure I will love it.' I was very woman-of-the-world in my bedroom on the *Twentieth Century* that third day of April 1943. Sounded nothing like me, of course.

The train trip was totally happy, comfortable, different. Three days to get used to the possibility of a whole new life. Then, at about noon on the third day, Los Angeles. The station was large, but nothing like Grand Central. The minute I got off the train I knew I was in new country. There was an immediate air of informality. After I passed through the gate a man came up and identified himself as an associate of Feldman. We were going to the Feldman office in Beverly Hills, where the man himself would be waiting to greet us.

As we left the station area the streets looked so white, palm trees on either side, and it was all so clean. I'd never known there were cities as physically clean and pure-looking. Beautiful. Many automobiles, no noticeable taxis, no streetcars, some buses. Not many people on the streets — that I found very strange — and no skyscrapers. We finally arrived at our destination, the California Bank Building on the corner of Wilshire Boulevard and Beverly Drive — a tall building compared with the others around it, but not tall by New York standards. Luggage was left in the car and we went to meet Feldman. The agency occupied an entire floor — there were individual offices on either side of the corridor and at the end a large corner office which housed my future, who was to return from lunch in ten or fifteen minutes. Various men ambled in. Finally, a very attractive man — dark hair, gray at the temples, mustached, very suntanned, in a gray flannel suit — walked toward me and said, 'You are Betty Bacall. Come on in.' In I walked. He made it very, very easy. His mouth curled up at the corners as though he were on the verge of a smile. After I told him about the trip, he said he'd reserved a room for me in a hotel in Westwood Village for the time being. He asked if I could drive a car. 'Drive a car?' I thought. 'I've never even considered it.' He said, 'Don't worry, there will always be someone to drive you here or wherever you have to go. I'll set up a lunch with Howard for tomorrow. Would you like to have dinner with me tonight?' 'I'd love it!' 'Okay, why don't you get settled in your hotel? I'll pick you up at seven thirty.'

He made it all simple, had a sense of humor. I liked him immediately. The man who'd come to the station accompanied me to the Claremont Hotel. Still spotlessly clean streets, palms and other trees, the shops small and shining, small buildings in Beverly Hills and on Wilshire Boulevard that had several apartments in each. It was so unlike my home city. The Claremont was a small white hotel off Wilshire, inside Westwood Village. The village looked charming from the car — I'd explore after unpacking.

I signed the register and was led to a small double room upstairs — my first time with a room all to myself in a hotel. My first time not having to share a closet or a bathroom. I could look out my window and see people (not many) walking around a small arcade across the street. Greenery and flowers all around. This California was incredible. It was like a resort. Did anyone work here?

Charlie Feldman picked me up at 7:30 and took me to a restaurant in Beverly Hills. The evening must have gone well, for in a letter to my mother dated April 7 I wrote:

Dearest Mommy —
Here I am, honey, at the start of my second day in California and I'm off to have lunch with Howard Hawks and Charlie F at two o'clock. Some fun! It will be my first meeting with Hawks.

And mother — Charlie is a darling, a perfect angel. He wanted to give me more money yesterday, but I told him I didn't need it, if and when I do I'll tell him. After all I've made a bargain and I'd like to stick to it as much as possible.

My test will take place sometime next week because Charlie thinks I should have my teeth fixed first. But we'll wait to see what Hawks says first. And don't tell this to anyone but Charlie adores me. He thinks I'm wonderful, vital, alive, refreshing, full of fire, intelligent and a few other things. And those, sweetie, are direct quotes. He says that he thinks I'll be great and that he'll do everything possible for me. So baby, maybe you'll come here after all. Here's hoping! I'll let you know as soon as anything definite happens one way or the other . . .

The letter went on, oozing love and joy and excitement. It showed her how very young I was. How Charlie Feldman could have said or felt or meant all of those things, having known me for one day; I could not explain. He was a flirt and he meant some of them — and he obviously moved fast.

On April 7 I was driven to Charlie's office. We were to meet Howard Hawks at the Brown Derby on Wilshire Boulevard, a block from the office. I was very nervous and Charlie knew it. At the Brown Derby we were led to our booth. After a few minutes a very tall man with close-cropped gray hair and broad shoulders came in. Charlie said, 'There's Howard.' He came over and we were introduced. I was shaking. He was very imposing. Spoke very deliberately, asked me a few questions. Said he'd liked the pictures in *Bazaar* — wanted to know if I'd had any acting experience at all. I told him very little, told him what it was. Charlie mentioned my teeth — having them fixed, straightened a bit or capped, I guess he meant. But Hawks did not feel that was necessary.

He told me what he wanted to do — a simple test. He'd pick the scenes. He couldn't have been nicer. And he frightened me — I was terrified I'd say the wrong thing. We finished lunch and headed back to Charlie's office. I shall never forget walking behind Charlie and Howard, who were talking and talking and taking forever to walk one block. I thought then, 'God, why don't they move? Do they always walk so slow?' I was trained in the speed school of the East, where there was never time to do all you wanted to do, so you always walked quickly — just short of a run, as though you had a real destination. I could have walked ten blocks in the time they took to walk one. Well, I'd better get used to it. My future was in the hands of these two men.

Back in Charlie's office Hawks asked me if there were any particular parts I would feel comfortable playing for the test. I couldn't think of any, I told him — I had been asked to understudy Claudia on tour, but hadn't accepted. I would prefer to leave it up to him. I was taken back to Westwood with nothing to do for the rest of the day. I walked around more of the village, then wrote about ten letters home.

I thought about Hawks and what an odd person he seemed to be. He was not a demonstrative, relaxed sort of man. He was inscrutable, speaking quietly in a fairly monotonous voice. He seemed very sure of himself. Charlie called me at day's end to tell me that Howard liked me and that we would make the test the following Friday.

The sun shone every day. The most perfect weather I had ever known. Balmy air, incredible clear blue skies. Everyone seemed to have a car. As I was beginning to find out, life in California was impossible without one.

I waited around the office for Charlie, talked to some of the other agents; in a couple of days I became a regular fixture in that office. When Charlie came in I would ask for news of the test. When would I know what the scene would be? When would I see Hawks? He said, 'Take it easy' and laughed at my impatience. I always wanted to know everything right away, no horsing around. Charlie said I'd see Howard on Monday — the weekend was coming up and no one did anything on a weekend. He took me out for an early dinner one night and asked if I'd like to come up to his house on Sunday for lunch and the afternoon. Absolutely, I said, how would I get there? 'I'll come and get you, of course.' It was beginning to get to me, always having to depend on someone else for transportation. In Westwood, having no car was impossible — I was stranded.

Back in my room I'd carry on conversations with Charlie before the proverbial mirror. I had a terrible crush on him. He had a wife, but I thought their life together must be odd if he could have dinner without her. My idea of marriage was that a husband and wife did everything together from the end of a workday on. I had a lot to learn.

Mother called me on Saturday morning, anxious to hear everything. She felt so far away, she *was* so far away, but I couldn't tell her anything definite. It's always difficult to explain delays, what takes time. Especially when you're not sure yourself.

On Sunday Charlie took me to his house. It was on Coldwater Canyon, which is still Beverly Hills but not the flats. The house couldn't be seen from the street. He brought me out to the poolside, where his wife, Jean, was sitting. She was beautiful — blond hair, dressed in gold gabardine slacks, a white silk shirt, and three strands of pearls. She was very friendly and open. How could Charlie not have dinner with her every night? The house was marvelous. Spanish, all on one floor, beautifully and comfortably furnished. Outside up some steps was the pool and poolhouse. Did people really live like this?

We had lunch outside. What total luxury! To have your meals out of doors in the sunshine. It was God's country.

Jean had been a Ziegfeld girl when she was very young and, I was later to learn, had had many men at her feet. Understandable. Of course I told her all my hopes and dreams — that I prayed the test would take place soon because patience was not my strong point. She was reassuring, knew how hard it was to be in California and not know anyone — I was to feel always welcome there, call on her anytime.

The next ten days were endless. On the phone at least once a day to Charlie, so frustrated — postponement after postponement. One letter to my mother dated April 15:

Now you won't hear from me until Saturday or Sunday of next week for the simple reason that the test has been postponed to Wednesday. But don't worry, sweetie, I'll call you just as soon as I know the results.

And on April 21:

Mommy darling, I know how hard it must be for you to wait for word from me. But they do things so slowly here. Always taking their time. And if you're nervous, just imagine how I feel. I have no insides left. But if it flops I won't be the first actress who couldn't crash Hollywood on her first try. . . . The only assurance I can give you, baby, is that I'll do my best. All I ask of you is patience and if nothing happens to bear with me.

I had seen Howard a couple of times more. I read scenes for him. He took me to lunch and told me about his directing experiences with various actresses. It was always what he said to them, or to Howard Hughes, to Jack Warner — he always came out on top, he always won. He was mesmerizing and I believed every story he told me. Once he made some remark about a Jew and I turned cold. I'm sure I paled visibly, but he didn't seem to notice. 'Oh, no, don't let him be anti-

Semitic. God, don't let me come all this way and have it blow up in my face. It just couldn't happen now.'

I told Charlie about it. 'What will I do when he finds out? What will *he* do?' Charlie laughed and said, 'Howard just talks. Don't worry about it, he and I are friends, have been for years.' They didn't move in the same social circle, however. I was panic-stricken.

The day before my test I was driven out to the Warner Bros. studio to see Howard and Perc Westmore, head of the make-up department. After all this waiting, something was going to happen at last. Driving to Warner Bros., new territory for me — Sunset Boulevard, the Strip, with its famous nightclubs, restaurants, Schwab's drugstore, where Lana Turner was supposed to have been discovered, along Highland Avenue to Burbank down a curved road to WARNER BROS. printed in large black letters on buildings (which turned out to be sound stages) on enormous billboards, to the main gate. Here was the home of Bette Davis, Muni, Flynn, Sheridan, Cagney, Bogart, Greenstreet, Lorre — the list was long. There were many separate buildings looking like houses which turned out to be executive offices, dressing rooms, make-up department, music cutting rooms, wardrobe. The car stopped at a small house with the name HOWARD HAWKS hanging over the door like a doctor's shingle. Opposite him was another bungalow with the name HAL B. WALLIS on it. I was led into Hawks' outer office and announced by a secretary. The inner door opened and out Howard came with a smile. He put his arm around me and said, 'You're going to make your test with a young man named Charles Drake. You'll meet him after lunch and we can go over the scene.' Howard had decided that *Claudia* was right for me, so we were doing a scene from it. He walked me over to make-up so that Perc Westmore could have a look at me and said, 'You know, Perc, the test is tomorrow morning, see what color Betty will need, and that's all.' Westmore took me into his room, sat me before his make-up mirror, and examined my face. He said, 'Ummhumm' and pushed my hair back. 'We can pluck your eyebrows and shave your hairline, straighten your teeth.' I was terrified and very upset. I said I'd like to call Howard, which I did practically in tears and re-peated it all. I said, 'You don't want that, do you?' He said absolutely not and spoke to Westmore, saying, 'I want her exactly as she is, nothing changed, a light natural make-up for tomorrow.' Perc understood, he only thought some of those touches would be an improvement. But no, Howard had chosen me for my thick eyebrows and crooked teeth and that's the way they would stay.

I went back to Howard's bungalow and he took me down the street to the green room for lunch. The green room was for the actors — round tables, walls adorned with large photographs of the stars. It was full. Next to the green room was a large commissary for crew, extras, etc. There was also a large dining room at the end of the lot where the brothers Warner and their producers ate. Wherever I went around the studio my head was on a swivel. This was where movies were made. There was so much to absorb. It looked almost like a private home in parts — trees, lawns. It was so much more complicated than I had thought, so much grander.

Howard told me that make-up people were used to doing someone over, that Perc was very good at his job but just had to be told. 'He probably thought I wanted you to look like Dietrich. If they try anything tomorrow — to change your hair or anything — don't let them. Tell them I want you to look just the way you do now.' I was relieved. Of course Howard knew how frightened I had been. What would they have done if I hadn't called him?

We went back to Howard's office, where

tall, blond, handsome Charles Drake was waiting. He was a young hopeful at Warners — Howard had used him in *Air Force*. We went into Howard's office and read the script — I knew it, actually. Of course I was nervous. It was strange to play a scene with a complete stranger. I was trying to impress him, to impress Howard. Howard gave me a little direction along the way, we didn't make any physical moves, but he talked about interpretation. Finally he said, 'Okay, you'd better go home, study and get a good night's sleep. You'll have a long day tomorrow.'

I thanked him and thanked Charles Drake and was driven back to Charlie's office, a complete and utter wreck. I was to stay the night at Jean and Charlie's and be picked up the next morning at 7:30, so I went back to my hotel, got my toothbrush and pajamas (I always wore pajamas), and was taken back to the office, where I studied my scene until Charlie had to go home. It was hard to keep my mind off the importance of the following morning. Would I be good enough, would Howard like me? 'Think of the scene, remember what Howard told you when you rehearsed it in his office.' I could only do my best. But what if my best wasn't good enough? Like all things in my life, it became crucial, a matter of life or death. I've never understood less than an extreme. I somehow got through dinner with Charlie and Jean, though I couldn't eat. They both kept telling me, 'You're in the best possible hands with Howard. He wants it to be good, he will take enormous care. Don't *worry!* It's going to be all right.' God, how I must have bored them.

Jean took me to the spare room where I was to spend my last hours. The next day the long, slow march would begin — the switch would be pulled. I kept repeating the scene over and over to the mirror, the wall; my stomach was jumping so, I felt so sick, I had to crawl to the bathroom to throw up. Did everyone go through this, or was it just me?

Back to bed, mind racing — it would not stop. Howard's face flashing before me — what did he really think? And the Jewish business? If I was asked I'd have to tell the truth. Coward! It's awful to be so frightened. I finally went to sleep. A knock on the door — 7:15 already. I jumped up, threw cold water on my face, quickly dressed, grabbed my script and was ready. I wanted to get to the studio, start to work. I loved to act — it was just that this was a whole new thing to me — I'd learn the methods — 'Don't panic — don't panic.' Jean had slipped a good-luck note from her and Charlie under my door. I walked out the front door into the sleeping world. It was so peaceful — morning dew, sunshine, birds — a beautiful day. Would it be a lucky one?

The studio car was waiting — I was on my way — over Mulholland Drive down to the San Fernando Valley to Warner Bros. I was taken back to that make-up department. My hair was washed and set and I was put under the dryer. Someone brought me a cup of coffee. There was a lot of activity in the make-up department between seven and nine. All actors working in the movies being shot were there. All the leading actors. A shooting day begins at 9:00 a.m. and ends at 6:00 p.m. I was introduced to Dennis Morgan, Gary Cooper, Ann Sheridan. It was exciting to see those stars getting ready for work — exciting just to see them.

At about nine o'clock I was taken out from under the dryer and sent to Perc Westmore's room to be made up. He was doing Ann Sheridan, so I had to wait awhile — tests came second to actual filming. Finally Perc was ready. I sat in that chair again and he started on me. He was very friendly, but I don't think overly pleased with not being allowed to redesign my face. He said, 'Wouldn't you like your eyebrows a little thinner and rounded? I think they'd look much better, no one on screen has eyebrows as thick and angular as yours.' I said, 'No — Howard wants it this way. Perhaps he'll want to make some changes later.' (But I didn't believe that — the way I was was the way I was and nothing would really change that.) He did put false eyelashes on me, which I hated. I asked him to cut them — I wanted them shorter than my own so they'd never be seen — but he left them a little longer. He said they would help.

Then my hair had to be combed out. Everything took much longer than it was meant to, particularly the first day. I was afraid my hair would be too curly. No one had ever set it before — I always did it myself, I was used to it. And I wanted the wave in the right place on the right side — starting to curve at the corner of my eyebrow and ending, sloping downward, at my cheekbone. Of course it *was* too curly, my hair always acted up when I didn't want it to. I was getting more and more nervous.

Finally they were finished. The sound stage, Stage 12 (they were all numbered), was enormous. Going through a door that says DO NOT ENTER WHEN RED LIGHT IS ON, which means that filming is in progress. I entered this dimly lit stage and saw Howard. He kissed me on the cheek, said, 'You look good, how do you feel?' 'Terrified,' said I, 'nervous.' There was a camera, but not like the Rolleiflexes I had known, rather, a large apparatus with a seat behind it which moved. And a cameraman and quite a few other men in the area — the 'crew.' They had been lighting another girl — 'Have I been replaced already? Don't panic' — who turned out to be a stand-in for me. So many strange people — so many new faces — so much equipment for this one scene between two people. Finally Howard said, 'Okay, let's try a take.' Please, God, don't let me be sick. Howard was marvelous — spoke softly, trying to soothe me and get the best out of me. I felt as secure with him as was possible for me to feel, given the circumstances. A letter dated May 3 to my mother:

My test was more fun, Mommy. I got to the studio at 8 for hair and make-up. Flirted with Dennis Morgan (the wolf), said hello to Cooper, had a chat with Sheridan and got on the set at 11:30. Went over the scene a few times with Howard. Then the first 'take.' 'Shot' until 1:30 — broke for lunch — saw Errol Flynn in the commissary and dove under the table. Got back on the set at 2:00 — 'shot' until 4:00. And I loved every minute of it. I had a dressing room and a stand-in, a hairdresser and a make-up man, the best photographer at Warners, an 11 page scene and Howard as a director. I had what every star has. A scene for a test is never more than 2 or 3 pages — stand-ins, dressing rooms, etc. are unheard of. So I was really a very lucky girl. Everyone told me that what I had only one out of 10,000 girls gets. So — there you have it.

Saw the test on Wednesday. It's the weirdest feeling to see yourself move around and talk. I didn't think it was exceptionally good. I didn't look beautiful. But Howard and Charlie said it was excellent. Anyway, I'm the first girl Howard has ever signed personally and Charlie says I'm his protégée.

After the test was over I was full of bravado, name-dropping like crazy and very blasé. Actually Howard's decision to sign me was made very quickly when one thinks how slowly things were usually done out there. And how quickly I accepted Charlie and Howard as my mentors — how quickly I shifted gears from East Coast to West.

I wrote endless instructions to my mother, and a letter asking for an honorable discharge from Equity as I would not be doing stage work for a while. I had sent Uncle Jack a copy of my contract with

Howard — seven years starting at $100 a week, moving to $1,250 in the seventh year. I would have to send Mother money to buy me the things I asked for — and her ticket. I thought it was costing me a fortune to live — $17.50 a week just for rent and about $20 for food. So I'd have to get a salary advance. I was very happy, though. But I didn't analyze it at all, it almost seemed the normal course of events. I had left New York one month before, filled with anticipation but uncertain of what the result would be — and here I was, after four weeks, accepting a life in California as though it were the most natural thing in the world.

Four days later, on May 7, another letter to my mother.

Well, here it is honey — the news you have been waiting for so long.
Lv. New York Sunday May 16 — Commodore Vanderbilt — 4:20 p.m. Car 177 — Roomette #5.
Arr. Chicago — Monday, May 17 — 9:20 a.m.
Lv. Chicago, Monday — 12 o'clock — Bedroom A Car 198 — Santa Fe — Chief.
Arr. Pasadena 11:15 a.m. Wednesday. May 19 — L.A. 11:50 a.m. Is that clear, sweetie? As for taking Droopy

out, you can do that at the various stops. I will meet you at the station, so look for me . . .

At the end of the letter —

And I'm not going to have you working — at least for a few months and then if you want to you can. But not immediately. You're going to rest while you have the opportunity. And don't forget that.

For a minute there our roles were reversed. I was going to take care of my mother for a change. I was taking over — giving the orders, making the decisions. I found an apartment in Beverly Hills — 275 South Reeves Drive, just two and a half blocks from Charlie's office. Four rooms furnished with a private entrance, for $65 a month. That set-up would never have existed in New York for twice the price. Until I got a car, which I could not exist without, I could easily walk to the office and around Beverly Hills. It was ideal. More space than Mother and I had ever had.

Howard had told me that he intended to wait for just the right part for my introduction to movies. He expected me to work on my voice. And he unfolded more stories about what his approach was with actresses — with Carole Lombard in *Twentieth Century*. She didn't know how to react to John Barrymore in one scene: Howard asked her how she herself would behave, she told him very differently from the script — she'd kick him, scream at him. Howard said, 'Okay, do that.' She did and it worked. Howard always knew how to handle women in movies. That's how he told it, and I suppose it was largely true — the results proved it. As time went on I realized he too had quite a fantasy life. Either consciously or unconsciously, he wanted to be a Svengali, and he was that to me at the beginning.

I hung on his every word. I was afraid of him — he seemed to have no highs or lows, but I would not have wanted to see him lose his temper. And he was so sure of himself. He had decided there would be no interviews. No press at all for a while, and I shouldn't be seen too much by people in the business. He thought my first name should be changed and he'd work on that.

I ran to Charlie constantly, telling him things Howard had told me, and if I had any questions, I asked him. I thought he was the nicest, most generous man I had ever met. He arranged for me to have driving lessons, said he'd help get me a car when I was ready. He sent the railroad tickets to Mother. He would take no commission from me until I made a lot of money, so I never signed an agent's contract with him. But he did own half my contract with Howard.

I moved into Reeves Drive a few days before Mother was to arrive. I wanted to have everything in perfect order for her — food in, clothes in closets and drawers. I was so excited with the apartment — it was so clean, everything was so clean — the food was so fresh and so beautiful to look at — oranges, lemons, and grapefruit hanging from trees. So that's how they grew. Fantastic! The markets were so big and beautiful. Mother would never believe that people lived all year around in a place like this. It was like being on a lifetime holiday.

At the station when I saw her I screamed out, 'Mommy!' — rushed to her and hugged her, kissed her, squeezed her. How much I had missed her — life was so much better when she was with me. Droopy remembered me — jumped up and licked me. I had so much to tell Mother. 'Wait till you see what it's like — it's all so beautiful — and sunny and blue sky. You'll love it.' I rattled on and on. She was happy, of course, but much less hysterical than I, much less given to extremes. We headed for our new home, with me pointing out places of interest as we went, stopping at last on that lovely tree-lined street with the white stucco buildings and red tiled roofs. She breathed in — made a sound of 'Oh, it's lovely' — and I led her up the stairs to our little nest. We had a lot to catch up on. Did life change so quickly and completely in five weeks? Yes, my dear — it changed so quickly and completely in five minutes.

Mother and Droopy and I settled in very nicely, happy in our apartment. We became instant Californians, except for the waiting around — I never could get used to that. I finally completed my driving lessons, took a slightly nervous test, but passed and applied for a license. All I needed now was a car.

I had to go to court with Howard to have my contract approved because I was a minor. There were a couple of photographers around and my first almost professional publicity photograph was printed in the California newspapers. I was launched. But none of it seemed quite real. It was a fairyland for the living and with all new people and movie make-believe. I don't suppose I ever sat down and applied it to life as I had known life. Limited though my experience was, and God knows it was, New York was real and California was not. 'Twas ever thus.

In a used-car lot near Charlie's office I found a 1940 gray Plymouth coupé for $900. I thought it was heavenly. The price certainly was. I told Charlie about it — he immediately lent me the money to pay for it. The office made all the arrangements and I was a car owner. Not bad for eighteen and a new kid in town. I had my license — now Mother had to learn. The car was freedom. No more depending on anyone to get any place. A relief.

There were many lunches and much time spent with Howard. He wanted me to drive into the hills, find some quiet spot, and read aloud. He felt it most important to keep the voice in a low register. Mine started off low, but what Howard didn't like and explained to me was, 'If you notice, Betty, when a woman gets excited or emotional she tends to raise her voice. Now, there is nothing more unattractive than screeching. I want you to train your voice in such a way that even if you have a scene like that your voice will remain low.' I found a spot on Mulholland Drive and proceeded to read *The Robe* aloud, keeping my voice lower and louder than normal. If anyone had ever passed by, they would have found me a candidate for an asylum. Who sat on mountaintops in cars reading books aloud to the canyons? Who did? I did!

Howard wanted to have some good, special pictures taken of me. He knew a super photographer named John Engstead and set a day for us to do it. They would be taken at Howard's house, which I had never seen. I might even meet his wife, 'Slim,' whom he spoke of so often and who had been the one who showed him my pictures in *Harper's Bazaar* in the first place. I was given directions on how to get there and finally found it. My sense of direction has always been wanting — that is, north, south, east, and west direction, not life direction.

He lived in Bel-Air on Moraga Drive in the most beautiful house I had ever seen. It was a ranch-type house, all on one floor, with beamed ceilings, beautiful wood floors, antique country furniture — rich and comfortable and tasteful. The grounds were large. There were stables — both he and Slim rode. There was a pool. And I met Slim — a tall, thin, incredibly beautiful and unusual woman only seven or eight years my senior. She had great personal style. I was led back to her bedroom, which was gigantic — like a bed-sitting room; her dressing room had more shoes than I had ever seen — handbags on hooks — open shelves filled with sweaters — a room-size closet filled with clothes of all descriptions — an enormous bath.

Howard's bedroom, dressing room, and bath adjoined it. Did kings live any better than this? He and Slim had decided what I should wear — some things of hers, one or two of mine. One dress was silver lamé. John Engstead arrived with cameras, and my first portrait sitting began. The backgrounds were an enormous fireplace, a chair — all very simple. He was marvelously easy to work with — not unlike Dahl-Wolfe. I didn't spend much time with Slim that day, but I liked her immediately, though I did feel shy with her. I thought both people and the house they lived in overwhelming. The portraits were the best I'd ever had, and still are.

After a few months Mother got restless and found a job around the corner from Reeves Drive that was pleasant and not too taxing. She was more efficient than anyone her bosses had ever known — they felt lucky, and they were. She learned to drive — badly. She got a license, but was what is known as a careful driver, hugging the curb at thirty miles per hour. She was always nervous behind the wheel, stemming from an accident she'd had when she was a girl when some chickens — some chickens? — somehow flew through a window of the car in which she was riding, causing glass to break and providing her with a lifelong scar on her arm. I wasn't a hell of a lot better.

So the weeks went by — and the months — and I hounded Charlie every day — 'What does Howard have in mind? When will I go to work? I'm going out of my mind not working.' I was merciless. He tried to pacify me — 'When Howard is ready, that's when you'll work.' Charlie was going to co-produce a film with Howard made up of different stories concerning the war amalgamated into one. One episode concerned a young Russian girl who parachuted into a field and met a soldier — it was short, but they were thinking possibly I could play that. What a thought!

Meanwhile, Howard would have me come to Warner Bros., where I started to work with the music coach, Dudley Chambers. Howard thought I might sing. He took me onto a set where Lewis Milestone, the famous director, was making a film with Anne Baxter and Farley Granger. He introduced me to Milestone and we watched a scene being shot. And more stories were unfolding — what Howard had said to Katharine Hepburn on *Bringing Up Baby* — how he and Cary had thought of something marvelous to do in a scene — the dialogue between Howard and Rita Hayworth on *Only Angels Have Wings*. How he had given Hayworth her first break, but she hadn't listened well enough, so he didn't want to be bothered with her after that. She was damn good in it nonetheless.

Howard's record spoke for itself. I learned much later that he had always wanted to find a girl from nowhere, mold her into his dream girl, and make her a star — his creation. He was about to begin. When I would ask Howard if he had anything specific in mind for me, he was noncommittal.

He said he thought he'd like to put me in a film with Cary Grant or Humphrey Bogart. I thought, 'Cary Grant — terrific! Humphrey Bogart — yucch.' Howard's idea was always that a woman should play a scene with a masculine approach — insolent. Give as good as she got, no capitulation, no helplessness. Oh, he had something in mind, definitely, but it would be a long time before I knew what it was. A perfect example of Howard's thinking was *His Girl Friday*, which was a remake of *The Front Page*, but changing the star reporter to a woman — Rosalind Russell. And it couldn't have worked better.

The next six months were spent in reading aloud, studying singing, listening to Howard, meeting some people whose names had been mythical to me — and mostly heckling Charlie about work.

Jean Feldman was an old and close friend of Cole Porter. She told me that on Sunday nights (or was it Thursdays?) he always had a few soldiers who had no place to go — no home nearby — to dinner and always invited young actresses to dine and dance with them. We went one summer eve in 1943. Cole Porter lived in Brentwood, in an unpretentious but beautiful house on Rockingham Avenue. He was a fairly small, very neat, very elegant, well- and soft-spoken man who made me feel completely at home. His taste was impeccable — the food at his house was incredibly good, immaculately served. It was incredibly good fun and the soldiers were thrilled to be there. Drinks were always served early, and in summer out-of-doors — then food — then dancing. I became a regular — it was the continuation of my Monday nights at the Stage Door Canteen, only slightly more luxurious. I started off calling him Mr Porter, but he insisted on Cole. He walked with a cane — Jean told me of his ghastly accident with a horse, how he was constantly in pain and never complained, never mentioned it. There are all kinds of courage. I had marvelous times in that house.

One day I was having lunch at his poolside and was the last to leave. Finally he walked me to the door. At that moment the door opened. Standing there in white shirt, beige slacks — with a peach complexion, light brown hair, and the most incredible face ever seen by man — was Greta Garbo. I almost gasped out loud as Cole introduced me to her. No make-up — unmatched beauty. It was the only time I saw her at anything but a distance.

I had also been to Howard's house a few times for dinner. I had gotten to know Slim better — liked her more at each meeting. She was clearly very, very bright, very original in looks and thought, and very straightforward. And with humor. They all had that — particularly Slim, Jean, and Charlie. That saved me. I could put up with anything if I could laugh.

Howard's friends were Victor Fleming, the director, and his friendly wife, Lou; Harry Carey and his wife, Ollie; Johnny and Ginger Mercer; Hoagy Carmichael; Lee Bowman and his wife, Helene; Hal Rosson — great cameraman; Gary Cooper. There were many more. Some of them, including Van Johnson, used to race motorcycles up and down mountains on Sundays. It was on one such day, I believe, that Van Johnson was seriously hurt. Howard admired Van's perseverance — the fact that no accident would stop him. I was introduced to people slowly — Howard didn't want me to be seen too much, particularly before I'd done anything in films. One night in the fall of 1943 Howard and Slim gave a really big party — Bing Crosby, Bob Hope, Charlie and Jean (Charlie being the only known Jew who seemed to have gained entrance to Howard's private life). I stayed close to the piano, listening to Johnny Mercer singing his and other songs, Hoagy Carmichael playing the piano. Lee Bowman was a terrific dancer and I spent a lot of the evening dancing with him and flirting, of course. At one point I was near the piano, dancing by myself — in my own world, but aware of Hawks and others at the far end of the room watching me out of the corners of their eyes. There is strength in being a new young face thrust into a group of people too used to one another. I guess I used that. I wanted something of my own, and, failing that, was willing to flirt outrageously with a man like Lee Bowman. I went a bit far that night and Helene Bowman was less than thrilled with me, for which I could not blame her one bit. Lee took me home — somewhere along the way it was daylight, and I remember sitting on a diving board in my evening dress and then dancing with him. Harmless, and I enjoyed it completely. And that's as far as it went. Howard and Slim thought the evening was a great success as far as introducing their protégée was concerned. They were pleased. That's all that mattered to me.

Elsa Maxwell gave an enormous party at Evalyn Walsh McLean's house, and Jean and Charlie took me. *That* was a star-studded evening. Mrs McLean was wearing the Hope Diamond, which just looked like an enormous piece of glass to me. The women were all in flowing gowns, adorned with their best jewels; I was in a short tailored dress and sat on the steps in a corner, feeling very alone but watching in awe the movie stars — old, medium, and new — greeting each other and vying for center stage. Names — names — names, and I had to pretend to be cool. I managed until one of my heroes, Robert Montgomery, sauntered over. Robert Montgomery — I couldn't believe I was meeting him. He sat on the steps and talked to me — actually flirted with me. I thought him wildly attractive. It was time for me to leave, he took me to my car, asked me for my phone number. I gave it to him. He said, 'Too easy.' It never occurred to him I might be an innocent virgin who hadn't a clue as to what he might have in mind. I suppose those men were used to women giving themselves gladly. Nothing could have been further from my mind. That was one of my first experiences with the game that was meant to be played between men and women. I knew nothing, but nothing, except how to go so far and no further. I wanted my romance to be the real thing — total — so I was not good material for that part of the Hollywood scene.

Such was the extent of my social life until the end of 1943. That September I was given a nineteenth-birthday-party lunch by Elsa Maxwell, to which Jean, Hedda Hopper, Mrs McLean, and a few other people were invited. It was a nice thing for her to do. She had a cake for me, and Hedda Hopper wrote a small piece in her column about it. That was my first mention in an important Hollywood column. Was I impressed with myself!

One day before the year's end Howard asked me to come out to Warner Bros. He had been working on an idea that had been germinating for some time in his head. He had told me about his friendship with Ernest Hemingway, about their manly pursuits — hunting, shooting together. And fishing, natch. He owned the rights to a book of Hemingway's that I had never heard of called *To Have and Have Not* and had thought he would someday make a movie of it. He wanted to use Humphrey Bogart as the male lead. Bogart was making a film called *Passage to Marseille* at the time and Howard said, 'Let's go down on the set and see what's going on.' Not a word about the possibility of my working. The *Passage to Marseille* sound stage was enormous and bare. Howard walked me over toward some light where the set was and the next scene was being lit by the cameraman and his crew. Michèle Morgan was sitting on a bench on the set. Howard told me to stay put, he'd be right back — which he was, with Bogart. He introduced us. There was no clap of thunder, no lightning bolt, just a simple how-do-you-do. Bogart was slighter than I imagined — five feet ten and a half, wearing his costume of no-shape trousers, cotton shirt, and scarf around neck. Nothing of import was said — we didn't stay long — but he seemed a friendly man.

My first California Christmas was eventful only in that the sun was shining and it was swimming weather, as opposed to the white Christmases I had known. Howard and Slim gave me a beige gabardine suit and a brown silk blouse, which I never took off. Jean and Charlie gave me a silk scarf and a white silk shirt. They were the best-quality clothing I'd ever had and I was thrilled with them. Mother and I spent the day quietly and cozily, calling New York and speaking to the family. Wrote to everyone else. It was our first holiday time completely alone, but we were in California after all and that wasn't too bad.

Just after Christmas I was called to the studio by Howard and he gave me the only present I wanted from life. It was a scene from *To Have and Have Not*. He was going to make the movie — he had Bogart — it would start in February 1944, and he wanted me to test for it right after the first of the year. I read the scene — it was the 'whistle' scene. I was to do the test with John Ridgely, an actor under contract to Warner Bros. whom Howard had used before and liked. I couldn't believe it. Was it really true I might actually get a part — go to work? I was on cloud ten — a very high, comfortable cloud, far from reality. He had mentioned the possibility of using me to Humphrey Bogart and it was fine with him — he'd been shown my first test, of course, and would be shown the second. Bogart was in Casablanca entertaining the troops and would not return before mid-January. Howard said he'd rehearse Ridgely and me every day, but nothing was definite — a lot depended on the quality of the test and Jack Warner's approval. It was very generous of John Ridgely to test with an unknown — he was getting good parts at Warners and was offering his time with nothing to gain but goodwill. Another example of an actor's generosity to another actor.

Not a word was to be said to anyone until a decision had been made. Charlie knew, of course, and when I called him, hysterical with joy, he laughed and said, 'See, I told you something would happen when Howard was ready.' In response to questions I dared not ask Howard (I could ask Charlie anything), he told me he thought my chance of getting the part was good — that Howard would not be making the test unless he thought so too.

I stopped everything but study from that moment on. The character's name was Marie, but the man, Harry, called her Slim. It was a good scene, very adult, sexy — much better than anything I had ever hoped for, with a great tag line about whistling. I'd do the best I could and Howard would guide me — I trusted him completely.

After that we rehearsed every day in Howard's office — Sundays, New Year's Eve, New Year's Day. John Ridgely would sit in a chair opposite Howard's desk, and I had to sit on his lap and kiss him. I was self-conscious and very nervous. Howard told me how to sit and where — made me do the whole thing while he watched. Kissing is fairly intimate — to do it with a man you hardly know and with your mentor watching and your future hanging in the balance is enough to put fear into the heart of a fairly experienced actor — to a novice like myself it was utterly terrifying. And I desperately wanted to be good for Howard — I couldn't bear to have him feel he'd signed a dud.

Howard took me to wardrobe, chose a dark shirt and jacket, put a beret on my head, and told me the test would be the next Tuesday. He drummed into my head that he wanted me to be insolent with the man — that I was being the forward one, but with humor — and told me about yet more scenes he had directed other actresses in to give me examples of the attitude he wanted. I hung on his every word, trying to figure out how the hell a girl who was totally without sexual experience could convey experience, worldliness, and knowledge of men.

On the day of the test I was my usual spastic self. Rose at 6:00 a.m., got to make-up before seven. Over-anxious. Hair and make-up done, with no alterations suggested this time. On the set before nine. Howard looked at my make-up and hair — called Sid Hickox, the cameraman, over. Howard knew how he wanted the scene photographed — *me* photographed. He wanted a mood created photographically. The molding was beginning for real. Who knew what kind of Frankenstein's monster he was creating?

I got into my costume. John Ridgely was ready, and we started to rehearse the opening of the scene on the set. We worked quietly, with Howard watching and the crew very much in the background. The day went well. It was a marvelous scene — Hickox was terrific — and Howard gave me such care. He was kind, affectionate (for him that would mean a smile, a hand on my shoulder, nothing too overt). He made me feel secure. At day's end I felt good about it. So did Howard. All that remained was to see the scene on film and get the verdict. More waiting, more anxiety.

The remainder of the week crawled by. I was on the phone to Charlie daily for news: When would Howard see the test? I drove that man crazy.

On Monday Howard saw the test and Charlie was present. Each of them called to tell me he thought it was good. Howard would show it to me on Wednesday. Another crucial Wednesday in my life! I drove to the studio with my heart in my mouth. In Howard's office I met Jules Furthman, a writer (he didn't look like a writer) who was writing the screenplay of *To Have and Have Not*. Howard took me to the projection room and as I slid low in my seat he ran my test. I was no judge then, nor would I ever be, of myself on the screen.

Every fault — and there were many — was magnified, every move, look, the way I read a line — it all made me want to hide. But when the lights came on, Howard turned to me with a smile and said, 'You should be pleased. Jack Warner saw this yesterday and liked it, so things look pretty good.' I was afraid to believe it might happen. I'd know in a few days — if I could last that long.

Finally I got the call. Would I come to the studio for lunch with Howard? And then he told me — the part was mine. He and Charlie would have to sell half my contract to Warners or they wouldn't give me the part. But it was a great break, and to work with Bogart, a big star and good actor, could not be luckier for me. Actors of his stature were not often willing to have a complete unknown playing opposite them.

But I must say nothing yet about the part or the picture. Howard had plans. He wanted to find a good first name to go with my last one. Was there a name in my family that might be good — what was my grandmother's name? Sophie? No! He'd think of something.

He wanted me to continue working on my singing — continue reading aloud for my voice training — practice shouting, keeping my register low. He thought the picture would start at the beginning of February. After those months of waiting, it was finally happening. I was bursting with joy.

Mother was so happy for me — she knew how lucky I was. She had met Charlie several times, Howard once or twice, felt I was in good hands. She wanted to go back to New York, and as I was going to be working constantly from then on, it seemed a perfect time. She wanted to see the family. She missed her friends. Lee. So off she went, leaving me to my new life and my total preoccupation with it.

At lunch in the green room one day Howard told me he had thought of a name: Lauren. He wanted me to tell everyone when the interviews began that it was an old family name — had been my great-grandmother's. What invention! He wanted me to talk very little — be mysterious. That would be a departure. If there was one thing I had never been, it was mysterious, and if there was one thing I had never done, it was not talk. I had a lot to work on.

There was another woman's role in the picture and Warners had insisted that if they were to give me the lead, Howard had to use a girl they had under contract and had hopes for: Dolores Moran. Howard acquiesced. He was also going to use Hoagy Carmichael. Hoagy had never acted in his life, but Howard had the perfect part for him — Cricket, a piano player in the night-club of the hotel in Cuba where most of the action took place. He'd play while I'd sing. (While I'd *what?*) They were good friends and Hoagy loved the idea. Howard had thought everything out very carefully indeed. He was tailoring everything to complement what he wanted me to be, and out of that would come his dream realized, his invention — emerging perfectly out of his mold after the proper baking time of all the right ingredients.

One day a couple of weeks before the picture was to start, I was about to walk into Howard's office when Humphrey Bo-gart came walking out. He said, 'I just saw your test. We'll have a lot of fun together.' Howard told me Bogart had truly liked the test and would be very helpful to me.

I kept Mother up to date on develop-ments, sending lists of people to call with the news — Diana Vreeland, Louise Dahl-Wolfe, Nicky de Gunzburg, Tim Brooke — with instructions to keep it to themselves. I couldn't write to anyone — only Mother!

Call Fred Spooner — tell him I saved $48 this week and will try to do the same next week. Had to spend $20 on a new clutch for my car. . . . Send me slacks. . . . Send me this — that — everything. . . . Sat opposite Bette Davis in the Greenroom the other day — she stared at me — maybe she thought I looked familiar — Ha! Ha! Went to dinner and to see *Casablanca*! — watching Bogie [whom I barely knew]. The picture isn't scheduled to start until Tuesday now — but frankly I don't think it'll begin until a week from tomorrow [that would be the next Monday]. They have to change the locale from Cuba to Martinique. Political difficulties, because as it stands now, characters and story don't reflect too well on Cuba. Have been working hard at the studio every day. I think I'm going to do my own singing! [I'd been having singing lessons every day.]

The picture didn't begin until the following Tuesday. I had tested the wardrobe — hair — make-up. Sid Hickox had photographed them with Howard present, experimenting as he went, as Howard wanted me to look in the movie.

Walter Brennan had been cast in a large part, Marcel Dalio, Walter Surovy (Risë Stevens' husband), Sheldon Leonard, Dan Seymour — of course Hoagy. I went into the set the first day of shooting to see

Howard and Bogart — I would not be working until the second day. Bogart's wife, Mayo Methot, was there — he introduced us. I talked to Howard, watched for a while, and went home to prepare for my own first day.

It came and I was ready for a straitjacket. Howard had planned to do a single scene that day — my first in the picture. I walked to the door of Bogart's room, said, 'Anybody got a match?,' leaned against the door, and Bogart threw me a small box of matches. I lit my cigarette, looking at him, said 'Thanks,' threw the matches back to him, and left. Well — we rehearsed it. My hand was shaking — my head was shaking — the cigarette was shaking. I was mortified. The harder I tried to stop, the more I shook. What must Howard be thinking? What must Bogart be thinking? What must the crew be thinking? Oh God, make it stop! I was in such pain.

Bogart tried to joke me out of it — he was quite aware that I was a new young thing who knew from nothing and was scared to death. Finally Howard thought we could try a take. Silence on the set. The bell rang. 'Quiet — we're rolling,' said the sound man. 'Action,' said Howard. This was for posterity, I thought — for real theatres, for real people to see. I came around the corner, said my first line, and

Howard said, 'Cut.' He had broken the scene up — the first shot ended after the first line. The second set-up was the rest of it — then he'd move in for close-ups. By the end of the third or fourth take, I realized that one way to hold my trembling head still was to keep it down, chin low, almost to my chest, and eyes up at Bogart. It worked, and turned out to be the beginning of 'The Look.'

I found out very quickly that day what a terrific man Bogart was. He did everything possible to put me at ease. He was on my side. I felt safe — I still shook, but I shook less. He was not even remotely a flirt. I was, but I didn't flirt with him. There was much kidding around — our senses of humor went well together. Bogie's idea, of course, was that to make me laugh would relax me. He was right to a point, but nothing on earth would have relaxed me completely!

The crew were wonderful — fun and easy. It was a very happy atmosphere. I would often go to lunch with Howard. One day he told me he was very happy with the way I was working, but that I must remain somewhat aloof from the crew. Barbara Stanwyck, whom he thought very highly of — he'd made *Ball of Fire* with her, a terrific movie — was always fooling around with the crew, and he thought it a bad idea. 'They don't like you any better for it. When you finish a scene, go back to your dressing room. Don't hang around the set — don't give it all away — save it for the scenes.' He wanted me in a cocoon, only to emerge for work. Bogart could fool around to his heart's content — he was a star and a man — 'though you notice he doesn't do too much of it.'

One day at lunch when Howard was mesmerizing me with himself and his plans for me, he said, 'Do you notice how noisy it is in here suddenly? That's because Leo Forbstein just walked in — Jews always make more noise.' I felt that I was turning white, but I said nothing. I was afraid to — a side of myself I have never liked or been proud of — a side that was always there. Howard didn't dwell on it ever, but clearly he had very definite ideas about Jews — none too favorable, though he did business with them. They paid him — they were good for that. I would have to tell him about myself eventually or he'd find out through someone else. When the time came, what would happen would happen, but I had no intention of pushing it.

Howard started to line up special interviews for me. Nothing big would be released until just before the picture, and everything would be chosen with the greatest care. *Life*, *Look*, Kyle Crichton for

Collier's, Pic, Saturday Evening Post. Only very special fan magazines. Newspapers. I probably had more concentrated coverage than any beginning young actress had ever had — due to Hawks, not me.

Hoagy Carmichael had written a song called 'Baltimore Oriole.' Howard was going to use it as my theme music in the movie — every time I appeared on screen there were to be strains of that song. He thought it would be marvelous if I could be always identified with it — appear on Bing Crosby's or Bob Hope's radio show, have the melody played, have me sing it, finally have me known as the 'Baltimore Oriole.' What a fantastic fantasy life Howard must have had! His was a glamorous, mysterious, tantalizing vision — but it wasn't me.

On days I didn't have lunch with Howard, I would eat with another actor or the publicity man or have a sandwich in my room or in the music department during a voice lesson. I could not sit at a table alone. Bogie used to lunch at the Lakeside Golf Club, which was directly across the road from the studio.

One afternoon I walked into Howard's bungalow and found a small, gray-haired, mustached, and attractive man stretched out on the couch with a book in his hand and a pipe in his mouth. That man was

211

William Faulkner. He was contributing to the screenplay. Howard loved Faulkner — they had known each other a long time, had hunted together. Faulkner never had much money and Howard would always hire him for a movie when he could. He seldom came to the set — he was very shy — he liked it better in Howard's office.

Howard had a brilliantly creative work method. Each morning when we got to the set, he, Bogie, and I and whoever else might be in the scene, and the script girl would sit in a circle in canvas chairs with our names on them and read the scene. Almost unfailingly Howard would bring in additional dialogue for the scenes of sex and innuendo between Bogie and me. After we'd gone over the words several times and changed whatever Bogie or Howard thought should be changed, Howard would ask an electrician for a work light — one light on the set — and we'd go through the scene on the set to see how it felt. Howard said, 'Move around — see where it feels most comfortable.' Only after all that had been worked out did he call Sid Hickox and talk about camera set-ups. It is the perfect way for movie actors to work, but of course it takes time.

After about two weeks of shooting I wrote to my mother — she'd read one or two things in newspapers about my not having the first lead opposite Bogart —

Please, darling, don't worry about what is written in the newspapers concerning first and second leads. You make me so goddamn mad — what the hell difference does it make? As long as when the public sees the picture they know that I'm the one who is playing opposite Bogart. Everything is working out beautifully for me. Howard told Charlie the rushes were sensational. He's really very thrilled with them. I'm still not used to my face, however. Bogie has been a dream man. We have the most wonderful times together. I'm insane about him. We kid around — he's always gagging — trying to break me up and is very, very fond of me. So if I were you, I'd thank my lucky stars, as I am doing and not worry about those unimportant things. The only thing that's important is that I am good in the picture and the public likes me.

I don't know how it happened — it was almost imperceptible. It was about three weeks into the picture — the end of the day — I had one more shot, was sitting at the dressing table in the portable dressing room combing my hair. Bogie came in to bid me good night. He was standing behind me — we were joking as usual — when suddenly he leaned over, put his hand under my chin, and kissed me. It was impulsive — he was a bit shy — no lunging wolf tactics. He took a worn package of matches out of his pocket and asked me to put my phone number on the back. I did. I don't know why I did, except it was kind of part of our game. Bogie was meticulous about not being too personal, was known for never fooling around with women at work or anywhere else. He was not that kind of man, and also he was married to a woman who was a notorious drinker and fighter. A tough lady who would hit you with an ashtray, lamp, anything, as soon as not.

I analyzed nothing then — I was much too happy — I was having the time of my life. All that mattered to me was getting to the studio and working — my hours of sleep just got in the way! From the start of the movie, as Bogie and I got to know each other better — as the joking got more so — as we had more fun together — so the scenes changed little by little, our relationship strengthened on screen and involved us without our even knowing it. *I* certainly didn't know it. Gradually my focus began to shift away from Howard, more toward Bogie. Oh, I still paid full attention to Howard, but I think I depended more on Bogie. The construction of the scenes made that easy. I'm sure Howard became aware fairly early on that there was something between us and used it in the film.

At the end of the day of the phone number, I went home as usual to my routine: after eating something, I looked at my lines for the next day and got into bed. Around eleven o'clock the phone rang. It was Bogie. He'd had a few drinks, was away from his house, just wanted to see how I was. He called me Slim — I called him Steve, as in the movie. We joked back and forth — he finally said good night, he'd see me on the set. That was all, but from that moment on our relationship changed. He invited me to lunch at Lakeside a few times — or we'd sit in my dressing room or his with the door open, finding out more about one another. If he had a chess game going on the set — he was a first-rate chess player — I'd stand and watch, stand close to him. Physical proximity became more and more important. But still we joked.

Hedda Hopper came on the set one day and said, 'Better be careful. You might have a lamp dropped on you one day.' There was a column squib in the *Hollywood Reporter*: 'You can have your B&B at lunch any day at Lakeside.'

Bogie took to calling me more often. He had two friends named Pat and Zelma O'Moore. She had sung 'Button Up Your Overcoat' in a Broadway show, but had since retired. Pat O'Moore was an Irish actor whom Bogie had befriended — he worked in Bogie's films and others when there was a part. They had a small boat which they kept in Newport in the slip next to Bogie's. They lived in a small trailer camp in town. Bogie took me there one night and we all had dinner together, but he couldn't do that often. Other nights he'd call very late — sometimes one or two in the morning — and come over to my apartment. It was an unusual role for Bogie. He was not by instinct or practice a cheat or a liar. He told me about his marriage — how he had more or less fallen into it. He'd been married twice before. When he was in his twenties, he'd been married to a famous Broadway actress, Helen Menken. Always his wives had been actresses — always wanting to continue their careers, always putting that first.

After Helen, he married an actress called Mary Philips. When they'd been married for seven or eight years he accepted an offer to come to California, and he wanted her to come with him. He didn't believe in separations and he also didn't believe in following women around. But she insisted on following her career on the stage and he said, 'Okay, but don't stay away too long.' She did. He met Mayo — fell into something with her (drink and bed, I should think), warned Mary to come out, then went to Chicago, where she was in a play with Roland Young. He got there, found that they were having an affair, and that was the end of that marriage. He felt he had to marry Mayo — he was a marrying man, she expected it, it was the gentlemanly thing to do, so he did it. And it got worse and worse. They were known as the Battling Bogarts — almost every evening wound up with her throwing something at Bogie, trying to hit him and succeeding most of the time. She'd stabbed him in the back with a knife on one occasion and he had the scar to prove it. He said he had to drink — it was the only way he could live with her. She was jealous — always accused him of having affairs with his leading ladies — always knocked him as an actor, making sarcastic references about the 'big star.' She'd sung 'More Than You Know' in a Vincent Youmans musical, had been successful and was a good actress — but drink took over and the minute there was a third person present, she'd start on Bogie. He wasn't crying the blues to me — he accepted it. He didn't like it, but that's the way it was and he couldn't do anything about it.

I said nothing to anyone about seeing Bogie outside the studio. But anyone with half an eye could see that there was more between us than the scenes we played. I'd listen for his arrival in make-up in the morning. He'd get there about 8:30 — he wore no make-up, just had his hair blacked in a bit in front where it was getting thin, but he'd come to see me having my hair combed out. Sometimes we'd go to the set together. I'd always leave my dressing-room door open so as not to miss him if he passed by. There was never enough time for me to be with him. In the picture I wore a black satin dress with a bare midriff that was held together with a black plastic ring. One day I cut out a picture of Bogie and fitted it into the ring — walked over to him casually on the set until he noticed it and laughed. Our jokes were total corn: 'What did the ceiling say to the wall?' 'Hold me up, I'm plastered.' . . . 'Do your eyes bother you?' 'No.' 'They bother me.' . . . And I'd make my gorilla face, which consisted of putting my tongue under my upper lip and dropping my jaw. All silly but marvelous. And he taught me constantly in scenes. We had one scene in which I had been teasing him — he was to take me out the door because he wanted to have a bath — stop and kiss me before being interrupted. He told Howard he'd seen the Lunts do something in a play once which he felt would work for us. After the kiss I was to run the back of my hand up the side of his face, which needed a shave, then give him a short, quick slap. It was a most suggestive and intimate bit of business. Much more so than writhing around on the floor would have been. And in rehearsals of other scenes he'd sometimes add something — a word or a bit of business — that would throw me. He'd say, 'Just to make sure you're listening.' He taught me to stay on my toes at all times.

By now Howard of course knew something was going on and he didn't like it. As we neared the end of the picture, he summoned me out to his house one night. I was petrified. Just he and his wife, Slim, were there. He sat me down and began. 'When you started to work you were marvelous — paying attention, working hard. I thought, "This girl is really something." Then you started fooling around with Bogart. For one thing, it means nothing to him — this sort of thing happens all the time, he's not serious about you. When the picture's over, he'll forget all about it — that's the last you'll ever see of him. You're throwing away a chance anyone would give their right arm for. I'm not going to put up with it. I tell you I'll just send you to Monogram [the studio that

219

made the lowest form of pictures at that time]. I'll wash my hands of you.' Of course I burst into tears — tried to control myself, which only made it worse. Slim said, 'But what do you do, Howard, if you're stuck on a guy? How do you handle it?' She was trying to help me. Howard would have none of it. 'You just play the scenes, do your work. You can laugh and have a good time, but just remember that when the picture's over, *it* will be over.' I told him I didn't want to disappoint him, I was trying hard, I loved the work. Bogie had been wonderful to me and we had so much fun together, but I'd try to be better — 'Honestly, Howard.'

I was so upset when I left — in such a state. I was sure he'd send me to Monogram — that my career was over before it had begun. And didn't Bogie mean anything he had ever said to me — was it all just for the picture — just empty talk — did he really not care about me? I cried all night. The next morning I was a mess — eyes all puffy and red. I had to put ice on my face at 6:00 a.m. and again when I got to the studio — I didn't want anyone to see that I'd been crying. I was determined to behave differently. Howard had almost convinced me. After all, Bogie was a married man, he had nothing to lose by flirting with me, it was all frivolous. Only Bogie was not a frivolous man — I knew he wasn't — and he wasn't cheap. I was confused, terribly upset, and scared. Bogie greeted me as usual, only I was different and tried not to be. But he knew instantly. 'What's wrong?' 'Nothing,' said I. 'C'mon — has Howard been talking to you?' I nodded — 'I'll tell you later.'

Later that day when it would be least obtrusive I went into Bogie's dressing room and told him what Howard had said to me. He stroked my hair and my face and said, 'No, Baby, he won't send you to Monogram — don't you worry, you're too valuable to him. He just can't stand to see your attention diverted from him, that's all — he's jealous. And I do mean what I say to you. We just must be very careful — I don't want you to be hurt. And if Madam [his name for Mayo] finds out, you *could* be hurt, and I couldn't stand that. But don't worry about Howard — his nose is out of joint, that's all.' And of course he was right — Howard was losing control and he didn't like that. And I owed him a great deal — he'd done everything for me, and though I was afraid of him, I did like him and respect him. But I'd have to be more careful of my demeanor.

A few days after that we were to shoot me singing 'How Little We Know.' That was to be a full day of me, Hoagy, a lot of extras, and no Bogie. I had prerecorded the song and was to sing the playback, which is not easy, particularly for a novice. Howard was satisfied with the recording, though he thought one or two notes might have to be dubbed later on. Bogie and I planned to have dinner together that night, with me cooking. The menu would be hamburgers, baked potato, and a salad. A cook I wasn't. He called me on the set in the afternoon — he'd call me at home later to make sure I'd returned.

At the end of that long day, Howard put his arm around me and said, 'You did a really good day's work, Betty, I'm proud of you.' That's the only true compliment he ever paid me. It was hard for him. I was pleased that he was satisfied — I thanked him — but he didn't know who I was on my way to as I left the studio.

How do you know when you're in love? I had no basis for comparison. Every emotional involvement I'd had before — like Kirk — I'd thought was love, but it wasn't. I was almost sure I loved Bogie — and more than that, that he was in love with me. We shared so much — understood so much about each other.

We started to drive home together, leaving the studio with Bogie in the lead in his car, me following in mine. We drove over Highland Avenue, turned right on Hollywood Boulevard to Franklin, then another right onto Selma Avenue, a small street that was curved and very residential — almost no traffic would pass through.

We'd pull over to the side and he'd come over to my car. There we would sit, holding hands, looking into each other's eyes, saying all the things we couldn't say at the studio. We'd sit on our street for fifteen or twenty minutes, dreading the moment of parting, then he'd get into his car and off we'd go, making the turn at Laurel Canyon Boulevard to Sunset Boulevard, continuing on until we reached Horn Avenue, where Bogie lived. As he made the turn, he'd wave his hand out the window — I'd do the same and go on to Beverly Hills. It was romantic — it was fun — it was exciting — it was all-encompassing.

I'd never known anyone remotely like Bogie. As he revealed more of his life to me, I realized that it had been complicated and rough. Though he'd never had children, he'd always had responsibilities. His father had died in his arms and left him ten thousand dollars of debt and a ring — gold with two rubies and a diamond — which Bogie always wore. His mother had been an artist — Maud Humphrey — and had drawn Bogie a great deal for children's food ads and books. Bogie had been known as the 'Maud Humphrey Baby.' She evidently was strong — a suffragette. He admired her, but she was not warm or affectionate. She died of cancer when she was seventy. And he had two sisters — Kay and Pat. Kay had been a gay girl during speakeasy days — laughing, drinking, burning herself out so that she died in her thirties. Pat had been the quiet one — madly in love with her husband and he with her — mother of a lovely daughter. Tragically struck down when a young woman by an illness that would plague her all her life — divorced and left with only Bogie to take care of her, emotionally and financially. Bogie looked after his sister always — loved her and was constantly saddened by the rotten hand she had been dealt. She was goodness incarnate. So, not including his three failed marriages, he had had burdens to bear.

He was a gentle man — diametrically opposed to most of the parts he played. He detested deceit of any kind. He had never had a secret relationship such as we were having. Our drives home, foolish jokes, kidding on the set, all the behavior of kids in love — he'd never known. Nor had I. I had so many new feelings all at once. I was in awe of him and his position of 'movie star.' I was aware of being nineteen and he forty-four, but when we were together that didn't seem to matter. I was older than nineteen in many ways and he had such energy and vitality he seemed to be no particular age. I was an innocent sexually — Bogie began awakening feelings that were new to me. Just his looking at me could make me tremble. When he took my hand in his, the feeling caught me in the pit of my stomach — his hand was warm, protecting, and full of love. When he saw me at the beginning of the day and when he called me on the telephone, his first words were always 'Hello, Baby.' My heart would literally pound. I knew that physical changes were happening within me — the simplest word, look, or move would bring a gut reaction. It was all so romantic — I would not have believed Bogie was so sentimental, so loving. I couldn't think of anything else — when I wasn't with him I was thinking of him, or talking about him. One-track-minding with a vengeance. My friend from *Johnny 2 x 4*, Carolyn Cromwell, came to stay with me for about ten days. She was madly in love with a music publisher named Buddy Morris, who was married with three children. So she'd tell me everything about Buddy and I'd tell her everything about Bogie. Talking our loves out loud made them seem more possible.

And I wanted to give Bogie so much that he hadn't had. All the love that had been stored inside of me all my life for an invisible father, for a man. I could finally think of allowing it to pour over *this* man and fill his life with laughter, warmth, joy — things he hadn't had for such a long time, if ever. My imagination was working overtime.

What would my mother think of all this? She knew nothing about me and Bogie. I hadn't even given her a slight indication — no doubt for fear she'd rush back to California too quickly. Without her I was free to think only of him, this man who made every day brighter because he was in it. Oh God, what would I do when I couldn't see him every day — when the picture was over? How could I live? But I would see him somehow. He wanted it as much as I did, I was sure he did. There was always a tiny element of doubt in mind about my luck. Early training. He had to love me — he had to!

So the days passed, and the weeks, and the movie would end soon. Mother came back from New York. I was happy to see her, but I knew that trouble would start when she found out about Bogie. I said nothing — just told her about the movie, how it was going, about all the interviews I'd been giving, about Howard bringing Paul Lukas on the set one day to surprise

226

me. One night when we were asleep the phone rang — Bogie, of course. He'd gotten out of the house after a big drunken fight with Mayo — would I meet him around the corner? I never hesitated for a second — whenever he called, I was there. I jumped into slacks and sweater. Mother stuck her head up: 'What's going on? Where are you going?' Me: 'I'm going to meet Bogie. I have to. I'll explain it all to you later.' She: 'Are you crazy? Get right back into bed!' When my mind was made up, my mind was made up. 'I will not get back into bed. *Please,* Mother, don't worry.' And out the door. Into my car and around the corner to Rodeo Drive and Wilshire Boulevard. There was Bogie with Jimmy Gleason, whom he'd met at some bar. I ran up the street — arms open wide, hair flying — to Bogie's smiling face and safe embrace. We sat in the car for a while — Gleason didn't know or care what was going on — it was just that Bogie had to see his Baby. What it felt like to be so wanted, so adored! No one had ever felt like that about me. It was all so dramatic, too. Always in the wee small hours when it seemed to Bogie and me that the world was ours — that we were the world. At those times we were.

I got home about an hour later. Mother awake, of course, saying, 'Get to sleep —

you have to work tomorrow.' Furious. The next day after work I had to explain a lot of it to her. She said, 'But he's married — he's been married three times. What kind of a man is that — with a wife — who'd be seeing a girl twenty-five years younger?' 'I know all that, Mother. You don't understand. He's unhappy — his marriage is lousy — his wife's a drunk and a mess. He loves me.' 'Of course,' said Mother, 'why shouldn't he? A girl so young and beautiful. Who wouldn't?' She didn't trust him for one second. Bogie was her contemporary. I was *her* Baby. He'd had three wives, he drank a lot — what kind of man could he be, except no good? *Her* early training.

'When you meet him you'll see how different he is than what you think.' But she didn't expect to meet him. She knew that something big had happened to me and she knew that nothing would stop me. But she wasn't ready to relinquish her position just yet — certainly not without a fight. She wanted the best for me, and Bogart wasn't the best. And I owed Howard a lot — I wasn't to forget that. I couldn't just forget everyone else because of Bogart. Obviously she was right about that. And yet that's about what I was doing.

To Have and Have Not was almost finished. Howard was happy — Warners was — Charlie was. Bogie and I were happy with the movie, but miserable at the thought of our separation. It had to come — Bogie was going to his boat at Newport Beach. That was what he loved — the sea. It meant health and peace to him. And he would have to pacify Mayo. She'd mentioned me too many times, and though that was part of her pattern, he wasn't about to take any chances.

My falling in love had definitely taken over and put the biggest, most exciting thing that ever happened in my work life into second place. I didn't realize — not really — what the movie might mean. I hadn't seen any of it cut together, and in any case couldn't have understood what would happen to me as a result of it.

Finally it was the last day of shooting. We'd film the last scene and do publicity stills. It was a big set and a big lighting job. Hoagy at the piano. Me with him — extras — Bogie saying goodbye to Marcel Dalio — Walter Brennan moving with Bogie — me wriggling across the room to Bogie — him grabbing my arm — all of us walking away — fade-out. Bogie and I went to Burt Six's studio for stills — first Bogie alone, with me behind camera making faces, joking, then the two of us. Bogie knew just how to do it. We played our own scene, which was very Slim-and-Steve anyway — we had become them or they us almost from the beginning. Terrific fun — exciting — vibrations beyond description. It was pretty funny, my playing this woman of the world, this know-it-all, experienced sex-pot — me nineteen years old and actually knowing nothing, a true innocent, but blessed with the good sense and humor God and my family had given me, plus the willfulness and determination to get what I wanted.

Howard's voice saying 'Cut — print' brought the most memorable and important eleven weeks of my life to a close. Bogie said goodbye to everyone. I was going to have dinner with Howard and Slim that night, a celebration of sorts. I walked outside the stage with Bogie, stood by my car, and put my hand straight up in the air, smiling as Bogie drove away. It was hell — I was so unhappy. But I was determined to be brave, seemingly devil-may-care, my attitude being 'Everything's going to be okay. We'll see each other again any minute.' But the emptiness when he left! I felt as though everything that had given me care and support was being taken away. When would I see him — when would he call? How could he stand to be with *that* woman — how could he stand not to be with me? Questions on questions. Talking to myself again.

I was such a single-minded person that I

really did not understand there were other possibilities. If you were separated from someone you loved, how was it possible to derive pleasure from *anything?* How could you enjoy sports — a meal — other people? How was *anything* in life bearable away from your loved one? I had been super-charged the last several months — my first movie and all that went with it, compounded by falling in love. Every moment had been used — every part of me had been functioning — my mind, my make-believe self, my ambition, my romantic side or core — feelings of physical desire and pain that I had never known — a true awakening. I was beginning to leave girlhood behind, beginning (at last) to move toward womanhood.

Howard was really very happy with the film. And with the celluloid relationship between Bogie and me. Originally the script had involved an attraction between Bogie and the character Dolores Moran played. But halfway into the film Howard ran some of our scenes cut, showed them to Bogie, and with Bogie's help had come to the conclusion that no audience would believe anyone or anything could come between Slim and Steve. So scenes were adjusted accordingly and all of mine made stronger and better. You can't beat chemistry.

Howard was also happy with me, being sure the romance with Bogie had come to a close and that he was in control again. We didn't discuss it in depth, Howard just said he was glad I had come to my senses — 'You can have a good time and not throw your career away doing it.' Bogie was a terrific actor, our scenes together had worked marvelously, he had always known they would. (And he had. How, I'll never know — unfailing movie instinct, I guess.) But Bogie had been married to this hard-drinking, tough lady for a long time and he liked it. He certainly would never leave her.

The jury was still out on that one, but Howard could be right. In spite of everything I had told myself, everything Bogie had told me about life with Mayo, and all that had passed between us verbally and physically, I knew there was a chance Howard was right.

I had much to fill my days — more interviews, portrait sittings. Slim and I were photographed on Moraga Drive for *Harper's Bazaar*. We had become good friends, although the shadow of Howard loomed large for both of us. She had to live with him and I had to work for him, so I never talked freely about Bogie. She knew I was involved and instinctively felt that Bogie was, but, being more grown-up than I, thought it was just a love affair that time would take care of. She was very proud of me and protective of me. I could never really connect with Slim and Howard's relationship. They seemed temperamentally different — Howard was clearly crazy about her, but, undemonstrative as he was, I never felt a sense of fun or sex between them.

About a week after the movie wrapped, I received my first letter from Bogie. He said how unhappy he was because I was not with him.

> I wish with all my heart that things were different — someday soon they will be. And now I know what was meant by 'To say goodbye is to die a little' — because when I walked away from you that last time and saw you standing there so darling I did die a little in my heart.
>
> Steve

I mooned for days. Of course I couldn't write him. I just hoped against hope to see him and had to wait for that phone to ring. It finally did. Bogie was in the Coast Guard during the war and was on duty once a week patrolling the shore. During the course of the night he would have a free hour, so we decided that I'd drive down, spend the hour with him, and drive back. It was the only time we could be sure of having together — far from ideal, but a damn sight better than nothing. So each week I'd drive down, most of the time with Carolyn, my devoted, patient, and understanding friend. The drive to Balboa took over two hours. I'd go to the gate — they'd tell Bogie I was there — we'd sit in his car, holding hands, talking, looking at each other, kissing. We'd exchange letters — I'd bring one down that he would read after I'd gone, and he'd give me one that I would read on the way home and twenty times after that. It was high adventure — very romantic, frustrating, and young. What any two people madly in love would do. Bogie's letters were all on the same themes: how much he loved me — how terrified he was of my being hurt — how he wanted to protect me — how wonderful of me to take that long drive to see him for so short a time. A few examples.

Baby, I do love you so dearly and I never, never want to hurt you or bring any unhappiness to you — I want you to have the loveliest life any mortal ever had. It's been so long, darling, since I've cared so deeply for anyone that I just don't know what to do or say. I can only say that I've searched my heart thoroughly these past two weeks and I

234

know that I deeply adore you and I know that I've got to have you. We just must wait because at present nothing can be done that would not bring disaster to you.

And a week later:

Baby, I never believed that I could love anyone again, for so many things have happened in my life to me that I was afraid to love — I didn't want to love because it hurts so when you do.

And then:

Slim darling, you came along and into my arms and into my heart and all the real true love I have is yours — and now I'm afraid you won't understand and that you'll become impatient and that I'll lose you — but even if that happened, I wouldn't stop loving you for you are my last love and all the rest of my life I shall love you and watch you and be ready to help you should you ever need help.

All the nice things I do each day would be so much sweeter and so much gayer if you were with me. I find myself saying a hundred times a day, 'If Slim could only see that' or 'I wish Slim could hear this.' I want to make a new life with you — I want all the friends I've lost to meet you and know you and love you as I do — and live again with you, for the past years have been terribly tough, damn near drove me crazy. You'll soon be here, Baby, and when you come you'll bring everything that's important to me in this world with you.

One Saturday he had to be in town for a little while on business. So naturally he came to my apartment. We were together for just a couple of hours — my mother stayed away, which was really good of her considering the degree of her disapproval.

Then the June 14 letter:

Darling, sometimes I get so unhappy because I feel that I'm not being fair to you — that it is not fair to wait so long a time — and then somehow I feel that it's alright because I'm not hurting you, not harming and never shall.

I'd rather die than be the cause of any hurt or harm coming to you, Baby, because I love you so much.

It seems so strange that after forty-four years of knocking around I should meet you, know you and fall in love with you when I thought that that could never again happen to me. And it's tragic that everything couldn't be all clean and just right for us instead of the way it is because we'd have such fun together. Out of my love for you I want nothing but happiness to come to you and no hurt ever.

Slim darling, I wish I were your age again — perhaps a few years older — and no ties of any kind — no responsibilities — it would be so lovely, for there would be so many long years ahead for us instead of the few possible ones.

And he always cautioned me to stay away from the Hollywood folk — the ones who thrived on gossip and other people's troubles. I had started so well on my career, and the more successful I became, the more people would try to latch on to me. Don't ever do anything cheap — don't ever hang around with people who do cheap things.

On July 5 the following communiqué was sent to the Warners staff on both coasts from their head of publicity, Charlie Einfeld:

Polish up the picks, shovels and pans for the gold mine on the way in Howard Hawks' production of Ernest Hemingway's *To Have and Have Not*, which we sneaked last night and which is not only a second *Casablanca* but two and a half times what *Casablanca* was. Here is a story of adventure and basic sex appeal the likes of which we have not seen since *Morocco* and *Algiers*. Bogart terrific, never was seen like this before. Lauren Bacall, new find of ours playing opposite Bogart, distinct personality who positively will be star overnight. Nothing like Bacall has been seen on the screen since Garbo and Dietrich. This is one of the biggest and hottest attractions we have ever had. If this sounds like I'm overboard, well I am.

I was not allowed to go to the first preview, but Charlie Feldman told me about it. It went fantastically well — all the audience-opinion cards were great. Howard was very happy — Warners were thrilled — and I would be a big hit. It would be almost a year before I understood what this meant. I didn't know what a studio and its publicity department could do, plus a director of Howard's stature who was totally behind me. Being a star to me only meant my name in lights. I was completely unaware of what publicity would bring.

They had a second preview about ten days later and Howard and Charlie took me to it. It is weird to see a movie that you've worked on scene by scene all put together. First the opening titles and credits and the music. I was so nervous and so excited. I was uncomfortable watching and hearing myself, but seeing Bogie's and my scenes together, I was able to relive all the moments we'd shared on the set — all the funny, silly things we'd done. And I knew how far the relationship had traveled by each scene. I could have spent weeks seeing the film over and over because it brought me close to Bogie again. But the audience reaction threw me — I had not expected so much laughter, so much sheer enjoyment, from strangers. It would have been wonderful if Bogie had been there with me to see and hear it all. Maybe one day we could see it together. I couldn't wait to tell him about it.

After the preview I stood in the background with Charlie Feldman while Howard talked to Charlie Einfeld and some other Warner people and they looked at more opinion cards. Then Howard and Charlie F. took me for coffee and asked how I liked it. I told them as best I could. How could I help but love something that had changed my whole life — that had given me the chance to realize my dream of being an actress and had introduced me to the man I had fallen in love with, who had to be the best man who ever lived. It was a marvelous night. I felt really close to Howard, so relieved when he smiled, when he seemed satisfied. I wanted his approval, and when he gave it, I felt terrific. Charlie Feldman I always felt good with. He was a friend I could trust and talk to — but not about Bogie. I couldn't talk about him to anyone but Carolyn yet.

The picture was going to be released in October. Until then I would do only what Howard and Warners, with Howard's approval, wanted me to do. Warners owned half of my contract, but Howard had the final word about his discovery, and he still wanted me to keep a low profile. After the picture came out, I'd have enough to do. So again I found myself waiting for something to happen. Fortunately, my head was so full of my life with Bogie — living from phone call to phone call, from meeting to stolen meeting — that my career took a back seat. My focus was Bogie — I dreamed only of him, of our being together forever. I wanted to give him the fun he'd never had, the children he'd never had. I wanted to show him that it was all possible. I wanted to believe it myself.

At four one morning the phone rang. Bogie was a little drunk. 'I'm walking back to town. Come and get me — I'll be on Highway 101.' My mother thought I was completely mad when I started to get dressed. She was furious. 'You can't jump every time he calls. He'll have no respect for you. Let him know that you won't meet him any hour of the day or night. He's taking advantage of you — it's ridiculous.' But I would not be stopped. It was raining, but I didn't care. I was in love, I was on my way to meet my man — that's all that mattered. I rushed to my car and started out. Pitch dark and me not a great driver and with no sense of direction. Somehow I found Highway 101 — I'd driven it often enough on my Coast Guard nights. My Plymouth was such a light car that in rain and heavy wind it would weave from side to side. How in hell was Bogie walking on a highway in this weather? I drove for more than an hour — it was beginning to get light. The rain finally let up. I kept hugging the right side of the road, looking frantically for Bogie. At last, as the sun rose, I caught sight of him — unshaven, wearing *espadrillas,* and with a large sunflower in his lapel. We were about a half-hour out of Newport — I don't know how he'd got there. I slammed to a halt, rushed out of the car — there was no traffic — and into each other's arms we fell. It was the funniest, craziest thing he'd done so far.

He was exhausted — directed me to drive to the O'Moores' trailer. He'd called them and we were expected. It was a

241

Sunday morning. I loved being with these friends of Bogie's. There was no strain — we didn't have to pretend anything. I had gotten to know Pat and Zell rather well — they were my lifeline to Bogie — I could ask how he was, what he was doing, what was happening — what did they think would happen — what about Mayo, what was he like with her, anything like he was with me? They were his friends, not hers. Zell had coffee made and we had a good leisurely breakfast. A friend who had the trailer next to theirs was away and had said they could use it, so Bogie could take a nap later on if he wanted to. He talked about his sister and how well she was doing — talked about his sailing. He had two small-class sailboats that he used to race in Newport all through the summer. Bogie loved sailing — everything about it. It made him feel so good to be on the water — painting, varnishing, anything to do with a boat was food to him, health. He talked about the fight he'd had with Mayo — he'd had to get out, couldn't stand it anymore. After a while it was clear we wanted to be alone. We had to be. We had been sitting in dressing rooms, in automobiles, hiding for so long. We went to the trailer next door. It was the first time we'd had complete privacy — no anxiety about phones or doorbells ringing — we could do

242

or say anything we pleased — it was our nest — it was the most natural thing in the world — we were so happy — we were so in love — it was beautiful. I shall never forget that day.

Bogie had to return to Newport, as he didn't want to leave his sister. Pat would take him. I cried as he drove away.

I would see Bogie again that Wednesday — Coast Guard day. In his July 12 letter he wrote:

> Sunday was so beautiful, so sweet, my dearest, and you were wonderful to come to the rescue of poor befuddled me — I was just about ready to give up and die under an oil well when I saw your blessed face — never was so glad to see anyone, and I must have been a beautiful sight. And then that lovely day with you darling — and the moments that were ours alone to cherish always in our hearts.

Throughout this period I had to keep telling myself it would all come true for Bogie and me. I never believed that marriage was a lasting institution — for obvious reasons spawned in my childhood. I thought that to be married for five years was to be married forever.

Mother was not a cynical woman — on

the contrary, she had fantasies of her own, romantic dreams. But she was horrified at the thought of a married man chasing me — much less a three-times-married man. She didn't trust Bogie at all. When from time to time I would read her passages from Bogie's letters expressing his worry and care for my well-being, she'd only say, 'He *should* say those things.' She knew how headstrong I was, but she lectured me anyway about character — his, if he had any, a man who cheated on his wife, and mine for getting mixed up with him. 'He should have waited until he was free if he loves you so much.' She just didn't understand at all — she didn't know him, didn't know all the problems. I did — but as there always was an element of doubt in my head, her talks fed that element.

She and I had gone to another preview of *To Have and Have Not* with Charlie and Howard and she was flabbergasted. It must have been a shock to see one's pure and innocent daughter behaving like a wanton, life-bitten woman of the world. Of course both of us wrote the entire family all about the movie — they were waiting breathlessly to see it. None of them knew anything of Bogie and me. Grandma, who was true Old Country, would have been very upset. As far as her values went, Bogie had nothing going for him — he was too old for me, he'd had three wives, he drank, he was an actor, and he was Goyim. So I wrote her my usual letters — all about work, California — and we sent pictures to her. She hadn't been very well and she missed her darling granddaughter — my year in California was the first in nineteen that she hadn't seen me at least twice a week, except for school and camp. She needed her children around her and she had had them for most of her life. I always thought of what she might think or say when she saw me in the movie or if she learned about Bogie. Kirk had always been her favorite because he was Jewish. I hadn't told Bogie I was — it had never come up, and religion as such was not important to him.

The first week in August it had been arranged that I would drive down to Newport and stay on Pat and Zelma's boat for a couple of days. A dangerous decision, but Bogie wanted me to see Newport — to feel the atmosphere that he had described to me so many times and loved so much. I loved the idea — forbidden territory is excitement incarnate.

I would be kept under wraps and below until the boat moved away from the slip. Mother was so worried: 'If his wife catches you down there, it will be just awful.' The understatement of the century.

I drove down in the morning. Bogie would keep Mayo occupied until I was safely aboard. There was no danger of her leaving his boat as long as he was on it. The whole scene was really a B movie. Funny now. When I got there, Pat gave me a letter from Bogie. It turned out that Mayo had to go to town the next day for an entire twenty-four hours, so I'd be with him all that time. Glorious!

I had never been on a large boat before — my sea-going life had been confined to rowboats and canoes. The O'Moore boat was a power boat that had bunks, and a galley (kitchen) and a head (john). It was thirty feet long, which made it almost ocean-going to my city-bred eyes. Being aboard was like playing house. Not really roomy, but very nice. The yacht basin was a series of boats of all sizes separated by small wooden walks called slips at the water level or just above. I'd never seen so many boats — my God, were there that many people who lived on the water?

The next day Bogie came on board for lunch. It was so wonderful to see him, to be with him again — to touch him. Mayo had to go to the doctor — she had broken her foot, falling down drunk, of course — had been in a cast, and had to be checked out. What a windfall! Bogie pointed out his

246

boat. It, too, was a power boat, about thirty-six feet. He thrived on small sailboat racing — had already won two cups that summer, which gave him more of a kick than any movie could have done. He loved competing and being accepted as a sailor by other sailors. He greatly resented their resentment of actors — their attitude of 'For an actor you're a good sailor.' But Bogie did not play at sailing and they knew it — he knew all the rules of racing, had read every book ever written about it, and, best of all, he could do it well — and each cup he won proved it.

He kept saying, 'This is why I love sailing — the sea — the air — it's clean and healthy and away from the Hollywood gossip and leeches.' It was a beautiful, clear, sunny day. Bogie had told me he might work with Howard again — Howard had talked to him about a Raymond Chandler story, he wanted to put us in another picture together right away. Bogie was having contract arguments with Warners and was worried about the outcome. He wanted some security and, after *Casablanca* and *To Have and Have Not*, was in a good position to renegotiate. He couldn't decide anything about Howard's project until that was settled. If we could work together again, we could be together again. What a lovely, happy thought.

That night Zell cooked dinner on the boat, but Bogie decided he wanted to take me over to the yacht club for a drink. 'You're crazy,' said I, 'we'll have nothing but trouble if Mayo finds out.' 'She won't,' said he, 'we'll just go for one — they're my friends, not hers.' There seemed to be no choice — if Bogie's mind was made up, that was that, there was nothing to discuss. So I put on a navy flannel shirt of Bogie's over my sweater and pants — took a deep breath — put my hand in his and went. He had a little putt-putt — a small boat with an outboard motor — and we traveled across the harbor in that. He took me into a dimly lit room with a bar on one side and an outside deck right on the water. There were only a couple of people who were friends there — it was a quiet night at the club. As he had several pet names for me — Charlie, Chuck, Junior, game names — he introduced me very casually to a couple of his sailor pals. They were slightly mulled — I meant nothing to them anyway. I was just a girl, they didn't think anything of it. But I was nervous — really wanted to get the hell out. I didn't want trouble and felt very much an outsider. After a very long hour we left. On the ride back — it was cold and dark — sitting just in front of Bogie, I had to ask the question that had been so much on my mind — I had to get it straight. Did it matter to him that I was Jewish? Hell, no — what mattered to him was *me*, how I thought, how I felt, what kind of person I was, not my religion. He couldn't care less — why did I even ask? He couldn't really understand my anxiety, but he'd never felt it himself — he wasn't Jewish. Being singled out for such a thing was inconceivable to him. It was a big weight off my shoulders — I was relieved to have it in the open, it had been lurking too long in the unfinished-business department of my mind.

Bogie stayed on the O'Moore boat that night. The next day he had to go back to his own — Mayo would return sometime during the day. I was going to stay the day and drive home late. Around lunchtime he came over to say goodbye to me — we were always saying goodbye — and suddenly Pat called down, 'Christ, Mayo's heading this way.' I thought I'd drop dead from fright. There was nowhere to go. Bogie shoved me into the head, where I sat holding on to the door with my heart pounding so loudly I was sure it could be heard all over the boat. I could hear them talking — I heard her say, 'Let's sit down and have a drink.' Oh God, don't let it happen now — I was so scared I was shaking — what a hopeless confrontation that would have been. The O'Moores said they had to go onshore to get something — Bogie said he wanted to go too — at last they left. Pat walked down the dock with Bogie and Mayo — Zelma came down, called to me that the coast was clear. When I could come up on deck, what a relief to be able to breathe the air again! I couldn't wait to get away. Newport Beach was not the place for me. I hated the hiding. I didn't want to return until the all-clear was the all-clear for all time.

Bogie got to a phone the following day: 'That was a close call — whew!' He said that Mayo was suspicious — not of specifics, but in general. His Coast Guard duty would be over in a couple of weeks, and he'd be in and out of Balboa getting his business affairs straight. I went down there one more time for one of our trysts. He was not happy. He said Mayo was going to stop drinking, or at least was going to try, and he had to give her that chance. It was the only civilized thing to do. He loved me as much as ever, but felt we should lie low for a few weeks. He'd call me.

Meanwhile Howard had started to prepare *The Big Sleep*. I kept busy with singing lessons — Howard wanted me to sing again, 'Baltimore Oriole,' he wouldn't give up that fantasy. Bill Faulkner was working on the screenplay. I saw a lot of Howard at the studio and of Howard and Slim at night as well. But I hadn't seen Bogie for a few weeks. Maybe Mayo was behaving herself. Maybe they'd stay together. Every negative idea I'd ever had came to the fore. 'But,' I kept saying — there was always a but — 'he does love me — I know he does — you don't love someone so much one minute and stop the next.' Oh, I had a hard time of it — I was so unhappy, depressed, worried. How could I work with him again if he didn't love me? I'd have to — but how could I?

My Uncle Jack wrote Mother that he and Vera had seen a preview of *To Have and Have Not* — they were very proud and pleased. He'd been apprehensive because he thought the publicity was building me for straight sex — he was happy there was some humor in it too, for he was convinced, as was my Uncle Charlie, that my forte was going to be comedy. At the end of his letter — dated September 15 — he also said, 'Mother is not well again and I don't know how long she is going to last. I would arrange for her to see the preview no matter what it cost if I weren't convinced she wouldn't live through it — the emotional strain would be too great.'

On the sixteenth a box of flowers was delivered to my door. A note inside read, 'Look who's twenty — Steve.' He'd remembered. I was teary-eyed — my first red roses — he did love me, he was just trying to do the right thing by everyone, trying to be fair — he was too good, too kind. But oh, I missed him. Thank God for my friend Carolyn. She could moan to me about Buddy and I could moan to her about Bogie. We had some swell times moaning together.

Grandma was living with Rosalie and Charlie. When Jack's letter arrived, Mother and I called her there. She was happy to hear our voices, but she sounded very weak — a shocking sound to me. I wished I could be with her. She had sent me a birthday card — 'To my darling Bettelein.' The warm feeling of unjudging, protective family love cannot be equaled. I told her she had to see the movie — I'd have a screening set up for her in New York. Mother said she'd be coming to New York with me soon, so we'd all be together again.

On the afternoon of Wednesday, September 20, the phone rang. I was alone in the apartment — Mother had gone out with a friend. It was Charlie, telling me that Grandma had died. It had all happened very quickly. Tell Mother there's no point in her rushing to New York — the services will be tomorrow. Jack got on the phone — Vera — oh, I wanted to be with them. My poor darling Grandma. And how would I tell Mother?

I was destroyed when I hung up. My Grandma, I'd never see her again — the first time I'd lost anyone I loved. It all seemed impossible — how could there be a world without Grandma? She was so much a part of my life, I couldn't conceive of it. I tried to pull myself together — I looked awful. I listened for Mother, heard her coming up the stairs. She knew something was wrong the minute I opened the door. I was shaking — I couldn't stop, I couldn't help it — how do you tell your mother that *her* mother is dead? That was the beginning of a traumatic pattern in my life.

I told her Rosalie and Charlie had called. She immediately said, 'Grandma.' Yes, I said — put my arms around her and as gently as I could told her what they had told me. She cried, but tried to hold herself in check for me. She was strong in that way, used to not giving in to her emotions. She told me — it was too queer — she had gone with her friend to a palm reader. The woman had said she was going to have some bad news — the letter M was prominent in her palm.

Why is it that on the eve of great success disaster always strikes? Grandma knew that good things were happening to me, that I was on my way, but she could not live long enough for me to share it all with her.

Mother and I spent the next several days on the phone to New York. She needed very much to talk to her brothers and sisters who were all gathered at Rosalie and Charlie's. She needed to talk about her mother. So she and I talked a lot about Grandma — it was very sad on Reeves Drive that week.

Jack wrote us about Grandma's services and how happy our many cheery letters and my impending success had made her. He also told us of passing the Broadway theatre where *To Have and Have Not* was to open in three weeks — to see what photographs and ads had been put up. He was satisfied with all he'd seen — Walter Brennan and I were the only ones featured, with Bogart starring. He would check the coming attractions so he could see the kind of build-up Warners were giving me. They had sent out a release on my life, largely put together by Howard, stating that I was the child of American parents of several generations and implying that I was from Society. Jack knew there was nothing to be done about it, but neither he nor Charlie liked it. He couldn't know that it would all be set straight before long — not intentionally, but because I could never lie for long. I lied too badly.

I was frenzied over what might happen when the picture opened in New York. My imagination had a field day. I couldn't stop thinking and talking about *To Have and Have Not* — even though it had been finished six months earlier, it was the only tangible thing in my life at that point. I hadn't seen Bogie or spoken to him for weeks — and was very unhappy. I knew he had agreed to be in *The Big Sleep*, which was to start shooting in early October.

I was at the studio one afternoon, sitting outside Howard's bungalow getting some sun while waiting for him, when I heard a car draw up and a door slam. It was Bogie. I started to shake uncontrollably. He walked up to me, said, 'Hello, how are you, Slim? I didn't expect to see you here today.' He was nervous — I was monosyllabic — we were both so unnerved by the meeting that we couldn't say anything personal. There was too much to say, so it became nothing to say. Bogie said, 'I have a new car — come take a look at it.' After all we'd been through together, that was all we could talk about. I looked at the car — a blue Cadillac, his first — said something brilliant like 'Pretty color,' and then 'I have to go to wardrobe.' He was going to see Howard for a minute about the picture. After he went in, I went to the nearest ladies' room and just trembled. There was so much I didn't know — didn't understand. Was he really going to stay with Mayo? I refused to believe it. But when would I have the answer? I'd have to pull myself together before the picture started, that was for sure. I waited for about fifteen minutes, then headed back for Howard's bungalow. The blue Cadillac was gone — Bogie was gone. I went to Howard's office. He was looking at wardrobe sketches for me — told me which he liked — his taste was impeccable, and I wouldn't have disagreed with him anyway. He also wanted to try me with my hair up for one scene. Everything would be tested as usual. Had I seen Bogie? 'Yes,' I replied. 'He looks good — a summer at Newport agreed with him.' 'If you only knew, Howard,' thought I.

To Have and Have Not had opened in New York and my entire family had gone to the first evening show. They'd been to a preview, but of course had to go into a regular theatre and hear the audience reactions. Uncle Bill wrote me that he loved everything I did in the film — he saw so much of the me he knew. They all knew I was a great mimic, so there was no surprise for them when I mimicked Dolores Moran. Uncle Bill was a scholarly, imposing man — difficult in that he expected a great deal from you. He wrote,

We are all very happy at your instantaneous success. We hope that it will not

256

change your basic character. If anything, it ought to make you more devoted, thoughtful and generous to your mother. She made the opportunities for you long, long ago — and at no small sacrifice to herself.

Funnily enough, on that same day Charlie wrote to me:

My darling, it is not easy to put into words my emotions and mental impressions since you leaped from obscurity to fame. It's all great fun and excitement. I'm happy for you but I'm a little afraid because I worry about your personal happiness. Success is an important part but only a part of happiness. You must make no important, irrevocable decisions until we have talked them over preferably face to face or at least by mail. Feel free to write and confide in me because I believe I can help you. Experience is an important factor in dealing with life and 20 is too young for experience.

He went on to describe how they had sat in the loge, $1.60 apiece — how they'd laughed — how the audience had laughed — how I was a perfect foil for Bogart. 'This means Warners, Hawks and Feldman need you as much as you need them. This means you can maintain your faith and personal integrity and individuality regardless of their prejudice.' I must be grateful — eternally grateful to them, but the press had leaped overboard because of me, not them. My forte was comedy.

Your voice, its timbre, its low register, its rare quality, is ideally suited for Bogart roles. But all this just increases the gap between 20 and 45. Remember the precious quality of youth which makes you vital, young and vibrant is out, extinct in 45 and plus. Don't miss the lesson of this simple arithmetic. You see, I cannot see you professionally apart from your personal life because more than anything else in this world I am intent that they blend into a mixture of wild, ecstatic happiness and permanence. Remember, you need no one. As long as you keep your feet on the ground, smile, gracious 'Thank you' with no trace of vanity, conceit or swellheadedness, you can travel the whole distance of life under your own steam.

I bought the *News* — your first newspaper review — after dinner. A good one. I was so pleased and proud. You are my daughter. You are so unspoiled, so beautiful. Don't ever spoil.

Remember Granny and make your Mommy proud and happy and make her an integral part of your success.

So he knew something. Mother must have written that she was worried about me and that unknown-but-had-to-be-no-good-for-me quantity called Bogart.

I see now in my middle age how aware they were from the heights of their middle age of the dangers of being twenty — of decision-making in innocence and inexperience. That they who knew nothing really of the movie business should know what the pitfalls might be does them credit. But that both Charlie and Bill mentioned Mother astounds me. Did they really think I didn't know how much I owed her — that I wouldn't want her to share in my success? I had always been headstrong, selfish, but at my worst I never turned away from my mother — and I never stopped needing her.

I'm fascinated and still unenlightened when I think of certain of my family now — Charlie especially. I see that he was a father figure — I see his worry, his love for me, his wit and his own need for approval, his need for his own mother. He always seemed the most vulnerable one to me, I guess that's one reason I loved him the most. But I see too how solid they all were — what a firm base I had to grow from. They adored my fame and all that went with it, but their basic life values didn't change. If they bragged, if they displayed my photograph in an office or at home, it stemmed from personal joy and pride in me. Not one of them ever used me for anything at any time. Even now as I live through my life for a second time, I am warmed and strengthened by reflecting on them. In moments of doubt (which are many) and insecurity about one's future (which is more present than not), if I think about Charlie and my mother and my Uncle Bill, the lows and highs of their lives and how they dealt with them, it helps me to ride over the rough spot in the road. I was profoundly lucky to have such a family to draw upon.

So *To Have and Have Not* transformed me from a nothing to a combination of Garbo, Dietrich, Mae West, Katharine Hepburn. I was the greatest discovery since . . . I made Bogart sit up and take notice . . . I was a new face to deal with on the screen . . . I was the answer . . . Hooray! So proclaimed the press. I was everything Howard Hawks had always wanted. My name would be on everyone's lips all over the country, my words would be immortal — my God, what was I going to do about the me that was buried beneath all that, the me that I was stuck with, that was real? How could I live up to all that — how could anyone? Fortunately, I was unaware of the huge impact. As long as I stayed in my little apartment on Reeves Drive with Mother and Droopy — as long as I worked and didn't go out too much — I would remain so.

We started shooting *The Big Sleep* on Tuesday, October 10, 1944. My first scene was my first scene in the picture — the first day of shooting — with my hair up. I played it very cool on the outside, which was hard, since anyone could see my hand shaking every time I lit a cigarette or held a glass. I had to pour a drink in the first shot — my typical luck. As the bottle hit the moving glass, I wished I were dead. Bogie saw it immediately and joked with me a bit. We had the same camera crew, luckily, and I stayed very close to Howard that first week — that seemed to be the only way I could deal with it.

Bogie asked me to stop on our street on the way home so he could talk to me. God give me strength!

I played the yet-to-happen scene as I was driving toward Selma Avenue. I handled myself beautifully — it's always easier when you're playing both parts. The blue Cadillac was waiting. I stopped just behind it. He got into my car. I huddled against my door on the driver's side — mustn't get too close. He told me that the last few weeks had been the most difficult of his life. How many times he had wanted to call me, how much he had thought of me, how much he did love me. I must try to understand. Mayo said she'd stop drinking, she'd try. She'd failed before, but he had to give her a chance.

I said I'd have to respect his decision, but I didn't have to like it. And we needed so much to be together. He was unhappy, I was — even Mayo was, I guess. But I wanted what I wanted and when I wanted it. Patience is not one of my shining qualities, it never was. All I could do was the best I could do. There was no way Bogie and I could be in the same room without reaching for one another, and it wasn't just physical. Physical was very strong, but it was everything — heads, hearts, bodies, everything going at the same time. After our talk it became easier to work, no time at all before we were back at our old joking, ribbing Slim-and-Steve status. I was more guarded than he was, but only at the beginning. After about two weeks of shooting, the phone rang late one night. Who else? I met him. We went back to my apartment. He couldn't bear being away from me any longer. He'd had a fight with

Mayo, of course. She'd been drinking when he got back from the studio and things went from bad to worse. He had to get out of the house.

One night he called from his house to hear my voice (he said), he'd been drinking heavily. He really was in rotten shape. Depressed, upset, worried. One of the worries that plagued him was the difference in our ages. He could be my father, I'd never stay with him, it couldn't last.

Peter Lorre, who had been on the set during *To Have and Have Not*, was a very close friend of Bogie's. His wife-to-be was a beautiful German actress named Kaaren Verne. They were good to be with and cared what happened to Bogie. Peter was totally unlike his movie self. Very, very intelligent, knew a great deal about medicine, a first-rate horseman, drank a good deal but it never got out of hand. His ranch was one of our havens. Burl Ives was a close friend of Peter's, and on more than one occasion when Bogie and I were there Burl was too. Playing his guitar, singing, and drinking. I had never been around drinkers before. I had never learned to drink myself. I wondered if I ever would. To be thrust into that atmosphere when you are twenty is really traumatic. I didn't have a clue about how to handle it, so I just went along and watched — I'd learn the hard way. I'd always talk to them as if they were sober, which resulted in no communication.

All these friends and acquaintances of Bogie's were his contemporaries. I was like a sponge. As I was able to take direction and absorb and learn quickly, so I was able to on a social level as well. This was lucky because there would have been no way for me to have a life with Bogie without adapting to his friends and his way of life, so different from mine. It's one thing to love a man and do all the things he does with him, it's quite another to function in the same way with strangers. I accepted it all as it came and didn't really question it. First things first, the rest would take care of itself.

About three weeks into the picture Bogie left home and checked into the Beverly Hills Hotel. The press moved in, he made a formal statement: trial separation — no, it had nothing to do with me or anyone else. Mayo said she loved Bogie and would try to get him back. I said not a word, but I was so happy. He'd left, he'd finally left! My mother was not so pleased — be careful, remember he was still a married man. Bogie and I made arrangements to meet in his hotel room. I'd have to arrive late and go in the back way, trying not to be seen. It was decided that Carolyn, whom he'd never met even when she'd driven me down to Balboa, would come with me, so it would look less obvious. Illicit love can be fun — especially at twenty. I parked my car away from the hotel. Carolyn parked hers. We sneaked through side doors, down a corridor, laughing all the way, knocked on the appointed door, and were let in by a slightly disheveled but anxious Bogie. He was suspicious of my girlfriend. She was intimidated by him. They were both on the defensive. I wanted them to love each other — they did, but not that first time. She had to call Buddy, who was in New York. She asked to use the phone and insisted on paying for the call. Bogie refused to accept. A battle of words ensued. Carolyn was adamant, gave him a five-dollar bill, which he proceeded to set fire to. Charming. I had no toothpaste. Carolyn went out to get me some. Hard to believe that I was actually thinking about toothpaste at a time like that. The hotel adventure was fun, but trying not to be seen was not. Every time someone knocked on the door — room service or the maid — I hid in the closet.

It was not the best of times. Howard didn't know exactly what was going on, but he knew he didn't like it. He had Slim call me one day to tell me that Howard didn't know she was calling, but that I really should straighten myself out — he was really sore at me and I was a fool to antagonize him — I should tell Bogie that this whole thing might finish my career, and certainly would as far as Howard was concerned. Slim said she was sure I could figure out a way to handle it without turning my life upside down. I knew Howard was standing right there as she spoke. But how in hell *can* you handle love without turning your life upside down? That's what love does, it changes everything. My life would never be the same again. I didn't want it the same. But I was always torn. On the one hand, my career, my future, my life's dream and wish. On the other hand, Bogie, my love, first and total, also my possible future, now just at its beginning, going great some of the time. I didn't want to anger Howard, I was terrified he'd do something awful, like sending me to Monogram. Yet I had to see Bogie, I had to be with him. I was consumed by that feeling. And I couldn't cope with either one of those monumental happenings, much less both.

About a week after Bogie had moved to the hotel, he came into my make-up room when I was getting ready to go to the set. The make-up department knew what was going on and everyone discreetly left the room when one of us walked in on the other. I was due on the set in about fifteen minutes. Bogie looked at me and said, 'I've gone back.' The tears didn't wait an instant: 'But why?' 'I had to, the doctor said Mayo was sick, an alcoholic and in very bad physical shape, she had to go into a hospital. You wouldn't even throw a dog out,' he said. The tears kept coming, the eyes got redder, the make-up was being ruined, eyes puffy. I had to work. How could I be photographed? I couldn't go on the set like this. He'd have to stay with her until she was well. I went to the john, had a good cry, got some ice and pressed it to my eyes. I couldn't even cry without everything going to pieces. I was a mess. I got to the set, the make-up man and the hairdresser said nothing, just kept the ice coming, wrapped in towels. I got into my costume, stalling as long as possible so I wouldn't look as if my life had just crashed.

Somehow I got through that day. Howard said nothing. The press were barred from the stage, but he knew Bogie had gone back home. He'd be glad when this picture was over. Thank God I didn't work every day.

The local newspapers were full of Bogie's reconciliation, which made me want to die. My poor mother didn't know what to do. Obviously Bogie was a son of a bitch, she hated to see me so miserable.

In spite of my personal anguish, the movie was great fun. A marvelous cast, and we all liked one another. One day Bogie came on the set and said to Howard, 'Who pushed Taylor off the pier?' Everything stopped. Howard, no one, had the answer. Taylor was the mystery chauffeur in the film. His disappearance was what brought Marlowe (Bogie) on the case originally. Howard sent a cable to Raymond Chandler asking him. *He* didn't know. *The Big Sleep* was a whodunit's whodunit. Intricate, intriguing, mysterious, filled with colorful characters, many of whom made one-scene appearances. Everything added to the aura of the film. And no one ever bothered to figure it out. It was a great detective movie and great fun to watch. Still is.

Howard was peculiar — and very self-assured. If ever Jack Warner or Harry Warner or any other executive came on the set to see how the work was coming, Howard would stop shooting. He'd never make a fuss, never say a word. He knew he was being checked and he wouldn't have that, so he just stopped. They finally caught on to the fact that they were holding up production. When they left, he started again. Howard told me that whenever a producer walked on a Jack Ford set, Ford would go to his dressing room until they'd gone.

One day a memorandum came from Jack Warner: 'Word has reached me that you are having fun on the set. This must stop.' Howard told Bogie and me that Warner was an incredible monster to deal with. It would take experience for me to ever try, I'd never understand a man like that. Bogie had been suspended from Warners many times for refusing to act in bad films. Jack didn't seem to care about quality, or protecting his talent. All he knew was that he was paying his actors and they had to work — he didn't care if a film was good or bad for them, there would always be someone else when a career went down the drain. When we were filming *To Have and Have Not*, Bogie introduced me to Jimmy Cagney. Cagney said to me, 'If you can survive even seven years at Warners, then you can conquer the world.' It took a while, but not too long, before I knew what he meant. But at this point I still trusted Jack Warner; it didn't make sense to me that he would want to put me into anything but the best. And, in any case, I had Howard to protect me.

Mayo came out of the hospital after a week. She knew the marriage was on its way out. She was desperately trying to hold on, and Bogie was helping her. It was sad and it was hopeless. I understand it all much better now than I did then. Just as I thought I was able to cope with the situation, something else would happen to throw me off balance.

Bogie could not bear his life with her. She hadn't been home three days before the drinking began. It was all right for the first day and then all hell broke loose.

About three o'clock one morning my phone rang. I was dead asleep — so was Mother — I had to work in the morning. Bogie was at home and very drunk. 'Hello, Baby.' 'Where are you — where are you calling from?' 'I'm at home — I miss you, Baby.' The next voice I heard said, 'Listen, you Jewish bitch — who's going to wash his socks? Are *you?* Are *you* going to take care of him?' I was numb — I stood there, scared to death and horrified, with my mouth open — holding the phone away from my ear, afraid to say anything. My mother said, 'Who is that? Hang up the phone.' After more vilification and Bogie shouting, 'Hang up the phone, God damn it!' to her — I hung up. Unnerved, to say the least. So she knew about me — all our care to avoid this, all for naught. What would happen tomorrow?

Mother was livid. 'How could he subject you to that?' 'Mother, he was drinking — he's miserable.' She was in a fury — there was no excuse, absolutely none, nothing would ever come of this but trouble. 'Why should you start your life like this? If he were decent and really cared about you, he would never allow you to be in this position.' There was no rationale. I could never persuade her, and I couldn't defend him with total conviction this time. Mother and I fought many times through this period. I, being stubborn, refusing to admit to being even slightly wrong, would storm out of my house. Sometimes in the middle of the night I'd get into my car and just drive, to get away.

When I got on the set next morning there was no Bogie. I decided to change before asking questions. Finally at around 9:30 I walked over to Howard. 'Hello, darling,' he said. When I moved toward him, he was always receptive and affectionate in his way. He said, 'Bogie called — he's going to be late.' Okay. To fill up the time, Howard dreamed up shots that Bogie wasn't in. Being on time was compulsive with Bogie — part of being a professional, having respect for your craft. But he missed that day. Purely and simply drunk. A friend called Howard later and said Bogie'd been up all night and felt and looked lousy — he really was not mentally or physically able. 'Okay,' said Howard, 'forget it — we'll shoot around him.' We did what we could, but it wasn't enough for a full day's work. I was a mass of confused emotions. If Bogie'd been drinking, he'd have to rest at home for a while. What kind of a life did he lead? I could not envision living with anyone like that — it was so far from *my* relationship with him, which, with all its problems and rough times, was based on hope. Starry-eyed, but hope nonetheless. His life with Mayo seemed to be one hangover after another — only destruction and ugliness.

Howard summoned me to his house again. Mother drove out with me and waited in the car. I was being called on the carpet, Howard fighting for his Svengali role. 'Look, I'm not going to go on with this. I can't have anyone under contract who won't listen to me. Bogart likes his life — he likes the drinking and he likes his wife — you're throwing away a whole career because of something that's just not going to happen. You're a damn fool — I'll just sell your contract — I can't be bothered anymore. If I'd known anything like this could happen, I'd never have signed you. So you'd better make up your mind — this is your last chance.' More tears. Reason told me I must stay with Howard — but reason had nothing to do with any of it. I was emotionally gone. I needed Bogie — I felt I had to be with him — I couldn't help it, there was no alternative. I was being pulled in all directions. When I was with Bogie, it all became clear — he was so wise, he was so sure of how life should be lived — he made it seem simple to understand, and he was on my side. I trusted him totally — he could convince me of anything.

Howard and Slim did everything to distract me. Slim called to invite me to dinner one night. 'I've got the most dazzling man you'll ever meet in your life for a fourth — once you meet him, you'll forget all about Bogart.' The man was Clark Gable, in uniform. Imagine meeting Clark Gable — one of these larger-than-life people that you pay your carefully saved money to see. He *was* dazzling to look at, but he stirred me not a bit. I tried to flirt a little, tried to be attracted to him — but it didn't work. He was just a pleasant terrific-looking man without an overabundance of humor who had incredible dimples and was named Clark Gable. There were no sparks flying that night. He even took me home — Clark Gable in uniform standing at the foot of the stairs to my apartment on Reeves Drive — in the moonlight. He kissed me good night, smiled, and walked away. Nothing, but nothing.

Bogie came back to work and told me of his adventure. He'd been out all night drinking. At 7:00 a.m., unshaven, he was

273

walking past houses on some street, looked through a window, and saw a woman preparing breakfast for her family. Imagine seeing a Bogart face staring through your window at that hour of the morning. The husband went to the door, asked him if he'd like to come in for a cup of coffee. So he sat with the children having breakfast — they adored it. Nice people — and they never saw him again.

He also told me he'd had a talk with Mayo. He wanted out definitely this time, it would never work, but he'd really have to be careful — her doctor said that not only was she an alcoholic but also somewhat of a paranoiac. One more complication. He would speak with his manager, Morgan Maree, about the financial settlement. Before that he'd have to get things straight with her — get her to agree to go to Reno. Then we could think about our life.

It was happening — it was really happening. I couldn't believe it, but I did. Even before it happened. Because it had to.

The picture was finally finished. Bogie gave me a present — my first gold bracelet — an i.d., with my name on one side, 'the whistler' on the other. Slim helped him choose it. Relations were somewhat strained between Howard and me. He sensed he had lost. The girl he had invented was no longer his. I can see now how he must have felt. Having invested his time, money, and talent in an unknown, on the point of realizing his lifelong dream of creation — and standing to make a good deal of money — he would not be thrilled at having it all blow up in his face. Why in hell should he have been patient and understanding? No reason — I wouldn't have been, had positions been reversed, yet I expected *him* to be. Also I knew he had a sneaking feeling for me. I remember someone on the picture stopping me on the lot one day and saying, 'You know, you ought to call Howard. You ought to ask him for a date.' 'Why?' asked the foolish girl. 'Because he'd like it. He likes that — and he really likes you a lot. You could go over to his private office. Nobody would know about it.' Boy, I was slow. It took some time before I realized what he was talking about.

Nevertheless, Bogart snatched his discovery away from him — his plans blew up in his face. He had an incredible ego, but there was no good reason for him to like what happened, or to put up with it. He even suggested to Bogie once that he get a room in the Ambassador Hotel, downtown, away from the Beverly Hills scene. That was the way to have a little outside fun.

But Bogie was the last man on earth to make that kind of suggestion to.

During *The Big Sleep* I met more of Bogie's friends. One of them was Mark Hellinger. Hellinger had been a newspaperman in New York during the speakeasy days. He had fallen in love with a *Ziegfeld Follies* girl, the beautiful Gladys Glad. The story was that during their courting days Mark would write columns to her — when things were not going well, he'd write very sentimental stuff to woo her back. He was a movie producer now, he was known for his capacity for drink and for getting everyone else drunk — he could drink a bottle of brandy and a bottle of seventeen-year-old bourbon on the same day and it would never show. He drove a big black Cadillac with the license plate MH1. He wore gray suits, gray shirts, and white ties. Always a gray fedora. He knew many hoods, liked something about some of them — the glamour, mystery, power, who knows? Went to the racetrack. Was known for his extravagant tipping — ten bucks to a parking attendant, twenty to a waiter — always carried a lot of cash and started to shell it out on arrival anywhere. He never let anyone else pick up a check. That was his game. He'd go to any lengths — calling in advance, bribing captains, anything — so no one else could pay the check. A sweet, vulnerable man — a good friend, loved by all. He always invited strays to his house for Thanksgiving and Christmas dinners. Mike Romanoff, Bugsy Siegel, Al Smiley, a Siegel friend, their wives or girls. Bogie and I had our first Christmas dinner together there. I remember thinking how charming Bugsy Siegel and Al Smiley were — soft-spoken, polite. When Bogie told me Bugsy was underground-connected, I couldn't believe it.

Mark and Gladys lived in an enormous house up in the hills on LaBrea Avenue — an electric gate, swimming pool, tennis court, projection room, the works. But the house was always dark. You'd enter an enormous living room with almost no lights on, cloths covering the furniture — move to the den where the bar was — *that* was lit, but the place was not comfortable. Gladys would come into the bar late, after guests had arrived, in full make-up and tinted glasses. A tall, beautiful woman, very sweet, always a little under the influence of booze or tranquilizers I thought, and I think her two small children were always a little frightened of her. She spoke very softly — sitting around a dinner table, one would always see the man next to her leaning over very close. I thought it was that they thought she was devastating, but Bogie told me it was because they couldn't hear her, and she was always talking about the canned goods — how many cans of Campbell's soup were in the basement.

Howard felt *The Big Sleep* needed another scene between Bogie and me — one of those titillating *double entendre* scenes — but he'd wait until he'd cut the film. Meanwhile, Warners wanted me to make my first trip to New York since *To Have and Have Not*. I was ecstatic at the idea, I hadn't been back in a year and a half. They would arrange it all — with Charlie Einfeld planning it, there'd be lots of publicity. He wanted me to go to Chicago en route — to the National Press Club in Washington — revisit Julia Richman High School — give tons of interviews. That was okay with me, and I'd see my darling family again — I couldn't wait for that. But there would be no Grandma — what would that be like? It was planned that I'd leave on February 2 on the *Super Chief*, with Mother and Droopy and Jack Diamond, our publicity man on *The Big Sleep*, who'd become a friend.

Jack was a great pal of Walter Winchell, who was then known all over the world — he was a unique newsman, gossip columnist, radio commentator with machine-gun delivery. He was out in California for a couple of weeks and told Jack he'd loved me in *To Have and Have Not* and wanted to meet me. So one Sunday night Jack took me to the radio studio to sit in on the broadcast and go to dinner afterward. This was the big time — meeting Walter Winchell! He was a friend of Mark Hellinger as well, and I took quite a ribbing from Mark about it. So did Bogie. Mark would say, 'Look out — Winchell loves young girls, loves to go dancing — he might make you forget Bogie. He's turned more than one girl's head in his time!' Bogie was not crazy about the notion, but it did come under the heading of publicity and he didn't want to deprive me of anything that might give me a boost. As I was sitting in the glass booth listening, Winchell came to his 'Orchids to You' section — a couple of minutes devoted to praise of someone. I heard my name and blushed purple. He was complimenting me on my performance and saying, 'Look out for Bacall — hold on to your hats — she is something!' Winchell was a good newspaperman but a vain man, convinced he could change the course of world events — slightly deluded, but never mind. He also fancied himself a ladies' man. He had a slight crush on me — and, sure enough, Mark was right, we went dancing at the Mocambo. He mentioned me again on his broadcast and broke precedent later by devoting an entire column to me titled

'Bacall of the Wild.' I was flattered and it did me a lot of good — perfect fodder for Warner's publicity department.

Bogie stayed away from home another ten days, then gave it one last try with Mayo over Christmas. He had given me my first gold watch, with a gold chain strap. He put it on my wrist himself. Then, after the holidays, he left Mayo for good. He said they had agreed on a settlement and had retained lawyers. It was walking a tightrope whether she would agree to go to Reno or not.

Bogie was back at the Beverly Hills Hotel. We hid at The Players for dinner — it was on Sunset Strip just opposite the Garden of Allah and was owned by Preston Sturges. We were there one night with Jack Diamond and Walter Winchell, I in gray trousers and a navy boat shirt of Bogie's. Not a planned dinner. It made me very nervous to go out publicly, but Bogie felt it was okay if there were others present and we didn't stay too long. I was slouched low in the booth, hoping not to be seen. Winchell said, 'Wouldn't you love to go to New York and be in a play?' 'Yes,' I said, then realized what I'd said and followed it by a quick 'No.' Bogie pounded his fist on the table, furious that after all the trouble he was going through, I could even think of going away. 'You goddamn actresses! If that's your plan, go ahead and go — forget about me.' I was filled with remorse — tried hard to put it right. Said I'd just been joking, which I had.

Bogie was hypersensitive during this period, the only time his sense of humor faltered. He was turning his life upside down, and I didn't understand all the complications of that. To me it was very black-and-white simple. His anxieties about me were manifold — the age difference, which was never out of his thoughts — and the fact that I was just beginning my career. Would I want to give it up? Should I be asked to? But there was no way he was going to start a life with me if I had any doubt as to what came first with me — marriage or career. And the property settlement. He'd worked all his life for the little he had — he hadn't accumulated much, but half would go automatically to Mayo. As I'd never had anything to divide up, how could that have meaning for me? I would pay lip-service to understanding — would think that I did — but I didn't. Bogie knew damn well that if I stuck with my career, a marriage to him could not succeed. 'If you want a career, don't get married. You can't have both.' I was sure I wanted nothing but to be Mrs Humphrey Bogart. I said I was prepared to give up work, and I believed what I said.

Bogie made his final move — into the

Garden of Allah, a famous group of old Spanish bungalows that housed Robert Benchley, Charlie Butterworth, Nunnally Johnson, Dorothy Parker, John O'Hara when in town, Arthur Sheekman, Thornton Delehanty, John McClain. Alla Nazimova, the mysterious Russian actress, lived there and I think owned it. It boasted a great bellman who delivered mail, provided booze when needed, and knew something of the life of everyone who resided there. He was slightly under the influence himself a good deal of the time, but no one seemed to care. Bogie took a bungalow facing the swimming pool — large living room, bedroom, small kitchen and dining area. Very comfortable.

At this time Mary Chase's play *Harvey*, about an invisible rabbit, was a great success in New York. As I was supposed to be what is laughingly called invisible, I was tagged 'Harvey' by Bogie. A girl of many names in that year.

Life was more and more falling into place. Louis Bromfield, one of Bogie's oldest and best friends, and Louis' secretary, George Hawkins, a round, mustached, outrageously funny man, were to be in Los Angeles very briefly. Bogie had told me all about Louis' Malabar Farm, with its thousand or more beautiful acres of Ohio farmland. Louis had started his literary career brilliantly with his tetralogy titled *The Green Bay Tree*, *Possession*, *Early Autumn*, and *A Good Woman*. Later he had written *The Rains Came*, which was a big hit and sold to films, had become a farmer, a working farmer, and fallen so in love with the soil that his writing thereafter took second place and suffered accordingly.

Bogie's and Louis' political philosophies were diametrically opposed, but that did not interfere with their friendship. Bogie felt that Louis worked his farm, cared about farmers, understood about them — and that his politics were the result of intelligent thought. Based on that, they must be respected. Louis was a very tall man of enormous charm and good humor. We got on well immediately. It was odd to see Bogie in the company of such a man — it made his past life much clearer to me. I could comprehend, in part at least, why Bogie always said the Twenties were the 'good old days' — much more fun than the Forties.

By this time many arrangements had been solidified. Bogie was going to Malabar with Louis and George for a couple of weeks, then to New York, where he would wait for me and where I would meet his New York newspaper friends and '21' friends. I was going to the Racquet Club in Palm Springs with Mother for a rest before taking off on my personal-appearance tour. Bogie had ordered a ring for me from his friend John Gershgorn, the Beverly Hills jeweler. It would be ready before I left.

We could be together all the time now — or almost — but still had to be careful not to flaunt our relationship in Mayo's face. Bogie had to make sure that she would agree to stay in Reno for six weeks without once coming to L.A. One twenty-four-hour period away would negate even five weeks in Reno and she'd have to start all over again. But the wheels had begun to turn — it was only a question of time now. So the cynics were wrong. My mother made her truce with Bogie — an armed truce, but she accepted it. How could she not? She saw how happy and how much in love I was. Bogie, Louis, and George left on the *Super Chief* in mid-January 1945. I had bought Bogie a small bronze rabbit to signify Harvey's presence at all times. We signed and exchanged several photographs — he took his to Ohio, mine rested on display in Reeves Drive.

The separation was bittersweet — to be apart for a minute was painful, but the knowledge that we'd be united in two weeks made it bearable. As I read Bogie's letters, which were frequent and long, I realized how much he had shaken up his life.

Now that he had left wife number three, he was free at last to look forward to something again. He hadn't believed anything good would ever happen in his life again — that he would have children — or love — or want anything as much as he wanted us to have a life together. He wrote to his business manager, Morgan Maree, about his settlement with Mayo, and he sent me a copy of the letter. He was careful that I should know every step, understand that I could go to Morgan for help at any time. I saw that he had completely exposed himself emotionally, that he was as vulnerable as a child — as prone to jealousy and anxiety as any kid in love for the first time would be.

I *was* a kid in love for the first time. It was easy for me — I knew nothing about pitfalls. I was giving nothing but myself and I could do that without a qualm. Never in my life had or has a man cared so much for me, wanted so much to protect me, surround me with life's joys, share everything. It made me want to return the care — to show him it was possible to be really happy with a woman, to give him children. I was determined to do that.

There were things in the press during those two weeks — that Mayo wanted him back, that she had no intention of divorcing him. I was upset by all of them. I'd cut out the clippings and send them to him. He'd reassure me — more of the Hollywood crap from the gossip leeches whom he despised, who couldn't exist except for us and didn't give a damn what they wrote or whom they hurt as long as it was a story.

Cole Porter's song 'Don't Fence Me In' was on the *Hit Parade* and Bogie's first wire to me said, 'Please fence me in Baby — the world's too big out here and I don't like it without you.' No one has ever written a romance better than we lived it.

I counted the seconds we were apart. Palm Springs was two weeks further away. I must have driven Mother crazy — I could not think or talk of anything but Bogie. When I appeared on the cover of *Life*, I was excited — and by all the other covers — but at the center and all around me was Bogie, and everything else disappeared far into the background. My breath depended on his. I could not have believed such completion. Nor could he — if he'd been in love before, he was obsessed now. He even forgot the twenty-five years between us and I never remembered them. When he'd been so concerned about the age disparity, he'd said to Peter Lorre, 'It can't last — she's much too young.' Peter said, 'You'll have maybe five years. Isn't five years better than none?' Bogie agreed that it was, and that helped him to decide. God, how lucky I was — Bogie might have been toying with me, just out for a love affair, or I might have been with someone who wanted to use me. But here I was, twenty years old, and I really had it all. And it was more or less handed to me. I hadn't had years of struggle and deprivation — my struggle seemed a lot to me at the time, but it was nothing, if not over-dramatized. I hadn't starved, I hadn't really supported myself before California. I'd had to be careful with money — I knew about work — there were no luxuries — but I'd never really suffered for my art. I was to learn something about that much later.

On February 2, 1945, Mother, Droopy, and I boarded the *Chief* to Chicago. I was wearing Bogie's ring, which John Gershgorn had delivered the day before I left. When we arrived in New York, all hell had broken loose. Bogie, drunk the night before, had told Earl Wilson about his Baby — 'I love my Baby — I miss my Baby.' Baby ('The Look') Bacall was splashed prominently in the New York newspapers and all around the country. It must have made a big hit with Mayo. As I disembarked from the train in Grand Central Station, I was surrounded by about twenty reporters and photographers and police. 'Give us the "Down Under Look," Baby.' 'What have you got to say about marrying Bogart?' 'Are you going to see Bogart?' 'How does it feel to be back in New York?' Me: 'I just got here — I don't know anything about Mr Bogart — I haven't seen him for three weeks — I'm not planning to marry anybody.' I didn't know what the hell I was saying. They sat me on suitcases — had my head on a swivel going from photographer to photographer — the rat-a-tat barrage of questions. And we were supposed to be subtle, keep a low profile. Fat chance!

I couldn't believe the mob. All of Grand Central was people — on every stairway, all screaming and pushing. I had a cordon of police around me — there was someone to take Mother and Droopy to a waiting limousine. It was mayhem — it was Einfeld.

I had to see Bogie right away. The Warners man told me he was waiting for me in his suite, but I'd have to see the press first. Oh God — Bogie would be in a rage. I was taken to my suite — my first suite — in a New York hotel. The Gotham — Bette Davis' hotel! There were flowers everywhere — I'd never seen anything like it. And the press — questions and more questions, and me trying to field them. I absolutely denied a forthcoming marriage — Bogie and I had agreed to that. He always said if they asked personal questions, don't answer — 'Fuck 'em if they don't like it.' All well and good in theory, but impossible in practice. And the women of the press: 'What a lovely ring — is it on your engagement finger?' It's on my Finger finger! 'Have you spoken to Bogie? When will you see him? How does it feel to be a star overnight?' And on and on. Bogie was calling. I'd gone into the bedroom, saying I was going to the ladies' room. He wanted me up there right now — I couldn't, room full of press, please be patient. 'Fucking Warner Brothers are running your life!' It was the worst Marx Brothers comedy imaginable — press agents dashing in and out of the bedroom. I couldn't remember anyone's name, I didn't know what questions I was answering half the time, I wanted to go upstairs — and, as usual, I was shaking with nerves. I hadn't expected anything like this — I'd thought it would be neat and tidy, one reporter at a time. I didn't know then how Charlie Einfeld planned things. There was a reason he was considered the best.

Bogie called every ten minutes. After almost an hour I was finally able to get away — I said I needed a bath. I rushed upstairs, leaving Mother to unpack and call the family, who were all coming to the hotel for a drink. I got to Bogie's door, turned the knob — he was sitting on the sofa with tears streaming down his cheeks. We threw our arms around each other. He'd thought I might have changed my mind — that, after thinking about it, I'd decided against marrying him. Even he, who was so sure of what he was, could be insecure. I was undone by the sight of him. Suddenly I had to reassure him — suddenly I was in control — he was so moving, simple, sweet. He took the ring off my finger and put it on slowly and surely to stay. He knew he'd gone too far with Earl Wilson, but he couldn't change that now. And Inez Robb, a top newswoman from International News Service, had interviewed him that morning. Bogie refused to lie, so, having said what he'd said to Earl, he said a bit more to Mrs Robb. He knew Warners had many interviews planned, but it had been agreed upon beforehand that I would have all my nights free. Bogie was taking me to '21' for dinner — our first in New York, alone, in front of everyone. But he promised to come up and meet my family, though he was less than enthusiastic, resenting anyone that took me away from him for five minutes.

Charlie and Rosalie, Jack and Vera, Bill and Renee, even Albert and Min from

Connecticut — only no Granny. I hugged them all — it was so good to see them again. Oh, I loved them. They couldn't wait to meet Bogie, of course — they were impressed, and Rosalie had always had a crush on him.

He finally walked in — introductions all around — Bogie very much on the defensive. He was older than Charlie and Jack — he was older than all of them except Bill. My cousin Marvin was at West Point, and Albert walked up to me pointing his finger at my chest, telling me I had to go up to see Marvin. Bogie just loved that — he said, 'She does what I do and that doesn't include West Point. She doesn't have to do anything.' That was not the best of meetings. He did like Jack, who was reserved but worldly — Charlie, who was funny and whose personality connected more with Bogie's than anyone else's — and Bill, whose voice he loved. Bill should have been a rabbi, Bogie always said. Rosalie and Charlie wanted us to spend one evening in their apartment, which we agreed to. It would be private, at least. Bogie said, 'Christ, you've got more goddamned relatives than I've ever seen.'

So the New York trip was on its way. At '21,' I met John O'Hara, and Quentin Reynolds and his wife, Ginny, whom I adored immediately. It was also at '21' that I was introduced to Moss Hart, who said, 'Congratulations on your success — you realize, of course, from here on you have nowhere to go but down.' He turned out to be a prophet.

Bogie took me to Bleeck's — the Artists' and Writers' Club, just under the New York *Herald Tribune*, hangout for newsmen. It was there the Saturday Club met — lunch for three hours — drinks, of course — and there I learned the match game. It was played very seriously by all, and I was only allowed to be a spectator at first. It was based on one outguessing and tricking the other. Each player had three matches in hand — would keep anywhere from none to three — and the next player had to guess the total. Wrong guessers were eliminated one by one, losers bought rounds of drinks, and it was important. I was finally allowed to play — the only woman thus honored — and, lucky for me, I played well. I loved going there — the atmosphere was a combination of bar and country cottage, everyone knew everyone else, they were very, very bright men and they allowed me in. So I was part of something new and something that was Bogie's.

Of course, I called George Kaufman. He had written me at the end of 1944:

Dear Peggy [he still didn't know my name],

This is a fan letter — you are superb. No one is more pleased than I at your success and in an unaccountable way I take quite a little pride in it.

George Kaufman

He finally got my first name straight — was a bit chagrined at his *faux pas,* but joked about it. After that we never came to New York without seeing George. I never stopped looking up to him.

We went to the theatre — fans outside the hotel day and night — professional autograph seekers, photographers and press dogging our moves — it was all new to me and I must admit I liked it. I couldn't truly relate it to myself, but it was fun. Yes, I liked it. And why not? To have left New York anonymously less than two years before and return with everyone after me all the time was quite a change. I was well aware that Bogie was responsible for most of it, but that didn't make me enjoy it any the less.

He wanted to see every old friend he'd ever had — all the people he'd been unable to see because of Mayo.

He took me to see Clifton Webb one afternoon. Beatrice Lillie was there, as well as Clifton's mother, Maybelle. The stories about her were myriad. It was said that when Clifton was a baby she used to carry him around with a lace cover over his face so he wouldn't be contaminated by the air. That she was tough about his contracts and stood outside the theatre when he was opening in a show to make sure the light bulbs spelling his name were screwed in above Ethel Waters'. Bogie said Clifton had been in love with Mary Hay, a dancing partner, and would have married her had it not been for Maybelle. She had a hen-cackle laugh, wore pearls, walked with a stick, and stayed up at all parties with all his friends — really must have wanted to be his wife. Clifton had undergone analysis for eight years and this day said that the doctor had told him his problem was his mother, to which Bea Lillie replied, 'We could have told you that years ago and saved you a lot of money.' Clifton told me that first day how happy he was to see Bogie happy at last, that he'd known Bogie since the Twenties — he, Noel Coward, Marilyn Miller, Jeanne Eagels had all been friends — and that Bogie was always a gent. He'd never believed any of the stories he'd heard about him during his last wild marriage. From that afternoon on, Clifton became a constant source of friendship, and remained a part of my life until he died.

Bogie's first wife, Helen Menken, was having drinks and *hors d'oeuvres* for a group of Navy men who'd been wounded, and invited us both. Bogie told me not to worry, she was a nice woman, they were friends, and she was looking forward to meeting me. That's more than I could say about meeting her. But we went, and she was attractive and friendly. I remembered spending much of my childhood listening to her on a radio soap opera. She told me it was not Bogie's fault their marriage failed — it was hers. She'd been a fool, but now she was overjoyed he'd at last met someone who could make him happy. Years later his second wife, Mary Philips, told me the same thing. So in the eyes of all ex-wives except the third, he was a gent.

Warners had arranged for me to go to the National Press Club luncheon in Washington. Because I wanted to be with Bogie and had his backing, I refused. I took on his tone with them very early on. My refusal brought my first telegram from Jack Warner:

Dear Lauren, very surprised to hear you declined to go to Washington. According to arrangements made by our New York publicity department I think you should play ball. And know you will do this after my asking you to cooperate.

Hope you having lovely time. Kindest personal regards, J.W.

It was the first of many play-ball-and-cooperate wires I was to receive from Warner over the next seven years. Charles Einfeld was in New York, would go with me and would get me back by nightfall. I liked him, so did Bogie, and deep down I really felt I should go, so I did. It was fun to be in Washington again — this time a hit. I had a good time with the press. The club was jammed that day — Vice President Truman was coming over. When he was introduced — after me! — he sat down to play the piano, which had conveniently been placed onstage, Charlie, who was standing off to one side on the floor, edged toward me on the corner of the stage and said, 'Get on the piano.' I felt a bit silly, not being Helen Morgan or even close, but I did it. Cameras started flashing. The Vice President and I exchanged a few words, and the resulting picture hit front pages all over the world within a few days. Charlie Einfeld was worth every cent and more that Warner paid him. Truman was not wild about the picture after he became President, but I loved it.

During the wild Baby publicity initiated by Bogie, Alex Evelove of the Warners publicity department sent a wire to Bogie saying he was very upset about it all, considering that Bogie was, after all, a married man, etc., etc. To which Bogie wired back: 'Perhaps you'd like me to return to help you with your Errol Flynn problems.' Errol at that time was being sued for rape by two under-age girls who'd been on his boat. Unsavory publicity in those days. The morals clause in all actors' contracts could give any studio an out if it so chose. As Flynn was a big star and his problem was in keeping with his glamour and reputation as a dashing lover, Warners ignored it.

It snowed one night in New York, and Bogie and I left the hotel after everyone thought we'd retired. We walked along Fifth Avenue, then did something I'd wanted to do since I was a child. We took a hansom-cab ride through Central Park. It was the only time during those two weeks that we were not followed.

Louis Bromfield and George Hawkins had been in New York with Bogie and stayed on a few days after my arrival. They left ahead of us, as the plan was that we stop at Malabar en route to California. I couldn't wait for that.

My return to New York had been triumphant, much more than I could have dreamed. I saw all my old friends — Fred Spooner, Betty Kalb, Joanne Tree, who had become close my last year of pavement pounding. Had a drink with Max Gordon, who was so pleased for me that he might have done it all himself. Betty K. came up to the hotel one afternoon — I could only see her and my other friends between interviews and Bogie and family. She had married an actor named Gene Barry and was madly in love with him. They had no money, so she was doing everything — cooking, laundry — but she loved him, knew he'd make it one day, and was happy.

One of the big events was my trip to Loehmann's. My old saleslady, Ruth Rothman, had spoken to Mrs Loehmann, who had gone to Norell and others to get models for me. At 7:00 a.m. Mother and I took off for Brooklyn — Bogie was horrified, but it was the only way, the store opened at nine and mayhem always followed. Three racks were put around me, the fourth wall held a mirror, Mother sat in a chair. Ruth had everything lined up and I started putting on and taking off — like old Seventh Avenue days. The buys were fantastic, and for once I could afford some things I wanted. I still was limited financially, but compared to two years earlier I was Barbara Hutton. That trip became one of my favorite things each time I was in New York. It was like going to old friends. I wish it all still existed — it was warm, cozy, crazy, totally un-chic, and it always brought me back to my origins. Mrs Loehmann sat upstairs in her rooms, and I'd go up to tell her what I had bought and have a cup of coffee with her. I never wanted to let go of that part of my life, because it was mine, and because it's impossible to have times like that after success. Success gives and takes away. I just tried as hard as I could to hold on to what was being taken away.

My time with my family was not enough. On departure day they all came for farewells, and I hated to leave them. I had a really fantastic set of uncles and aunts — they more than made up for my having no father.

From the moment the *Life* cover story and other big stories were released, my father started to give interviews. He was living in South Carolina — I hadn't known till the newspapers told me. During *The Big Sleep* he sent me a wire telling me not to marry a man so much older than I, and his interviews were full of his disapproval of Bogie. I was upset, naturally, and I suppose the old childhood hurt and resentment surged to the fore — it took fame for me to hear a word from him. Mother was always upset when his name was mentioned in the press, but there was nothing we could do — he wanted recognition and he took it. The confusion about my last name was revived, but there was nothing I could do about that either. Howard must have learned about all this and felt I had deceived him.

We took the train to Ohio, where George met us in an old station wagon. It was cold and the ground was snow-covered. We drove to Lucas, a tiny town, and on to Malabar Farm. The house was filled with beautiful antique French country furniture and seven boxer dogs and one cocker spaniel — and Louis, larger than life, his wife, Mary, their three daughters, and his white-haired matriarchal mother. Mother and I were put into one room, Bogie another, and I divided my time between the two. Malabar was more beautiful than Bogie had described it in his letters. I was agog. The food was wonderful, the atmosphere really back-to-the-earth. There was rationing because of the war, but one couldn't tell with the fresh eggs and great slabs of butter that the day started with. Louis had really been an innovative farmer. It was he who invented contour plowing and who believed so strongly and worked so hard for soil conservation and six inches of topsoil. The world of agriculture thought very highly of him. There were roaring fires, screaming games of hearts, Bogie and Louis' affectionate ribbing of each other about Hoover and Roosevelt. There were dog fights under the table during dinner and boxers breaking wind at all times.

Louis took me all around the farm, and in a barn, for the first and only time in my life, I saw a calf being born. It was a happy, healthy, peaceful way of life. I envied them all. That time was so happy — free from care and pressure — one of the most totally blessed periods I have ever known. George and Louis insisted that when the time came we must be married in that house. What a lovely idea! They took Mother and me in as their own. I hated to leave, but I carried away with me the picture of a house Bogie and I would build and live in one day on that farm. The picture was complete with me in apron carrying milk bucket. My imagination was always unchained.

Mother and I returned to the quiet and calm of Beverly Hills. Quite an adjustment after the mad three weeks we'd just spent. Bogie was comfortable in his new Garden of Allah digs. He was spending much of his time meeting with Morgan Maree and his lawyer. He would see Mayo only a few times more — all but once in the presence of lawyers. The once was to confirm that she was going to Reno for a divorce. He knew the spilling of the beans in New York had not helped, and he wanted to antagonize her no further. He was also beginning to prepare for an April start on *The Two Mrs Carrolls* with Barbara Stanwyck. The rest of his time was spent introducing me to more of his friends. As I divided my time between the Garden of Allah and Reeves Drive, meeting them was easy. I couldn't spend every night with Bogie, but I did spend some. We still had to be damn careful, do nothing to upset Mayo. There was no telling what she might do — in her paranoia, anything was possible, and if his adultery became public, no divorce for seven years. California law then, I believe. And Mayo had to be kept sober so that she'd stay the six weeks in Reno without a break. Mayo's mother and Bogie liked each other, and that helped.

Among the unforgettable characters I met at this time was the great humorist Robert Benchley — funny, kind, and vulnerable. He could be seen early mornings heading for the studio in his derby and black overcoat, briefcase under his arm, clearly trying very hard to walk in a straight line and not fall in the pool, thereby revealing the terrible hangover which everyone knew he had anyway. One night Bogie and I returned to the bungalow after dinner, with him wide awake, wound up, and wanting company. 'Let's call Benchley.' 'But it's too late, for God's sake — it's after midnight. He'll be asleep.'

Just then the phone rang. 'I was just thinking about you,' Bogie enthused, 'we were just going to call you. You're the one person we wanted to see. Am I glad you phoned! We'll be right over, Bob.' We crossed the pool to Benchley's bungalow, knocked on the door. When the familiar voice said, 'Come in,' we opened it to find Bob sitting in his favorite chair with one yellow light burning. He looked at us with tears in his eyes. 'What's the matter, Bob?' said Bogie. 'Didn't you want us to come over?' 'Of course I did, but I didn't *expect* you to. If I *hadn't* intended to see someone, I would have spoken with the same enthusiasm you did when I called.' What a sad and telling comment on the life of that funny and generous man. He was lonely — it was that simple. Bogie said that as a drama critic, Benchley had never been cruel to actors. No Woollcott or Dottie Parker barbs. Bob never wanted to hurt anyone. The Garden of Allah was the perfect background for a drinking bachelor. There were always pals — almost always someone to call or see. When all the displaced New Yorkers gathered in one place, it was fascinating to me — Dorothy Parker (who disarmed me by speaking softly and sweetly), Johnny McClain, Benchley, Butterworth, Thornton, Delehanty — freelance magazine writer. They all liked each other, all had much in common; they wrote, had wit, drank, were all lonely, all a little sad. There was never a feeling of competition — I remember what struck me was their mutual enjoyment, their camaraderie. They laughed a lot, and their hands never held an empty glass. There were nights I wanted to go to sleep, but no — Bogie wanted to stay up. They laughed and laughed — I laughed too — I wanted to go to bed, but I wouldn't have missed their agile, quick, original, witty dialogue for anything. It did cross my mind that the reason they laughed so much was that they drank. Not falling-down drunk — they just drank steadily. How on earth was I going to cope? For all my flaming youth, the simple fact was that I couldn't keep up with them.

The first time Bogie took me to Sam and Mildred Jaffe's house (Sam Jaffe the agent, not the actor), Mildred almost fainted from shock when I said I didn't drink. She'd never seen Bogie with a non-drinking woman. The Jaffes were two great and immediate pluses in my life. Mildred was a great beauty — black hair pulled tight in a bun, high cheekbones, large sloe eyes, a mysterious, half-Asian look. They really knew and cared about art — painting and sculpture — and were the first to make me aware of it. They were the great family in

Bogie's life — everything was built around each other and their girls. Sam was Bogie's agent and friend.

It had been so long since Bogie had been able to have friends to his house that now he wanted it all the time. Not parties — just the ease of people sitting around talking, drinking, without ashtrays flying through the air.

Mayo was to leave for Reno at the end of March, which meant that with any luck the divorce would come through at the beginning of May. Hurrah! Morgan Maree, whom Bogie loved because he was totally honest and trustworthy (rare in that town), had worked the settlement out fairly. It was costing Bogie a lot, given California's community-property law, but he thought it was worth it. He was a worrier about money and not a spender. He was not instinctively extravagant. The boat was his only luxury — expensive, but it meant his health and peace of mind. He relied on Morgan to see there was enough money for it. He wanted no details.

Jack Warner decided he wanted to put me in a picture called *Confidential Agent* with Charles Boyer — the director was Herman Shumlin, who had directed only *Watch on the Rhine* on film before, as well as having done it on the stage. I was not mad about the script or my part — Bogie didn't think much of it either, although he thought a lot of Boyer. But to cast me as an aristocratic English girl was more than a stretch. It was dementia. However, I decided to let Jack Warner make the decision. He wouldn't want to put me in anything bad, he cared about my career — anyway, it was a test: I'd see how much he cared. So I started to prepare for it, though there wasn't a chance that this New York-bred girl who'd been hacking around the garment center and Broadway could ever really prepare to be that English aristocrat. I just didn't know enough, hadn't a clue as to how to be British, and Shumlin never gave me a clue. So I remained my awkward, inexperienced, miscast self.

Bogie, about to begin *The Two Mrs Carrolls*, took me down to his boat one weekend. He couldn't wait for me to meet all his sailing friends and be a part of the life that meant so much to him. I wanted to love it, to do it all right — I wanted everyone to like me. There was so much to learn — cooking, for instance, about which I knew nothing. The boat people, or I should say the Yacht Club people, were mostly nice and friendly — all firm, long-standing Republicans — what Bogie called 'private people.' All wealthy, and almost all of them thought actors were freaks. I was a curiosity and looked upon with some disfavor by the wives. The husbands were always happy to see a new young girl — that's why I was looked upon with some disfavor by the wives.

Our first night down there consisted of boat talk — Bogie showing off his 'Baby' — me trying to find something in common with someone. This was really foreign territory. The evening wore on, the drinking continued, the talk got muddled — finally we got into the putt-putt and rode out to his boat, anchored in front of the yacht club. It made me apprehensive when Bogie drank a lot. I continued to talk to him as if he were sober — being reasonable, expecting him to be. I don't know what happened this time — when or how the click in his brain took place — but suddenly he was fighting with me. I got more and more frightened. He started slamming his fist on the table, crying 'You goddamn actresses are all alike.' The more I tried to cajole and pacify him, the worse he got. I started to cry. He shouted, 'Don't give me that crap. The hell with you — I'm leaving.' And he got off the boat. As I heard the outboard motor chugging away, I cried even harder. I didn't understand why he had lost his temper — I went over and over the whole evening and still couldn't latch on to any reason. I'd never seen fury like his — unreasonable, lashing out. I

307

hated it. I was trapped on the boat, and I was terrified that someone might have heard us shouting. I couldn't bear to live like this, but I just didn't know what to do. How can anyone explain what drink can do to people? You just have to live through it and figure it out for yourself as you go along. I cried half the night, solving nothing.

Very early in the morning Bogie returned. He was filled with remorse — didn't know why he'd behaved that way — he would never hurt me — he must have lived through so many years of drinking and fighting that he had simply continued that pattern last night. He was miserable about his failings, and again I had to reverse positions and reassure him. I finally figured out some months later that in his cups he had confused me with Mayo and acted accordingly. I remained alert over the next months, watching for signs on drinking nights. But it was not necessarily the same things that set him off, so there was no way for me to be prepared. Mark Hellinger used to tell him he drank like a kid, mixing his drinks — Mark drank one thing all night and stuck to it. Bogie would have Rob Roys before dinner — or martinis, which were always deadly (one is too many and two aren't enough) — beer with dinner — Drambuie after.

It was a lot for twenty years old to handle. I don't know how I did, except that when you're twenty, it never occurs to you that you can't.

Howard's initial instinct was confirmed. *The Big Sleep* was cut and being scored, he did need one more scene between Bogie and me. The scene would be one of those sex-by-inference scenes — locale, a smoky bar. He could cut it in easily and it would only take a few days to shoot. I hadn't seen Howard for a couple of months — my relationship with him and, more sadly, with Slim had faltered. He was friendly, though, and the scene, written by Jules Furthman, was a good one. Everyone was professional on the set — smiling, warm, but impersonal. The days went well — made me wish for another film for the three of us — but that was not to be.

I appeared on an overseas broadcast with Bob Hope and Bing Crosby, and shook as much as on the first day of shooting my first film. There was a large audience, and I remember Bing standing next to me with his arm lightly around my waist, knowing my nerves and letting me know he was there helping — and Bob Hope doing handstands in front of us.

Mayo had been in Reno for two weeks

when word reached Bogie she had come into L.A. Hurried calls to Morgan and the lawyer — 'Christ, can't you make her stay there? This will go on forever.' And some of the gossiping press — Jimmy Fidler, the trade papers —would not leave us alone. All in all, it was a very nervous, tentative time. Mayo was prevailed upon to go back, but those two days in Los Angeles lost us two weeks, since she had to start all over again. Bogie was worried. When he drank worried, the results were not terrific. He feared that maybe it wasn't going to happen for us, that something would go wrong, so he'd lash out at me on the defensive. It was only serious for a moment, but he certainly kept me on my toes.

At last the six weeks in Reno were coming to a close. If all went well, Bogie would be free on the tenth of May. He started to make plans. Calls to Louis Bromfield and George. We wouldn't have any time — he didn't want to wait until he'd finished his movie. With all my talk about how he'd been married all his life, how he needed his freedom, I didn't want to wait either. So it was finally decided. We'd leave California on a Friday, arrive in Ohio on Sunday; on Monday, May 21, we'd be married, and on Tuesday we'd start back to California. That way they'd only have to shoot around Bogie five days, and I could start *Confidential Agent* the following Monday.

We were walking on air. The wedding would be simple and short. George and Louis would arrange blood tests, license — everything. Bogie and I went to Gershgorn to choose our gold-chain wedding bands. We were photographed at the studio. Jack Warner gave me a 1941 black Buick convertible as a bonus, and I felt very glamorous, particularly with the top down. My family were all very happy for me — they liked Bogie enormously after New York and felt he'd do everything to make my life a good one. Mother was excited and teary — she'd stay with us round-trip and then go back East for a while. I found a very simple pale-pink wool suit, Mother a brown silk dress, for the wedding. Charlie Einfeld told Bogie that *Life* wanted to send their top photographer in the train with us. 'Great,' said Bogie, 'maybe he'd like to photograph us fucking.' That took care of that. The press were having a field day. I'd go to Bogie every day and hold up five fingers, four, three, and so on, to signify days left before he was trapped. Tony Martin had recorded a song called 'Mrs Me' months before and Bogie and I played it constantly — it was very hokey, very romantic, sentimental, but we were all those things, so it was perfect for us. At long last we didn't have to be careful anymore. We could go anywhere together, holding hands for all to see. Miraculously, we found a house on King's Road in the Hollywood Hills above the Strip. It was on three levels, very modern and completely furnished. I fell in love with it — the great view, patio with lawn on the second level, above the bedroom, and large study on the third. There was no land, but I wasn't thinking of land then. We couldn't take occupancy immediately, so we'd stay at the Garden of Allah until we finished our pictures.

Nothing could go wrong for us. All of Bogie's friends — who had begun to be *our* friends — were happy about it. There was nothing to mar our joy. I immediately became part of Bogie's generation — being the chameleon I was, it automatically seemed the thing to do.

We boarded the *Super Chief* on the eighteenth of May with photographers at the Pasadena station to send us on our way. We'd spoken to Louis and George, who had told us Mansfield and Lucas, Ohio, had never seen anything like the multitudes of press that were gathering there. The Bromfield phone never stopped ringing with requests for permission to pitch tents on the farm grounds — they had to call the police to keep crowds away, and George was the man to deal with all of them. Louis was busy being photographed in old corduroy pants looking like a farmer. He loved the fuss. They never had a better time.

George and Louis met us at the station and we headed for the farm. Arrangements had been made for a doctor to come over that night for our blood tests, and the next morning we were to be at the courthouse at 9:00 a.m. to get our license. The press were being held in abeyance as much as possible. There was no way for them not to be there after the ceremony, and a couple of them got into the house before, but the police would keep all strangers off the premises. Such excitement. The Bromfield kitchen was alive with activity — almost everyone connected with the farm had an assignment. The Dragon, as Louis called his mother, sat through it all strong and fierce. Hope, the Bromfields' second daughter, would play the Wedding March as George and I walked down the long, curved stairway. He was giving me away — Louis was best man — Mother was my matron of honor. The house was shining, every table waxed, brass polished — it was truly beautiful. Bogie and I were ridiculous, holding hands like teenagers (I almost was one), we mooned and swooned —

there has never been a more perfect time.

Judge Shettler arrived. He said he felt honored to be marrying us and he explained what the ceremony would be: very short, simple, but very real. 'Cherish' was to be substituted for 'obey.' He was a lovely man. How could I think otherwise? He was going to join me to the man who meant everything in the world to me. I couldn't believe my luck. I knew the sweetness and gentleness of Bogie better than anyone. He was an old-fashioned man — laughingly he'd referred to himself as a last-century boy, having entered the world on Christmas Day 1899. I felt as though I owned the world, and I did. My every dream and hope, and far beyond, were to be realized. I couldn't have wished for a man as incredibly good as this man was. And even so I didn't realize every quality of Bogie's on that day. He was to surprise and delight me continually in the ensuing years.

The happy house went to sleep at a late hour — it was not a night for sleep. We managed a few hours. I had to rise to roll up my hair so as not to frighten the groom. My last hours of what was known as single blessedness. I wrapped a scarf round my head and off we went for the license. As I had stayed the night in Lucas, I was acknowledged a resident — a prerequisite.

Again photographers. All went smoothly — Louis and George signed the piece of paper, and back to the magical farm to prepare for my giant step into a new life. My suit was pressed and hanging in my room. I was beginning to get nervous. I took a bath — laid out my something blue (a slip with my name embroidered on it), my something old (Bogie had told the press that would be him, but it was my identification bracelet that he'd given me), something borrowed (a handkerchief from Mother), and something new (everything else I wore). The wedding was to be at high noon. Bogie, dressed in gray flannel — I refused to see him before the wedding, being superstitious — was pacing downstairs, succumbing to a martini before the ceremony. Mother was helping Mary Bromfield set things up and asking me if I needed anything. I put my arms around her before getting dressed and gave her many kisses and told her how much I loved her. After her trip East, she was going to live in California for the time being. She liked it, and why not? I loved having her close by.

I was finally dressed, though running to the john every five minutes — make-up on, hair combed. Time was moving very slowly until suddenly, all at once, it was five minutes of twelve. George was knocking on my door. 'Are you ready, Baby?' I was Baby to many friends by that time, though no one said it quite the way Bogie did. I opened the door, we hugged each other, I gave him the ring. I was so nervous — began to shake. 'Hope's at the piano, ready to start. Bogie's very itchy standing with Louis, who is also very itchy. Everyone who works on the farm is assembled at the back of the entry hall — the family in front. Shall I give the signal?' Okay, I said. While he was signaling, I made my last dash for the john — my kidneys were no help that day. In the bathroom I could hear the start of the Wedding March. Oh God, why hadn't she waited? Later George told me Bogie had looked up and said, 'Where is she?' George's romantic reply: 'Hold it — she's in the can.' I emerged — Hope started again — and George and I started our descent. My knees shook so, I was sure I'd fall down the stairs. Bogie standing there looking so vulnerable and so handsome — like a juvenile. Mother as nervous as I, trying to keep her eyes from spilling over, a smile on that sweet face. Little Ellen and large Ann Bromfield, Mary, Hope, the cook — all those faces. Prince, Louis' favorite boxer, was the only dog allowed in. My knees were knocking together, my cheek was twitching — would any sound come out when I had to say 'I do'? We turned the corner. When I reached Bogie, he took my hand — the enormous, beautiful white orchids I was holding were shaking themselves to pieces; as I stood there, there wasn't a particle of me that wasn't moving visibly. The Judge was speaking — addressing me — and I heard a voice I'd never heard before say those two simple words of total commitment. Bogie slipped the ring on my finger — it jammed before it reached the knuckle, the trembling didn't help, and then it finally reached its destination. As I glanced at Bogie, I saw tears streaming down his face — his 'I do' was strong and clear, though. George wisely kept my ring for Bogie on one of his own fingers through the ceremony, so it went very neatly onto Bogie's. As Judge Shettler said, 'I now pronounce you man and wife,' Bogie and I turned toward each other — he leaned to kiss me — I shyly turned my cheek — all those eyes watching made me very self-conscious. He said, 'Hello, Baby.' I hugged him and was reported to have said, 'Oh, goody.' Hard to believe, but maybe I did.

Everyone hugged and kissed everyone else and more tears were shed. Bogie said it was when he heard the beautiful words of the ceremony and realized what they meant — what they *should* mean — that he cried.

Then all hell broke loose with the press. Cameras were whipped out, the outsiders were let in, the cake was brought out — three beautiful tiers, with a bride and groom standing under an arbor on top — and we were photographed from all angles — cutting the cake with Louis watching, me feeding Bogie a piece, George and I, Mother with both of us, all of us together. Some newsman asked if I was going to continue my career or stay home and raise a family. Bogie said, 'A lot of people would like to know that, including Warner Brothers.' 'And what do *you* think about it, Mrs Bogart?' 'Oh, I love you,' I said, 'you're the first one to call me Mrs Bogart.' Champagne was flowing — we all went outside for more photos — Louis finally could stand the blue suit no longer and changed into his dirty, old-man-of-the-soil corduroys — and newsreel cameras followed us around the farm. The Judge got very emotional — wished us a really happy life — told us to never forget the words of the service, and, with tears streaming down his face, gave me his Phi Beta Kappa key. The only shadow cast that day was from the trees. It was clear blue sky all the way — as I was sure our life would be. I couldn't forget Bogie's tears. Every time I looked at him I welled up. How had I lived before him? I couldn't remember my life before him — it all ran together, like watercolors. It seemed that everything that had ever happened to me had led to this day with him. I don't know whether it was his particular personality, his strength and purity of thought, or whether all brides feel that way. Probably a combination. I had no doubt that this happiness would last forever. I could not imagine living a minute without him. From now on I would not have to — we were together now, like the man said, 'till death do you part.'

The day continued on that high. We eked out every last drop of Midwestern air and sky — of farm and cooking smells — boxer dogs. Prince, who had calmly lain on the Judge's feet during the ceremony, had knocked up Folly, Bogie's bed companion on his first trip to Malabar without me earlier in the year. One of the puppies was to be our wedding present from Louis. That and one acre of land. I'd tossed the bouquet from midway up the stairs — Hope had screechingly caught it. Carolyn called from California to congratulate me — having had a fight with Buddy. She, having been with him for two years, was still unmarried — and here I was, after little more than a year, Mrs Bogart! Wires from family kept arriving — the excitement never ended.

We hated having to leave, but the following day, after profuse thanks to family and staff and one last look, with a promise to return soon, we left for our train. There was so much ahead that it was probably the only time in my life I was able to leave a place that housed people I loved without a wrenching pain. So the newlyweds headed back to California united at last and ready to live happily ever after.

Back in California, I faced fully for the first time that I was a big girl now and really was not going to live with my mother anymore.

The Garden of Allah was primed for our return. Benchley, Butterworth, McClain, Delehanty, and Parker had bought a cake, and once again the champagne flowed. A pile of telegrams greeted us. And phone calls from the studio — Bogie's work call and my wardrobe call. A sentimental lot. Wedding presents were being sent to the new house, which we'd be getting into permanently in about a month's time.

It was fun to be at the Warners studio as man and wife. Everyone we passed congratulated us — there didn't seem to be anyone even slightly against our union. Except Howard, of course, from whom we heard nothing. I visited Bogie on his set when I wasn't working. I couldn't go through a whole day without seeing him.

We were a happy, laughing pair.

Confidential Agent started shooting. Charles Boyer was a marvelous man, a first-class actor, but plagued with insomnia. If he had four hours' sleep, it was a celebration. He led a quiet private life, but liked chess, so when Bogie came on the set they played. Herman Shumlin would take no advice from anyone — he even tried to tell Charles, an expert, how to play a love scene. He would not allow me to see the rushes and gave me none of the help which I desperately needed. One would have thought — hoped — that someone, somewhere, would have cared whether I conveyed some sense of the character I was playing, but there was never a suggestion from Shumlin that I alter my speech, change an inflection, convey a particular attitude. From 'You know how to whistle' vamp to British upper-class girl might have been achieved by Lynn Fontanne, but sure as hell not by me. At twenty, I was far removed from either character, but the wry, earthy girl of *To Have and Have Not* had humor, which was always a part of me — whereas the British broad was totally straight and dreary. No way — no way possible to deal with her. I was one unhappy girl. After two pictures with total protection, I was on my own. One small problem: I didn't know what the hell I was doing. The facts were that I was a novice — had no experience — had everything to learn. I had come to Hollywood with only what I was born with, and Howard had known how to use it. Between him and Bogie I was submerged in tender loving care. But with Herman Shumlin — much ego and no communication — it was hopeless. I tried to reach Herman, but couldn't — didn't know how to ask Charles — only Bogie's visits to the set gave me any sense of myself. I knew the result would be negative. And I was furious that Jack Warner had been so careless with me. By this time Howard and Charlie Feldman had sold the other half of my contract to Warner Bros. for a purported million dollars, so I was really isolated. I was still able to beef to Charlie, who was always kind and remained my agent — he promised to keep an eye on the film and talk to Shumlin and Warner.

Bogie's sister Pat was coming out of the hospital and at last I would meet her. With my imagination I assumed that anyone who had had a breakdown would look peculiar. Despite assurances to the contrary, I was apprehensive. Pat was coming to the Garden of Allah to spend the day with us. Arrangements were always made by her doctor for her to live with an ex-nurse and friend of Pat's whom he knew. That way she felt secure, and any sign of deterioration would be recognized and dealt with before harm could be done. Frances Bogart Rose, known as Pat, was a tall, strongly built woman — easy to visualize on a horse — who bore a strong resemblance to her brother. She was very shy, totally sweet, and totally normal in her behavior. My fears were unfounded — I couldn't have been more wrong. Bogie was tender and gentle with her and she adored him. She was so happy that he was happy at last and that she had a sister.

I spent most of my time watching and listening — not completely at ease. But she was quiet and gentle — and, with all her size, somewhat delicate and obviously vulnerable. Bogie kept her informed about her daughter Patricia, when he knew something. Patricia was about my age — she and Pat corresponded, and Pat lived for the day she might see her. She dealt with her anguish in extraordinary fashion. The hurdle between us was jumped easily and she always spent a good deal of time with us when she was out of hospital, but she never lived with us. Bogie did not believe in in-laws living with husband and wife, and he didn't believe in anyone dropping in, relatives, even mothers, included. His rule was absolute: Call before and wait for an invitation. His home was sacred, and privacy to be respected.

There was the house to get ready and look forward to. Bogie's cook, May Smith, who'd worked for him on Horn Avenue, wanted to stay with him. Aurelio Salazar, his gardener, felt the same, and a Jamaican butler named Fred Clark, who was more British than Peter Sellers doing the Lord Chancellor. What a group to inherit — but I jumped in with both feet. I never knew how to deal with servants as such, never felt I was better than they — but I did feel they should do what they were paid to do, just as I did. In that I was demanding and, I suppose, a pain in the ass more than once.

So we moved into our honeymoon house in King's Road. To me it was heaven. May was a great cook and helped teach me menus. A tall woman who always wore a pink camellia over her left ear and a large smile, she'd raised two sons — one was a musician, one worked for the police department. She was independent — never complained, gossiped, criticized — she was like a second mother to me and I adored her. She really loved Bogie, knew his culinary tastes, which were limited, and only wanted to please. Her pride and personal dignity were tremendous — you had to respect her. Fred insisted on calling us M'Lord and M'Lady with a half-smile on his face. He was star-struck — bright, sunny, sometimes fresh, but would never remain a butler; just vamping till ready to make his move. But he was fun — he'd pick up Bogie's secretary, Kathy Sloan, every morning on Sunset and drive her to the house to deal with the mail, phone, anything Bogie might want. Kathy was a nice woman, worked hard, was devoted to Bogie. Her one peculiarity: she never walked into the kitchen — insisted on having her lunch on a tray.

Life fell into a semblance of routine. We finished our respective films and Bogie planned his big moment — showing me Catalina. I was filled with anticipation — I so wanted to adore it all. A beautiful summer weekend and off we went. Food was bought — I was going to cook a great dinner. I asked May how to cook string beans — twenty minutes in boiling water, I was told. I couldn't wait. I loved playing house, alone — just the two of us at sea in the moonlight, surrounded by silence — so romantic. We left Newport — the trip would take about two hours. Bogie showed me how to steer the boat. I fixed lunch down below, which was fine for the first five minutes — then, with the ocean swells and the motion of the boat, my stomach was visited with just a touch of queasiness. Please, God, don't let me be sick. I brought the lunch topside and I was all right — on small cruisers the stove is often in a corner of the main cabin near the door leading to the deck, so some air is always traveling through. I ate — my first mistake. Waves of nausea began to overtake me. I was tense, afraid Bogie would notice — and that made it worse. Finally I just sat in the open air in the stern, gas fumes floating past my nose, turning greener and greener, with Bogie at the wheel showing me glorious Catalina. I couldn't be too enthusiastic — afraid to move or say much for fear of throwing up — so I sat with a sickly smile on my face till we got in the lee of the island and the ground swells stopped. Finally the nausea passed. Poor Bogie — this meant so much to him, and, like all things that one builds too high in one's mind, it was a letdown. We moored in Cherry Cove — pretty, well protected, very calm. It had a small beach. Pat and Zelma brought their boat over — there were a couple of sailboats moored — I handled the boathook while Bogie handled the boat. There was much boating terminology to learn. (That was the year I learned everything at once: how to be a wife, run a house, sail a boat, cook, and not trust Jack Warner.) As soon as we moored, Bogie would have his first drink, that was custom. So we sat in the sun with the boat

326

very gently moving — I wished it would stay still — and Bogie telling me that once I got used to it, once I had my sea legs, I'd feel terrific. I hoped he was right. He was Navy-trained — hurricanes didn't bother him.

I prepared the string beans — put the water on to boil — and when it did, I turned the fire off and twenty minutes later announced dinner. What a fiasco. That remained a joke for years. Bogie did finally face the fact of my squeamishness, but went on believing that I'd improve with practice. Once I was there I always loved it — it was just the getting there I hated. Bogie taught me to keep my eye on the horizon — if you did that, the nausea would pass. Stare at an immovable object. God knows I tried, and it did get better after a time. I only wanted to be with him anyway, and I was determined to enjoy everything he enjoyed.

November brought the release of *Confidential Agent.* It was a disaster. The critics said they'd made a mistake — I was not Garbo, Dietrich, Hepburn, Mae West all rolled into one, as they had thought. I was just terrible me and should be sent back where I came from. As brilliant, exciting, and glorious as I had been just a few months ago, that's how amateurish, tedious, and just plain bad I was now. At the same time George Kaufman had directed a play in New York called *The Next Half Hour* and he was creamed by the critics. I ought to send him a wire, I told Bogie, saying we'd make a great pair. Bogie said, 'Do it.' Great not to lose one's sense of humor about oneself. Thank God I had Bogie. Well, Moss Hart had been dead right — I fell from the top of that ladder with a resounding crash. And it was the last time Jack Warner made a choice for me.

I wonder if critics realize how destructive they are. Imagine if I had not been a happy new bride — with that distraction and the support and guidance of my experienced husband. If I'd been alone, I could never have survived. Lucky for me I threw myself so violently, so single-mindedly, into the big things of life. If I hadn't been so consumed by Bogie, the thrusting of me onto the national scene with such a vengeance would have been uncopable with. Not having really hit that higher-than-a-kite high, I didn't have quite so heavy a crash. I realized early on how limited the critics' knowledge of actors is, how they do not recognize where an actor's contribution begins or ends. I remember that when *The Big Sleep* was released a year later they said: Ah, that's more like the first Bacall we loved (they hate to be wrong) — she's good in this one — we like her again — let's not judge too quickly — we'll see what happens. What they didn't know, of course, was that *The Big Sleep* was made before *Confidential Agent*. At the time, I didn't realize how much damage had been done, but after *Confidential Agent* it took me years to prove that I was capable of doing anything at all worthwhile. I would never reach the *To Have and Have Not* heights again — on film anyway — and it would take much clawing and scratching to pull myself even halfway back up that damn ladder.

Just about that time I received a lengthy letter from my father telling me the 'Truth' about my parents' divorce. According to him, he had been the maligned and mistreated one — he had washed my diapers and bathed and fed me — he had given my mother everything — her family had turned on him — it was he who was responsible for what I was today. He signed the letter 'your Father,' then his full name. The letter was typed — dictated, no doubt. What was worrying him was that he had no answers if questions were posed to him about me. The letter upset Mother greatly. We sent it to Uncle Jack, who had all the files on my father. His history was unsavory and spoke for itself, as did his neglect of me and his sudden rebirth. It was always unsettling to me to hear from him, mainly because I had given him little thought in my growing-up years except for the fact of his rejection of me, which was my constant companion. To have him suddenly reappear full of negative opinions about my choices made waves on my smooth sea. I didn't have curiosity about him then — I was resentful — I knew Mother and my family well enough to be absolutely certain they'd invented nothing. Their goodness and love stood tall and strong. Mother's worry seemed to be that if I ever saw him, he'd make a scene, and now that I was famous he was capable of calling press conferences — doing anything to gain recognition. Maybe I inherited my sense of the dramatic from him.

The letter was filed and ignored. My life was happy and full — my days of needing a father had passed — there was no ground upon which I could ever meet him now. Sad in a way, but when a man chooses to forget his child, he can expect the same behavior in return. It's not deliberate, it just happens. The damage was done long before.

One afternoon I was waiting for Bogie to come home from a day at the races with Mark Hellinger. The phone rang — it was Mother, distraught. She'd stopped at a market in Beverly Hills to pick up some food for dinner. Droopy and Puddle, his daughter, were with her. As they emerged from her car, the dogs were hit immediately by another car — your average hit-and-run driver. Droopy was dead and the puppy hurt. I burst into a flood of tears. Where was Bogie? I needed him! Finally — late — he called. He was crocked. 'Hello, Baby, meet us at LaRue's, Mark and I are there now.' Wonderful! I cried into the phone about Droopy — it had little effect. I should have known that a day with Mark meant a day with Johnnie Walker. I was furious with Bogie, but after more tears pulled myself together and got to the restaurant. Mark was smiling and happy — happy that Bogie was loaded and happy to see me. I got no sympathy from anyone. It was a night to forget. We ended up in the home of some silent film star — up until dawn — Bogie drunker than I'd ever seen him and drunker than he'd ever be again. He didn't know where he was, and only every now and then would he relate to me. I hated what that much liquor did to him — I still hadn't learned to drink, still hadn't learned how to deal with people who did, still was twenty years old. It all made me feel angry — and inadequate and uncertain. I was fiercely jealous of Bogie. He never gave me cause, but partly due to my insecurity, and partly due to the fact that I thought him so dazzling, I was certain every other woman did — and many did. I never showed it, but I felt it. That morning he was finally poured into the car and I drove him home. The vision of Droopy lying dead was still in my mind — I only wanted Bogie to fall asleep so I could call Mother. After getting him yet another drink and getting him downstairs — no easy trick — he did pass out. I felt only relief.

Mother and I went to the Pet Cemetery in the Valley. A woman straight out of Charles Addams greeted us and asked if we would like to go to the Slumber Room to see our dog. All her talk was very solemn, at a whisper. There is often something funny at every sad occasion — in this case, she was it. We followed her into the Slumber Room, where dogs of all types were lying asleep in open coffins, one mutt in a box lined with tufted satin. Droopy lay with his head on one paw just as he'd slept in life. I reached out to touch him — he looked so alive I thought he might be — but I touched stone. I quickly pulled my hand back and we quickly left the room and made arrangements for his burial. So, sadly, ended that chapter of my life.

Bogie was a Christmas baby, so I decided to give him a surprise party on

Christmas Eve. He always did his Christmas shopping the day before and would come home at around six. We were supposedly going to Hellinger's house for dinner. Our house had a Roman tub, about four by eight feet and five deep. I gathered Benchley, Butterworth, McCain, Nunnally, Hellinger, Delehanty, Sheekman, Pat O'Moore, Ray Massey — about twenty in all — and made them stand in the tub. They looked funny and silly, all with glasses in their hands, crushed together in a blue sunken tub — an unlikely sight. When Bogie came in I greeted him with a drink as usual. The tree was lit, the living room looked festive. It was very sentimental — our first Christmas as man and wife. Bogie wanted to go downstairs, but I said that something was wrong with the Roman tub — could he take a look at it first? I led him toward the door, opened it, turned on the light — all those ridiculous faces gathered in a bathtub shouting 'Surprise!' completely threw him off balance. It was the only surprise party he'd ever had — he couldn't get over it. The evening was a success. I was a nervous hostess, but there was good food (all made by May), plenty to drink, and good friends. Bogie was like a kid — touched that I would go to all that trouble, touched that people cared enough about him to gather together.

He'd never had occasion to test that before. It's odd when I think of it. Here was a totally successful man of forty-six who'd never had a party in his own home, never had his house filled with friends, people who genuinely liked him. There were so many things for me to find out about Bogie — information uncovered at unexpected moments; just as I thought I had him figured, something new caught me unaware. Astounding — there were so many, many layers to this man that, as well as I knew him, I'm sure I never uncovered them all. I remember him handing me my Christmas present, saying, 'I got tired of seeing all that tobacco in your bag.' He was shy. The gift was a beautiful gold cigarette case with a ruby clasp and the inscription 'For Mrs Me who never need whistle for Bogie.' Out of the corner of his eye, he watched me open it, and when we looked at each other, trumpets sounded, rockets went off. We really loved — we had every hokey, sentimental, funny, profound feeling there was to have. I loved presents, and I gave Bogie many always — half-birthday, half-Christmas — he'd grown up being cheated of them. He never bought me more than two things — usually one of them was extravagant. I always bought him something relating to the boat — something for his gold watch chain — clothes. He didn't want anything. He didn't care for jewelry — he wore his wedding ring on one hand, his father's ring on the other, a watch and key chain, very occasionally cufflinks, and that was that. But I loved to shop for him — I had never bought anything for a man before. And I had never had any money until now. Carolyn and I always spent several days Christmas shopping together. This year we bought our first ornaments for our first trees — she and Buddy had finally gotten married that September. Christmas still seemed funny without snow, but I'd overlook that.

Bogie hated New Year's Eve — that was the one night he refused to get drunk, just because everyone else did. Ornery. Our circle of friends was enlarging. Bogie had taken me into Ira Gershwin's home — his wife, Lee (for Leonore), and Bogie had lived next door to each other in New York and had kind of grown up together. I was very much in awe of and at the Gershwin house. Milling around would be Oscar Levant, Harold Arlen, Arthur Kober, Harry Kurnitz, Judy Garland, Lena Horne, Groucho Marx, Harry Ruby, Arthur Schwartz — the list was endless. They were friends, all bright, musical, and creative, mostly funny — that house was the warmest, most welcoming and sought after in Hollywood, and it played a large role in my California life and after. George Kaufman and Moss Hart were there when in town, Harold Arlen would play and sing, Ira would sing. The more often I went, the more time I'd spend beside the piano. I knew all the lyrics and my spirit was part of their music. And I finally met the mythical John Huston. He'd been best man when Jules Buck married my friend Joyce, so I'd met him briefly then, but that was before I was Mrs Bogart and I don't count that meeting. Huston was another original. Aside from his extraordinary talent, he's always been a personal mesmerizer. About six foot five, very thin, a man of soft voice and careful speech who seemed to travel loosely through life. He adored Bogie and vice versa — he was very funny, but devilish and socially undependable. I discovered this gradually. I was accepted immediately by him because I loved his friend. He didn't like women much on their own.

The next few years were the happiest of my life — I was really on a cloud. My life revolved entirely around Bogie. Though I worked a little, there was no doubt what took priority. We both changed as our lives together grew closer — we were so close that there was never a notion in anyone's mind that anything or anyone could come between us. Our commitment was a life commitment.

Bogie and I made our third movie together — *Dark Passage* — and went to San Francisco for a month of location shooting. My first time in that beautiful city. We lived at the Mark Hopkins Hotel and spent many evenings at the Top of the Mark looking over the entire city and the Golden Gate Bridge. We generally lived a quiet, private newlywed life there. Toward the end of shooting, back in the studio, I became aware of Bogie's nerves — if the phone rang, he'd tense up, didn't want to answer it, didn't want to speak to any except the closest. He'd noticed a bare spot on his cheek where his beard was not growing. The one spot increased to several — then he'd wake in the morning and find clumps of hair on the pillow. That alarmed him. It's one thing to be bald with a rim of hair, an actor could always wear a hairpiece, but without the rim it would have to be a full wig. The more hair fell out, the more nervous he got, and the more nervous he got, the more hair fell out. In the last scene in *Dark Passage* he wore a complete wig. He panicked — his livelihood hung in the balance. A visit to the doctor was in order. He never went to doctors. The verdict was that he had a disease known as alopecia areata — in lay-

337

man's terms, hair falls out as a result of vitamin deficiencies. He was plain worn out — the years of mistreating himself in bars and an unsteady diet had added up to this. It would grow back, but he'd need B-12 shots twice a week — scalp treatments — more food — in general, more care. That was a relief to us both. His next film was going to be *The Treasure of the Sierra Madre* with John Huston and he'd have had to wear a wig for that anyway.

George Hawkins and Louis Bromfield had given us a boxer dog as a wedding gift. We immediately named him Harvey — after me and that rabbit. He was a fantastic dog — actually he was not a dog at all, he preferred people and understood them. The first night we had him we locked him in our bathroom with newspaper all over the floor. He cried all through the night until I finally thought the hell with it, and let him into the bedroom. He never made another sound — nor did he mess the room. Harvey was the protector of the house and of us. If Bogie and I argued, he'd go to one, then the other, growling at us, trying to make us stop. If he saw a suitcase being packed, he'd lie at our bedroom entrance with his back to us — he'd have nothing to do with us if we were leaving him. We tried to take him to the boat, but he didn't know what to make of it.

Standing on the slip, I called to him to get on board, snapping my fingers, saying, 'Here, Harvey,' whereupon he followed my hand and landed in the water. But the boat was too confining for him, so we gave up and his first time was his last.

We had also bought a new house. I was determined to have a baby and Hollywood Hills was not the place in which I wanted to live and bring up children, nor would there be room in our current house. I loved to have six people to dinner, and the space wasn't right. And now I wanted land — I wanted to plant flowers. I'd been learning from our gardener, Aurelio, who loved the earth and watching things grow. Finally Bogie agreed that I could look. I found an enchanting house way up Benedict Canyon — not at all developed then, real country. It was owned by Hedy Lamarr, who said she'd give it to us if Bogie would make a movie with her. Bogie preferred to pay for the house. It was a house of tremendous charm, all on one floor — eight rooms (one a natural nursery), a pool, and an area in back for ducks, chickens, and turkeys. A minuscule version of Malabar. We both loved it — bought it and moved in. Carolyn and Buddy had moved to Coldwater Canyon, not too far from us.

The same year Bogie became the proud

owner of the *Santana*, a racing yawl said to have been a designer's mistake because she had a perfect hull. She was designed by Sparkman and Stevens and built by the Wilmington Boatworks. Her name represented a strong, hot wind that blows off the desert onto the Pacific. Bogie had wanted a sailboat from the beginning, long before I knew him, but couldn't afford it. Dick Powell, another lover of the sea, had bought the *Santana* from William Stewart, who had had her built, but Dick had terrible sinus problems and needed dry climates, so he had to sell. The *Santana* could be sailed by two people. We went out for a Sunday sail with Dick Powell and June Allyson, who were married by then. The sea did for Dick what it did for Bogie. He became lightheaded — singing, laughing. He didn't want to part with her. But Bogie was in love. If ever I had a woman to be jealous of, she was the *Santana*. Her sleek lines, the way she moved in the water. He learned everything about her from the first plank laid, every race sailed — she'd won the Bermuda race when Bill Stewart owned her. When Bogie bought that boat he was enslaved — happily so — and truly had everything he'd ever dreamed of. We took her to Catalina alone the first weekend of summer. I was at the wheel — Bogie raised the sails. The bulk of my sailing knowledge was gleaned from that boat. I was less squeamish on the *Santana* — sailboats are steadier than cruisers, and with the auxiliary motor turned off, the sail to Catalina was quiet and beautiful. Only when the wind was slack did she slap with the swells, as did my innards. The crossings were fun. I'd go up to the bow and watch the dolphins playing as we plowed through the water — and flying fish. Only in California could a fish fly, I thought.

On our second married Christmas I gave Bogie his second birthday party — no surprises this time. In our new cozy house, with our many more friends, including Hellinger, Huston, the Nunnally Johnsons, the Gershwins, Marees, Jaffes, Tony Veiller (writer) and his wife, Grace — plus the first group — it was a smashing success. Bogie had given me a large box and insisted I open it. I couldn't imagine what was in it, so I tore it open with the imbibing friends gathered round — I gasped — it was a mink coat. He'd ordered it from Bergdorf Goodman, and embroidered next to my initials on the lining was a very small mink. The coat was a beauty. I put it on. Mark said, 'Have you ever walked barefoot on a mink?' God, no, this was as close as I'd ever been to one. So I threw it on the floor, took off my shoes, and walked on it.

Harvey stepped on it too. Bogie was livid — he grabbed it from the floor — was this all it meant to me, after all his planning, how dare I throw it on the floor! He'd had a few, which explains his distorted thinking. Mark said we were kidding, it was all his fault. I said of course I loved it. I threw my arms around him — but he'd have none of it. It was touch and go for a while there.

By this time in my young life, I'd discovered aquavit. I liked the taste of it, and with ice it would last awhile. Bogie said it was too strong — schnapps, meant to be drunk straight with food as an apéritif. But I drank it before dinner and after, which was okay for a while until it made me sick and then I stopped. Christmas Day we always had milk punches made with bourbon, which I liked because I couldn't taste the bourbon and Bogie liked because they helped his hangovers.

Life was very, very full and very, very good. I was suspended several times, as Jack Warner wanted me in certain films whose scripts I hated. I tried to see him at the studio — explain to him that I wanted to work, but didn't feel the parts he'd chosen were right for me. Jack was always ill at ease, especially with actors. Once when he was having Errol Flynn problems, he was in the private dining room with some producers among whom was a new handsome man by the name of Robert Buckner. Jack said, 'Goddamn actors always want more money — I can make anyone a star. Just give me blank film. Look at him —' pointing to Buckner — 'I could make *him* a star — easy — but then he'd start asking for more money. Goddamn actors!' Then he got sore at poor Buckner. It was said Jack used to talk back to the rushes — when he'd watch Bette Davis crying, he'd say, 'That's it, Bette — pour it on — money in the box office,' and when he'd watch Bogie, he'd get tough: 'Go get 'em, Bogart — let him have it!' When I'd try to reason with him, Jack would lead me to his office window, point to the sound stages below, and say, 'Would I have all this if I didn't know what I was doing?' Then the formal telegrams would start coming — first one from Jack asking me to play ball and cooperate, the second from Roy Obringer, the Warner lawyer, quoting from paragraph whatever telling me in legal terms to report to work for whatever film. Followed by notice that in accordance with clause such-and-such, I was hereby suspended for refusal to work. That meant no pay. Once the film was recast and started shooting, I could send a wire saying I was ready, willing, and able to go to work and they'd have to put me back on salary. It was a game, but there was no way to avoid it. Once Warner had made up his mind an actor was to be in a certain film — good or bad — that was it. The actor was under contract and there was no way Warner would pay the s.o.b. if he didn't work. If the part was lousy, no matter. With each rotten script I thought of Cagney's words to me when I started.

If we weren't in New York at World Series time when one of my home teams had won, we'd be listening on the boat or have baseball lovers to the house. I'd always loved the game and it was such fun going to the games in New York. Quent Reynolds and Ginny began to figure strongly in our lives — Quent was always ready to go to the ballgame (he was a Toots Shor–Joe DiMaggio pal). Not many women went, but I always did. It made me feel I was still a New Yorker. Although we tried to get to New York twice a year, our time there was always frantic — going to the theatre almost nightly, dates for lunch, drinks before theatre, after — it was the only way to see everyone, and it was exhausting.

As I was learning more about wifery — enjoying friends, having dinners at home, gardens — I was learning more about the man I married. He hated calendar occasions — Mother's Day, Valentine's Day, birthdays, even Christmas. He resented being told by florists and candy makers that he had to buy a present, that it was expected. Much more fun and meaningful to buy a gift for no reason at all. When he'd had a long lunch at Romanoff's and ended up drinking too much and getting home late for dinner, he might buy me some expensive bauble — a clip that was a cuckoo clock, all sorts of gold gadgets. He always said there's no excuse for being late — drinking notwithstanding, of course — it takes two minutes to make a phone call. He took the two minutes.

And he educated me about Hollywood — about the press and the truth. If you tell the press — or anyone in Hollywood — the truth, it throws them, they don't know how to deal with it. He was dead right about that. Also that all through one's life one meets — and, in our business especially, is exposed to — attractive people. The circumstance of seeing them every day, playing love scenes, going on location can make a love affair very tempting. But you must always weigh a quick romance against what your life is — think whether it's worth the risk. It almost never is. And he would chide me: 'Long after I'm gone you'll remember this and see that I'm right.' And long after he's gone I have remembered all of it and he was always right. It could be infuriating at the time, but he had experienced and observed enough to *know*. It's incredible to me as I think back now — at about the same age he was when he told me all those things — to realize how much wiser he was then than I am now. Much of my knowledge of people comes from seeds planted those many years ago and grown strong, though not always straight, in the years since. He would say, 'Never damage your own character. To have a love affair breaks a bond between husband and wife — and even if your partner doesn't know about it, the relationship must be less open, so something very important will never be the same. And you've cut into yourself more than into him.' He was preparing me for temptation because of my youth and my lack of exposure — at the same time, I suppose, there were apprehensions in his subconscious. Small clues as to his vulnerability were left for me all through our life together and even after.

Bogie had decided to enter the *Santana* in the Honolulu race, the first since the war. He'd lined up his crew, all guys who had sailed with him before. The plan was that I, with the other wives, would fly to Honolulu to greet the boats as they rounded Diamond Head. Bogie had his heart set on it and I couldn't wait to go to Honolulu. But first we were going to Mexico for *The Treasure of the Sierra Madre*. It was to be shot, in the true Huston tradition, in locations not easily accessible. *Treasure* was a marvelous book by B. Traven and John had written a very good script — and had cast, in addition to Bogie, his father, Walter Huston, a devastatingly attractive and witty man and beautiful actor. Plus Tim Holt and Alfonso Bedoya, a great Mexican actor. Everything augured well. Bogie was to wear a wig, although his hair was growing back slowly but surely, and John had promised Bogie he would absolutely be finished by the last week in June to be ready for the Honolulu race. No question about it. Bogie had hired a cook for the race, lined up his crew, ordered some very expensive sails from Kenny Watts, and was looking forward to it like a kid meeting Santa Claus for the first time.

Our headquarters were in a lovely watering spa called San José de Purua, a few hours out of Mexico City. The Mexican crew were friendly — they sang nightly on their way home from work. We learned to drink tequila and went bowling almost nightly with Walter, John, John's new wife, Evelyn Keyes, Tim, and some of the crew. Only the food was a disaster — a whole fish with bulging eyes that looked raw would be served, or a rubber turkey.

Finally, after talking it over with John, I decided to order some canned soups, hams, baked beans, and the like, to provide something edible and reliable. My first night in the kitchen with the ham was a joke — I'd told two Mexican helpers to cut the skin off the ham, and while I was organizing the beans and stewed tomatoes they proceeded to cut all the fat off it too. With toothpicks I put it all back on, as well as cloves. The ham worked out and I was the location heroine. It was mostly good fun except for the moments John displayed his disdain for women — his wife in particular. Poor Evelyn would say something and John would say, 'What? What was that, Evelyn? Now, wait a minute — I want everyone to hear this' and Evelyn was on the block. Any casual, innocent, occasionally thoughtless remark was magnified and she was made to look like a fool. It was humiliating. He'd say, 'Here's Betty seeing to our dinners, in the kitchen with the cooks, and all you can do is complain.' I didn't envy her, married to John. He was brilliant, he was fascinating, he was fun — but stay a friend. Better still, a friend's wife. I loved Bogie, I was a good wife, so in John's eyes I could do no wrong. Evelyn managed for a while. She must have learned a good deal and emerged stronger and wiser.

As the shooting went on and the crew

sang more and worked more slowly, Bogie worried more and more about finishing in time for the big race. He prodded John, kept reminding him of his promise: 'God damn it, John, I've planned this for months — move faster.' John tried, but his first concern was the picture, and he liked Mexico and was in no hurry to leave. (Needless to say, the Honolulu race had to be canceled.) One of the reasons they worked as well as they did together was that John needed Bogie to keep him paying attention. He tended to lose interest as a picture was coming to a close. And Bogie always said that if an actor normally went just so high, John would always make him go higher, find things in himself he never suspected were there.

The great matter of riveting interest to me was Walter and John together. They'd evidently gone through some years of little or no communication. John had been a very good boxer, then a writer — had led a rather disorganized life, and Walter had thought he might never work at anything long enough to amount to much! But by the time of *Treasure*, Walter was deeply proud of his son. And John idolized his father. What's more, in *Treasure* he gave him the acting role of his life. They were like a couple of kids together — they made each other laugh, they enjoyed and understood each other's wickedness. They were alike in many ways. I was still learning about John, and it was a revelation to see that he was capable of feeling strongly about another human being. Walter Huston was a hard man not to love. Bogie and he worked wonderfully well together — Bogie was always happier working with first-class actors. He thought acting was a noble profession and was proud of being a member. Peter Lorre used to call much movie acting 'face-making,' and Bogie's feeling was that many film actors, young stars, were face-makers. The ones who weren't, like Spencer Tracy — those he admired.

After Mexico the location moved to Bakersfield, California, for two weeks — hot and dry. Murder in June and July. It was there that John told Bogie late one night, 'The trouble with me is that I am forever and eternally bored.' They'd been talking about life — John envied Bogie his. I always thought it was a sad and revealing remark, diagramming the internal war raging within him.

In the fall of 1947, investigations started in Washington led by Congressman J. Parnell Thomas, head of the House Un-American Activities Committee. His target was Hollywood, but his goal was headlines for himself. A Congressman named Richard Nixon was a member of the Committee.

We became aware of it gradually. Members of the Committee held hearings in California to which were called well-known people of various political persuasions, including Robert Taylor, Gary Cooper, Elia Kazan. The Committee grabbed space on the front pages of newspapers throughout the country and the world. Those people saw Communists under every bed. They were convinced that they were the only true Americans — the rest of us were infiltrating films with un-American thoughts, the beliefs of foreign governments. There was now a blacklist alive in Hollywood — some of the most talented and creative writers, directors, and a few actors were deprived of the right to work, though they were guilty of nothing. Studios were terrified. It suddenly became risky, even dangerous, to be a Democrat. Fear was rampant — the ruling emotion. Some writers had been subpoenaed to testify, among them Albert Maltz, Dalton Trumbo, Alvah Bessie, and refused to cooperate. Along with others including Adrian Scott, producer, and Eddie Dmytryk, director, they were called the 'Unfriendly Ten.'

Some of us Democrats began talking about it among ourselves. There was a large meeting one night at the Gershwins' which found most of the biggest stars, directors, writers in the business present — Judy Garland, Eddie Robinson, Burt Lancaster, Willie Wyler, Billy Wilder, John Huston, Philip Dunne, Harry Kurnitz, Danny Kaye, Gene Kelly, Bogie and me, and many, many more. It was the birth of the Committee for the First Amendment. After various people rose to speak, it was agreed that a formal petition must be drawn up and sent to Washington. Parnell Thomas was getting carried away with the publicity — more and more people in the industry, and the industry itself, were suffering, to say nothing of the Bill of Rights. The petition said,

We, the undersigned, as American citizens who believe in constitutional democratic government, are disgusted and outraged by the continuing attempt of the House Committee on Un-American Activities to smear the Motion Picture Industry.

We hold that these hearings are morally wrong because:

Any investigation into the political beliefs of the individual is contrary to the basic principles of our democracy;

Any attempt to curb freedom of expression and to set arbitrary standards of Americanism is in itself disloyal to both the spirit and the letter of our Constitution.

There were five hundred signatures. And the press became aware of us and of our thoughtful, sane protest against the activities and methods of the Committee. There was also a Republican and Democratic Joint Committee of Hollywood for Preservation of Civil Liberties. Another group in New York with a long list of signatures was protesting as we were — among its distinguished members was Helen Hayes. It was a disturbing and frightening period in Hollywood. Everyone was suspect — at least, everyone to the left of center.

One night a group of us were asked to go up to Willie Wyler's house to hear on a telephone set-up from some of the people in Washington what was going on there. It was a cry for help. I remember Adrian Scott describing the gavel-pounding of Mr Thomas and the way the cards had been stacked against everyone there. They wanted a group of us to come to Washington to give them moral support. Oh, I became very emotional about it. It was my first grown-up exposure to a cause, and my reaction should have clued me in as to how cause-prone I could be. We all listened very carefully. There was no talk of Communism — from our point of view, Communism had nothing to do with it. It had to do with the Hitlerian tactics being employed. I was up in arms — fervent. I said to Bogie, 'We must go.' He felt strongly about it too, but at first I was the more outspoken. My reaction was based on emotion: How dare that bastard Thomas treat people this way? What was happening to our country? He must be stopped. What kind of a world were we living in anyway, and what would happen to motion pictures? A lot, as we'd all find out later — a lot more than we thought at the time, and the effects were longer-lasting than any of us dreamed.

So it was decided that a group of us would fly to Washington — John Huston, Phil Dunne, Ira Gershwin, Danny Kaye, Gene Kelly, Paul Henreid, John Garfield, June Havoc, Evelyn Keyes, Marsha Hunt, Jane Wyatt, Sterling Hayden, Robert Ardrey, Jules Buck, Joseph Sistrom, Richard Conte, David Hopkins (a publicist son of Harry Hopkins), Larry Adler, Bogie, and me. Huston and Dunne were to be the official spokesmen. Howard Hughes offered us a plane for our trip.

The night before our departure a meeting was held at Dave Chasen's restaurant at which Willie Wyler told us we must not look like slobs. We were representing a lot of people in the industry, we must make a good impression — the women were to wear skirts, not slacks; the men, shirts and ties. It was so exciting — there's nothing like the charge you get out of being one of a group of people doing the same thing for the same reason — pure in thought and purpose, on a crusade. It's a fever. You feel so strongly, you're certain you can carry anyone — everyone — along with you.

Bogie released a statement about the trip:

This has nothing to do with Communism. It's none of my business who's a Communist and who isn't. We have a well organized and excellent agency in Washington known as the FBI who does know these things. The reason I am flying to Washington is because I am an outraged and angry citizen who feels that my civil liberties are being taken away from me and that the Bill of Rights is being abused and who feels that nobody in this country has any right to kick around the Constitution of the United States, not even the Un-American Activities Committee.

There was a petition for redress of grievances addressed to House Speaker Joseph Martin, Jr — we were to march to the

Capitol and present it to him.

The plane stopped along the way to Washington and some of us made speeches to waiting crowds. We were a serious group — reasonably well-informed, bright, and we all cared. John, Bogie, Danny Kaye, Gene Kelly, and I made most of the short speeches. At the end of mine I was sure I could run for office and, what's more, be elected. The airport crowds were large and vociferous — cheers went up — God, it was exciting. I couldn't wait to get to Washington. Wouldn't it be incredible if we really could effect a change — if we could make that Committee stop? Innocence is guileless and trustful. I was due for a big surprise.

The press greeted us at the airport and asked us to pose for pictures in front of the plane. Later we saw that the name of the plane was the *Red Star*. Coincidence or design?

We settled into the Statler Hotel. John Huston told the press we had not come to attack anybody, nor to defend the unfriendly witnesses. Just wished to fight the growing voluntary censorship in Hollywood.

We were to attend the hearings the next three days, hold press conferences, present our petition at the Capitol, meet with some Senators and Representatives for advice in the battle for freedom — and, hopefully, see President Truman.

We were led into the hearings, a back row being reserved for us. Following us continually were photographers and reporters. At the center of the raised platform sat J. Parnell Thomas, gavel in hand. As the witnesses were called, they refused to answer the charge of being a Communist. Our friend Quentin Reynolds, who was covering the hearings for *PM*, wrote, 'There is no doubt that the storm of criticism heaped upon the rather shiny pate of Mr Thomas by the press of the country has had a chastening effect. A dozen times Mr Thomas has said that the witnesses are not on trial: that the Committee is a mere fact-finding board.' And then Robert E. Stripling, the Committee's counsel and its chief inquisitor, spilled the beans. 'You have been charged with being a Communist,' Stripling told Alvah Bessie, 'and now you are being given a chance to answer that charge.' The witnesses were treated as defendants in a trial — bearing no resemblance to what Mr Thomas said the Committee function was. When witnesses such as Bessie, Dalton Trumbo, and Albert Maltz were asked 'Are you a member of the Communist Party?' and refused to answer, they were exercising their rights as defined in the Bill of Rights. They wouldn't answer whether they were members of the Screen Writers' Guild either. Political affiliation was not the business of the Committee, but Stripling demanded a yes or no answer, would not allow the witnesses to make statements of their own — and Thomas was gavel-happy. I couldn't believe what was going on — that jerk sitting up there with his title had the power to put these men in jail! It was frustrating to watch. I was full of sound and fury, sounding off at the drop of a hat. Our press conference was attended by representatives of every important newspaper in the country. Huston was holding forth in one corner. Danny Kaye in another was saying, 'It's like walking out on a stage and being given the raspberry before you open your mouth.' Gene Kelly, Bogie, me — and so forth. And I remember May Craig, a tough and terrific newswoman from Maine, saying, 'But didn't you know what it would be like in Washington? Didn't anyone tell you? You are so naïve.' We certainly were. Some of the questions put us on the defensive — we had to admit we didn't know whether any of the witnesses were Communists, and suddenly that became the important thing. But we weren't defending Communism (which in any case had not been outlawed), we were defending something else. I was so fired up that I wrote a piece for the Washington *Daily News* that appeared on the front page.

Exclusive: By Lauren Bacall: 'WHY I CAME TO WASHINGTON'

Perhaps I'm the girl whom some Americans remember as having said a certain line in a certain picture.

If I am, and you know me, then let's forget about it for the moment.

I'm speaking to you now as a person who shares the same rights any of you do — those given to an American citizen.

It's possible that in all the excitement and confusion, our purpose in coming to Washington has not been made clear. But I would like to take this opportunity to speak to you as an individual — as someone who has a job and gets paid for it, and wants to see that that job is protected.

I have been reading about the investigation by the House Committee on Un-American Activities with a great deal of interest and a certain amount of fear. I am a person who has always believed in the First Amendment to our Constitution, which gives us the right as Americans to freedom of speech and freedom of political belief.

According to what I've read, it seems to me that those freedoms are being jeopardized, and it's always been my feeling that when you're attacked, or your job is threatened, you ought to fight back. You ought to do something about it.

So I, together with other members of the motion picture industry, decided we should come to Washington and see if there wasn't something we could do.

Well, I want you to know that I attended two sessions of the hearings and it frightened me. When I left the House Office Building I couldn't help but feel that every American who cares anything at all about preserving American ideals should witness a part of this investigation.

You may think it's very easy for me to make a trip to Washington — that I can afford it. Well, that's beside the point. Believe me when I tell you that what's going on here can happen to you.

I don't want to alarm you, but I think you should be aware of the dangers that arise out of investigations like this that follow the procedure that this one has followed.

When they start telling you what pictures you can make, what your subjects can be, then it's time to rear up and fight!

It starts with us, but I'm sorry to say I don't think it will end with us.

If this committee succeeds in indicting people without giving them a chance to defend themselves, then they can stretch out their arms and reach all industries all over the United States.

Before I go further, I want it clearly understood that I'm not defending or attacking any of the witnesses who have appeared or will appear. And I am not questioning the committee's right to ask any questions it sees fit. I am questioning its right to ask questions and allow only monosyllabic answers.

As you no doubt know, a person's reputation is as valuable and sacred a thing as his life. When one is attacked on such a grand scale, and the whole world can read about the job he does and the beliefs he has, his very livelihood is threatened.

You know, most of us in the motion picture industry can last only so long. Maybe 10 years, and then somebody new comes along. So we hold the time we have very dear. If this investigation continues along the lines it has followed up to now, our homes and families are as good as gone.

So it's nothing to be treated lightly. The only way I can think of to point up the seriousness of this is to explain to you what will happen to the motion pictures you go to see two or three times a week.

You have no idea of the fear that has overtaken Hollywood.

A producer is afraid to produce, a director is afraid to direct, and a writer is afraid to write for fear anything he might say or do will be controversial to the point that he might be accused of the same thing that the witnesses who have been called here have been accused of.

Which means in simple language that good adult entertainment flies out the window and shallow water flows in the door.

Westbrook Pegler was staying in the same hotel. He wrote pieces on Hollywood glamour people who came to Washington and didn't know what the hell it was all about — how Bogie tipped a waiter fifty cents (which horrified Mark Hellinger, who made a continual joke of it, even writing a check for the amount to reimburse Bogie for his extraordinary educational expenditures). Much of what he said was twisted, though none was taken too seriously except by his devotees — not even the suggestions that we were better on screen back in Tinsel Town than in politics in Washington. What we didn't realize until much later was that we were being used to some degree by the Unfriendly Ten, in that our focus was subtly altered to defending them individually and collectively.

We left Washington still caring as much, but with a bit of the wind taken out of our sails. We never did get to see Truman, who — wisely, from his point of view — did not wish to involve himself with our group. The whole trip was exhilarating, but there were repercussions. It was suggested to Bogie that he issue a statement saying he was not a Communist and had no sympathy for Communists, and denouncing the unfriendly witnesses. This he refused to do. Less than two years earlier, ironically, the world had been praising Russia and American women had knitted sweaters in the great drive for Russian war relief. It still stuns me, the speed with which ideological shifts take place.

On our next trip East, Bogie did see someone high up in the Hearst organization and made clear to him the reasons for our protest. The Committee had had that much effect, and Bogie was furious that he'd been convinced of the necessity of any kind of explanation. He took no oath, swore to nothing, just made his stand clear — and did he resent it! I don't know now whether the trip to Washington ultimately helped anyone. It helped those of us at the time who wanted to fight for what we thought was right and against what we knew was wrong. And we made a noise — in Hollywood, a community which should be courageous but which is surprisingly timid and easily intimidated. The movie people were all worried about their bank accounts hurting. The effects of that investigation were far-reaching and lasted a long time. Some went to jail — many had to leave the country, since they weren't allowed to work — families, marriages went down the drain — many panicked to save their own skins and lost the respect of both sides. Those in favor of the investigation were very self-righteous and asserted their Americanism as though they were the only patriots. Why do so many Republicans think they are all that stands between America and destruction? There was much exaggeration and distortion, and for quite a while many people relinquished their political opinions or at least stopped voicing them.

Mark Hellinger had had a heart attack earlier in the year. We'd gone to see him in the hospital — he was grayer-skinned than ever, but said he felt great. He'd have to cut down on his drinking was all — one bottle a day instead of two. He never would expose himself, never wanted a serious talk about his life, which he knew left much to be desired. He knew that we knew — that was enough. Bogie taught me something about friendship. He never pushed it — he demanded truth and loyalty, but he understood shortcomings, and accepted people more or less as they were. Whereas I wanted to know everything, be told everything — I made huge demands on my friends.

During that year Richard Brooks entered our life. He'd written a terrific book, *The Brick Foxhole*, come out to Hollywood, and ended up at Universal writing screenplays. A fantastic fellow, full of extreme opinions — he would never own a foreign car, have a swimming pool, wear a tie — no bigger house, no falling into the Hollywood trap. Bogie named him the Angry Writer. We became close friends, went to each other's homes regularly, Bogie and Dick were on the phone often. Bogie loved Dick's anger, said it would be great if he could keep it, but sooner or later he'd succumb, wait and see — first the swimming pool, and the foreign car would not be far behind. Dick vehemently denied such a possibility.

Mark left Warners and moved to Universal to produce pictures, the first being *Brute Force*, which Dick scripted. Bogie loved other people's first reactions to Dick. Never had they seen such anger — that kind of anger and palm trees did not go hand in hand. Bogie just sat back and let Dick sound off — and laughed. Those days were fun. Until December 21, 1947, when Mark Hellinger died. He was only forty-four years old. A terrible shock. I remember driving to his funeral — Bogie, John Huston, and I. I couldn't stop talking — nerves — until John finally said, 'Will you please shut up!' When he said it, you had no choice. The funeral had nothing to do with Mark. It was my first funeral and it was religious, which Mark wasn't. The only good thing about it was the eulogy delivered by Quent Reynolds — what he said and the way he said it. There was an open coffin, and I, like a fool, looked. It was awful — the man in that box had a face like Mark's, though colorless and drawn, but it wasn't the Mark I knew and cared about. Bogie said, 'Don't do it again — better to remember him as he was. Once you're gone, you're gone. I hate funerals — they aren't for the one who's dead, but for the ones who are left and enjoy mourning. When I die, I want no funeral. Cremation, which is clean and final — my ashes strewn over the Pacific. My friends can raise a glass and exchange stories about me if they like. No mourning — don't believe in it. The Irish have the right idea — a wake.'

By this time our Christmas Eve party had come to be expected by our friends, and I had planned it before Mark's death. I had our brick patio cellophaned in to accommodate the guests — seventy people or more. We all drank to Mark — our first Christmas without him.

Early in 1948 we started *Key Largo*. Dick Brooks collaborated with Huston on the script. He watched every move John made in work — John was his model. Only, what John had was hard to learn — he was born with it. It was a good collaboration, and the cast was fabulous — Eddie Robinson, Lionel Barrymore, Claire Trevor. I had met Ethel Barrymore and was in total awe of her. She was an extraordinary woman — a great star, a great actress, beautiful, part of a unique acting family. Happily, she took to me, allowed me to be her friend until the end of her days, and we invited her to dinner several times. A friend had sent us four records of John Barrymore delivering Shakespeare soliloquies. One night Ethel was coming to dinner and Bogie thought she'd love to hear them. I wasn't so sure, but he said, 'John was always her pet, let's surprise her.' As she entered the house, Bogie put on one of the soliloquies. At the first sound of her brother's voice she said, 'No, turn that off.' It was an awkward moment — one of the very few times Bogie's instinct did not serve him well.

Bogie and I had the straight parts in *Key Largo*, but with John at the helm there was no question of not doing it. I was longing to work with John — my career had not been booming. And I'd just been taken off the suspension I'd earned by turning down *Romance on the High Seas*, which ended up giving Doris Day her first break. And *Stallion Road*, another winner that Alexis Smith finally made. It was uphill at Warners for most of us.

We rehearsed *Key Largo* for three weeks. Karl Freund was the cameraman — one of the best. Lionel Barrymore played my father and was in a wheelchair at all times, which I had to manipulate. Lionel pretended to be a grouch who needed no one. He had been confined to a wheelchair for some years and his legs pained him almost unceasingly. More than once I frantically looked at John when I'd hear Lionel moaning, but Lionel never said anything — wasn't even aware he was making a noise. Eddie Robinson was a marvelous actor and a lovely, funny man, Claire Trevor a wonderful actress and woman. I used to pour tea in my dressing room every afternoon and serve cookies. Lionel looked forward to it and worried if it was late — that there might not be any. We'd all gather round as he regaled us with theatrical stories. Eddie did 'Molly Malone' with a Yiddish accent which was wildly funny. I listened raptly to all. In the film, Lionel had a scene in which he was to draw himself out of his chair defending Franklin Roosevelt. As it happened, in real life he hated Roosevelt. John told us to watch how he gritted his teeth when he had to praise him — John loved stuff like that. Yet Lionel was marvelous in that scene — he was an actor first and foremost. *Key Largo* was one of my happiest movie experiences. I thought how marvelous a medium the movies were, to enable one to meet, befriend, and work with such people. What a good time of life that was — the best people at their best. With all those supposed actors' egos, there was not a moment of discomfort or vying for position. That's because they were all actors, not just 'stars'.

Carolyn and Buddy Morris had their first child and we'd still had none. I went to see Red Krohn, Carolyn's doctor, to make certain I had no problems. Even Bogie went to see him — I was determined he was to be a

369

father. And once I made up my mind — !! Finally both Red and Bogie agreed I must take it easy — relax — it would happen. Meantime think of the fun we'd have. Bogie's great observation was that making love is the most fun you can have without laughing. Although I calmed down, I went on watching the calendar for pregnancy signs. I finally caught on to saying nothing to Bogie, as he made it clear that sex was fun and at no time should anything clinical enter the picture.

We'd taken our usual trip to New York and celebrated our third anniversary. I remember saying we'd never had a honeymoon, to which Bogie rightly retorted, 'You've been on a three-year honeymoon — ever since we've been married.' Then I missed a period. I rushed to the calendar, marked it, and prayed. I counted every day until I missed the second. I'd had a false alarm once before.

I called Red Krohn and went in for my rabbit test. He called me: 'Yes, ma'am, you are pregnant.' I rushed to see him, he examined me and said absolutely — it would be around the end of December. The joy — the joy! I'd have to set the stage for Bogie's homecoming that evening — he'd faint when he heard. He didn't faint. I don't know what happened, but after I told him, we had the biggest fight we'd ever had. I was in tears — this moment I'd been hoping for, waiting for, was a disaster. I should have learned right then never to act out a scene before it's played. Bogie was full of sound and fury signifying that he hadn't married me to lose me to a child — no child was going to come between us. The next morning he wrote me a long letter apologizing for his behavior, saying he didn't know what had gotten into him except his fear of losing me — a child was an unknown quantity to him. He didn't know what kind of a father he'd make. He was so afraid our closeness and incredible happiness together would be cut into by a child — but of course he wanted us to have a baby more than anything in the world, he just would have to get used to the idea. He'd spent forty-eight years childless, and had never really considered that being a father would ever become a reality at this point in his life.

Jack Warner had been trying to get me into a picture called *Storm Warning*. I didn't feel it was right for me, but I wanted to work. I thought if I talked to him, perhaps some changes could be made that would enable me to be in it, so I didn't intend to tell him about the coming baby.

Hedda Hopper had been told by one of her spies that I'd been to see Dr Krohn. She called to ask if I was going to have a baby. I denied it — it was none of her business, I thought. She said, 'You're not lying to me, are you, Betty?' Those ladies were drunk with power during those years. I said, 'No, I'm not,' and hung up. I was always uneasy talking to those ladies — they had been allowed their power by the studios and they wielded it unmercifully. I told Bogie of the call and he said, 'Forget it — the hell with her.' The picture was never fixed — I was put on suspension — the story of the coming of the first Bogart heir was released, and I was denounced by Hedda in her column as caring more about money than I did about being a mother. We didn't speak for a year after that — oh, she could be a bitch.

Mother had been working in England for a year, but now she was back in California. She never discussed her private life with me, so I only knew she'd enjoyed England but was glad to be home. In the summer of 1948 she took a trip to New York and returned in August. For some reason she wanted me to find her a room in a small hotel nearby. I did and went to help her unpack. While she was unpacking, I noticed a small diamond ring on her finger. I said, 'What's that?'

She never stopped taking the clothes out of the suitcase while she said, 'Oh, that's an engagement ring.'

'What?' I screamed. 'Who?'

She laughed that shy laugh of hers. 'Lee.'

'When did he come back into your life?' I knew she'd been in love with him and that they'd split up. But now he was back and she'd loved him all those years and never said a word. What a woman. So Lee Goldberg, Marshall of the city of New York, attractive, good man whom I hadn't seen in years, was going to be my stepfather. That's why she wanted the room. Sneaky. He was coming out in September. Bogie and I decided to give them the wedding at our house.

There was so much going on in 1948. Bogie went on a boat race one weekend and I shall never forget how much I missed him. I was so much in love with that man that when he left I felt a pain in my heart. I actually did. He was so much my life that I literally couldn't think of anything else — had to catch my breath when he went away. Whenever I hear the word *happy* now, I think of then. Then I lived the full meaning of the word every day. Since then it has been elusive.

Harry Kurnitz gave Bogie a baby shower. If you can imagine Mike Romanoff, Paul Douglas, Dick Brooks, Jean Negulesco, Collier Young, Nunnally Johnson, Irving Lazar choosing baby presents for Bogie. It was funny — Dusty Negulesco, Ida Lupino, and I got dressed in our husbands' clothes and crashed the party late in the evening. It was a little drunk and very sentimental. My own baby shower was smaller, more sedate, more traditional.

On September 14, 1948, Judge Edward Brand stood in our living room, with Bogie best man, me, matron of honor, and married Mother to Lee. As I stood there with the unborn Bogart putting a foot out here, an arm there, I thought of all the years my mother had waited for her shining knight to appear, never once making me aware of her yearning, only making me feel that what happened to me was what mattered. Had she ever given up as Bogie had, or had she always hoped? Never mind — her dream had come true, and when the Judge said, 'I now pronounce you man and wife,' she put her hand to her chest and let her breath out with an exclaimed 'Oh.' I knew that she couldn't believe it had happened at last — that the tension of no compromise was over, that she would have a man to focus her love on, the love she had so much of. We had champagne and caviar, drank many toasts, and sent the bride and groom on their way — a slow honeymoon by car back to New York. At last it seemed that everyone in this impossible world had what they wanted.

Bogie formed his independent company called Santana Productions and started his first film, *Knock on Any Door*, with Nick Ray directing. He'd been working hard and was enjoying being his own boss. And I was reveling in my pregnancy. When a child starts to move inside you, it is the most fantastic feeling. God, I felt smug. I gloried in it — in every stage of it. And, of course, I was convinced that all these emotions and happenings were peculiar to me — had never been felt before. I was active all through the nine months — had almost no discomfort — loved watching my stomach move around. I couldn't get over the miracle that one person can live inside another person. I still think it's a miracle. Nothing original there.

On the morning of January 6, 1949, I awakened early. I felt strange, but wasn't sure if I should start timing the pains or not. They weren't the kind of pains I expected. I casually looked at the clock and sensed a beginning regularity to them. I said nothing to Bogie, who kissed me and happily went off to work. As soon as he'd gone I sat up and started to watch the clock. When the pains seemed fairly regular I called Red Krohn, who said to wait awhile — 'When they're coming every five minutes call me. I'll be here.' He was the only man who mattered to me on that day. I moved to the living room with my Baby Ben clock and at last the pains started to come at five-minute intervals. The phone rang — May told me that Sheilah Graham wanted to speak to me. I said 'Hello,' and while my eyes never left that clock I heard her voice say, 'Tell me, is it true Bogie had a child by another woman?' 'No,' I answered and hung up. I called Red again, who told me to come to the office. I remember dressing and feeling very vague as I walked down the path, waving goodbye to May, saying I'd be back later. I drove to Red's office, still vague, and on examining me, the pains now coming at three-minute intervals, he said, 'We'd better call Bogie — you're going into the hospital.' I was still sitting on the examining table when the door opened suddenly and a panicked, green-tinged Bogart face appeared. I don't know what he expected — to find me hanging upside down by my heels? This was new territory for him. Red gave Bogie instructions, about hospital signing in, entrances, etc., and said we should get right down there, he'd meet us. Poor Bogie. He was so worried, he was afraid to touch me for fear something would go wrong. I wasn't a bit worried. As he drove me to the hospital, I told him about Sheilah Graham's phone call. I thought he'd go mad — he called her every name in the book. 'Wait till I get hold of her, I'll fix that insensitive bitch.' It obviously wasn't true, but suppose it had been and she'd made that call? 'Why the hell didn't she call *me*?' He was nervous enough driving — terrified something would happen in the car. He kept saying, 'Are you all right, Baby? We're almost there, Baby.' His face was ashen. It was much easier to be me than him that day. I was signed in, and while I was being prepared, he paced. Red brought him to the labor room to sit with me. He wore a green gown to match his face. He took my hand in his, oh, so gently — he was so helpless, so sweet, so scared. As I took my hand away to hold on to the bars of the bed above my head as instructed, he turned even greener. He didn't know what to do — after a few minutes he asked if I minded if he waited outside, he couldn't bear to see anyone he loved in pain. Things happened very quickly after that — two hours later, at 11:22 p.m., Stephen (after Steve in *To Have and Have Not*) Humphrey Bogart was born. Red showed him to me in the delivery room. He was beautiful — all six pounds, six ounces, twenty inches of him. Bogie was waiting for me when I was wheeled from the recovery room to my own room. So relieved to see me smiling at him, talking to him. I was still gaga from the anesthesia, but I knew my man when he looked at me with tears in his eyes and said, 'Hello, Baby.' It was the fullest, most complete moment my life has known.

Bogie had a son — after forty-nine years of living, there was another Bogart on earth. And I was a mother. Every dream I had had for my life with Bogie had come true.

He went to Chasen's to pass out cigars. No cliché was overlooked. Early the next morning he came to the hospital before work and we called Mother and Lee. I was ready to have another baby immediately, I felt so good. Dr Spivek, our pediatrician, was at the hospital at 7:00 a.m. and came in to see me with his report on the perfection of Steve. He told me what formula Steve was on — I'd be able to feed him myself. He warned me not to be afraid of handling the baby — he wouldn't break. 'Enjoy him.'

Telegrams, flowers, phone calls started pouring in. Mother was coming out immediately to see her daughter and her first grandchild. My girlfriends visited me afternoons, Bogie and others at night. Dick Brooks brought his camera to the hospital and photographed Bogie looking through the glass at this first child. It was a happening to all our friends as well as to us, no doubt about that. Steve's arrival was well recorded.

And the exhilaration — I could have climbed Mount Everest. No postpartum depression for me! Never, never have I felt as I did then. The first time I held that baby was overwhelming. This entire complex being, twenty inches long — I examined every fingernail, tried to count his eyelashes — the smell of him — the feel. I was twenty-four and an only child, but I took to feeding and handling Steve as though I'd spent my life doing it. Whoever first said it was right — clichés are clichés because they are true. It was instinct. I was a natural-born mother (with my own child).

Two days before I was to bring my baby home, Los Angeles had its first snowfall in fifty years. I remember sitting in my hospital bed and looking out the window — I thought I was imagining things. What a great dividend — only right for the child of Eastern-born parents! I couldn't wait to get home. I could have a baby every nine months if it was this easy! I hoped Bogie was as happy as I was. As for me, I knew that I had it all — and Bogie had given it to me.

On January 11 the ambulance took Steve and me home. As we were carried to the front door, there on the lawn was an enormous snowman which Bogie had spent half the night building. It was odd to see snow covering camellia bushes. I was taken to our bedroom, Steve to his at the other end of the house. We had an intercom rigged so that I could hear every sound in the nursery — could talk to the nurse if I wished. It was kept on at all times. Harvey was crazy with joy at my homecoming. Dr Spivek said to let him in the bedroom when Steve was with me — not to shut him out, make him jealous. Even Dr Spivek treated Harvey as human.

I kept going in and out of the nursery every five minutes. Steve's nurse was not crazy about that, but she had to learn right from the start that I intended to do most things for my baby — that I had no intention of turning him over to anyone.

My first morning home I was having breakfast in bed when Bogie went off to work. Before he left, he stopped in to see his son — I had the intercom on and suddenly heard in a soft, new voice, 'Hello, son. You're a little fella, aren't you? I'm Father. Welcome home.' It was so unexpected — so moving. He'd never been faced with a tiny creature of his own before. He wasn't sure what to say to him or how to say it. He was just letting him know that he was there — that he'd do his best and was glad to have him. Lucky Steve. Lucky me.

Friends came to view the son and heir. Gifts arrived. Someone sent us a Maud Humphrey baby book, bound in pale pink silk, with lovely Maud Humphrey children on every other page. And Stephen was a replica of his father, the *original* Maud Humphrey Baby. We had asked Louis Bromfield and Ginny and Quent Reynolds to be Steve's godparents. With Bogie being a non-practicing Episcopalian and me a non-practicing Jew, we had no plan to do anything about formalizing Steve's religion at that point.

A week after Stephen's birth Bogie sent a twenty-dollar check to President Truman, accompanied by a letter asking him to please endorse the check and return it as a keepsake for Steve. A couple of months later the check arrived with the following:

Dear Mr Bogart —
I am returning the check which you sent me endorsed to Mr Bogart, Jr.

I hope you will buy him a savings bond with it and put it in his educational fund with my compliments.

It is a rare instance when I find a man who remembers his commitments and meets them on the dot.

Harry S Truman

The beginning of the Truman story was the

fall of '48 when Truman, campaigning for the Presidency, came to California for a rally. At the dinner preceding it, where I sat next to him, he and Bogie made a bet on the baby's sex — Truman said a boy, Bogie said a girl. Bogie lost.

The receipt of the Truman letter caused much excitement. What a nice man he was! The letter and the check immediately went into a frame, where they rest to this day, property of their rightful owner, Steve.

I fear my life began to revolve around my son. I wanted to do everything for him. When the nurse took a day off after the first three weeks, I slept in the nursery (Bogie didn't care much for that) and just kept looking at that beautiful child.

There was no question of my going to the boat in the winter, weather being what it was, but finally Bogie prevailed upon me to go for a weekend. I hated to leave Stephen — was afraid I'd miss a new sound or look, sitting, standing, something. But I went and enjoyed it — we were lucky with the weather and it was lovely to be with Bogie alone. I remember making a remark Bogie found unforgettable. As I looked around me at the beautiful sea, the white landing with its small beach, the clear water, the sunshine, I sighed contentedly: 'Who needs money when you can live like this?' Bogie howled.

He knew I hated to leave Steve, but I reassured him about our boat life — I'd happily go with him, but please not every weekend. The problem of owning a boat is that it's there and so expensive to keep up, you have to use it. That left us no alternatives. I would have liked going to the desert occasionally, but you couldn't leave that glorious, expensive craft sitting alone and unused! I always loved the ocean, but would have preferred a beach house to a boat. That idea was never entertained. The *Santana* was beautiful, the life healthy and good, but I was always torn. It seems from the beginning I was torn — I wanted a career and I wanted Bogie, then I wanted both and a child. When I worked, I wanted to be home and vice versa. The truth is that I wanted it all — all the time. And God knows I tried to have it. And God knows I almost did.

I was going to work again, so we had to find a permanent nurse. We were lucky, lucky, lucky. A great woman named Alice Hartley, Canadian, turned up. She was stocky, regular, easy. What convinced Bogie was the way she dealt with Harvey and Baby — the mate we'd bought for Harvey — when they jumped on her as she tried to get into the house. No nambypamby flower she — no babying of Stephen — she was full of love and good humor and the loneliness all such ladies had, with the difference being that she'd been married, had a daughter and a beau. The beau traveled — the daughter lived in Canada — she liked and wanted to work. She and May got along well — May was welcomed into the nursery, so there was not a moment's strain in the house. It was a family, as it should have been.

My movie was *Young Man with a Horn*, directed by Mike Curtiz (who called actors 'actor-bums' — he was quite a character), and co-starring Kirk Douglas and Doris Day. I hadn't seen Kirk in years. In 1946 Bogie and I met Hal Wallis on the train heading East. I told Hal about this fantastic actor who was in a play in New York — Hal had to see him, he was so talented. To Hal's credit, he did see him and signed him. From then on Kirk had been in California with Diana and their two boys. We worked well together, liked each other, talked over old and new times, and flirted — harmlessly. Unhappily, the movie was nowhere near as good as it should have been. Strange — there was I being directed by the man who had directed *Casablanca*. He wore riding boots often, lost his temper occasionally — but only at those who were vulnerable. He was just a tiny bit weak and he was brilliant with the camera.

He would tell me how much he loved Bogie — 'How is dahling Bogie? Such a wonderful actor.' Bogie and Peter Lorre had actually almost convinced Mike that there were weekend actors, but that did not include them — *they* worked Monday to Thursday, then the weekend actors took over. A funny idea and Mike almost fell for it.

Bogie was making another Santana film at Columbia, so we compared notes at night, but not too much. Unless there was particular trouble or a fascinating anecdote, Bogie believed in leaving his work behind at the studio. That was fine with me. Even during filming we'd have a couple of pals in for dinner. One night I'd planned a terrific menu for a group of eight friends, one being John Huston. Came 7:30, the invited hour, and they started to arrive — always time for a couple of drinks before sitting down at table. Eight o'clock, all there but John. At 8:15 I said we had to sit down or the squab would be ruined. John never showed. I was livid and told Bogie, 'Friend of yours or not, I'm never asking him again.' Bogie said, 'Look — you've got to learn to take people as they are. John is fun — better company than most — but not too reliable at times. Social events aren't that important to him. Enjoy him for what he is. He's not going to change.'

About a week after that we went to some gathering at the Beverly Hills Hotel and John was there. Bogie went over to him and said, 'My wife won't speak to you, she's really sore — you'd better fix it.' John came over to me, put his arms around my rigid self — 'Hello, honey' — then wheedled, cajoled, charmed, laid it on till I was limp. I looked up at him and thought, 'Bogie's right — what the hell, he's an original — there'll be no one like him again — he's crazy and funny and brilliant, and better a life with him in it than not.' So I laughed with John — Bogie joined in — John had accomplished his mission. If he thought you weren't with him, be you friend's wife or bartender, he'd turn on that charm and work like hell till he'd won you over. That accomplished, he'd leave — it was just to prove to himself that he could do it. He proved his point, but still no sitdown dinners in my house.

We'd become friendly with David Niven and his ravishing Swedish wife, Hjordis — began to see a lot of them, and Dorris and Nunnally Johnson, whose son Scott beat Steve into the world by a few months — Nick Ray and his wife, Gloria Grahame — Joan Bennett and Walter Wanger — Jean and Dusty Negulesco. Those plus all the old group — and visiting New York chums. Our house was a happy one and friends were always glad to be in it.

Steve was growing hair — teeth — was more adorable and lovable each day. It was very hard for me to be away from him — as with everything else in life, motherhood was no half-measure for me. There is no question that work took third place after Stephen's birth. I fear he became number one — Bogie two.

I took it all naturally and totally. Nothing unusual about that, I suppose. I loved walking into that nursery, breathing that rarefied baby air. I loved to feed him — to hold him. When I gave him his bottle he always grasped my little finger with his hand and held on very tight. I wondered if my mother had felt the same when she was feeding me. Being a mother is a fact — when you have a baby you become a mother. Simple. I turned to Jell-O when Stephen looked at me, smiled at me, fell asleep in my arms or with his head on my shoulder. All else was blotted out at those moments. Of course it changed Bogie's and my life. We not only weren't two anymore, we were four, because there had to be a nurse — more so that I could be with Bogie than for any other reason. He didn't want our relationship changed — he became just the littlest bit jealous. He wanted my attention in the evenings, and when he talked to me he wanted my mind all there. I still hung on his every word, but I was willful, too — and if I wanted something badly enough, I usually got it.

For the first time in my life I didn't have to worry about money. It's amazing how quickly I put my first nineteen years of budgeting behind me. If I liked a pair of shoes, I didn't buy one pair — I bought six. I wanted everything perfect in our new home, so I bought ashtrays, cigarette boxes, gradually began taking an interest in antiques. Every table was covered with things. Mother used to go to auctions and came up with a huge ancient Bible for me which I proudly displayed in our living room. That tickled Bogie. He said I wanted instant tradition — that the Bible and all the antiques made me feel more secure, as though I'd been collecting for years instead of months.

We were happy people of fame and fortune then. I met no one who might have threatened my marriage. If I flirted harmlessly on occasion, I was only doing what I hadn't done when I was younger. We were becoming a more and more popular pair — the word was getting around that it was fun at the Bogarts'. Everyone looked forward to our Christmas parties, and the year Steve was born I began one more tradition — our anniversary party. That was terrific fun. The weather was always warm — women looked pretty — flowers were in bloom. There was always a mixture of East and West coasts — our New York writer friends, any pal who was in town, and some chic, some not-so-chic movie folk. We never had a member of the press present — we wanted our friends to relax, have a good time and not look over their shoulders every five minutes. I adored giving those parties — always tried to think of something a little different for the menu. It was all part of my wife-hostess role — and, of course, people were brought into the nursery to view the perfection that resided there.

Gradually two not so normal people were beginning to live fairly normal lives. Though I must confess that, now as then, I have never known what 'normal' is. Perhaps it means regular — trying to make order out of chaos. Imperceptibly our lives took on a pattern. Bogie's drinking habits improved. He moved away from mixed drinks and from mixing his drinks. Not to say he stopped drinking, but he got much less angry when he did drink. He liked life more and he was beginning to feel more secure in our marriage. But you had to stay awake married to him. Every time I thought I could relax and do *everything* I wanted, he'd buck. There was no way to predict his reactions, no matter how well I knew him. As he'd said before our wedding, he expected to be happily married and stay that way, but he never expected to settle down. He liked keeping people off balance. He was good for me — I could never be quite sure what he would do.

We made our first trip to New York away from Steve in September. Miss Hartley was steady as could be — there were no apprehensions. It was World Series time. And *South Pacific* was a big hit on Broadway. I was more than a little enamored of Ezio Pinza — me and every other woman who heard him sing and saw him perform. We saw the show, went backstage after. Bogie led me into Pinza's dressing room, we were introduced, then Bogie just left me there. I went into my shaking routine with Pinza — totally tongue-tied was I, and furious with Bogie. It was a typical Bogart maneuver — 'She's so mad about him — sure — let her have him.' Oh, what a smart man he was. He knew the illusion was better than the reality, though in this case the reality wasn't bad! After I told Pinza I knew the entire score of the show and congratulated him on his beauty and talent, there was nothing more to say. Thanks a lot, H.B.

One night we had dinner at '21' with some friends, including Billy Seaman, an old drinking buddy of Bogie's. It was a long dinner — much booze consumed — and the three of us walked back to the St Regis Hotel. Then Bogie wanted to go somewhere for a drink. I did not. I tried to get him to come upstairs — he'd have none of it. Oh, he made me mad when he was drinking and stubborn — although he didn't need drink to be stubborn: when he made up his mind, that was definitely that. I marched upstairs — he and Billy went off for their nightcap. About four in the morning Bogie awakened me — with an enormous stuffed panda on either side of him, wearing red Stork Club suspenders — to tell me there'd been a little trouble and he thought we'd hear more about it the next day. The next day started about four hours later when an assault summons was delivered to Mr Bogart in person — at 8:00 a.m. Those people do rise early.

He decided Uncle Charlie should be his lawyer. Charlie loved it — it was one of his all-time favorite trials. The press had a field day. It seemed Bogie and Billy had bought two pandas at the Stork Club, taken them into El Morocco, sat down with them as their dates. The Morocco publicity man and a gossip columnist who was always trouble got Robin Roberts, a young woman around town, to try to take Bogie's panda. As she grabbed it, Bogie gave her a shove, saying, 'Get away from

me — I'm a happily married man.' She
fell — and sued. When Bogie was asked if
he'd been drinking, he replied, 'Isn't everyone drunk at 4:00 a.m.?' He always felt
the whole world was three drinks below
normal anyway. When asked if he'd hit
her, he said, 'I'd never hit a lady — they're
too dangerous.' If he hadn't been a hero
before, the panda incident made him one.
Our Hollywood friends loved it — wires
came by the dozen — they all wished
they'd been in New York. Charlie's argument in court was that Bogie was defending his property — that this woman
was just looking for publicity and using Bogart to get it. She'd arrived in court all
done up with two black-and-blue marks
painted on her chest. Charlie was impas-
sioned. The Judge summed up, 'Mr Bogart
was protecting his rightful property and
using sufficient force to do so. Whether he
used too much is the question. There is
not enough evidence — summons dismissed!' The crowd outside the courtroom
hailed Bogie — they loved him for protecting his rights. Bogie hailed the decision
and his lawyer. We all had lunch at '21'
and Steve and Scott Johnson each got a
panda. The reason Bogie never got into
any real trouble was that his derring-do
was always innocent. He just didn't like
hurting people. No wonder he was every-

one's hero. All through our life together, the most fun was where he was.

Bogie had a joke dream — that a woman should be able to fit into a man's pocket. He'd take her out, talk to her, let her stand on the palm of his hand, dance on a table; when she got out of order — back in the pocket. And she could be made life-size when desired. And despite how wonderful he was, there were times when I would have liked to do the same thing to him.

We were back in California and on the boat when news came over the radio that Walter Huston had died. We rushed back to town. Walter had been staying at the Beverly Hills Hotel — we'd all been together just a few nights before. It was all sudden and very sad. I was more than ever aware of John's very real love for his father. John Huston's life had not been based on attachments. He felt things, of course, but I don't believe that a life blow had ever been dealt him until Walter died. There was a small service, with a bust of Walter on a stand and Spencer Tracy reading the Twenty-third (my favorite) Psalm. It was beautiful and moving. There was a moment about halfway through when a deep, half-muffled sob emanated from John. A chilling sound. I looked at him and thought of him differently from then on. I was very glad he was married now to lovely Riki Soma and that she was to have a baby. John had done everything but that, and he wanted someone in his image. It was one of the things he envied Bogie for. One ending — one beginning.

I was in my last Warner Bros. picture in 1950 — *Bright Leaf* with Gary Cooper and Patricia Neal, directed once more by Mike Curtiz. 'Coop' was one of the most attractive men I've ever seen, with his cornflower-blue eyes. He was a pro, but not always on time. One morning he was late and Mike was livid — so much so that he screamed at me. He wouldn't dare let go at Coop, knowing he'd just walk off the set. Now, I have never handled myself well in screaming situations. I become inarticulate, usually cry. On this occasion with his ranting and raving — 'Goddamn actor-bum!' — I took myself tearfully to my dressing room. Finally Coop arrived, not all that late, and Mike was all over him: 'Gary, dahling, how are you — how do you feel?' Coop knew that Mike was full of it, but played the game.

Jack Warner kept giving me terrible scripts and I kept going on suspension. He was one of the most ill-at-ease human beings I'd ever encountered. When you'd try to talk to him about the script (which he'd probably never read), he'd crack a joke.

When you'd try to reason with him, he'd tell you how hard he worked — how the only reason he didn't come to the studio early in the morning was that he waited for his wife, Ann, to wake up so he could have breakfast with her. It was well known that he adored Ann much more than she did him. That side of him was sad — but his uneasiness with actors made it impossible to have any reasonable exchange. I tried to get Charlie Feldman to persuade him to let me out of my contract, but it was no deal. I was also getting restless about Charlie. He was a pal of Jack's and Darryl Zanuck's and wanted to produce — I felt I'd been with his agency too long and nobody there gave a damn about my career. A funny thing happened to my career after the first few years of being Mrs Bogart. Funny-peculiar. Everyone thought I was terrific personally, but they stopped thinking of me as an actress. I was Bogie's wife, gave great dinners, parties, but work was passed over. It was very frustrating. I wanted my career to go on. From the beginning Bogie had made it clear that he would never inter-fere — never try to get me into one of his pictures, never make it a condition of his working. He'd give me advice if I asked, but he never called a producer or director to try to get me a job. He went along with the director's choice always. It became apparent to me that, overjoyed as I was to be Mrs Bogart, I had no intention of allowing Miss Bacall to slide into oblivion.

John had spoken to Bogie about *The African Queen*. Bogie had never wanted to go to Europe — just had no curiosity about it — but I was longing to go, to see and do everything. Bogie liked his life as it was; going to New York was all the traveling he wanted to do. Finally Sam Spiegel told Katharine Hepburn that he had Bogie and John — told John that he had Bogie and Katie — told Bogie that he had John and Katie — and *The African Queen* was put together. I was wildly excited, but Bogie knew that John would find the most inaccessible spot in Africa as a location and he dreaded it. We planned to go early in March, by ship, to Paris first, then London, before filming began. The only thing I hated was leaving Steve, who would join us with Miss Hartley in London after Africa.

Mother was on her yearly visit to California, early this time, for Stephen's first birthday party. One morning I received a call from Uncle Charlie telling me that Jack had died while on holiday in Jamaica with Vera. I would have to tell Mother. God, why was it always I who had to tell her? Jack was the baby of her family, only forty-four years old. I remember looking out my bedroom window and watching my mother walk toward the front door, looking forward to a smiling baby and her prize of a daughter. I opened the front door. She knew, as she always did, that something had happened. I hugged her and blurted it out. A gut sound came from her — she must get back to New York. The phone calls started. When one of a family goes, and the youngest at that, the remaining members get even closer for a while. I'd been close to Jack — I shed many tears over his death. And I loved Vera and felt so for her. I grasped my husband very close to me through that.

All ghastly shots were completed — farewell parties given — passports gotten, including Steve's and Miss Hartley's.

We were leaving on a night flight to New York. Miss Hartley and Steve came to see us off, as well as Lynn Spiegel and Carolyn's mother, since Carolyn was on the plane too. I have a pain in my solar plexus when I remember how it felt to leave Steve behind — you suddenly say to yourself, 'Why the hell am I going — what am I doing?' Then, of course, you *know* what you're doing — you're going with your husband, who believes in no separations in marriage, who is working. Your life with him cannot stop for your son. And —

admit it — you want to see those unseen places. So the brain whirs — the heart tugs — the gut aches. I must have turned around a hundred times to look at Steve and wave and throw kisses and get teary-eyed.

In those days there was a stop in Chicago en route to New York. When we landed there, a man from the airline came aboard and said there was a phone call waiting for us. What could it be, for God's sake? It seemed that as our plane became airborne, Miss Hartley, with Steve in her arms, had had a stroke and was taken immediately to the hospital. Steve was fine at home, Lynn and Carolyn's mother were with him. My poor baby — poor Miss Hartley. I asked them to notify Dr Spivek and tell him I'd call them on arrival in New York. Bogie and I were in shock. How terrible — that seemingly strong, feisty woman. As soon as we got to the St Regis, we called home — Miss Hartley was dead. She had never regained consciousness. May was her sturdy, reliable self and knew just what to do for Stephen. I called Mother and told her. I had a sore ear from hours on the phone that first day. Mother volunteered to go out immediately — Lee could join her in a few weeks. Dr Spivek did not feel I should return. He would interview nurses, tell me whom he liked best,

I could interview her on the phone — it was only a few months. Bogie wanted me to stay with him. If the doctor said it was okay, I mustn't worry — and with Mother there, no problem. I was worried about my baby — I wanted to be with Bogie — I wanted to get to Paris, London, Rome, Africa — too many things to want.

Dr Spivek found an English nurse with excellent references. I interviewed her from a phone booth in '21' — a long, long interview. She sounded all right. I talked to May — Kathy — they were to report to me regularly. Mother would leave the day after we did. I tried to talk to Steve on the phone, but he would have none of it. Was I doing the right thing? As the doctor said, 'Steve will be fine. You may not be, but he will be.'

So we boarded the *Liberté*. Atlantic crossings are romantic happenings, no doubt about that. Your world is on that ship for five days — nothing outside can touch you. Bogie was in his element. I was surprised how much of my high-school French came back to me. Bogie was very proud of me speaking the language. It was very halting, but they understood me — vocabulary small, accent good. I felt mysterious and exciting speaking French. We docked at Le Havre, where a car and driver were waiting, and started out for the most beautiful, romantic city in the world — Paris. Our driver spoke English and was to stay with us all the six weeks we were there. We stopped at a roadside café in Rouen for ham, cheese, and the most incredible of French breads. Very early in the morning. Immediately I could see how artistic the French were — the simplest food looked beautiful, the furniture, even farm furniture, had its own unique flavor and tremendous style. I told the driver to warn me before we reached Paris so I could prepare myself. I was breathless with anticipation. The green of the French countryside was unlike any green I had ever seen. Suddenly he said, 'You can see the Eiffel Tower — in about ten minutes we'll be in the center of Paris.' I held Bogie's hand tightly — I couldn't believe I would finally be there. I must have been French in another life, or why did it mean so much? And then there it was — Arc de Triomphe, Place de la Concorde, the Seine, Louvre, Left Bank — the beauty of it! My eyes were not big enough to take it all in. And then the Place Vendôme and the Ritz Hotel, where we were going to live. Paris seemed so open — no crowded New York streets, no skyscrapers — the Paris sky so blue — our suite at the Ritz so romantic. After settling in a bit, we met Harry Kurnitz, who'd lived in Paris since the blacklist. We started out to see some of Paris on foot with him, stopping at the famous Café de la Paix, where you were supposed to see everyone you knew if you just sat there long enough. To sit at a sidewalk café having coffee or a drink — the sound and sight of France all around. The Champs-Elysées was incredible — the chestnut trees — how could one city attain such perfection? Who had dreamed it up? Who had made it all come true? I wanted to see every corner of it. Harry took us to the Tour d'Argent on the Seine for dinner, with Frank Capra and Art Buchwald. The restaurant had an arrangement with the city that Notre Dame could be lit at their request. And there was this girl from the Bronx, Brooklyn, and Manhattan sitting in Paris at a window of the Tour d'Argent with Notre Dame, especially illuminated, to one side and the Seine and the lights of the bridge below.

I was speaking French — Kurnitz was ordering dinner — and I felt sick. I couldn't eat — my first night in Paris and I couldn't eat. Not possible. My stomach was gone. Bogie took me home to the Ritz, where I collapsed in a storm of tears. It was all too much — the anticipation, the realization. I was too keyed up — emotion took over. There has never been a time since then that I haven't had a gut reaction to that city.

After my emotional release, every day was nonstop sightseeing — we went to every museum, Versailles, Fontainebleau — started our friendship with Anne and Art Buchwald (who became Bogie's chess adversary) — went to the racetrack — flea market — Dior — the press dogging our steps. My French improved daily and I bought everything in sight. We'd walk down a street and strangers would shout, 'Humphrey Bogar' and make like a machine gun. And Bogie, who had never wanted to travel, loved Paris — appreciated all the beauty, the pleasure. When it came time to go, I wasn't ready. I have never been ready to say goodbye to Paris. I am in love with the Arch of Triumph — aside from the Lincoln Memorial, it is the most moving monument my heart has beat to. I cannot explain why — it does something emotional to me and I cannot see it often enough. From any angle, at any time of day, in any weather, it stands for something strong and true and beautiful.

We went to London on the boat train, the first and last time I've done that — the rough Channel did not agree with me one bit, but the Golden Arrow that took us to Victoria Station did. Two countries so close and so totally different. After Paris, London took getting used to — Paris was fantasy, romance — London seemed unadventurous, solid, quaint, filled with pomp and circumstance. In both countries Bogie made a stir wherever he went — his mere presence attracted crowds and press. In California, stars are taken for granted — they're everywhere — so I was unprepared for the reaction that greeted us abroad. It wasn't for me, it was most definitely for him. Bogie had always said it takes ten years to become a true star. Definition: that wherever you go, anywhere in the world, you are recognized. He was, and I was impressed.

Sam Spiegel, John, and Peter Viertel were in London, so work seemed closer. There was a press conference at Claridge's for which I got myself all done up in a Balenciaga suit and Katharine Hepburn stole the show in her pants. I still hardly knew her, was in awe of her, and certainly didn't know what to talk to her about. I just hoped she'd like me — we had eight weeks together ahead of us in Africa.

Our next stop was Rome. At our first glimpse of it from the air Bogie fell in love. The color — it was all sepia tones, the red earth — he couldn't get over it. For twenty-six years I had been ignorant of this other world, but for Bogie it had been fifty-one years. You hear the names — Paris, London, Rome — but you don't really know they exist, not really know it, until you can view them with your own eyes and stand on their earth with your own feet.

Rosalie worked for Boys' Town of Italy and had introduced us to Monsignor John Patrick Carroll-Abbing. He promised to arrange an audience with Pope Pius XII for us. We had four days in Venice first. From the time the airplane put down, the Venetian press followed us across the Grand Canal in a parade of boats. It was so funny — they were taking pictures of us, we were taking pictures of them, every move was recorded. Our first visit to Piazza San Marco found us surrounded by mobs of people — fans and press — but none of it could mar our impression of that fairyland. Nothing about that city was disappointing.

We returned to Rome to prepare for our audience with the Pope. With my Jewish background, I was ill prepared. The consensus of opinion was that I should do what everyone else does — in a 'private' audience there are anywhere from ten to forty people, depending on how private the private audience is. We were both excited — not only by meeting the Pope, but at entering the holy Vatican walls. The concierge had a selection of black veils to lend for the occasion — it was a business. We were collected at the hotel by a representative of Monsignor Carroll-Abbing and, with veil and photographs of Stephen in hand, took off for our adventure. We had to relinquish our invitation at the door, and no amount of pleading on my part would make the man in charge give it back. We were led into the Vatican Museum, then through a long hall of treasures to the Sistine Chapel, then into an enormous room called the throne room, whose ceiling was made of gold from the United States. After a while a guard came in, called us, with about ten others, and took us through five rooms, each smaller than the one before. We finally came to a very small one to await our moment — it was very quiet and I was holding tight to Bogie's hand to calm myself. A cardinal came in and gruffly motioned us to stand back against the wall — very intimidating. We were in a semicircle. Another cardinal and a monsignor entered, and right behind them His Holiness. I had expected trumpets, but there was only silence. Everyone knelt and then rose and he started to greet each individual. He was smaller than I expected — all in white except for red velvet slippers. Each person knelt and kissed his ring. I was transfixed, and as he approached me, he stared at me so intently — took my hand and did not let it go — that when I tried to kneel I found that my rear was against a table and I couldn't move. He asked both Bogie and me what we did and where we were from — Bogie showed him pictures of Steve and he blessed them and us, and gave us a medal. I was hypnotized by the peaceful aura he seemed to emanate. And he did really give me a lengthy, steady, burning look — so much so that that evening at drinks Bogie's joke was, 'Don't be surprised if you get a call from the Vatican saying the Pope wants to see you again!'

Leaving for Africa, we arrived at the Rome airport to a battery of press and klieg lights. Katie Hepburn was nowhere to be found — the rumor was that she was already on the plane, but someone had looked and not found her. After a while Bogie, clever fellow, whispered to me to get on board and look in the ladies' room — I opened the door and there was Katie laughing uproariously at having outwitted the press. We sat chatting for a while, then to our horror the newsreel man with the klieg light climbed on board. Katie stayed locked in the loo — Bogie and I were photographed to pacify the man — the doors closed — Katie emerged — and via Sabena Airways we were on the first leg of our trip into darkest unknown Africa. Our destination was Léopoldville, the capital of the Belgian Congo. I don't know what I expected of the Congo — grass huts, drums beating — but one thing I did *not* expect was the Congolese press and the American consul waiting for us when we landed. Bogart and Hepburn were certainly known throughout the world; if I'd had even the slightest question, it was dispelled. We drove through the village. There were huts, but not grass ones — a great white Mohammedan church with a green dome in the center — women dressed in marvelous bright cottons, and each carrying something on her head and a child on her back, walking very straight.

We were in a hotel for the night. Before dinner I took a bath. As I was sitting in the tub — an ordinary tub — something made me glance over my shoulder. There at the joining of the ceiling to the wall by the door was a scorpion. I didn't want Bogie to know I was terrified. I got out of the tub carefully — so the scorpion wouldn't hear me — and picked up the slatted board that was on the floor in place of a mat. I had to get that creature before he reached the floor. I hurled the board — in a lightning move the scorpion came down the wall and ran to escape through the door. With Bogie saying, 'What in God's name happened?' I related the drama. He went after the beast, trapped him, and killed him. I was destroyed — my first day in Africa. Bogie set me straight: 'Listen, if you're going to have an attack every time you see a bug, you'd better get on a plane and go back. You're in Africa now, sweetheart — bugs and animals everywhere — get used to it.' 'I never will,' I thought — but, 'Of course I will, darling,' I said, 'it just took me by surprise.' Ha!

Next stop Stanleyville on the Congo River, where Sam Spiegel and Peter and Gigi Viertel were awaiting us. Our hotel was called the Pourquoi Pas. Why not, indeed! It was clean — food good — they even had a golf club nearby as pretty as any in the U.S., and the village here was deep into Africa. On our first afternoon there was a celebration for us — natives dancing in costume; painted faces and bodies. The streets were mobbed. It was very hot and humid. We sent our clothing back to London and ordered safari clothes — and tin trunks so that the dampness wouldn't seep in. Even with the rain, the temperature never varied — always *hot*. Easy to see why one might go mad in the noonday sun.

Finally we bade farewell to the Pourquoi Pas, crossed the Congo River, and boarded a train for Ponthierville. It was a Toonerville Trolley kind of train with an engine, two passenger cars, two freight cars, and a tin boat. We passed many villages, noting that they became more primitive as we moved deeper into the Congo. From Ponthierville we moved into Biondo. After an hour's ride we arrived at a small river. The car rode up onto a raft consisting of four large pirogues — four men pole the raft across the river. After another hour's ride we arrived at our camp, where John was awaiting us (in the bar). We stayed up until 1:00 a.m. listening to John talk about Africa and elephant hunting. He wanted to take me on a shoot — 'You must only remember to stay downwind of them — if one of those big tuskers senses foreign matter in the air, you're a goner.' He was in love with the country and animals and the hunting life — all very Hemingway macho. We fell into bed exhausted under our mosquito netting, but not to sleep before Bogie made it clear that I was going on no shoot with John, who, he maintained, could not hit his hat. Bogie disliked the idea of killing animals anyway.

Our camp was an amazing feat — eighty-five natives had built it in eight days, from pure jungle. The bungalows, of which we had one, were made of bamboo and palm leaves, with small screened windows and curtained closets. Patio with hand-made furniture of the same ingredients. There was one large building with dining room for the company — and an adjoining bar. There was a company mascot — a tiny monkey named Romulus (after the film production company). Outdoor privies and showers. The showers consisted of a tin barrel overhead filled with water. When a chain was pulled, the water came out through specially constructed holes.

At first Katie seemed nervous and talked compulsively. She and I still didn't know each other well — at the time I couldn't appraise her. I concluded her talking stemmed from being a woman alone, in an inaccessible part of the world, at the mercy of Huston and Bogart, about whom she'd heard all sorts of stories, the least of which was that they drank. I thought she was apprehensive — was trying to make it appear that she could handle any situation, that she knew all about men like them. As it turned out, she could — and she did. She talked to me about her family, about her work in theatre and the movies. It really took guts to travel so far without a friend or companion. I had no idea what she thought about any of us. Our friendship would happen slowly. But very surely. And would become one of the most affecting, influential, and treasured friendships of my life and for always.

While the three of them went off to rehearse, I set about trying to make a home.

Everything was so damp there was little to do — our floors were Mother Earth, with a few mats scattered about. Bogie and I had our own boy named Caballa, who fetched for us and pressed for us. We had drinking water to brush our teeth in, a basin to wash in, and that was it. There was nothing to do but read, write, eat. We decided first night out that it was advisable not to ask what we were eating — we didn't want to know. I had a list of fifty basic Swahili words to study and darts to play after dinner. It was not animal country — I had my usual run-in in the shower with a flying bug, but I rose above it. Katie and I began comparing ant bites — even with the mosquito netting those little things inexorably found their way to human flesh, leaving large red welts in their trail.

We had two days of heavy rain. Sam Spiegel arrived at two one morning, having been stuck on the raft crossing the river en route to the camp. When the weather broke we went downriver on a large towing boat like the *African Queen* to try it for maneuverability. Each of us had a native fanning with reeds to keep the flies away. On the first day of shooting it rained, finally clearing enough for us to go to the river and head for the location. The local chief arrived dressed to kill (not literally), with feathered hat, red blanket between his legs, medals, knives, bracelets, medallions, spears. He'd been led to believe that he was to be in the film. On the basis of that, he'd put all the locals to work on our camp — without him nothing would have been possible, in addition to which he provided the daily labor for the boats, the camera raft, the camp, everywhere. He boarded the *African Queen*, uninvited, with wife and child. After setting up the next day's work (as there was no sun again), we returned to camp on the *African Queen* — leaving the chief behind. To pay us back for our bad manners, we ran out of gas and had to be towed by the raft.

When the filming finally did begin, the trip downriver was a riot. Besides the *African Queen*, there was another boat like her for towing and filming, a raft with camera equipment and crew, and Katie's dressing room, which was put together with bamboo. She carried a large mirror so that she could check her costume — it broke in half early in the shooting. Instead of forgetting about it entirely — being a pro, knowing it was a necessary object — she carried the larger half herself for safety's sake and for the remainder of the location. The woods was our loo and Katie and I would trudge out as the spirit moved us, standing watch for each other. The natives didn't know what we were about. When a match was struck and a flame followed, they'd mumble in Swahili. They didn't know what a camera was for. I would sit at a typewriter in my shorts, that alone a freakish sight to them, and as the keys hit, they'd look at each other and chant in Swahili — I knew they thought it was voodoo. We must have looked very strange to them — I certainly did, in my shorts.

The work was very slow, the sun very hot. Tempers flared once between Bogie and John. When it rained, John would go off hunting, but Bogie wanted him to pay attention, God damn it — be practical and figure out what to do if the weather proved insurmountable. John really became a white hunter in Africa — he believed he *was* one — and he adored it; he didn't care how long he stayed. That was John. Bogie was different — he wanted to be back in civilization. He had a life that he'd built, nurtured, cared about. John's seemed to be wherever he was with whatever film he was making. He liked moving about. So they complemented each other, and the resulting work was always their best. John was fantasy — Bogie reality.

Appendage living was not my style, so to be of some use I took over the lunches — they'd been a mess. I had two native

413

helpers, who didn't much like taking orders from a woman — and my being a white woman compounded the felony. I got very nervous and started doing more and more of the work myself rather than listen to so much angry mumbling. Actually, I wasn't nervous — I was scared!

The shooting went smoothly for a few days, with only minor delays caused by no gasoline in the *African Queen* or the launch, or sighting a green mamba that turned out not to be a green mamba, or various crew members falling in the river. The river was full of disease — one serious one called bilharzia, caused by people relieving themselves in the water and their skin being attacked by worms that worked their way under it. Fortunately, the company escaped that one.

Morning and evening I would see Katie sitting on her patio writing letters on a legal pad. One morning she seemed very upset, so I asked if anything was wrong. Very wrong — her dear friend Fanny Brice had died. Katie is a private, private person whose standards of behavior are very high, and she must have felt very much alone a good deal of the time. I couldn't have borne not having anyone to tell my secret thoughts to — I guess she used letters to relieve herself of some of her burdens, but that couldn't be enough. She was an actress — a fine one, a successful one, a big, big star on stage and screen — but the rest was a mystery. Until we became real friends, that location must have been lonely for her, despite her happy nature and essential optimism.

And the physical obstacles! One morning we were being towed on the raft while camera and crew were being towed by the *African Queen*, on which Bogie and Katie were playing a scene. I remember John's face suddenly turning away from the scene to the tugboat — in making a turn, the raft had jammed into some trees, taking the canopy of the mock-up with it. The boiler nearly fell on Bogie and Hepburn — Guy Hamilton, John's assistant director, held it up and burned himself. Lamps almost fell — it was terrifying, a miracle that no one was hurt. In true British tradition, the camera kept grinding.

The day after that, John came over to our bungalow to have coffee with us before leaving for the location. We were rising at 6:30 by then to try to get in a whole day's work, seven days a week. Guy Hamilton walked over and whispered in John's ear. John stopped for a second and said, 'I can't believe my ears, would you say that again?' And Guy repeated, 'The *African Queen* has sunk.' The natives had been told to watch it, and they did — they watched it sink. We rushed down to the river's edge, and, sure enough, there was the poor *African Queen* on its side, full of water. Some work could be done with the mock-up while Guy and fifty other men pulled the old *Queen* out of the river and set mechanics to work. We sat around, watched, took pictures — and Katie and I left the raft early to visit a coffee plantation. When we returned, the propeller had been removed and was being hammered into shape, with an ingenious native bellows made of wood and palm leaves fanning the flame. Through the next couple of days a minimal amount of work was done — the crew were exhausted, but not one temper was lost. They were really a fantastic bunch — almost no complaining, patient and all pitching in to help, whether it was their job or not, still cheerful despite all the obstacles and still doing Class A work.

The *African Queen* was working again — hallelujah! So there was only maneuvering up and down river and the raft to control — trying to avoid being trapped by logs which might or might not rise up out of the water along the way.

Katie and I returned to camp that evening, went to our respective tents, and ran out screaming. Our bungalows had been invaded by thousands of ants — a thick carpet of them on the floor, in our clothing — terrifying. The legs of our cots were put in cans of kerosene. It would only be a matter of days before the ants took over completely — the company would have to leave. Fortunately, there were only a few days more of shooting on that location. Our native boys had to stay up all night to keep fires burning to stave off total invasion. I shudder even now when I remember it. Soldier ants are large and move quickly over and into everything. Any territory is theirs from the moment they enter it. Nothing could stop them. Even elephants get out of their way. I was no elephant, and *I* certainly wasn't going to hang around. The chief arranged a musical farewell for our last day — the natives again doing their dance number, going off madly in all directions. At one point I joined in with my bdingo in hand, and with their drums we had an old-fashioned jam session.

As we headed for Ponthierville, we passed a bamboo forest. Katie said, 'Stop the car, I've always wanted to sit in the middle of a bamboo forest.' I thought Bogie would explode. Here was everyone trying to get out of there, and Katie wanted to sit in the middle of a bamboo forest. But the car stopped and out she got — as did I. 'What the hell, while I'm here I might as well see what a bamboo forest is like — I may never get another chance.' It was very still and very beautiful.

We reached Ponthierville at about the same time as the brave *African Queen* generator and towboat, which had chugged their way down the river. Spent the night on a paddle boat. It was still hot, muggy, and noisy and we had to rise by 6:00 a.m., so we didn't sleep much. But it was heaven compared to those ants.

Through all of this Bogie's nerves got frayed from time to time. He never stopped worrying about whether we'd ever get out of Africa. John loved Africa, Katie loved it — even I did, except for missing Steve. No wonder Bogie was frazzled — he had visions of months going by and there he'd be, still working with John. Anything was possible. One member of the crew had a bad attack of appendicitis. I was the only one, doctor included, who had brought antibiotics. I turned them over to him and they saved the day for the poor Englishman, who was rushed to Stanleyville calmed down eventually; he'd been away in London and had no idea what everyone was going through, in addition to which on his first night back in Africa he'd been bitten by something and had a large, ugly, and painful boil on the back of his neck. I told Sam I'd work out lunch menus and see that the food was in order. The crises over, the work on the movie continued and I tried to keep myself occupied. I guess I wrote to everyone I knew on that trip — devoted Nunnally Johnson, Harry Kurnitz, and my mother kept me looking forward to mail.

Africa was definitely getting to us. With the exception of about five people, the crew felt awful. Even I, who had been lucky up to that point, was beginning to feel odd. At about 2:30 one afternoon the long-awaited cry arose: 'Burn the village.' With that it started — natives running in all directions, huts flaming inside and out, pieces of roof flying straight into the air. Then the rains came, so we had to stay until the following day. At last the final day of shooting in Butiaba, and off we went at 5:30 a.m. for the Murchison Falls. After going up the river, we entered the Victoria Nile and I had my first sight of crocodiles and hippopotamuses. Navigating the Nile and avoiding sandbars was a tricky business and maneuvering a paddle steamer no easy task, but we reached our location spot without a major crisis.

After six weeks of scruffy beard, Bogie shaved. I'd almost forgotten his face, it had been so long since I'd seen it. He looked wonderful, though a few pounds lighter from the great African diet. They were only able to shoot half a scene because, yet again, the rains came. That was to be the daily happening, so John, aptly named The Monster by Bogie years before, would have to be prodded to start shooting at eight instead of nine. There were continued meetings between the camera crew and John, searching for ways to simplify the remaining work. So many of the crew were confined to bed — some with dysentery, amoebic or straight, some with undiagnosed illnesses, a few cases of malaria — that the film had to suspend shooting for three days. Even Katie had to take to her bed — she was a sick lady, nauseated all the time, but never complained and never missed a day's work. God, I admired her! She had opinions, voiced them, and stuck to them, sometimes drove Bogie crazy — mainly, I think, because they were so alike, and also because he knew she'd stay in Africa forever if need be.

I went mad trying to invent things to do during those three days. I'd rise at seven to go out in the small boat to photograph game. I'd been warned how dangerous it could be, that if one of those hippos I thought were so cute got under the boat, it could easily be overturned and the crocs would come in for a hearty meal. The element of danger was always there and I always dared it.

Finally work got under way again, and

with that a visible rise in spirits. I played Florence Nightingale — in short, Loretta Young — to the crew who were still confined to their beds. Talking — they telling me about wives and girlfriends and England; writing letters for them sometimes. Oh, they wanted to go home. I just wanted to see Steve — he was two and a half now, I'd missed four months of his growth. I had been able to push my pain to one side for a while, but no longer. I thought about him and yearned for him all the time, but was afraid to count the days for fear something would happen. John was still convinced that Departure Day would be July 15. I cabled Mother to arrange Steve's departure for London on July 20. But with all these changes, who knew what would happen?

The mail brought us a letter from Mother enclosing a small clipping announcing that Mayo had died. I told Bogie, who said only, 'Too bad. Such a waste.' I asked him why. He said she had had real talent, she had just thrown her life away. I wondered whether he was sorry not to have stayed with her. I was still such a little girl, such a fool. Nothing could have been further from his mind.

A cable came the following day announcing the birth of Angelica Huston. There was great excitement, and champagne was drunk and cables sent off to Riki, the proud mama. John was bursting with pride. A birth and a death.

There were only two more days to go. None of us could believe it. And we were right not to. John suddenly decided he'd like three days more. Bogie was in such a fury at his lack of foresight — and at Katie, who he thought was aiding and abetting John — that I thought he'd explode. John made a convincing and moving speech to the crew, was articulate as always, dramatic, almost brought tears to the eye. The crew continued to prove how exemplary they were. They said they'd stay with John, but felt it all could be speeded up. A solution was found. All sound could be done Saturday and Sunday, and all props and electrical equipment could leave Sunday night — only the camera would remain. So John, Katie, and Bogie stayed to shoot until noon Monday, which would get them to the airport at Entebbe in time. I left with the crew Sunday night to have a day in Entebbe — and there was a cable from London telling us that Steve would arrive there July 21. I could begin to count the hours.

When we arrived in London, Steve wasn't there yet, but it would only be one more day. My stomach was fluttering. I checked his room to make sure all was as should be, put some of the small stuffed animals around that I had bought in Africa, and struggled through the next twenty-four hours. Bogie and I were interviewed, had lunch at our favorite Caprice, a long dinner at Les Ambassadeurs with Orson Welles and Sam Spiegel, stayed up late — I was much too excited to sleep anyway, all I could think of during dinner was 'This time tomorrow I'll have my baby boy.'

We got up at eight, left the hotel at nine, arrived at the airport at ten to clear Steve's trunk through customs. The head of the airport arranged for Steve's plane to taxi to the number-one entrance used by the royal family — Bonnie Prince Charlie had been there a few days before. Now it was Bonnie Prince Stephen's turn. At 11:55 the plane arrived. I never had been so nervous. The gangway was pushed up, the door opened, and there was Steve. The minute he saw me he made a face, the kind he always made to me. He came down the gangway, smiled at me. I picked him up and was in heaven. Bogie looked very emotional. Steve remembered us and talked constantly. We hadn't heard him talk that much before. We were a family again. The African adventure behind us, we had to concentrate on being together now.

The best thing about that last six weeks in London is that we got to know London itself. Slowly I began my love affair with that city. And we made some lasting friendships. First, the Oliviers, who were appearing together in *Antony and Cleopatra* and *Caesar and Cleopatra*. Larry and Vivien made it easy, as if we'd been friends all our lives. Our mutual affection had happened instantly in California. It was right and rational then and continued to be ever after. Of course, Bogie and I were relaxed again — we had our son with us, the tensions of the location were behind, we enjoyed these people, felt good with them. Bogie was so impressed with Larry as both director and actor. Spencer Tracy had always said that Larry was the greatest actor in the English-speaking world. The more we saw of him, the more we agreed. Mind you, I knew very little, so that my judgment may have been colored by personal feelings, but with my sponge-like approach to every atmosphere, I was learning. Bogie really did know exceptional acting when he saw it, and through years of experience he had vast knowledge of the theatre. He said whenever he saw something really good in New York or London, he'd feel a great urge to return to the stage. But then he'd weigh his life in California — the boat, the sea, outdoors — and decide that meant more. He didn't really want to uproot himself. But he was a good enough actor to want to extend himself. It was always my feeling that if the right play had come along at a bad moment in his movie life he would have taken the plunge. But his movie career was flourishing now — getting better every year — so artistically he had satisfaction. As long as the quality was high and he could work with the best directors, he was happy to stay where he was.

I still can't believe the people I met — from friends we made and kept, like Margot Fonteyn, Robert Helpmann, Richard and Sybil Burton, Emlyn Williams, to T. S. Eliot, whom we met one night at the Oliviers', a quiet, charming man who seemed to be totally unimpressed with himself. It was incredible to me that at twenty-six I was meeting the best in so many worlds. In all the arts. Such luck. I took it in stride because I was married to Bogie, I guess, or because I didn't have sense enough or was too young not to. Or perhaps because these people themselves were so hard-working, so caring and involved in what they did, that they were open and welcoming to Bogie and me. They worked hard because they had chosen to, they were professionals, and they marveled at others' good work. It was a great lesson. Whenever I am asked about competitive acting, professional jealousy, all that pettiness, I have only to reflect that the best actors, dancers, writers are not like that, they are too busy learning, improving, moving forward, trying to bring more to their professions. And they appreciate and admire other people who are good at what they do.

Bogie worked on *The African Queen* until two o'clock in the afternoon we were to leave London. Steve and I went to the studio for lunch and said goodbye to the crew. We all had been through a lot together and even though I hadn't been in the film, I had been there through all the hard times, so we shared a common bond, and leave-taking was emotional. I had seen a rough cut of *The African Queen* — a very exciting experience. There was no doubt that it was special, and Bogie and Katie perfect throughout. I knew it was a high for Bogie — John and I had talked about it in Africa. He felt that Bogie was better in this film than he had ever been. It was that perfect marriage every actor dreams of — script, director, and co-star. We said goodbye to John and Katie — we'd see them soon in California — and headed for Southampton and the *Ile de France*, a last look at England for a while and my last five days of speaking French. Now that

that world was open to me, it would be a permanent, ever important part of my life.

It was time to go home, to Benedict Canyon and to my career, which I'd ignored for this long period — I'd been sent a script by Fox, but wouldn't leave Bogie and they couldn't wait. Back now to what life was all about. Bogie couldn't wait to see the *Santana*, and all our friends would be waiting for us. It was a good feeling to have left so much warmth behind and to have as much to look forward to.

So we settled back into our California routine and I found myself relieved to be home. My life there was where I felt safe. We gave our usual Christmas Eve party and I really outdid myself at that one. *The African Queen* was released in California, received with wild enthusiasm and much Academy Award talk for all concerned. Katie had rented a beautiful house that had once belonged to Charles Boyer, I think. She never would go out to dinner, but she did enjoy having two or three good friends come for a meal. One night she had Spencer Tracy, James Cagney, Bogie, and me for dinner. The three actors were contemporaries — each had left his individual mark — and they liked and admired each other. As they exchanged stories and reminisced, Katie and I sat spellbound. That is the only time I can remember that we both shut up. We just sat listening, and I, for one, felt privileged to be there. Bogie always said that if he were asked to choose the best actor in movies, Spence would win hands down — and without question the greatest movie personality ever seen was Cagney. It has passed through my mind that, in a way, he too thought it was pretty terrific to be with Spence and Jimmy that night.

Spencer was a man I had come to know slowly. We had adjoining booths at Romanoff's when he had his regular Thursday night dinners there — and he'd come to our house more and more as the years went by. Even to a couple of our big parties.

He had great humor — real, true wit, was highly intelligent — an avid reader. A total professional who had no patience with self-indulgent actors. His face had everything in it — many lines, smiles, love, wickedness, sensitivity, wisdom. The sight of Spence was always an experience. If it was unexpected, it lifted my spirits, made me feel warm; if the meeting was planned, that day was invariably a better day than the one before. Spence's endless, unrelenting charm and sweetness were accompanied by an undercurrent of tragedy and torment. He and Bogie shared many attitudes and opinions. Complemented each other — they also shared their time.

I might say Spencer always affected me the way the Lincoln Memorial does — except that he was not a monument, too human, too real. But he was larger than life — a special event at all times to me, one of my life's rarer bonuses.

Cagney I never knew. He never was seen socially anywhere — lived a very secluded life. But a nice man and interesting and original. He and Spence had known each other for years — were members of the Irish Club that included Pat O'Brien, John Ford, Frank Morgan, and more.

It was an unforgettable night. Katie and I sat on the floor — at their feet, of course. I remember thinking Katie was like a little girl — so thrilled to be in the company of these men, to know them. She hung on their words with a look of wonder and unending pleasure on that great face. I had thought she would be used to all that by now — but not at all. It was my first inkling of Katie's naïveté and vulnerability. I knew even then what a happy addition she and Spence were to our lives — later I would find that they were to be much more than that.

Stephen was three years old and giving both of us more pleasure with each passing day.

He was a beautiful boy — a loving boy who loved being with his father and mother. Bogie couldn't wait for the day he could take him on the boat and to Romanoff's for lunch. One day Bogie and I were having breakfast when Stephen came in, on the verge of tears, saying, 'Mommy, I can't walk — it hurts.' I pulled his pants down to discover a bulge in his groin. I panicked inside and called Dr Spivek, who said it sounded like a hernia — keep him quiet until he got there. When he arrived, he examined Steve, saying, 'This will hurt a little, so hold his arms and legs.' He had to try to push the hernia back up to see if it would pop down again. I held Steve's arms, Bogie his legs. The poor baby was screaming — Bogie could not look at him, turned green as he had in the labor room with me. I thought he would be sick. The hernia did drop down again and Dr Spivek told us Steve would have to have surgery. Not my baby — who'd ever heard of a three-year-old with a hernia? It's very rare, a weakness some few children are born with. Dr Spivek said we could not wait — it was the kind of hernia that could strangulate. The following morning we took Steve to Cedars of Lebanon Hospital, the place of his birth, trying to explain it to him so he wouldn't be terrified. The hysterical gibberish all frightened parents speak. Poor Bogie — it seemed even harder on him than on me. Thank God he was working. Steve was very brave. Scared and brave. When he was wheeled into the operating room, I thought my life would end. To see this tiny body on one of those tables with a sheet up to his chin — they had the grace to attach a large red balloon to the table to distract him. After what seemed an interminable time but was actually about an hour, Dr Spivek came out of the operating room to tell us everything was fine — operation a success — and it had been necessary. I thought that table would never come out, but it did — with the red balloon still flying. We rushed over. Steve opened his little eyes and smiled — 'Hello, Mummy, hello, Daddy' — and we walked to his room, me suddenly shedding tears of relief, Bogie in control but with an expression on his face I had come to know well. When moved, he would make a funny, almost chewing motion — a way he had of keeping himself in check, I think.

On the day I was to bring Steve home, there was a terrible rainstorm. It had started the night before, but I was determined to get him out of that hospital. So we went, and the ambulance managed to make it to our house. Bogie had stayed in the Beverly Hills Hotel for fear of not getting to work, but was due home that night. There was a party at Louella Parsons' —

he would stop by, then come home. Ha! He stopped by all right — a couple of hours later she called and told me Bogie was fine and not to worry. Then Bogie called, said he couldn't make it up the canyon. I said, 'Funny, Aurelio made it.' Bogie had got a little looped and stayed bravely near Sunset Boulevard, helping cars that were stuck get unstuck. I was furious — but Bogie was Bogie. He knew Steve and I were safe, so he had his small moment of adventure. He was a totally dependable man on ordinary days and in a crisis, but once the crisis was over, the relief he felt was so great that he had to have a drink.

Actually, he'd been drinking less and less, but he was still unpredictable — that way I was a little off balance, could never be quite sure what he would do. He hated to be taken for granted and had no intention of allowing it. He had spoiled me so much, had given me freedom to grow — he knew so much better than I did how continual exposure to new people and atmospheres would change me. For instance, I went through a period of enjoying parties. I liked getting dressed up. Kept buying new clothes — Christ, I had to wear them. And I loved to dance. As my security in life grew, so did my sense of self. Once when we were going to a big party at Sylvia and Danny Kaye's, Bogie was very angry with me and when we arrived, he pulled in the brake, slammed his fist on the dashboard, and said, 'Damn it, I am not an escort. I'm not here just to take you to parties and take you home. Get it straight — I'm your husband.' That must have been a moment when I'd gone too far, when I did take him for granted. Not consciously, never consciously.

1952 found me pregnant again, and Bogie, Katie, John, and *The African Queen* being nominated for Academy Awards. Marlon Brando and Vivien Leigh were also nominated for *A Streetcar Named Desire.*

As Award time grew closer, friends joked more and more about Bogie's acceptance speech. They were certain he would win. He was just as certain Brando would. But he played along with Swifty Lazar, Mike Romanoff, Niven, Dick Brooks, Spence and Katie. He was going to announce that he owed nobody nothing — if he'd got the Award, he'd got it only because of his own hard work and paying attention to his craft! He had been nominated before, but this time it seemed different. I was convinced he'd win, though harboring a tiny corner of doubt because of Brando. Katie and I had a replica of the tiller of *The African Queen* made for the big night and had it inscribed with one of her lines in the film: ' *"Nature, Mr Alnutt, is what we are put in this world to rise above —"* Baby, Rosie. '

When the big day came, all our pals were as keyed up as we were. The idea of awards was diametrically opposed to Bogie's concept of non-competitive acting. He said so loud and clear in the press, because such things are meaningless for actors unless they all play the same part. But let's face it — you still want to win. As long as it is the highest accolade one's profession can bestow, it is an honor — public recognition by one's peers. That night seemed endless until they got to the best-actor award. What would I do if he lost? I was in my fourth month, but had managed to squeeze myself into the only original Christian Dior dress I would ever own. Finally Greer Garson came onstage to present the best-actor award — *Streetcar Named Desire* had already won best supporting actor and actress, Vivien had won best actress. Poor darling Katie, I had so wanted her to win. Greer started calling the names — Marlon Brando, Humphrey Bogart, Fredric March, Montgomery Clift, Arthur Kennedy — and the winner is — I was squeezing Bogie's hand so hard and holding my breath — Humphrey Bogart, for *The African Queen*! A scream went up in the audience. I leaped into the air — thought I'd have the baby then and there. Bogie kissed me, walked to the stage amid really wild, enthusiastic applause and hurrahs, and said, 'It's a long way from the Belgian Congo to the stage of this theatre. It's nicer to be here. Thank you very much.' And then proceeded to thank John, Katie, Sam, the crew, saying, 'No one does it alone. As in tennis, you need a good opponent or partner to bring out the best in you. John and Katie helped me to be where I am now.' He was very emotional, and very humble. He had really wanted to win, for all his bravado — when push came to shove, he did care and was stunned that it was such a popular victory. He had never felt people in the town liked him much and hadn't expected such universal joy when his name was called. Bogie had everything now — a happy marriage, a son, another child on the way, an ocean racing yawl, *Santana*, success, and the peak of recognition in his work. We called Katie when we got to Romanoff's. After all they'd been through together, and the way they worked together, it would have been wonderful if they both had won. She was adorable and sunny and as good a sport as anyone could be, a woman who would never let you down. It was a night to celebrate for Bogie.

As I had proved with Steve, I was not your average expectant mother. Again it was not pickles at four in the morning that I wanted — this time it was another house. We didn't have room for the new baby in Benedict Canyon, we would have to build on a room, so as Bogie threw his hands in the air, I went house-hunting and fell in love with the most beautiful house — French colonial, whitewashed brick, beautiful rooms, balconies, trees, and a tennis court. No pool, but plenty of room for one. It was much grander than anything we'd had before or hoped to have, for that matter, but once I'd seen it I could think of nothing else. Bogie thought it was beautiful too, but much too rich for our blood — it was not a house one would expect to see actors in. 'However, if you want it, if Morgan Maree says it's okay, it's okay with me.' We bought the house — see what I mean by spoiling me? By this time my taste in furniture was totally for antiques — French or English. Only the upholstery could be modern. (Bogie insisted on comfortable chairs to sit in — with our gang, it wouldn't do to have to worry about the fragility of the furniture.) I went to work with almost demonic energy.

I felt less well than I had with Stephen — my feet and ankles swelled and I tended to feel faint — but I never had any real trouble and was very happy with my new house. Bogie always said all he needed was one room, anything more than that was beyond him. He'd had his early theatre training in hotel rooms — that's where he began his lifelong habit of tucking his trouser cuffs in a bureau drawer so that they'd hang straight and not need a press. That always made me smile — he did it as neatly and naturally as his morning shave.

I went into labor late in the afternoon of August 22. The drama that preceded Stephen's birth was not to be repeated. Bogie was nervous, but not quite so bad as the first time. I hugged and kissed my cherished Stephen and told him the next time he saw me I'd be home with a brother or sister for him — he expected one his age or at least his size. So down we trotted to good old Cedars of Lebanon Hospital and went through much the same routine, except that this time Bogie did not join me in the labor room. The second Bogart was a little slower in coming into the world and the anesthetic was a little slower in being given — always the case with second children, so as not to stop the contractions. At 12:02 a.m. Leslie Bogart arrived — Bogie and I had decided that a girl would be named after Leslie Howard, his first mentor and my imagined love. We kept the first name and eliminated the last. So we had a beautiful daughter. Bogie was awed once more by the magic of childbirth and filled with admiration for my female capability. His joke had been 'Be like the peasants — give birth in the fields — toss the kid over your shoulder and keep going.' Spoken aloud to make him feel it was all going to be easy — as much for him as for me — and to still our anxieties. Afterward he said, 'And you are called the weaker sex!'

Bogie's reaction to a girl was not the same as to our boy — he was always gentle, but he looked at Leslie as if she were a fragile flower. He was almost afraid to touch her. Bogie had never thought he'd have children, much less a wife he loved who loved him. I knew he was thinking these things. There he was with a son and daughter, and the wonder of it was humbling — a far cry from his early analysis of marriage: 'I sometimes wonder if the fucking you get is worth the fucking you *get*.' I always wanted to make a needlepoint pillow with that on it. His progeny gave him yet another reason for life and work — there was so much he wanted to teach them, to show them. I had proved to him that I was right, that he was not too old to be a father. You never are. And they were lucky to have *him*.

Leslie and I returned to our new home, where Steve gave Leslie a curious look, but wasn't that interested. Whenever I fed Leslie he'd come in and watch, but he wasn't wild about the attention being paid her. We had a nurse for Leslie. I never believed in not taking care of our own children, and yet if I'd done that, I'd never have done anything else. And I suppose I didn't really have the patience. I was with them a lot, but every day, all day? I couldn't have done it. I guess I was still too itchy to be moving in my own life. There were still too many unexplored areas.

A few days after Leslie and I came home, Mildred and Sam Jaffe came to visit. We started on politics — it was Presidential election year. Dwight Eisenhower had been the man each party wanted for its candidate, and Bogie and I had been among many who had gathered in Madison Square Garden to encourage him to return from Europe, where he was Commander of NATO. I, along with the rest of America, liked Ike; I wanted him on our — the Democrats' — side. But it was not to be. Then there was talk of a new man on the Democratic horizon — the Governor of Illinois, Adlai Stevenson. He'd been singled out by Truman at a Jefferson-Jackson Day dinner and besieged by the press with the usual questions. Are you going to be a candidate? Has President Truman asked you to be the nominee? We watched the Democratic convention, saw him nominated, heard him make his speech. It was a sound I hadn't heard in politics since F.D.R. — a cultured voice and perfect diction. But I still was disappointed that that great father figure, Ike, was not to be our candidate. Now Mildred Jaffe sang the praises of Stevenson. She urged me to read John Bartlow Martin's book on Stevenson, and a few days later she brought it to me. It painted a picture of a man of enormous integrity, purpose, and wit — and I was always a sucker for anyone who could make me laugh, laughter being the best sound there is. Adlai Stevenson had humor and seemed to apply it to politics as well as to life, and the level of his humor was high. The book made me want to know more about him.

Dore Schary, Don Hartman, and Bill Goetz were giving a garden party in September when Stevenson was due in California. Its purpose — to introduce him to film folk and to see who would support him. I accepted the invitation to meet him. Bogie did not. At the party, Stevenson stood on the receiving line. One by one, we were led up to him, and as we reached him, the flashbulbs would go off to record

440

the Historic Moment. I said a few nondescript words — he said something witty — we laughed and had our picture taken. He was friendly, open, warm, on first meeting.

I remember a very well known producer saying to me that afternoon, 'If you're smart, you'll keep your mouth shut and take no sides.' It was five years after the House Un-American Activities Committee investigation, but now, with the McCarthy fear, Hollywood seemed terrorized. I had never considered myself particularly brave, but I thought then, 'What have we come to if I can't voice my preference for Adlai Stevenson? Would it be worth living here if I couldn't stand up for him?' He was the candidate I was going to support, Eisenhower smile or no Eisenhower smile. Bogie was still for Ike and was due to go to Denver with Darryl Zanuck for a Republican rally. I was sent a wire asking if I would appear at a rally in San Francisco for Stevenson and do a day's campaigning in the environs. I thought about it and answered yes. I wasn't working, my children were thriving, nothing seemed as important as the election. People were fiercely taking sides. Many of our friends were for Eisenhower, and it was hard to argue against him, but instinctively I knew Stevenson was special — a rarity. Something was happening inside my head. I had to go to San

Francisco. Bogie began to waver, and then a few days before I was off to San Francisco, he made up his mind, called Zanuck, and told him he was going with Stevenson. Darryl wrote Bogie a letter saying:

> My old friend Wilson Mizner once explained to me the futility of combating the inevitable — he also said that one single strand of golden hair from the head of a beautiful woman is stronger than the Atlantic Cable.
>
> Love and XXX Francis

It was the first time I had made a strong decision that went against my husband. We'd disagreed — had our fights like everyone else who lives with anyone else — but I'd never gone off on my own so definitively on an issue so public.

From the day we went to San Francisco, my life and I myself began to change. I was insanely caught up in the excitement of campaigning — lunches, rallies, motorcades, platforms, college campuses. We were assigned to a car a couple behind Stevenson's. Crowds waving and screaming — it made me feel I was running for office myself, I got very pushy: no one who didn't have to be was allowed ahead of me in the motorcade! We flew back to Los Angeles on the Governor's plane, me talking to him all through lunch. His press secretary, William McCormick Blair, asked if we'd be able to campaign in the East, and I said yes before Bogie had a chance to hesitate. We had a week at home with Stephen and baby Leslie and I put on my own campaign to try to sway people, get them to switch to Stevenson. I sold tickets in Romanoff's to raise money, which Mike in his most royal tones asked me not to do in the restaurant — Mike was a pure Eisenhower man. But I had no patience with anyone who was not for Stevenson — everyone *had* to be. I became fierce — I was obsessed — he *had* to be elected. I could think or talk of nothing else. We'd listen to his speeches, hang on every word, cut out any quote from the newspaper. There was none of the usual campaign hyperbole. For example, when Eisenhower said, 'I will go to Korea' — and many thought he won the election right there — Adlai told me he had thought of saying that too, but felt it would be too much of a grandstand play.

Our job was to help attract crowds, as Stevenson was still relatively unknown in much of America. I was sure that the more people saw and heard him, the more would vote for him. I didn't believe for a moment that he spoke over the heads of the 'ordinary man.'

We flew East for the final lap of the

campaign in New York and Chicago. At every speech from the beginning — every platform, breakfast, lunch — Stevenson would catch my eye and wave and smile at me. To my fantasizing mind he seemed so vulnerable — so passionate about people and their needs — everything both Bogie and I believed in. Clifton Webb said he looked like Dwight Fiske. Fiske, I gathered, was a society piano player, somewhat effeminate, before my time. I didn't find that funny. Fun was also made of his wave — and they had a point about that, though I would never admit it. It was his built-in modesty, he just held up his hand slightly modestly and halfway and waved, while Eisenhower raised both arms and looked sure and great and like a winner. Everything went just right for Eisenhower — even when Nixon's finances came into question. The Democratic National Committee published proof that Nixon had access to funds provided by friends — less than a week later he vindicated himself on national TV, talking about his dog, Checkers, and his wife, Pat, with her Republican cloth coat, and proving to the American people's satisfaction that he was an honest man. Ha! Eisenhower went beyond that — even beyond Joseph McCarthy — on his train at a whistle stop in Chicago, not defending his great friend and former commander, General George C. Marshall.

Bogie said he had a funny idea for a cartoon. He'd be standing at our front door with a child on each side and rain falling heavily and Stephen would say, 'Daddy, where's Mommy?' Bogie, looking sadly into space, would reply, 'With Adlai.' It was a funny idea and I laughed, but Bogie knew that I had been deeply affected by Stevenson and, for that matter, he had too.

At every stop of the campaign train, we'd be introduced one by one to the waiting crowds — first Bob Ryan, then me, and then Bogie, and we'd each say a few pertinent, rah-rah words about our candidate. Then Adlai would be introduced and speak for perhaps ten minutes. The grind was rough, starting at 8:00 a.m. and lasting into the night. My memory is that he rarely had time to polish a speech before he had to speak it. Although he had great speechwriters, he himself wrote much of what he said. I always saw him with a yellow pad and pencil, furiously writing away up until the actual moment he was to speak.

Bogie and I left the train before it got to Grand Central Station in order to rehearse for the Madison Square Garden rally. Robert E. Sherwood had written some marvelous things and got the best people in

New York to appear — he cared so much, another extraordinary, exceptional man. It was good to see Bogie and Sherwood together almost twenty years after *The Petrified Forest*. No wonder Bogie talked so often of the good old days — with people like Bob and Madeline Sherwood constantly in your life, they would have had to be good. I flowered with these people — I drank in their attitudes, their spirit. Of course Stevenson had been labeled an 'egghead' by the opposition. The people around him, like Sherwood and Arthur Schlesinger, were eggheads as well. They were intelligent, and they cared more about the national good than about themselves. There was no one closely involved with Adlai Stevenson whom I didn't admire.

Bogie and I went to Chicago for the final rally. In the car en route to the station Arthur Schlesinger told us that Adlai had decided what he would say if he lost. I said, 'How can he think of such a thing now? He's not going to lose — he can't — he's needed too badly. Now is this country's chance for something better — they'll realize it!' As Bogie said, 'The American people always do the right thing finally. As they proved with Truman.' They *had* to do it this time too.

The Governor invited us to Springfield, Illinois, for the election returns. Bogie was horrified at the idea — he wanted to go home. I said we had to go — I couldn't not be there, it meant everything to me. I begged — I pleaded — I won. But first we had to vote. So we did something truly crazy. We flew to California — attended another political affair at the Biltmore Hotel — collapsed at home with our babies (though, to be truthful, my mind was not on them) — listened to Adlai's final campaign speech on election eve — rose at seven the next morning — voted — and flew to Springfield. We checked into an old hotel where everyone was gathered. Bogie felt lousy — had a virus, we thought — so he went to bed. But, having come this far, I was not about to miss anything.

After Bogie had everything he needed — or that he could get in that hotel — and knowing I had one foot out the door anyway, he told me to go out with the others for the disaster ahead. Dutch Smith, an old, close friend of the Governor's, took me to the Executive Mansion. In a room on the first floor, a few people were quietly gathered. There was no air of victory — Jane and Ed Dick, old Lake Forest Stevensonites who had worked tirelessly during the campaign — Buffie Ives, the Governor's sister, came in for a while — Ernest Ives, her husband — Bill Blair — Arthur Schlesinger in and out. The Governor was in a private room watching the returns. It was a ghastly night — that quiet in the air that signifies doom. The results got worse and worse, and I worried about Adlai. Dutch said he was all right, he could deal with this defeat. I couldn't — none of his friends could. I just sat there in deep depression, staring glassily at the television set, unbelieving. The people did *not* always do the right thing, or they could not have turned away from this man! I could feel the cracking of my heart. Dutch came over and whispered that we'd better get back to the hotel — the Gov and his family would be going there soon. And a message came from the Governor saying that he would like Bogie and me to come for lunch the next day in the mansion. Lunch! He thought of everyone, always — everyone but himself.

We rushed back to the hotel. There was a crush of people, of the press — everyone's face was drained and tense — there was noise, but it was the noise of desperation. The Governor appeared with his sons, his sister and her husband, the Dicks, and Bill Blair. He looked hurt and pale — tired and brave and very alone. 'Someone asked me as I came in, down on the street, how I felt. And I was reminded of a story that a fellow townsman of ours used to tell — Abraham Lincoln. They asked him how he felt once after an unsuccessful election. He said he felt like a little boy who had stubbed his toe in the dark. He said he was too old to cry, but it hurt too much to laugh.' I, along with everyone else, was dissolved in tears. It was a devastating time, yet the words he spoke suited the occasion perfectly, as his words always did. I sobbed my way back to our room, where poor Bogie, who had run out of quarters for the television set, was suffering with his virus compounded by my agony. He was upset — though clearly not as much as I — and relieved that the whole thing was over and he could go home. I told him the Gov had invited us to lunch. I was heart-broken — for the world and for myself. I adored Adlai Stevenson, I suppose I even worshipped him. He instilled that feeling in many — loyalty, adulation. He brought out the best in me, or at least I thought he did. He made me feel I knew more than I actually did, that I was valuable. He broadened my horizons — made me more aware of human dignity and the plight of people everywhere. Until Adlai Stevenson, I was a perfectly happy woman with a husband whom I loved — a beautiful son and daughter — some success in my work — a beautiful home — money — not a care in the world. His entrance into my life shook me up completely.

I fell into an unhappy sleep and awakened early. Bogie felt better and was raring to leave, but he decided to take it easy until lunch. I went downstairs after packing, and Bill Blair walked into the hotel and asked me to come back to the Executive Mansion with him. I asked him how Stevenson was this morning and he said fine — as well as could be expected, up early and actively pursuing his gubernatorial tasks, plus many others resulting from the election campaign. As I entered the mansion the Gov was coming down the stairs. He put his arm around me and I said, 'How are you?' and he said, 'More important, how are *you?*' I was a wreck, as he could plainly see. He asked if I had ever been to Lincoln's tomb and house. 'No,' I said. 'But you must go, you must see it. Take a car from outside and go — then come back and we'll have lunch. Bill, see that she gets in the right car.' Even then, on the morning after losing the Presidency, he could plan a sight-seeing tour for a constituent-admirer. So I went to the tomb of that great man, and to his house with its rocking chair, and I thought, though I was certainly in awe of Lincoln, 'Perhaps Stevenson is as great a man, and perhaps America has missed its finest moment and will never know it.'

Bogie met me back at the mansion. We

climbed the stairs for a preluncheon drink — only Bill Blair, Buffie and Ernest Ives, Jane and Ed Dick, and Stevenson's sons were there. Mrs Ives had not seemed overly fond of me — she was very possessive of her brother, acted as his hostess in the Governor's Mansion and would have done so in the White House. She could see how deeply I felt about him and perhaps felt that he might be susceptible. Drinks were a bit strained — what was there to talk about really? Life has to go on. The Gov kept the conversation going — talked to Bogie, who described his frustrating night with the coin TV — and we went into lunch, all but young Borden there. The only sign of testiness from the Governor came as we were all seated and in walked Borden, the Gov saying, 'Late as usual.' Adlai's sons were good boys all — from what I could gather, the divorce had had its greatest effect on the middle son. Not a happy situation, and not easy for Adlai to deal with alone. We spoke of California, and Adlai wanted to know about Africa, and about how the film world had felt about his candidacy. Purely social talk — but it was enlightening to watch his control, his ability to sit at the table for a fairly normal lunch on so totally abnormal a day. When it was time for us to leave, he said he hoped to be in California, and we invited him to stay with us any time, hoping it would be soon. We were at the top of the stairs. Bogie went ahead, having thanked the Governor and wished him luck. I said my goodbye and he hugged me. I got very teary and started down the stairs. At the foot I turned around and smiled and gave him my big wave. He was standing there smiling in return, saying, 'Someday come again and we'll put our feet up and talk.' I was determined not to have him vanish completely from my life.

On the trip home I was far away from Bogie, my thoughts on the man I had left behind. I tried to imagine his life. I had found out as much as I could from his friends — anyone who had known him in the last few years. In my usual way, I romanticized. He needed a wife, obviously — his sister had taken the official place of one, but he needed someone to share his life with. I fantasized that I would be a long-distance partner — a pen pal — a good friend whom he could feel free to talk to about anything. A sympathetic, non-judging ear. It took me a long time to dissect my feelings, but at that moment I felt a combination of hero worship and slight infatuation. This campaign had disrupted my life completely. I was flattered to have been included — flattered to have been singled out by Stevenson as someone a bit special. I was, after all, just twenty-eight years old — I'd just had a second baby and had been preoccupied with domesticity for the last couple of years. My career was at something of a standstill. I needed to dream — I needed to reach out, to stretch myself, to put my unused energies to use. My choices up to then had been Bogie or work — now they had expanded to political life, to bettering the world and its people, or at least to advancing and being connected with a great man who was capable of doing something about it. It takes one person who cares desperately — who has real passion about something big — to unleash one's own comparable passions. And Adlai was so articulate. He offered me a mentality that encompassed not just his world or my world, but all the world. That had never been offered before. It wasn't that I was dissatisfied with Bogie or loved him any the less — it was that Stevenson could help a different, unknown, obviously dormant part of me to grow. Bogie was fully aware of my state — Stevenson had affected him in somewhat the same way, except he was a man and — being a balanced, controlled human being — unlike me, he didn't go to pieces. Nor did he revel in the fantasy life I have always lived, where anything or everything is possible.

It was not easy to come down out of the

clouds and back to reality. Catching a virus of my own helped. I had to take to my bed for a couple of days. And Christmas was approaching — Mother and Lee coming out to see the new grandchild — Bogie's fifty-third birthday party — Steve's fourth birthday party. And Bogie was going back to work.

Our Christmas Eve party in the new house was a rousing success. Even Spence Tracy came. Everyone kidded me about Adlai — I not having been subtle at all. Strangely, many hinted that he had been taken with me as well. I did nothing to dispel the notion. Let them think what they liked — they would anyway — and besides, I was flattered.

George Cukor had told me about a play by Zoë Akins called *The Greeks Had a Word for It*. He said it was very funny and had a terrific part for me. As I had a new contract with 20th Century-Fox for a picture a year, I told Darryl Zanuck about it. He bought it, and gave it to Nunnally Johnson to write for the screen and produce. Nunnally called me at home one afternoon to say he knew I could play comedy, but there had never been film on me actually doing any; would I mind very much testing a scene so that Zanuck and he could see real footage? It was not a question of my ability and, of course, I'd get the part. . . . It was an awkward conversation — I was not thrilled at the idea of a test — but because it was Nunnally, I agreed. I remember hanging up the receiver and telling Bogie about it, and Bogie saying, 'You'll never have a friend as good as Nunnally. Don't ever lose him — hang on to that.'

So I made the test, which Jean Negulesco directed, and got the part. The film was titled *How to Marry a Millionaire*, to be filmed in Cinemascope, a new widescreen process which Fox owned and which Zanuck intended to rock the movie business with. *Millionaire* was to start shooting around February of 1953 — at the same time Bogie would be in Italy for *Beat the Devil*. I wanted to go with him, but I would have to make *Millionaire* or forget my career altogether. Anyway, I'd agreed to do it. But it would be our first separation in eight years of marriage. We talked it over — he felt I should do the movie and join him when I finished. He was very good about it — *Millionaire* was the best part I'd had in years.

Before Bogie left for Rome we discussed the religious future of our children. As neither of us was a church-going practitioner of any religion, we hadn't thought it important to make a choice. However, our decision to send Steve to Sunday School at All Saints Episcopal Church because his friend Scott Johnson went there had proved to be the right one — Steve really looked forward to going. But he couldn't continue without being a church member. Bogie's feeling was that the main reason for having the children christened was that, with discrimination still rampant in the world, it would give them one less hurdle to jump in life's Olympics. I, with my family-ingrained Jewish background, bucked it — it felt too strange to me. True, I didn't go to synagogue, but I felt totally Jewish and always would. I certainly didn't intend to convert to Episcopalianism for the children, or to deny my own heritage. At the same time I knew how important it could be to a child to have a religious identity. So we agreed that as long as our positions were made clear to Reverend Smith of All Saints', we'd go ahead and have it done. Bogie kept reminding me that I must put aside my feelings — that of course the children would know they were half and half, but their feelings were different from mine and always would be. So it was settled. We chose Ruth and Paul Zuckerman to be Leslie's godparents, Ginny and Quent Reynolds and Louis Bromfield to be Steve's. As they couldn't fly out, Dorris and Nunnally Johnson were surrogates. If it had been allowed, they would have been godparents as well. Unhappily, Bogie was in Europe when the actual christening took place. It was a lovely ceremony. I held Leslie, six months old, who was perfect — fascinated by the stained-glass windows and silent throughout. Stephen, standing alongside me, was very funny. When Reverend Smith sprinkled water on his head, he said, 'I don't like the drops,' and as the ceremony drew to a close, when Reverend Smith said, 'He shall enter the house of the Lord,' Steve spoke out loud and clear, 'If he wants to come in — then let him come in.' All ended on a happy note, but I still felt odd, church procedure being totally foreign to me. Yet I was glad about having done it for Stephen and Leslie — and determined that they would always be aware of their Jewish blood. In the light of what we had to face four years later, I can only say thank God I did go through with it.

A week after Stephen's fourth birthday party Bogie was to head for New York and Rome. I went as far as New York with him for a few days of our usual madness in '21,' at the theatre with the Reynoldses, Zuckermans, O'Hara, the Harts, Kaufman — always keyed up and fun. And my family, whom Bogie did truly enjoy. At drink time our hotel suite was a constant flow of relatives and friends. We were invited to a cocktail party and dinner for Adlai Stevenson given by Ronnie and Marietta Tree, but the date was after Bogie's departure. I was thrilled at the thought of seeing Adlai so unexpectedly soon, and was not at all sad to be the only Bogart present. I'd intended to stay on a few extra days anyway to see family and friends and to shop at Loehmann's. Our parting was hard and sweet and filled with promises to write. 'Take care of yourself.' 'Be good.' 'Be careful.'

The party and dinner for Adlai were a great success. He was in A-1 form — happy to be in New York seeing his new friends again. After dinner we sat in a small group. Marietta recited a beautiful poem. Bob Sherwood stood up, turned up the collar of his jacket, looked sadly round at us all, and gave his rendition of 'Brother, Can You Spare a Dime?' I used to do a joke imitation of 'Wonder How It Feels' from *South Pacific*, singing both parts, Pinza's and Mary Martin's. Either Bob or Mado Sherwood told me, 'Do it for Adlai, Baby.' Adlai waited with a smile and a bit of a taunt for me to deliver. So I did it — and was a much better Pinza than a Martin. I was terribly self-conscious and embarrassed. I've always marveled at people who can simply sing a song, even badly — make a speech — anything — in a room full of people, and not be bothered by it. I can do it from a distance, as an actress, but not as myself. Bob Sherwood said some words about Stevenson — what he had meant to us all — what great quality and spirit he had brought into the campaign and into public life. Adlai talked about how grateful he was to all of us, what his aims had been, how he had hoped to raise the level of political dialogue, how he hoped he had succeeded to some extent. All this was spoken very informally, with drinks in hand — we all were sentimental. And there was laughter and jokes, and finally Bob and Madeline and Adlai and I piled into one cab, stopped by the Sherwoods' for one drink, and then Adlai dropped me at my hotel. I wanted to talk with him alone, to talk personally, but there was no chance. Though I wasn't certain that he would get that personal with me, the implication was that he would — he did like to flirt, and he did like to be admired, and he did know that I was very young and had a solid crush on him. I guess he was pleased — he did nothing to discourage it. I left him with the promise of seeing him in California the next month. He was coming out to raise money for the Democratic campaign deficit — it would be the jumping-off spot for his trip around the world. Bill Atwood, another new friend, thanks to Adlai, was accompanying him for *Look* magazine, as was Bill Blair, his friend and right hand. Something to look forward to.

I returned home to prepare for my role of Schatze in *How to Marry a Millionaire*. Marilyn Monroe and Betty Grable were to be in it as well — it was about three girls looking for millionaire husbands, and it was funny, witty, even touching. I hadn't really known either of my co-stars before and hoped the association would be a good one. It was strange, Bogie not being there. I was selfish — pressing on with what I wanted to do and very brave as long as he was around to back me up, but in truth I was not all that brave. I enjoyed being able to do as I pleased for a while — it was good to go to sleep when I wanted to, study my lines for the next day without having to worry about dinner for Bogie. It was especially good because it was temporary.

As Cinemascope was a new experiment for everyone, it was difficult. One had to keep the actors moving and not too close together, as the screen was long and narrow. You shot longer scenes in Cinemascope, five or six pages without a stop, and I liked that — it felt closer to the stage and better for me. Betty Grable was a funny, outgoing woman, totally professional and easy. Marilyn was frightened, insecure — trusted only her coach and was always late. During our scenes she'd look at my forehead instead of my eyes; at the end of a take, look to her coach, standing behind Jean Negulesco, for approval. If the head-shake was no, she'd insist on another take. A scene often went to fifteen or more takes, which meant I'd have to be good in all of them as no one knew which one would be used. Not easy — often irritating. And yet I couldn't dislike Marilyn. She had no meanness in her — no bitchery. She just had to concentrate on herself and the people who were there only for her. I had met her a few times before, and liked her. Grable and I decided we'd try to make it easier for her, make her feel she could trust us. I think she finally did. I had only a few conversations with her. She came into my dressing room one day and said that what she really wanted was to be in San Francisco with Joe DiMaggio in some spaghetti joint. They were not married then. She wanted to know about my children, my home life — was I happy? She seemed envious of that aspect of my life — wistful — hoping to have it herself one day. One day Steve came on the set and was doing somersaults on a mattress. She sat on a stool watching him and said, 'How old are you?' He said, 'I'm four.' She: 'But you're so *big* for four. I would have thought you were two or three.' He wasn't, and was confused (so was I, so was she), but kept turning his somersaults. There was something sad about her — wanting to reach out — afraid to trust — uncomfortable. She made no effort for others and yet she was nice. I think she did trust me and like me as well as she could anyone whose life must have seemed to her so secure, so *solved*.

The Stevenson dinner was in February. He and Bill Blair were to go to Palm Springs afterward for a few days of sun and rest. I had a couple of days off at that time and decided to go down there too, staying with Buddy and Carolyn. Stevenson, on the dais with Dore Schary and others, caught my eye — or I caught his — or we caught each other's. I went up to the dais before the speeches to say hello to Dore, but actually to speak to the man sitting next to him. We were photographed together and exchanged some chat later in the evening — at those dinners you have to settle for that. I told him I'd be in the desert, which seemed to please him no end, and he said we'd have lunch and dinner together. I left feeling very high, with my imagination going at full tilt,

462

and headed toward Palm Springs that weekend.

It was a perfect time of year for the desert. My first night down, there were about eight of us at dinner. Adlai was in high spirits, and after dinner we all went to a small club. The music was dreamy — everything I needed, with my hokey love of ballads and my head full of romance and fantasy. I recall turning to Adlai, who was next to me, and asking him his favorite song. He replied, 'The Battle Hymn of the Republic.' There was always laughter with him. And there were always people around. He was going to have to see some Chicago politicians for Sunday lunch and he did not look forward to that. They were typical ward politicians of a kind he did not favor, and he told me I had to come to that lunch to ease the pain. I was included in all his activities, which only fed my fantasy. But he and I really did get along very well. I learned that he seldom read books — novels almost never — and I wondered how he had such a command of language and how he knew so much without reading. He talked to me as though I knew and understood as much as he did — as he had when we were all on the campaign train and once, passing in the corridor, he turned to Bogie and asked, 'Was it Christ who said, "Be ye perfect"?' He endowed us with gifts we did not have. We played tennis — each time I missed a shot, I cursed, and he would say, 'Always the lady.' He asked me about my life. I savored every second. The truth is that I had fun with him — and it was a new kind of fun. I was certain he needed continued encouragement — not just from professional politicians, but from the rest of us. He had to realize how important he was. I was as selfish as many others in that I didn't want him lost. I wanted — for my own sake — to have my hero governing this country. He was my first emotional hero since Roosevelt, but Adlai wasn't a father figure as Roosevelt had been for me. He was someone I could look up to — his mind excited me — and his flirtatiousness encouraged me. And some of his friends and the people around him also encouraged me — they said it was good for him to have me around, he enjoyed my company, felt easy and relaxed with me, I took his mind off his heavy responsibilities. Almost anything that was good for Stevenson I was all for. So, short of leaving husband and home — which I had no desire or intention of doing — I would see him when I could and keep the thread of my presence alive in his consciousness. I left Palm Springs reluctantly. If the weekend accomplished nothing else, it had proved to me that my choice had been right — that Adlai Stevenson was someone worth putting myself on the line for, worth fighting for.

The next couple of months were occupied with work and planning to join Bogie in Ravello. He had written me long letters — the first since our courting days — describing the beauty of that part of Italy and the film's progress. A writer named Truman Capote had been hired to work on the script. Bogie's observation about him was, 'At first you can't believe him, he's so odd, and then you want to carry him around with you always.' He was the hardest worker Bogie had seen in ages and he loved that. There were Huston script problems, compounded by assorted others — one being that Bogie and George Sanders, driving to a location, had hit a stone wall. Bogie had bitten into his tongue and had to have several stitches. I was upset and worried — I never thought of Bogie having anything wrong with him — but he called me and through a lousy connection assured me that all was well.

Leslie was now eight months old and growing prettier every day. She had not been a beautiful baby, just very pixie-looking, but things were changing before my eyes. She was so different from Steve — Women's Lib notwithstanding, girl babies are very different from boy babies. She adored her brother, who was almost totally uninterested in her except for being curious when she tried to stand up or speak, and who only wanted to know when she'd become a playmate. I had them photographed together and rushed the pictures off to Bogie so he could see the changes in his offspring.

How to Marry a Millionaire was finally completed — everyone was pleased with it — and I was off to meet Bogie. Unhappily, due to our delays, I would have to meet him in London and miss Italy altogether. My loss. I was excited at the prospect of Bogie after three months and curious as to what it would be like when we first met each other — a shame it would have to be in public.

In those days one slept in a berth on a plane, the flight to London taking nine or ten hours. About an hour before London we ran into some bad weather and we arrived late. By the time we landed, there was no time to go to the hotel before lunch. I was met by someone on the *Beat the Devil* staff and whisked to the Savoy Hotel and into the lunch room, where Bogie was seated on the dais. Someone was making a speech of some sort. I was put into my seat, also on the dais — not even allowed to kiss my husband hello. There were a couple of people between us. Bogie looked at me with the funny chewing motion he always made with his mouth at emotionally high moments. I smiled at him and was fascinated at how nervous I was — shaking almost as much as I had on that bench outside Howard Hawks' bungalow. The thrill was far from gone. After eight years of marriage the excitement was as strong as ever.

Bogie had been offered the part of Captain Queeg in *The Caine Mutiny*, which was to be produced by Stanley Kramer with Eddie Dmytryk directing. He wanted to play that part and through his keen awareness of emotional upsets he had an insight that few actors could equal. Columbia wanted him badly, but didn't want to pay him his top salary. Bogie was so angry at this — he said, 'This never happens to Cooper or Grant or Gable, but always to me. Why does it happen to me? Damn it, Harry [Cohn] knows I want to play it and will come down in my price rather than see them give it to somebody else.' Strangely, Bogie always had to struggle, even though he was one of the biggest stars the motion picture industry had ever produced. None of it came easily. He was never in a position to ask for a lot of money on a take-it-or-leave-it basis, because he wanted to do good things and couldn't walk away from excellence. There was to be a three-week location in Honolulu, where we'd never been, and we could take Steve. The cast was good — Fred MacMurray, Van Johnson, Jose Ferrer. But most important, Bogie really wanted to be Queeg. So he gave in. The theory always was you should never let a producer know you want to play a part because that gives the producer the upper hand; he knows he can get you for less money and that's all that interests him. A hopeless position for a caring actor. I've had the same problem in my own career — I've always lowered my price when I really wanted a part. It's a foolish thing to do — if they want you, they want you and they'll pay — but most of us have such frail egos we think we can always be replaced, so we capitulate. Insecurity plays a strong role in an actor's life. With all of Bogie's self-assurance as a man, he worried as much as Spence, or most of the other fine actors and stars I knew, about being replaced. And actually this vulnerability was one of his most attractive qualities.

So back to California and the children. Bogie worshipped his little daughter, she seemed so delicate to him. He showed what an old-fashioned man he was — he treated her like porcelain, and always told Stephen he must do the same. That was often not Steve's inclination. Oh, I loved having two children. We were a family — more so with two than with one. That was my storybook idea of families, besides which I had long ago decided I was not going to subject my son to being an only child as I had been.

1953 was a very good year for us. Bogie worked continually and in good films, I went back to work after three years in a movie that became a big success, and we traveled a good deal, seeing old friends, making some new, solidifying some in between. We were in England for my contemporary, Queen Elizabeth's, coronation — witnessing the British at their best and most endearing in the rain, a mad, exciting, totally unforgettable week. I still marvel at her capacity to perform that lengthy, electrifying, magical ceremony. We had our health — our union — and family life was thriving. I had been asked by Fleur Cowles, who was then married to Mike Cowles of *Look*, to write a piece for the magazine. My theme and title was 'I Hate Young Men.' I was paid a token sum and wrote it totally myself — my first commercial writing venture, and very important to me that it be done well. I listed the qualities that I admired and found attractive in men, and named six men who, despite the pressures and frantic pace of the times, had managed to keep their wits, personalities, and humor about them and retain their sanity. The men were Adlai, Robert E. Sherwood, Nunnally Johnson, Alistair Cooke, Louis Bromfield, and John Huston. Their reactions to the piece were funny. Sherwood wrote that since the article came out he had been the most hated and scared man on the boulevards; it was obvious, he said, why I picked the other five — 'Stevenson because he is literate — Johnson because he is witty and wise, Cooke because he is debonair, Huston because he wears funny caps and Bromfield because he is a Republican (just to show how bipartisan you can get) but there could be only one conceivable reason for your choice of me — my malicious animal magnetism. That thought inflames the fellows around this town and terrifies the dames.' Adlai wrote that he was not sure how becoming the state of lowered lids and self-conscious confusion is for a man both humble and sophisticated, charming and simple, wise and humorous: 'What can I do? My clay feet are showing, what a task you have given me, and what a task you have given yourself, for now you will be consigned like sufferers before you to write and write.' (He wasn't quite correct on that score.) Bromfield wired 'Thanks kind remarks — *Look* article excellent and professional except Bromfield under-estimated.' Alistair: 'Humble, dignified and humorous thanks from the junior member of the Bacall club but where do you get that turn of the century stuff?' I have no record of any word from Huston. He was in Europe. The last few sentences I wrote about him were, 'Figuratively speaking, of course, he has left his friends' bodies strewn all over the world. Wherever you might be for the moment, you have his undivided attention and all his thoughts: that is, you have them until he feels the need to move on. So there you are with egg on your face — and lucky to be, I say.'

How to Marry a Millionaire was released in November and I was to go to New York for the opening. Never one to refuse a trip to New York, I accepted — it was for less than a week and Bogie was working, so it was fine with him. That opening was fun. I was led across Broadway from one theatre it was playing at to another by New York police — many searchlights, big crowds. Mother and Lee were there, and I enjoyed being the focus of attention. I knew the film was good, and success does give one a lift. Dutch and Ellen Smith had invited me to their home in Lake Forest, Illinois, for a weekend on my way home. Adlai would be there and would come to dinner with some other friends. I accepted eagerly, sure that

Bogie would be pleased. We talked almost daily and I told him about the invitation. He was furious, said, 'Absolutely not' — he wanted me to come home. I said it was perfectly harmless, it meant only two days more, and I had already accepted. He was in a rage and slammed down the phone. Somewhere in him was anxiety about my feeling for Adlai. It had come out before and would again. He had held himself in check most of the time, but when it got to be too much he let loose. I went. It was a lovely dinner and I was glad to see Adlai again. All very proper, though it was clear I adored him. I told him how I happened to be there; he asked after Bogie, as he always did. It was a different world, that world — the people were very friendly, but I was an outsider. The next day there was a luncheon for Adlai to which I was also invited. Buffie Ives was, as usual, less than glad to see me. She asked me how my husband was, and my children — very pointedly. I was flattered that she might consider me a threat. She came over and tried to drag Adlai away — he said he'd be right over, that he was talking to me. He was somewhat intimidated by her, and I think he used her to get him out of places he didn't want to be. She may have been an annoyance at times, but he needed her and they were close. In any case, that afternoon was clearly not a situation he wanted to be rescued from.

Early in the evening Bill Blair drove me to the airport and we stopped at the Governor's farm in Libertyville to say goodbye. I couldn't see the grounds at night, but the house was warm, cozy, and unpretentious. One of Adlai's devoted followers and backers from 1952 — I can't remember her name — was there. I wasn't thrilled with that — but he gave me a big warm hello and she glared at me in a less than friendly fashion. I became more aware each time I saw him how many assorted women were vying for his time and attention. It's touching to think of in retrospect. I mean, this man was not anyone's notion of a Don Juan, no sex symbol, not a seducer, yet he was capable of dangling so many ladies, keeping them interested, grateful for his time, and each thinking that she was the One. I guess we each brought out something different in him — and we all flattered him, and he needed that. And he did the same for us. All the women were married, therefore safe. I remember only one who was too overwhelming — that was Marlene Dietrich. She became enamored of him, as we all did — wrote to him, called, got him to escort her somewhere public once, but never again. She came onto the set of *Millionaire* one day to tell me he hadn't called her — she couldn't understand why — if I saw him, would I please ask him to call? 'Of course,' I said, knowing that I wouldn't. I did mention her, half kidding, and Adlai, not saying anything derogatory, just laughed — said she was a charming woman but too much for him. He never gave too much, just enough to keep you wanting more. And yet he was a life-enhancer. Being with him awakened a whole other part of yourself.

1953 was also the year I declined to place my feet in the cement at Grauman's Chinese Theatre. It was to coincide with the *Millionaire* opening. The day I was told about it, I said to Bogie that it seemed to me anyone with a picture opening could be represented there, standards had been so lowered. Bogie, loving a chance to puncture Hollywood's ego, said, 'Why don't you refuse?' Joe Hyams, sensing a story, agreed. I, welcoming the idea of a new cause, however minor and short-lived, decided I *would* refuse. Joe said he'd print my statement in the *Tribune*, and I wrote, 'Before I came to Hollywood, Grauman's Chinese was something very special to me — it meant not only achievement — it was the Hall of Fame of the motion picture industry and the people in it were unforgettables and irreplaceables.

I don't think of myself as either — I feel that my career is undergoing a change and I want to feel I've earned my place with the best my business has produced.' That statement made newspapers across the country and, along with all the other news stories, was forgotten the next day. Time went by, I wasn't asked again, and so twenty-five years later, a tourist or aspiring actor going to Grauman's Chinese to see the legendary stars' footprints will not see mine — or miss them.

Bogie had signed to do Joe Mankiewicz's *Barefoot Contessa* in Rome, starting in January 1954, which meant three months or more there. I didn't want to leave the children for that long, so we agreed that I would follow in three weeks. Despite the fact that Steve was a January baby, he was allowed to enter school (kindergarten) a few months before his fifth birthday — Westlake was a school for girls, but the kindergarten was coeducational. Bogie and I went to stand in the background on his first day. There was this small boy sitting at his own little desk — of course he looked adorable, like a little man. I looked at Bogie and saw his eyes filled with tears watching his son starting on the road to growing up, learning independence — it caught Bogie unawares. I think he had never believed he'd be seeing a son of his doing anything at all — ever.

So he left for Rome and *The Barefoot Contessa*, and I headed for New York a few weeks later. The day before I was to leave for London, Frank Sinatra called to ask if I'd mind carrying a coconut cake to Ava Gardner, who was in the film with Bogie (apparently she liked coconut cake). We had started seeing Frank the year before. I don't recall quite how the friendship began — he was alone and not happy, neither work nor his personal life had been going well, so we'd had dinner with him a few times and he'd been to our house. Close friendship was still to come. On the morning of my departure from New York the cake was delivered to me in a large white box — unpackable, of course, so I took off with the coconut cake permanently attached to my hand to keep it from getting crushed. I stayed a night in London, and then Bogie was at the Rome airport to greet me. The care he took of me — that he was still excited to see me, still looked forward to me — I marveled at his ability to keep our relationship fresh. He took me and my cake box to the Excelsior Hotel and I asked him to tell Ava Gardner I had brought it. He told her — she did nothing about it — so two days later I decided to take it to her before it rotted. I didn't know her and felt very awkward about it —

who knows what has happened between a man and a woman when it goes sour? Bogie had told me the picture was going well and that Ava had many people with her all the time, including her sister and a bullfighter named Luis Miguel Dominguin, with whom she was in love. I took the damn cake to the studio and knocked on her dressing-room door. After I had identified myself, the door opened. I felt like an idiot standing there with the bloody box — there were assorted people in the room and I was introduced to none of them. I said, 'I brought this cake for you — Frank sent it to me in New York, he thought you'd like it.' She couldn't have cared less. She wanted me to put it down on some table she indicated — not a thank-you, nothing. I stood there very much out of place and finally managed to get away. I was furious with her and never did get to know her on that film, but have a little since and like her. Her reaction had only to do with Frank — she was clearly through with him, but it wasn't that way on his side. I never told Frank the coconut-cake saga, he would have been too hurt. Bogie always said the girls at M-G-M were so pampered, so catered to, that they were totally spoiled and self-indulgent. But she was professional about her work, and that's all he cared about.

Our time in Rome was fun. Howard Hawks, Harry Kurnitz, and William Faulkner were there preparing for *The Egyptian*, and a group of us, including Edmond O'Brien, also in Bogie's film, would go around the corner from the Excelsior to Harry's Bar for dinner. Invariably Bill Faulkner would be sitting alone at a table. He was such a shy man — Bogie or I would go over and ask him to join us and he was so grateful for company that he'd stay with us until we left. One night Howard gave a dinner at a great Italian restaurant called Passetto. I was seated next to Kurnitz and opposite Bill. With my usual tact, I said, 'Tell me, Bill, why do you drink?' Bill, in his soft Southern drawl said, 'Well, with one martini ah feel bigger, wiser, taller, and with two it goes to the superlative, and ah feel biggest, wisest, tallest, and with three there ain't no holdin' me.' An enchanting and revealing answer. I suppose the fact of his being a small man had always bothered him, probably started him drinking. He was a charming and gentle man, and very serious. He was telling us what he planned to do after he finished the script: 'I thought I'd drive through the Loire Valley — tasting the wine of the country as I go.' I remember Kurnitz telling us that Faulkner was poured off the plane on arrival in

Cairo. After a few days of not seeing him around, Harry decided, as they were collaborating on the script, to stop by Bill's hotel and visit him. He knocked on the door — a nurse quickly left the room, which had a few empty bottles on the floor. Bill was sitting up in bed. Harry said, 'Well, Bill, it's good to see you — how are you doing?' 'Just fine, Harry — ah just can't seem to shake this cold!'

My two months in Rome consisted mainly of walking the same streets over and over again to keep myself busy while Bogie was working. At night, when Bogie got back to the hotel, I was full of energy and raring to go — but he, of course, had to work the next day, so we'd go to dinner and hit the sack. Still, whenever he had a few days off, we'd go to Florence or Venice, and he loved Italy as much as I did. But our time there was finally over and it was back home, via London and New York. Oh, how I wanted to see my children — the best part of going away was opening my own front door. Everything I really wanted was there.

We were deluged with phone calls from our friends welcoming us back, and we started seeing everyone. Lee and Ira Gershwin gave a large party for Leonard Bernstein, whom we'd never met. He was ravishing to look at, with enormous vitality, energy, and a great sense of fun. Bogie and I were dazzled by him, though if it came to a contest I would have won. Lenny sat down at the piano, I sat at his feet, everyone sang their old and new songs. I was in my element — there was almost nothing I enjoyed as much as sitting by a piano, hearing and singing songs. One of the rituals at the Gershwin house was the playing of new scores by the men who wrote them, as Harold Arlen and Ira himself did that night with the score for *A Star Is Born*. Judy Garland and Sid Luft had moved to our street, two houses away from us — their daughter Lorna was about six months younger than Leslie, so we had all become very chummy strolling back and forth between houses. Judy had just finished *A Star Is Born*, with Sid as producer, and we were all looking forward to it, feeling that at last Judy, after her many professional and private ups and downs, was about to realize her dream and win an Academy Award for her performance, proving to all the cynics that she was still very much an artist. So everyone that evening was 'up,' and the party lasted until the wee hours. Lenny Bernstein was in Hollywood to see *On the Waterfront*, as Sam Spiegel wanted him to score it. He and I were very much attracted to each other, I don't know why — we were both happy with our mates.

Anyway, Bogie and I saw a lot of him from that night on — he'd come to the house for tennis, drinks, dinner. He was always work-consumed. Bogie said that he was a genius — that he would always be on the move, had to do what he had to do. He was right, of course. Once when he knew Lenny was coming to town, Bogie said, 'Oh, I can't take that sitting on the floor, playing the piano all night, I'm going on the boat.' With Lenny it was always music until three in the morning. It was fun — it was new, and all my life I have been prey to anything new. Besides, at Hollywood parties, women were ignored. If you weren't the hottest, most successful kid in town, men stayed away from you and talked among themselves about the movies they made — about the picture business. Women did not feel like women, we were just there. So anyone who paid special attention became a necessary part of one's life. I used to think that if we had been free souls, Lenny and I might have run off together. Another childish fantasy. As Bogie said, 'Lenny has too many things to do in his life to be a satisfying mate. You'd probably have a great time for a weekend but not for a lifetime.' That's where the twenty-five-year differences in our ages showed. He had the patience and trust in me to let me grow. He knew I was an innocent, never having had the chance to spread my sexual wings, so he allowed me my intermittent crushes. He had taught me early that all through one's life one meets people whom one is attracted to — sure, it's fun, but that's when you decide whether one weekend is worth it. I never dared. Not only did my nice-Jewish-girl syndrome get in the way, but I knew that Bogie — however much he loved me — would put up with flirtation, but if I ever really did anything, he would leave me. He valued character more than anything, and he trusted mine — I knew that and it kept me in check.

Time decided it was time for a cover story on Bogie. In the piece Bogie sounded off on all his favorite subjects:

WOMEN — They've got us — we should never have set them free [last-century man, remember].

MONEY — The only reason to have money is to tell any SOB in the world to go to Hell.

FATHERHOOD — It came a little late in life. I don't understand the children and I think they don't understand me and all I can say is thank God for Betty. [Is it any wonder I loved him?]

MANNERS — I have manners. I was brought up that way, but in this gold-fish-bowl life, it is sometimes hard to use them. A night club is a good place not to have manners.

He talked about how much better he felt when working — 'Puts me on the wagon.'

John Huston and a few friends were sitting around one evening and he asked if anyone had the desire to relive part of his life. Only Bogie said yes — 'When I was courting Betty.' (Is it any wonder?)

We opened an Edward R. Murrow *Person to Person* season that September. Great excitement in the household then — we were wild Murrow fans, stayed home every Sunday night for *See It Now.* Anyone who lived during that time had to be aware of Murrow's dedication, character, and purity of soul. He changed the face of broadcasting, and had as much to do with McCarthy's downfall as anyone in government. On *Person to Person* we took him through our home, talked about me on Truman's piano, Bogie's being the Maud Humphrey Baby, and Bogie's future project, *The Man Who Would Be King.* Bogie's definition: a project is what it's called until you get the money together. Huston had talked about Bogie and Gable doing this film in the Himalayas — another inaccessible Huston location and another dream unrealized until 1976, when Huston actually made it, but with Sean Connery and Michael Caine. Stephen and Leslie, dressed for bed, made a brief appearance — even Harvey and his family were seen coast to coast. I was a nervous wreck as usual, but, as always, once it was over I wanted to go back to the beginning and do it all over again.

That summer and fall began our close friendship with Sinatra. We began by seeing more of him through others — then he started to visit us and we to visit him. Bogie always liked Frank — he enjoyed his 'fighting windmills' and Frank made him laugh. It was not a great career time for Frank, though getting better steadily since *From Here to Eternity*. He was lonely and still in love with Ava Gardner — I do believe it was the first and only time that someone else had done the leaving. Frank was attracted to Bogie and to Spencer Tracy — he admired them as men and as talents, and being with them gave him a feeling of solidity that his life lacked. He was a restless man, totally incapable of being alone. He really came alive at night, due to a lifetime of training as a band singer. Frank had an apartment in a great building on Wilshire Boulevard which belonged to Gladys Belzer, mother of Loretta Young. On his way to being superagent, Swifty Lazar lived in an apartment next to Frank's. Whenever Swifty gave a dinner party, we were there and Frank often was too — the two bachelors were always free.

A Star Is Born opened in October — a big old-fashioned Hollywood opening. Sid and Judy were giving a gigantic party and, as friends and neighbors, we were of course invited. Bogie and I were not ones for openings — too many lights, people, and, worst of all, cameras, and to get all done up just to sit in a movie theatre seemed silly. But this was not the usual opening — because of Judy. She was a complicated woman of tremendous wit and intelligence who had survived a distorted childhood and distorted marriages and relationships that had left their mark. But she and I became good friends. She was fun and, when we'd sit quietly of an afternoon or evening, great company. It was hard for her to think beyond herself — it had been that way for too long. But *A Star Is Born* was made in spite of the cynics' predictions, and it was Sid who helped her get through. Whatever quirks he may have had, he was very good with his children and he did take care of Judy through some rough times that could not have been easy for him. The movie was a real comeback (I hate that word, but for want of another) for her, and at last she seemed happy — had a lovely home, Liza and Lorna with her, nothing could go wrong.

Bogie had four films released that year. Cary Grant came to the house one afternoon and remarked, 'You get all the good parts now, Bogie — how do you get so many of them?' Bogie's answer was 'Because I keep working.' He felt that work breeds work, and you're bound to get good things if you keep at it. So that our life (thank God) was far from being one enormous party. Most of our free time was spent at home. Our idea of a perfect evening was dinner on trays in front of the television. We had a great comfortable sofa with an enormous coffee table in front of it — our trays would be set on the table — I'd serve — and if Bogie liked the menu we'd have a wonderful evening. He'd sit at the end of the sofa nearest to the TV — I'd stretch out at the other end with my feet on his lap. We enjoyed our cozy evenings alone — we guarded them. Only my occasional urge to go to a party would get Bogie out — otherwise he was perfectly content to stay at home every night of the week. What he did enjoy was lunch at Romanoff's. When he wasn't working he'd go almost daily and take Steve from time to time. Often he'd play chess with Mike into the afternoon. Unless Bogie was on the boat, he was at somewhat of a loss when he wasn't working.

We both started the new year with

jobs — Bogie in *We're No Angels* with Peter Ustinov and I in *The Cobweb*, my first time at the legendary M-G-M. It was also the year of the new Thunderbirds, and Bogie and Cooper and Gable each bought one — middle-aged hot-rodders. The new sleek look appealed to them all.

Judy was expecting another baby, she'd told me months before; was so excited about it, so looking forward to it. Maybe this time she'd have a boy! And she was nominated for an Academy Award for *A Star Is Born*. So was Grace Kelly for *The Country Girl*, and though she was riding very high at the time, we were sure Judy would win.

Frank stopped by our house for a drink the night Judy was taken to the hospital. We had a rule by then: If the light over the front door was on, we were home and awake and a chosen very few could ring the bell; if not, we were not receiving. Frank had started coming almost nightly — clearly we provided some sort of stability for him — and wherever he'd been for dinner or with whom, he still felt the need to check in. Bogie said some time later, 'You don't think he comes to see *me*, do you?' Bogie was sure I was the attraction. But I was only one of them — Bogie sold himself short.

The night Judy's baby was born Frank

was going to the hospital to see her and asked me if I wanted to come along — Bogie was working the next day, so we went without him. Frank had brought some kind of stuffed toy for Judy. We saw her after she came out of the recovery room, still fuzzy from the anesthesia, having indeed mothered a son. We kissed her — Frank gave her the toy — it was a lovely moment, very sweet and thoughtful of Frank, and it meant a great deal to Judy. The Academy Awards would be given while she was still in the hospital. The TV networks had sent crews to wire the room, get cameras in — men were hanging outside her windows placing cables, lights, God knows what. The big night came and we were all gathered around our sets praying — and Judy lost. She carried it off beautifully, saying her son, Joey, was more important than any Oscar could be, but she was deeply disappointed — and hurt. It confirmed her belief that the industry was against her. She knew it was then or never. Instinctively, all her friends knew the same. Judy wasn't like any other performer. There was so much emotion involved in her career — in her life — it was always all or nothing. And though she put on a hell of a front, this was one more slap in the face. She was bitter about it, and, for that matter, all closest to her were.

That year I was in *Blood Alley* with John Wayne — to my surprise warm, likable, and helpful — and William Wellman's salty and terrific directing.

And then Bogie and I were offered a live telecast of *The Petrified Forest* for Producer's Showcase — a two-hour special, with Fred Coe producing and directing, Tad Mosel adapting Robert Sherwood's play. Henry Fonda was to play Leslie Howard's role, Bogie his original one of Mantee, and I the girl. It was a simple, romantic, ingenue role, unlike anything I'd ever done, and all *live*. God — like a play! We said yes. I was totally terrified through the entire three weeks of rehearsal. I recall David Selznick telling me I was crazy to do a live show — 'If you make a mistake, you make it in front of three million people.' But I had long since decided I had to take chances with my career. I remembered Bogie telling Judy, when she'd sit in the living room saying she had more goddamn talent than anyone in town, 'Talent's no good in a living room, you've got to get out there and do it.' I knew I had to take risks; if I fell on my ass, I fell on my ass. And certainly no one in the film industry would let me try anything new. So we did it. I'd never spent time with Fonda before — he was a rather withdrawn man then, ill at ease. But great to work with —

professional, generous — the start of my admiration for and devotion to him. Scared as I was, it was wonderful working with pros like Hank and Bogie, even wonderful working in this new medium of television, which seemed to have a corner on the worst features of movies and theatre combined.

When we were finally ready to go on the air and I heard the countdown — 10 9 8 7 6 5 4 3 2 1 — my heart was pounding so hard I was sure it would be picked up by the mike. But I seemed to sail through with flying colors, my friends were surprised and pleased, and, most important, Sherwood liked me. I had a tremendous sense of accomplishment, which was my first clue as to how much I would enjoy acting onstage now. After the show we gave a party at our house. Everybody was so relieved, they got drunk. We had a rug with a pattern of large squares, and at one point in the evening I looked down and saw Hank curled up peacefully inside one. He looked so comfortable that I decided to join him, which I did on an adjacent square. The last thing I remember was being carried upstairs, and Bogie being absolutely furious with me for passing out.

The Desperate Hours was going to be filmed by Willie Wyler. Bogie wanted to play the gunman — the first Mantee character to come along in years. To have Bogie and Spence in the same picture was everyone's dream. But one day Bogie told me there was a billing problem with Spence — naturally, they had both had top billing for many years. Bogie said, 'I don't give a damn. Let them work it out.' The result was an X (the agents were having fun with it), and the way they'd drawn it, it looked like Spencer Bogart and Humphrey Tracy. So it never worked out, which saddened Bogie. If it had been left to them the result might have been different. How I would have loved to see them work together! Fredric March played the part, a marvelous actor, and Bogie enjoyed working with him. But Bogie and Spence, all the feelings they had for one another, plus their talent — that would have been extraordinary to see and to record on film.

David and Hjordis Niven, Mike and Gloria Romanoff, Swifty, Frank, Judy and Sid, Bogie and I formed a group known as the Rat Pack. In order to qualify, one had to be addicted to nonconformity, staying up late, drinking, laughing, and not caring what anyone thought or said about us. Spence was only an honorary rat, because he lived a secluded life, but his heart was in the right place. We held a dinner in a private room at Romanoff's to elect officials and draw up rules — Bogie's way of thumbing his nose at Hollywood. I was voted Den Mother, Bogie was in charge of public relations. No one could join without unanimous approval of the charter members. Nat Benchley, a visiting rat from New York, drew up an insignia for us — a large group of rats of all shapes and sizes in all positions. What fun we had with it all! We were an odd assortment, but we liked each other so much, and every one of us had a wild sense of the ridiculous. The press had a field day, but we had the upper hand.

Noel Coward was going to appear in Las Vegas for the first time at a nightclub in The Sands Hotel. The Sands was where Frank always played; he had an interest in it. Frank liked to fly his friends into Vegas, not a place most of us Rat Packers frequented. He really enjoyed being head man, arranging everything in his territory. Looking forward to Noel, we all flew up to Vegas and were met by hotel representatives; luggage was whisked off to appropriate suites filled with booze. Then drinks, dinner, all arranged by Frank, with a hundred dollars' worth of chips for each lady. And a front table for the opening, stocked with the usual Jack Daniel's (which I'd started drinking a few years before and Frank had switched to), Scotch, vodka, etc. Frank forgot nothing.

I shall never forget watching Noel Coward walk onto that stage. He was holding a mike and — I couldn't believe it — he was shaking with nerves. After all his years and years of experience and accomplishment, he was still nervous. He'd been apprehensive about appearing in Las Vegas — would they understand his material? Would they care? He needn't have worried — he had a huge triumph. We were there for two more days, saw Noel's show nightly, met at Frank's suite each noon for drinks and laughter. Funny, but Frank, who was known to have several girls around, didn't have one with him that time. As a matter of fact, he seldom brought a broad (his word) when he met with us. We all flew to Frank's house in Palm Springs for the weekend, and Noel came down for his day off, courtesy of Frank. Noel played and sang his songs, Frank sang, they were both in top form — imagine what that song fest would have been worth recorded! Frank took us over in Palm Springs as he had in Vegas. No one was ever bothered with a bill for a hotel, for a meal — that was Frank's way. It made him feel good; it was his way of entertaining us — in his home as he had been in ours. And he had company — he wasn't alone.

Then back to reality. Bogie enjoyed that convivial, crazy, party-holiday atmosphere for a while, but he wasn't one to pass his time aimlessly for very long. We were all good friends, but the Vegas-Palm Springs life was Frank's life, not ours.

When Noel closed in Las Vegas, we gave our first pool party in his honor. All the Hollywood people he cared about were there. I, the nervous hostess who was always demented about everything being exactly right, decided that Noel had had enough grand dinners. Ours would be very American, very California, so we had a barbecue going at one end of the pool, with hamburgers and hot dogs and salads, and Good Humors of every variety for dessert. Noel loved it. It was a happy night. 1955 was full of happy nights and days.

We took Steve out on the boat with us one weekend and I was so terrified he'd fall overboard, we agreed that next time Bogie would take him alone on a men's weekend, leaving the anxious mother home with her daughter. Bogie was amazing with Leslie. I used to love watching them together. He didn't know quite what to do with her — he would gaze at her with wonder in his eyes. She was delicate, she was a girl, so he would be delicate with her. He was a gentle man, not overly demonstrative, yet when he looked at his daughter you could see him melt. He became totally vulnerable.

Bogie finally did take Steve out on the boat. When he returned, he told me that when they got to Catalina, they went out in the dinghy to set their lobster trap, then back to shore so Steve could play on the rocky beach for a while. Steve wanted to go on playing, so Bogie said he'd come back for him and rowed off. A few minutes later Steve called out, 'Daddy, wait for me,' and started to swim to the boat. He was only six and a half years old, but, by God, he made it. Bogie was so impressed. 'The little guy's got spirit,' he said. They became very close in those few days together. That was the test period, and Bogie intended to teach Steve to sail and take him with him often. Steve loved it, did what he was told to do on board, and felt very grown-up being with his father.

Mother and Lee were about that summer. Lee always went on the boat with Bogie; Mother stayed home with me and the children. She adored those children. It was good to see her so happy. Her marriage could not have been better — Lee was a good, kind man who took care of her, and she was mad about him; they took trips together, laughed together. Mother had a wry wit that I hope I inherited. Bogie's sister Pat also got along wonderfully with Mother and Lee. She was with us a lot when she was out of the hospital, and she was out for longer and longer periods of time. We were a family, and it seemed that the quality of life had improved for all of us, that nothing could blight that condition.

Bogie and I went to New York in time for the Rocky Marciano championship bout in September. I always looked forward to a trip to New York, but that year we'd moved around a lot and I really missed being in our new house. I'd got the garden just the way I wanted it, the pool and the poolhouse made it perfect, and with the tennis court we really had everything there. There was no reason to leave. But Bogie had contracted to do *The Harder They Fall,* a fight picture, and because he was playing a reporter the studio had gotten him ringside seats. He sat with the press. One of the reporters there, an old friend of Frank's, said — with affection, mind you — 'Frank's a last-rites pal. If you get hit by a truck, he's right there with an ambulance, everything, but how often do you get hit by a truck?'

I'd been offered a part in a movie called *Written on the Wind* — a lot of money for three weeks' work. It was a soap opera with Rock Hudson, a hot new star. My career had not been flourishing, yet again, and when I told Bogie about it, he thought I should do it if the set-up seemed right. It had a big budget, a good cast. I'd never done anything quite like it before — a really straight leading lady, no jokes, so I said yes. But I was able to go to Chicago with Bogie for a few days' location shooting as my picture wouldn't need me until November. And one afternoon I had tea with Adlai. I was still somewhat in awe of him, although we had strengthened our relationship through the written word. I was brave on paper, setting down whatever seemed important to me. Face to face, I was less outspoken. He took it all in good humor.

Poor Bogie was under the weather in Chicago. He'd always been a cougher. From the first day of shooting *To Have and Have Not*, between 'rolling' and 'action,' I'd heard him cough. Often sitting in a theatre he would cough when there was silence on the stage or an actor was speaking quietly. It was sometimes irritating. At times he'd cough in a way I've never seen before or since — in a series, unable to catch his breath. His explanation was that he'd always had a sensitive throat. In Chicago he saw a doctor for a vitamin shot — he couldn't miss a day of work, after all. He got through the location work and was soon back to his old self after we returned home. He continued his filming there while I began mine.

Noel had sent me a cable asking if I'd play Elvira, the ghost in *Blithe Spirit*, on television with him. I was terrified, but of course said yes. To work with Noel Coward was an opportunity not to be missed. As television was still fairly new and I was so scared, I wouldn't have dreamed of starting rehearsals without knowing my lines. Anyway, Noel insisted on it. It wasn't easy to learn them while shooting *Written on the Wind*, but I did my best. Claudette Colbert was to play the second wife, Ruth, and Mildred Natwick was to recreate her original Broadway role of Madame Arcati. Noel was directing as well as acting. He'd had some trouble with his leg, but was going to be full of shots so it would be okay.

Noel arrived in California early in December, and we began our three weeks of rehearsal. On the first day, all but Claudette knew their lines. She and Noel were old friends — she's a terrific lady and a good actress — but she liked to work with script in hand. That did not suit the Master at all, he had specifically requested that we be word perfect, so an edginess began between them. They were both right, but when working with Noel you did it his way. The edginess grew. He said, 'Look at Betty — she's been filming, yet knows her part perfectly.' That only made me want to kill myself. One day during rehearsal he lost his temper — Claudette still had the script in hand — and said, 'That's the wrong line.' Claudette said, 'You've got me so nervous I'm saying the lines backward.' Noel: 'And that's exactly how you're playing the part.' She'd had her clothes made by Balmain, as she always had — and insisted on being photographed only on the left side of her face. Noel thought both sides were the same — she'd made a successful career thinking otherwise — and he had no intention of turning the sets around — oh, it was a wonderful three weeks. I tried to pacify Claudette, who was really and rightly very upset and nervous; I had no argument with her — everyone was nervous about live television anyway. Then Noel decided we had to have an audience in the studio and he would invite them. That meant Hedda, Louella, and every big star you could think of would be there. Panic. I said, 'Of course. I'll die, but of course.' Noel ran a tight ship.

So *Blithe Spirit* was performed 'live' in front of a name audience of about one hundred people, and — thank God — it went off without a hitch. Relations between Noel and Claudette were still strained, but the performance was a success. Our dressing rooms were swarming with people afterward — Quent Reynolds was in town and came with Bogie, Judy, Merle Oberon, Clifton Webb, Liz Taylor. I felt very good about this show — was mad about my gray ghost make-up, enjoyed doing it, was less nervous than in *Petrified Forest*, though still nervous enough for four. Bogie was proud of me. He said, 'You must look at your print of it. [Part of my deal was to get a print.] You used every moment — stayed "alive" even when you weren't speaking.' In other words, I had stayed in the part throughout — continued to think, though silent. To have Bogie so positively approving was an event. He only said what he meant — he never lied to me. He had told me years before that as a young actor he'd been in David Belasco's office one day when a playwright was coming in to see the famous producer-director. Mr Belasco sighed and said to Bogie, 'It's a terrible play he's written.' But when the playwright came in, Belasco praised him — told him he'd liked the play, but that he had too many productions scheduled to think of putting it on for some time. Later Bogie asked Belasco why he had lied. 'When you know someone can do much better, then you criticize and make him go back and write and rewrite. But when you know it's the best he can do, then you praise him.' That attitude had nothing to

500

do with Bogie's comments on *Blithe Spirit*; he had been all too critical on other occasions!

Clifton gave a large party for Noel before the TV show and told me that Hedda was going to be there. I'd had nothing to do with her since she'd printed some lousy remarks about me, as well as trying to keep John Wayne and Bill Wellman from hiring me for *Blood Alley*. Clifton had decided it was time we made up. I'd been drinking martinis — don't ask me why. Clifton put one arm around Hedda and the other around me. 'Come on, you two, make up — this is ridiculous.' He hated people he liked not to like each other. I fumed at Hedda, told her she'd been a bitch to try to keep me from working. She said, 'You're right, I was. Why don't you give me a kick?' Whereupon she turned around and I kicked her in the ass — most unladylike, but very martini-like — whereupon everyone laughed loudly and a truce was declared.

We all went to Frank's in Palm Springs for New Year's — a lovely way to start the year, with close friends who loved one another. Noel went back to town on Sunday for some reason I don't remember. The Romanoffs were staying till the next day — the Nivs and us were going back. That night as dinner came to a close, Frank, looking sad, begged us to stay on. Not begging in the true sense, but begging in Frank's sense — looking very forlorn and alone. I thought, 'Oh, the poor guy, we should stay.' I looked at Bogie and he said, 'Sorry, old pal, we've got to get back to town.' In the car going home, I said, 'We should have stayed.' Bogie said, 'No, we shouldn't. You must always remember we have a life of our own that has nothing to do with Frank. He chose to live the way he's living — alone. It's too bad if he's lonely, but that's his choice. We have our own road to travel, never forget that — we can't live his life.' As always, Bogie was dead right. He stood behind his choices, and, persuasive as Frank could be, he could never make Bogie forget who he was. That intractable sense of self was Bogie's greatest strength and certainly one of his greatest attractions for his men friends — to say nothing of his women, to say nothing of future generations.

1956 was to be the year that Bogie and I were to make our first film together since *Key Largo* eight years before. Warner Bros. had bought John P. Marquand's novel *Melville Goodwin, U.S.A.*, a love story about a military man and a Clare Boothe Luce–type woman. We were both looking forward to it. We'd been married ten and a half years by then. Life seemed very good indeed.

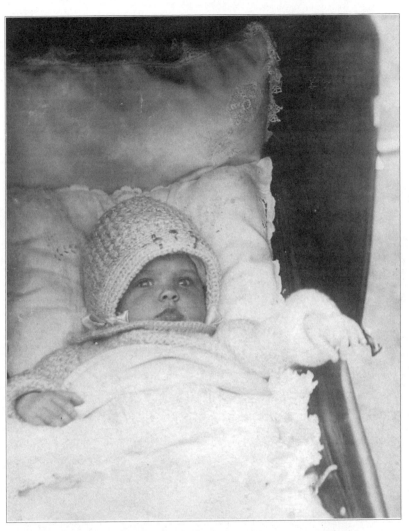

Infant me in baby carriage, 1925

Alone

Alone at
Highland
Nature Camp,
Lake Sebago,
Maine

Nine- or ten-year-old me
at Highland Manor School

With my mother
at camp

At camp
(middle of front row — of course), 1937

At the Night of Stars
with Burgess Meredith, 1941

Hostess at the Stage Door Canteen.
John Carradine is at the mike, 1942

With Uncle Charlie

Mother and Lee

The Family, 1943: Vera, Jack, Renee, Bill,
Grandmother, Charlie, Rosalie, Mother

Being pulled and
tucked by Diana
Vreeland, 1943

Modeling photo in
Harper's Bazaar, 1943

The famous
cover of
*Harper's
Bazaar*,
March 1943

Lauren Bacall, 1943 [Cover of Harper's Bazaar, March, 1943]. Photograph by Louise Dahl-Wolfe © 1989 Center for Creative Photography, Arizona Board of Regents. Collection Center for Creative Photography, The University of Arizona

My screen test for *Claudia*, 1943

Experiments with hairstyles for
To Have and Have Not tests, 1944

'The Look' — shot by John Engstead at Howard Hawks's home, 1944

'The Look' — great red dress, 1944

Opening
scene in
*To Have and
Have Not*,
1944

A
publicity
still from
*To Have
and Have
Not*, 1944

With my
first dog,
Droopy,
1945

On Harry Truman's piano, National Press
Club, Washington, D.C., 1945

The Big Sleep — on the set with Bogie, John Ridgely and Howard Hawks, 1945

With Bogie on the lot during *The Big Sleep*, 1945

514

Our wedding: Louis
Bromfield, Bogie, Mary
Bromfield, Mother, me,
George Hawkins and
Judge Shettler,
21 May, 1945

Sailing on Bogie's
beloved *Santana*,
1947

On location for *The African Queen*
with Katie and Bogie, 1951

With Adlai
Stevenson,
1952

The New York premier of
How to Marry a Millionaire, 1953

At lunch for the Oliviers: Laurence Olivier,
Clifton Webb, Dick Sale, Vivien Leigh, Joan
Bennett, Charlie Feldman behind Bogie and
me, Mary Anita Sale next to Charlie, Najda
Gardiner leaning on me, and Reggie Gardiner
sitting next to Maybelle Webb, 1953

The family visiting Bogie on the set of
The Desperate Hours, 1955

Bogie
with
Leslie,
1955

With Steve on *Blood Alley* location, 1955

With Leslie in a dancing mood, 1958

Our Christmas card the year Bogie died, 1957

Vogue magazine
by Louise
Dahl-Wolfe,
1957

With
Frank
Sinatra,
1957

With Slim Hayward and Ernest Hemingway
in Spain, 1959

With Jason before our wedding, 1961

And then with Sam on the set of Jason's film
A Thousand Clowns, 1965

With Leslie,
Malibu, 1965

With Robert and Ethel Kennedy
backstage at *Cactus Flower*, 1967

With Yves St. Laurent on my 1968 television special — the start of a valued friendship

Applause — 1970

My second *Life* cover, 1970

Receiving my first Tony — for *Applause* — from Walter Matthau, 1970

Katharine's gift to me on winning my first Tony Award, 1970

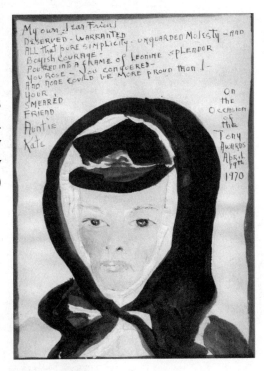

My own dear Friend
DESERVED - WARRANTED - UNGUARDED MOLESTY - AND
ALL that PURE SIMPLICITY - BOYISH COURAGE -
POURED INTO A FRAME OF LEONINE SPLENDOR
YOU ROSE - YOU CONQUERED -
AND NONE COULD BE MORE PROUD THAN I -
YOUR,
SMEARED
FRIEND
Auntie
Kate

On
the
Occasion
of
the
Tony
Awards
April
1970

Murder on the Orient Express, 1974

With Sam, Jardin de la Climitation,
Paris, 1974

With darling Peter Stone — first day of
rehearsal for *Woman of the Year*, 1981

At Roddy's house with Leslie and Sam

With Phyllis Newman and Adolph Green
celebrating my birthday in Paris, 1989

With John Gielgud at my
house in the Hamptons

With George and Joan
Axelrod having a jolly time.
Photo by Roddy McDowall

Me with
George Axelrod

At Veronique and Gregory Peck's home after receiving the Cecil B. DeMille Award for Outstanding Achievement in Motion Pictures at the Golden Globes, 1993

With Gregory Peck in *The Portrait* for TNT, 1993

With Alec Guinness in *A Foreign Field* for the BBC, 1993

Receiving the Commandeur des Arts et Lettres with Dustin Hoffman receiving Officier, 1995

Winning the great César presented by Alain Delon in Paris, 1996

With Barbra Streisand and Jeff Bridges, 1997

Me leaving
my Paris
hotel, the St
Simon, with
M. Gil, my
driver, 1997

With Sam and Sidsel Robards,
1997

In my hotel suite on the night of the State Dinner with Steve, Sam and Leslie, 1997

Bill and Hillary Clinton and my family — Barbara Bogart, Erich Schiffman (son-in-law), Stephen Bogart, Leslie Bogart, Sam Robards and Sidsel Robards. Kennedy Center Honors, 1997

Kennedy Center Honors — with Charlton Heston, Edward Villella, Bob Dylan, President Clinton and Jessye Norman, 1997

Kirk Douglas crushing me at the Deauville Film Festival — *Diamonds*, 1999

With Alexander Cohen on the opening night of *Waiting in the Wings*, December 1999

With Lars Von Trier on the *Dogville* set, 2002

With my son
Steve at the
Birth premiere,
2004

Nicole Kidman
et moi at the
New York premiere
of *Birth*, 2004

Bogie came home one day and told me he'd run into Greer Garson at lunch. Greer had said she didn't like his cough and that he must go to see Dr Maynard Brandsma, her doctor, an internist at the Beverly Hills Clinic. She'd actually dragged him there for an examination. I was so used to Bogie's cough that I hadn't been aware of any change. He'd been off his food a little, but that wasn't unusual — he said that sometimes his throat burned when he drank orange juice. Not enough to do anything about it. I should have realized at once that the mere fact that he'd consented to go with Greer to a doctor was indicative of something serious. But any time I ever mentioned a doctor to him, Bogie bristled, so he wouldn't have listened to me in any case. The doctor found his esophagus a bit inflamed and wanted him to come in for a sputum test in a few days. Bogie had his sputum test and Dr Brandsma said he'd call in a few days with the results. The whole medical scene was foreign territory to both Bogie and myself, so we didn't pay too much attention.

The Desperate Hours opened and we went to the big premiere, which also honored Willie Wyler. Bogie had loved working with Willie again — Willie always made you try harder, go beyond yourself. His and

Huston's methods were different, but they both stretched real actors.

And we were having great fun shooting our wardrobe tests together for our new picture — mine was to be very chic, mostly designed by Norman Norell. I couldn't believe Bogie and I would be working together again after so much time. The crew were all familiar to us — Warners was another home in a sense, we knew it so well. Our sense of play, of bouncing off each other, was so great that the test was almost like playing a scene — we were Slim and Steve all over again. The picture would begin at the end of February, and then in the spring Bogie was going to make *The Good Shepherd* at Columbia for his own company. It was a sea story by C. S. Forester and Bogie was excited about it.

The doctor called Bogie in for another test — a bronchoscopy. The sputum test had produced some irregularities, and the bronchoscope would reach down into the esophagus and take a sample of tissue. After that, Dr Brandsma suggested we go down to Palm Springs for a week of rest and see how Bogie's throat felt. It still didn't seem ominous to us — like an infection of some kind. Yet Bogie's appetite had definitely decreased. It bothered him to swallow. He was so thin to begin with — 155 pounds soaking wet, as he said — that he could ill afford not to eat. Frank generously offered us his house, so down to the Springs we went. After the week was up, Brandsma wanted to make another sputum test but we were still not too worried. I just knew that Bogie wasn't up to snuff and was disturbed by his inability to swallow much solid food.

At the end of the week Bogie was still unable to eat. During the best of times he was easily put off by food, but with swallowing problems he really had an excuse. He had probably lost a few pounds already.

We returned to town and Bogie immediately went to Brandsma for the sputum test. Again there were some irregularities, and Brandsma would be able to make a definite diagnosis with the results of this test. Two days later he called and said the movie would have to be postponed — Bogie needed surgery — would we both come to his office in the morning? It still did not seem threatening, I don't know why — ignorance of medicine, I suppose. The following morning Dr Brandsma explained that the first sputum test had shown some irregular cells which had made him suspicious; the biopsy had borne out his suspicions by showing malignant cells in the tissue; and less than two weeks later the second sputum test had shown more than twice as many unhealthy cells as the first. There was no question that an operation was called for. Bogie asked if it couldn't be postponed until after the movie was completed — we were to start in a week or so. 'Not unless you want a lot of flowers at Forest Lawn,' said Dr Brandsma. 'We were very lucky to catch it so early — it's not often that we can in that area.' It could not wait. He knew the best possible surgeon — Dr John Jones, who had developed the blue-baby operation as well as the J, so named because the incision for the removal of one rib is in that shape.

I was stunned as I listened to the doctor, but I was totally uninformed about cancer, and my ignorance kept me fairly calm. Bogie was not pleased about postponing the picture — 'It'll cost the studio too much.' Brandsma said again, 'If you don't have the operation, they can all go to your funeral.' It was undramatic, rather matter-of-fact, though not cold, but Brandsma realized after even such short exposure to Bogie that he was not to lie to him.

All I understood was that Bogie needed an operation — nothing else. Dr Brandsma and Dr Michael Flynn, a throat specialist also at the Beverly Hills Clinic, had gone over everything together. They would talk to John Jones, and Bogie and I would have to meet him. We had no choice — the operation would take place as soon as possible. We went home dazed, but neither of us panicked. As always, Bogie's attitude was: what has to be done has to be done — no need for dramatics. I took my cue from him.

The next afternoon the doctors came to see Bogie. John Jones was one of those rare doctors who communicate instantly their compassion, dedication, and mastery of their craft. Both of us liked him immediately — he inspired utter trust. He told us rather simply what the operation would be, said that we were indeed lucky the malignancy had been detected early. He would arrange for Bogie to enter the Good Samaritan Hospital the following Wednesday and surgery would be performed the following day. We explained to Steve and Leslie as best we could that Daddy had to have something removed from his throat — it wasn't serious, but he'd be away for a couple of weeks. Steve naturally didn't understand. Leslie, being three and a half, certainly didn't. How could they when even we didn't?

Our pals had to be told. We were going to Frank's for the weekend, and the Rat Pack — the Nivs, Romanoffs, and Swifty — gathered with us that weekend. Everyone was in top form — Bogie joking about his surgery, he and Swifty ribbing each other (mind you, Swifty was terrified of illness). That weekend no one did anything but make Bogie laugh, trade funny remarks with him, and generally behave normally as only great friends know how to do. Later I was to know how horrified they all were at the thought of his illness. His not being in perfect shape had never occurred to anyone who knew him.

We returned home Sunday night — Bogie had business to clear up with Morgan Maree. There was so much to do I had no time for emotions. I wasn't really afraid — I didn't realize what there might be to be afraid of. Bogie was sweet and loving as always — perhaps a little quieter. As I think of it now, he seemed a little remote, as though surrounded by cellophane, a material not very strong but strong enough to protect him. Wednesday, early in the afternoon, the limousine came to pick us up. Bogie kissed and hugged the children and Harvey. The night before we'd all stayed very close together — not a prelude to tragedy, just close and good. It was the twenty-ninth day of February 1956. As we headed toward the hospital, Bogie very shyly and quietly took my hand and said, 'Funny, I've never spent much time with doctors. Now I'll probably spend the rest of my life with them.' A small smile. I smiled back at him and said, 'No, you won't — they wouldn't dare.' We had to keep our humor — that was the essence of us as individuals and as a pair.

Bogie's room was good-sized, but a hospital room is a hospital room — no way to make it look like anything else. We also had a small adjoining room for me when I wanted to stay overnight, for the phone, etc. Not knowing what was really going to happen, plans were out of the question.

I remember they had to shave Bogie's chest to prepare him for surgery. We ate almost nothing. Who could have an appetite? Dr Jones came by to tell Bogie not to worry and to make clear what to expect. He and Dr Brandsma had decided he would have to remove his esophagus and shift the stomach around so they could attach it to the tab that was left. They would go in through the chest, necessitating the J operation and removal of a rib. Also cut the vega nerve, which controlled digestion, so that when he was able to eat again he would notice that food dumped quickly into his stomach; until he got used to it, it might make him feel a bit nauseated. With all the explanation, all the care, it was still just words. Words I had never heard before — wished I wasn't hearing then. Impossible to comprehend such things until they have taken place. Both doctors were calm and reassuring and kept telling us how lucky we were to have caught the cancer so early in that not easily detectable spot. What they did not tell me until much later is that this was one of the worst possible places to have cancer, because it moves so quickly to the nearby lymph nodes, and after that they have no way of knowing where it may travel.

Surgery was to take place at seven the following morning. Bogie and I were left alone. We were both quiet — there was not much to say, really, but again there were no dramatics, no Bogie saying, 'If anything should go wrong,' no instructions. That there was no choice we knew, but didn't suspect it was the beginning of the end. All I knew was that for the next three weeks the center of my life would be in this drab, impersonal room. I sat on the bed — Bogie was on, not in, it — I took his hand. It was awkward, almost. He must have been frightened. There was no discussion of the seriousness of it — he felt he'd have a few bad days and then be okay. I told him I'd be with him, not to worry about anything. As if that were possible. After a while he said, 'Well, I guess I better get some sleep, take these pills the nurse left.' 'Right, darling. I'll go home, see the children, and I'll be here before you go to surgery.'

We kissed good night. 'See you in the morning. If you need anything — if you forgot anything — I'll bring it tomorrow.' 'Night, Baby.' 'Night, Baby.' And home I went. So strange leaving him behind in the hospital. But I had to see my babies, that would make me feel better. When I got home I went in to Steve and told him not to worry — 'Daddy is fine. I'll call you from the hospital tomorrow' — and we hugged each other tightly. I tiptoed into Leslie's room, kissed her. She was peacefully asleep in her hand-me-down crib. I went downstairs to the kitchen — told Jay I'd be rising at six to get to the hospital, that Mr Bogart was fine. So on March 1 I got up at dawn, had a last cup of coffee, and headed downtown. The press had been told that Bogie was entering the hospital because of a swelling in his esophagus of an inflammatory nature — nothing about cancer, very played down. I'd spoken with Mother, Nunnally, the Nivs, Spence, Jaffe, Swifty, Maree, said they could reach me at the hospital late in the day. I'd told Mother I would call her — she was very worried.

I was used to that hour of the morning when the city was quiet, but it was quieter than ever that morning, and I felt very alone. I reached Bogie's room as they were preparing to take him in to surgery. In a hospital gown, tightly tucked into the sheets, nurses everywhere — it all became very real and frightening. I hated to see him there. The last pill had left him very groggy, but he knew me — smiled. I smiled back, leaned over and kissed him. I walked down the corridor with him as far as they would let me go and then went back to his room to wait. I don't remember how I got through that day — hundreds of cups of coffee, hundreds of cigarettes. Called home and spoke to Steve and Leslie, called Mother later in the morning. Dr Brandsma was the first one — obviously, as he wasn't the surgeon — to come in and see me. He said that all was going well, that Bogie would be on the table a few hours more. Wasn't there something I had to do, somewhere I had to go? Only here, I said. The phone kept ringing. How many times I said the same things over and over — but better than having no one to say anything to. With each passing hour I became more and more aware of the value of our friends.

Dr Flynn came in. The operation was going very well. He had watched Dr Jones perform the J. The esophagus had been removed, two lymph nodes had been removed, tissue samples were going to pathology. They would have to open the abdomen to get at the stomach — two operations at once. God! First they said he'd be down at one — then they said at two.

Why was it taking so long? Finally, at about five or five-thirty Dr Jones came down in his green surgical gown. Bogie was in the recovery room. All had gone well — he'd be down in about an hour. Dr Jones had been on his feet since seven that morning; Bogie had been on the table for nine and a half hours. How could a body take that much? I was told they had removed the malignancy, and that I should try to get some rest, I'd need my strength when Bogie was recuperating. They'd give me a very mild sleeping pill, the mildest there was, as I was unused to them. But I wouldn't sleep or even go out for something to eat — not until I saw Bogie safely in his room. Of course I had planned to spend the night in the adjoining room — the next few nights. More phone calls — Mother, Huston from somewhere in Europe, Swifty, Niven, Spence, Frank, the Jaffes, Nunnally, the Gershwins. What could they do? Did I want to come over — to have dinner — anything, anytime — no notice — we'll be here. Everyone sweet, thoughtful, understanding. I called home to tell Steve that all was well, but I'd be staying with Daddy tonight.

The room was dark — it was dark outside. I'd been sitting in the adjoining room with one light on. Corridors quiet, but with all the whispering and tiptoeing that goes on in hospitals. Suddenly the sound of wheels — the door opening — nurses — bottles hanging from everywhere, tubes — Bogie with that terrible black thing in his mouth to keep him from swallowing his tongue — lying on his side — his left arm and hand, hanging through the raised side of the bed, swollen to four times their normal size. My God, I was so frightened. He looked so unlike Bogie — still mercifully unconscious. Why so swollen? Because he'd been in that position for so many hours, it would be back to normal in a day or two. At least he was there — I could see him — he was breathing. Bogie had come through — his body had undergone a great deal in those nine and a half hours, but his heart was strong.

'Go out for a bowl of soup or something,' said the doctors, 'he won't come to for hours.' 'But I have to be here when he does.' 'Don't worry, you will be, you're safe for a long while.' So I went out with Morgan.

But I couldn't stay away for long — too frightened that he'd wake up and not find me there. I was out of focus anyway — tense, exhausted, afraid to see him again looking like that, yet having to be with him. Why hadn't anyone prepared me for that sight? They were used to it, it was part of their business. I went back, crept down the dimly lit corridor. The nurse said he was still asleep. I tiptoed in and really looked at him again. Poor baby — all those tubes, those bottles — what was the body under the blanket like? It would all be better in the daylight, wouldn't it? There was so much I didn't know. The night nurse told me to go to sleep — she'd call me when he woke up. It was only nine-thirty.

I didn't take the Seconal and I didn't really sleep — I wanted to be ready if I heard voices next door. Sometime during the night I heard something — shot out of bed, opened the connecting door — the nurse was at Bogie's side. He was still out. He'd come to for a moment and lapsed back into sleep. 'Is he all right?' She told me to try and relax — the next couple of days he'd be more asleep than awake, and if I dashed in every time I heard a sound, I'd fall apart. She knew exactly what to do, what to expect. I knew nothing. I was at her mercy — afraid to get too close, afraid to touch Bogie for fear I'd do something wrong. Standing in that darkened room, looking at my husband in that bed. He was enclosed in another world, protected not by me, but by those raised bedsides, with those bottles and tubes sustaining life, the nurse (two that first night) trying to make him comfortable, checking his pulse, blood pressure, God knows what — writing things down on his chart hanging at the foot of the bed . . .

Sometime during the next two days the routine began to alter. The shades were raised — Bogie was awake — we held each other's hands — he was rolled to an almost sitting position. Dr Jones came in to check on him two, three, four times daily — Brandsma and Flynn twice at least — interns — more nurses bringing whatever they had to bring. The second morning the suction machine was rolled in, its purpose to clear the lungs of mucus so pneumonia wouldn't set in. When it came in I went out. Bogie hated that machine. The second time he used it I heard him pleading, 'Please — no more.' For him to say those words it must have been horribly painful. He had a high threshold of pain, wasn't one to complain. I went into his room and asked the nurse to stop. Why did he have to go through that — hadn't he been through enough? She was tough — said, 'He's lucky to have this machine. Before it existed, patients used to die after surgery. This is saving him from lung congestion, pneumonia — he has to have it.' She was a good nurse, I suppose. But not simpatico.

Sometime during that period I got home, saw my children, changed my clothes, brought a nightgown and robe to the hospital. I don't know what I did then. I was on the telephone constantly, it seems — friends from all over calling. Mike Romanoff and Dave Chasen offering to send food in so we could avoid the hospital fare. Flowers, fruit, letters pouring into the hospital. I would show them and read them to Bogie. He was stunned that so many people in our business cared, even people he hardly knew — Fred Astaire, Duke Wayne. He couldn't get over it, that so many took the trouble to write, call.

Finally the suction machine disappeared for good. Bogie was feeling much better, looking much better, though still bandaged heavily and being checked regularly. Hand and arm did return to normal. His cough had not disappeared, though it had diminished. One evening I was sitting with him — it was early, about a week after surgery, his wounds had been healing well — and he started to cough. As I got up to ask him if he wanted some water, I suddenly saw blood coming through his abdominal bandage. Absolutely terrified, I put my hands on the bandage, trying to hold everything together — and keep calm, not let Bogie see how panicked I felt. Thank God, at that moment an intern walked in and saw me there — I must have had a ghastly expression on my face, something shouting *Help!* The nurse called over the speaker —

I heard the word 'STAT,' which means on the double — emergency. Bogie was taken upstairs immediately. John Jones was luckily present. Bogie had coughed his stitches loose — his abdominal incision was healing on the outside better than on the inside, and a couple of the well-known racking Bogart coughs were all it took to open him up again. I was utterly destroyed. I'd done the right thing through luck — I don't know how, I've never been any good at the sight of blood — it just happened that way.

Bogie was quickly in and out of surgery for the repair job and there were no more dramas like that.

I was constantly bending the doctors' ears, asking endless questions: 'How long before he really feels well? Did you really get it all? When will he be able to work?' On and on. The pathology report had shown a malignancy in one of the lymph nodes that had been removed, and the consensus was that X-ray treatments would be necessary. Not as soon as he returned home, but within a few weeks. It was a preventive measure; they had got all there was, but this was added insurance. They wouldn't say anything to Bogie just yet. They had grown fond of him and they admired him. He did everything he was told — never complained. He had books to read, an occasional visitor. He wanted to get well — he wanted to go to work. He'd lost weight after surgery, but he would put it on again after he got home.

Our friends were marvelous. I will never forget how Swifty Lazar, who was profoundly frightened of illness and hospitals, insisted on coming to pick me up one evening after Bogie was asleep. It is as clear a picture as though it were happening now — I stepped out of Bogie's room into the dim corridor and as I quietly walked to the end of it, I could see Swifty standing hat in hand — green of complexion from apprehension — waiting there, looking even smaller than his five-feet-four. He had made the superhuman effort — done something he'd never done before and, in the name of friendship, had come through. The great lesson that you learn at such a time is whom you can count on and whom you can't. Who your friends really are. I remember all too well who didn't come through.

John Huston came to town and wanted to see Bogie. We arranged a surprise — Bogie would be in the john and I would get Huston, who was waiting outside. By this time Bogie was strong enough to deal with it. The nurse saw that Bogie stayed in the loo. I brought John in from the corridor. He got into Bogie's room and when

Bogie emerged, John was lying under the sheet in his bed. It was funny — John's machine-gun laugh, Bogie's understated one. Two really good old friends so glad to see one another. Later I walked John to the elevator and told him as much as I knew. He was in America for only a few days. 'Bogie's going to be all right, honey — he'll be fine, just fine — we'll make *The Man Who Would Be King* yet.'

Suddenly it was homecoming day. I was given my instructions by the doctors. They would visit regularly and a nurse would come during the day to do whatever Bogie needed done. He was on the road to recovery. He felt much better — he was eating carefully, small amounts (never hard for him) several times a day, experiencing the 'dumping' process as predicted, but the muscles would strengthen with use and eventually adjust. He'd have three weeks before starting X-ray.

Home was humming with activity and expectation. The children, so excited about Daddy's coming home, were briefed by me about no jumping all over him. Harvey would have to be kept at bay — May, Aurelio, Kathy, the butler were getting everything in order, looking forward to having us both back home. I was overcome with joy at the prospect of turning my back on Good Samaritan Hospital. That last day was a high point — Bogie so happy to be going home to normalcy — to get ready to work, to see his boat, be with his children — to be part of life again.

We had a gay dinner in his hospital room that night, catered by Chasen's, then I was going home to get everything ready. He would arrive by ambulance in the morning. We were both excited about the next day, such a simple thing to be so excited about — going home. I kissed him good night — 'See you in the morning and don't be too late.'

It was strange being in our bed again, knowing I could wake up to a leisurely breakfast — I had been living by the clock for weeks. I was keeping Steve home from school so he'd be there to greet Bogie. Up early. I paced, kept looking to see what time it was — he was due by eleven. Nervous as a cat, I kept checking the same things over and over — only Bogie's favorite foods were to be prepared for him, plus a food supplement tasting like malted milk. The bed was ready — the room looked beautiful — books, magazines, glasses within easy reach. There was the sound of a door slamming. I rushed to the bedroom windows — he was there. I called Steve and Leslie — Kathy and May were at the door — we waited upstairs and as he was being brought up the stairs he looked up and saw me with a child on either side. With that old emotional chewing gesture of his, he said, 'This is what it's all about — this is why marriage is worth it.' I smiled down at him, on the verge of tears, suddenly realizing that he was too — and realizing how much he'd been through, and how far away coming home must have seemed to him, and how good it was to have him back. Then he became the old Bogie again as the attendants helped him to bed. 'I've been trying to tell these guys how great it is to be married — that you can't beat having your wife and kids there to greet you, that there's nothing like it.' They'd been giving him an argument, all in good fun — but he was right. The only thing better than having your wife and kids waiting for you was to have your husband returned to you, where he belonged.

The next few weeks Bogie was stronger every day, coughing less, smoking filtered cigarettes for the first time — 'These are pretty good, aren't they?' — feeling well. The worst was behind him. Only food was a problem. He was eating some, but the dumping process was not helping his appetite. Yet he tried hard — food was the way to strength and gaining weight.

Flowers, books, booze, letters, phone

calls kept coming, and friends to visit with him. He wasn't ill, just recovering from surgery. His spirits were terrific — the Damoclean sword was the X-ray. It was explained that they'd removed the cancer, but in case something was floating around that shouldn't be, the X-ray would kill it. We had to do as advised — the doctors knew a lot more than we did. My encounter with the medical world filled me with wonder, admiration, frustration, and fury. The doctors were all good men, the best in their fields, but I always felt there were things they never mentioned. Those inscrutable expressions! There were no definite answers, they didn't *have* the answers, there was so much they just didn't know in the practice of medicine.

It would be an eight-week X-ray program on the million-volt machine — there was only one in the city. Five days a week. Bogie would feel a bit nauseated — the effect was cumulative — but after it was over he'd be fine. Even this program was accepted by us without panic. We believed what they told us. His color was coming back, he did feel quite well and cheery. And I reflected his attitudes completely — it was so good to have him home again, to see him in our own bed again, to have him next to me again. Steve and Leslie were in the room every afternoon and evening, watching television with us. Harvey was remarkable. He was in our room daily, of course, and knew — don't ask me how he knew — not to jump on the bed, on me or Bogie. He was so gentle and concerned. He would sit alongside the bed on Bogie's side and Bogie would pet him and talk to him. Then he would just lie in front of the fireplace so that he could clearly see who came in the door and watch Bogie.

On a Friday, three weeks after Bogie came home from the hospital, he and I drove down to that machine just to see it before the treatment was to begin. The technical expert was there to explain the workings of it. I was not allowed in the room with the machine — only to look through a square of glass in the wall. The room was bare. In the center was a long narrow metal slat and overhead, pointed toward it, a large round metal object that looked like something from outer space. It was eerie and frightening — the atmosphere so heavy. Bogie explained it all to me afterward. The machine aimed its beam at the tiniest point in Bogie's chest — wherever the medical team had felt would be the most vulnerable to cancer — while he lay on that slab, and for a very few moments one million volts of X-ray were concentrated into that area. The machine was frightening-looking; the procedure was frightening as well.

Louis Bromfield had been ill early in that year of horror — something to do with his stomach or liver. We'd spoken to him when he returned to Malabar from the hospital — strange that he and Bogie were having health problems at the same time. One afternoon just about at the time Bogie was to start his X-rays we were sitting at home when the phone rang. It was Ellen Bromfield — Louis had just died. He had been home, feeling better, and suddenly it happened — dead at sixty. When I hung up, I told Bogie. Bogie looked quietly straight ahead of him.

Bogie wanted to go to the boat for one day, as he knew he wouldn't be able to for the next eight weeks. He wanted to go because he loved it. The boat was his health, his safety, and we wanted to make sure that it was being cared for. So we drove down on Saturday for a few hours. We didn't take the boat out — he wasn't up to that — but it meant so much to him just to be there. It was strange seeing Bogie on the *Santana* but not springing around. Usually he was filled with joy from the moment he stepped aboard, trotting down the gangway, even singing. Not this day, however. The spring had been taken out of him.

Monday came, and Bogie left for his first

treatment. I did what I had to do at home, busying myself with an ordinary day, trying to get back into some semblance of the old routine. Walking around the garden with Aurelio, seeing how all my plants, flowers, vegetables were doing — what I needed or wanted to add or replace. Going over food with May. She knew Bogie had to eat — together we tried to figure out every small thing that would appeal to him.

The first week of X-ray wasn't too bad. Bogie did not react violently — he was far from enjoying the experience of coming face to face with that threatening machine, but he didn't feel very nauseated at first. After two weeks he began to feel lousy. Tired, of course — it was a debilitating procedure — and he began to feel more nauseated and lost his appetite totally. He was determined to come downstairs to dinner every night even though he didn't eat. We had trays before the fire. He could manage the liquids and some foods in small amounts. He'd suddenly ask for a boiled egg or creamed chipped beef; when it arrived, he'd eat a tiny portion. He wanted to eat, but when he saw the food he just couldn't. He still had a drink before dinner, or an occasional beer. May would tempt him with his favorite steak tartare. Anything and everything was tried. Some days he'd manage more than others. I kept asking the doctors how he would ever gain weight this way — how the hell could you eat when you wanted to throw up all the time?

I remember Bogie coming home from a treatment and heading slowly right for the stairs — not even attempting to come into our room downstairs. He just said, 'I think I'll go upstairs and lie down awhile, Baby — I'll come down later.' I didn't know quite what to do. I could only guess how he felt — Bogie wasn't one to dwell on such things. He forced himself to sit in that room with me every night. That was our place — before surgery. I tried not to ask him continually how he felt, but it was hard not to — there was so much I wanted to know. The doctors had told us what the X-ray would do, but that doesn't help you day to day. Bogie had to go through it physically, and I had to watch — neither of us really knew what was going to happen until it did. All we could do was deal with one day at a time until the eight weeks passed. A man's illness is his private territory and, no matter how much he loves you and how close you are, you stay an outsider. You are healthy.

Occasionally Bogie would make me go to dinner at a friend's house. Because he wasn't up to it, he said, was no reason why I should stay home all the time. Secretly he wanted me with him constantly, just to know that I was there, but realistically he felt I had to get out once in a while. So I did — once in a while, but not for long.

My career had come to a dead stop. No one offered me anything — I was caring for Bogie. Finally a film came along that I wanted to do. Dore Schary was producing, Vincente Minnelli directing, Greg Peck in it, and they wanted Grace Kelly. But she was in Europe preparing to become Princess Grace of Monaco. So I called Dore, told him I could play it, wanted to, and when I cut my salary in half, he finally said yes. It was *Designing Woman* — a lovely, funny script, a terrific part, and I was happy about working. Felt lucky to get it. I wasn't sure about leaving Bogie to work, but he wanted me to.

Though Bogie was up to nothing physically, his head had never stopped working. He was concerned about *The Good Shepherd*. Would Harry Cohn hold it for him? Sam Jaffe and Morgan brought him full reports. Of course Cohn would hold it for him — he only had to advise the Navy of a postponement, Bogie was not to worry. Cohn felt sure Bogie would be able to start in the fall — would gain his weight back by then.

It must have been toward the end of May that Morgan told me Bogie would have to draw up a new will. I shuddered at the thought. 'Why? After all he's been through, why is it necessary?' 'Look,' said Morgan, 'I'm his friend — I love the guy — but I'm also his business manager. He may be all right, but he may not. It doesn't look too good — I've talked to the doctors — and it must be done while he's in shape to understand it. I would be delinquent in my job if I didn't insist on it being taken care of now — it would be unfair to him and unfair to you. He wants to see that you and Stephen and Leslie are taken care of properly. We have to do it the right way. We have to do it without delay.' I asked how he would tell him. He said, 'Don't you worry about that — I'd tell him matter-of-factly. He hasn't made a new will in years and it should have been done months ago, but because of his surgery we had to wait. Now he's well enough to deal with it.'

So the words were spoken at last: 'It doesn't look too good' — he might die. I felt ghastly. I didn't want to see Bogie discussing his will — it was so horrible, so devastating a picture. I could not think in terms of Bogie not living — it was just totally unacceptable. So I heard the words and put them from my mind. They constantly hovered in the back of my brain, but as long as there was breath and life in my husband, I flatly refused to bring them forward. It was the only way I could continue the game.

By the end of the eight weeks Bogie felt really bad — weak — no chance of gaining a pound. 'He'll feel so much better after two weeks.' The hell he will! It seemed that to recover from the effects of the X-ray treatment takes as long as the treatment itself takes. That meant Bogie would be in the clear in July. Bogie weighed himself every day. No change. I kept telling him to wait awhile — once every two weeks was plenty — it was tough to get started once you'd lost. He finally did feel better. It was in August, I think, that things began to improve. Frank was going to play at The Sands in Las Vegas and he planned a birthday party for me in September — the Rat Pack — he'd have a plane to bring us up there, natch. Bogie said, 'Sure, it'll be fun.' I didn't need convincing.

It was also in August that I started to prepare for *Designing Woman*. I was still apprehensive about leaving Bogie every day, despite the improvement, but I couldn't wait to go to work. I'd never worked with Greg Peck and was looking forward to that.

Bogie was definitely feeling better — the effects of the X-ray finally left him — he was ready for a weekend on the boat. He wanted to sail to Newport and take Steve. A couple of his sailing crew friends would be along — it was warm — it would be good for him. And Steve was anxious to go with his father — these last months had been hard on him. It had been an unnatural time, unfathomable to a seven-year-old. Bogie called me from the boat, as he always did: 'Hello, Baby.' His old hello. He felt he was on his way. I felt so too.

When Bogie came home that Sunday night I heard his car enter the driveway — I got his drink ready as I always had — he walked smiling into our Butternut Room in his sailing garb, hugged and kissed me, and announced that he had gained one pound! It was like being handed the sun.

The next day Bogie called Morgan and Sam, telling them he was beginning to gain and *The Good Shepherd* could probably be planned to start two or three months from then. They were happy to hear it, but said there was no rush — Harry Cohn could easily put off the Navy until we were sure of dates. Bogie hated not working — holding up production. He was so encouraged by that added pound, he was sure it would be a daily recurrence. For a couple of weeks our life was almost normal — no lunching at Romanoff's or dining at Chasen's, no partying, but good friends came by for a drink, and we even fed a few on trays with us. Frank and Swifty in particular — Frank almost nightly — fell into the pattern of ringing the doorbell if the light was on. The nights were never late — Bogie still wasn't up to that, and he wanted to keep getting stronger so that he could return to work — but the atmosphere was more cheerful. I began going to Metro daily for wardrobe — *Designing Woman* was to start shooting in mid-September.

Sometime during that summer Harvey became ill — he coughed a lot and seemed to have difficulty moving quickly. Definitely not his spry self, and off his food. The vet concluded that Harvey's heart was weak, that he must have had some kind of attack that went unnoticed, and said I'd have to find a way of keeping him from climbing the stairs more than once a day. How do you tell a dog to slow down? Bogie was as upset as I was. We pampered him more than ever — tried to explain the need for a new routine. We couldn't have loved him more — from the beginning he'd had as much care and love as a child. I tried to explain to Steve that we had to be more careful with the dog — not too much play, don't get him excited.

Leslie had her fourth birthday party out of doors — twenty children, all as usual.

We spent Labor Day weekend on the *Santana* and had a quiet, happy time in Catalina. The weather was beautiful and, as always, Bogie was happier on the boat than anywhere.

Bogie had not gained an ounce since that famous pound. But he was still feeling stronger and trying to eat more, and at least life was proceeding somewhat normally. Drs Brandsma and Flynn still checked in, but not on a daily basis, and it was a relief not to see them — I'd had enough of doctors, nice though they were. Arrangements were finalized for my birthday in Las Vegas — Cole Porter, Swifty, the Burt Allenburgs, Martha Hyer, the Romanoffs, and the Nivs were to fly up together. Bogie had decided to withdraw — he wanted a long weekend on the boat, would go to Newport, taking Steve along.

I flew to Vegas with the group — I think we were there for Frank's opening, but I'm not sure. The place was packed — our group was at a long table down front facing Frank and the mike. He'd had a cake made, three-tiered with 'Happy Birthday Den Mother,' gave me a large stuffed horse for me and my children, introduced me and sang 'Happy Birthday' to me from the stage. I was called to the phone — it was Bogie to wish me a happy birthday. I hadn't expected it and screamed with excitement and pleasure. Should I have gone with him? I kept wondering. I was escaping from reality until that call — I must have needed the noise, the extravagance and general insanity of Las Vegas, the feeling of no responsibility, the feeling that life was being lived. We all stayed up too late — Kim Novak was Frank's date and we were all photographed cutting my cake. It was fun, like the days before February 29. I returned home to find Bogie waiting for me in the Butternut Room — a bit edgy and resentful, whether because he couldn't go or because I did, I'm not sure. Finally he calmed down enough to hear who'd been there and what we'd all done. He was somewhat jealous of Frank — partly because he knew I loved being with him, partly because he thought Frank was in love with me, and partly because our physical life together, which had always ranked high, had less than flourished with his illness. Yet he was also crazy about Frank — loved having him feel that our home was his home. Knowing Bogie, I suspected he was beginning not to feel quite so well as he had been. He told me Steve had been marvelous on the boat — responsible, capable — everyone was crazy about him. Bogie couldn't wait to teach him how to sail — told Steve, 'We men will go sailing. Leave the women — Mommy and

Leslie — at home to wait for us.' Steve loved it — felt important and special. It was good for them both to be together.

I started *Designing Woman*, coming home with my nightly reports. Our first day's work was at the pool of the Beverly Hills Hotel, and Bogie brought the children to watch for a while. He stayed to one side — the still man photographed only Steve and Leslie with me. Greg and I had days of shooting on a sailboat — Bogie was there on the *Santana* and Greg and I went aboard for lunch. That movie was one of my happiest film experiences. It had one of my all-time favorite lines — 'Open your eyes, Maxie, and go to sleep.' It was also a godsend. Greg and I played characters very much in love, working in different worlds, fighting a lot. In one scene I was leaving him after a fight, running on a cobblestone street in spike-heeled shoes — and of course proceeded to fall and sprain my ankle. It was a romantic movie and I seemed to be constantly running toward Greg or away from him, so I had emotional and physical release to compensate for keeping everything inside at home.

One afternoon I came home to find Bogie in a state of rage. Dorothy Kilgallen (one of Bogie's least favorite columnists and Frank's number-one hate — she was truly vicious) had printed in her column that Bogie had been moved to the eighth floor of Memorial Hospital, where he was fighting for his life. I wouldn't have believed that even she could be so rotten. The press for the most part had made it a point not to mention anything about Bogie's health since his surgery, except that he was on his way to recovery and would start *The Good Shepherd* soon. He was horribly upset. Why wouldn't he over-react — who had more right? He'd been struggling for so many months to gain weight, to feel better, to function. The phone started ringing. Of course the fact that there was no Memorial Hospital in Los Angeles was only one minor inaccuracy! Bogie sent a wire to Kilgallen saying, among other things, 'Unless you start checking the facts you're apt to wind up on the nineteenth floor of Bellevue.' His comments to the press were, 'The fact that there's no Memorial Hospital didn't bother me so much, but that eighth floor was what got me sore. Pretty damn ominous.' He was determined to straighten it out. He put in a call to the night editor of the *Journal-American*, Kilgallen's paper — in a way, it was the old Bogie stirring things up, not letting the lie prevail, not letting the cheap gossip press — the leeches he loathed — get away with anything. Joe Hyams had called to check the story. Bogie in a fatigued and feeble voice said, 'If you want to do me a last favor, come right over.' Joe of course arrived immediately, to find Bogie slumped in his chair, waving a letter he had composed. Joe promised to print it word for word as he had written it. As Bogie started reading it aloud — 'An open letter to the working press' — the phone rang. I got it — it was the editor — Bogie took the phone and shouted into it, 'Do I sound as if I'm fighting for my life? God damn it, don't you check your stories? You just allow that bitch to print anything,' and on and on he went — unrelenting, shouting, finally hanging up totally exhausted. As he pulled himself together and got his breath, I sweetened his drink, and after some forced conversation between Joe and me, he was able to go on with his letter.

I have been greatly disturbed lately at the many unchecked and baseless rumors being tossed to the people regarding the state of my health. Just to set the record straight, as they say in Washington (and I have as much right as anybody in Washington has), a great deal of what has been printed has had nothing to do with the facts. It may even be necessary for me to send out a truth team to follow you around.

I have read that both lungs have been

removed; that I couldn't live another half-hour; that I was fighting for my life in a hospital which doesn't exist out here; that my heart has stopped and been replaced by an old gasoline pump from a defunct Standard Oil station. I have been on the way to practically every cemetery you can name from here to the Mississippi — including several where I am certain they only accept dogs. All the above upsets my friends, not to mention the insurance companies. So, as they also say in Washington, let's get the facts to the American people — and here they are.

I had a slight malignancy in my esophagus. So that some of you won't have to go into the research department, it's the pipe that runs from your throat to your stomach. The operation for the removal of the malignancy was successful, although it was touch and go for a while whether the malignancy or I would survive.

As they also say in Washington, I'm a better man than I ever was — and all I need now is about thirty pounds in weight which I am sure some of you could spare. Possibly we could start something like a Weight Bank for Bogart and believe me I'm not particular which part of your anatomy it comes from.

In closing, any time you want to run a little medical bulletin on me, just pick up the phone and, as they say in the Old Country — I'm in the book.

Joe felt that he had been duped — Bogie was not drawing his last breath — but Bogie, as Joe was on his way to the car, pointed a finger at him: 'You promised — you gave me your word,' so Joe was forced to print it.

Bogie never, from the beginning, believed in disguising the nature of his illness. 'Why should I? It's a respectable disease — nothing to be ashamed of, like something I *might* have had.' 'No worse than gallstones or appendicitis.' 'They'd all kill you if you didn't catch them soon enough — the way people act, you'd think that cancer was as bad as VD.'

Around that time Bogie started complaining about a pain in his left shoulder. He never mentioned anything unless it really hurt. It was treated rather as if it were a pulled muscle. I remember him reaching back and showing me the spot — my trying to massage it — his saying it felt better. From then on he talked about wanting to work more than anything else. 'But I couldn't do it thirty pounds underweight.' He was deeply discouraged about not gaining weight. I kept repeating that he would — just give it time.

The pain persisted. He went to see Dr Brandsma and came home with the diagnosis. It seemed to be a pinched nerve — in the healing process this often occurred. As it wouldn't go away, both Dr Brandsma and Dr Flynn re-examined Bogie and gave him some pain-killing pills. His appetite lessened and he lost more weight — nothing drastic yet, but enough to cause concern. After a while the pills didn't help. Bogie was resting upstairs one evening, and before they went up to see him they talked to me downstairs. They were afraid the cancer had returned.

There was only one choice: nitrogen mustard. That treatment, while severe, if not killing, often arrested the spread of the disease. It would mean four or five days in the hospital. They would tell Bogie it was treatment for the scar tissue — more words that I didn't really understand. He accepted what they said — no questions but obvious ones. 'Will the treatment solve it?' 'Absolutely it should. It's strong, but we've seen it work before.' Then they explained in detail how scar tissue formed in an area after extensive surgery, very often crowding a nerve, pressing in on it, causing pain. There were no lies — they couldn't lie to Bogie, they knew he'd know, so they skirted around the truth. It was announced to the press that Mr Bogart was entering St John's for treatment of a nerve-pressure condition 'due to excessive scar formation following previous surgery. Pills given to alleviate pain cause lack of appetite.' It was also printed that he would check in with a chess book, some detective thrillers, a bottle of Scotch, and his portable chess set.

The sun was shining brightly when we arrived. I carried his case — he walked, but with effort. That night he felt pretty good. They had given him some treatment, but the real thing would start the next day. Meanwhile they had alleviated the pain with special compresses, heat, and some intravenous medication to dissolve the scar tissue. He wasn't happy to be in a hospital again, but the atmosphere of St John's was fairly cheery and there was to be no surgery this time. Actually, I think it was a relief to him in a way to be able to stay in bed — not to carry on the pretense that everything was fine. He would be taken care of, not feel he was inconveniencing everyone at home; he hated to impose. Dr Flynn was at the hospital that evening and walked with me to my car as I left. He told me the chances were good that the nitrogen mustard would work, and that in any case it was the only chance — the last chance.

I was terribly depressed as I drove home.

So little was known about cancer: there was surgery, there was X-ray, cobalt, nitrogen mustard — and that was it. I could feel the doctors' frustration, though, as John Jones kept saying, 'We must do everything we know how to do. As long as the patient's alive there's a chance. Research is being conducted all the time — one day suddenly there'll be a cure, as with penicillin. One day there was no penicillin, the next day there was . . .' But I was sick of talking to doctors — of listening to words and phrases I didn't know the meaning of, of seeing no solution, of having hope become despair in a matter of hours, of being at the mercy of it all.

Frank was constant with his phone calls and visits to Bogie — and it wasn't easy for him. I don't think he could bear to see Bogie that way or bear to face the possibility of his death. Yet he cheered Bogie up when he was with him — made him laugh — kept the ring-a-ding act in high gear for him. He did it all the only way he knew how, and he did it well.

The five days Bogie was in the hospital he didn't feel too bad — a little listless, and not eating. They plied him with liquids like grape juice, which he liked, and the sustagen malteds, but he had lost more weight. The night before I was to take him home I had a meeting with the doctors.

They told me he would be weak but otherwise all right — they wouldn't be able to give me a true prognosis on the nitrogen-mustard treatment for at least a week, probably more. They didn't think I'd need a nurse unless I wanted one so I could get some sleep, but I knew Bogie would hate having a nurse around and as long as no medical attention was required I could handle it.

The next day I got him into his clothes, although they hung on him. He was so happy to be going home. The nurse wheeled him almost to the car — he walked the rest of the way, apologizing for leaning on me. It was being in bed and not eating for five days. 'Once you get home we'll fatten you up, Baby. The pain in the shoulder is gone now — you'll be fine. Besides, I love you to lean on me — it's the first time in twelve years. Makes me feel needed.' We got home and very slowly climbed the stairs. He would lie down until dinner and then come down to the Butternut Room, where we'd eat and watch television. I helped him into his pajamas. While he rested I did whatever I had to do — told the children to try to keep the noise down while Daddy was resting. They went in to see him before he came downstairs. It was almost enough for them to be in the room — they kissed him but didn't climb on him or make any noise. At their dinnertime Bogie and I started downstairs — had a drink together. We had something on trays which I ate and Bogie didn't. The children had gone to bed. Bogie and I were on the sofa in the Butternut Room, having coffee, watching the box. I was worried about how he felt, but I couldn't ask: he hated that direct question beyond description. What could he answer anyway — lousy? He got up to go to the bathroom, which was no more than eight feet away — I tried not to watch him, not obviously at least. He looked strained. I heard the door open after a few minutes and as I turned to look at him he just disappeared. I jumped up — oh God! — I rushed over to him — he had fainted and was out cold. I screamed for the butler, told him to carry Mr Bogart upstairs to bed. I was hysterical. I rushed for the phone and could hardly dial Dr Brandsma's number, my hand was shaking so. I screamed into the phone, 'He fainted — why didn't you tell me something like this could happen?' I ran upstairs to see Bogie, who had come to — composed myself, saying, 'It must be a reaction to all the medication you've had — don't worry, darling.' What could I say? He couldn't understand what had happened — was worried, even frightened, though he never said he was either. I told him to try and sleep — that if he hadn't come downstairs, it wouldn't have happened. Anything to try to soothe him. I didn't know what I was saying.

Soon Dr Brandsma arrived. I waited downstairs while he examined Bogie. I was still a basket case, in a state of semi-trauma, and I clearly looked it, for when Brandsma came downstairs he took me by the arm and sat down on the sofa with me and proceeded to talk to me like a child. 'Look, Betty, I'm sorrier than I can say that this happened. There was no way of our knowing. The effects of the nitrogen mustard are cumulative — they just knocked Bogie flat all at once. He should have come home with a nurse, but I was hoping we could get away without one.' But why had it happened — would it happen again — what would it be like tomorrow — how could I prepare myself to take care of him? 'We have to take it one day at a time. I think he should have a nurse, perhaps a male nurse, until the treatment wears off and he's stronger. A male nurse could carry him down the stairs.' My heart sank — Bogie would be upset by that. I said, 'Let's try it a day or two without one. The butler can carry him down. If I can't manage, okay, but you'll have to explain to Bogie that you feel it's a good idea and why.' I was looking for constant reassurance from Brandsma — any ray of light. I never thought in terms of this being the beginning of the end either — it was just another temporary crisis. After that experience I dealt with our life minute by minute. But I was scared.

I made some ground rules. Whoever wanted to visit Bogie had to call and ask what would be the best time, and I didn't want too many at once, no matter how close friends they were — it was too much of an effort in his present condition. His second day home Sam and Mildred Jaffe came over. Mildred hadn't seen Bogie for a while and on entering the room I heard her gasp — she couldn't help it, she was so shocked at the sight of that figure in the bed. Having seen him daily, I hadn't realized how drastic the change had been. I glared at her, and as we were walking down the stairs after their visit, I told her, surprised at my fury and my ability to articulate it, that if she couldn't control herself she must not come again — that the point of friends coming to visit was not to commiserate over his illness but to cheer him and get his mind off it. Of course she apologized profusely, hugged me, kissed me — she was like a mother to me. I loved her a great deal, but I was steely about this, determined that it must never happen again. Mildred said she could see him and contain herself, but only if there were other people in the room.

After a few days I had to agree to a male nurse. Bogie was still weak — he got out of bed every day and walked across the room to sit on our chaise-longue, and he'd go to the bathroom, but it was better if someone was close by to help him if he needed it. The male nurse was young, strong, not entirely sensible, and had the personality of a flounder. One afternoon I walked into the bedroom to find Bogie very agitated. In raised voice to the nurse: 'What do you mean, no improvement? What do you mean, my appetite stays the same — that there's no weight gain? Of course there's no weight gain. That takes time . . .' and on and on. That nurse had shown him his own chart. I could have killed him — demanded to know why he'd shown it. 'Well, he asked to see it.' I wanted no one around who might make extra waves in Bogie's life, so it was agreed that the nurse would be there no more.

I had finished *Designing Woman*, and *Written on the Wind* had just opened in the East. As I said, it was a soap opera — Rock Hudson and I always knew that — but it turned out to be a very successful one. I remember Bogie stretched out on the chaise reading a review, me squatting alongside — and his saying, 'I wouldn't do too many of these.' His standards were as high as ever.

We were able to get the really good nurse Bogie had had in Good Samaritan. She made him feel very safe and was easy to get along with — did whatever was necessary for Bogie without making him feel a total invalid, and she had some wit, praise the Lord. The doctors came every day, Dr Brandsma literally morning and evening. We tried to have people for drinks upstairs in the bedroom, but Bogie wanted to be in the Butternut Room when his friends came. Swifty was one of the few who saw Bogie upstairs — he came before official drink time, armed with a story or joke to bring a smile to Bogie's face. Bogie didn't like being carried. At last it was worked out that we would put a chair in the dumb-waiter — an old-fashioned one that was very roomy. Aurelio removed one board to give him more headroom and we used a wheelchair. Downstairs he would transfer to his favorite orange chair and drink with his buddies. He could walk, but it was hard for him — he just was not strong, and there was no point in wearing himself out unnecessarily. It was a neat arrangement, though not a happy one. He looked so frail sitting in that dumbwaiter, and it was a dark, though short trip. It couldn't have been anything but very unpleasant, but he wanted to do it — he insisted upon doing it. That cocktail hour became the high point of his day. Friends would phone to book themselves between five and seven and I'd try to keep it to two at a time. Niven often came directly from the studio in full make-up on his way home — the regulars could always come in, though they never came without calling. It became more and more apparent who was not a regular. Dick Brooks, for instance, a close friend who had almost been invented by Bogie as a character — Bogie had certainly influenced his life in every way — did not come for a long time. I was furious — and I voiced the fury once. Bogie's comment was, 'Well, don't be too hard on him — some people just don't like to be around sickness.' Too damn bad, I thought. Dick could have swallowed his distaste in the name of friendship. I was fierce — I admit it. I had taken on some of Bogie's color, gaining strength while protecting him. There was no way for me to understand or to forgive the ones who fell short of the mark. There was no way for me to forgive Dick. I think he finally did come once, but he was shamed into it — probably I put him on the defensive. But I didn't care about him — I cared only about Bogie; I cared about his not being let down. Had positions been reversed, Bogie would have been there. And Swifty, who had a true phobia about sickness and cleanliness, rose above it out of friendship — out of his high regard for Bogie. Clearly it was the fact of Bogart — indomitable, indestructible, always-there Bogart — suddenly not having strength, physical strength. No one wanted to face that fact. And Bogie through those last weeks made an extraordinary, super-human effort, keeping the talk going — he did much more than his doctors thought within the realm of human possibility.

Raymond Massey came to town and visited — they were longtime friends and colleagues. Ray started the visit avoiding any talk about Bogie's illness, but Bogie turned the tables on him by saying, 'Wait till you hear what happened to me — it was awful,' describing his operation in detail and asking if Ray wanted to see his scar. By the end of the visit it was Ray who needed cheering up.

Christmas was not far off. David and Jennifer Selznick came over one afternoon — David very concerned whether everything that could be done for Bogie was being done. Shouldn't I maybe call in another doctor? Get another opinion? In this great country of ours, wasn't there one mind who knew more than any other? He was sweet and loving, and I was grateful.

Oh, how I wished there were one mind that had the answer! I told him I had asked the doctors the same question. They all had said no — if it made me feel better, I should by all means bring in someone else, but they had discussed Bogie with some of their colleagues, and it was agreed that they had done all that could be done. David understood — said he'd like to give Bogie pictures of me and the children for Christmas, and would I mind if John Engstead came over to photograph us? What a lovely idea. I didn't know how to make Christmas and Bogie's birthday even halfway normal, but I would have a tree and many gifts for the children, even gifts for Bogie.

It was around this time that the three doctors sat me down in the Butternut Room. Brandsma was the spokesman. 'I'm sure you'd rather know the truth, wouldn't you? I'm sure you know already. Bogie cannot last much longer. We don't know how he's lasted this long. The nitrogen mustard didn't work — we would certainly have seen a difference by two weeks after he'd had the treatment. We really didn't expect it to work, we just hoped.' 'But isn't it possible,' I asked, 'that it might still have some effect?' I knew there was no answer they could give me that I wanted to hear, yet I still asked the question. I didn't accept, *couldn't,* the fact of Bogie dying. I heard the words — answered accordingly — but that was all. I had continually asked the nurses, 'Isn't he better today? He ate a little more — isn't that a sign of improvement?' They shook their heads. There was no way he would get better — it was just a matter of time.

Brandsma advised me to begin to think about arrangements, to prepare myself and figure out what I would need and from whom. I remember looking pleadingly at these men who held my husband's life in their hands — John Jones, wonderful and dedicated, saying, 'I've done everything I knew how to do — I hoped I'd gotten it all, but clearly I didn't.' They were all sad — they admired Bogie so much. I didn't know what to do. I thought of K.C. On some excuse, I left the house one afternoon and drove to All Saints Church and sat in Rev. Smith's office, telling him what the doctors had said. 'So I suppose it will happen sometime soon — it could be days, weeks, no one is quite sure. K.C., he is not a religious man in the churchgoing sense, but he's very religious in the life-everyday sense. He believes in the Ten Commandments, he believes in the Golden Rule, and he's lived his life by them. So if you'd just think about it, so when the time comes you'll know what to say . . .' I knew K.C.

would help with the children. He had a gift of communication with the young which was to be envied — they loved and trusted him.

I don't remember repeating my discussion with the doctors to anyone else. Mother and Lee were at the house daily, but they spent more time with Steve and Leslie than with Bogie. I suppose one reason I kept silent was that voicing it might make it happen. I know I didn't articulate even to myself that he would leave me soon. As long as he was breathing, could talk, I felt our life would continue. I knew the word *death* — but I'd never really been in the presence of it.

I knew he wanted to be cremated, but that too was only a word. How much preparation could one make when dealing not with fact but with emotion?

He still shaved every morning — on a tray in front of a mirror, with an electric razor. I don't know what he saw in that mirror, but he never turned away. So how could I?

Spence and Katie came to visit almost every night — about eight-thirty, after everyone else had gone and Bogie was back upstairs. He looked forward to their visits — so did I. They behaved as they always had: Spence pulling up a chair at the foot of the bed, using our bench as a table for his coffee — Katie on the floor. Spence telling jokes — kidding around as he always did with Bogie. I don't know how he managed, but he did. Much later Katie told me that he was shattered before each visit and shattered after. While he was there it was no different from the way we had all been in better days. I loved those people so much — they were both so solid, so complete, so unqualified. They helped me as much as they did Bogie.

I remember Carolyn picking me up one afternoon to go Christmas shopping. As we were driving away from home, I said, 'If anything happens to Bogie, I'll never get married again — never.' Her reply was 'Never say never.' She was right. But despite such apprehensions about a future without Bogie, I never sat down and thought to myself, 'He's going to die.' I never thought each day could be his last — or that I would waken one morning and find him gone.

By that time we had two nurses. When the pain increased, the doctor prescribed something. I don't know what — morphine? Bogie was so thin by then that every time a needle touched him it left a mark — there were fewer and fewer areas that were in the clear. One afternoon he got out of bed and, with only his pajama top on, pushed the wheelchair across the room to the chaise. His will to live was so strong, he forced his body to do what it was incapable of doing. The sight of him walking away from me — he was skin and bone, I don't know how he stood up — was devastating, heart-breaking.

When Brandsma came, Bogie would ask careful questions — no life-or-death ones. 'Why was I in pain after the last treatments?' 'The scar tissue hadn't completely dissolved and was pressing on a nerve.' Bogie knew you had to eat to stay alive, but he couldn't. The malteds came twice daily — coffee, water, liquids mostly. He just couldn't get food down — he would chew endlessly a bit of toast. His plea to me was always the same: 'If I could just work.' Because if he worked he'd be okay.

I often left the room when the doctor was there, hoping Bogie might say something to him he wouldn't say to me. I'd ask Brandsma endless questions afterward: 'What did he say — what did you tell him — what does he think?' Finally Bogie began having trouble breathing. The doctor told me we should have oxygen in the house — he told Bogie it would make it easier on him while he was trying to gain strength, an occasional whiff was a great pick-me-up. Even I should try it — it's terrific. Nothing was terrific. But two enormous green tanks came, one for upstairs, one for down. I was shown how to work them — not too complicated. I took some and it *was* good. Bogie tried it — he didn't make a fuss — another indignity which had to be borne. It made him feel easier and he used it from time to time — more often each day.

One afternoon Steve and Leslie were in our bedroom playing. Bogie was on the chaise — he just watched them. When they went for their baths, he said, 'Don't have them in here too often, Baby.' He didn't want them to see him as he was, or he didn't want them to remember him as he was. Or, he couldn't bear to look at them knowing he wouldn't be around for the rest of their lives.

It is extraordinary that not once did Bogie ever say a word to me along the lines of 'If anything should happen to me' — or 'When' — or 'I know.' We continued the game of its being nothing more than a bad virus. Bogie set the tone, and his attitude was such that I had to play along. He said to me once, 'If you're okay, then I am — if you're upset, then I am.' So there was nothing for me to do but be okay.

He was still presiding over the cocktail hour. He'd started drinking martinis again which I made with dry sherry — he liked that better. Probably he could taste them more than Scotch. His lungs must have been filling up, because he spat a lot. Instead of having to ask for a tissue constantly, it was easier for him to have a receptacle. The nurses provided a stainless-steel one, hideously kidney-shaped and hideously clinical-looking. It would sit on the table next to him when he was downstairs and beside the bed when he was up. A couple of people were having drinks — I don't remember who, but they must have been good friends. I was sitting on the sofa opposite Bogie, having just handed him his drink. As I looked across at him — conversation was proceeding — he just sat there, sipping his martini, interjecting an occasional word, using the steel spittoon. He looked so helpless, so vulnerable, so uncomplaining, that I had to walk over and put my arms around him. I didn't say anything — it was something I had to do. His reaction was immediate. Almost brushing me away, he said, 'Don't do that, Baby — there's nothing I can do about it.' That was as close as he ever came to saying anything pointed about his illness.

He was a complete shut-in — had been since St John's. He'd even said that he was. Once when he was sitting downstairs, Steve and Leslie ran into the room wanting to watch TV. As Leslie ran by, he reached out and stopped her — sat her next to him and kissed her fingers and held her hand in one of the most gentle, loving, and moving gestures I have ever seen . . .

We got through Christmas — I don't remember how, but we did. I gave Bogie a portable radio, new pajamas, a smoking jacket — I don't know what. There was nothing festive about the day. Steve and Leslie opened their many presents and loved that, as any child would. Bogie loved the pictures Engstead had taken — we used one for our Christmas card — and he became fifty-seven years old. By next year all would be well and we'd be having a party once again. New Year's Eve we had champagne and caviar and drank toasts to each other in the bedroom with Mother and Lee.

Huston was back in California and came every day, regaling Bogie with stories of the filming of *Moby Dick*. Everyone came in ten-minute shifts — I told them that, no matter what Bogie said, ten minutes was all he could take at a time. There were exceptions — Spence and Katie (who were always there when no one else was anyway), Huston, Morgan, Nunnally, Swifty, Niv, Romanoff — the closest.

Clifton Webb, an old friend of Bogie's and close to both of us from the beginning of our marriage, had been in Italy making a film. He returned around the end of December and called immediately — wanted to know all about Bogie — had been told he was very ill again and wanted to see him. He became very emotional, kept saying, 'Oh, poor Bogie — I can't bear it,' got weepy on the phone. I told him he could not come unless he could hold himself together, that seeing Bogie after so many months would be a terrible shock to him, but Bogie was very alert and would notice the slightest suggestion of emotion. Clifton shouldn't come alone, I thought — better with a friend. He finally came with George Cukor, who had been before. I was very apprehensive and stayed with Clifton and George as Bogie was wheeled into the room. Clifton got through it somehow, but as Bogie was being wheeled out of the room, Clifton totally collapsed — started to cry, moan. I was trying to keep him quiet so Bogie wouldn't hear him. One had not only one's own emotions to contend with, but also those of friends who couldn't deal with the facts. Clifton was a special friend — and cried easily — so there was no point in being angry with him. That afternoon, however, he was definitely more of a problem than Bogie ever was.

One day Sam Goldwyn and Willie Wyler came for drinks. By then Bogie was no longer being transferred to the big chair, he just stayed in the wheelchair. The nurse stayed downstairs in case he needed any-thing. There was general talk. Bogie sud-denly beckoned for the nurse — pulled up one pajama leg, exposing his pathetic frail limb — he needed a shot. No fuss. Gold-wyn was stunned to see the thinness of that leg. Bogie didn't see his face — Goldwyn slowly turned away — the conversation was somehow kept going till the shot was ad-ministered. That was the only time Bogie ever did anything like that in anyone else's presence. He apologized briefly, but said he'd needed it for the pain — he was okay now. No dramatics. I marvel at him every time I think of his conduct. He suffered such humiliation from his disease — his poor body had been driven further by his will to live than it was ever meant to go, but still he would not give up. The only thing different I noticed those last few weeks was that he wanted me with him all the time. If I was downstairs visiting a friend, talking with a doctor, whatever — the phone buzzer would ring: 'Can you come up for a while, Baby?'

One morning Jack Warner called and wanted to know if it would be all right to visit Bogie. I was very much surprised, but I said, 'Certainly, Jack.' I gave him a time to come and told Bogie, who was touched that Jack would make the effort — and an effort it was. At the appointed time, the doorbell rang and there stood Jack in Homburg hat. Awkward, nervous, ill at ease. He removed his hat and kept turning it around in his fingers. He said, 'I won't stay long — I wanted to see Bogie — I've always liked him — admired him. I've heard what a time he's had.' I took him upstairs, where he stayed with Bogie for about fifteen minutes. I stayed in the room. Bogie had to put him at ease — of course tell him that his first film would be for Columbia. A gentle ribbing — Bogie wouldn't step too far out of character. And Jack tried to tell some kind of terrible joke. I'm sure he died a thousand deaths during that visit, but he showed up, and that counted for a great deal. He thanked me for letting him come — he felt good about having done that. And I was grateful to him. Bogie said, 'Jack's not a bad guy — he's just so uncomfortable with everyone. He has to make jokes to prove he's regular.' Whatever his reasons, it was one of the better things Jack did.

Louella Parsons asked if she could come. Bogie said sure. She had been a good friend — not a friend friend, but a columnist friend. With the exception of Kilgallen and a couple of other New York items, the press had been respectful of his privacy during his illness. About a week before he died there'd been a rumor in the East that his death was imminent and when the wire services and newspapers called to check, Bogie's words were, 'What are the ghouls saying about me now?' Joe Hyams had come over to check the rumor that he was in a coma — always ready to give Bogie a place to let off steam publicly. He told Joe, 'You can say that I'm down to my last martini. The only thing I'm fighting is to keep my head above the press.'

Our routine had been the same each day for months. I kissed him good night before I went to sleep in the little nap room next to our bedroom — wakened each morning to kiss him good morning — had my breakfast with him. The doctor came — the nurse was there — Harvey came up every day and always walked over to Bogie and stayed with him for most of the day. The children were in school except during the holidays. My conversations with the doctors were always the same. Bogie was getting weaker — I had noticed that when he sipped his grape juice through a glass hospital straw his hand shook, and when he put the glass down on the table his focus was less good. I'd talk to the nurses about it, to the doctors — they said it was because of the pain-killing drugs they were giving him. Since that day in the Good Samaritan Hospital when he asked them to please stop the suction machine, he had not uttered one complaint. I don't know how we all got through those days — the routine saved us, I guess. Somewhere in there Steve had his eighth birthday party, not a large one, but he had his best friends and a cake and presents — I ran some sixteen-mm. film for them. The essential thing was to do as many normal things as one possibly could. Steve and Leslie saw Bogie every night — kissed him good night — they knew he was there.

One day when Dr Brandsma came in, Bogie said, 'You know, I don't seem to be getting any better. I'm getting worried. Am I getting worse or is it what you expect?' He gave the doctor his arm.

'I would say it's about what we expect.'

Questions like that left me unsure whether he really knew he was dying. If there is anything good to say about cancer — and I don't really think there is — it is that its victims always seem to feel they have licked it. Yet he never asked direct questions, questions that would require definitive answers.

On Saturday, January 12, Spence and Katie came to visit in the evening. They stayed for about forty minutes — maybe more. It was their usual kind of visit, Bogie really enjoying them — except that he was a little less concentrated, his focus a little less good. If they noticed his shaking hand, they never let on. I walked them down-stairs to the door and went back up. Bogie wanted to watch *Anchors Aweigh* with Gene Kelly and Frank on television. We watched it and enjoyed it. Bogie wanted me on the bed with him — next to him. Whenever we were alone in the evening it was always side by side with the television on, there was nothing new about that. Then he said, 'Why don't you sleep here tonight, Baby?' It was the first time that request had been made. 'Of course I will. I hadn't because I felt you'd be more comfortable without me.' Actually, he felt freer about waking up at night without me on the bed — he didn't like to disturb me! Even at that stage he told the nurse he wanted his wife to stay with him that night. They both looked at me as though I didn't have to — shouldn't. But of course I would stay — I *wanted* to stay with him. I could hold his hand. I always loved holding Bogie's hand even in its frailty. Odd how important holding a hand can be — how reassuring.

That night was a night never to be for-gotten of total restlessness — of Bogie picking at his chest in his sleep — of his feeling he had to get up and then not — of constant movement. I was awake most of the night and could see his hands moving over his chest as he slept, as though things were closing in and he wanted to get out.

The only thing that became more apparent to me that night was an odor — I had been noticing it as I kissed him. At first I thought it was medicinal — later I realized it was decay. Actually I didn't realize it — I asked the nurse what it was and she told me. It was a strong odor — almost like a disinfectant turned sour. In the world of sickness one becomes privy to the failure of the body — to so many small things taken for granted, ignored. I reacted not with revulsion but with a caving in of my stomach.

And I was frightened by the mystery of it all. Why did Bogie have to go through a night like that one? Hadn't there been enough torture? Did it all have to gather itself together and pounce on him like this?

Sunday morning Dr Brandsma came early. I was dressing to take the children to Sunday School. Before we left, Bogie said, 'Doc, last night was the worst night of my life — I don't want to go through that again.' I took the children, came back upstairs with the morning paper. Bogie was sitting up, very shakily moving the electric razor over his chin. I sat with him, had coffee — he still couldn't forget the night before. I asked him if he felt better. 'It's always better in the daylight.' Sunday School was short, I had to collect my babies — I said I'd be right back and kissed him as I always did. Newspapers later printed that he said, 'Goodbye, Kid,' making it seem overly dramatic and pointed. It was not like that — it was just 'Goodbye, Kid,' in a most ordinary way under most extraordinary circumstances. He did say, 'Hurry back,' to which I answered, 'I'll only be gone long enough to pick them up and come home — ten minutes at the outside.' I arrived at the church and honked my horn at my offspring, who hugged K.C. goodbye and ran to the car. We buzzed home and on arrival we all went upstairs, they to wash for lunch, me to tell Bogie I was home. He was dozing — the nurse whispered to me that he seemed somewhat comatose. 'What the hell does that mean?' 'We don't know yet — not for sure. If he is in a semi-coma, he may come out of it — if not, he'll sink into a deep coma.' I looked at him — he looked as though he were just sleeping and would waken after a while. The house was very still. Mother was there — she was marvelous about everything, kept out of the way, spent most of her time with the children, but sat with me when I needed her. The doctor came back — I let him in, said I'd wait downstairs. A couple of friends called — I told them Bogie was resting, I'd talk to them later. The doctor came down and we walked into the Butternut Room. Bogie definitely seemed to be in a coma. He might come out of it, but the doctor didn't think so. It was normal after last night. I asked him to explain. After I told him what Bogie's movements had been through that night — hands picking constantly at his chest — he said, 'That's what happens just before one dies. People feel claustrophobic — it seems as though everything is closing in. And everything is. It's their last fight — the restlessness — the thrashing.' A fight to be born, I thought — a fight to die.

'But,' I said, still grasping at straws, 'he might still have a chance.'

'Yes, but I don't think so,' he said. 'He's fought harder and better than anyone I've ever seen. He's lived longer than we had any right to expect. He should have been gone four months ago. Medically, that is. But his will to live was so strong he fought it off. His will is not enough now.'

'Oh, God, I can't believe it.' I started to shake — no tears, just shaking, hardly able to get my breath. 'What shall I do about Steve? Would you say something to prepare him?' Just then I saw Steve and called to him to come in. 'Come here, darling — sit by Mommy.' I was in the orange chair — big enough for both of us. 'Dr Brandsma wants to talk to you for a minute.' That small boy — that beautiful

boy, just eight years old a week before —
sat on the edge of the chair, a little
hunched over, head tilted back a little, almost as if trying to avoid a blow, and
looked at Dr Brandsma.

'You know, Steve, your daddy has been
very, very ill.' Steve nodded. 'We've been
doing everything to try to make him better.
He's tried to get better. But sometimes
that's not enough — his illness is very
strong.' Steve nodded. 'He's asleep now.
He may go into a deeper sleep. He may go
into a sleep so deep that he cannot wake
up.' Steve nodded again. 'Do you know
what I'm trying to say to you?' Steve
nodded again.

I had my arm around him — I was
shaking all over. Steve didn't cry, didn't
say one word, just looked at the doctor and
nodded, never changing his expression.
'Do you know what the doctor is saying,
darling? Do you understand?' Another nod.
I hugged him and said I'd be with him in a
few minutes. He ran out of the room. Dr
Brandsma was destroyed. To have to tell a
little boy that his father was dying. I almost
broke down — didn't because I have some
kind of gauge in me that keeps me from
doing it in front of anyone. And I couldn't
crack up now — how would I get through
the day? How would Mother, Steve, Leslie
deal with it all if they saw me go? I

couldn't. I just lit another cigarette and kept on shaking. Brandsma said it was the hardest thing he'd ever had to do. I told him I wanted to take Steve up to our bedroom to see Bogie — to see him sleeping quietly. Did he think it would be all right? He did, but why? I wanted Steve to see Bogie again and not be afraid. To feel that Bogie was taking a nap. I brought Leslie into the bedroom just so she could see that her father was asleep. I felt she was too little to sit quietly. Would it be all right to talk to him? To hold his hand? What might happen? I was so frightened. 'Yes, you can talk, though he may or may not hear. You will get no response — but it's all right to do whatever you want to do.'

After he left I went upstairs to see if there had been any change. The nurse said no — she was taking his pulse regularly, checking him. And why would I want him to wake up? He'd suffered enough — he was at peace now. Better for him to stay in that limbo of oblivion.

I looked at Bogie again — went very close. He was sleeping — every bone clearly outlined — not a flutter of an eyelid. It was a sleep of life, different from the one to come later. I told the nurse I was bringing my son in, to please leave us alone.

I found Steve and asked him if he'd like

to come into the bedroom with me to sit with Daddy for a while. I explained that Daddy was in a deep sleep — that there was nothing to be afraid of. I was sure it would be of some comfort to see his father sleeping peacefully, almost normally.

Hand in hand, Steve and I walked into the bedroom. There is an aura of another world in a room that holds someone on the brink of death. One moves quietly and carefully, as if in awe of that terrible unknown. I gingerly sat on the bed — more frightened than Steve. What could happen — would Bogie sit up and fall back down dramatically? I don't know why I was frightened, what my apprehensions were based on, but my imagination took charge. I'd seen too many movies. Steve came close to the bed. I took Bogie's hand in mine — he seemed to react — to squeeze it in return. I sat Steve on the edge of the bed and we two held Bogie's hand and sat there looking at him and thinking our thoughts. I didn't say to myself, 'He's dying.' He was just sleeping a sleep further away than any I had ever known. There was nothing to relate to. I didn't think, 'Is this the culmination of a life? Is this how our marriage ends? Is this man, full of life and fun, really going to leave us forever?' I just felt a total sadness, and as I looked at my small son, whom I loved so much, I thought of the unfairness of it all. Why should he have a burden this great to bear so early in life? Leslie was four — too young to have as many tears — life was simpler for her now. Steve was just old enough for complications to begin. Hers would come later. After about fifteen minutes we left. Steve leaned over and kissed his father's cheek — I did the same. It seemed a perfectly natural thing to do.

Then more calls. I told Morgan and whoever else was on the other end of the phone that it looked as though Bogie was in a coma, we weren't absolutely sure how long it might last.

Brandsma returned in the evening. He told me Bogie could conceivably remain in a coma for days — did I want to keep him alive, just breathing, though he might be a vegetable? I didn't think Bogie would want that, and Brandsma said he felt it was the last thing Bogie would want. There was nothing to do at this moment anyway — just wait. He could be reached any time during the night. Not to hesitate. Mother knew, May knew, Kathy, the butler, the nurse — there was nothing to say — we all had to wait. There would be no cocktail hour that day. I don't remember now who came over — one or two friends must have. I called Katie to tell her and Spence not to come that night. Early in the evening I looked for Steve and found that he had gone back into our bedroom to see Bogie. When I asked him why, he said, 'Because I wanted to.' I tucked him into bed, heard his prayers — did the same with Leslie, having told her Daddy was sleeping all day. She said, 'Will he wake up tomorrow?' 'I don't know, darling.' Christ, I had no answers. How do you prepare your children when you can't prepare yourself? I went to the nurses. They were not very hopeful, not hopeful at all. They were both staying through the night. They changed the bed — moving Bogie to one side while they placed the clean sheet on the other. They were so efficient. It was out of my hands. They had taken over — pulse — blood pressure. Bogie was just lying there in that sleep, the decay permeating the room and everything in it. I wanted to stay on the bed next to him — I was afraid to, but I wanted to. They said, 'No, you should get some sleep. We'll only disturb you as we do things for him.' So somewhere around midnight I kissed Bogie good night — this time, for the first time, in eleven and a half years of married life, with no response from him — and went into the little nap room. I lay down on the bed, and for the first time in almost a year I sobbed and sobbed and sobbed — months and months of tears. I let it all pour out, saying, 'Please don't let him die — please don't let anything happen to him — please let him live,' over and over through my sobs until I slept.

Suddenly I was awakened — the nurse gently shaking me. 'Mrs Bogart, it's all over. Mr Bogart has died.' There was that special yellow light coming from the bedroom — that light that goes with death in the early hours of the morning. 'When?' 'About five minutes ago. Dr Brandsma is on his way. You may come with me now.' I got up — numb, worn out — put on my robe — the robe I had worn in *Dark Passage*, our first movie together after we were married, the robe I had worn Saturday night when sleeping next to Bogie. The nurse had her arm around me as we walked through the door of the little room into our bedroom. I saw Bogie lying in bed — mouth slightly open — hands on the outside of the sheet — the outline of skull and face clearly drawn. I moved toward him — the nurse's arm still around me, trying to guide me out of the room. I couldn't really believe it. I was afraid to touch him — I kissed him on his cheek, it was not yet cold. Someone else was present — that unknown someone who had taken over. The nurse kept saying, 'Come on, you mustn't stay.' Much later I realized that terrible things happen to the body, not to be seen. I let her lead me out, looking back over my shoulder at Bogie lying in our bed — on what had always, until his illness, been my side of the bed — sleeping that other sleep. I must not wake the children. I would go downstairs to wait for the doctor. I was in a trance. The doctor's car drove up. The house was silent — it was dark outside — I let the doctor in and told him I'd wait for him downstairs. I turned on some lights — I didn't even know what time it was. I went into the kitchen to make some instant coffee — brought in a cup for me, one for the doctor. He came down and told me all arrangements had been made — he had called Forest Lawn and they were on their way. It was unreal. I'd wait until morning to call Mother, I wanted her to have an undisturbed sleep. I called Morgan and told him — he said he'd get dressed and come over. I had to let the newspapers know, but I didn't want their people around the house. I called Joe Hyams, who asked if I wanted him to inform the wire services, etc. 'Yes, please, Joe — if you would.' I didn't want to wake Katie or Spence. I called the Nivens and told them. David was working, but would come after work — Hjordis would come in the morning after the children went to school. It was about three o'clock in the morning. There would be so much to do. I didn't want the children to wake up before they had to — I would tell them individually — oh, God, how would I tell them? The nurse came downstairs, told me how very sorry she was, but how it was better for him — he might have stayed alive and in a coma for a week or more — he had suffered so much, it was a release for him. I wanted to know how she'd known he was dying. She said she and the other nurse had been checking his pulse every twenty minutes — suddenly it got so fast they couldn't count it — his temperature went up — it happened very quickly. She hadn't meant to hurry me out of the room, but she'd felt it was better that I didn't linger, better I didn't remember that final picture too vividly. But it was a picture you would never forget. I have never forgotten.

The doorbell rang. It would be the men from Forest Lawn. Somewhere, sometime, Morgan and I must have decided Forest Lawn was the place, even with all the jokes about it. What difference did it make, really? Dead is dead. Dr Brandsma said the men would like to see me before they went. I walked to the door. A man in the usual black suit was standing outside, and in a corner of the courtyard was the black hearse, the rear doors open and facing in my direction. And a large white sack in a funny shape was at the opening of the doors. As the man offered his condolences I saw that sack. 'What is that!' 'That is Mr Bogart — I'm very sorry, Mrs Bogart,' in that practiced sympathetic voice. Bogie in a sack! How horrible! I'd thought he'd be taken out of the house on a stretcher, lying as if he were sleeping — not thrown into a sack as if nothing. But he *was* nothing. That was not Bogie — the heart and the mind were Bogie. When they went, only flesh and bone remained. And to these men it was a business. They did this every day — many times a day. Still — why couldn't they have waited? That picture too has stayed with me ever since, and will as long as I live — and in the nightmares I had for months after, that white sack was in evidence. 'Why,' I asked the doctor and the nurses, 'why did they take him like that?' 'You shouldn't have seen it — but that's the way it always is. Bogie doesn't know, but you shouldn't have seen it.' I'll say I shouldn't have!

I was moving in a daze. I talked — I listened — it was only about Bogie. It was numbness that took over, certainly not acceptance. I didn't analyze anything — all that came later.

As dawn approached I went into the kitchen. May was awake — I went into her room and told her — she cried — we hugged each other. We'd been through so much together — she loved Bogie so much. Those last months she'd asked no questions, just did everything she could do. First class.

The nurses were ready to go. They had done all that they could do in every way, they had been wonderful. They too had thought Bogie a marvelous man and an incredible patient.

I had to tell the children. I went upstairs, opened Steve's door — he was awake, lying in his bed. I sat down and hugged him very hard. 'Oh, darling — I am so sorry to have to tell you this. Daddy died early this morning — he stayed in his sleep — felt no pain.' Steve just lay there and rubbed and rubbed his eyes — made fists of his little hands and rubbed his eyes hard, back and forth — they were red and wet, but he did not cry. 'Is he in heaven?' 'Of course he is, darling — he'll be watching us, so you must be very brave and strong. He was so proud of you — never forget that, and that he loved you very much.' What could I say — how can you tell a child? How can you tell your son that from that day forward his life will never be the same — that there will never be a way to fill that gaping hole? Never. I said it the best I could — I was so worried for him — I knew nothing except to love him. I told him I would get Leslie — bring her into his room for a few

609

minutes. That beautiful little girl who was worshipped by her father. I took her out of her crib, sat her on my lap, and told her in much the same words that Daddy had gone to heaven, that we wouldn't see him again, that he loved her very much. I brought her into Steve's room, where we sat on his bed, the three of us together, and just said we must always love one another. Leslie cried at the thought of not seeing her daddy again, not understanding anything else. I wanted them to be close together — to help one another. It was a lot to want. I called my mother, who was just getting up — it was still only about 7:30 — told her.

Harvey came upstairs, walked into the bedroom, walked over to the bed — first the side Bogie had been on, then the other — then into Bogie's dressing room. He knew something was very wrong. He walked to the bed again — looked at me as if he understood — and stayed there.

It was a big black headline in both morning papers. Joe had done well and had kept the press away.

Mother arrived, more upset than I'd ever seen her.

And poor Pat, who was in the hospital, called me in tears. 'Poor Bogie — he was the best brother — husband — father. What will I do without him? Why did he have to go first?' She was shattered — she was the only one left of their family.

Phones started to ring — telegrams and flowers started to arrive — people started to come. It was Monday, the fourteenth of January, 1957 — three weeks after Bogie's fifty-seventh birthday.

K.C. came over to see the children. Talked to them, soothed them.

I would have to think about a service — a eulogy. Would Spence deliver it? I mentioned it to Katie when she came. She'd ask him, but she didn't think he'd be able to — physically able to.

Mike and Gloria Romanoff arrived, James and Pamela Mason, Dorris Johnson — Nunnally was down south and flew back immediately. When I thanked him, he said, 'I would have walked.' Leland Hayward and Slim Hawks (to whom he was now married), the Negulescos, John Huston, the Jaffes, Swifty, Hjordis — the house was swarming with people. I remember sitting at our coffee table in the lanai with Morgan and others, figuring out the course of funeral events. Jess Morgan (of Morgan Maree's office) had gone to Forest Lawn for cremation arrangements. While we were sitting there he came back and told me they tried to sell him a casket for five thousand dollars, which he'd thought was outrageous. So he had chosen a very simple pine box — not the cheapest, a nice one, but as it was going into the crematorium, there was no point in extravagance. He said I would have to go there to choose an urn — he would take me the following morning.

Spence called me and in a most pleading voice said, 'I couldn't deliver the eulogy — I just couldn't — I wouldn't be able to get through it. I loved old Bogie. I could do it for someone I wasn't that emotional about, but not for dear Bogie. Please understand, darling.' Of course I understood. Darling Spence — he was too close — he cared too much.

Uncle Charlie and Rosalie called from San Francisco to say they'd be coming down. Betty Comden and Adolph Green called from New York. Ginny and Quent Reynolds, Ruth and Paul Zuckerman, were flying out. Frank was in New York at the Copa — he called — he'd probably come back for the funeral.

I decided that John Huston should deliver the eulogy. I asked him if he would — he said of course. We were standing in the hall talking when I heard Steve, who was lying on the floor at the head of the stairs, calling to me through the banister railing, 'What is the date, Mommy?' He was writing something. I went upstairs to find that in a little agenda book he had, he had written: 'January 14th — Daddy died.'

I decided the service would be on Thursday the seventeenth, and that Bogie would be cremated while the service was taking place. I wanted no flowers — only contributions to the American Cancer Society.

The lanai and the Butternut Room were filled with friends — just sitting, giving support — quietly talking — recalling moments with Bogie — even some laughter. So much activity, there was no time for tears. I moved through it all zombie-like.

Bogie had always said he wanted no funeral. Quick cremation and his ashes strewn over the Pacific Ocean — he'd always loved the idea of a Viking funeral. I told Morgan I wanted to follow his wishes — to go out on the *Santana* and leave what was left of him in the ocean that meant so much more to him than land. Morgan told me I couldn't do that — it was against the law. Now the law has been changed, but then it couldn't be done. Morgan also felt that Bogie was too public a figure, and that there should be a place for his children to go to in later years, a place to find him. I was confused and torn. Did I have an obligation to keep a permanent place above ground? Perhaps so — though, to me, Bogie's legacy on film was greater than the greatest monument could have been.

Toward the end of the first day the crowd began to thin out — David Niven came from work and there were a few others. I don't know how I stayed awake, but I did. It was life's longest day for me. It would be my first night alone — my first night without Bogie on this earth. Mother offered to stay overnight, an offer I leaped at. 'You can sleep in the little room,' I said. 'Where will *you* sleep, then?' 'In our bed. I have to start sometime — it might as well be now.'

I sat with the children through their haphazard dinner — they were distracted, not hungry. I told them to eat only what they wanted. There was no point in insisting on a real meal — May was in no shape to cook it, they were in no shape to eat it. I wanted them to go to school the next day, I thought it would be better for them. I had spoken to Steve's teachers, explaining he would be out Thursday, tried to make them aware of what he was going through. I'd alerted Leslie's school. I counted on the sensitivity of others. They all seemed to understand.

Everyone had left by ten o'clock. The radio and television news were full of talk about Bogie. Special programs were being planned. I had asked Kathy Sloan to subscribe to a clipping service during that first week so I could put together a scrapbook for the children.

I had put Steve and Leslie to bed, listened to their prayers as they added a P.S.: God to please take care of Daddy and a God bless Mommy only. They were tired, but all the activity in the house had keyed them up. The adjustment would take time — maybe forever.

At last Mother and I headed for the bedroom. That odor still hung in the air. Strange to have no nurses, not one familiar face, no sound after so many months. The bed looked larger than it was, and emptier. Every corner of the room seemed darker. Bogie's dressing room stood as it had been left — closets and drawers brimming with clothes, some never worn. My head was filled with all that had to be done — what music should be played? All the people to be invited to the house after the service to drink their toasts to Bogie. And Forest Lawn awaited me in the morning. Of course it would be against the law to strew ashes across the ocean — how else would funeral homes make their money?

I slept — badly, but I slept, strangely aware of being back on my own side of the bed. That odor was still hovering. Was it really just this morning that Bogie had died? It seemed forever ago.

I woke up very early and went immediately to the children. I was worried about

Steve. He got up, dressed, spoke little. I told him Lee would be there when we got home. He and Leslie had their breakfast, their nurse took them to the school bus and came back saying that there were photographers outside taking their pictures! I couldn't believe it — was it really news to photographers that two small children were on their way to school on the day after their father had died? I wanted no photographs — how in hell could their lives go on like this? I called Joe Hyams, my press intermediary, very upset — asked him to try to find out who they might be.

Jess and I left for Forest Lawn — I had never been there before. The road that leads to it is a turn to the right just before the Warner Bros. studio. Funny to see the studio sign first (our beginning), then head toward death. There are acres and acres of green grass, headstones, bronze plaques, before you enter the building area. We entered a small building and were met by a man with a polished, professional manner — a man used to grief and prepared to take full advantage of it. We were led into a small, dark room with just one yellow bulb burning. There were four different bronze urns on display. The man in a slow, sympathetic (even if it was real I wouldn't have believed it), mournful voice told me the price of each, gave me his recommendation. I chose one of them — I only wanted to get out of there. And would we follow him, please — he thought he had found a lovely spot for Mr Bogart. He took his keys and led me to a small garden with high walls — it was called the Garden of Memory. He opened an iron gate. There were little bronze doors about the size of safety-deposit boxes. The niches behind them were fairly deep. Large enough for more than one urn. The man showed me the size of the plaque, asked me what I wanted on it — I told him just 'Humphrey de Forest Bogart' and the dates of his birth and death. He said, 'Would you like me to print it here?' pointing to the top of the plaque. 'There's room for all of you.' I almost hit him — honest to God, is there no limit? Get me out of this place! 'And you see,' pointing to a small glass vase perched alongside the plaques with a pathetic flower in it, 'you can have permanent care all year round for just a small fee.' You're not going to trap me into that, you bastard. These people get you in your grief and misery and sell you whatever they can at the highest possible prices. Bogie had left behind some of his cynicism with me. That, plus my own, kept me alert enough to keep saying no. And I was angry at the world — 'no' was my best friend. At last it was done. There must be a better way . . .

When I had got home, there were friends waiting for me. Frank had called and would call again. My friends felt I should get away after Thursday, that I had been shut in for months, that it would be good for the children to be in another place with other associations for a while. When Frank called again, he offered me his house for two weeks. After talking it over with Mother and Lee, I decided to try it. They would come with me.

At a final discussion with Morgan and K.C. about the service, it was decided to have K.C. read the Twenty-third Psalm. I chose music that was not gloomy. I would bring magnolia leaves from our own trees — have a few white roses — and on the other side of the altar, in clear view, I wanted to place the model of the *Santana*. No decision could have been better. As I think back on my life after Bogie died, I think that choice was the last sane one I made for many months.

Jess, who had gone to Forest Lawn to finalize everything, came back with a message to me from another ghoul there: 'Please tell Mrs Bogart that if she would like to see her husband, he looks wonderful.'

Drs Brandsma and Flynn came to commiserate, to offer solace, though there was none, to talk about Bogie. People are never quite sure whether the bereaved want to hear the name of the one that's gone. I did, I couldn't speak at all without mentioning his name; he was so much my life, so much our home. And by talking about him constantly, I might convince myself that he had only gone away for a boat race . . .

On Wednesday, the night before the service, there was to be a very special radio program. It was to last an hour, and consist of many Bogie interviews. I hungrily searched for any and all programs relating to him. I didn't want to forget — I wanted to hang on. I remember sitting at the small table in the window of the dining room where we often had lunch. It was nine or ten o'clock at night, the children were asleep. The program began. Bogie's voice was coming through. A few of us sat around the table listening — those inflections, those chuckles I remembered so well. I couldn't speak. Everyone there — Mother especially — watched me for a reaction. None was visible. At the end I walked to the pantry where May was standing, having been listening to the same program. I fell on her warm, welcoming body, sobbing out some of the misery, frustrations, and tensions of the past year. I couldn't cry that way with Mother — she would have fallen apart with me. I didn't have to hold anything in reserve with May. She had been in that house every day those last eleven months, had known Bogie longer than any one of us, and she was May — all wisdom, all understanding. I hadn't expected the tears — they just came.

Rosalie and Charlie had arrived that day. Oh, I was glad to see them. My Chach — how lucky I was to have him there. His presence helped so much.

The family and John were gathered at home by 10:30 — the service was scheduled to begin at 11:30, the church was five minutes away. John was nervously pacing. He had shown me some of the eulogy the day before, but I had not seen it all. The cars were waiting. We came downstairs, hugged and kissed those who were waiting. It was time to go. The children, John, and I were in the first car; Mother, Lee, Rosalie, and Charlie in the second; May, Kathy, and Aurelio bringing up the rear.

As we entered the church I could see that there were mobs of people all around. It was reported that over three thousand people lined the streets. At 12:30 there was to be a minute of silence at Warner Bros. and 20th Century-Fox. The church was packed, I recognized a few faces closest to me, tried to smile as I took my seat in the front row. I looked at the altar with the model of the *Santana* standing alone, proud and clear. It was a moving sight, much more than any casket would have been. Katie told me she was the first one in the church, arriving early to avoid the press, and in a skirt, not her usual trousers. Devoted Katie, and when she saw the model of that boat she completely dissolved. The fresh green of our magnolia trees, the white roses were just right. K.C. stood up and spoke his words about Bogie and God. He recited the Ten Commandments because Bogie had believed in them and lived by them. And he read Tennyson's 'Crossing the Bar.' Then came John. I feel compelled to quote verbatim from what John spoke that day. He said it better and more personally than anyone else could have. As I watched and listened to him, I thought of the influence Bogie had been in his life — how their careers had grown together, how each had made an impact on the other. I had always instinctively felt that the two people who most affected and involved John's emotional life had been his father and Bogie. How hard it must have been for him to put those words together, written from his deepest heart, and speak them aloud. I treasure them, knowing how difficult it was for him to allow those feelings to surface.

Humphrey Bogart died early Monday

morning. His wife was at his bedside, and his children were nearby. He had been unconscious for a day. He was not in any pain. It was a peaceful death. At no time during the months of his illness did he believe he was going to die, not that he refused to consider the thought — it simply never occurred to him. He loved life. Life meant his family, his friends, his work, his boat. He could not imagine leaving any of them, and so until the very last he planned what he would do when he got well. His boat was being repainted. Stephen, his son, was getting of an age when he could be taught to sail, and to learn his father's love of the sea. A few weeks' sailing and Bogie would be all ready to go to work again. He was going to make fine pictures — only fine pictures — from here on in.

With the years he had become increasingly aware of the dignity of his profession — Actor, not Star: Actor. Himself, he never took too seriously — his work most seriously. He regarded the somewhat gaudy figure of Bogart, the star, with an amused cynicism; Bogart, the actor, he held in deep respect. Those who did not know him well, who never worked with him, who were not of the small circle of his close friends, had another completely different idea of the man than the few who were so privileged. I suppose the ones who knew him but slightly were at the greatest disadvantage, particularly if they were the least bit solemn about their own importance. Bigwigs have been known to stay away from the brilliant Hollywood occasions rather than expose their swelling neck muscles to Bogart's banderillas.

In each of the fountains at Versailles there is a pike which keeps all the carp active, otherwise they would grow overfat and die. Bogie took rare delight in performing a similar duty in the fountains of Hollywood. Yet his victims seldom bore him any malice, and when they did, not for long. His shafts were fashioned only to stick into the outer layer of complacency, and not to penetrate through to the regions of the spirit where real injuries are done.

The great houses of Beverly Hills, and for that matter of the world, were so many shooting galleries so far as Bogie was concerned. His own house was a sanctuary. Within those walls anyone, no matter how elevated his position, could breathe easy. Bogie's hospitality went far beyond food and drink. He fed a guest's spirit as well as his body, plied him with good will until he

623

became drunk in the heart as well as in the legs . . .

Bogie was lucky at love and he was lucky at dice. To begin with he was endowed with the greatest gift a man can have: talent. The whole world came to recognize it. Through it he was able to live in comfort and to provide well for his wife and children.

His life, though not a long one measured in years, was a rich, full life. Over all the other blessings were the two children, Stephen and Leslie, who gave a final lasting meaning to his life. Yes, Bogie wanted for nothing. He got all that he asked for out of life and more. We have no reason to feel any sorrow for him — only for ourselves for having lost him. He is quite irreplaceable. There will never be another like him.

My arms were around Steve and Leslie. I kept looking at them from time to time to make sure they were all right. I glanced at Mother, in whose face was written the greatest pain I'd ever seen. Then K.C. rose again and asked us all to stand and recite the Twenty-third Psalm. Then to kneel for the final prayer. The music was by Bach and Debussy — one of Bogie's favorite composers. I brought my children to the kneeling position with me. They had behaved beautifully. Had they understood any of it? At least they could see how many people cared about their father. And I hoped it was reassuring to see Niven, Swifty, Mike, Nunnally ushering friends down the aisles. When they were older, they might read John's words and understand better. And then I thought: 'At this moment the cremation is happening.'

It was over. We rose and headed for the side door. We got into the car and headed home.

It seemed that everyone in the church had come to the house. Mike Romanoff had sent cassoulet, salads, cheese, booze, and waiters by the carload for Bogie. It was like a party — almost. Everyone came to me first, drink in hand, then talked among themselves. Marlene Dietrich kissed me and gave me sympathy. I remember Dr Jones sitting at the table with Brandsma and Flynn, drawing on a piece of paper, going over the surgery again to see how it had been done, searching for more knowledge, assuring himself that the way he had done it had been the only way. Danny Kaye came up to me and said, 'You have no idea where you are.' I suppose he was right, but I kept moving through it all as though I knew what I was doing. And Spencer was there, and Kate, and the Jaffes, the Johnsons, the Marees, Jimmy

Van Heusen, the Gershwins, the Pecks, the Dick Powells, Bogie's captain Pete, the Wylers, the Goldwyns, Bill Blair (representing Adlai), Bogie's hairdresser, make-up men, nurses, studio heads, neighbors. Betty and Adolph, after the wire and the phone call, just arrived the day before the service — they had to be with me — what true friends! The house was alive with voices, laughter, plates of food, drink. I moved from one to another like a hostess. Odd stories of Bogie and moments remembered, outrageous, funny, infuriating, brave, all that Bogie was. He'd left his mark, all right. Steve and Leslie were running in and out. As long as there were people, as long as there was noise, we could manage. In the midst of it all, Frank called from New York — he had not been able to come — to ask how I was, the children — he'd call later to find out what time we'd be leaving for Palm Springs.

The high-comedy part of the day came from the American Floral Association. The papers had printed my request that there be no flowers — instead, contributions should be sent to the American Cancer Society in Bogie's name. Whereupon the floral group got carried away and sent me a telegram. As I opened what I thought was another condolence wire, my mouth dropped open: 'Do we say don't go to see

Lauren Bacall movies?' That gave me and all who saw it the one true laugh of the day.

It was so good to see those rooms full of people again — to hear laughter. And it was all about Bogie, all for him. He wouldn't have believed so many held him in such high regard. He wouldn't have believed the more than a thousand telegrams from all over the world; from old friends like Jack Buchanan, Noel, Moss Hart, George Kaufman — new ones like the Oliviers, Cookes, Schlesingers — from people who had met him once — or never. From children of friends, like Bill Hayward from Lawrenceville, where he was in school. From many like Max Gordon, Irving Berlin, Howard Lindsay, who'd known him when he started in the theatre; tennis champions Pancho Segura and Tony Trabert; Aly Khan; Governor Knight of California, who'd met him once or twice; Cole Porter, Jerome Robbins, Averell Harriman. It was staggering.

I took all personal letters with me to Palm Springs to read when I had time. I would write a personal note to everyone who had sent a wire or letter. And all the clippings would have to be sorted out for the scrapbooks. I was very organized — I managed better when there was a lot to do.

Buddy and Carolyn Morris lived in Palm

Springs and Steve and Leslie would have their Steve and Chris to play with. The Nivens were coming down for a weekend with Cary Grant. So we wouldn't be too dismally alone. Sun and, hopefully, sleep would help us all. The children loved the desert — we went riding, swimming — but I started having nightmares, waking up in the middle of the night hearing Bogie talking to me — seeing his emaciated body upstairs, calling to me over the balcony — seeing him dead in our bed. One night, in a cold sweat, tears covering my face, hearing a thud and looking downstairs to see that misshapen white sack in the entry hall. The doctors had given me pills to help me sleep — not true barbiturates, Miltown at first, I think — but I stayed depressed. I couldn't get used to not seeing Bogie, not talking to him. I started to read the letters I had brought. Sterling Hayden — 'There are those who say our maker has things all worked out for us and whatever happens is for the best — there are times when I can't agree and this is one of them.' Fred Astaire (whose wife had died of cancer not long before Bogie) — 'I know so very well what you're going through.' Sailing companions Ken Carey, Bob Dorris, Bob Marlott — remembering the joy on the *Santana*, their admiration and respect for Bogie the sailor, the side of him they were privy to — his love of the sea — how much he had given — how they wished they could do more. John Cromwell — telling me tales of early theatre days shared. A man from *Photoplay* in New York quoting Louis Bromfield when he told Louis he was leaving Cleveland for Hollywood: 'The only good thing I can say about Hollywood is Bogart lives there.' Ed Murrow — 'There are times when people who work with words know that they are futile — this is such a time. Someone once wrote, "There are no pockets in a shroud. The dead hold in their hands only what they have given away." Your husband gave much.'

Harry Cohn writing that last May he had been apprised of Bogie's illness and 'I became determined then and it became an absolute command at Columbia that nothing would be discussed at this studio concerning any change of plans re *The Good Shepherd*. It was to preclude any possibility of a leak to any column or paper. The only thing allowed was a change of date. It was my desire and Columbia's that Bogie never suspect even the possibility of his not making that picture — and this was the reason I was afraid of making a personal visit to him — I was concerned that a slip of the tongue or facial expression when I saw him might give me away — and to give him any disheartening doubt. It was the least we could do for Humphrey Bogart — would we had been able to do more.'

And there were many more. From John O'Hara, impressing upon me the priority work must take above all else. From Howard Lindsay and Russel Crouse with their memories of Humphrey. From actors who didn't really know him. From Charlie Blair, dear friend, who had flown Bogie around Italy during the war, and flown Steve to meet us in London — saying how he'd learned from Bogie and because of him dared his record-breaking solo flight over the Pole — Bogie had convinced Charlie that anything was possible. From the president of his fan club for fifteen years. From Herb Shettler, the judge who married us. They all spoke of Bogie's spirit — his heroic character — his laughter and his wanting to help others. Some of them made me cry — some of them still do. The impact of his death was great. I want whoever reads these words to have a sense of Bogie — what he was, the personal mark he left on many varied lives. I clung to the letters — they kept him close to me.

On the surface the children were enjoying themselves — I was amazed at what resilient creatures they were. One day Leslie said to my Mother while I was out riding with Steve: 'Why did God take my daddy away?' Mother was nonplussed — could only think to say, 'God needed him.' Whereupon Leslie replied, 'Did He think it was more important for Him to have him than his children?' Mother couldn't answer that — indeed, who could? So in that four-year-old head, all kinds of questions were being asked.

One night while the Nivens and I were having dinner at Cary and Betsy Grant's house, David took me outside. He had lost his young first wife many years before and knew grief. He put his arm around my shoulder and said, 'There is no panacea for this kind of loss. Just know that every day it gets the tiniest bit better — suddenly one day you can put it in a different perspective. You'll never forget Bogie — nor would you want to. You'll just one day be able to put him in a different place in your life.' I never forgot what David said. Of course it had been deeply ingrained in me by Bogie not to mourn — that it did no good for the dead and was just self-indulgent. That was all well and good to say — not so simple to practice. But it almost forced me to keep things inside — and by keeping them inside, lengthened the time for me before I was able to put them in perspective.

The two weeks came to a close. I packed

up the children and myself, and with Mother and Lee we headed back to reality. Lee would go back to New York and Mother would follow soon — I told her I'd have to learn to deal with life as it would be from now on. The children would be in school, I had endless letters to write, and I would have to think about work. I doubt that many producers thought of me as an actress at that point, I had been so much Bogie's wife that last year — except for *Designing Woman*, I had not been near a studio. And no one seemed to be breaking down the door for my services. I hated that casual sloughing off of me — or of anyone, for that matter.

I had decided the children and I would have dinner together in the dining room from now on. At least routine could be understood. One night just before Valentine's Day, while at the table, Stephen said, 'I know, Mommy, I know how we can surprise Daddy — we can all shoot ourselves and be with Daddy on Valentine's Day.' I was shocked and unnerved. What had been going on in that young mind? I tried to stay close to Steve — it seemed to me that he felt the loss very deeply, but who really can say who feels what and at what age? I'm sure I was neglectful of Leslie in my over-concern about Steve, and that I made many mistakes, but I could only do what I could do with the arrival of each day. All our nerves were frayed and would be for months to come — for years. All of our lives had been indelibly scarred. Whenever Steve was angry with me, more often than not it was 'I wish Daddy were here instead of you.' I asked Dr Spivek about it — the other doctors — they all said it was perfectly natural, that Steve was full of resentment because his father had left him, that he probably felt he had done something wrong to make his father want to leave, that his father hadn't loved him. So I tried to make up by loving him too much. As long as Mother could stay, I went back to leaning on her — I felt less alone in the house. When I had to see people regarding Bogie's will — talk to anyone who came — answer letters — she more than took up the slack. And of course she was wonderful with the children.

I didn't have a clue what I was doing. I got up in the morning, talked on the telephone, ate meals, saw friends at home, played with the children — did what had to be done. I was breathing, but there was no life in me. I couldn't think of the future, I could only think of the man I had lost — the man who'd given me everything, taught me about people and living, with whom I had found my way of life. How could I continue alone? How would I fill the days — to what end? He had taken so much with him.

A letter from Moss Hart refused to start with the usual words of sympathy:

Perhaps what no one's said is that in spite of the death, you're a lucky woman. You've had 10½ [actually it was 11½] years of marriage with a fine man — not many women can achieve that in the sense that you and Bogie did. You and you alone were the one person in all of his life that Bogie loved the most tenderly and most deeply — that he took the most pride in and that he relished and enjoyed above all other human beings. It is a lucky woman indeed who can enrich a man's life to the extent that you enriched Bogie's, and now is the time to remember that. You are lucky too in the flowering legacy that Bogie left you in Steve and Leslie — a part of himself that is and will continue to be a constant reaffirmation of his life and not Death — and it is because I believe in such affirmation that I feel that in the realm that lies beyond your present sorrow you will find comfort in having had those wonderful years together. They do not come to everyone but they came to you — and Bogie — and to have had them is to have defeated Death and to have had life at its best.

I read and reread that letter endlessly. Of course I had been lucky — I had always known that — but Bogie hadn't been, to die so young, and in such a way, leaving Steve and Leslie without the privilege of knowing him. The days continued, but with no point of view. The two small children became my focus — if I hadn't had them to help me keep some semblance of sanity, God knows what I would have done. As it was, I did little right. I could do for Bogie, but it would be many years before I could do for myself. And the nightmares continued.

I knew I would not be able to keep the *Santana* — it was pure Bogie anyway and should be used and sailed by a man who loved it as Bogie had. I would have to go down there, though, to collect Bogie's belongings. So I arranged it for a Sunday and took Steve and Leslie with me. It was not a day for sailing, but I wanted to go out anyway, so we started up the engine and we motored around the bay. It would be my last trip on board. So strange to be there without Bogie. As we moved around the bay on the cold, gray day, past familiar yachts of friends, pictures of sunnier, happier days flashed before me. When we got back to the dock and I'd sorted everything,

I took a last look below — another on deck — another walking up the gangway to the car. It wasn't only the *Santana* I was saying goodbye to, it was goodbye to a kind of life — a facet of Bogie I'd shared with him, and a way of life I'd never know again. It was the last time I saw that sailor's dream, the fifty-five-foot yawl *Santana.*

There was also Bogie's dressing room at home to deal with — how I dreaded that. Everything in it reminded me of some occasion somewhere. I didn't want to do it quickly, and yet what was the point of keeping all his things when they could do someone some good? Finally I made myself do it — when the children were in school. I set aside everything I thought would fit Lee — gave Aurelio some things — gave Kathy anything her grown-up son could use — saved all handkerchiefs for Steve — kept some silk shirts for myself. It was ghastly. I tried to psych myself into a business-like approach as I fiercely emptied cupboards and drawers. That odor was still in the air. It took quite a while for me to recover from that day.

Even home had less meaning — all the things in it so assiduously collected, with such love, all meant to last forever because we were to stay there forever. What did it mean to have these tables and chairs, these cups and saucers — what good was it? And I had thought, 'This is permanent.' It was ridiculous to accumulate things, to feel that possession gave safety — it's true of neither people nor things. Every object signified some portion of life with Bogie — I had brought nothing but myself to our marriage, and except for some original Maud Humphrey sketches which belonged to Bogie, everything we had lived with I had found since May 21, 1945.

And Steve was having problems at school. The teacher complained that he seemed withdrawn, but that suddenly during a class he would stand up and scream — very difficult to manage. What the hell did she expect? There he was surrounded by his school friends, hearing them talk about their mothers and fathers; he couldn't do that ever again. I thought teachers were supposed to understand, have compassion, help. Did she expect him to behave according to her idea of normal?

At home he seemed much as usual, though a bit edgier — a bit more withdrawn. I had his friends over to play as often as possible, and Steve and Leslie went to their houses — lucky to have so many neighbor children. Every effort was made to keep the days normal. The home atmosphere was all right during the day, but at night — at dinnertime — it became tough. It was not an atmosphere of gloom, exactly, that pervaded the house, as much as the feeling of heaviness, emptiness — of a big something missing. There were no terrible crises with Stephen or Leslie, only the same one. I was mostly concerned with Steve — so much too much with him that I almost forgot my little girl. As I think back on Leslie's mien, she just got quieter. All our emotions were raw.

Dore Schary had asked me if I would travel for three weeks to Boston, New York, Washington, Florida for publicity on *Designing Woman*. It was to open at the end of March. If I would go, it would take me through Easter, and Stephen and Leslie could come with me. I leaped at the chance — it was work of a sort, and a reason to be in New York, to see family and friends. A reason to leave Mapleton Drive. And it would give me something to look forward to.

Frank wanted to give a small dinner for me with only my closest friends before I was to leave for New York. He invited about ten people, including Spence and Kate. As they never went anywhere together except to our house through Bogie's illness, I didn't expect them to say yes, but, to my everlasting gratitude, they did. Katie even wore a dress, and I was so moved to see them sitting there in that living room, making that effort out of friendship — their sweetness was indescribable.

I was making a little progress. One afternoon I went to All Saints Church to sit and think. I was not — am not — a religious person. I would like to believe there is a God — I want there to be — but I'm not sure. Yet it seemed the only place where I could sit undisturbed for as long as I liked and think my own private, confused thoughts. There was an aura of peace in that church, a calm I needed badly. And it was familiar, yet not. It answered my need.

I arrived in New York on April 1. It was my first time out publicly since Bogie's death less than three months before. The press were welcoming and warm — the picture was enthusiastically received everywhere — no questions were asked about Bogie, only about the children.

I was so happy to see my family again — I really needed them. And I did not lack company; I was pampered to within an inch of my life. For the first time in my professional life, I was functioning as an independent actress, as a single woman. And since I loved *Designing Woman,* I felt better about my work than I had in years. The dark area was that Bogie was not around to share my pride — I had so wanted him to see me in it, to give me his approval.

It was strange to be out in the world again, unprotected. But it was good. It made me aware of the existence of other things. Adolph Green took me to see *Bells Are Ringing*, which had opened just before Bogie died. We went out afterward with Sydney Chaplin, who was in the show. We'd been with Betty Comden and her husband, Steve Kyle, met up with Harry Kurnitz and Marty Gabel and Arlene Francis and the George Axelrods along the way, ended up singing songs from the show at dawn on Fifth Avenue. My God, it was fun — the most carefree time I'd had in over a year. The whole time in New York was filled with excitement — unplanned, loose, easy nights. There was no time to think of what the last year had been. I thought this must be what David Niven had meant. 'I feel all right — I can't believe it — is it possible I'm going to be all right from now on?' I believed it then — fool that I was.

Frank called several times to see how I was — when I would be coming home. He was the only unattached man I knew, and I was glad he was around. I suppose that, without realizing it, I was starting to depend on his phone calls.

Adlai had called also, and asked me to

bring Steve and Leslie to his farm in Libertyville for Easter Sunday. I was thrilled — knew they would love it, knew that I would. He came to New York, too, and I saw him at a small dinner. He took me back to the hotel, came up for a nightcap, and talked to me about my life, and about life in general. He was so full of care and thought — I adored him, and felt lucky to have a tiny part of that great heart and mind.

Everything went right on that trip — friends, family; the critics liked the movie, I liked talking about it; I made my usual trip to Loehmann's with Mother to buy acres of Norell samples — for what I don't know. If I bought, perhaps I'd have places to go — people to see — a life to lead. From the day I could afford it, I've shopped too much. As my mother used to say as she looked at my hundred pairs of shoes, 'How can you ever wear them? You only have two feet!'

Suddenly it was time to head for Chicago and home. I never liked saying goodbye to Mother, but she'd come out to see us in a few months. Except for Bogie, she was my most solid rock of love and security, and though the balance had shifted away from her during my marriage, it was shifting back.

Stephen, Leslie, and I took the *Twentieth*

Century to Chicago. We were met by a car on Easter Sunday morning and headed for Libertyville. As we pulled into the driveway, Adlai opened the front door. He laughed — kissed me hello — hugged the children. I was overjoyed to see him — he always made me feel better than almost anyone else. It was as though my brain shifted gears when I saw him — I reactivated the better part of it. He'd planned the day for Stephen and Leslie, had hidden eggs around the house for an Easter egg hunt with a prize for the winner. There was a terrific lunch — I remember Adlai's ravenous approach to food, as though each bite would be his last. A substitute for other gratifications, I'd always suspected. We had a marvelous walk in his woods after lunch. His love of the land was clear — his longing to spend more time there, lead a life there. I felt his loneliness acutely through the light banter. He was affectionate with me — concerned about my frame of mind and any plans I might have. We had tea before the fire — an unpressured day, unusual for each of us, and one of the best I'd had in a long time. The children felt immediately at home. I hadn't known until then that Adlai could do that.

After a night at the Ambassador East in Chicago we flew home. The three of us were very close. We'd gotten through our first holiday without Bogie.

Home looked beautiful. It had been good to get away and it was good to get back — until I went upstairs. I still half-expected to see Bogie in our bed, and remnants of that odor hung in the air. But I felt better than I had before leaving.

There were flowers from Frank to welcome me home.

Soon afterward there was a closed-circuit prizefight — the middleweight championship. Sugar Ray Robinson and Gene Fullmer. Frank had bought a row of seats in some theatre and invited me to go. He had meticulously striven to keep his private life out of the news — not easy when you are a natural news-maker. I had never thought much about celebrity after the insane exposure I'd had at the time of *To Have and Have Not* and my marriage. Bogie was a natural news-maker too, almost everything he said or did making a very loud noise in the press. I just lived my life, and the press and I had for the most part been on good terms. I gave no thought to being noticed on such a quiet evening, even with Frank, but when we emerged from the theatre there were photographers waiting, and the resulting pictures ended up in newspapers around the world. It was my first public outing in Hollywood — the first time Frank and I were linked, even tentatively, in a romantic way. I could never figure out how they knew I would be there. Much later I remember telling a friend I couldn't understand why the press cared so much about Frank and me — why it made such a stir. This friend looked at me unbelievingly. 'Don't be a fool — you and Frank can't go anywhere without causing a commotion. Individually you make news, but together it's insane.' The next eight months were to prove him right. Indeed, the next months were filled with intense and difficult moments of every kind.

One afternoon Harvey became ill — he lay down and started to foam at the mouth. I got him into the station wagon, had the vet alerted, and raced over to the Valley, shaking all the way. Harvey stood up in the back of the wagon with the white foam all around his muzzle, looking as though he didn't understand what was happening. I kept saying, with quavering voice, 'It will be all right, Harvey — lie down,' kept talking to him while I couldn't breathe, frantically trying not to hit a tree or another car. After examining him, Dr Winston said he'd had a heart attack — that he should stay quietly in the kennel for a couple of days. I hated to leave that dog. The next day I could see he was even weaker. The doctor said, 'I know how much you love Harvey — he's a great dog. He's had a good, healthy life — you don't want to see him disintegrate. It would be a terrible thing for him to have to be confined. You can take him home if you want to in another day or so, but you must seriously consider putting him to sleep.' I said I'd call the next day. Before leaving, Harvey had happily licked my face, telling me how glad he was to see me and how much better he was. About thirty minutes after I got home he called: 'Harvey just died — he was happy — he'd just seen you, had just eaten his dinner and lay down and died. Lucky for him.' I was destroyed, collapsed in tears. My Harvey — another big piece of my married life gone.

In August, Harry Kurnitz offered me his penthouse in New York. I'd never lived like a bachelor girl in New York in the summer when the city was empty. I decided to try it for two weeks. Steve was still in camp, Leslie in a play group — I'd return in time for her birthday party.

Harry's apartment was perfect — tiny, with a balcony, on the corner of 75th and Park. It was fun to be in New York when only real workers were there. I had my little flirtations — and Mother. Walking in the city at night with the streets so empty made me feel as if I owned it.

Mother and I spent most of the days together. She loved going around with me. She'd come into Manhattan to meet me and we'd shop for the children — linen for my bed — antiques. My nights were my own secret adventures. A couple of mornings after our last shopping expedition she called me. 'Can you come? I'm at Doctors' Hospital.' Her voice sounded funny, faraway. Then silence. I panicked — didn't even know where Doctors' Hospital was. I looked it up, rushed over, and, after hysterically questioning every nurse in sight, found her — in an oxygen tent. I shall not forget walking into that room, seeing her lying there, face to one side under the plastic tent, towel on her forehead. Unconscious. It was so unexpected. No warning. I started to shake. They — those faceless theys, I didn't even know her doctor's name — told me the first forty-eight hours were crucial. We'd just have to wait. I found a phone. The family started to arrive. Lee — white-faced. Charlie and Rosalie. Renee. I just stood at the foot of the bed, looking at my mother. What had happened? How had it happened? Why didn't I know more? Would she be all right? I was so frightened. I prayed all day — all night — whispering to myself, 'Please let her be all right — please.' I stood vigil with Lee in that damn hospital for forty-eight hours. The bad lighting —

whispering corridors — uniforms — waiting. She was going to be all right. She'd had a massive coronary, the kind Eisenhower was to have. Six weeks in the hospital, a couple more at home. She was a good patient. She wanted reasons for what had happened to her, to give me clues to prevent it ever happening to me. She'd unpacked an enormous barrel of china the day before — 'Take a lesson from me, Betty — never do that — never lift anything.' She was always after me to stop smoking — 'If I can stop, anyone can.' I stayed for two weeks until she was well out of the woods, but she wanted me to get back to the children. 'You can't leave them for too long — Steve will be coming home from camp — Leslie's alone.' Also I was going to work again — at last. Not a marvelous picture — a remake, sentimental — but Negulesco would direct and we loved working together. It was to start at the end of September. *The Gift of Love.*

Once I was home, Frank and I became a steady pair. We flew to Las Vegas for *The Joker Is Wild* opening — he took me to the *Pal Joey* opening in town — at all his small dinner parties I was the hostess. People were watching with interest. It seemed to everyone — to his friends, to mine — that we were crazy about each other, that we were a great pair; that it wouldn't last; that

Frank would never be able to remain constantly devoted, monogamous — yet that maybe with me, he *would*. My friends were worried I'd be hurt — he wasn't good enough, couldn't be counted on for a lifetime. But just then it was all going smoothly. I sat in on some of his recording dates — I was the center of his life at the moment. At least I thought I was — I felt I was. It seemed perfect, no way for it not to work. And I was happy. Surface happy.

I can't really remember how it all began — there must have always been a special feeling alive between Frank and me from earlier days. Certainly he was then at his vocal peak, and was wildly attractive, electrifying. And Frank had always carried with him not only an aura of excitement, but the feeling that behind that swinging façade lies a lonely, restless man, one who wants a wife and a home but simultaneously wants freedom and a string of 'broads.'

The last few months of Bogie's illness he was away working off and on. If in town, he came over at least twice a week. When he didn't come, he never failed to call. Toward the very end he seemed instinctively to be there at the key moments. Having lived the better part of a year in the atmosphere of illness, I guess I not only began to depend on his presence — the voice on the other end of the phone — but looked forward to him. He represented physical health — vitality. I needed that. Unwittingly I must have begun to feel that illness was all there was. It had become a way of life. Bogie had always paid an overabundance of physical attention to me — he had incredible energy — he was life. I was used to it, and I needed it.

I don't know what I became during Bogie's illness. I wasn't aware of any change in my behavior — only more protective of him. I paid total attention to everything to do with him. But a part of me needed a man to talk to, and Frank turned out to be that man. He was life as usual — I was not. I was a healthy young woman with tremendous energy. Work was a channel. People, fun, activity — I needed them all for health. I didn't feel consciously deprived — resented nothing — even had worked for part of that time; God knows what would have happened if I hadn't had that as some release. But there was the odd hour of the odd day when I wanted something normal — a normal conversation. That need was magnified a thousandfold by the time Bogie died. So that my dependence on Frank became greater and greater. It wasn't planned. It simply was.

After Bogie's death I focused all my remaining energies on my children. To somehow keep life going — to have something to smile about even for a minute. The house had been so quiet for so long, then so noisy for the week after Bogie's death, then so quiet again. The nights especially. I had never known that kind of quiet before. Or that kind of aloneness. I felt as though a large chunk of me were missing. I felt physically mutilated.

I wanted it all to come back. I wanted to wake up smiling again — I wanted something to look forward to — I hated feeling that my life was over at thirty-two.

If I was included by friends at any small dinner, it was natural for Frank to pick me up if he was going. He was alone too. And he always made me feel better — I was even able to laugh. He was a good friend. We enjoyed being together. He was helping me, looking after me. Swifty Lazar was another who was alone — who from the beginning made it his business to stop by my house daily. His devotion and care for me went beyond friendship in any ordinary sense, and I needed him and valued him and would forgive him any slip in years to come for what he had been to me when I was desperate and without hope. But Frank answered a more basic, unarticulated need. When I was in New York and he called all the time to see how I was, I loved those calls. Even began to feel rather girlish — giddy. There was a man somewhere — a man who was alive — who cared about me as a woman. I came to expect those calls — to wait for them. And somewhere in my subconscious I intended that they would happen every day.

The fact of my being alone was crucial. Up to that time there had been either my mother or Bogie to lean on. Now there was no one. If I'd stopped to verbalize that, I'm sure I couldn't have functioned. Would have been paralyzed with fear. All these years later, I see how hopeless it was from the start. How there was no way for me to think straight, how there was no way to really feel anything positive — like loving; no way for there to be a solid, good future for me and Frank. I was silently asking more than anyone has a right to ask — burdening him with my terrors, my unspoken demands. Had he been sure of himself and his own life then, it might have worked. But he wasn't.

We continued for several months as close friends — he attentive, me overly receptive. Then suddenly he didn't call at all for over a week. I couldn't understand it — again someone lost, again alone. I tried to rationalize it, didn't discuss it with any of our friends, but I was miserable.

Everything hurt. I loved my house, yet I

couldn't walk into the Butternut Room without seeing Bogie in a chair — or our bedroom without seeing him in bed. And there was the weekly nightmare that would literally have me waking up screaming. I didn't know what to do. I had no work offers, though maybe with *Designing Woman* in full release that would all change for me.

I wanted a life. I didn't want to stay home simply waiting for Steve and Leslie to get back from school — have dinner with them in that quiet dining room, with three large, empty, quiet rooms waiting for no one after dinner — a little television with them before bedtime — then me with myself — *by myself* — to read, to stare out a window or at nothing, to cry. Worst of all, I suppose, to possibly have to face what my life really was. I wish I had stood in the middle of a room and just screamed — screamed until there was no scream left. Instead I continued bottling up all emotion.

People always ask what you'd change if you had your life to live over again. I wouldn't change a lot of the unhappy times because then I would miss something wonderful. But I would change that period like a flash — *me during it* — how I behaved with Stephen and Leslie, either short-tempered or over-affectionate — avoiding everything I could that had to do with Bogie, with my past life — my insane desire to get out of my house. As if that could erase anything.

After a week of talking to myself — explaining to myself why Frank hadn't called, why it all had suddenly stopped, carrying on imaginary conversations, what I'd say to him if I saw him, etc. — the phone rang. Frank on the other end telling me — just telling me as though I'd understand — where he would be taking me every night for the next week. I was so happy to hear from him that I pretended I did understand. I'd find out why later. But with Frank, forget about 'why.'

I can only guess he'd taken that week to work out his feelings about me and decide whether he could take me on or not. That's when our relationship really changed. No promises were made — it was just a fact. We were together. Where he was asked, I was. A couple.

People react in funny ways. My friends, who secretly felt this would not be a good choice for me, accepted us as a pair — thought it was serious. Except for my most intimate friends, they probably thought I could take care of myself. Frank's friends, on the other hand, warned me not to push — thought I would be better for him than vice versa, and, knowing him, didn't think he could last in his new role of fidelity. And some of the wives of his friends were strangely possessive toward him and not crazy about me. I was not just an arm decoration, not one to sit in a corner waiting for him to give me a smile or a sign that it was time to leave. I was too much of an individual for that — too established as a positive half of a positive pair.

I didn't really know where I stood with Frank. I expected him to call — I expected to see him nightly, to become a permanent part of his life. I never understood the love game, I could never play hard to get. I had been married to a grown-up. Bogie knew what he was about and he wanted to know where he stood; if a woman loved him, he felt better, stronger, not threatened. Frank, on the other hand, liked to be kept off balance. I was the wrong girl for that.

But he made me feel I was the one for him. Maybe that was his art — or maybe for a time he really thought I was. We'd planned a great Fourth of July — he'd charter a boat, invite three other couples on board. It sounded wonderful — Frank had introduced me to a world of charter planes and boats filled with his friends. Then, a couple of weeks before the Fourth, he withdrew again. Became remote — polite, but remote — off on his own. I couldn't figure it out. Did it mean the Fourth was off? That I wasn't invited? I had to make plans, I did have two other lives I was responsible for. Should I corner him, ask why? Frank was bad when cornered — better not. Again rejection. My insecurity moved to the forefront once again, took over. Frank was capable of a scene, and I dreaded scenes. A friend of his said, 'Just sit tight — do nothing — be pleasant and pretend it doesn't matter. Your life will go on.' I followed that advice and it was right. But it was hard to do. Every time Frank acted this way I'd feel sick — scared — awkward.

Certainly none of my friends understood that kind of carrying on. If you loved someone, that was it — you were together all the time unless there was a fight. Something specific. But with Frank, forget specifics. He'd had so many scars from so many past lives — was so embittered by his failure with Ava — he was not about to take anything from a woman. 'Don't tell me — suggest' — God knows how many times I heard that. But I didn't know how to suggest.

It seems ridiculous now. It was so painful then. It embarrassed me to have to say I didn't know if I'd be with Frank on a night when people were sure I would. It threw them off. Had there been a quarrel? No. Then why? I was miserable. Of course. I couldn't think of anything else. My mother always said that was my trouble — over-concentrating on any one subject. Zeroing in. I tried to change me and I couldn't. It was too deeply ingrained.

Then suddenly another phone call — the Fourth was on again, as if nothing had happened — no explanations. I swept all doubts under the rug and was in heaven. I loved being with him. I felt like a woman — no man had ever made me feel more wanted and more rejected, all in a week's time.

This time I was determined to be cool. I succeeded for a while — it worked like a charm, but it had nothing to do with the kind of woman I was or am. When things started going well, I was on such a high. All my juices were flowing, I felt so alive. I refused to remember how low the lows had been. It was just that commitment was such a big step for him. When it got *too* big, he backed off. Simple. Sometimes he would sing his songs to me — irresistible. When he was away working clubs — far away, that is — he called constantly. He seemed to need me as much as I did him. A few of my friends were terrified I'd marry him — knew I was riding for a fall. But I had the bit in my teeth and there was no stopping me.

I sold my house — had my gardener dig out all my clivia plants and take them to

Frank's house, as they were his favorite color, orange. I knew if I moved out of that house he'd feel better. He never mentioned it, but I knew Bogie's ghost would always be there — always coming between us. I had to erase it — I would never have a future unless my surroundings changed. I didn't realize then that you take yourself with you wherever you go.

The house I moved into was nice enough, it just had nothing to do with me. I got rid of half my furniture, my silver, I didn't know what I was doing. Before leaving Mapleton Drive I gave a slam-bang Halloween party. 'The Ball O' Bacall.' Frank was adorable — got there early, acted as host without being asked. It was a great party until the end, when something clicked in Frank — I don't know what it was. He suddenly wanted to leave. Felt trapped, I guess. Fortunately, only a few diehards were left by then.

As a couple we were combustible. Always when we entered a room the feeling was: Are they okay tonight? You could almost hear a sigh of relief when we were both smiling and relaxed.

I was quite consistently happy for several months. I didn't know what would happen between us — I only knew that when Frank's moods didn't take over, life seemed good. I had many sagging moments, when a wave of Bogie would wash over me, but that was mostly when I was alone. I tried to push him out of my mind. I only could think of Frank. And I thought of him too much. So that I could crowd Bogie out.

All through this time Steve and Leslie were always happy to see Frank. They'd been used to his frequent visits long before their father died, he'd been part of the framework of their lives. He gave them lovely presents, but thank God I never said anything to them even suggesting permanence.

The simple truth was that I just didn't know where I stood. And though I tried not to push him in words, I must have been unable to stop myself. I don't know what I was afraid of — that he'd lose his temper? Not call me? I guess all of that. I was totally vulnerable then, my only thought was to please him. I was changed — life had changed me.

But it hadn't changed Frank. He was still Frank — adoring one day, remote the next. We got through Christmas beautifully — had a lovely Christmas Eve at his house. We were planning New Year's Eve in Palm Springs. He told me what food to buy — more than fifty friends were coming to his house. I was excited. Playing house, going to the market as though I were Mrs Him.

What a babe in the woods!

That never-to-be-forgotten New Year's weekend I was to act as hostess for Frank at a party at the new Romanoff's in the Springs until Frank got there from town. About ten of us, all having a fine time. I remember his arriving — my getting up to greet him — his saying to everyone, 'Doesn't she look radiant?' I remember feeling so happy. The next day he wanted me to go home. No specific argument — that click again. Of course I was in tears, wanting to be there, thinking of everyone expecting me to be there. I made up my mind it would be better to stay and not to have to answer questions later. I can't believe my naïveté.

But I was one unhappy lady. Having decided to stay, I was stuck with it. That night should have shown me the way once and for all — unhappily, it didn't. As friends came in, I put on my best smile, but of course they sensed that something was wrong. Frank stayed near the bar most of the night — I didn't dare go near him. It was a full disaster. So painful — with friends all having a good time, my closest ones shifting their eyes from him to me nervously — that volcanic atmosphere. A nightmare.

That was the first time Frank really dropped the curtain on me. A chilling experience. I still don't know how he did it, but he could behave as though you weren't there. He drank heavily, which led me to believe he wasn't very happy himself. I had to try to rationalize his behavior. I absolutely could not comprehend his ability to ignore me so totally.

With civility and nervousness I got through the following day. When he took me home that night, I knew it was over, at least for a while. I was due to make a life-saving trip to New York to publicize the not very good film I'd just made. Of course he didn't call to say goodbye. I tried hard to make excuses for him, telling myself it was all because of his unhappy past. It seems to me that by concentrating so much on Frank, I left no time for facing facts. Except at night, when my subconscious took over.

One afternoon in New York I came back to my hotel from an interview and there was a message from Frank. He had called from Philadelphia, he'd call again. He did — almost as though nothing had happened — saying he'd be coming through New York en route to California and could I have dinner with him? I was calm — on the surface — and said that I could make it only because I had early publicity to do the following day and had been planning a quiet evening alone.

He was waiting for me when I got to the

bar downstairs. I was friendly, though not overly so. We talked like two friends who had insane electric currents running between them all the time. I seemed stronger in New York, away from the Hollywood scene. I had my family there — extra security — really, the only security I could count on. And I was busy, which always helps. More independent. I drove to the airport with Frank. Although we'd been out in public, there seemed less of a chance of publicity in the East. The press had really been bugging both of us in California. I recall a wire-service man on the Coast saying, 'When are you and Frank getting married?' and me pleading to be left alone, asking why they wouldn't stop. He said, 'We'll keep at it until you do or you don't.' Even I was getting paranoid about the press. I'd always thought I could handle them — I'd been taught by the master. But the pressure was strong.

At that moment I felt in a position of strength with Frank. I told myself that I expected nothing, but I knew I wanted everything. Though his erratic behavior was very much a part of him, I flatly refused to face what it might portend for our future together. I probably thought that if I didn't face it, it might go away — that was the unrealistic hope. All I wanted was for my life to continue as it used to be. My fantasizing was so great that I didn't realize there was no way that could happen. Now I can see that I was trying to erase Bogie's death — pretend it had never happened — that he had never happened. The pain of that loss was so excruciating, I wanted to deny its being. Impossible — ridiculous — but real at the time. Had anyone suggested that my motive was to eliminate Bogie from my life, I would have lashed out at the liar. It takes so long to understand things, so much time wasted.

Frank was wildly attentive while I was in New York, keeping close tabs on my return to California. The night I got home he came over to see me. He didn't know how to apologize, but he was fairly contrite, at least for him. He said he had felt somewhat trapped — was 'chicken' — but now could face it. 'Will you marry me?' He said those words and he meant them. Of course all my barriers fell. I must have hesitated for at least thirty seconds. Yes, I thought to myself, I was right all along — he couldn't deal with it, was afraid of himself, but finally realized that he loved me and that marriage was the only road to take. I was ecstatic — we both were. He said, 'Let's go out and have a drink to celebrate — let's call Swifty, maybe he can join us.' I questioned nothing. That was my trouble — one of my troubles. Fortunately, it was nighttime, so the children were asleep and I didn't tell them anything.

We were going to meet Swifty at the Imperial Gardens on the Strip — a Japanese restaurant facing the Garden of Allah. On the way, we started to plan — we'd have to add rooms to Frank's house for the children. That house high on a hill — never meant for small children — I tried to imagine it all. Something wrong in the picture, but I dismissed it.

Holding hands, we walked into the bar and sat down in a booth where Swifty was waiting for us. When Frank told him we were going to get married, I don't think he took it seriously. He thought it a 'great idea,' but didn't believe it — until Frank started to plan the wedding. 'We'll get married at the house and instead of our going away, we'll have our friends go away.' He knew the way he wanted it — he didn't ask what I might want. He wasn't dictatorial, he just had his plan and it never occurred to him I might not accept it. I didn't disappoint him. I was too happy, and I loved his taking over, that being one of my most acute needs.

A young girl came over for autographs. Frank handed me the paper napkin and pen. As I started to write, he said, 'Put down your new name.' So 'Lauren Bacall' was followed by 'Betty Sinatra.' It looked funny, but he asked for it and he got it. I often wondered what became of that paper napkin.

Frank was leaving for a singing engagement in Miami — we'd work everything out on his return. Mum's the word until then.

I was giddy with joy, felt like laughing every time I opened my mouth. My face radiated happiness. I said nothing to anyone, but now I knew — my life would go on. The children would have a father, I would have a husband, we'd have a home again. I had been right to move away from Mapleton Drive. I'd have to get rid of more stuff — no way for all my belongings to fit into Frank's house. It was a hard secret to keep — I was about to burst — I wanted everyone to know. But I kept my mouth shut.

Emlyn Williams opened in his Dickens evening at the Huntington Hartford Theatre. Frank was away, Swifty took me. All Hollywood was there. At intermission, before I went into the ladies' room, Louella Parsons stopped Swifty and me, asked me if Frank and I were going to get married. Being a lousy liar, I said, 'Why don't you ask him?' and kept moving. My heart leaped at the question. Why would she ask that? Louella so often gave the impression of vagueness, of being slightly out of it. On my return I saw Swifty still talking to her — just as I reached him, she disappeared. Swifty said nothing, and I thought nothing further about it — was just relieved not to see her. On the way home after the theatre and supper we pulled up to a newsstand for the early edition of the morning paper. I saw enormous black letters jumping out at me from the *Examiner*: SINATRA TO MARRY BACALL. I gasped — oh my God, what a disaster — how the hell did that happen? How could Louella have printed that? 'My God, Swifty. You told her — are you crazy? Frank will be furious!' Swifty just laughed: 'Of course I told her — I didn't know she'd do this. I just said I happened to know that Frank had asked Betty to marry him. So what? He did! What's wrong with saying it?' I said, 'It wasn't up to you. You're coming home with me right now and calling Frank — I don't want him to think I did it.' I was so insecure it was pathetic.

When we phoned Frank, Swifty told him the news, but didn't make it clear that he had been the culprit. It was a great joke to Swifty — 'Ha ha, the cat's out of the bag now, old boy.' I got on the phone briefly, saying I was ready to kill Swifty. As I recall, Frank was not overjoyed, but at least he was prepared for the coming onslaught of the press, and he didn't chastise me. I must have sounded contrite, though I had no reason to be. I was just frightened of making waves. Hopeless for any relationship, much less a marriage. But he said nothing to prepare me for the next and final step in our saga.

The following day, of course, my friends started to call. I told them all I didn't know, there was no final decision yet. So somewhere in the back of my foolish head I recognized a major problem. Slim Hayward called from New York and asked, 'You're not going to do it, are you?' I said, 'Maybe — I'm not sure.' Her memorable remark was, 'Well — everyone is entitled to one mistake.'

I told my mother that he had asked me, but that the story was premature. I still didn't go into anything with the children except to say there was a story in the paper about Frank and me that wasn't true — protection in case someone at school mentioned it. It was a hectic time. I was not quite walking on air — rather limping — Frank hadn't called for a few days, so the operative word was apprehensive.

Finally one night the phone did ring. It was Frank saying, 'Why did you do it?' Me: 'I didn't do anything' — heart pounding. He: 'I haven't been able to leave my room for days — the press are everywhere — we'll have to lay low for a while,

666

not see each other for a while.' 'What?' I screamed silently. 'What are you saying, Frank? What do you mean?' Foolishly I was pleading to be forgiven for something I'd had no part in. 'I won't hear from you again?' Disbelieving, but realizing how important this conversation was. I was incapable of being reasonable — still all open nerve ends — still unprotected — finally having to begin to face that.

There was nothing left to say to Frank. He was three thousand miles away, his attitude remote. Clearly he thought I'd given it away — he couldn't deal with the press, they were driving him crazy, and under this circumstance the pressure was too great. He felt trapped. I tried to rationalize his feelings — couldn't — but he'd be back in a couple of weeks and we could figure it out then. I didn't know that this was to be my last phone call from Frank — the end of our exciting, imperfect, not-to-be love affair.

From a friend, I don't remember who, I heard he was back in Los Angeles. Swifty had dinner with him — Swifty, the perpetrator of it all. Frank was speaking to him, but not to me! I was so hurt, so miserable. When a party was given, Frank would be asked — I would not. Bill and Edie Goetz asked us both once, a month or so after his return. We had one person between us at dinner, but Frank didn't acknowledge my existence. He did not speak one word to me — if he looked in my direction, he did not see me, he looked right past me, as though my chair were empty. I was so humiliated, so embarrassed. Nothing would bring my sense of humor back — it deserted me that night and for some time afterward. I would have preferred him to spit in my face, at least that would have been recognition. I couldn't deal with this — there was no way to understand it. We had been such friends for so long, how could he drop the curtain like this? I was under a permanent cloud then — trying to excuse him to others, pretending I understood — but others had seen his behavior before. No one just drops someone without discussion. It was such a shock, that cold slap in the face in front of everyone.

I felt so on the defensive. To be rejected is hell, a hard thing to get over, but to be rejected publicly takes everything away from you. Adlai Stevenson once said you must never take a person's dignity from him. I understood now what he meant.

I spent night after night in tears, hearing from time to time about Frank's activities — dinners, girls, work. I was suddenly an outcast, and there was no one really to talk to. Carolyn — my one friend who was *my* friend, not part of the Hollywood group — was unforgiving of his behavior, and at least I could say sane things out loud to her. One weekend a few months later I was staying in Palm Springs with Carolyn and Buddy. There was some kind of open-air concert Buddy had to go to — Frank was to sing. I thought I'd have to learn to deal with it eventually, might as well start, so I went with them. While Frank was singing I put on my usual front. After the concert Buddy went to get his car, I got separated from him and Carolyn, wanted to leave, to avoid seeing Frank, and found myself face to face with him. He looked right at me again as though I were not there — not a flicker of recognition — called his group — got into his car. The blood ran to my face, then away. I felt sick. My humiliation was indescribable.

I did everything I could those next few months to try to make a life. What was I doing living in a rented house anyway? It had nothing to do with any part of me. I belonged nowhere — to no one. I faced more realistically each day the passing of Bogie. It was almost as though he had died twice.

Frank and I did not meet again for about six years. When we finally did, it was at a party Swifty gave, funnily enough. Frank came late from a TV show, beefing about TV's incompetence and demands, foul-humored. Mia Farrow was waiting for him — they were not married then. We exchanged superficial words — he drank a lot — became furious with Swifty, who was sitting at another table — let him have it verbally. Then he pulled the tablecloth out from under the glasses and plates, and amid the crash and spillage he shouted furiously at Swifty, 'You — you were responsible for what happened between her and me!' I almost laughed. It was Frank's way of admitting finally that he did know it was Swifty and not me who'd spilled the beans. Some beans!

As I look at it all now, it doesn't seem possible it happened as it did. I see that under no circumstances could it ever have worked. I expected more from him than anyone has any right to expect of another human being — loaded him with more responsibilities. No one could have remained upright in that circumstance. We used one another in some crazy way.

Actually, Frank did me a great favor — he saved me from the disaster our marriage would have been. The truth is he was probably smarter than I: he knew it couldn't work. But the truth also is that he behaved like a complete shit. He was too cowardly to tell the truth — that it was just too much for him, that he'd found he couldn't handle it. I would have understood (I hope). Well, he's paid for his lacks in his life — okay, it's his life — but why the hell did I have to pay for them too?

Anyway, it turned out to be a tragedy with a happy ending. Now, after a slow start, we are back on some sort of friendly basis. We don't live the same kind of life or think the same kind of thoughts anymore, but I'll always have a special feeling for him — the good times we had were awfully good.

In the middle of this terrible year, when Mother was in California resting after her heart attack, the phone rang early one morning. Mother was due at my house in an hour or so. It was Rosalie: Charlie was dead. Oh God — not true — not him, not my Chach. She was distraught. He had just returned from a trip — they'd had a delicious evening together, ending up in bed, and on completion of the act of love, he was dead. Rosalie couldn't believe it. Through the night she kept shaking him, talking to him. Useless — he was gone. He was young — only fifty-three. To lose him was unbearable.

How would I tell Mother? What a pattern in our lives — first I'd had to break the news to her of Grandma's death — then Jack's — then Bogie's — now Charlie's. And with Mother's heart condition . . . I called a marvelous doctor in Beverly Hills, Rex Kennamer, who knew her case — I'd had to have someone to call since her attack. He said he'd come right over — give her a shot — keep her calm. I was not to tell her before he got there. I stared out the window at the driveway, watching for his car or hers — shaking from head to foot — trying to stop my tears, to forget my own loss.

At last a car — it was the good doctor, thank God. He got his shot ready. I decided to say he'd just stopped by to see how we all were — had been in the neighborhood. Another car — Mother. I opened the door, hugged her — small talk — I don't know what I said. She wasn't suspicious — she liked him, he was a nice man, a perfect doctor. I brought her into the living room, sat her on the sofa next to him. 'I have something to tell you, Mama' — my heart was breaking for her, for Charlie. 'What?' she said. 'What?' — knowing it was disaster. But which disaster? There had been so many. The doctor gave her his shot to calm her down. 'It's Charlie, Mama. Rosalie called — he died —' A sharp intake of breath — a moaning 'Oh' and tears. She said, 'We must go — I want to go to New York!' My poor mother — she became the matriarchal figure after Grandma, not because of seniority, but because it was she who believed that keeping a family together was the most important thing on earth. Now she didn't even consider her terror of flying. We threw things together, boarded the night plane.

The next day in New York, Rosalie kept saying over and over, 'But, Betty, what do you do about the pain? I have this pain' — pointing to her heart — 'and it won't go away. Is it like that for you? What do you do about it?'

The funeral was the following morning — the casket would be open. My first reaction, remembering Hellinger, was that I would not look. But that evening, friends and family around, the casket at the end of the room, I found I was drawn to it — I wanted to see my darling Charlie once more. Charlie who held so much of my formative years in his hands — who took so much of my love with him. So I walked quietly toward the bier with some trepidation — and there he was, looking much the same as he had in life. As if sleeping; not waxen. I just stood there looking down at him, the years and moments with him flashing before me. I could not bear the thought of never seeing that face again. I had lost the two great male influences my thirty-three years had known.

The next day, on the drive to the ceme- tery, Rosalie was sitting in the back of the car, I was in the jump seat, and she said again, 'It's this pain — it won't go away — what can I do about it?' The pain was the wrenching of Charlie from her. Like sur- gery. I could only tell her, 'It takes time — it takes a long time. Bogie's been gone a year — it takes a long time.' I didn't dare say, 'Maybe that pain never goes away.'

That April Rosalie was coming through California. I was in Palm Springs staying with Buddy and Carolyn. She stopped by the house to see the children and called me from there. She'd been traveling for Boys' Town, was on her way to Las Vegas, then home. She sounded very up, but the pain, she said, still wouldn't go away. I'd be in New York soon and see her — I loved her, wished she could stay until I came back, but she couldn't. 'Okay, darling — see you in a month or so.' The next day Mother called from New York. There'd been a mid-air collision over Las Vegas — Rosalie was in it — there were no survivors. Three months to the day after Charlie died. It didn't seem possible, such incredible timing, yet if she would have had to live with that pain, was she better off? Better off dead?

Was there to be no end to disasters? For two years they had come non-stop —

Bogie, Charlie, Rosalie, Mother's attack, Frank. I couldn't bear it. I had to go away. I knew I should get out of California, there was no future for me there, but I still couldn't make the decision. Slim called me saying that she and Leland Hayward had to go to Europe in the fall — Leland was going to negotiate with the Baroness von Trapp for rights to what would become *The Sound of Music*. She'd been after me to get the hell out of that dead place — 'It's not for you.' I knew she was right — I was miserable, tense, desperate — Europe would help. She suggested Spain, and finally we agreed to make the trip together.

Slim was fantastic. She had been responsible for changing my life. Now, some fifteen years later, she was pulling it together for me. She knew I was desperate. The best things about Slim were her gift for total friendship, her original, inquiring mind, her great sense of fun, her willingness to accept her friends as they were without judging them. She never pushed, she just said what she thought — you could take it or leave it. She was loyal and she was funny. That trip with her was the beginning of my being saved, the first step toward facing and dealing with my life as it truly was — not as I wished it were.

Being in a new country, with an unknown language and all new people, filled me with abandon. We did everything. I drank whatever was put before me, ended up watching and half-dancing flamenco through more than one night — had a continual hangover and never stopped moving. I even played a scene out of a Marx Brothers comedy one night in our hotel suite, with Slim sitting in her bedroom reading a book and me being chased around the living room by a Spaniard. I kept stopping at her door en route, saying, 'I'm still on my feet.' It was an incredible time — new fun, madness — and I didn't think of Frank. I felt like a woman for the first time in ages, being admired and desired as a woman, having value.

After two weeks we headed for Paris, where Leland joined us. Then Munich. When Slim and Leland went back to New York, I returned to Paris. I'd been sent the script of a film to be made in London the following year. I said I'd go to London to meet the producer and director. While in Paris, Vivien Leigh called to tell me she wanted to give a party for me. Whom did I want? 'I only want to see you and Larry — you don't have to do anything special for me.' But she insisted, so I left it to her.

On arrival in London I learned she was heading toward another breakdown — still playing *Duel of Angels* eight times a week, but having gained a great deal of weight. The party she wanted to give had turned out to be for more than one hundred people. She had taken over a nightclub for it.

Larry asked me to lunch at the Ivy. He was honest, simple, and terribly sweet as he explained that the party was Vivien's doing, not his; that of course he would go because of me, but he wanted me to understand the situation. He was going to California to be in a film and would not come back for a long time, and when he did, it wouldn't be to Vivien. The marriage had been heaven the first ten years — hell, the second. Now it was over. But she needed her friends — he wanted me to stand firm and close to her. He felt such concern for her, such pain at the ending of it all. But he knew he would not survive if he did not get away.

He took me to see her play, in which she was wonderful and beautiful, overweight or not. Backstage she greeted us with champagne and non-stop talk, then we left for the party, which was overrun with cameras — at the entrance and upstairs, where I found myself in a receiving line with Larry on one side and Vivien on the other. Every name in the English theatre was present — old friends, new friends-to-be. Flamenco dancers, orchestra, up till dawn when the dregs — being Brian Bedford (in the friend-to-be category), the Burtons, the Kenneth Mores, Jack Hawkins, and a few others — were dragged to the Connaught or somewhere for scrambled eggs by Vivien, who was possessed of a manic energy and total inability to sleep — all symptoms. Watching her and Larry that night, it was hard to believe they were the same two people whose life had once seemed so idyllic. It brought into sharp focus the luck Bogie and I had shared, and the almost guaranteed-to-be-unlucky union that Frank and I had escaped!

I happily agreed to do the film, which would take several months, with locations in India and Spain, interiors in London. I would put Steve and Leslie in the American School, and I went to see the headmaster, who made it all seem easy and attractive. Work is what would determine my life from now on — six months in England (I wasn't allowed more by their laws).

By the time I got back to California I knew I would leave there for good. I had spent the last several years in misery and desperation — I couldn't have done anything right there. And now I'd discovered there was a whole big world for me to live in — something I had never even suspected until that trip. Naturally I was a little apprehensive after fifteen years in California, but why stay, for God's sake? Out of the thirty friends I thought I'd had, there were maybe eight true ones — better to know that, but painful to learn. Had my whole *raison d'être* been Bogie? Wasn't I myself worth anything? I was so confused, so demoralized, I had to find out who I was, make a place for myself — my own place. I'd been protected and spoiled for so long, it was almost a way of life. It was time to grow up — learn to stand alone. I had to get out from under being 'Bogart's widow.' That was not a profession, after all — and there would be no hope of a new beginning unless I fought for one.

The children too needed a fresh start. I sang London's praises to them, describing the palace, riding in the park, the zoo. May would come with us, and I'd register Steve and Leslie in New York schools for the following September, just in case we ended up there. And on January 9, 1959, I left for London to start a new life with the two people I loved most in the world, my children.

We were met by a barrage of press. Steve hated being photographed. From the day Bogie died, he instinctively turned away from cameras. I was welcomed with open arms as Bogie's widow, and as someone who loved England and had many friends there. We had one day to familiarize ourselves with our new home, which my old friend Joyce Buck had found for me. Then up at dawn Monday morning for the children's first look at the American School in Regent's Park. Again photographers waiting — I'd asked the headmaster to prevent their entering the school, and he was only too pleased to comply.

So we were immediately thrust into our new lives — having to run before learning to walk. Just as well. It was snowing — very cold — not good for May, but she bundled up and together we found our local fishmonger, butcher, greengrocer, all within a block of each other and our house. May, who had only been out of the U.S. once — to Honolulu — had the greatest adjustment to make, but she never complained. I arranged for French tutoring, for piano lessons. On the weekends it was sightseeing — the changing of the guard, which Steve and Leslie adored — the zoo — Portobello Road — museums. It was all an adventure, and discovery was fun. My friends were marvelous, as always — when you have a friend in England, you have a friend for life. The Mores and Jack and Doreen Hawkins became close chums. Rex Harrison was playing in *My Fair Lady* at Drury Lane and Larry Olivier was in California, so Vivien, Kay Kendall, and I became a steady threesome.

The press couldn't figure out why three ladies went everywhere alone — the facts of Rex's working and Larry's absence not occurring to them. I was preparing for my film, *Flame over India* — we'd shoot a week in London, India for six weeks, Spain for another six, and wind up again in London. Except for leaving my babies, I couldn't wait to see India for the first time.

Life was falling into place. I was still lonely — still missing Frank — but enjoying England, and getting stronger. Half of life's problems disappear when one's head is healthy. I yearned for someone to belong to, but I didn't brood. There was too much to do and see.

I was asked to appear at the Royal Command Performance — Alec Guinness's film *The Horse's Mouth* was chosen. I was very frightened, though I only had to be introduced and stand on the stage with Maurice Chevalier, Richard Todd, Richard Attenborough, and several others, and sing a song I hoped to remember then and can't now. Cole Lesley, Noel's secretary, took me there — I was so nervous standing on the receiving line waiting for the Queen Mother that I made him get me a drink. He presented me with a glass of water which turned out to be vodka, on which I almost choked — a funny evening. You can tell yourself it's nothing to meet royalty — they're only people, like our President — but it's something nonetheless. I was bedazzled by the Queen Mother and her diamond tiara. If my mother could see me now!

We did wardrobe tests and started shooting at Pinewood Studios — old, beautiful. The large dining room for casts and crews had a bar, unheard of in Hollywood, so civilized. In England acting was an honored profession. I loved working there. I fell easily into the English rhythm — less pressured, much saner than any I'd known. No ring-a-ding-ding.

Kay Kendall and I became very close. She was such a funny woman and so, so beautiful. One night at a party she told me about having gone to her doctor about bumps in her groin — she was longing for a baby — said, 'I'd thought I'd bought the building' (British expression for dying), but no, he gave her some explanation, she was all right. She and I went to Rex's closing night of *My Fair Lady* — an exciting, moving evening. I remember looking over at Kay and seeing tears streaming down her cheeks. It was months after that, on my return from location, that I heard she had leukemia — she had indeed 'bought the building.' Another unreasonable injustice — why always the best people, while the shits of the world go on?

Jock Whitney, our Ambassador to Great Britain, invited me to dinner at the Embassy. Fred Astaire, an old buddy of his, and his sister, Adèle, were there. Fred, recalling old times, demonstrated a bygone happening by dancing a few steps ending with a flourish on a sofa, and reminisced with Jock — wonderful fun. I was having a happy time until I was called to the phone. It was the children's nurse — I'd been robbed. That took care of that evening. I rushed home to find Scotland Yard there and every piece of jewelry I owned, including everything given me by Bogie, stolen. The thief had come in through a window — Steve's window while he was sleeping, thank God he didn't wake up — tiptoed into my bedroom, and quietly emptied all my drawers. May and the nurse, on another floor watching television, had heard nothing. The Yard men told me they knew the culprit — a man called the Fly, who climbed the outside of houses till he found an open window. They recovered a good deal of the jewelry, though not all the irreplaceable sentimental pieces, and I hired a detective to stay in the house every night. As I would be away for a couple of months, I wanted no anxieties about the safety of my children. The Man Upstairs wasn't through with me yet.

Mme Pandit, Ambassador to Great

Britain, came to have tea with me, bringing along a list of places to go, things to see, food to eat, and a copy of *A Passage to India*. Her Sikh in his pink turban stood guard half a flight below. I felt very clever telling Kenny More and Lee Thompson, our director, how much more I knew about India than they did. We agreed to have Mme Pandit's highly touted chicken tandoori (roasted in paprika) on our first night in New Delhi. (When we got there and ordered the long-awaited chickens, they appeared — three red skeletons on a platter. Must have been an off night for chickens. We laughed and laughed.)

On arrival in Bombay, our first stop, I felt the impact of a totally different world. There is no way to imagine it — veiled women in saris, red dots in the center of their foreheads; colored turbans on men dressed in white; cows — sacred, of course — walking in the street. The streets teeming with humanity. In India, awareness grows of how many people are alive on this earth. We get so caught up in our own worlds, we forget. And some of us never know.

Jaipur, where we were to spend most of our time, is ravishing — known as the Pink City, all buildings being painted a desert pink. We lived in a hotel that had been the summer palace of the Maharajah — that was my first exposure to ceiling fans, and to peacocks strutting on the lawn outside my balcony. Strolling down the main street of Jaipur's bazaar in my loud-printed Pucci pants and shirt, camera slung over my shoulder, arms covered with plastic bracelets, I was stared at by the inhabitants. This crazy woman! They'd never seen one in trousers, moving with such freedom — when they saw me coming (which was often, loving bazaars as I do), they would stare and laugh. I didn't care. I was in a place far from anything I'd known, my attitude was open, abandoned; it was high adventure and I loved it. Everything fascinated me. In a conversation one day, my driver said, 'You know, we are a very poor country.' 'Why, then,' I said, 'do you have so many children?' Whereupon he just shrugged his shoulders and with a smile said, 'It is God's will.' No basis for discussion there. I was so full of curiosity — so anxious to see all I could see — that I was even impervious to the heat. I went to see a woman in Delhi who told my fortune — she was so convincing I almost believed I might really be a blade of grass or a butterfly next time around. And I met a wise old man who sat guru-like on a raised platform in his house, greeting people who had been sent to him or whom he had known in another world. At the end of the location Kenny More and I had a few free days and went to the Taj Mahal. I had been told to see it by dawn, dusk, moonlight. The automobile ride to Agra showed farmers winnowing wheat — a camel walking around a well bringing up water — everything primitive. We stopped for a jam session with a dancing bear, and the vultures sat and talked among themselves intermittently all along the way. There is always the fear that a wonder of the world can't live up to expectations. Not so. The Taj Mahal was breathtakingly beautiful — if anything, better even than I'd been told. Beauty like that is too dazzling to be imagined.

I left India, with the assurance from another fortune teller that I would return, and headed for Rome. Two days there, then London to see my children before the Spanish location — they were well, thank God, and Mother was coming over to spend some time with them.

In Spain, Slim Hayward suggested we drive to Málaga, where Ernest Hemingway and his wife were staying with the Bill Davises. Oh, I'd love to meet him at last. Slim and Leland were having problems. He was due in Madrid soon, but something was going on, she wasn't sure what; they'd had problems before, mostly due to her having to take so much responsibility for his children's extreme crises. She was never one to shun responsibility of any kind, but she felt his failure to pay attention was out of order. They were his children, but he had a curious habit of going to sleep when problems arose.

We got to Málaga. She called the Davises, spoke to Papa H., who immediately invited us to dinner, saying he and A. E. Hotchner would come to collect us. I was eager to meet this larger-than-life character. He really turned on the charm — calling me Miss Betty, saying he'd heard about me from Slim, and he'd admired Bogie, and my behavior during Bogie's illness made me okay in his book. Naturally I hung on his every word, and naturally Mary Hemingway, knowing him, was not too pleased. They were talking about hunting. She asked me if I was a good shot — leaned over, saying, 'Maybe you'd like to come with us sometime,' placing a bullet on my plate. I didn't blame her — obviously he'd given her a bad time in the past; just as obviously, his ego required feeding. A woman alone can't win with wives. It's a problem I've had all of my single life, and there's no way to fight it. But I've never had conscious designs on married men, and I'm certainly less of a threat than most women, if only because I don't really know how to go about such things casually. Only relationships that are total are possible for me.

Slim left for Madrid, and I went on to Granada. A few days later Leland called me to ask if I would read a new play by George Axelrod that he was going to produce in the fall. A great part for me. His enthusiasm was infectious, so I said of course I would love to. He would send it down immediately and call me from New York, where he was heading. I couldn't figure that one out — he'd just arrived.

I read the play, *Goodbye Charlie,* as soon as it arrived and thought it was very funny. I'd been pondering my next move after my six months in London. I couldn't move Steve and Leslie every six months from school to school, country to country; I'd have to settle somewhere. The stage had been my first love, an unfulfilled dream. I'd be terrified, but I was a chance-taker — I wanted to find out if I could do it. And it was the best reason I knew for a move back to New York. So when Leland called, I said yes. He told me he'd plan a long tour out of town and not too close to New York so we'd be spared the early opinions of the press — he wanted me to have time to feel secure on stage. The idea of the play was of two close men friends who spend a lot of their time screwing other men's wives, but who'd rather be with each other than with any woman. One of them, Charlie, is shot escaping through a porthole. His punishment is to be returned to earth as a woman — and thereby hung the play. It *was* funny, and I was high on the entire plan.

I called Slim in Madrid to find her in a shattered state. Leland wanted a divorce. I felt so bad. I loved Slim and had never seen her like that before. There'd been rumblings that the new lady in Leland's life was Pamela Churchill, ex-wife of Randolph Churchill, but neither of us could believe it. I went back to London to finish my film and be with my children, mother, and friends, make arrangements for the summer, and start thinking about the fall.

George Axelrod and Leland rang from New York — they'd thought of Sydney Chaplin, who was living in Paris, for the leading man in *Goodbye Charlie*. George wanted to see Sydney and me together; they'd both come to London.

I felt good to know definitely what the future would be. A new chapter. And I was ready.

I said goodbye to Cadogan Place, all the local shopkeepers I'd become attached to, to my friends — and to London. I wished I had a proper reason to stay there — once you've lived in that city, it's a hard place to leave. But there was suddenly a great deal to look forward to and I was full of hope. I was only sad to leave my friend Slim, who for the first time in the years I had known her was disjointed, purposeless, and except for her daughter Kitty, whom she adored, without a center to her life. We shared vulnerability, Slim and I, and I understood her fragility only too well. It brought home to me even more clearly how lacking in focus a life can be without work. It would be queer to embark on this unknown venture without her support and presence — she had been so much a part of my career, from its first shaky step. We said a teary goodbye at the airport, and me and mine boarded the plane.

We were met in New York by Mother and Lee, George and Leland, and acres of press, who seemed to care that I was settling in New York and returning — if you could call it that — to the theatre.

After settling into the apartment which Joan Axelrod had found for me, I started to prepare for the stage. Daily voice lessons with Alfred Dixon, who'd coached everyone from Mary Martin to Katharine Hepburn — making peculiar sounds, trills, learning to speak from the diaphragm . . . I felt like an idiot at first, very self-conscious, but I knew I'd better damn well learn as much as I could before we started rehearsals or I'd be in big trouble. Leland had booked an eight-week tour, and, as promised, we started in Pittsburgh, where no one from New York would go. Then on to Cleveland, Detroit, Baltimore, gradually moving closer to New York. (We played the Nixon Theatre in Pittsburgh and the Ford Theatre in Baltimore — an indication of things to come.) We'd spend our last two weeks in Philadelphia, where New Yorkers *would* go, and open in New York in December. Mainbocher, who had quite a bit of theatre experience, would do the clothes, and George would direct the play — a first for him. Leland, a very persuasive man, had convinced me that we could have no one better than George. 'Look at John van Druten, who directed his own plays so marvelously.' Leland was so sure, and I trusted him. And George was my friend. They both knew a hell of a lot more about the theatre than I did, both had nothing but consecutive hits, so who was I to question? I had my instinct and my taste, would say what I thought in the area of acting; but for a woman of strong opinions, supposedly outspoken and in control, it's odd that I was quite prepared to do things almost entirely their way; to more or less turn myself over to them. Was it my basic desire to trust, be guided, be helped — as with Hawks? That may have had something to do with it. And of course I was a novice in the theatre, whereas George's favorite line was 'I'm in the hit business, baby.'

They did take care of me. Leland instructed me to use his office as much as I needed, and provided a secretary to oversee my life while in rehearsal and on the road. I weekended in the country with Joan and George. She sent me lists of everything and anything I might possibly need in the city — where to go, whom to call; found me a nurse for the children. I felt warm and welcome.

Rehearsals began. As we moved along, Sydney and I found some things that didn't work as well as they might. Sydney was very articulate about them and convinced me of some I wasn't sure about. We worked well together, liked each other. One night after a late rehearsal we went out for a drink and mulled over the problem of the play. Sydney had it all figured out, and had an idea how to fix it. My feeling was that we couldn't go to George without a constructive suggestion — no good just to spot a weakness. We called him around eleven o'clock, asked if we could come over to talk. Of course, he said. Over we went and told him our reservations. He listened politely and carefully — ideas were exchanged — but it was his play. He felt we had to play it the way he wrote it, get before an audience, before changes were made, but he would certainly consider our criticisms.

Rehearsal time in a play is unique. Your life becomes the play, the character — all else is secondary. Actually, all else gets in the way. Anyone not connected with the play is hopelessly outside. You rehearse eight hours a day — study lines at night — dream of it. The last week you go on a twelve-hour rehearsal schedule — meals go by the boards, everything does except the play. Actors and directors become closer than husbands and wives, everyone is working toward the same end. It's not a self-serving period at all, it's the most creative time for an actor, the most exciting and rewarding. For the first time in my adult life I began to call on all my resources as an actress. To really use myself.

I had no qualms about leaving the children home, because Mother was there and May was there, and they were at school, every day. Nothing else mattered, no other worries to distract me.

Our first stop — Pittsburgh. Finding our way around on the set for the first time. No matter what is explained beforehand, how many models are shown, you never really know where you are until standing on the stage, on the set.

I remember Leland's voice from every nook and cranny of every theatre saying, 'Louder, I can't hear you.' He'd warned me he was going to do that — stop me at every word if necessary, so I would never forget to speak out.

The day of the opening George and Leland told us not to worry about the notices. Pittsburgh audiences were unused to theatre, particularly new theatre. This was a time for us alone, to see what worked and what didn't. Easy to say, but I was one nervous actress. I got through the play shaking all the way. The sound of an audience was strange — laughs came for the first time — no laughter where we expected it — but the performance finally ended. They applauded and I felt very high. From that night on I was to be forever hooked on the theatre. Back in my dressing room, as I started to sit, my elderly and rather vague dresser pulled the chair out from under me, and when George and Leland and Pamela Churchill (who'd just arrived on the scene) entered my room, they found their star flat on the cement floor, unable to move. They helped me up (my tailbone really hurt), said the play went terrifically, I was terrific — like a thousand-watt bulb, said Leland. The local critics were not mad for the play, but were for us actors. I was X-rayed, found I'd cracked my coccyx, and was confined to a special corset for three weeks. Better to happen at the beginning. The only good thing about Pittsburgh was that I got a new dresser.

The next eight weeks were consumed with rehearsing all day, with constant changes, with performing. George would type up the changes at night, deliver them for the morning rehearsal. We'd work, pages in hand. On nights when changes were to go in, we'd sit in our hotel rooms — me with Sydney's understudy, he with mine, going over and over the new words. Nothing is more difficult than trying to un-learn a scene or a speech. Sometimes on-stage you get half the old and half the new lines. Sydney had a hellish time with the new lines — warned me he was a slow study, and if he went up mid-scene I couldn't look to him to maneuver us out of trouble; his only hope was to try to re-member. One night he did go up — just looked at me, started to stutter, started making it up as he went along. Only actors know what actors go through — one is so naked, so vulnerable, onstage. It was the start of my awareness of the danger in acting — the constant risks — of putting yourself out there on the line and maybe getting shot down.

The Baltimore press was unfavorable to the play. Washington's best critics had come to review it, also unfavorably. Our business was great — sold out everywhere — but Washington critics know plays and their criticism coincided with that of all the previous critics: the fault lay in the play. Poor George was a wreck, rewriting constantly, directing. Alas, directing was not his forte. He's a highly intelligent man, with great humor, sensitivity, and kindness, but he's a playwright — he expresses himself better on paper and he was too close to the play, he couldn't have judgment about it. Leland would go away for a few days to return with a fresh eye. In Philadelphia, our last stop, Sarah Marshall, daughter of Herbert Marshall and Edna Best, came in to replace Cara Williams in the most important supporting role. She was a first-rate actress and comedienne. We had only two weeks left before opening in New York at the Lyceum Theatre, where I'd auditioned for *Franklin Street* so many years earlier. We had to freeze the play soon so we could play it and refine it without further changes. George promised us it would be frozen one week before Broadway. He went back to New York for a few days to get some perspective — he'd been working too many hours, sleeping too few.

At last George turned up in Philadelphia with a big last scene, to go in only a few performances before New York. I thought it was good, so did Leland. Even Sydney felt it could work. It was a lot for me to learn — a two-page monologue. We rehearsed it during the day. It was to go in the next night. I didn't object to the rush, my feeling being that if it was going to be, the sooner I learned it the better. It was all part of the creative process of the theatre. Oliver Smith's wonderful set, so good to move around in, was a big help to that final scene.

The night the new scene went in I was in a terrible state of nerves — so many words, so much to remember. I have to say it was probably the best performance of that play I had ever given or would ever give. It was one of those nights when everything works. We all felt very confident.

Sydney was admirable and helpful, as always. It's such a good feeling to share a stage with someone supportive, for whom you have great affection. He and I really liked each other, respected each other, but no romance. He'd had that experience once and never again. A love affair with your leading man or woman is not easy. If there's an out-of-town fight — and they're inevitable — it grows out of all proportion, and you still have to look each other in the eye eight times a week. Hopeless. So it didn't happen with us — I was much too preoccupied, and he was in love with Noelle Adam, a beautiful French dancer.

Then my first exposure to the assigning of opening-night seats, a matter of great importance then. Who would sit where? There had to be laughers next to the critics. Leland and George choreographed it. Who was on whose guest list? We had many of the same friends, which helped. Adlai wanted to be there, and I wanted him, of course. Alistair and Jane Cooke and David and Hjordis Niven, the Reynoldses and Zuckermans, would also be my guests. And my mother and Lee, who had to have the best seats, to say nothing of Stephen and Leslie.

Opening-night audiences are traditionally ghastly — critics who dissect; friends over-anxious, either laughing too loud or too often; professional opening-nighters, there to see each other not the play. There's seldom a true reaction to a play. At my most relaxed (which is most people's most tense), I can't bear to know who's out in front — just one friend unnerves me. This audience was almost entirely friends — plus Adlai. God!

The curtain went up — the play started well — laughs in the right places. I made my entrance to tremendous applause which only made me quiver more — I had to lift a bottle of Jack Daniel's to my mouth to take a drink and almost knocked my teeth out because of the shakes. We played our first scene, in which Charlie (me), trying to convince George (Sydney) of his identity, recalled a time only the two of them could know about and described the moment of truth in the stateroom in bed with his host's wife, where, upon trying to escape through the porthole, Charlie was shot. The scene ended with me turning to George, saying, 'Look, look,' and opening my trenchcoat with my back to the audience. One could feel the men in the audience turning cold. From then on, it was uphill. They tried to like it, but the concept was so unattractive to them that they couldn't react properly to anything else.

George and Leland came round at the intermission to encourage us. 'It's going great — just play the play.' The adrenaline was flowing to such a degree I felt wonderful.

The curtain came down to great applause. Still shaking, Sydney and I hugged each other. There were photographers outside my dressing room, which was so full of flowers no visitor could get in. Hundreds of telegrams, gifts. I quickly changed for the photographers, but Adlai was my first sight on emerging. He kissed me, congratulated me — said something witty, of course — but was self-conscious with all the cameras around. Niven, Betty and Adolph, Alistair and Jane, so many friends pouring out love. It was a high point. I'd found new territory. I felt good about being there, and they felt good that I was there.

At the party after, before the reviews came through, I was standing at the bar with Moss Hart. I know now, of course, that he realized the play wouldn't go. He said, 'Don't take personally anything you might read — you should feel very good about tonight, your first time onstage in a leading role. You're good. You can do it and you should be proud of yourself.' Here I was, home, eighteen years after I started out. Finally I was starring on Broadway — my name was in lights — and it had been every bit as exciting as I dreamed it would be. But waiting for the reviews was hell. When they finally arrived, Sydney opened the *Tribune*, read one paragraph of Walter Kerr's review, and said, 'Well, let's see what the Knicks are doing.' The critics definitely did not like the play, though they did like the actors. I was welcomed as a movie star who handled herself well on a stage. Movie stars are suspect on Broadway — are we just dabbling, not taking it seriously? We're not of the theatre. It takes a long time to be accepted. But I still felt good. This play was a beginning.

George took a terrible beating critically and it sent him into a decline. He'd worked so hard, put so much of himself into *Goodbye Charlie*. He'd been the critics' darling since *The Seven Year Itch*. Their harsh words really hurt him. It put a strain on our relationship for months until his wound healed.

We ran for three months to full houses, but audiences did not like the play. We closed because the advance was dwindling.

At one performance I knew someone special was out front, but didn't know who — from the rumbling backstage, it must be someone important. Toward the back of the orchestra I saw a shock of white hair. I was afraid to think it might be Spence and Kate — they would never come together, and he'd never come at all, I didn't expect that. But when the curtain came down, into my dressing room walked Katie — adorable, warm, loving — full of compliments. And then the door opened again and in he walked. I threw my arms around him — he'd actually come to the theatre and sat out in front through the whole play. It moved me beyond words. Oh matchless, uncommon, wondrous beings.

New Year's Eve, Quent Reynolds picked

me up at the theatre. We were to appear on a late TV show, then go to Lee and Paula Strasberg's party, where everyone in New York theatre would be. I was liking my life in my old town a lot. I felt no yearning for California. My Sinatra scars had not quite healed — he actually called me backstage one night to ask how I was, but I never saw him. I loved being on the stage — felt good there. And, most important, I felt I'd finally landed someplace where I might belong, might enjoy my days, might be able to relax. For the first time in years I felt I might have a future.

Quent and I arrived at the Strasbergs' — a sardine crush. And there was an actor I'd met once, before my trip to Spain. Leland and Slim, Jerry Robbins, and I had gone to see *The Disenchanted*, and backstage they had introduced me to the star, Jason Robards. Audrey Hepburn had told me once while I was still in California that I should meet him, that I would like him. The second time I saw him was that New Year's Eve. He was feeling no pain, and we hit it off instantly. He stayed with me until I left. Rex Harrison called me the next day to say that his last view of me had been talking to Jason as he was burning my shoulders with his cigar.

Jason was rehearsing *Toys in the Attic* at the Hudson Theatre, a block away from the Lyceum. He sent me some notes written on the envelope of his first rehearsal pay — a smart seventy or eighty dollars. He was quite dazzling — and a little crazy. A remarkable actor and unlike any I'd ever known. Everyone thought he looked like Bogie, but I never did and I still don't. The flirtation began, was fun. Nothing is more fun or exciting than the unknown — the possibility of something . . .

He was a pure theatre man and considered by his peers to be a rarity — a great talent — someone who brought something indefinable to every role.

What followed next wasn't surprising. He picked me up at the theatre one night for supper. It was a Tuesday night, the first time I'd heard an old theatrical adage — beware of Tuesday and Friday nights, a natural pitfall because they precede matinee days. To many of us who were daring and a little crazy, an obvious night to stay out late. He was completely sober that night — rather shy, quiet, and very attractive. He had three children, two of them within a year of Stephen and Leslie, one a good deal younger. We gravitated toward each other immediately. My need for someone having been denied for so long, it was impossible for me to turn away. In the course of that night I found out that his three children were the result of his first marriage; that he had married again, but it wasn't working. My history with married men is peculiar, considering my early training. Mentally I had it straight — it was wrong to become involved, to have anything at all to do with a man who belonged to somebody else. If he didn't like it where he was, let him get out of it and then come around to me. With all of that firmly implanted in my brain, I found that, with the exception of Frank, every man I was really attracted to had a wife. Was it because all the best men were already taken? Was it some underlying, mysterious, subconscious wish to screw up other people's marriages? Or was it simply that the few men I was drawn to who were simultaneously drawn to me had married young? For whatever reason — it happened. I suppose Jason and I could have stopped seeing each other, but we didn't. It wasn't a daily contact — he'd call at odd hours of the morning, slightly looped. We'd meet in the Palace Bar around the corner after my show, a place full of characters with a very simpatico bartender — not unlike Harry Hope's bar in *The Iceman Cometh*. It became our hangout. Jason was a drinker. My interpretation was that he drank out of unhappiness — a logical conclusion from past experiences. His show went to Boston, and he called me from there often and late. I was being drawn deeper and deeper into a relationship with him — looking forward to his calls, hoping for them. I was in desperate need of someone to love — someone to belong to. Having lived through a few relationships, I do know now that I have endowed the men in my life with the qualities I wished them to have, rejecting whatever qualities they actually possessed that interfered with my romantic notions. Patently unfair to them.

Having left California, I seemed to have lost some of my career identity in the transfer to New York. At least, I felt as if I had. The identity given me by a complete life with an extraordinary man who was also a star seemed to have been buried with him. Perhaps it had been. A lot of it. I'd found fame, fortune to a degree (certainly it was, compared to what I'd arrived in California with), an entire life connected to another person's life, had spawned two children — and returned to New York emotionally raw, still looking for recognition, identity, and love. Though I never consciously entered a room looking for a man, I knew one when I saw one. Jason seemed a totally natural happening — and an inevitable one. He was not only attractive and wildly talented, he was unpredictable; there was an element of danger, which I suppose always keeps me awake, among other things. And he was new.

His reaction to me had nothing to do with my name or fame. Much more important, we each had children, and all of us seemed to have a common need to be a family. Built-in-brothership for Steve and Jady, sistership for Leslie and Sarah, and care for David.

Toys in the Attic opened in New York at the end of February, and from then on we saw each other more and more. We'd send notes to each other through our dressers — silly, romantic, funny cards. One rose. Nights he would call late and arrive at my apartment still later. He often stayed over.

Charlie closed March 19. It was an unhappy day for us all. The backers more than made their money back — sold it to films — but there was no advantage in going on investing money in a loser. Leland was philosophical; George, devastated, took off for California. I, on the other hand, though the run had been short, gave no thought to being anywhere but New York.

I became more and more involved with Jason. A few friends dropped hints about his drinking — 'Are you sure you want that?' I didn't accept it as a problem. A couple of times he'd behaved erratically with me — not showing up, once calling me Mrs Bogart. I chalked it up to a life of struggle — his first marriage breaking up; his first wife having had a drinking problem herself; his children sometimes neglected; his youngest son, David, being born partially blind; his helping his father, whom he adored but who had given up in his forties; his feeling of rejection by his mother. A black childhood and young manhood. Plenty of reason to drink. Like many other women, I was sure that if his life were different, he would be too. Naïveté, thy name is me.

One Saturday or Sunday morning, Steve was in bed, and when his door opened and Jason walked in, Steve's face broke into an enormous smile. It was as if he'd seen his father again. I've never seen anything like it. His face had not lit up like that since Bogie's death. Jason and I wanted our children to meet, to become friends. Both sides were receptive, both had something missing.

I adored him. He read poetry I'd never heard before — we drove to a nearby beach with the children on a Sunday — I went to Stratford, Ontario, with him for a weekend, where he'd played Hotspur, to see his pal Chris Plummer and others in the company. Our time together was exciting, romantic — I felt adventurous, light of heart. Everything was new. It was the beginning of my second life — the New York theater chapter. Goodbye Hollywood, hello Broadway. And I had a new man to focus on entirely — I would savor every minute of it. And to make it all perfect, one of 'our' songs was 'All My Tomorrows' sung by — can you believe it? — Frank Sinatra.

I suppose I convinced Jason I would make everything fall into place, that I was the true haven for him and for his children. Once I found him and made up my mind that this was what I had to have, I would not give up. Utter tenacity — no way I would let go. At times when he was drinking heavily he would fight me, saying he wanted no part of me or my life; take off into the night. If he didn't call in a day or two, I'd get to him.

One night Ginny Reynolds gave a party, and after his show Jason and I went to her apartment. At one point he decided to leave. Ginny tried to make him stay, but he had other ideas. Her concern was me — she was wise to the ways of all kinds of men, and much more realistic than I. She told me Jason said to her, 'I don't feel it for her — not enough — it's not there.' Now, there's nothing anyone can do about that. But I wouldn't accept it — he was loaded, he didn't mean it, and he didn't say it to me. I wasn't about to let him off the hook. Later on he said he hadn't meant it.

When Jason drank he was somebody else. Not a fighter, but a singer of songs, a reciter of poetry. He didn't care where he was, though on instinct he would wind up in Greenwich Village bars — a holdover from *The Iceman Cometh* and his Village life with his first wife and three children. Or the Palace Bar, or any of a number of other theatre hangouts. In our wooing days it became something of a game to me — the places were new, the people were new. Though I drank enough to get me through an evening and into the wee small hours, I never fell into a drink problem myself. Never had the stomach for it — and never wanted to cut out from the world anyway.

As much as I loathed drunkenness, I found myself able to get through those times because of what Jason was when sober. He had an ingenuousness about him — charm — shyness. He was tremendously warm and appealing. He was a man who could love. He'd felt such guilt about the end of his first marriage that he gave away almost every cent he had ever made or ever would make. And often he would end up in his old apartment sleeping it off or having breakfast with his children. It wasn't any romantic feeling for his ex-wife, but the children that brought him back.

She and I liked each other, and I know she was happy and relieved when the children were with me.

Decision had always been so clear to me before: if you loved someone, you went where that person went. Simple. And when a marriage was over, you left — clean and clear. Jason didn't think like that, it was never simple for him. Actually he began my awareness of the grays in life, the maybes. I was sure he loved me, I was sure we'd be married — the only question was when. The poor guy didn't stand a chance. And I could imagine a new life — a new baby. I wanted his child. I wanted one because of love and because I felt it would make all the difference to our life together — his, mine, ours.

And I became more theatre-oriented than I had ever been — exposed to the biggest talents our theatre has. Maureen Stapleton, Irene Worth, Jose Quintero, Chris Plummer, Anne Jackson and Eli Wallach, Thornton Wilder. I was so proud to be connected with Jason, with his talent; to be befriended by the finest of our actors, directors, playwrights.

There was an actors' strike in June, the first time in memory. Actors never struck — real actors couldn't bear the idea of theatres closing. Some plays wouldn't reopen. But it had to be done. There is a camaraderie among actors — special love and respect the good ones have for each other. They all take the same risks, have the same vulnerabilities. They protect one another, and in a crisis stand strongly together. I was allowed to enter that group, despite my Hollywood past. I wasn't truly one of them, but they let me in nonetheless, and I was deeply grateful.

Before I had convinced anyone I was seriously intending to become a permanent fixture on the Broadway stage I was exposed to the best — through Jason. I'd never known an actor more giving to others in his work — less judging, more loving. To him acting was based on that. He was a pro, he knew what he was doing, it all seemed to fall into place for him onstage. Of course, in O'Neill plays he became the character he was playing — O'Neill had that effect on him; his understanding of the writing was so total he might have invented Hickey, Hughie, James Tyrone. He has greater perception of O'Neill than any other actor anywhere has ever had — he might almost (if you can bear the melodrama of it, and I can) have been born to act his plays. Just by listening and watching Jason, by knowing how strongly he felt about interpreting each play, I learned.

And for all the black days I had with him, there were so many good days. We laughed a lot together — he believed in laughter. And he tried as hard as he could.

One day May was not feeling well. She wouldn't give in, wouldn't complain. I could see something was very wrong. I made her lie down. My doctor came and said she'd have to go to the hospital. It was her heart — she would have to have special care, tests. It was serious. She didn't want to go, she wanted to stay home, but she accepted the verdict bravely as she'd accepted everything in her life. She was a big woman, but she didn't look it sitting there in a wheelchair waiting for the elevator. I hugged her and kissed her. When the doctor called later, the prognosis was not good. May's heart was failing — she'd had another heart attack.

Around seven the next morning the call came. May had died. Her heart had been too far gone — her great heart. Oh, I didn't want to lose May — the last witness of Bogie's and my life together, the last thread. I dreaded telling the children. When they came home in the afternoon and headed for the kitchen, I stopped them, pulled both close to me and told them. Steve burst into tears, sobbed relentlessly. The dam had burst. It was the first time he had cried over loss — he'd held himself in for his father, that had come in other ways, but for May tears. When Leslie saw Steve cry, she cried — she'd lost as much as he. We spent that evening close together, talking about May. She would leave a hole that could never be filled. I would always think about her — always miss her. There's no replacement for anyone in this world.

As I'd only sublet my apartment for a year, I'd have to find another, unfurnished, and send for my stuff from California. I fell into one by accident. Someone told me about an apartment at the Dakota, the great old building on Central Park West with its high ceilings and enormous rooms. I took the apartment on sight. Jason came with me and loved it, though he was unused to anything that size. I had the furniture to fill it — he wasn't mad about that idea, but I convinced him. Chairs and tables are just chairs and tables, it's the people who use them who make the difference. And there was a room for each child — large enough to house Jady, Sarah, and David when they came. We were so much in love, there seemed no doubt we would live in that apartment forever. Together. Another forever.

There was still Jason's divorce, which took a long time. He was covered with guilt — the alimony demands were extravagant — his wife was bitter. I couldn't blame her for that. He was having trouble making the final move, packing his belongings. His wife had filed suit for divorce in October. For adultery, citing me. I had to think for both of us. I turned down work — nothing marvelous, but work. My mother told me I was a fool to turn down jobs — if I did it too often, they'd stop asking — but I couldn't leave Jason. Wouldn't. I was in love, I wanted to be with him, and I was terrified something would go wrong if I was away. My self-confidence had not gotten much stronger with the passage of time. And my children needed him — his needed me — we all needed each other in a home together. Blinded by emotion, over-concentrated, over-focused, I did everything to diminish the shadow of Bogie. Jason was not consciously upset by the legend, but when he'd had a few drinks something might come out. He was not a competitive man, he had his own secure place in his work — that's the only thing he felt sure of, the one place he had a total sense of responsibility — but with his past personal life such a mess, he needed my constant reassurance that it would be all right, that I loved him, that I didn't need my old life and the luxuries that went with it.

I joined him in California, where he was making a movie. He'd rented a small house so we'd have privacy. He'd told a reporter that he loved me and we would get married as soon as he got his divorce, and that was picked up by others of the press — a mistake. It only angered his ex-wife-to-be. But Jason had no idea of the ways of the press — he said what he thought — he'd not been in the news except as an actor. But it was different with me. In every item I was referred to as 'Lauren Bacall — widow of Humphrey Bogart.' And always some comment like 'A father for her children, or will he be able to fill Bogie's shoes?'

I met Jason's father, whom I liked enormously, and his stepmother, an ordinary woman with the usual ordinary prejudices. Jews for one. Jason, Sr, called Dad by all, was an attractive, witty man, rightly proud of his theatre work in the Twenties. He knew that his son's talent was extraordinary, as he knew his own was not. He and Jason sang together, drank together, adored each other — though I finally felt Dad used Jason. Dad and I got along immediately. He and Agnes, his wife, lived in a tiny cottage in the Valley. He didn't like to ask Jason for help, but he did. He was a disappointed actor — he'd known success once, decades before. It was an old actor's story — always sad, always a little unreal. When Jason was around, Dad would talk about the theatre again, feel a part of something he was no longer a part of. He had a new audience in me for his stories, his songs. The four of us went out to dinner one night. The Robards boys drank too much, became rowdy — general coarseness. I hated to see Jason like that, it had nothing to do with the Jason I loved, and if it did, I didn't want to know about it. Agnes and I finally got them home, where the drinking continued. Dad wasn't supposed to drink anymore — he had a bad stomach — but that night was horrendous. The only comedy relief was everyone on their knees searching for Dad's lost contact lenses. Under the influence of booze, they brought out the worst in each other. Jason was becoming unmanageable — he started to insult me, and when we got back to our house we had a knockdown, drag-out fight. I was frightened — this Jason was completely foreign to me — I only knew I had to get away. I managed to escape while he was making one of his long-distance calls — when drunk he called ex-wives, theatre friends, anyone. I got into the car and drove to the beach, as I used to do. It was the first time I seriously wondered about the kind of life I might have with Jason. If there were to be many nights like this one, it would be hopeless. When he wasn't drinking he was everything I wanted. When he'd had a few drinks he was still okay. But there came that unforeseeable moment when he became someone else. I still held to the thought that he was in a transition period — once our lives were permanently settled together, all else would fall into place. It was my first return to California since Bogie and the split with Frank — I wanted to see my friends, wanted them to meet Jason, they wanted to meet him. But I wanted them to meet him sober, at his best, the way I loved him, so that they would too. I wanted so much. In my mind I could take a man for what he was, but emotionally no. It was pure make-believe, wishful thinking, the fulfillment of my particular dream — impossible to isolate or analyze at the time. I remember Adlai saying to me, 'Are you sure? Remember, Bogie was a mature man. It's not going to get better after you're married, it's going to get worse.' All went ignored. I knew better than anyone.

I talked to myself a lot on that drive to the beach. Got out and walked. I felt very much alone. I couldn't bear the thought that this might not work out — I was in far too deep. I would wait before going back to town, give Jason time to sleep it off, do a little thinking himself. We had so much going for us, it couldn't all go down the drain. I called Dad — went over there for breakfast. Jason called to see if I was there. I told Dad to say no, which he didn't like doing. Finally, Jason, having called again, came around in the afternoon. He was tentative — sweet and so appealing — we talked it all out. He wasn't a man who wanted to discuss his drinking or bad behavior, but he acknowledged it, felt it was all wrapped up in his past. We did have our strong bond, and we were crazy about each other, so we went on, never really facing that problem that was to be the core of every trouble we ever had.

Back in New York Jason went into rehearsal for *Big Fish, Little Fish*, a play by Hugh Wheeler, John Gielgud directing and Hume Cronyn and Marty Gabel among those in the first-rate cast. It was a happy company, and they all loved John. I remember sitting in the audience during a run-through, watching the outline of that great Gielgud profile watching the actors. It was a funny, lovely play, unappreciated in New York. The run was short.

The next few months were taken up with plans for our future. Jason signed to make *Tender Is the Night* with Jennifer Jones, so it would be Europe for May and June, California after that. Steve and Leslie would go to summer camp and I would accompany Jason. The divorce settlement was made — Jason gave up everything, the second time he'd done that. He'd worked hard all his life and every cent he earned went to an ex-wife. He never begrudged what he paid for the children or to their mother, Eleanor, for that matter, but there was a limit. When you want freedom, you have to pay. But not that much — it just wasn't fair to him.

We took off for Europe, knowing the divorce in Mexico was practically a *fait accompli*. The papers had been signed in May. The British press took their pictures, wrote their stories: 'How does it feel to follow Bogart?' Wouldn't it ever end? I should have known better. As long as it's news, takes up space in a paper, of course not.

Just before leaving for Europe and *Tender Is the Night* I had discovered I was pregnant. We'd planned to spend a few weeks relaxing — I was anxious for my English and French friends to meet Jason. They were all happy I had found someone — someone wonderful who would be wonderful to me.

I told Jason about the baby and he was overjoyed. I said nothing to anyone else, least of all my children or my mother. Pregnant and not yet married — nice Jewish girls didn't do that. This one did. Jason was in good form most of the time in London and Paris. A couple of drinking nights with Jack and Doreen Hawkins and Kenny and Billie More. Both Jack and Kenny enjoyed drinking, got carried away sometimes, but in a good way — not the same way Jason did. My friends didn't pay much attention to Jason's way with booze, though they sensed — Doreen in particular — a difference. We saw Anne and Art Buchwald and Jim and Gloria Jones in Paris — had a great time.

We were in Nice waiting for the film to begin when Mother and Lee passed through. The night before had been a bit booze-ridden, so Jason was not in top form. But we spent the day together, and took Mother and Lee to a crazy Mediterranean restaurant where again the wine flowed — unfortunately — like wine.

The next morning Jason was feeling rotten, and with the sun shining happily above, he told me he didn't want to get married again. I was stunned and scared. The idea of an abortion briefly flashed through my mind, but it was too terrible to contemplate — and I wanted that baby. I told him I understood how he felt, with two broken marriages, children, too much responsibility, not a moment of relief, of freedom. I sat at the window looking out at the sea, the sun shining on it, trying to figure out what to do. Should I pack up and leave him now? What about the baby?

What a mess I was in, and no one to talk it over with. Extraordinary for a woman who seemed totally in control of her destiny, sure of what and who she was, the personification of strength. Here I was at thirty-six, emotionally shaky, with no defined future and no purpose except to prevail somehow.

Jason was to go to Switzerland for the first location shots on the film, and I went to Paris to think some more. At least I had a few friends there. I saw a lot of Annie and Art Buchwald, who were warm and welcoming as ever but who had their own lives, plus three children. Everyone had his own life. My dear — time *you* had one. I felt very odd-woman-out — no connection with anything but my expanding waistline, so there would be a connection soon. Jason called me, asked me to join him in Zürich, we'd work it out. So I went. We talked and talked and talked. He wanted our child too, didn't really want to let go, loved Steve and Leslie, decided he wouldn't know what to do on the loose. He got no argument from me. Our agent, Peter Witt, arrived. He said we could marry in Vienna — he'd be advance man as well as best, he'd set it up. I'd never been to Vienna, but Jason had and couldn't wait to show it to me — one place he knew that I didn't. We planned to go after Jason's last location shot in Switzerland. Jennifer gave us a wedding dinner on the eve of our departure — she was a wonderful, caring friend. She never asked questions; in true friendship, she accepted what was. If I wanted to marry Jason, she was all for it. She admired him tremendously as an actor and liked him personally — any reservations she kept to herself.

We were met in Vienna by Peter, who told us all the details on our way to the hotel. We had to meet the lawyer the following day, and the day after that I would be Mrs Robards. The meeting with the lawyer was in a large, dark room in a large, dark building. We sat nervously opposite him. He was not warm and friendly. The questions he asked were curious, to say the least. Religion? When I said Jewish, he looked at the other man in the room and then back at me. It might have been Nazi Germany. 'And your husband is dead?' 'Yes.' 'Do you have the death certificate?' 'No — but surely you know he is dead. Every newspaper in the world headlined his death.' I felt sick — I hated that man. 'But we cannot take your word for it. We must have proof.' I couldn't believe it. Don't tell me he didn't know Bogie was dead! 'And you, Mr Robards. Do you have a copy of your divorce papers?' 'No — I have a letter.' It was a disaster. Peter talked to the lawyer in German, ushered us out, said he still thought it would be all right. The next day was supposed to be our wedding day. Jason called America to find out about the divorce papers, whether they'd been sent, or would a cable do? We had our rings. I had my dress. But Jason had to return to America to go on with the picture, and between the divorce papers and the death certificate it didn't work. The officials would not be satisfied. I hated Vienna — I actually felt in danger there. The press were in the hotel lobby, and with Peter as interpreter we told them about our difficulties, tried to laugh them off. We'd marry in Las Vegas, the hell with them. A dismal trip — we were both drained.

After a few days in New York with the children, getting them off to camp, I followed Jason to California. We planned to spend the weekend in Las Vegas, in the bridal suite of The Sands. It would be queer to be married there. Because my first wedding had been so special, so personal, I never thought of the wedding ceremony in any other terms. I'd been a snob about Las Vegas weddings. Now I thought, 'What does it matter? It might even be fun.' We took Dad with us as best man — Jennifer Jones would be my matron of honor. We went for our license after leaving our things at The Sands and they said no. I couldn't believe it! Christ, *anyone* could get married in Las Vegas. But a law had just been passed about Mexican divorces, and the time between divorce and remarriage. So back we went to The Sands, where Jack Entratter had prepared the bridal suite, judge, wedding cake. What a saga! Was someone trying to tell us something? I felt as though the whole world were against me. I hated Vegas — my good times there were long since over. It was ridiculous to sit in that bridal suite, trying to pretend I wasn't destroyed, trying to salvage the evening with a joke, a drink. Even Jason didn't feel like drinking. There was nothing to celebrate.

Two defeated people returned to their flat in Westwood. We decided to go to Mexico the following week, but not until every law old and new had been checked backward and forward. The press in California were having fun with our bad luck, and I was beginning to feel jinxed. However, July 4 was the following week, and Jason and I found something marvelous in that for a wedding day, something to do with self-assertion, independence, with the entire country celebrating our wedding day.

On the day itself, we were in Mexico and the lawyer took us to the judge's chamber, if you could call it that. We signed what we had to sign and the ceremony began — in Spanish. Being a sentimental idiot, I was sure I'd be teary-eyed, but in Spanish I couldn't swing it. I just didn't understand what the judge was saying. But we said 'I do' and it was real — we were man and wife, and happy to be. We had a wedding lunch of tacos — one of my favorite foods — and tequila, with Mexican guitarists under a hot Mexican sun, and cabled our children, who were thrilled. David and Jennifer Selznick gave a large party, which ended slightly disastrously with Jason drunk and all of us up until seven in the morning. Slim called on our first married Sunday morning — she was so happy for me, and full of sentiment as I described my cooking breakfast.

Our time in California had been bumpy. I was pregnant and was delighted to get home to New York. My stomach was growing, it was odd being pregnant after nine years. Stephen and Leslie seemed to be looking forward to it — Leslie particularly. Steve adored Jason, adored having a man in the house, someone to call Dad. Jason was marvelous with children, and he loved to cook. I'd never done much of that, but I began to enjoy our doing it together — the family sport. We thrived, for the most part, only falling by the wayside on the nights when Jason didn't show up.

He'd done that for years, and it was very hard to break the habit. It happened in spurts. When he was good he was very very good, and when he was bad he was a disaster. I became tense and somewhat drawn, trying to keep it from the children and Mother. There were too many late nights — too much unpredictability. Poor Jason wasn't used to coming home after the theatre, and I was in no mood (or shape) to go bar-hopping every night. Sometimes he'd show up and I'd have supper waiting. Other times I'd be on the phone trying to find him. I put it all down to bad old habits, but it was taking a toll on me. I kept hoping it would get better. It *had* to.

Jason had not promised to change into another person. Yet somewhere in me — not somewhere, everywhere — I'd expected him to. It was all well and good and fun and exciting at the start of a relationship not to know when your lover would be turning up. It was quite a different thing not to know when your husband would be turning up.

My only experience had been with a man who knew exactly what he wanted. And I had known what Bogie had wanted — how far I could go, what he would put up with, what he wouldn't. Positions were now reversed. Jason was still finding out what he wanted, and there was no pattern to that. He wanted mostly to stay alive. Keep working. He had no preconceived notions on behavior. It did not interest me to make all the rules, yet I found myself doing just that — expecting too much, always being disappointed. I guess I didn't truly look at the man — I only saw what I wanted to see. Impossible. I thought I tried to adjust, and I did to a degree, but not enough. I wanted my husband with me, not in bars, not coming home all hours of the night, sometimes with strangers, to play records at seven in the morning. I didn't want the children to see it — I didn't want to see it myself. So I became more tense, held too much back, not wanting to face things as they were. I wanted to stay with my fantasy. Alas, I would not be allowed that luxury.

During this time Mother had taken to cutting out every article she could find pertaining to heart disease — any new discovery, any medical theory. She watched her diet carefully, she adhered to everything her doctor told her, but she'd had another setback. Not a bad attack, but edema, and she had to spend a couple of weeks in a hospital. Her doctor's brilliant observation to Lee and me was that she was not a well woman. 'Her heart has been badly damaged — it will only get weaker

727

— she has a year or two at the most to live.' I hated him — what he said, and the way he said it. Lee and I knew the damage her heart had sustained, but imminent death — no! Who was this doctor anyway? Mother had found him — she had faith in him, but we didn't. After going through a few months of hell with our secret, we convinced her to change doctors. I remember sitting next to her in my apartment, at that time deep into my pregnancy, feeling her warm reassuring hand in mine and loving her so much. To be without her was unthinkable. The prognosis of the next doctor was serious, but set no time limit on her life!

About ten days before Christmas, at around four in the morning, I felt the first pain. It couldn't be the baby — too soon — but I'd felt differently this time from the very beginning. The pains started to come more regularly. Jason had gotten home late, quite sloshed. When I told him of the pains, he said, 'Get into bed, darling, I'll bring you something on a tray. Don't move.' While he was crashing around the kitchen I called the doctor. It sounded like labor to him. 'Time the pains for half an hour and call again.' They got stronger and closer together. Jason loaded — the children (four of them) asleep — what a mess! He came in with the most ridiculous tray of food — coffee, eggs, half an avocado — if I hadn't been furious and scared, I would have laughed. He put the tray on the bed and it collapsed, with food and drink everywhere. God! I called the doctor again, who told me to take a cab and get to the hospital. While Jason was trying to put the tray back together and get me back to bed, I was trying to dress and tell him that we had to go to the hospital. We went to Leslie's and Steve's rooms and told them where I was going — not to worry; Steve smiled at me, much as he had at the age of three on Benedict Canyon when Leslie was born. I told the nurse to tell my mother where I was when she called in the morning. We got a taxi and started rumbling up the West Side Highway to Columbia Presbyterian Hospital way uptown. Jason was making not much sense, and I was frightened. My water broke about five minutes from the hospital. Wouldn't we ever get there? I felt as though I'd never had a baby — nothing that happened to me this time had ever happened to me before. The doctor was nice but really unknown — I didn't feel secure, I just wanted to have the baby. At the hospital I kept telling the anesthetist, 'It hurts — give me a shot.' He kept saying he didn't want to give me too much too soon. It seemed forever that we argued.

Then I don't remember anything until I opened my eyes to see four other pairs of eyes staring down at me. I was in the recovery room, and my jaw was hurting. It seems my jaw had locked, and as they'd thought I was coming out of anesthesia they had removed the depressor from my mouth, only to have me go under again. Four doctors had been trying to pry my jaw open and were about to perform a tracheotomy when my jaw relaxed and they could open my mouth. I vaguely remember being wheeled into my room, seeing Mother and Lee in the corridor. Jason's face looked tired but happy. And I was the mother of a seven-pound boy. It was December 16, 1961.

We had chosen the name beforehand: Sam. Not Samuel, not Sammy, just plain Sam. Middle name Prideaux, Tom Prideaux being Jason's cousin and Sam's godfather-to-be. I wanted Kate Hepburn and Carolyn Morris to be the godmothers. Katie said, 'Why do you want me? For heaven's sake, I'm no good at paying attention to children.' I insisted that five minutes of exposure to her was worth five hours of anyone else, so she agreed. During my time in the hospital I had a typical attack of the blues. Sam was a beautiful baby, of course, perfect in every way — but Jason showed up one night to visit and then not the next. The baby nurse I'd hired quit before she ever came, so I had to quickly interview another one in the hospital. That was my only truly lucky break. Hedy, the nurse who came, was quiet and sure — and understanding about people and life's problems. She was to stay a year and a half, and continue to take up the slack with Sam for the next ten years and more — a blessing on us all.

Jason was to pick me up at the hospital the morning of December 23. I'd called the night before to make certain he'd be there. I hadn't felt well this time — run-down, emotionally fraught. This had not been marriage as I'd ever conceived of it or known it. My adjustments were many, but the first months had been more down than up. That morning I must have called four or five times — first no Jason, then a drinking Jason. He was on his way up with a big surprise. Just dandy, I thought — our first day home with the baby and him three sheets to the wind. At last he arrived several hours late, and the surprise was that he'd hired a Rolls-Royce to bring me home from the hospital. I couldn't have cared less — better sober in a taxi. But press were waiting downstairs, and I put a face on for them. I didn't want Jason holding Sam — afraid he'd drop him. He insisted. To avoid a scene, I gave in, but I was nervous and upset — not an ideal state for a new mother. As we reached the foot of the steps leading to our elevator in the Dakota I started to hemorrhage. I got upstairs. Hedy was waiting and took Sam while I rushed to my bedroom to pull myself together — got into a nightgown and into bed. Nothing had gone right and I was anything but a happy woman. Why was it going so badly? I was in no emotional state to figure it out, but I did know that this was no way to be married. I had a husband whom I loved but with whom nothing went smoothly for more than two days at a time. We were certainly not your average newlyweds starting a great new life. Funny to think of it now — I never analyzed it at the time — I did not know in so many words what Jason expected of me. He did not object to my working — he did not object to me — he just did what he did, and as long as he was working I knew where he'd be a half-hour before his performance. His habits were the same after Sam's birth as before. I had just not been so steadily exposed to them before. How long could I last?

Jason was going into rehearsal with *A Thousand Clowns* by an untried author, Herb Gardner. That should help to straighten him out, I thought. We'd talked about his drinking up to a point. He recognized that it was a problem, but he would not go for help. He loved me — loved Sam — all the children. 'It will all work out.' So I held on to hope, ecstatic when he didn't drink, nervous when he drank a little, frantic and miserable when it took over. And resentful — often Jady, Sarah, and David would come for a weekend, and no Jason. I'd be left with the six children. I decided I would not lie to them — if they asked where he was, I'd answer, 'I don't know.' 'Will he be home for dinner?' 'I don't know.' I was angry, and it was years before I dealt with the truth of it. It was not malice or cruelty on Jason's part — drinking was, and had been, a part of his way of life for too long, and he had neither the will nor the strength to do a complete about-face.

It all came to a head in the summer of 1963. He'd had a two-day siege and come home feeling very sick. I had made up my mind by then that he would have to do something positive. Life was becoming unbearable. Success didn't help — reassurance — love — the children. Nothing did. And I was turning into someone I didn't like. I'd continually lie to Mother — try to keep her from coming over without telling her why. I'd gathered our friends at home for a surprise party for Jason's fortieth birthday, telling him only that a couple of people were coming by for a drink after his show. I had a cake all ready. When the clock struck two, it was clear he had made other plans — and who knew when he'd show up? A few stalwarts stayed, the others left. When he finally did walk in, loaded, I was in such a state that I grabbed a bottle of vodka, turned it upside down, and smashed it into the cake. 'Here's your god-damn cake!' When I realized that what I wanted to do was slam it over his head, that I was capable of violence, it frightened me so that I knew I would finally have to act.

Fortunately, the next day he was so sick he acknowledged that he needed help. I must try to get him a doctor. That was the first break in my black sky. He finally did find a psychiatrist willing to take him on and life became brighter — certainly more helpful.

Then in the spring Jason's father died — the one member of his family he really loved and had rapport with. That week was filled with sadness — the pathetic funeral that we tried to make a little better. Jason's mother and her husband came up from the desert. Jason hadn't been close to her for years, but would become more so from then on. He paid for everything out there. He was the provider; the one with talent, with quality.

And only a few weeks later, in June, my

firstborn, Steve, graduated from Buckley School. It was very moving to see my almost adolescent son about to enter his young-manhood phase. Next step, Milton Academy. Four years of living away from home, which we felt would be a healthy, happy experience for him. Watching him graduate, though, brought pictures of fourteen years before flashing to mind, and all the hopes and dreams that went with them. What a lot of terrible things had happened since to cloud those hopes, those dreams.

Jason signed up with the new Lincoln Center Repertory Theatre at a great financial sacrifice — Robert Whitehead, Elia Kazan, and Arthur Miller were starting it, a major repertory company in New York. It was something Jason believed in, and only with a star of Jason's stature involved could it prevail. The first play was to be Arthur Miller's *After the Fall*, directed by Elia Kazan. They were to open at the Washington Square Theatre, which would remain their home until the new theatre was built in Lincoln Center. Jason and I had discussed it — he would be bringing home little money, but we felt money was not to be considered in this instance. Neither Miller nor Kazan would be making any money either. Rehearsals would start October 1, so he'd have the summer to rest. We rented a house in Malibu.

It was time for me to pick up my career. The only thing producers seemed interested in me for was a television series, which I refused to do. The picture business made me feel like two cents — unwanted, unworthy. Very depressing. Well, I'd turned my back on it all four years before — I'd have to eat a little crow. But I couldn't beg for work — 'Look at me, I still look good, I can act. I'm not Bogie's wife or widow, I'm an actress.' I made a guest appearance on a *Dr Kildare* segment, a very popular show starring Richard Chamberlain, everyone's hero that year — including Leslie's.

I lowered my professional sights totally to start working in pictures again, and agreed to be in a truly tacky movie, *Shock Treatment*, whose only saving grace was that my friend Roddy McDowell would be in it and we could suffer together. The theory was that once I worked out there, they'd see that I seriously wanted to work and other offers would come.

Jason and I for the most part had a good summer. A few bad days, but he continued talking to the doctor on the phone. He was trying. And Sam was growing. He was beautiful, and he was funny. He made me laugh from the very beginning. His reactions were funny, he had true humor (not all children do). And my mother worshipped him. Actually, it was mutual — they were incredibly close.

Steve and Leslie went back to school in mid-September and Jason to rehearsals of *After the Fall* at the end of the month. I returned to California mid-November for another film, *Sex and the Single Girl.* A very good cast — Natalie Wood, Hank Fonda, Tony Curtis — but not a very good film. At that time it seemed we might move West, as I had been successful in finding work there. It was my only Christmas away from Stephen and Leslie and Sam, and I was feeling very sorry for myself, but there was no way to go East for one day with work on either side of it. I did make it back for the opening of *After the Fall.* Adlai was to take me. The day of the opening he explained that Mrs Johnson, the First Lady, had asked him to escort her — did I mind? He'd have to take us both. Wonderful — how could I mind!

The opening was a theatrical event. Jason's work was supreme — brilliant. And on January 26 of that year Jason and I were presented with the American Academy's award for achievement, with Adlai as the presenter — the Academy where I had had my precious year of training more than twenty years before. 1964 started very well, but the Lincoln Center people did not live up to their promise of no commercialism. Miller sold serial rights to the play to a magazine, the television rights too — movies too, I think — making a fortune. Here was Jason working his tail off, getting practically no money for an ideal that was being crashed to the ground. Sam Behrman had a new play, *But for Whom Charlie*, that was put into the repertory. It wasn't very well received, so there were more and more performances of *After the Fall*. The theatre was being run like Broadway. Very disillusioning. Jason kept on until his year was up, but he left feeling that he'd been had.

There was a Eugene O'Neill play, a one-acter called *Hughie*, that Jason had always wanted to act. I dreaded that, although he was the greatest interpreter of O'Neill in anyone's memory. Alas, he had more than a tendency to take on the personality of the character he was playing. It was a bad time for us, what with Jason's disenchantment with Lincoln Center, and Eugene O'Neill. He became erratic with the doctor — drink took over more and more with *Hughie* — I became more of a shrew. There were always odd children problems cropping up and I would have the responsibility of six thrust upon me suddenly. And there were money problems — never the fault of

Jason. He never stopped working. He'd do television specials to supplement his theatre work — he earned a fortune — but alimony ate it up. He resented there never being enough for us, but there was nothing he could do about it.

My fortieth birthday came and went — traumatic for me — and I went to Phyllis and Adolph Green that night. No Jason.

Hughie only played five weeks. In February, Jason was to take it to California. We booked into the Bel-Air Hotel. I was more rundown than I knew — almost on arrival I began to fade. I felt nauseated, could hardly sit up. Jason drove me to my doctor's office. The diagnosis was that I needed a lot of rest and fluids — my blood pressure was fluctuating badly, I was overwrought, I had to get into bed and stay there. Jason would be at the theatre nightly. He hated to be around illness, wanted no part of it. Sam had a cold and had to stay in bed also. Too much responsibility at once for Jason — he drank and stayed away.

Katie came over one afternoon, took one look at me, and pronounced me a damn fool. 'You're too thin — a wreck — you should be on the beach. The marriage is no good for you — get out, forget it, think of yourself again. You've forgotten about living.' She was dead right. I realized I'd been trying to beat the drink problem by talking logically, or by threatening to leave. Spence told me, 'No one ever stops drinking because someone asks them to. You can't make him stop — he will, but only when he wants to, only when he has no choice. I know.'

They were only telling me what I knew but had refused to face. I knew I would have to leave Jason eventually. I'd forgotten to notice the sky, the trees, flowers, grass — to just enjoy a beautiful day. I'd forgotten how to laugh, to relax, to have any sane social exchange. I had no peace. My only pleasure was my children. My reasons for staying with Jason, for keeping us together, had been them — and perhaps another reason was that I couldn't face defeat. I loved Jason when he was the Jason I knew he could be, but the other Jason took over too often. No life could be built on that. My physical breakdown had forced me to face it all as it was. No more pipe dreams.

By the time Steve and Leslie came out to California I was able to go out for a few hours a day. I talked to them one afternoon while we were driving somewhere — asked them how they would feel if Jason and I separated. They wanted to know why. I told them that we had problems, that he drank too much, that it wasn't working out. They hadn't seen him drinking often — hardly at all. His daytime sleeping had been presented to them as necessary due to theatre hours. If he came home on a Sunday afternoon, they never asked him where he'd been, they were just glad to see him. I didn't want to paint a black picture for them, didn't want to dramatize the depressing turn my life was taking, I just wanted to feel them out. And I was able to say it out loud for the first time.

I rented a house in Trancas until the end of the summer. Sam loved the beach, so did Jason, but I was thinking mostly of myself, of my health. A new addition to our family was Nanny, a young Danish nurse who was to devote eleven years of her life to our Sam. I was besotted with my small son — he gave such pleasure — I had to keep myself in shape for him, for all my children. I made no quick irreversible decisions, but I knew I had turned a corner. I had come back to reality and my priorities were clear. I was fed up with the life I led. And in the next months two deaths brought things ever more into focus — Quent Reynolds in March, David Selznick in June. Two men I loved and admired, two widows I felt great love and sympathy for. Each death brought me closer to those left and reminded me never to stop paying attention, never be careless, who knows who won't be here tomorrow? They also made it clearer and clearer that I would never go back to the early dark life with Jason. I had lost sight of the preciousness of time — had been living from midnight to dawn, sacrificing my own health, both physical and mental. I finally had to face some facts: that I had value as a human being — that alcoholism destroyed families, was not to be lived with — that I would not be destroyed, nor would I allow my children to be. I would have no patience with anyone who threw his life away. And not for a second would I allow anyone to throw mine away. The values came back — life's standards. Out of every disaster some lessons learned.

I would have to keep my career going. I was offered a part in *Harper* with Paul Newman — a kind of suspense film patterned after *The Big Sleep*, but without the same kind of part for me. Paul was the detective. I knew him, liked him personally and as an actor, and was more than pleased to have an opportunity to work with him. That would take up a month in the summer.

Joe Hyams was writing a book about Bogie. He wanted my blessing — wanted me to write an introduction. Knowing of Joe's attachment to Bogie, I agreed. The Bogie cult had begun in Harvard's Brattle Theatre early that year. They still have Bogart festivals, and the collegians of the day pack the house to see their hero. It was extraordinary that Bogie transcended generations, that the young could identify with him, recognize something in him that they admired and wanted to emulate.

I began to be asked my opinion of it. I had mixed emotions — I was very proud, thought it quite incredible that Bogie had been singled out above other movie stars as a folk hero for students. He wouldn't have believed it. But I felt awkward because of Jason. To be constantly talking of a Bogie who had been reborn made his presence loom large again. So I would try to bring Jason into the conversation, referring to his brilliance as an actor, making an effort not to deny Bogie but to put Jason in a different high place. It wasn't easy and I never quite achieved it, but I tried.

Jason had enough problems of his own — and we had enough together — not to need this extra added attraction. Yet there were Steve and Leslie, and I wanted them to feel pride in Bogie, to see young men and women, their seniors by not too many years, adore and admire their father. I, of course, didn't realize at once how tough it was to be Steve — to be Bogart's son. 'Was he really your father? What was he like? Did he really talk the way he did on the screen? Did he have a gun?' Steve felt isolated in a way — what kid wouldn't? — singled out for reasons of his parentage, self-conscious. I'm sure that more than once he wanted to change his name to Smith or Jones.

Peter Witt called from New York. David Merrick had a play he wanted to send me, to go into rehearsal in October. Jason was going to do *The Devils* with Anne Bancroft, starting in September, and I'd have a month alone at the beach with my baby. I read the play — *Cactus Flower*, a French comedy with Abe Burrows adapting and directing — and agreed to do it. It had been over five years since *Goodbye Charlie*, time to try the stage again. I wanted to sign for a year, Merrick wanted two. John Frankenheimer told me to keep myself free to do his next film — he had a good part for me in it — so I agreed to two years in the play, in return for which Merrick agreed to give me time out for the movie. I was still a believer.

On July 14th, early in the afternoon while I was heading home along the Pacific Coast Highway, sun blazing, the radio blaring, an announcement suddenly came over the air — Adlai Stevenson had dropped dead on a London street. I slammed on the brakes, almost hitting a few cars, took a deep breath, and pulled over to the side. Oh, no, not Adlai. Tears rushed to my eyes as I sat trying to absorb the news. Poor Adlai — never fulfilled, not appreciated enough, so much frustration, so much he wanted to do. Only sixty-five — yet it was quick, thank God for that. He'd been walking in Grosvenor Square with Marietta Tree — poor Marietta, what a terrible thing to witness. He was being flown home for a Washington funeral. A little late, I thought, to pay that kind of homage to him. I wanted to go to Washington. I felt a great emptiness again — not to have him to look forward to, a funny postcard, those eyes, that wit. That friendship. Too many losses — too many irreplaceables. No one I ever loved, it seemed, had had his full share of life.

I called Art Buchwald in Washington to ask him for details. Did he know where Arthur Schlesinger was? I received a wire from Bill Blair, I think, asking me to come. Arthur called, inviting me to stay the night at his house. Jason understood the state I was in. When I got to Arthur's house in Washington late at night, I found a note from him directing me to a room. Marietta and Jane Gunther were also there. Funny — three women who loved Adlai, who each had her own special relationship

745

with him, all there. He had an uncanny knack for keeping all of us, and more, dangling — happy for anything he threw our way. None of us had ever discussed our places in his life. Next morning we all hugged each other. We shared grief, the same grief. We sat around the table having coffee, talking of isolated experiences we'd had with Adlai — quoting conversations — each trying to reinforce her own importance. I thought to myself, 'I know things they don't know — I've been places with him they haven't been, shared times they haven't. I was more special than they know.' And they were clearly thinking those same thoughts. Women are a joke! (To say nothing of men!)

All I knew as I sat in the Capitol with the guard of honor surrounding his casket — as I looked at Buffie, who had lost the most treasured person in her life; as I looked at young Adlai, at Borden, at John Fell, at President and Mrs Johnson, Vice President and Mrs Humphrey, the Senate and the House — was that I had lost the last of three men who had changed my life. Bogie, Charlie, and Adlai — the three men who had contributed most to my growth. There would be no others like them to love, no others to bring about radical change in what and how I felt, saw, and thought. But each had left me with such richness! I would refer to them — each of them — for the rest of my life.

Jason was in rehearsal when we got back to New York. Steve returned to Milton, having spent his first working summer in the Trancas market; Leslie went back to the Lycée, and Sam to Central Park. Abe Burrows and I started to meet on *Cactus Flower* — casting, wardrobe. The first day of rehearsal came. The company was good. We had a new actor, Joe Campanella, who hadn't played a lead on Broadway before — no comedy as far as I knew. It was Merrick's theory that casting Joe would either work marvelously or not at all; that was the only chance he was taking with the play. A new girl named Brenda Vaccaro played the second part; Burt Brinckerhoff, the second man; Robert Moore in a supporting role. All good actors. I was my usual spastic self, but was relishing it. I felt I had value for the play and was wanted by the producer and director, not as though they were doing me a favor the way I always felt in pictures. The play took over my life as plays always do — learning lines, wardrobe fittings (I'd talked Norman Norell into doing my clothes, his first in theatre — I'd come a long way since Loehmann's). I managed to catch occasional glimpses of Leslie and Sam — it's really impossible to be anything but an actress when in rehearsal, but I wouldn't stop trying. I was used to that torn feeling. Our first out-of-town stop was to be Washington, D.C., then Philadelphia for two weeks. Not too bad and not too far away.

Jason was going to be in Boston with *The Devils* while I was still rehearsing in New York, and he'd open in New York when I was in Philadelphia. My head was into my work and my own life. They would come first now, and we'd see what the future would bring. I was making no plans of any kind, and I'd absolutely decided it was up to him which way our marriage would go — I wouldn't work against him, but I needed tangible evidence that his effort was real. I'd told him this plainly and I meant it for the first time — I wanted us to stay together, but on a different basis. It was up to him now. Ridiculous to give him ultimatums, when logic or reason had no bearing on the case. I only knew I'd tried everything I was capable of trying, and had finally reached a point where emotionally I had had enough, where there were no more threats — or compromises — to be made. A plateau. I at last had that strength — the positive work atmosphere obviously added to it, making me feel part of something again and cared about.

So I left for Washington, knowing the play was bound to succeed. I was nervous, but on opening night everyone's nervous. Ours went well, except that I knew there was a lack in my big scene with Joe. But the audience laughed a lot, and the curtain came down to enthusiastic applause. I was sitting in my dressing room about to remove my make-up when David Merrick walked in and said, 'You were great, but I'm going to replace Campanella.' David didn't talk to Joe. I felt sorry for him — one performance was no test, yet I suspected David was right. Joe had been miscast. It was fascinating to see a producer act so quickly — one of his values, I suppose; that's what made him good. No indecision. His reputation with actors was negative, he didn't like them, was impossible to get along with — yet he and I did get along. There was mutual respect. I liked knowing where I stood with someone; he liked pros. No one in the theatre could believe I liked him. 'Just you wait,' they said.

A couple of nights after the opening I was leaving my hotel for the theatre, stopped in the dining room to see if Abe was there, and found him and David sitting there with Barry Nelson, a good actor, expert in comedy, who'd come down to see the show. He liked it, and said he would take over from Joe. He expected billing with me over the title and I readily agreed.

I'd been solo before, but I didn't care. Merrick would not take my photograph off the *Playbill* cover, though, to make it the two of us; he had definite ideas about everything.

In the theatre when an actor is replaced, the whole company becomes paranoid. Who's next? Everyone was on his toes — best behavior. But we were enjoying the rehearsals because Barry had a true comic sense — what he did affected what we did, and it was all for the better. But grueling. Out-of-town tryouts are designed to kill actors — rehearsal all day, play at night, not enough sleep, brain working overtime.

One night after the show Abe took me to supper. 'I don't know how to say this — it's kind of awkward — but a man called William Perske called. He said he was your father.' I must have paled. The bad penny, and always at the wrong time — though I knew there'd never be a right time. 'What did he want? Why did he call you?' I couldn't figure that one out. 'That's what I didn't understand. He wanted twelve seats to the show. I'll see that he gets them if that's what you want, but I thought it was a strange call and I didn't want to do anything without checking with you.' 'I appreciate that, Abe. I tell you, I haven't seen him since I was eight years old! He had a hell of a nerve calling you — and twelve seats is ridiculous!' I could just hear him laying it on Abe. How dare he! I was furious and embarrassed — bad enough he had given interviews those many years ago, but now to involve people I was working with! 'You don't have to do a damn thing — I don't care if he comes or not — it's up to him.' And I resented the fact that, deep down, he felt he deserved something. Just because he was my father — an accident. He'd contributed nothing to my life except anxiety. Why did I feel obligated in some way?

One night I thought I saw the outline of a man in the audience who might be him, but I never knew for sure. I'd never be ready for that meeting, never know what to say, even what to feel. You can live your life — be responsible, bring up children — and still be totally unprepared to face a stranger who happens to be your father.

Jason had called several times to see how the play was going, how I was. He was not overjoyed with his own experience. He loved working with Annie Bancroft, but wasn't very confident about the future of the play. He said he'd try to get to Philadelphia. But I didn't want him in Philadelphia — I wanted to concentrate on my show.

We opened to good notices in Philly, and went on rehearsing days and playing nights — Barry was four weeks behind us in working on his part. Jason called to say he'd have a free day while they made the move from Boston, and announced that he was coming. I told him I'd rather he didn't, but, being contrary, he more or less told me to go to hell, that he'd come down anyway. Typical — when I wanted him, no chance; when I didn't, I couldn't keep him away. But still I didn't expect him to show up, knowing he'd be unwelcome.

On the Saturday night after the show I got back to my room and there was Jason. He'd come down on the train — was solicitous, bending over backward. I was not very responsive, maybe not very nice. I still cared about him, but I had started to care about myself again too. That made a tremendous difference.

Opening night at the Royale Theatre, where I had once excelled at ushering. December 8, 1965. Leslie was there with Mother and Lee (Steve was at Milton, Sam was too young). Once I got going, I had a good time. I felt good about this one, and so did the audience, but there were still the reviews to come. I welcomed all my friends backstage after the show. Abe was thrilled, and Merrick said, 'You're a clutch player — when it counts, like tonight, you're better than ever. The sign of a star!' I felt terrific. Mother sat onstage, trembling. She loved the play, loved me in it, was clearly prejudiced. Merrick hosted a small table at Sardi's, just for Abe and Carin Burrows, Barry, the French authors of the play, and me. Jason came to pick me up after the show, feeling out of place. When I entered Sardi's, there was the traditional greeting of applause and cheers — it has no bearing on the success of the play or its worth, but it's exciting for the actors. Sardi's always gets the morning papers first, hot off the presses. I spent most of my evening waiting — so much depended on this. Vincent Sardi came toward us with the papers — we all rushed to open them, then the rush to look for your name, to find the adjectives. Why we have to be told what we are by someone else, I'll never know, but we do. The show was a hit. Kerr was ecstatic: I was dazzling, I was a hit. Taubman of the *Times* found it hilarious — me hilarious.

I was one happy lady — walking on air. Everyone hugged everyone else — the closed corporation of a play. Jason felt left out. He was no part of our play, and *The Devils* hadn't been well received and wasn't going well. This was my night and I was enjoying it to the hilt — you might even say lapping it up. It was my first unequivocal hit. The next day there was a line at the box office, and the mail orders were heavy — people were planning months in advance. In a hit, once that curtain goes up, the waves of love that come across are loud and clear. In America, audiences are guided by the critics; if they're told to enjoy a play, they do — if they're told it's funny, they have smiles on their faces when they walk into the theatre.

In those first months every night was a party. Jason went to California to make a movie (*The Devils* had closed in January), and I was free to thrive on my success. I loved the play, really felt good onstage. I was fascinated by how much at home I felt. Theatre seemed a better medicine for me than films. I loved the continuity, the building of a performance from first act to last. I loved it because it was live, and because once that curtain went up, it was mine. An incredible feeling. When the audience is with you, you can feel it, you can pull it along even more. *Cactus Flower* was a very wearing show for me, playing it was like keeping a balloon in the air for nearly three hours. There's nothing tougher than comedy, and this was frothy and light, worked with an enormous amount of energy. I could never let up, not a moment to relax.

And I had many quick changes. Eloise White, my dresser, was working really hard — the changes in *Cactus Flower* were more like a musical than a straight play. Part of my deal was that Merrick would pay my dresser. Standard salary. I would add a bonus. Now I'd have to ask him for a raise for her. It was David's birthday and Abe had invited me to celebrate it with them after the show. David came into my room — a perfect opportunity, I thought, so I broached the subject. He exploded. The David Merrick I'd been warned about but had never been exposed to suddenly appeared. 'You're just like all the other damn actors. Never satisfied! When you make an agreement, stick to it. I thought you were different, but you're not, you're just like all the others.' And he stamped out of the room. For Christ's sake, the man is a maniac! That took care of that night's supper. He was in such a fury that he never came backstage again. I gave Eloise the raise myself, and David and I did not speak for the remainder of the run. Everyone who knew him said, 'He'll always be like that — we knew it would happen — we told you. He hates actors.' I could never understand his outburst. He was making a fortune on the play.

As happens easily with comedies, after a while they get out of hand. An actor getting laughs is apt to string out the scene to make the laughs last longer. It never works for long, it distorts the play, louses up the timing. Brenda was starting to do it, so was Barry. Now, I am a very disciplined performer — I work my ass off, and I believe in keeping a play, particularly a comedy, moving. I pride myself that my timing is on the nose. And I was tired and overwrought, all the tensions of the last five years adding up to my fraught state. On top of the rest, John Frankenheimer started to shoot his movie without a word to me. I could have killed him. I was committed to *Cactus Flower* for two years thanks to his promise and my stupidity. I said nothing to John about it for years, but I was upset, and wouldn't forget it. It wasn't malice on his part, just carelessness. Anyone in our business should know that one doesn't speak lightly to actors about work. Our futures are too precarious.

My holiday week was approaching — and about time. Jason had rented a beach house, so I went to California to collapse. I slept a lot, started to relax. The week's highlight was a big party Rock Hudson gave in his new house, which he'd bought from Sam and Mildred Jaffe, who'd moved to England. It was a house full of old memories and new people. Everyone was friendly, but I didn't feel part of the town at all. I enjoyed California living, especially at the beach, but it was not to be permanent again — of that I was certain.

The Bogart boom had been in full swing that year. All the books had come out, about six all told, including Joe Hyams'. I had written what I thought was a hell of an introduction to it, but I found the book disappointing. No one had done justice to the man yet. I agreed with Budd Schulberg, who thought John O'Hara should write the book. Or Nunnally. But it never happened — people were too caught up in their own lives, understandably. I'd been asked to write one myself, which I steadily refused to do, but Bogie's presence permeated my life once more. It took me twenty years to realize that I'll never get away from it — nor should — and don't wish to.

My second year of *Cactus Flower* was tough. I was physically tired and needed a real vacation, but I wasn't going to get it, so press on, old girl. Besides, everyone I ever knew in the theatre and films was coming to see it, which was fun. Great to be good in a show that's a hit. No apologies to make.

The main lesson learned during the run was that the stage was very much home to me. I loved it. To say nothing of the fact that I was offered the best in the theatre, as opposed to the least in the flicks. I was referred to in the press as the toast of the town, but it never went to my head. I remembered too well the story Bogie had told me about Helen Menken in *Seventh Heaven* being that year's toast of the town — until Jeanne Eagels came along a short while later in *Rain* to take the title. That's the business. No matter how high the peaks scaled, there's no guarantee it will last. But those two years belonged to me. No one could take away the kick I got when I happened to see the laughing face of Robert Kennedy looking up at me from the third row center, or was told by Jack Benny how perfect my timing was. Even John Huston seemed to show genuine enjoyment of my work.

Jason made several trips to California for films, and tried hard when home to be ultra-loving — a real husband-father. Sam was in first grade at Collegiate school, which was close to home. Leslie was still struggling along at the Lycée, and Steve was only home for holidays. Sarah, Jady, and David made fairly regular appearances, and we'd try to do as much together as we could. When Jason was good he was very, very good. He functioned better in films or at least in California than he did in the New York theatre. He drank in California, but the routine was not the same. There was something about theatre life — let's have a drink after the show, stop by for a drink, etc., and the endless bars and favorite hangouts. Too many established patterns. I couldn't and wouldn't be a policeman any longer. I did tell Jason that if he had to drink, I didn't want him doing it at home. I had put most of our liquor out of sight — I didn't care if I never had a drink. I was immovable about his never being drunk within our home again. I was not going to have Sam or Leslie see him like that.

Spence and Katie had started *Guess Who's Coming to Dinner*. It was Spence's first film in five years. He had not been well, he'd had ulcers, I believe — was always swallowing some terrible chalky substance. He was hospitalized in '66. Katie used to bring him homemade soup and sit with him until he slept, slipping in and out the side door of the hospital. No one knew about it except a few intimates. She never veered off course. I think the only reason Spence agreed to be in the film was that Stanley Kramer was devoted to him and would do everything to make it less taxing. Katie never took her eye off Spence — at his elbow unobtrusively if he should need anything. No danger of his wanting for a thing with her around. He had been apprehensive — he was so professional, he couldn't bear falling short of the mark in work. Learn the lines and hit your marks — the hell with motivation. They didn't understand how I could stay in a play so long. 'Like being in jail.'

Steve was to graduate from Milton in June of '67 on a Saturday — a matinee day. I asked my agent, Peter Witt, well in advance to broach the subject to David Merrick. Under no circumstances would I miss Steve's graduation. Let him sue! Peter told David — David said no — I cursed, fumed, said I'd go anyway. As the time grew closer, I got tenser and tenser, telling Peter to prepare David for my not appearing Saturday. Why, oh, why did it all have to be so damned unpleasant? Why couldn't producers be human beings? My son's graduation, for God's sake — once in a lifetime. I'd played *Cactus Flower* for a year and a half, never missing a performance — why couldn't this be settled reasonably in an adult fashion? I couldn't understand it then — I can't now. Of all places, in the theatre there should be human understanding, compassion, just ordinary sanity about life. Christ, we're not machines.

Finally Peter told me I would have to go to David's office to plead my case. David had to be in his God position, I in my servile one. Okay — anything for Steve. I pulled myself together and on the appointed day went to David's office. I wasn't going to grovel. I told him the graduation was something I could not miss and I had hoped he would be understanding and not make a Dreyfus case out of it. I felt the way I had as a kid, raising my hand in class to ask if I could leave the room. It was ridiculous. Anyway, he played innocent — 'Why didn't you come to me in the first place?' He would let me know. And later that day he called to tell me he'd provide a car to take me to and from the airport to ensure my returning in time for the night show. Total grace.

Earlier that week Spence and Katie had called to say they'd finished the film. Spence had delivered a ten-minute monologue non-stop without missing a line. He was relieved — proud of himself. Said Stanley had been terrific — thank God he hadn't dropped dead before he was finished, with Stanley uninsured! We laughed.

On the morning of June 10, Jason, Leslie, Sam, and I boarded a plane for Boston for Steve's big day. I couldn't believe the years had passed so quickly — that Steve had reached young manhood. He had grown up well, a good, really decent boy. He'd been affected by the burdens of his lost father and the Bogart name, but he was coming out of it all right. He'd enjoyed Milton, and there was less friction between us. My head was full of images of his birth — childhood — Bogie. So much of our lives unfulfilled. It was a hard day in that respect, yet I felt so good about him.

We'd been airborne some twenty minutes when Jason, sitting behind me, tapped me on the shoulder. 'A man behind me heard it on the radio — Spencer is dead.' But I'd just talked to him — he was fine! Oh my God — how is Katie? Of all places to hear it — no telephone, no details. But details weren't needed. The fact was enough. I was distraught. Spence so pleased he hadn't dropped dead during the film must have known something was coming. I was so worried about Katie. How do you come to terms with the end of thirty years of your life? The biggest and best part? It was hard to think of anything else. And yet a few hours later I managed to swell with pride at the sight of Steve taking his diploma. One life begins, one ends. So much life, excitement, hope for the future at a prep-school graduation. While, three thousand miles away, my treasured Katie had lost her best friend.

The run wore on and me with it. Barry left the show for a television series, Kevin McCarthy came in to replace him for a while, then Lloyd Bridges. And Brenda left. So

762

there was much rehearsing in addition to performing. On November 18 I played my last performance of *Cactus Flower*. The cast gave me cards and a lovely silver mirror for my bag. Jason lovingly sent flowers, gifts; he was very proud of me, full of tender, loving care. Now, for months I'd been thinking of nothing but getting out of the play. After the first eight months, the audience begins to change and acting and the energy required to keep the comic balloon in the air becomes more work than play. Two years in sheer drudgery — to keep a part fresh for that length of time gives ulcers and leads to exhaustion. Yet I had created that part and I wasn't crazy about anyone else claiming it as hers. And it had given me a place in the theatre — at least the beginning of one. But I couldn't go on playing it for the rest of my life. I left, hoping I'd get another part, but far from certain. In any case, the children would be happy to have me home for Christmas. Actors always work on holidays. But the only night I would rather be onstage than anywhere else is New Year's Eve. I hate that night — the old ringing in the new. Everyone consciously loves everyone else at the stroke of twelve o'clock, and an hour later antagonisms flourish once again.

Jason was going to Italy for a movie early in the spring of '68. I was definitely ready for that trip. He left about a month before

I did. Mother had a birthday in March and for the first and only time in her life she said she would like me to have a dinner party for her. She was impossible to buy things for, never wanted me to spend money. I was happy to give her something she wanted — a dinner would be fun. I had the whole family and did the whole thing — funny toasts, birthday cake, candles (not the correct number), presents. She laughed a lot. It was the only time I gave a party for her — odd, now that I think of it. She and Lee were married in my house, but I'd never given her a party. I'm so grateful I did that year.

Robert Kennedy was our Senator. I had known Jean, Eunice, and Pat for years and liked them more and more, and I had worked for Bobby when he ran for Senator. I found him really extraordinary — I had a gut reaction to him and I knew I was right. He had shown such capacity for change — such a great heart, I couldn't forget his reaction as he arrived in Atlanta after Dr King's assassination, nervously turning a rolled-up piece of paper in his hand, saying, 'I know what it is to lose a loved one in this way' — so moving. Eugene McCarthy had made a mark with the young in the early primaries, and Bobby couldn't decide about running for President. I was fiercely for him — we all, those who were for him, wanted him to make his statement. I fought anyone who disagreed with me, and when I got involved politically and emotionally I could not tolerate anyone who disagreed. Funny — I cared greatly about John Kennedy's election, and worked for him, but I cared more about Bobby. He touched me more. I felt so completely that he was the man we needed — the one who would make all the difference. Some who'd known him in Joseph McCarthy days and when Jack was President didn't trust him. But I did — he had changed, had had the courage to change and the capacity. I did what I could, what I was asked to do, for Bobby before leaving for Europe. There was to be a rally at Madison Square Garden on June 17 and I'd be back for that.

My trip to Europe was all right at the start — toward the end of it Jason and I were not getting along at all. I couldn't get away from him soon enough. He'd return to New York while I was still in Paris shooting a fashion special with Milton Greene and Joe Eula. I hadn't worked since *Cactus Flower* and the thought of Paris for five or six weeks was anything but painful. Preliminary preparations were made, we shot a few scenes, and then the student uprising took over. No way to continue working. Everyone was walking around with transistor radios glued to their ears for the latest developments. I was staying at the Lancaster Hotel, which was emptying rapidly of tourists. I managed to get one call through to the United States to tell the children and Jason I was safe. They couldn't get through to me at all. Mail was not going out or coming in. The hotel advised me to leave, the banks were about to close — it was not the moment to be in Paris. Sargent Shriver was our Ambassador at the time, thank goodness. He finally managed to find a station wagon that would drive Milton and me to Brussels, where we would board a plane. I headed for New York on June 5 — plenty of time to prepare for the rally for Bobby. I was able to call Mother and give her my flight number. She never failed to meet me at the airport, never tired of that first sight of her pride and joy. She was the one person in the world who missed me beyond all others. That night I was detained by customs, so I sent word to her to go home and I'd meet her there. Mother and Lee were waiting when I got home late, Leslie and Sam asleep. I was exhausted on a five-hour time change.

The same change opened my eyes at about six the following morning. I tiptoed into Sam's room to see if he was awake so I could hug him. He was sitting up with his radio on his lap, his face lighting up at the sight of his mama. He said, 'Mommy, Kennedy's been shot.' I couldn't imagine what had made him think about John Kennedy that particular morning. I said, 'I know, darling, but that was a long time ago.' 'No, Mommy,' he insisted, 'Senator Kennedy's been shot.' I turned his radio up, totally disbelieving — heard something about Bobby's shooting — ran wildly through the house, waking Leslie, Nanny — turning on the television in my room, where we all gathered. Then the whole hideous story unfolded.

We sat huddled around that set the entire day. Jason called from Spain, unbelieving, saying we had to get out of the United States, get the children into sanity. People everywhere who had been sure what Americans stood for were questioning everything now. As I looked at Sam, aged six — my beautiful, blue-eyed, yellow-haired boy — I realized that he had spent his entire life in awareness of assassination: of John Kennedy, then Martin Luther King, now Bobby; that there had been days of mourning, of funeral corteges on television, of wives left husbandless and children fatherless. Even at six he must have wondered if that was the way life was in our United States. If I as an adult felt insecure, anxious, nervous about the future, how must he have felt? Children are so instinctive, and Sam was hypersensitive to anything emotional. How could I tell him what a great country ours was? How lucky he was to be an American? How could any American feel lucky or proud during those years?

Dick Cavett called to ask if I would participate in his show that night. There would be four or five people talking about Bobby. I said, 'Now? It's so soon.' But he was right. Talk now, try to figure it out, say how you feel while the wound is open, the pain strongest. I did it — vented my anger, and my terrible sense of personal loss. The funeral was to be at St Patrick's Cathedral. I received a telegram asking me to go, and then continue on the train to Washington. Art and Anne Buchwald and I arranged to go to St Patrick's together. I would spend the night with them in Washington.

It seemed strange that everyone in that crowded cathedral had an emotional identification with Bobby. It wasn't a case of huddling together. It was standing shoulder to shoulder — completely open, completely naked emotionally. Ted Kennedy's eulogy was the most moving, most devastating, I had ever heard. When his voice broke, it became apparent that he might have lost more than anyone, that his burden was the greatest and he would be the most alone. And then in the silence as we all stood came the clear, pure sound of Andy Williams singing 'The Battle Hymn of the Republic.' Men and women sobbed. And then the final sight of Ethel and her children and the whole Kennedy family walking up the aisle. The pallbearers who had gone through Jack's experience, now carrying Bobby. I couldn't believe the Kennedy family's bravery and courage, and couldn't help marveling at their religious belief. And I thought of Rose Kennedy, who if she had borne only four children would now have none.

The train ride to Washington was what I imagine Lincoln's must have been like. All along the way, there were people watching, holding signs, paying tribute to the young man who had represented hope.

Ethel walked through the train, stopping to say a few words to everyone, to thank us for coming. What a person — what capacity — to be aware of anything but her own grief. The immediate family rode in the last car with Bobby most of the time. At one point Eunice and Jean came out. I talked to them, not about Bobby, just talked to these two stricken women who were my friends. Eunice was tense, but could talk — I was blinded with admiration. As Eunice was closest to Jack, Pat was to Bobby and Jean to Teddy. I was proud to know them, proud to have shared a moment of their brother's life. I remember Arthur Schlesinger saying to me, 'We have lost the only three people in public life we cared about.' And I knew he was right, just as I knew that I would never feel the same emotion again for anyone in politics.

In Washington the casket and the family were greeted by an honor guard as we rushed to Arlington for the candlelight burial. I saw that box being lifted into the hearse, and I could not believe that that young, virile body was inside.

The procession at Arlington was extraordinary. The world seemed to be there. We each held a lighted candle, and the sight of the flames winding down and around the pathways was moving beyond description. Art and Annie and I were able to stand near the family. All were numb, still unbelieving. As the ceremony came to a close, I noticed Ted Kennedy turn from where he had been standing and stop at John Kennedy's grave. From one brother's grave to another. That said more than a thousand words. Ted's life was there on that knoll in Arlington. And now even more burdens would be his.

At Hickory Hill, fifty or more friends gathered for a drink and a snack. The long line of children, each looking after the other down to the smallest — the two youngest happily unaware. The strength and courage of Ethel were remarkable — I stood in awe of them — and envied her faith. Standing on that lawn on that warm June evening, I reviewed the last time I had been in her house, when Bobby had taken me on a tour from pool house to playroom, through all the kids' bedrooms. On seeing the infant Douglas, I said, 'What a time he's been born to,' and Bobby said ironically, 'What a world!' Everyone had personal thoughts and memories; we all exchanged stories, we all felt lost. Our hero had been taken away from us. A President still had to be elected, but who could have a taste for it now?

After Bobby I felt detached from life, purposeless. I didn't seem to have anywhere to go, everything seemed pointless. Nothing was happening in my career — typical after a hit show. The film rights to *Cactus Flower* had been bought for Mike Frankovich to produce, with Walter Matthau starring, Gene Saks directing. Freddie Fields, my movie agent, was convinced I could get my Broadway part, though in Hollywood it doesn't necessarily or even usually follow that the creator of a role onstage carries it onto the screen. Another example of Hollywood's consummate creative thinking. How could I be right for it if I had created it? Asses!

I had to spend much of the summer in Paris for the fashion special, which finally would be filmed. Jason would return to the U.S. and go to Malibu, where we would meet in August. Steve was staying in Philadelphia. He'd done badly in his first year at the University of Pennsylvania, though not so badly as to have dropped out. I had been so preoccupied with my marriage, with travel, with being out of work, with Leslie and Sam, that I hadn't realized Steve was in trouble. Also, he and I had not been getting along well. I put it down to his wanting independence, plus the normal resentment a son feels for his mother until he finds his own female with whom to identify. It was a phase that would pass. I'd spoken to him on the phone and then hadn't heard from him for a while, so I wasn't sure where he was. It never occurred to me he was in any trouble. I thought he was just making his independent statement. My blessed mother, while I was in Europe, made it her business to find him — she was so much smarter than I. She called him, persuaded him to meet her on a streetcorner in Philadelphia, and convinced him to let me know where he was, to never lose touch. She reported all this to me, at the same time chastising me: 'How could you let any time go by, not knowing where he was living? He has to know that you care what happens to him!' She was right, of course. With her old-fashioned thinking about relationships of all kinds, she was amazingly adaptable and sensitive to the problems of the Sixties. She came through when it mattered most to Steve and to me. She always came through.

The television special on fashion in Paris was great fun. Leslie appeared in some of the scenes. She had grown into a beautiful sixteen-year-old girl — could have been a model in a minute if she'd been so inclined. Her Lycée years served her well in Paris. She was incredibly good with Sam, he was and is mad about her, and she and I were on the threshold of a good relationship. Sam spent all his time at the Shrivers', the Jardin d'Acclimatation in the Bois — amusement park — cum zoo — cum everything. I thrived in the Paris atmosphere, made new friends with St Laurent, Marc Bohan, Ungaro, and Cardin. My French improved and I was in the middle of all those collections! I had a new life during those eight weeks and made the most of it. I needed it badly — it kept the horror of the assassination far away, and made it unnecessary to face the problems of my personal life immediately.

The children and I arrived in California in mid-August, ready for a month of beach time. Jason was there. We had been growing further apart — certainly the drinking had been a large part of it, but beyond that it seemed we had less and less to share, with the great exception of Sam, who unequivocally adored his father and vice versa.

Freddie Fields had arranged a meeting between me and Mike Frankovich at Mike's office at the Columbia studio; Freddie was certain I would be cast in *Cactus Flower*. I wasn't certain at all. During our meeting Mike told me he wanted me, but that there seemed to be some question in the minds of Saks and Matthau. I couldn't conceive of that being true — Walter being a product of the stage, Gene too. We were all friends, though that had no bearing on anything. I felt Gene would go along with the majority wish, and Walter would get what he wanted. A few nights later, at dinner at Kirk and Ann Douglas's, Freddie stood up and announced to all that I'd been cast in the film. Everyone applauded, pleased for me. I asked Freddie if he was sure. Sure he was sure. I was happy — maybe this would be the turning point for me, back in a good film after so long. I'd resented having to play the Hollywood game, selling myself for a part that 'belonged' to me, or at least that I had created. It was humiliating, but I did it — and then it wasn't set at all. Ingrid Bergman had the part. I couldn't believe it — couldn't believe that I wasn't to play my own creation, couldn't believe Freddie had made that announcement. I felt ridiculous, unimportant, so unappreciated in that town, by everyone — producers and agents alike. In California my New York success meant less than nothing — they didn't think beyond the *Hollywood Reporter* and who was the latest hit. If you had ability, you could hang in for a few years; if not, tough luck, there'd be someone else coming along. It was up to me to force myself, with no help from the outside, to believe in me — unreservedly. To keep my standards high — and my sense of humor flashing.

Through all of this my marriage was falling apart. I was upset, angry, disgusted — but I knew what I wanted out of life by then, so I was not destroyed. There was no point in threats anymore. As Jason and I had discussed often in the past, one day he would take off and that would end it. He did — he disappeared for two days. Life is curious. I was looking for an envelope or a stamp one day while he was gone, went into a desk drawer, and there was a letter from his accountant, referring to money he had loaned a girl. I lifted that piece of paper and there, staring up at me, was a romantic letter to him from this very same girl. So the one thing I had never considered seriously had taken place. But that was it, and I was sure I could handle it with aplomb on his return. I knew the marriage was over — it had been over for quite some time — and this new fact was something I had no intention of living with. There is nothing deader than a terminal marriage. No reason to keep it going.

When he returned on a bright sunny morning, I said nothing. He took a shower and when he emerged I asked him how this girl was, having read her name in the letter. He was stunned — the last thing he expected. I said, 'There is really no point, Jason, in going on. It's over, so let's end it. Now, with dignity and like grown-ups.' I was actually very matter-of-fact, decisive, no histrionics. Jason recognized the finality and accepted it. He said he was sorry, what should we do? As he was returning to New York in three days to rehearse Joseph Heller's play, *We Bombed in New Haven*, it should not be too difficult. I insisted on one thing — that he must be the one to tell the children he was leaving and not coming back. Not Sam yet, Sam wasn't yet seven. I wanted Jason to go back to New York and clear his things out of the apartment so that trauma wouldn't have to be dealt with once we were home. I wanted it done cleanly and clearly — the best way for Sam. We would stay on in California for another two weeks, so it should be easy. But endings are never easy.

Those three days were mournful. We got through the days all right — the ocean helped — but the nights were a mess. Jason was very low. He told Leslie one afternoon — embarrassed, very sweet. Leslie wasn't deeply upset — she had always liked Jason, but had never depended on him. He and I would sit in the living room after dinner just looking at each other. He'd take my hand or I'd take his. I felt the need to bolster him somehow, to give him some hope for his future. We were both sad — an investment of eight years is a large one. I told him not to meet Sam and me at the airport, that it would be easier for Sam to walk into the apartment with no trace of Jason there. Then I could tell him, and after that Jason could. We would both make it clear to Sam that it was no one's fault and had absolutely nothing to do with our love for him. It would be hard — and it proved to be — but it had to be done. I wasn't sure of too much in my life at that point, but I was sure of that.

The three endless days went by and

Jason left. He hadn't had a drink. I enjoyed him like that — I mean I really liked him. But I couldn't live with him anymore. I reviewed much of our life together. It was clear that I had always wanted it more than he had; that I had taken on something I didn't understand; that many of the times had been good, many rotten; that I was sadder for Sam more than for me; and that if I'd listened to Katie, I would have had five more years in the sun. I was relieved when Jason went. I could do as I pleased, go where I pleased, no excuses to make.

I called home before leaving the Coast to make certain that Jason had moved out. He had not — couldn't find a place. I said he had to be out when we arrived, I couldn't go through that with Sam. Again I was fierce about it. Once the step had been taken, it had to be followed through. I should have been prepared for the fact that Jason wouldn't be prepared for the final step.

Sam was used to not being with Jason on a regular basis, but the fact of his not living at home even part-time would be a high hurdle. I told him on the trip back that Daddy would probably not be at home. That Daddy loved him very much, but sometimes grown-ups have to stop living together. That Daddy and I had decided to try living in different apartments.

That he would still see his father, that he could talk to him whenever he wanted to — like Jady, David, and Sarah. I wanted so much for Sam never to have a sad or insecure day. Jason and I agreed on that — that he was the only one of our children who was not screwed up due to childhood traumas, and we wanted to keep him that way. He was an open, loving child — it was marvelous to have a child who was not afraid to show love or talk about it.

Sam heard what I said, of course, but he didn't accept it.

I turned the key in the lock — opened the front door to what I thought was an empty apartment — only to find Jason walking toward me. I was furious, but couldn't say anything with Sam there. Sam rushed to his daddy, joyous at the sight of him.

The last few weeks of Jason's being at home were most peculiar. Here we had decided to end our marriage, but he still hadn't moved out, so we were sharing the same bedroom. All very civilized. I went out on my own — not with men, but with friends. He came home every night. The contradictory quality of our life was spellbinding. When I'd wanted him home, he wasn't; now that I was going out, not caring what he did, he was there. I wasn't thrilled with having to insist, but I was not willing to have this limbo go on and on. Jason did try to explain to Sam, much as I had, why the decision had been made. He would be in a play on Broadway, so within easy reach.

I had to prepare Sam's school for possible erratic behavior, and I talked to Sam's pediatrician (a wise, understanding man) about it. He felt it would be a good thing for Sam, if he had difficulty, to talk to a doctor. 'Better now than when he's seventeen.'

Mother's reaction to the separation was full of understanding. She was fond of Jason, in spite of her awareness of my unhappiness. One day she would say, 'It's all for the best.' The next, 'Sam will miss him,' and 'I'd think twice if I were you, Betty, he's very attractive, you know, there aren't many as attractive as he is.' Like her, I knew the pluses and the minuses. But so many times I'd been left alone to make our decisions, I might as well be single. Was it pattern or destiny having to bring up three children alone? And the constant pull between work and home — it is simple for some, but not for this kid!

Sam was happy at Collegiate, but he began to show signs of rebellious behavior. I tried talking him into going to the doctor, just to talk about anything he chose. He was remarkable for his seven years — very decisive. He couldn't be forced to do anything. Threats didn't work, deprivation of pleasure didn't work. He was his own person, and I admired him for it. He finally consented to go to the doctor. Fascinating to see a child psychiatrist at work, as I was allowed to do on the first visit. The child was turned loose in a room full of toys, and as he played, the doctor would casually ask questions that were not casual.

At our first Christmas without Jason, I had arranged with him to come up during the day to see Sam. Jason made the appearance, but emptyhanded. Sam had a gift for his father, so did Leslie, but Father had nothing. I'll never forget how one Sunday Jason joined Sam and me at a Chinese restaurant and Sam said, 'Why, Daddy? Why didn't you bring a present on Christmas Day?' Jason gave some feeble answer, but Sam wouldn't let him off the hook. He really cornered him. He couldn't understand it, and he wanted an answer. I'd never seen a child so openly put a parent on the spot, and I thought it terrific that he could do it, that he so clearly had the upper hand, and in a way was more mature than his father.

Mother and Lee became regular Sunday visitors and often came to dinner during the week. Sam would unfailingly say, 'Don't go home, Granny — why can't you stay? Are you staying for dinner?' He really made her feel wanted — 'He has heart,' she would say. He did and does — had and has always been an open person — he hadn't learned to protect himself at an early age as his brother and sister had had to do.

I started the New Year looking for a divorce lawyer. It was unknown territory to me — I had never thought I would be in that position. I was planning to make no unreasonable demands on Jason, I wanted it handled simply and undramatically. My friend, Joan Axelrod, found me a lawyer, and Jason had his, but he was doing nothing about it. Finally I got up the nerve to call him about it — not easy, but he was very nice on the phone, sensible, agreeable. If we'd been able to communicate that well from the beginning, we would have stayed together forever. After this conversation I was filled with doubt — almost considered not going through with it — though in my deepest heart I was certain it would be the best solution for us all. With my tendency to romanticize, I even thought that the divorce might bring us closer together. It was harder to let go, even being the instigator of the split, than I had thought it would be. And painful. There's no way to forget the good things — the promise of a life shared. And no way not to feel some sense of your own failure.

At least I felt that it was honorably done — that Jason would have a chance at a free life for the first time. The lesson of Bogie I had finally put into practice: in the face of inevitable, terrible happenings, how much better to hold on to one's character and hurt others as little as possible. The straight road. My only prayer was that, somehow, Sam could benefit. If we remained honest with him, he might be better able to cope with his life in the long haul.

The year would be a tough one. Jason was going to Rome after some work in Nevada. He hadn't spoken to Sam for months, and I was running out of excuses, but kept assuring Sam that when his father returned to New York he would surely see him. Sam always accepted the fact that separations from his father due to work were enforced rather than deliberate. Then I learned, after the fact, that Jason had been in New York without calling Sam. I was livid — called my lawyer, who in turn called Jason's, who'd also been unaware of Jason's visit. But Jason had told his accountant to go ahead with the divorce settlement. Sam had been fairly calm, but the impact had not yet fully reached him. I desperately hoped for Sam's sake that his father would break his pattern and not rush into another marriage — a pipe dream on my part, and I knew it, but I was still a great one for hoping. Damn careful I would be before leaping into another relationship. I'd done it once before for the wrong reasons — never again, I vowed. But the amazing thing about life, I've finally discovered, is that you really don't learn from past mistakes. You do logically, reasonably, but emotionally not for a second. Whether through stupidity, or my old habit of romanticizing and dreaming, I kept thinking, 'You never know what's just around the corner. It's been there once — twice — it has to be there again!' I was always ready for a bright, fresh start, and I didn't mean to waste one more minute. Patience was still not my strong suit.

Mother went into the hospital for pulmonary edema — she had been hospitalized for this before. Three weeks after she was released, she went in again. Each time it happened in the middle of the night. She would be so frightened — thank God the doctor was always available, and the hospital only five minutes away. She was advised as an extra precaution to keep a portable oxygen tank in the apartment. Oxygen was security. I spent a lot of time driving back and forth to be with her. Mother, the children, the divorce — a lot to occupy me, but, alas, none of it work.

Then, out of nowhere, I was approached about a musical version of *All About Eve*, to be produced by Joe Kipness and Lawrence Kasha, with a score by Charles Strouse and Lee Adams. The book was being written; nothing else was set.

I'd always been musical — one of my great frustrations had been my inability to sing. If I did this show, I wouldn't be dancing with Fred Astaire, but I *would* be in a musical. *Could* I do it? How do you decide if you can do something you've never tried before? I'd always gambled with my career, but would this be really going out on a limb! The idea was that I would play Margo Channing, the part played to perfection in the movie by Bette Davis. Wouldn't it be funny — funny in the proper context, I would hope — to be playing the same character as my childhood heroine? I heard the score — liked what I heard. I might fall flat on my face with this one, but I might not. I'd be terrified, but that was nothing new. It would mean a lot of work, but that could only be good. I thought and thought and finally decided to take the plunge. What the hell — with everything else in my life shaken up, might as well go all the way. I remember Moss Hart saying you have to shake up

785

your life every seven years — this was less than seven years, but a needed shake-up nonetheless. Once I said yes, I was terrified. Who to direct it? I'd need all the help I could get.

My first move was to start voice lessons. I arranged to work with Keith Davis, the voice coach who had helped me on *Cactus Flower*. And I'd go regularly to a decent gym until a couple of months before rehearsal, when I'd have to start serious body work. From all I could glean from experienced friends, it was stamina which would carry me through in the end. But at least I had a goal — a reason to get up in the morning. I would be totally disciplined, do absolutely everything I had to do. I picked Angela Lansbury's brains about what she had done to prepare for *Mame*. Angela — a damn good actress and a total pro — gave me the full lowdown on what a musical entails: nothing short of slave labor. There'd be no room in my life for anything else. But at that point I *had* nothing else, and no real expectation of finding it. Yet I was enjoying life alone, though very frustrated still at my inability to get a divorce. Jason was inaccessible in Europe and in no hurry, while I wanted it behind me. I needed that legal piece of paper — that public statement. Why was it so bloody important? Training. I'd been brought up on marriage certificates — divorces — proof positive of one's official condition.

I was at a low financial ebb — hadn't worked for a year and a half. If the show went well, I'd earn a lot, but until then I had to watch out. I wasn't used to thinking about money. Through my life with Bogie it had always been there; with Jason, though he never stopped working, most of his earnings went to past wives and growing children. Yet there'd always been enough. He paid his way — plus. People were under the impression I was a rich widow. Wrong! After Bogie's death, newspapers had published part of his will — over a million dollars — a fortune! Yes, but they neglected to mention that the government took over half. Why do you have to pay for dying? I do not understand, and no one will ever be able to explain to me why what you have earned in your lifetime does not belong to you to do with as you see fit. God knows the government gets enough in taxes while you're earning it. Incomprehensible. Anyway, what was left was half mine in trust and a fourth each for Stephen and Leslie. A cushion, but not enough to live on. And twelve years later the cost of living had risen considerably, and responsibilities continued. I wanted to go to Europe for five or six weeks before starting work on the show — my last fling.

The Nivens invited me, with Sam and Leslie, to spend two weeks at their beautiful villa at Cap Ferrat. And Sam Spiegel offered me his flat in London for as long as I wanted. So there'd be no hotel bills — just tourist plane fare, with Sam going for half. I could just manage that — a brief stop in Paris, then train to the Nivs.

Until we left on July 1 it was voice lessons three times a week with Keith and work on the score with Peter Howard, our conductor. I'd been working for a few weeks with Peter when Charles Strouse, the composer, walked in to listen to me. My nerves began to jangle immediately, but I'd have to sing in front of many — better start learning now. Just concentrate on your breathing — the meaning of the song — forget him. But how can you forget the man who wrote it and is now judging you? *Why wasn't I born with a voice?* But I sang, and felt it wasn't too bad — Peter, playing the piano, was giving me approving smiles. I didn't know Strouse well, and he seemed very serious to me. As I finished, he looked at Peter and said, 'She was flat on that note.' What a boost for my morale! I felt like a fool — inadequate — became defensive. 'If you wanted Streisand, you should have got her!' Peter was on my side — said I was doing well. I asked Charles to do me a big favor and not come around — it was too soon for him to listen to me. Months later I reminded him of that episode — he hadn't meant it that way at all, I had misunderstood. He'd known I could do it, he'd just wanted Peter to be aware of my weak spots. We had become friends by then, but at the beginning I was too fragile to accept that kind of criticism. I knew I wasn't a singer — I knew that everyone else knew it too — but by dint of hard work, perseverance, much encouragement, I was sure I could do it. I could act it. Just give me enough time.

Late in the spring Mother made another trip to the hospital — same problem, pulmonary edema. Again it happened late at night, again she asked the doctor, 'Is this it?' She'd had so many scares, poor love. What a way to live. This too was a short stay, but it's strange that I still didn't find her recurring edema ominous. It was just something that happened — that would be taken care of — and then she'd be fine. I accepted it as part of life. I hated hospitals, hated to see her in one, but as she behaved more with annoyance than with fear, I didn't become anxious.

Lee had planned a golfing weekend over Memorial Day. Mother didn't want to go, and Lee wouldn't leave her. She suggested she come stay with me, and I wasn't overly receptive. Not to excuse myself, but I was apprehensive about something happening, with only me to deal with the oxygen. I was plain scared. She was upset at my lack of generosity, and she had reason to be, but I was so emotional about her that I feared for my behavior under duress. It was the one time in my life I truly felt cowardly.

She said, 'Lee hasn't had a moment's peace for thirteen years. He works hard, he needs to get away and relax. How can you be so selfish?' She was right. I fell very short of the mark that afternoon. Of course Lee could go, of course she could come — I would love to have her. As the weekend approached, Lee brought her to my apartment — with her portable oxygen tank, which he showed me how to work. Preventive measures had to be taken. Nothing left to chance.

One of my mother's habits that I remembered most clearly from childhood was her rising at seven, taking a bath, and dressing immediately. She had always been ready to go off to work when she woke me up for breakfast. Now, some twenty-five years later, her routine remained unchanged. Very reassuring, that kind of steadiness. She stayed in my bedroom. My bed was enormous, and I wanted to be there if she rose during the night. And it was really fun having her there — I'd forgotten how much I enjoyed her. The first morning I woke up to find her dressed, with a cup of coffee in her hand, having seen Sam and Leslie off to school. They adored having her there, and she was mad about being with them so much. I was a daughter again, and it felt good; I'd been alone a long time. The second night she woke up in the middle of the night — I opened my eyes to find her sitting on the edge of the bed. I quickly got up, walked around to her side, put my arm around her, asked her if she felt all right. Did she want anything? Should I get the oxygen? No, she just felt a little weak — she'd be okay. She leaned her head against mine and we just sat quietly — mother and daughter — for about fifteen minutes. I stroked her hair, her arm, feeling very protective, full of love — and going over in my mind what to do with the oxygen if the need arose. She had never leaned on me before. We were very close together those three days. I so loved her being with me, I couldn't bear the time to end. The day Lee was to collect her, I wanted her to stay, but she wouldn't dream of it — she belonged with her husband. What a dunce I was — I could have had her many weekends. If I hadn't been so preoccupied with my own life, I might have thought of it. If I'd known how wonderful it was to have her in my house, I might have thought of it . . . If —

Steve came home from Boston University, to which he'd transferred, with the announcement that he was in love. Her name was Dale, and she was from Connecticut. He had to be with her — he wanted to spend the summer in her parents' home — he'd get a job. He was very emotional about her, desperate to be with her. I hadn't met her, but I'd never seen him like this. He wasn't working at school again. In his emotional outpouring came the extraordinary information that he'd been trying drugs in Pennsylvania — grass, acid — but that since meeting Dale he'd been off it all. I'd known nothing about his drug scene and was deeply shocked. Stupidly, it hadn't occurred to me that drugs had been part of his period of no communication at Penn. Naïve was I about this child of the Sixties. It was going on everywhere, why should Steve be unaffected? But there was no damage done, thank God. And if Dale had got him to stop, he must love her a lot. He seemed so young to me — he *was* so young: twenty. Came the awakening that I didn't know him as well as I thought I did. I didn't really know how he'd been spending his days, weeks, and months in college these last two years.

Neither college had been successful for him. He couldn't find his way, he didn't know what to do with his life. At that moment the only thing that mattered was to be with Dale. He lashed out at me with a resentment he'd been harboring for God knows how long. 'You've never been what I thought a mother should be. Never in the kitchen, cooking dinner — always working!' I'd thought he understood about my work. Some mothers stay home, keep house; some work. That is not what makes a mother. He was very immature. Was it all pouring out of him because he felt this emotional need? Did he really mean it, or was he just angry that I was there and Dale wasn't? Did he truly feel I'd been a rotten mother? I was faced with a young man who apparently had never understood what I was about at all — nor I him. He hadn't seen beyond his own needs and desires, but do children ever? I suppose I hadn't either with my mother. It takes a lifetime to understand a parent. I thought, 'Later, when he's not in such an emotional state, we can talk — I can find out more.' I knew his basic instincts were good, and I also knew he'd had a rough go, being his father's son. He never asked questions about Bogie, never wanted to know details. I tried — casually on the surface, knotted up inside — to give him pertinent facts as the opportunity arose. He accepted the facts, but didn't care to delve deeper, and I had the good sense not to push. 'Eventually,' I thought. Now I don't know if there will be an eventually. The one thing Steve has been consistent about is that *African Queen* is his favorite movie, and that he wants Bogie's Oscar. So, though he may have blocked out his father from childhood on, turned his back on his pain, he did really care about some identification.

Mother returned to the hated hospital on June 26, this time with an irregular heartbeat. I saw her every day. She thought she'd be out by July 1, but as that date approached, it was clear she wouldn't be. I had no intention of leaving for Europe before she was home, so I put off our departure to the fifth. Every day they said she'd be out the next — I didn't know what to do. She seemed perky, so I decided to go, but I'd put it off yet again. I drove Sam and Leslie out to the hospital so they could wave to her from the street. Children weren't allowed to visit, but as she had a room facing the front of the building we did the next best thing.

Finally came the date of departure. Mother went home that morning. I finished packing, got the children organized, and went to spend a few hours with her. We sat on her terrace. She wanted to make me tea — couldn't stand being waited on herself — but this time I made it. I wanted her to promise no exertion. I gave her my itinerary — told her I'd find the lovely cotton nightgowns she preferred — promised to write regularly. She said, 'No phone calls — I don't want you spending your money.' I hugged and kissed her goodbye and said I'd be back before she knew it. As I waited for the elevator, her front door opened. I was startled by that unfamiliar gesture. She said she just wanted to see me again — say goodbye again. I walked back, put my arms around her again, asked her if she was okay. Yes, of course, she just wanted to have another look at my silly face. The truth, I realize now, is that she didn't want me to go, but would never ask me to stay. I gave her a smile, a squeeze, and walked into the elevator.

Paris was as beautiful as ever, and after about a week we took the train to Cap Ferrat. The Nivens were waiting for us. It was marvelous to see them — I had missed my two good friends. And their villa was unbelievably beautiful, with a pool filled with sea water, and a garden and gazebo on the edge of the Mediterranean. I subjected David and Hjordis to my vocalizing — played them my tape of the score, sat every day on the pool deck facing the sea while barking my exercises and trying to sing my songs. Poor Mediterranean. Innocent couples riding their pedalos or lazing in the sun, private planes trailing advertising streamers, water-skiers — all were subjected to my sounds. But I was not intimidated. Nothing could stop me! It was a perfect visit — easy, full of laughter and health. And how good to know people you loved were alive and well in their own part of the world.

We went back to Paris for a few days. At Chanel one afternoon I was told Katie Hepburn was there. I let out a yell — ran into her dressing room, where we laughed and hugged each other. She was fitting her clothes for *Coco*, her first musical, which was to open in November. We decided we were both crazy doing musicals, but enjoyed the fact that we were doing them at almost the same time. And I'd be able to be at her opening.

We arrived in London with all friends at the ready. Plans for Sam to see everything in London — the palace, changing of the guard, the Thames, the zoo, Piccadilly Circus, the parks. Leslie's first beau, Tom Logan — son of Josh and Nedda — was in London, so she was in heaven. She was a smart sixteen when they met and they became instantly attached. At once she became noticeably more self-assertive with me. The old identity crisis — daughters trying to find out who they are, divorcing themselves completely from their mothers. It was the beginning of abrasive times between us. She wanted to spend her seventeenth birthday in London with Tom, which would mean staying a good week longer than I'd planned. But I had always loved London — had many friends to catch up with, and there was never enough time. It would be at least a year and a half before I could return.

I wrote more often to Mother than ever before. Long, newsy letters. She always wrote back. I remember one night wanting to phone her. Then I thought she'd spend half the time telling me how ridiculous I was to spend money I didn't have. One of her letters, in response to my decision to stay for Leslie's birthday, had much to say about why I was staying on — I'd been away long enough. Her handwriting sloped off toward the end, and I thought she must have been tired when she wrote it. She was in my thoughts constantly. I shopped for her everywhere, wanted to be in communication with her in some way daily — a letter, a postcard, a gift.

So I was glad to board the plane late in August to be with her again. Upon arrival home, my housekeeper said, 'Your mother's in the hospital.' Oh, not again, I thought. I dialed that ghastly number and reached her before lights out. She had gone in that day, sounded a bit tired, but was happy to hear my voice. The children spoke to her and I told her I'd come in the morning to spend the day with her. Later, Lee brought me up to date. She had gone into the hospital late in July — two and a half weeks after I left — and stayed for more than three weeks. Home just eleven days ago, now in again. He said he had almost called me to come home. 'Why didn't you?' She was adamant, he said; warned him not to dare call me. So he was afraid to — afraid she would be too upset. But I should have known. Not his fault — if I had called that night in London, I would have found out. Lee had planned to go upstate for golf on the Labor Day weekend, but he would cancel. I told him not to, that I would be with her every day. I was sure he needed to get away.

The next morning I gathered all the goodies I had bought her in Europe and headed for Brooklyn and the hospital. She was sitting up in bed waiting for me. Thin. I hugged and kissed her, showed her all her new lovelies, and helped her into a Paris nightie. She was scheduled for some new heart-scan test that morning, and when the nurse came in to take her down for the test, she said she wanted me to accompany her. In the room housing the special machine she was put on an angled table. There is a needle that moves on a graph, as in an electrocardiogram. I hated to see her on that steel slab, but she accepted what had to be done. No complaints. But this was her fifth trip to the hospital in six months.

Her doctor came to see her in the afternoon. I didn't much care for him. While a nurse was ministering to her, I walked down the hall with him. He said her heart had been steadily weakening, that the hospital would be short-staffed over this weekend and it might be better for her to be in intensive care. I said, 'Let's do anything but that — she hates it.' He said he'd try to avoid it, but was making no promises.

I stayed with her. She said the food was disgusting — how she would love to taste tunafish again! I was worried, I didn't want to leave her, but she needed rest and the children were home alone. I'd see her tomorrow. I hugged and kissed her again, but tried not to overdo it — she never liked one to be too demonstrative.

The next morning she seemed much the same. The ever-pervading atmosphere of gloom that exists in all hospitals was in full bloom. Mother had had her terrible lunch before my arrival — the tuna I brought would wait until tomorrow. I told her Sam was in good hands, so there was no problem about my staying with her. She was always worried about something — Sam's being alone; Leslie; Steve — what was he doing in Connecticut, what kind of girl was Dale; what was I doing — was I eating enough, was I sure I wanted the divorce from Jason. Endless worries. I was always uppermost on her mind — she was proud of me despite my being wanting in so many areas. I was always sure of love with her, yet always wanting her approval.

The doctor came again in the afternoon, and told me she'd definitely have to go into intensive care for the weekend. I told him I'd be there all day — go home for an hour, and come back in the evening. I'd go with her to intensive care at the end of the afternoon. He'd definitely check her. Her heartbeat was irregular and the day was hot; she might need oxygen to ease her breathing. She'd be better off in intensive care — there was no choice.

Lee came in the afternoon, hesitant about going away. She insisted that he go. I'd be there, nothing to worry about. He'd been living under such tension — never a full night's sleep, every time she stirred he'd waken, and every crisis had been in the middle of the night.

It was time to face intensive care. One

could already feel the absence of staff on the floor — the feeling of a long weekend.

The nurse helped Mother into a wheelchair and we started down the hall toward the intensive-care room. As she saw it, she put her hands up. 'Oh, no!' Almost a wail. I put my arm around her. 'It means nothing, darling. Don't be frightened — it's only for a couple of days because there aren't enough nurses. They're off for the weekend. Only to be certain there's someone always there to attend to you.' My heart was pounding, I was so nervous for her. We got her into bed with the usual screen on each side, to give her some privacy and so she wouldn't have to see the other patients. Intensive care is frightening. When she'd been there years before, at night the beds would be full, the next morning one or two would be empty. Death in the night. They allowed me to sit with her more often than the usual five minutes every hour, so it all seemed less critical. And she accepted it. I hung around, sitting on the broken-down sofa in the hall, waiting to be told I could sit with her again. It was grim. She'd said, 'Why don't you put on a dress — why do you always come here in pants? You look so much better in dresses.' She always wanted me to look my best. Tomorrow — I'd wear a dress tomorrow. When I kissed her good night, I said, 'See you tomorrow.' 'Don't forget,' she said, 'be here early.' I spoke to the intensive-care nurses — one a young man. She had wanted something, he hadn't been quick to give it to her. I was furious and I told him off — not to make a scene, but nurses in that unit were supposed to jump for the patients. That was the point of it. He seemed slow, casual. Can hospitals only get the dregs to work on holiday weekends? When I got home I called the doctor and asked him to check without fail so Mother would have what she wanted. I suppose he thought me hysterical, needlessly demanding. I couldn't have cared less. I'd had enough experience with doctors, nurses, and hospitals to take nothing for granted. The good were fewer than the bad, and the damn hospitals charge enough — anyone who paid those bills was entitled to demand anything.

The next day was hot — typical of New York at the end of August. I put on a dress, kissed my children — I'd hardly seen them the last two days — and took off. Mother was sitting up in bed, reading the morning paper. When she saw me she smiled and said, 'That's better, that's the way you should always look.' The dress. I sat on the side of her bed, the disconcerting monitor — that small screen with the thin white line moving up and down, recording her heartbeat — hanging overhead.

I spent the next hours in and out of that room. The doctor came at around six to examine her. I had to wait outside. He came out and told me her heart was very weak. They were putting an oxygen tube in her nose so she'd have no effort breathing. I said, 'Can I stay?' He said yes, but that it wasn't necessary, she was being cared for and should have total rest. Back in the room, Mother was arranging herself in bed, sitting up with that hideous green tube in her nose. She gave me a look I knew well — a do-as-I-say, don't-give-me-an-argument look. 'I'm going to rest — you go home.' 'I'd like to stay a little while.' 'I want you to go home to be with the children — I'll see you tomorrow.' I nodded assent, kissed her, hugged her, tube and all, and left with the doctor. As we went down the elevator and walked toward my car, I started with my usual assault of questions. He gave his usual answers. He did say she was weaker, and he couldn't say that she would get better. He said, 'I'm doing everything there is to be done. I'm available any time of the night or day — I live two minutes from here.' I said, 'Do you think I should stay?' He said, 'No, she wants you to be with your children. She'll sleep. Better to do what she wants.'

On the drive home I started to cry — and to talk. 'Oh, please let her be all right — please don't let anything happen.' I should have remembered my tears and talk those twelve years earlier on the eve of Bogie's death.

I got home and sat at the kitchen table, where Sam and Leslie were having their dinner. Sam, aged seven, came over, sat in my lap, put his arm around me, looked into my eyes. 'Why are you so sad, Mommy? I've never seen your eyes look so sad.' Trying to keep my voice steady, I said, 'I'm just worried about Granny, darling. She is very sick.' I had told Leslie what the situation seemed to be, but had spared Sam. He knew anyway.

I took off my dress — it was a hot night — and put Sam into bed. Around nine o'clock the phone rang. Leslie called me: 'It's the doctor.' I rushed for the phone. He said, 'I'm at the hospital — your mother has had another attack — you'd better come over right away. Come in the ambulance entrance on the side, they'll let you right up.' I was frantic. I had to call Lee. Leslie got the number as I threw on my dress. I grabbed the phone, told Lee what the doctor had said. I was on my way to the hospital — thought he'd better come back. He said he hadn't unpacked, was planning to come back anyway, he'd leave immediately. I rushed out of the house, got a taxi. I was shaking like a leaf. At the hospital, I ran in. They were waiting for me — for once no questions asked. I ran to the door of the intensive-care room. All was dark except for the light over Mother's bed. She was lying there — still had the oxygen tube, and there was a cloth on her forehead, some kind of metal plates on each arm and leg — electrocardiogram I guess. The doctor and nurse were on one side and I rushed to the other. I was so frightened. I picked up her warm hand and held it in mine. She was unconscious — a coma? Shock? I don't know. The monitor was still flashing its white line up and down. I never took my eyes off her — I just held her hand. But then I darted a look at the monitor. The line was straight now — it had stopped moving up and down. I looked at the doctor, who shook his head. 'She's gone.' That couldn't be. I leaned over and kissed her on the side of her neck — I heard the sound of a breath coming from her mouth. I said, 'She made a sound — what was that sound?' 'No,' he said, 'she didn't — that's normal.' I held her hand again, kissed her again, but I was terrified. Was this really death? Wasn't there some mistake? I didn't want to leave her, but I was afraid to put my arms around her —

afraid of that unknown. I just stood there — shaking — numb. A nurse led me out of the room. There was a small desk just outside. I sat on the chair and started to cry, leaning against a nurse whose face I never saw.

Finally I called Leslie and told her — told her to call Steve — said I would wait for Lee and then come home. I was numb. As I was telling the nurse I'd have to make another call and trying to compose myself, a bed was wheeled past me with a white sheet covering a form I knew was my mother. 'They're very quick about that,' I thought. How strange — a daughter watching the mother who had given her life lose her own. Is that what it's all about? I called Renee, her beloved only sister, told her. She gasped and said, 'Why did it have to be her — why couldn't it have been me?'

The doctor came out of the room and suggested I come to his house to wait for Lee. 'But he won't know where to go.' 'I'll leave word at the entrance,' he said. I wanted to be sure no one else told him about Mother. I must tell him myself, must be with him, so I went with the doctor to an unknown, rather formal apartment where I waited with the doctor and his wife. I couldn't understand what had really happened. It seems Mother told the nurse she felt nervous and asked her to call the

806

doctor. Nervous. My thoughts went back to Bogie — was it like the 'picking' he had gone through? The doctor had gone to the hospital immediately. The attack had started — she had no pain, her heart just couldn't take any more; it had been a miracle she had lasted as long as she did.

But why hadn't I been called sooner? And why hadn't this doctor, if he suspected this might happen, told me to stay? Why had he encouraged me to go home? Might I have gotten there in time to speak to her — for her not to have felt so alone? Had she had time for that — for fear? Everyone says we are all alone — we live alone, we die alone. It seems to be true.

The doorbell rang. I stood up — Lee. I started trembling again. He didn't know. 'Why are you here? How's Mother?' 'She's gone,' I said. He turned away, face contorted. I put my arms around him. 'Let's go home. You spend the night with me.'

Leslie was awake when we got home — composed, yet very upset. She, too, held herself in, did her crying alone. What a crazy family we were. Both Lee and Leslie said over and over that Mother had hung on, waiting to see me — she'd had to see me again before leaving this world. Why hadn't I come back from Europe sooner? But then would she have died sooner? It was after midnight when we got to bed. It had all happened in just a few hours. Just three hours before, my mother had still been alive. Such a short time to make such a difference.

I spoke to Steve, who said he and Dale would be down the next afternoon. My first reaction was, 'Why Dale? She didn't know Mother.' It was too personal a time. Yet I was glad Steve had her.

I slept fitfully, trying to decide how I would tell Sam, he loved and looked forward to her so much. Early in the morning I went into his room. I put him on my lap, and just told him, 'Granny has gone away — to heaven. Her heart just gave out.' He was very sad — hugged me, comforted me. His gift of love was a very special one. I thought of taking him to the funeral, and then I thought, why? I didn't want him to have that final picture of a coffin — I wanted him to remember his granny alive, full of fun and laughter.

We made arrangements. I had decided to speak to the rabbi — I wanted his words to be personal. If I couldn't speak them, I would write them for him to speak. There were the grisly details — the choosing of the casket — how do you shop for death? After that, Lee and I went to their apartment to choose her final outfit. Who invented that tradition — dressing up for never being seen again? It was weird walking into her apartment without her in it — knowing she would never be in it again. Going through her clothes, choosing something she favored. We went to look at the funeral parlor, at the impersonal room where the service would take place.

Aunt Renee came to my apartment. How close everyone becomes — how we hang onto one another, remembering everything from childhood on. I was an orphan — that realization came as something of a shock. No mother — never a father. There would never again be anyone who would love me without reservation — to whom I would be such a shining, glowing creature. Nobody's child. That realization would become more acute with time.

As we sat in the library talking — worn out, wrung out — the telephone rang. Jason, tipsy, from Spain. I was in no mood to humor him, I just wanted the divorce papers signed. As he rambled on, I cut him short: 'Look, I'm in no mood for your drinking. My mother just died and I can't talk to you.' He sobered up immediately. 'What? When?' Quickly I told him. He wanted to know when the funeral was. I told him and he said he was coming. I said, 'No — I don't want you there. Don't come.' He said, 'I'm coming anyway.' I was sure he wouldn't — didn't see how he could from that distance.

I went to my desk to write about my mother. Her persona was clear — that, of course, was the reason for the mutual love and respect between her and Bogie. They stood tall together. She was a truly selfless woman — no acquisitiveness, no greed, no waiting for payment for services rendered. No doubt, ever, where one stood in her affections — totally honest. Enormous vitality, zest for life, and constant awareness of others — with the importance of the preservation and protection of family looming largest. Her life had not been an easy one, but with every disappointment, every broken dream, she remained funny — her unrelenting sense of humor saved every moment of irritation or tension. I was an amalgam of her and Bogie. I knew that what she had implanted in me from the beginning was what had gotten me through up until then. She left me with all my memories, but she left me, and the pain would be mine forever. And I had never thanked her for everything.

The next day Steve arrived with Dale — our first meeting. She was pretty, quiet, sweet. It was an impossible time for me to meet the girl in Stephen's life. And dreadful for her — she was exposed to the entire family at once under the worst possible circumstances.

We drove to the funeral parlor that evening. The room was badly lit. Against the wall was the coffin in which my mother's body rested. I'd been offered the chance to see her — that same offer — 'She looks lovely!' Those people are mad. Of course I would not see her. Friends came, all who loved her. She had the gift of lasting friendships — twenty, thirty years. My sweet cousins Judy and Joan. Uncle Bill — strong, vulnerable loner. Uncle Al, her last brother, who hugged me with tears running down his face. They'd had their differences, but blood was thick; particularly Rumanian blood.

And suddenly I saw Jason walk in. I was stunned and yet it was right after all. Mother had cared about him and he obviously had about her. He had flown a long way. I rose and put my arms around him — it seemed natural. When Jason was cold sober, we understood each other very well. I was glad he'd come, and grateful.

Finally everyone left. I asked Steve and Leslie to wait outside. As Lee and I stood beside the coffin, I started to stroke it, wanting my touch to reach through to my mother. I broke down, sobbing uncontrollably — I wanted, so wildly, to open that casket and climb in with her. It was the most unbearable moment of my life. Poor

Lee stood there not knowing what to do, never having seen me in such a state. I could think of nothing but her. I wanted her to feel that I was there, with my love strong enough to reach her. To make up for all I hadn't done for her and wished I had, and some I had done and wished I hadn't. Losing is the hardest lesson in life, for once someone is lost, it is too late to change anything. So we are forced to live with and face our imperfections. Not easy, but there is no escape.

I was able to get through the following day's service having totally worn myself out the night before. The words sounded all right, though they couldn't ever say enough. I kept Steve and Leslie close and wondered how Lee would deal with his life from then on. Twenty years with someone is a lifetime, particularly for someone who waited so long to commit himself. They were perfectly suited, always answering each other's needs.

Jason left for Spain after the service. I thanked him for coming, and he promised to sign the divorce papers at last. Endings happen in tandem more often than beginnings.

This would be Lee's first night alone without Mother in the world. I wanted him to feel I was a haven where he would be welcome any time. I and mine were more his family, his own, than even his sisters and nephews and nieces. He felt more grandfather to Steve, Leslie, and Sam than he felt father to me — in truth, I never felt he was my father. I wanted to, but I had been too grown-up when he and Mother married — and Mother had always been my parental force. The dawning of being nobody's child would come stronger — loom larger — as the days, weeks and months went on. I would have to learn to live with it, though I did not expect to succeed.

I started the next day trying to settle divorce details. Might as well quickly follow one disaster with another. I would leave for Juárez, Mexico, on Tuesday, September 9 — get my divorce Wednesday. All papers were in order, Mexican lawyers set up, day's routine planned to the second. Divorce was an industry there, for God's sake. I was sent the revised script of *Applause*, which I would take with me. I wanted the divorce behind me — what I was really looking forward to was huevos rancheros for breakfast and tacos for lunch. (After all, I'd had them on my wedding day too!)

The flight was uneventful, giving me too much time to think. A woman from the lawyer's office was waiting for me on arrival in Texas, to drive me over the border to Juárez. She gave me the next day's rundown. It would all be over by five o'clock, with time out to fulfill my craving for tacos. As I lay in bed that night, I could only think of Mother. With tears streaming down my face I spoke to her. 'Mama, you would be pleased, I'm doing it now, I'll have a clean, free life again and I'll try to live it well.' The terrible truth of never hearing her voice again was devastating. I wish for it still. Over eight years have passed and I miss her just as acutely, think of her perhaps even more. The knowledge of death being part of life's cycle helps not at all. There is no way to prepare for the darkness of that pit of despair, the gaping hole that remains empty and gnaws constantly like an open nerve.

I forced myself to think of the future. Because of the children. And because of the show. *Applause* would be my first important work without her around to share it. The desolation, the nothingness, was not to be borne.

Exhaustion took over. I awakened to a bright Mexican sun — a blue sky and huevos rancheros. I walked around the hotel courtyard into a few shops to find souvenirs for my children. Everything was on schedule. When that same lady took me to the lawyer's office, I was reminded of *Treasure of the Sierra Madre*. He did not look unlike Gold Hat — green suit, yellow shoes, shiny black hair, and glistening gold teeth. He was efficient, took charge immediately, no nonsense. Who knows how many divorces he was to handle in a day? He told me what I had to do, had the paper for me to sign in the judge's office. It was over in half an hour — quick, impersonal. I was given my final papers, taken to a restaurant for homemade tacos, and put on the plane. I had arrived a Mrs, less than twenty-four hours later I was leaving a Miss.

It was a queer feeling — an eight-year-old marriage, wrapped up and thrown away in thirty minutes. Even wanting the divorce, it was difficult to go through. I felt the same as I had the day before, but I wasn't the same. My status had changed. My approach, my attitude toward men would be altered, and vice versa. And all because I had signed a stamped piece of paper. Who ever set it up that way? Bogie always said — and was he ever right — 'Marriage should be made difficult — and divorce easy.' It's the other way around in our society. Two minutes to be legally tied and endless months, sometimes years to be untied.

That Saturday I wrote to my mother.

Tonight you will have been gone from me two weeks. Dead. God, it is too unbearable. I cannot accept it — I cannot believe it — I cannot face it — I love you so much. But did you ever really know? I was so careless so much of the time. Is that what life and love for parents is — carelessness? But I always loved you so — and needed you and I am so empty now — I cannot go through fifteen minutes a day without thinking of you — I want to cry all the time — and I cry for you as well as for me — how rotten — how unfair for you to have been deprived of more years of pleasure — of doing — of seeing — of being. Darling Mother — what a good brave lady you were. How much care and love you had in you! How proud I am to be of you — how lucky I am to have had you — I only hope I can conduct my life as you would have wanted. I will play my opening night in the show for you. Oh Mama — will life ever be good again with you out of it? Will it?

The need to communicate was so strong, the need for a shoulder, for reassurance. I felt incomplete again — as though I'd lost a limb.

And there were so many decisions to make on the show. The director, Ron Field, was set — it would be his first time out as director, although he was an experienced, first-rate choreographer. Joe Kipness took me to lunch and told me about Ron. Since this was my first time in a musical, I had hoped for a director of experience, secure in all areas, who would prop me up if I faltered. I needn't have worried. When Ron and I met, he told me everything he had done in the theatre, and his feelings about *Applause*. Later he said he'd felt as though he were auditioning for a part. That hadn't been in my mind at all. He had faith in himself, real confidence, probably thought, 'Who the hell does she think she is? I have more theatre experience than she has!'

A settlement had to be made with the first writer — the decision had been made to replace him. The powers that be asked how I felt about Betty Comden and Adolph Green taking over. They were close friends of mine, and I'd always thought it dangerous to mix friendship with work, but it seemed a good idea nevertheless — they were so smart and funny and talented. First Betty called, then Adolph, to ask how I felt about their working on *Applause*. And soon it was all settled. Work on the script started immediately, and we were to go into rehearsal in November. Now I'd have to start taking a dance class, which I did with Ron's assistant, Tommy Rolla. It was a whole new world for me — trying to develop parts of myself that hadn't been used before. Training the body for endurance — to dance, to keep moving. My friends in the musical world had told me the toughness of what lay ahead. Jerry Robbins had said, 'You'll have to stay out of crowded, noisy rooms. Save your energy for the show. Find a nice guy and keep house, with quiet evenings for two.' Clearly the best way to get through any show — or any life, for that matter. But the work would be good for me. I was looking forward to being consumed by work, too exhausted to think. I felt compelled to write another letter to my mother.

It is four weeks that I am home. Four weeks in which you were taken from me — a happening I cannot accept or come to terms with at all — four weeks in which I got my divorce and will hopefully be able to shape my life again — with more care — more sense — more contact with reality. And four weeks in which Steve came home with Dale to tell me they were going to be married. How you would have screamed. But you would have been proud of Steve. (Am I really writing of you in the past tense?) He really seems to want the responsibility and she is a sweet, simple girl. They seem to love each other. But most important Steve is growing up at last and well. He wants Lee to stand up for him which would have pleased you and made you proud. So we will all go, Lee, Leslie, Sam and I — missing you badly. You know, since you have gone — Steve seems to want to be with his family more. So out of the heartbreak and misery of now — someone may be helped. That was what you always wanted anyway. What was most important to you. And so you shall have that.

Since your leaving I have been so disorganized. I cannot joke or find anything that is funny — I wonder if the old me will ever come back. I feel so vulnerable now — so ill-equipped to handle anything. Scary at 45. Maybe I, too, will grow up now. I do know that whatever I do — missing you — I will do it better. You left me so much.

I will work for you and all that you always believed I could do. I will do it more for you than I ever did for myself. You were my shining light really. It was not I. I needed you more than you needed me. How strange and horrible life is. So much comes into focus so late. The lessons are too hard. For the few moments of beauty — of joy — of discovery — there is so much pain.

You don't have to be frightened anymore, my darling Mama. Your rich, full heart has taken you to rest. I wish I could believe in a hereafter. It would be so comforting to know that you were able to see those you loved again — Grandma — Jack — Charlie — Bogie. And how rewarding it would be to think I would be with you again finally as I was at the beginning. Rest well, my love — you gave so much of yourself on this earth — and have left us all so enriched. If I can do half as well, what an accomplished life I will have led. Funny — I just thought — life is a four-letter word — death a five. It is just possible the latter is best?

That last obviously was written at low ebb. I never for one second have considered that that unknown other world could be better than this one. At any rate, it was the last time I addressed words on paper to my mother. I kept and I still keep a small picture of her near my bed so that when I turn to the left — reach for the phone, a cigarette, or just turn — I can see her face. If I am moved to say something to her, I can and do — and I feel better being able to see her as she was. Even sad, I feel better.

There had been so many changes those first weeks. So much adjusting to do. Steve and Dale were indeed getting married, and on the eve of Steve's wedding I was full of self-pity — as though everyone I loved were going away. I was alone in my bedroom. Leslie was with Tom. Before going to sleep, Sam, aged seven and a half, had told me that *he'd* be leaving soon. My first-born, over twenty years ago, really starting his own life now. I didn't feel that much older, but I felt so alone. No Bogie to share it with, no Mama. Those pictures flashing before my eyes from every movie I'd ever seen — a child getting married, mother and father always in attendance. There'd be only me at the wedding. I felt full of questions — Will there ever be a shoulder to lean on? What will life hold from now on? Only work, friends, problems. Was Steve frightened? I idolized that boy — had him on a pedestal from his first breath. I knew what a truly good boy he was, with fine, old-fashioned instincts like his father's. There was so much more of Bogie in him than he knew. I prayed he would find direction now — he'd had a long time of personal struggle for one so young.

I thought, 'I am too sad inside to know what I feel about Steve's marriage. It is a fact, and I will be there, and I will think how I was on that day when *I* was twenty, and wish for him some of the same happiness I had. But I am empty inside now. A terrible feeling. I wish it would go away.'

We all drove to Connecticut — a beautiful October day, sun shining on the bride-to-be. It was a short, simple service. I was far away part of that day — at my own wedding, Steve's birth, events in his life. He looked so young standing there, yet so sure of what he wanted. The wedding lunch was filled with toasts and laughter, picture-taking. At their chosen moment, Steve and Dale took off in a car with tin cans tied to the rear bumper. I looked at Leslie and at Sam, thinking, 'One gone — two to go. Or maybe not. Daughters are more apt to have a continuing relationship with their mothers. When a son goes, he goes.' But it wouldn't be long before Leslie took off too. She looked so beautiful that day — she is such a beautiful girl — and her mind must have been full of her own emotional life. She didn't talk much with me about Tom; she was mysterious. I was often not quite sure what she was thinking.

And then Sam — a smart seven and a half — planning his own departure. What a character!

I would concentrate totally on work from now on. I'd taken on an enormous responsibility — and a big chance. I had to be good in this show, better than ever before.

It would be the first time distractions would be at a minimum, the first time I had nothing to pull me away. And the harder I worked, the less I would think. Actually, from the time I fell in love with Bogie I had never been able to forget my personal life and zero in on my career. Now I would do it with a vengeance.

Ron thought it a good idea for me to learn a song that he would later choreograph, so I would get an idea of how to sing, move, and make sense all at the same time. I'd take a voice lesson with Keith Davis, then go up to Peter Howard's to work on the songs, then go to a dance studio for my exercises — half ballet — then practice the assigned song with a pianist. So it went, on a daily basis — hard physical work, concentrated. It's one thing to be musical, which I fortunately am; it's quite another to learn how to sing — to project — to *act* a song. To say nothing of trying to rid myself of my terrible shyness. I used muscles I didn't even know I had, took hot epsom-salts baths nightly. Everything hurt.

Betty and Adolph worked quickly, but they knew better than I that work would continue through our out-of-town tryout. Charlie Strouse and Lee Adams revised some songs, threw out others. As new scenes were written, they were read to

Charlie and Lee so that all the collaborators could decide on changes or adjustments. Creating a musical is complicated, a world unto itself, an experience that has no relation to doing a straight play. I learned that a song should be the culmination — the realization — of a scene, and because it is music it hopefully can reach higher than the scene possibly could without it. It was thrilling to be part of this birth. Exploring new territory is always thrilling — you never know what surprises lie ahead.

Auditions began. There were six key parts apart from Margo (me): Eve, Bill Sampson (Margo's lover), my hairdresser confidante, the producer, and Margo's and Bill's best friends. I sat in on many readings. It's so hard to know how to make a choice — some actors read marvelously and never get better, others read badly and become marvelous. Certainly if my own career had depended on auditions, I would have spent my life selling ties.

When it was boiled down to the final two or three actors for each part, there'd be a conference among Ron, the authors, the producers, and me. I always stayed low in my seat — far back in the theatre, of course — so as not to be seen. Ron was very sensitive to the actors, not making them stand too long under that glaring stage light. It boded well for his future as a director — and for our relationship over the coming months. Finding a girl for Eve was not easy. The final choice was an unknown girl, Diane Macafee — lovely-looking, with a beautiful voice. They all knew they were gambling — it could either be marvelous or not work at all. Then came the day of the leading man. There were two actors in the running, both new to me. On this last day Ron wanted me to get onstage with each of them so he could see how we looked together. I later learned the point to that — as my stage personality was strong, they had to have a leading man who held his own and wasn't wiped off the stage. The one who survived me got the part!

As rehearsal time drew near I was filled with anticipation. I had been preparing without let-up for three months, to say nothing of the time I'd put in before the summer. Ron set up the first reading of the play one evening at his house. We were to go into formal rehearsal the next week. I had already started to work with the dancers — become familiar with the dancers themselves, the total musical atmosphere, the word *gypsy,* signifying the kids in the dance corps. Gypsies know what they are doing, and Ron had gathered the best — all young, some ridiculously so. It was riveting to watch them learning the routines, stretching, pliéing constantly, studying themselves in the floor-to-ceiling mirrors. I was self-conscious at first, knew they were watching me — to see if I could do anything at all, I suppose. Sizing me up. But I was willing to try everything, and called upon my years of training to help me now. And I stumbled through, after a shy, hesitant start. The time I'd put in paid off; I was ready to learn — and it all came easier than I thought it would. Everyone helped. Gypsies are encouraging and generous, particularly when they see you're determined to really dance instead of faking it.

The vibrations were right and I could tell we would be a happy company. All of us got along well from the first reading; we liked one another. We had drinks after the last word was spoken — what a relief for all. *Applause* was on its way. A reality.

Our first day of rehearsal was December 22, three days before Christmas. Many preparations to be made for Sam, Leslie, and Lee. Steve and Dale were coming down — she was pregnant. It was our first year without Mother.

Our first day of rehearsal started off with the press. Ron and I did a couple of steps from my big number to the flash of bulbs, tossed off a few words, and they left. Now we could get down to business. I had been told something about each of the main actors. All the men were married except for the leading man, Len Cariou, who had a long-standing relationship with an actress. Thank God, I thought. I was always wary of actors, in or out of work situations (particularly in), but in this case there was never any thought of a possible involvement, which made the work even more of a joy. After the misery in my life since 1956 it seemed that at last the pendulum was swinging upward for me. I could sense the possibility of a life and a future — something to feel good about.

Every night, as soon as Sam was in bed, I took my script and tape into the library. There I practiced my songs aloud and studied my part. After I thought I knew my lines, Leslie would cue me. There was no time for anything else. I had never worked so hard — used so much of myself in mind and body. It required discipline and stamina. Lucky I had always had lots of energy.

Ron knew I was close to Betty and Adolph, and we all knew the dangers of friends working together. From the beginning, Ron was boss. I always felt there had to be a captain for a play or a movie, and I always felt the director should be that captain. So he handled it all. If a problem arose, I went only to him, and Betty and

Adolph did the same. It worked like a charm.

I had asked him not to tell me when they were coming to rehearsal, and to please try to keep them away until I felt surer of the part. I was nervous enough without them there, and they knew it. The day they finally did come, they slipped in unobtrusively — I saw them out of the corner of my eye and stayed away from them until we'd run through the entire first act.

It was a big test for me, rising above a lifetime of self-consciousness, of nerves, working in front of Betty and Adolph in the new medium of the musical in a brightly lit rehearsal room. I simply had to work overtime at burying my qualms. They were adorable — complimentary, understanding, simpatico. The first hurdle had been jumped with a few feet to spare.

Every day I seemed to arrive earlier and stay later than anyone but Ron. I was in all but two scenes in the show, and when those two scenes were being rehearsed, I was working on my singing or dancing, or having wardrobe fittings — always something, no time for sitting and staring into space. Yet it was exhilarating. When I plunge I do plunge; halfway is not my way. Unconditional commitment.

With each passing day I became more submerged in the character of Margo

Channing. Some of her frailties had always been mine, some became mine. It isn't that you truly turn into the character you're playing, it's that more hours of the day and night are devoted to work than to anything else. As rehearsals progress, your involvement becomes more and more absolute — the rest of your life gets crowded out. There's no way to forget your children, but you can come dangerously close. Friends in the business understand. Social life disappears and is not missed. All you want to think about, really, is the play, and the only people you want to see are the other players.

I had told Ron I'd torn a cartilage in my knee several years before. In the disco number, he'd originally staged the finale with the lightest gypsy, Sammy Williams, jumping into my arms. I didn't think more could happen to the damn knee, but I didn't want to push it. Ron wanted me to dance — to do a real number. I was all for that. We tried the lift a few times on top of a jukebox, but what with the jukebox rolling a bit, wires onstage, and other hazards, it was finally eliminated. Ron had scheduled a gypsy run-through the Sunday before we left for Baltimore. I'd never known what a gypsy run-through actually was. I found out. You run through the show — no costumes or sets or orchestra, only a piano — in a theatre filled with the casts and gypsies from other shows running on Broadway. It would give us our first exposure to audience reaction, and them a chance to see a new show in the raw. The prospect terrified me.

The date was January 18, the place the Lunt-Fontanne Theatre. I was dressed in slacks and turtleneck sweater. The theatre started to fill up. There was no curtain. The actors were shaking in the wings, the gypsies warming up way upstage in corners, using pipes as barres. I'd taken a voice lesson with Keith and done my warm-up with Tommy.

Finally it was time. Ron, as is customary, walked downstage to explain the set, time, and place. The show was supposed to open with television screens on either side of the proscenium. Peter Ustinov was our guest host for the Tony Awards — we'd filmed that bit in advance, my welcome by him, my presentation of the award to Eve. A new idea that we hoped would work. As I heard him say 'Margo Channing,' I made my first entrance. The applause was tumultuous — you'd have to travel far to find an audience equal in enthusiasm to gypsies and fellow actors. The theatre was packed, the audience insanely receptive. And I was doing something I'd always dreamed of doing — actually being musical in a musical comedy heading for Broadway. Professional dreams being realized after so many, many years. It was utterly thrilling. We all felt sure we had a hit. There really is nothing to equal in excitement a run-through like that. With no sets or costumes, the audience must use its imagination. They're privy to a new birth, the first unveiling of a creation. What a feeling to be part of it! At the last curtain call the stage became flooded with every musical director, producer, writer I'd known — and actors, all bursting with enthusiasm. I could have flown.

I left for Baltimore a day ahead of the company for my first orchestra rehearsal. That's another high. Even with all the early imperfections of the arrangements and musicians, hearing the score with an orchestra for the first time is something special. Our conductor, Don Pippin, was wonderfully helpful to me — one of the most important factors in a musical. The conductor, after all, is a leader and his ability to help or hinder is not to be measured. Don, luckily for me, was a helper.

The company arrived, the cast filtered in. We'd not seen one another for a couple of days — in the incestuous birthing of a show, that's a long time. I didn't want to miss any of it, I wanted to be part of it all, everyone's beginning.

For the next eight weeks, fourteen to sixteen hours a day, we were all — led by Ron — as close as parents and children, as lovers; we were dependent on one another emotionally, creatively — finding our way through the maze of changes, learning more about one another. Musicals, I was to learn later, are notorious for love affairs out of town. Everyone goes crazy, particularly the gypsies. Eight or nine weeks together — people start looking for partners. Not me. My head was into work only, into making it better. I was expending so much energy and emotion, I had none to spare. After rehearsals we'd walk back to the hotel, have a drink in the hotel bar, then hit the sack. Our first night in Baltimore, Len and I were heading toward the marquee on our way to a nightcap when we looked up and saw his name misspelled: 'Ben Cariou.' He was Ben to me from then on.

We previewed on Monday. First time in all the clothes. We'd staggered through a dress rehearsal, but it wasn't quite the same ballgame. Elizabeth White, my great dresser, and Jerry Masarone, in charge of my crowning glory, helped to calm me. I got through it, but so scared I was no judge of how it went. The house was full and the audience responsive. Just before you open, you always think it's a hit, whether it is or not. When you're that involved, how would you know? The next night we opened. The Baltimore papers were on strike, and we weren't sure which Washington critics would turn up. Our notices were not overly favorable, but the audiences loved us and business was splendid. We knew we had work ahead, and I was keyed up and ready for it.

Through all this time I kept myself aloof from Len. He was attractive and bright, a wonderful actor, a joy to work with. He seemed to be his own man, self-confident. We had fun and worked wonderfully well together. A natural situation in a somewhat unnatural circumstance. I had no intention — not the slightest — of any involvement. But given the parts we played, it was inevitable. Oh, it's difficult — you're together without a let-up — and we did get our parts and ourselves all mixed up. I knew we had a year ahead of seeing each other six days a week — an involvement could only lead to disaster, certainly for me. I couldn't let anything happen. Besides, he had another life, settled and happy. I wanted us to be friends. I wanted not a day to pass when we wouldn't be pleased to see each other. I wanted no strain. And I was unrealistic. I held him at arm's length for a while. But only for a while.

After the opening, the changes started.

There was a feeling of depression after the notices, but we had eight weeks ahead of us, time enough to make the show what we all knew it could be. Every day we rehearsed, every night we played. Before the Saturday matinee Ron came into my dressing room. I'd heard rumors that Diane Macafee was going to be replaced. I asked him about it and he said, yes, he felt it had to be. I said, 'Don't you think it's that out-of-town panic? The minute something isn't quite right, an actor is fired.' I was very troubled at the prospect. Ron said, 'Do you like Diane?' I said, 'Yes, I do.' He said, 'But you shouldn't — that's the problem. She should present a threat to you. That's why the show isn't working the way it should. She doesn't come across as all those things Eve Harrington must be.' I said, 'It seems so unfair.' 'Maybe it is. It's my mistake, but until I saw her in the show I couldn't be sure. Just trust me.' I had no choice — I'd believed him up until then, and I did trust him. But it didn't lessen the hurt I felt for her.

The pressure was constant. Rehearse all day — scenes, songs, dances; performance at night; drinks at the hotel, sleep; breakfast and start all over again. The routine out of town is killing, designed to finish actors off, but you keep going — on nerves, hope, and creativity. The adrenaline pumps on. An occasional call to my children to make sure all was well, but I felt, and indeed was, very removed from them. I'd have a weekend at home before Detroit, so they wouldn't feel totally deserted.

The first day we did the new opening number, everything went wrong — lights crazy, sets not working, sound off, everyone off. Pure disaster.

Ron walked into my dressing room before the next Saturday matinee, looking down at the floor. I had become very sensitive to him, felt very close to him. He knew I still felt badly about Diane — he did too. I told him I still felt uneasy about replacing her — there ought to be another way, less traumatic. He said, 'You think so? Just look in the fourth row center this afternoon. You'll see Gower Champion sitting there.' 'So what?' I said. 'So I'm being replaced,' said Ron. 'What?' I screamed. 'Over my dead body!' He had planned to go to New York during the matinee. I made him promise to stay, to come to my room after the performance and we'd take it from there. Five days ago we'd had a hit. One set of reviews, one negative word, and panic had set in. But there was no way I would continue with another director. Replacing Diane was awful enough, but replacing Ron was going too far.

After the matinee Ron was in my room

when the door opened and in walked one of Broadway's most successful producers, Alex Cohen. He hugged both of us enthusiastically. 'You'll all get Tonys! It's sensational — the most exciting show I've seen in ages — your work is marvelous!' Ron told him he was being replaced, whereupon Alex, after a few expletives, tore over to tell Joe Kipness the error of his ways. I took Ron to my hotel suite, Len joined us, sensing trouble, and we sat him down, ordered a drink for him, food for me, called Kippy and started raving. 'He's my captain — if the ship sails without him, it sails without me.' I ranted on and on. Of course I had another show to do, and Ron was terrified I'd lose my voice with strain. Finally Joe said, 'Gower just came down to visit, he's passing through, we're old friends — as a matter of fact, he's meeting me in the bar in a little while.' 'Oh, he is, is he?' I thought. My position was clear. I called my agent and told him the story: 'If Ron goes, I go. Make it clear to Kippy!' I was livid. The theatre — God! So much insecurity, so many people thinking change means better. Ridiculous! How in hell can you be talented one minute and, because of a critic or two, lose it all?

After I hung up, I said to Ron, 'Let's go to the bar and say hello to Mr Champion.' Ron paled. We were all fragile people just then. Just before entering the bar, I put my arm through his — Len was on the other side — and in we walked. Big smile to Kippy and Gower. When Gower said, 'Great show,' I patted Ron on the shoulder and said, 'It's all because of him — I don't know what I'd do without him.' I did everything but flutter my eyelashes. And that was the end of that.

Replacing Ron would really have done the company and the show in. With his second wind, renewed faith, Ron plunged ahead. More changes, more meetings with Comden and Green, Strouse and Adams. The changes were concentrated in large numbers like the party scene, involving the whole company. As much as possible, scenes that Eve was not in. There was so much to do, it didn't matter, except that we were unable to work in sequence. At last I got the word — Penny Fuller was to replace Diane. The day she arrived, Ron called me into his room to meet her. We got along immediately. She knew what a tough situation it was, what ambivalent feelings are involved in firing and hiring. Penny was great to work with. So skillful. Our scenes had another dimension, no question. It was very exciting. Funny how imperfection can be thrilling. It's the possibilities of what may come, what might be, that make you tingle.

After Baltimore, Len and I drove back to New York. It was very late, but before heading for our respective homes we just had to drive by the Palace Theatre. There was my name up there, and the enormous logo above the marquee — bigger than I'd ever dreamed it could be. I felt like a kid again looking at that theatre — that theatre which had housed some of the greatest variety artists in show business. I might become part of its history. Unbelievable.

After a hectic happy day with my children I headed for Detroit. My mind was only on the show — I'd never thought I would look forward to Detroit with such enthusiasm.

We opened on February 19 and Ron read me the reviews. After the opening we'd had a cast party fraught with drink, manic gaiety, and some strain. Margo Channing was beginning to get to me. I had been too keyed up, so naturally now felt too let down. The insecurity of Margo was becoming mine and, added to my own, it laid me very low. The reviews were excellent, though not quite so glowing as I would have liked. I became full of doubts. 'Maybe it isn't there — maybe it'll come later. Maybe, maybe . . .' Ridiculous to have to be assured by a stranger that you're good, but I wanted all those adjectives. Is it pleading for affection as in childhood? Or simply wanting approval, also as in childhood? I felt quite alone. Totally vulnerable.

At the end of four weeks we had made many changes in the show, rehearsing daily and playing at night. One night my voice went. I was terrified. It was clearly because of too much work and too little rest. I was taken to a throat doctor for treatment. When the star takes ill, everyone becomes very nervous — including the star. I didn't rehearse for a day or two, but I didn't miss a show and was back to normal by week's end.

My spirits started to climb. With all the changes — a line, a speech, part of a song, a move — dressing room, quick-change room plastered with yellow paper delineating each change, act by act, scene by scene — how one head can retain it is a mystery. Except that somehow it becomes possible. You have to do it, so you do. There were six versions of the party scene. Len was given a new ballad ten days before we closed in Baltimore. A new version of a group number. And my final song went in with a new tag scene five days before our closing in Detroit. But at last the show was frozen.

Press interviews were interspersed — some good for New York, some not so good. One jerk wrote a piece having a conversation with me as though Bogie were present and commenting. I had refused to answer questions about Bogie. I made it clear before agreeing to an interview that it was to deal with *Applause* and me, nothing else. It was time. If they didn't want to talk to me about me, the hell with it. I wanted my own life, my own place. Bogie had been dead for thirteen years, I'd had another marriage and a divorce, I had embarked on a new road. I had to stop looking over my shoulder all the time, and I didn't want anyone looking over it for me!

By our last week in Detroit I felt there wasn't a bad moment in the show. I'd never felt so good in a part, nor worked so hard, nor functioned so well. And emotionally I became Margo Channing more and more. The reality of New York — children, my own home, Len's life there — was just around the corner, but fantasy was where I was living, and I wanted to stay in it as long as I could. The theatre is insidious. All my professional life I'd been warned not to confuse a part I was playing with myself. I was able to avoid it in films, less in the theatre, and out of the question in *Applause*. I was having a marvelous time, so why not? And when in hell had I ever heeded warnings? I was the only one who would be hurt — though I didn't really believe it at the time. Lives take on a pattern in spite of your conscious effort to break it. Before Bogie my emotional life hadn't worked — and after, God knows, it certainly hadn't. Yet the hope remained — the ability to enjoy, to trust, to give. I refused and still refuse to believe that my first love — my happy marriage of eleven and a half years to Bogie — was the beginning and end of that experience. I demanded and still demand the possibility of another good relationship before my time is up. Having tasted the fruit, I flatly refuse never to taste it again.

At this point in my life, just before the opening of *Applause*, I would say I was at my peak, mentally and physically sharper than ever before. Using every bit of me. Determined to be the best I could be. New York was approaching — final rehearsals, technical rehearsals, readying ourselves for the first of four previews before the opening. All so exciting and frightening. And then opening night — Sunday, March 30. I've never seen so many flowers, so many telegrams — an avalanche. On one dressing-room wall Larry Kasha had framed *Life* — I was on the cover, my second time. A surprise. Friends from everywhere thought of me. Only one person would I not hear from, and she lived in the back of my mind, never leaving it. This one was for her.

Voice lesson, body warm-up, more vocalizing. Concentrate on the part. You cannot shake — it's going to work, try to enjoy it. It's time to walk out on stage and deliver. As I made up, I went over all the changes to make sure I forgot nothing. Liz had the usual tea and honey at hand. The call 'Half-hour' on the speakers. Ron came in with a beautiful necklace of small gold hearts. It was the biggest night either of us had ever had, the culmination of so much work and love. A new beginning. 'Fifteen minutes.' Charles Strouse and Lee Adams dashed in to wish me luck, Betty and Adolph too. Leslie, Sam, and Lee were out front along with many friends. 'Five minutes.' Masarone gave the hair a final lift. Oh God. Len came into my room to take me upstairs, a routine that had become regular for us. He knew how nervous I was. 'Places, please.' Take many deep breaths — remember what Keith told you. Stand in the wings. The overture — that's what a musical has that is so incredible, that gives such a lift, that hits you in the pit of your stomach. The rustle of the audience, the theatre packed . . .

The show began. My entrance was coming up — 'Margo Channing.' I walked onto the stage — huge applause — the show moved forward from scene to scene,

Len and I working together like a charm, Penny — the whole company terrific. Yes, I was frightened, but I loved it. And this one was for my mother.

At the interval Ron came back happy. It was going well, better than ever. Second act the same — everything worked, even the sets, nothing stuck, all ran smoothly. Then the finale. Ron had staged exciting curtain calls, like a musical number. The whole company took theirs, and when they parted I was standing upstage, back to the audience. On cue I swirled around, arms in the air, and walked downstage for my bow. A thrill to do, and an added high for the audience. We took many calls — opening-night enthusiasm, but the show was good, we all knew it. Then photographers back-stage, dressing room full of people, changing for the traditional trip to Sardi's — I wasn't about to miss that — and then Kippy and Kasha were giving an opening-night party at Tavern on the Green.

Sardi's and the Tavern were an extension of the Palace — excitement upon excite-ment. Then the first reviews. Clive Barnes singing my praises. A hit. Leslie and Lee there to share it — all my New York friends. Ron read the reviews aloud — we might have written them ourselves, they were so good. Dancing in the streets — hooray! Then suddenly, sitting at my table,

I was on the verge of tears. Too much tension — geared too high — nowhere to go but down? Who knows? Mother, more than likely. I'd gotten what I'd always wanted, I was an enormous hit, the show was an enormous hit, but the hole was there, that cavern that would never be filled. I could forget it most of the time, but that night I had been totally vulnerable on the stage and went on being so off it.

Yet this was definitely my time. There were no qualified reviews, at last I had the adjectives I'd been waiting for. Walter Kerr was so flattering I blushed on reading his words. He said what I'd worked so hard to have said — that I was not just a movie star dabbling in the theatre. I was a full-fledged star of the stage. Thank you. The compliments were wildly extravagant and I reveled in them. It was almost like being discovered for the first time. I had a new career, a musical career. And the audiences were fantastic.

Len and I were still involved with each other, although real life changed our habits considerably. Of course I, being a romantic and unrealistic, wanted it to continue. It couldn't. There were times we were together, and that was always terrific fun. He loved all my friends and many aspects of my life. And eight times a week we were those other people — Margo and Bill. As long as that remained, our involvement would go on too. He was many years younger than I — as with our characters in the play. It all fell neatly into place. Yet he was a curious combination of social inexperience and a very mature, settled man. He had planned his life, figured out what he wanted, how he wanted to live, and would fight against anything threatening his plans. Meeting me had thrown him a little off balance and he didn't like that. I remember showing him a line in Chapter 13 of John Fowles' *The French Lieutenant's Woman* — 'A planned world . . . is a dead world.' He wasn't crazy about that. I never could figure out how such a young man could be so closed to personal change when here was I, having lived many lives, always open to new people and things, possibilities, adventure. I still cried into my pillow over relationships. I don't believe he did. Every other week I'd give myself a good talking to — 'Forget him except at the theatre. Part-time lovers are not your bag. Never have been, never will be. He'll go his own way — he has to — enjoy your time together, don't fret about the rest.' Sometimes it worked, sometimes not. Mostly not. But it had to, for the sake of the show. And he never lied to me. He was not careless with me — just careful of himself. He'd been straighter, more honest, than most men I'd known, which is why I could never stop liking and respecting him. That's why we are still happy at the sight of each other. It's a good feeling to be glad to see someone you were once mad about. I haven't had it about many.

During our first month the Tony nominations were announced — the show, Ron, Len, and myself nominated, plus one of our supporting actors, Brandon Maggart. I was so excited! I couldn't believe it. At last, my very first nomination for anything, anywhere. Katie was nominated too, for *Coco*. Of course I wanted to win, but Katie — my friend, one of the women I admired above all others, set apart, and such a truly wonderful actress. I adored Katie so — it was ridiculous, actors in competition for a prize. But what a prize! It shouldn't mean so much, but — admit it — it does. As long as awards are being given, it's better to get them. Katie and I joked about it. She wouldn't go to the award presentation, she'd never gone to any function like that. Laughingly she said, 'If I win, you'll accept it for me, won't you?' And how I would! I was sure she *would* get it. Why couldn't we both get it, damn it?

Jason had married again. I wasn't on the greatest terms with him, felt he'd been very careless about Sam. I prevailed on him to tell Sam about the marriage himself. Certainly Sam had been hoping from the beginning we'd get together again. That was his own hope — he hadn't been led into it by either one of us. Now he accepted the new marriage, sort of. Well, he had to. I had made it clear to Jason that when he saw Sam I wanted him to see him alone, not yet with his new wife, not with his other children. Sam worshipped his father, and needed time alone with him. With Steve away, Jason was the only man in his life. I was sometimes at home when Jason would come to take him for the afternoon, but I wouldn't stay — it had to be a special time for the two of them, alone. Sam continued to astound me. I recall his coming into my dressing room after a matinee, having seen the show from the wings, saying to me, 'Who is your new playmate, Mommy?' He'd only met Len once or twice.

The Tony Award show was some night. My dressing room in the Palace was afloat with friends coming in for a drink. Then to my seat in the audience for the early awards. God, I was nervous. Cecil Beaton won the costume award for *Coco*. We didn't win anything until Ron's name was announced — first for choreography, then for direction. I screamed — we all did — my voice was totally shot. And I still had my number to do.

Then Walter Matthau — another irony — announcing best performance by an actress in a musical. The names of the nominees — my heart thumping, then stopping altogether. Opening of the envelope. And I heard it — 'Lauren Bacall for *Applause*.' I screamed again, jumped out of my seat toward the stage. My friends in the audience were on their feet stamping. I could only make foghorn noises of shock. I'd never won anything before — some actresses did, not this one. I finally gathered myself together enough to thank Ron and the company of *Applause* and the authors for the biggest, best love-in of my life. By the time I was to wind up the show with 'Welcome to the Theatre' (from *Applause*, of course) I had almost no voice. It was an unforgettable night for me. Totally rewarding. It left me exhausted — and happy.

From the age of nineteen I had been made aware of the pitfalls of awards. And, as my career moved on its zigzag course, I never contemplated winning one. I still don't think actors, directors — any creative artists — should be pitted against one another. There is the high in winning, the low in losing — and the human frailty of resentment that the loser feels toward the winner. That uses up energy where it should not be used, energy that is needed.

For the real stakes in the theatre are high — they are life stakes. That's what I love about it. You gamble with your life, and that's a gamble worth taking.

Still thinking back to that Tony night: I was a winner, but I was alone, and that was a glaring fact of life to me. Crazy to look at it that way? Of course I'm crazy — but alone is definitely alone. Work is essential to me — really using myself, really functioning, body and mind at their best — but it only heightens my emotional needs, it doesn't lessen them.

The night after the Tonys, the show went fantastically. The audience knew I had won, and the opening scene itself was all about the Tony Awards, so the applause on my entrance had two meanings. That communication between actor and audience is incredible fun — the lift it gives is indescribable — but again, it basically deals with emotions, with people. And there's nothing like it. It's love. But it ends when the curtain comes down. I remember that after Johnny Negulesco saw the show he said, 'You can never have a high like this anywhere else — you don't need a man, there isn't a man alive who could ever make you feel the way that audience makes you feel.'

Wrong!

There *is* a man alive, I'm sure, who

might make me feel that way. The only question is whether or not I will find him.

Nonetheless, from a work point of view, *Applause* continued to be the most rewarding experience of my life. I just wanted to have everything.

There came the devastating night of Friday, July 31. At the beginning of the disco number, as I raised my right leg for a high kick, my left leg buckled — a rip-like thunder to me. The kids thought I had slipped, then realized it was something else and caught me before I hit the stage. I knew something terrible had happened, but kept on going in the show, God knows how. I was filled with terror. The leg buckled another couple of times, without warning. The doctor was waiting for me in my dressing room at the interval. My knee started to puff. I started to cry. All I could think was that my brief moment of glory was over — I might be incapacitated for weeks. Len came into the room, helped put make-up on the white tape that was holding the hated Ace bandage in place. One of the young doctors told me to call Dr James Nicholas' office on Monday so that he could examine my knee and prescribe my future course of action. That was to be the beginning of one of my luckiest medical associations.

I missed no performances, but we eliminated the disco scene until we could hear Dr Nicholas' diagnosis — which was that I had torn the other cartilage in that knee. Treatment was prescribed. The doctor impressed on me the necessity of keeping the muscles around the knee strong — only possible by working with weights. The disco would have to be dropped from the show for three weeks, and I'd have to wear the bandage until the swelling went away. Later I discovered that Dr Nicholas was Joe Namath's doctor, as well as doctor for dozens of other athletes who had a knee, elbow, or foot problem. And they were followed by Nureyev, Baryshnikov. . . . Dr Nicholas kept me from surgery and from missing a performance, and I could never be grateful enough. I've been lucky so far — got through almost five years of *Applause* and a few after without a major mishap. No more taking my body — or luck! — for granted.

The first time the disco went back in the show I was very nervous. Had to think of that knee constantly, figure out where to put my weight, how to favor the right leg, without the audience being aware. I worked with weights before my daily body warm-up and I go on doing it to this very day.

One night at the interval I was told that Bette Davis was in the audience. That she had said she would come on two conditions: (1) that she did not sit up front, and (2) that there would be no pictures. I almost died. God — the creator of Margo Channing in *All About Eve*, the definitive performance. My childhood idol was in the audience watching me play *her* part.

I had never known her well at Warner Bros. — had only seen her a few times there. I was apprehensive about meeting her afterward — about how she would feel, what she would think of the show, of me. I opened my dressing-room door in answer to her knock and there she was — my dream, my fantasy actress. Every part she had ever played — and I loved her in all of them — flashed before me.

I offered her a drink, which she declined — she had to get back to her daughter in Connecticut. She sat on a chair, not on the love seat, which might have indicated she would stay awhile. I stammered something about how ridiculous it was for me to be playing her part. She said, 'Funny — I'd never thought of this as a musical.' She was reserved, polite — rather closed. And I was uncomfortable. My admiration couldn't be lessened — I was just personally uncomfortable with her. After a few more exchanges she rose to leave. Her last words were, 'No one but you could have played this part — and you know I mean that.' I thanked her and she left. There was so much more I had wanted to say to her, but I was too self-conscious, and her reserve kept her in check. If we'd had fifteen minutes, it might have been warmer, I might have made her realize how much her being there had meant. That woman who was the biggest woman star in motion pictures in the Thirties and Forties, Garbo notwithstanding, actually took an ad in the Hollywood trade papers saying she was looking for a job — was ready, willing, and able. That that should happen is the horror of this business.

And now she is being appreciated as she should be — saluted by her peers, her contribution to film recognized as unique. That's part of the glory of this business.

So the months went by, the Palace Theatre filled to capacity at every performance, well-known people from all walks of life coming backstage unexpectedly. It was always rewarding, always gave me a lift. One of the most unforgettable nights that I still think about, and will always, was about six weeks after opening night. Noel Coward brought the Lunts. They stayed in the dressing room — I wouldn't let them out. Len sitting at Lynn Fontanne's feet — me hanging on to Alfred Lunt's every syllable — Noel enjoying it all. Three people whose contributions had been immeasurable and everlasting. One night Paul Lukas came — aged, white-haired, still good to look at. My mentor of thirty years earlier. He was proud of me, he said. 'So you finally have done what you set out to do.' Sitting in my dressing room, I could picture vividly the reverse scene at the Martin Beck Theatre — all our conversations. I had forgotten nothing. And it was a good feeling, to remember.

The problem with a hit show, of course, is that the longer it runs, the harder it is to perform. Outsiders don't understand that. To keep it fresh — to have each new audience feel you're doing it for the first time — that is the discipline of the theatre, that's what's tough. No matter how you feel — sick, unhappy — you have to forget all that and just go out on the stage and do it. That's the greatest lesson one learns, the important one.

I had decided early in *Applause* that I would not plan my social life. If someone invited me to supper a week, even days, in advance, and had to know definitely, I would reply, 'Then don't count on me.' I had never lived my night life loosely, but I knew it was time for a change. How did I know if I'd feel like going out that night? Or, indeed, if I wouldn't get a better offer? Not socially better — emotionally better. It created problems with some friends, but I decided, 'The hell with it — I'm going to be selfish and only do what I really want to do.' It was time in my life for that. I'd lived so many years on other people's demands — husbands, children. It was time for me to live on my own.

My whole day was geared to that day's performance. Not too much time on the telephone — bad for the voice. Plenty of rest — nap from four to five. Eat something on a tray — red meat preferably, but not too much — at five. Voice lesson at six. To theatre by seven for body warm-up and work with the weights. Ready to make up at eight for an eight-thirty curtain. When we were on the experimental seven-thirty curtain, everything moved up an hour. My only time to play was after the show — that was for me and I was going to keep it that way. I put out so much on-stage, I had to do my own thing when that curtain came down. I've never regretted that choice and have continued it since. That is the extent of my self-indulgence.

I paid a price for my choices — more times than I care to mention I spent evenings alone. Funny how people you know sometimes come to see a show and don't come round afterward, thinking your dressing room is full, that you're busy. On those nights I often was sitting in my room praying that someone would knock on my door.

One night the Duke and Duchess of Windsor came round full of compliments, sent flowers the next day. I couldn't tell him how I'd cried as a little girl when I heard his abdication speech on that ancient Atwater Kent radio. I was still impressed by people — a onetime King of England in my dressing room, complimenting me! Proof positive that being an actress enables you to meet more people from more parts of the world — fascinating people, accomplished people — than any other profession on earth. It made Adlai Stevenson possible in my life. John Kennedy. Robert Kennedy. I still can't get over how lucky I have been to know men like that.

Toward the end of the first summer's run, I had to face the fact of Leslie's leaving the nest. She'd spent her whole life in a French school, and she wanted an American college. I had thought she would choose to go to the Sorbonne or to Italy — what I would have chosen had I been Leslie. But she was her own person — as willful as I — and that was that. She would spend a year in a Boston Art School and feeling that was not her calling would go to Boston University as Steve had done, and see if she could deal with the American way of learning after ten years at the Lycée. She was in search of her identity — logically had to find it away from me. I remembered watching her head for Boston — all eighteen years of her — and knowing she was more than figuratively walking away from me and toward her own life. Our relationship had gotten better and better, closer and closer. I found myself able to confide in her some of my personal frustrations; she listened well, her thinking was true and straight — no nonsense. She was developing into quite a somebody and on her way to being my best friend.

And Jason and I were still not on the best terms. He was unable to deal with Sam as I felt he should — he didn't see him enough, call him enough. He was still struggling with his own life. I wanted him to make it absolutely clear to Sam that we were not going to be one happy family again. That remained Sam's fantasy, and he was having great difficulty separating fantasy from reality. I was worried about him, and his excellent pediatrician suggested that he should see that child psychiatrist. But Sam was too smart to be shoved in any direction, so I had to explain to him that this man was a doctor, and that he could tell the doctor anything he wanted to about anything that bothered him, about anyone, and it would never be repeated. I had to say casually, 'It might help you to feel better. Worth a try.' He agreed to meet the doctor, and after the first meeting agreed to see him once a week, on the basis that if he wanted to stop, he would stop. I accepted his conditions. The sessions helped Sam a great deal — so much so that as summer approached, he said he wanted to stop for a while and go to camp; he'd start again in the fall if he felt the need. The doctor and I agreed — let's see what happens, maybe he can handle his emotions better. Time would be the teller of that tale.

We celebrated our first year of *Applause* with a cake-cutting ceremony in front of cameras on Broadway. A year already, and what a year. I was an emotional wreck, my inability to be casual about my personal relationship with Len had taken its toll. I was very thin — in good physical shape, really, but emotions were taking over more and more often and I was getting a drawn look on my face. There were still high spots, though. One night at intermission there was a knock on my dressing-room door. Elizabeth, my dresser, opened the door and there was Ethel Merman. As I gasped, she charged into the room, saying, 'Where's the can?' Merman the definitive musical-comedy star — in my opinion, the best that ever was. She lifted you right out of your seat, she was that exciting. Out she came, saying, 'You've got to stop doing *this*,' as she hit her chest with her fist. In 'Welcome to the Theatre,' the first-act curtain number, I hit my chest several times and she said that each time my body mike would send a resounding roar through the theatre. No one had mentioned it before. But at the end of the show she did tell me she liked me. I hope she meant it.

The night Joe Mankiewicz came to the show I went to supper with him and his wife. *All About Eve* was his brainchild — he had written and directed the film — and he was totally possessive about it. He was happy to see how much of his work had been kept in our show and liked it better than he had anticipated. A great relief to me. He is a man of no small talent and no small accomplishment, and I wanted his approval.

About a month after the show's anniversary, Len asked me out for supper. It was a Saturday night — well chosen so I would have Sunday to recover. Out we went, happy as could be. When he took me home we had a nightcap and then he dropped his bomb. As gently as he could — as sweetly — he told me he was leaving the show in three weeks. He was going to play in repertory at the Guthrie Theatre in Minneapolis. He felt it was time for him to do something else, and he'd wanted me to hear it from him. I was stunned — it was totally unexpected and I burst into a flood of tears. I had become more emotionally dependent on him than I had realized. I had thought I was handling the situation, but clearly I was not. Another ending. I felt the bottom of my world dropping out — the world of *Applause*, which had become more my world than anything else in my life. There I was on this ferris wheel, dangling in mid-air, with no support beneath me — frightened and beginning to feel sick. We sat in my library until dawn, talking, talking about the year, the work, our involvement with each other. His feelings about me were not to be taken lightly either. Of course I understood the logic of his decision, and, from his point of view as a young actor, the necessity for it. But understanding didn't make me like it. And I would have to stay with the show for another few months. By then I had agreed to go to St Louis to play *Applause* at the Municipal Opera, an outdoor theatre seating twelve thousand people, the week of July 4. How could I play it with another actor? Bill Sampson was Len — there would never be another Bill Sampson for me. That's what separates me from the real lady stars — I don't want to be supported by an actor while I take all the bows and enjoy my vehicle. I don't believe in vehicles. I want to share the stage. That's what theatre is to me — sharing. I love my solo curtain calls — don't misunderstand — but I don't want to be out there all alone, and I never will.

It was traumatic for me — that night, that shock. *Applause* had given Len his first lead in a Broadway show, and we'd grown together in it. Nothing would be quite the same for me. It wasn't just a show, it was a crucial portion of my life. And he had been such a strength to me, on and off the stage. He knew me so well, was aware of my weaknesses. Even after the success of *Applause*, I still had to fight my past life. Whatever people have made me in their heads — both from my movie career and my marriage to Bogie — is an obstacle to now. They want their memories and fantasies kept intact — they're not interested in the person I am. Every man needs his own identity. His ego will not allow him to be thought of as an appendage to an actress. And though I have never lived my private life like that, I have not found a man secure enough in himself — grown up enough, if you will — to take his chances with me because he knows and values me as I am.

Well, there's not a damn thing I can do about my past life. It has been lived — it is past — it has contributed largely to what I am, what might attract a man to me or interest a man in me. But it is not now — not today. I am still fighting for the right to be thought of as I am, the way it is, not as anyone else's image or idea of what I am because of parts I played when I was nineteen. It's been a losing battle so far, it may always be, but I won't give up. Not then — not now — not tomorrow.

I finished my Broadway run in *Applause* sixteen months after it opened. Len had left — there was another Bill Sampson and I dealt with it professionally. Then a month in Europe trying unsuccessfully to reorient my head and lighten my spirits. But how can two years of unrelenting, totally demanding work, plus my mother's death, plus my divorce — how can all that be wiped away in one month? I returned to re-rehearse for a national tour of *Applause,* the emotional highlight of which was playing in Los Angeles. 'At last,' I thought, 'I'll show them — ten years later — that I have talent, that I am good, that they were wrong to sluff me off.' Opening night there was my most nervous night in all those months of playing Margo. It revealed to me once again how much importance I had placed on proving my worth — leaving my mark on that community. What did I expect — that all those who had rejected me would appear as one to beg forgiveness? They couldn't have cared less. My friends — the real ones — came. The others didn't, couldn't be bothered. The theatre was too far away and their minds don't think beyond grosses. What's in the trade papers? Whose footprints in cement? But mine — remember? — aren't there!

I took the show to London for a year, returning for the second time to a city I had slowly learned to love, filled with people I had loved for a long time. But this time I would be on the London stage — not only allowed to breathe the same rarefied air as Olivier, Richardson, Gielgud, Scofield, and so many more, but welcomed by them, by all. They wanted me to love their island. So I embarked on another new beginning in a small, cozy, perfect house — perfect for Sam, Nanny, and me — with a reason to be there.

So I flourished in the land of royalty, gentility, creativity, and friendship. *Applause* opened. Not all the critics loved the show, but they did me, and there's no one who would not respond to that. I felt loved — whether it was the woman they thought I was, who had evolved over twenty years into my Margo Channing, I am not sure. I only knew that the praise for my work was unequivocal and I was not about to ask questions. People came — audiences responded — they let me know they were glad I'd traveled those three thousand miles. I reveled in it. And then I fell in love with a married Englishman. Unexpectedly, but definitely. And after six completely happy months the relationship was brought to a devastating end through circumstance — bad timing — bad luck. For a while I hated England, felt betrayed, blamed the country, not the individuals. Felt trapped. I'd been working nonstop for five years — too hard — too long. Being Margo Channing had been my greatest theatrical gift, and being Margo Channing had taken its toll. Then along came Sidney Lumet with an offer for *Murder on the Orient Express* with a blinding cast of star actors. So one English year was to stretch into two. With that film experience came not only new friendships but the happiest work experience I'd had in my movie life since the beginning. And the raw hurt — the pain of another emotional ending — became somewhat dulled.

Steve and Dale came over for a two-week visit — I bought a beautiful dog, Blenheim, for Sam — and I loved my life in that, for me, enchanted city. The city is clean — the parks are green — everything about the less-pressured English life I loved. Best of all, I had Sidney and Sandra Bernstein and their children for Sam's and my English family, with whom we always felt wanted, needed, and loved.

But in America, Watergate was in full flower. My only news came from limited TV coverage and newspapers. I wanted to know more — every detail. Having always been violently anti-Nixon, I wanted — felt the need — to be in America. I wanted to be certain Nixon would be removed. I wanted to be there to see it. Yet whenever I heard a loose English remark about the languid pace with which Watergate was being dealt, I found myself defending my country. So it was time to go. And there were Steve and Leslie — plus a Bogart grandson I hadn't seen in two years. And Sam's father was in America — Sam should not be deprived of him.

Finally, there was no real reason to stay. My work was over. And I had avoided the competitive world of my birthplace as long as I dared.

I had one place to live that was my own, and that place was the frantic city of New York. So back I came, with endless luggage — crates of possessions to be shipped — Sam — and Blenheim. I didn't know what would greet me on arrival, it was almost like exploring new territory. But there was really no choice. It was time to fight the battle of work in my own country, and to face my own reality, which was not England.

But even after months in New York I was miserable. The culture shock on re-entry was enormous. The soot, the noise, the filth in Central Park, the pushing and shoving. I was happy to see my children and my friends — they were happy to see me — but I could only think of England and wish I'd never left it. And re-entry was hard on Sam as well. His two years away from Collegiate School had left him in a terrible academic hole. The work was harder — he couldn't handle it — he asked to go back to seeing the doctor. I asked him why. He said, 'I think I need help.' So we floundered — disjointed, disoriented, misplaced. No good work was in the offing. I rode on the joy of the *Orient Express* for some time — happily, for it brought England closer to me.

Jason was in *A Moon for the Misbegotten* on Broadway. I took Sam to see it. Jason was brilliant. I was so happy for him. He had learned a terrible lesson along the way. He had stopped drinking, his marriage was good, he had one new daughter and another baby on the way; that would make an even half-dozen. At last we became good friends. Whenever he'd come to get Sam for a weekend, dinner, whatever, Jason and

I would sit and talk about work, about life. He was a good man — a wonderful man — I liked him, even loved him as a friend. He was worth the time, even the pain, invested. So my first instincts about him were right. He dealt wonderfully with Sam, was dependable, could talk over Sam's problems. He understood — he had compassion. He'd always had that. And Sam was happy to see us enjoy each other's company, though he knew it was on another level now. Some rewards come late.

That first summer in New York, with Sam away at camp, I still had no direction, still hated being back, felt isolated. That was when I decided to write this book. I had always loved words, always had more writers as friends than anyone else. I felt I might be able to do it. Maybe this was the time. Maybe it would help me to discover something about myself, to add it all up. What I am — and why. How I got there.

Statistically I fell into the broken-home category — brought up by one parent, my mother. Through pure luck — the luck of face and body, and having them noticed by others at the right time — I was given an opportunity to reach the highest of all highs at the age of nineteen. Howard Hawks invented a personality on screen that suited my look and my sound and some of myself — but the projection of worldliness in sex, total independence, the ability to handle any situation, had no more relation to me then than it has now. With that I was also given a personal life fuller than I had ever dreamed I would have, or, needless to say, have had since. At the age of twenty I had grabbed at the sky and had touched some stars. And who but a twenty-year-old would think you could keep it? When it all went — though the career was more down than up almost immediately — why did I keep going? Why didn't I fall prey to the obvious pitfalls of life — booze, drugs, withdrawal? I would say that being loved unselfishly by two people had a hell of a lot to do with it. My mother gave to me constantly. And her support, her nurturing of me, her constant encouragement, together with the strength of our family and my own character, my ability to laugh at myself — all that is what made it possible for me to deal with Bogie, a man with three marriages in his past and twenty-five years on me.

And Bogie, with his great ability to love, never suppressing me, helping me to keep my values straight in a town where there were few, forcing my standards higher — again the stress on personal character, demonstrating the importance of the quality of life, the proper attitude toward work. To be good was more important than to be rich. To be kind was more important than owning a house or a car. To respect one's work and to do it well, to risk something in life, was more important than being a star. To never sell your soul — to have self-esteem — to be true — was most important of all.

All this was so deeply implanted in me that I couldn't go down the drain. I am the sum of those two people and my beloved Uncle Charlie. Going back through my life until now, the Jewish family feeling stands strong and proud, and at last I can say I am glad I sprang from that. I would not trade those roots — that identity. I have learned that I am a valuable person. I have made mistakes — so many mistakes. And will make more. Big ones. But I pay. They are my own. What was not real in Howard Hawks' version of me is not real now. I remain as vulnerable, romantic, and idealistic as I was at fifteen, sitting in a movie theatre, watching, *being,* Bette Davis.

I'm not ashamed of what I am — of how I pass through this life. What I am has given me the strength to do it. At my lowest ebb I have never contemplated suicide. I value what is here too much. I have a contribution to make. I am not just taking up space in this life. I can add something to the lives I touch. I don't like everything I know about myself, and I'll never be satisfied, but nobody's perfect. I'm not sure where the next years will take me — what they will hold — but I'm open to suggestions.

and Then Some

First and always, to my children, and then to my grandchildren — Bogarts and Robards — next and future generations with abiding love for all

Has it really been twenty-seven years? I can't believe it. Time flies even when you're not having fun. Having come this far — having lasted this long — longer than I expected (I grudgingly have to thank my father's side for the longevity factor) — things of assorted sizes and shapes have happened. Perhaps not as filled with highs as the previous, say, fifty years, but there has been variety — some joy — some sadness inevitably — and lots of laughter. That's because in my cockeyed way I think life is a joke. I write the numbers down — twenty-five — fifty — but the truth is we're only here for a minute. But what a minute!

Upon reaching your seventieth year, life begins to shift. First comes the shock of it — my God, am I really seventy? I don't feel that different. But I sure as hell am. All my life I've just kept on going, never thinking of years, numbers. Going from one job to another. Suddenly — WHAM! The body still functions pretty well — a few bumps in the road along the way — but the body has gotten a bit larger — horrors! When you face that, can the gym be far away? Okay, I accept the fact of regular exercise entering my life. I still remember my twenty-four-inch waist lasting for my first fifty years. Don't torture yourself, I whisper — forget it — throw away the tape measure — maturing has taken over. I've never been a sedentary person anyway, always on the move, only now with supervision. It's trainer time. Although always active — in the theatre you have to be fit — now I have to set aside time, give up at least half a day for gym and physical therapy. Knee problems from *Applause* days — back acting up intermittently — torn rotator cuff in my shoulder (I'll never pitch again) — and on and on — you name it. My body needs attention. Boring, yes. Necessary, yes. I am always singing that song, 'My Body lies over the ocean, my Body lies over the sea. My Body lies over the ocean, oh bring back my Body to me.' Keep the humor going. The need to work remains — movies, theatre, TV — I don't care really. As long as it's good — interesting — new — I love new — it will take me out of myself and into someone else. Always a pleasure.

Work has continued to be paramount in my life. From time to time one of my sons — Steve or Sam — asks me why I don't take it easy, spend more time in Paris or London or anywhere in Italy, places that I love. There seems to be never enough time to do everything you want to do, go everywhere you want to go. My answer is simple. My goal in life has always been to work. I wouldn't know what to do with myself if I had nothing to do but wander. So I continue to search and hope for the next job — in a way I suppose it enables me to think and to look toward the future. To think there is a future.

You know, the early part of one's life — family, hopes, dreams, first love, first job, first child, first everything, actually, and the realization of all that — seems the most interesting for the reader. Accomplishment of one's goals, how you got where you wanted to get, is always fascinating. But I realize now, having moved beyond that point, that there is something to be said about what happens after you've reached your goal — both professionally and personally — if indeed you ever do truly reach it.

My change of focus was taken over twenty-seven years ago by the all-consuming book tour — all over the world wherever *By Myself* was published. I was thrilled to go — I am still thrilled to go — particularly if the cities (countries!) are unexplored territory, meaning my first-time exposure. They were all different — requiring focus and concentration on my part — language adjustment — would you believe me speaking Japanese? — even Australia, Ireland, Scotland — the lilts were different, the rhythms not the same. I had to stop at the end of one country, take a step back and try to absorb the sights and sounds of the next, winding down from the heady experience of success and popularity all over — an experience, by the way, that I had never had before. Especially going solo, leaving myself wide open to questions of intense privacy — friendly and un-, some journalistic chips on shoulders, some embracing, some truly interesting — and some making me feel better than others.

After the final emptying of suitcases, shutting off the intense travel of a book tour — the travel for fun goes on, taking some time to be aimless — something wonderful happened. My friend, playwright Peter Stone, asked if I had ever thought of being in another musical, his idea being *Woman of the Year*. I had not. He wanted to rewrite the movie for me, so one night we went to his house, he set up the projector, fed the film into it — and away we went into the world of Spencer Tracy and Katharine Hepburn — and the world of politics and sports and the conflicts that followed. Peter told me he had mentioned the idea to John Kander and Fred Ebb to do the score — how did I feel about that? Robert Moore possibly to direct — how did I feel about that? Tony Sharmdi to choreograph — again, how did I feel? I felt fantastic about all of that but as we didn't really know one another, we felt a meeting was in order. I really wanted to meet them anyway, particularly Kander and Ebb whose work I had always admired — still do to this day and will forever more. I love those guys. I did, however, find it rather queer that having played the Bette Davis role of Margo Channing in *Applause*, I was now going to tackle the role my great friend Katharine Hepburn had played in *Woman of the Year* — my God! How could I dare take this on! Though *Applause* had been a gigantic success with rave reviews and my first Tony Award, I knew in my heart that the fact — the reality — was that audiences would never think of Margo Channing as anyone but Bette Davis, and the same would be true of Kate in *Woman of the Year*. Because no matter how good the shows were — and they were terrific — no matter how good I was — the film would always be there for future generations. The theatre is live. You see the show — you love it — you never forget it. But future generations will never see it.

In spite of the self-imposed obstacles —

the memory of Kate, for one, and my own lack of confidence — I jumped in hook, line and sinker! I started my old routine — singing lessons, dancing, stretching, learning lines — all months ahead of casting, much less rehearsing. I was thrilled to be working again, thrilled with the people involved and loving the casting process. Being in on it was always exciting — sitting in a darkened theatre, far enough away from the actors auditioning — so as not to be seen yet able to see. Peter, Kander and Ebb were there, Comden and Green — my close, close friends who were writing the book of the show — were there, Bob Moore, our director, was there. All heads together after each audition, deciding the possibles worthy of a callback, the others quickly dismissed. I always felt a pang when an actor was rejected, having had that painful experience too many times myself.

I've always had qualms about sitting in judgment on my fellow actors. I know only too well how difficult and painful auditions can be. No matter how much faith we have in our abilities, the nerves are ever present and the fear of rejection paramount — rejection being the defining feature in the life of an actor. And it never goes away; no matter how many years have been invested in performing, how much accomplished, an actor's life remains tentative. So why do we choose it? Because we have to do it, we were trained to do it and we love doing it. Yet we stay with it after endless disappointments and heart-breaks. Why? Because there is always the hope that the next time will be different. We will make it! Well, sometimes we do — if we have a lot of luck — and more times we don't. I've never been able to figure it out. Am I a masochist? *No.* I just have always wanted it badly enough to hang in there and I never stop hoping. Even now, after all these years, the fears, the testing, the failure never goes away. But when it works — WOW! There's nothing like it. All that other negative stuff falls away — it's more than worth it! And after all, it is that childhood dream and prayer come true.

Once the bug bites you, you are a goner. Even at the end of a long tour when you are counting the days, checking them off on your calendar as I did at the end of the *Woman of the Year* tour. Even then, after a short rest, upon buying a ticket for a new play, sitting in a darkened theatre facing the stage instead of being on it — even then I feel a twinge, a twinge of yearning to be up there again, in the play. Because the stage is the actor's — it belongs to him. Movies don't. Movies belong to the director. No matter how good you are —

no matter how spectacular your performance might be — it is not up to you — the director decides and with his nippers might cut out your favorite scene. He decides. Of course, if he's a good director he wants a good performance from his actors but he is not out to glorify them, he is out to glorify the whole movie. Nothing personal, you understand. Still, it's fun making movies — if they're good, of course they always have to be good — in spite of the endless waiting. It is very much the 'hurry up and wait' syndrome. You hurry up to do your touch-up for the next scene, then you head for the set — ready, an assistant director by your side — and guess what? The camera is not quite ready for one reason or another; often the director is changing the blocking which means readjusting the lights. So the wait is on. But, no matter — with film, you use different parts of yourself and you learn to deal with the waits.

Something new has been added to the daily routine of each day's shoot and I must admit I find it somewhat humiliating. From the moment you arrive on the lot — the car door is usually opened by a waiting second or third assistant director who has a piece of plastic in his ear to which a plastic cord is attached (to be invisible, which it is not) that in turn connects to something he holds in his hand which looks like a telephone but is not — and *it* starts. 'She's here,' he murmurs into the no telephone — and from there on every step along the way is marked — 'we're on our way to her dressing room' — 'hair and make-up are there for her' — like the FBI–CIA reporting my every move. Then 'How long will it take you to get ready? He [the director] may want to rehearse. So start the hair and make-up and we'll let you know when he's ready on set.' It drives me wild. If there is one thing I am sure of it is that I am a professional. I'm there to work and I'm mostly on time. But I hate to feel spied upon. I don't know who dreamed this idea up but whoever it was, was not fond of actors. Mainly it has nothing to do with work — everything to do with schedules — money. It always boils down to money. Sadly.

The Nineties were surprisingly good and productive years for me. My professional life became satisfyingly varied after *A Foreign Field* in 1993. There were four and a half months on the rue du Cherche-Midi in Paris while making Robert Altman's *Prêt à Porter*. Living in Paris was total bliss. Working there made me feel like a resident. The Cherche-Midi is a great street in the

7th arrondissement on the Left Bank, an area I have frequented for years. But to wake up every morning and stop at the Cafe Alexandre for a hot chocolate while waiting for the studio car to pick me up, is one of life's grand pleasures. Paris affects me like no other city in the world. I gasp at the sight of it at night — all lit up — the Eiffel Tower — Place de la Concorde — Arc de Triomphe — Notre Dame — the Sacré Coeur — after rain with the pavement glistening — it is all too breathtaking to even try to describe. I've always had a gut reaction to it, from my first glimpse of the Arc de Triomphe in 1951, that feeling has remained with me, made my heart beat faster each time I enter the city. It is the city of light and unimaginable beauty. It's a funny thing about Paris and indicative of the French way of life as compared to ours but no matter what the weather — rain, shine, killing heat and no air conditioning — no matter what the time — during lunch, pre-dinner, during and after dinner — every bar and bistro is packed with people of all ages talking, smoking, drinking, laughing — sharing their lives. What better way to live? Nothing fancy, everything human. So many years ago I remember my wonderment when Vivien Leigh, my good dear friend, told me she couldn't bear to have a year go by without having been to France. Now I know that feeling all too well.

A couple of years ago I almost went a full year with no Paris. That is major for me. I have decided that I need to be there. It feeds my spirit. Not only the brandy, but because I have many friends there and know the city so well, especially the Left Bank. I feel very comfortable there, that I belong there. Call it escape if you like but it truly isn't. I am attached to Paris, the good, the bad, the beauty. And over the years — the days, weeks, months I've spent in all kinds of weather — the city has never let me down. I have never been disappointed — it has always lived up to my expectations, my remembrance of times past (to steal a phrase). The new illumination of monuments and buildings of the past few years — its artistry and the sense of pride that Parisians take in their city — has surpassed anything I might have imagined. And yet, with my familiarity with the streets and squares of Paris, I am still discovering corners, small cafés, gardens — it still surprises — it still makes my heart beat faster.

In the spring of 1995, I had just arrived in Paris — was sitting snugly in my bed looking forward to two weeks in my favorite city when my agent called. A script was on its way — *From the Mixed Up Files of Mrs. Basil E. Frankweiler* — a movie for television — to start shooting in two days. I had to answer immediately, say 'yes' or they had to get somebody else. Typical. Nothing convenient about my profession. So I read the script and liked it. My son Sam mentioned that *From the Mixed Up Files of Mrs. Basil E. Frankweiler* happened to be his favorite book in his younger years. I said 'yes' and started repacking my unpacked clothes and headed for Los Angeles. They *had* to turn in the product by a certain date and all was in readiness — that's the nature of the business. My late friend John Schlesinger described Hollywood as being 'a temporary place, buildings disappear like fortunes and reputations, the instant dispensability of all of us working in movies. Underneath the facade of promises is all the frustration. At the studio, people dress to prepare for fantasy but they are treated like commodities.' That was a profound and ultimately sad analysis of the movie business to a large degree. John was a brilliant director — deeply intelligent, sensitive and interesting — another witty and loyal friend.

The fun of the film for me was the unfolding discovery of the story. I had never heard of it before yet it was familiar to most elementary school children. In the television production, the two young actors were particularly good. Child actors are often difficult to work with for many reasons — usually parents who hover over them during work hours — coach them — push them. There are few parents who handle their children's careers as Shirley Temple's mother did. Somehow, while being the biggest star in the Hollywood firmament from the age of four or five to her entering the awkward ages and pulling away a bit, Shirley managed to have a sane, private, totally un-Hollywood childhood. I have worked with child actors on several occasions. Studying the parents' behavior on set taught me a thing or two in my scenes in this movie. Some of the kiddies are very spoiled — not their fault — but not the 'Frankweiler' children. Despite the fact that, practically on arrival in L.A., I was standing in the shower at four o'clock in the morning washing my hair — heading for my first day of shooting — it turned out to be fun. A happy experience with the Sam connection very much in the foreground of my sense it would be a plus for many a child. And something for the grandchildren to enjoy.

Paris would come again at a later date. After L.A., I headed to New York — home — an almost impossibility for me. I wanted the theatre, to be on stage, but in what? Where was the play? Imagine my delight when my old friend, Duncan Weldon, called to invite me to Chichester on the south coast of England for the 1995 summer festival. He suggested *The Visit*, a Frederic Durenmatt play that I had seen many moons ago with the great Alfred Lunt and Lynn Fontanne. They made even the most feeble play look like a masterpiece. *The Visit* is far from feeble, but it is a very difficult piece that many an actor does not like. Not because it's challenging but because it is dark, diabolical, interesting though slightly depressing. However, I jumped in with both feet. It sadly turned out not to be my favorite experience onstage.

Bogie had introduced me to the Lunts on a trip to London in the early Fifties. I was in awe of them in every play I saw them in — they were true theatre magic. Because of my unreal memory of the Lunts' brilliance, it was my fantasy to have Paul Scofield (the number one actor of his generation, and perhaps all those that followed) play the Alfred Lunt part. He graciously declined, saying he never liked the play. That slowed me down a bit. One of my many faults — and a major one — is to read into a play qualities that perhaps are not there once I've said 'yes' to it. I tend to trust the wrong people at times and my instinct goes awry.

Being in completely new theatrical surroundings, though I'm quick at adjusting, I still had to learn how to work physically on a thrust stage. Most stages are elevated from the audience with a curtain separating them, thereby keeping the actors in a play in their own special world. A thrust stage has no such curtain, rather it juts out into the audience creating a sense of immediate contact with the actors and the play. In the case of Chichester, the space was large with many seats, which generally works well with that size audience. Having seen many Chichester productions, I think I only had the sense of it being real, wonderful theatre. I also think in some ways, as it was so new to me, I was in awe of the past — the British actors I admired more than many American actors. I had had the privilege of seeing the classics, like Shakespeare, all acted by Olivier, Richardson, Gielgud, Guinness, Scofield. And I could never live up to them or the women — Vivien Leigh, Maggie Smith, Joan Plowright, Edith Evans. Jumping over these hurdles — not necessarily clearing them — I struggled.

The cast was good, all experienced in the thrust venue, the director too. We did not communicate well, unhappily. I think he thought of me too much as a movie star, so did not direct me to a large degree. I, in turn, was a fish out of water. I became quite frustrated and did not know who to go to for help. The director is so much the key to an actor's performance for guidance, the giving of confidence, the support. When that fails, I withdraw, playing it safe. That's never a good thing to do, neither for a performance nor for emotions. Finally my performance was, I think, quite uneven. Good in some scenes, not so in others. Once committed to a project, though, you're stuck, aren't you? The result, unfortunately, was that the fun (and even in a grim play such as *The Visit*, there can be moments of fun) wasn't really there. Thank heaven for Johan Engels, a brilliant top-rated costume and scenic designer of world operas and ballets as well as theatre. He became my friend and my tower of strength.

My spirits did not soar, which was my first and only experience with that. Usually there is some saving grace in the theatre — usually the theatre itself. Just being part of it is enough. With a shaky self-confidence, it was uphill for me for a good part of the run. It's experiences like this one that make me wish I am as tough as I'm sometimes thought to be. The company was fun. Though I never really got very close to them, there was a sense of general camaraderie. I almost always have had a positive feeling among the actors in all the plays I have been in. This was no exception. It was different, but it doesn't take away from the work that we all did to play the play and give the audience its money's worth. Looking back, the rough edges have worn down to some degree and though not a professional landmark for me, it was still the theatre, part of a well-known festival in England where I love to live and to work. The final judgment is I am glad I did it. I learned a thing or two and I was out there, not necessarily functioning at my best, but definitely functioning — I was out there. I was working.

The perks were that Harold Pinter was appearing in another theatre at the Festival at almost the same time so I could spend some time with him and his wife, Antonia Fraser, two people I became very attached to in 1985 during our *Sweet Bird of Youth* months together. *Sweet Bird of Youth* was a great high for me — first because I was able to speak the words of Tennessee Williams — a great poet and playwright — and because I was directed by Harold Pinter — another great playwright. Harold, being an actor — a good one — himself, was a marvelous director — great and articulate with actors. We hit it off immediately. The entire experience, from our six weeks out of town — in England, that meant Bath, Brighton, Plymouth — all new theatres to me, all enthusiastic audiences — to ending up in London at the Royal Haymarket Theatre inhabiting the dressing room of Gielgud, Olivier, Ralph Richardson, Alec Guinness — all theatre greats — very exciting for me. The play was well received, as was the company. We had a sold-out run of more than six months in England and then went on, this time with an Australian cast, to play four and a half months in that country. Though it was a difficult role, unlike any I'd had before, it was bliss from beginning to end. It was the beginning of a lifelong friendship between Harold and Antonia and myself and I am more than grateful for that. Happy times then and ever since.

On returning to New York, my career took an unexpected turn. Barbra Streisand was going to direct and star in a movie called *The Mirror Has Two Faces*. I was called to go to her apartment and read a scene with her, playing her mother. You see that for actors auditions never cease. You still never make it. No matter what you call it, I was still being tested, judged. And the time had come — face it — you are a character actress, which actually I always had been anyway, not a leading lady. Well, if I could have more parts as good as the one in *The Mirror Has Two Faces*, it was fine with me. I was very excited at the prospect of working with Barbra and being directed by her — my first time to be directed by a woman. I had known Barbra since her Funny Girl opening night when she took my breath away with her singing, acting, funny, touching magical self. So I went to her apartment on the appointed day at the appointed hour, as nervous as when at seventeen I had had my first audition.

It was to be my first visit to her private home and I had no idea what to expect. As Barbra is a perfectionist, I knew it would be filled with lovely things — fairly uncluttered and very neat. It was all of that, mostly English furniture, much white upholstery. One thing I did notice was her affection for dolls and doll china — mostly antique and expensive. She herself was dressed in white, all comfortable, at home kind of clothing — pants, scarves hanging loosely. She took me around the apartment, all attractively done, all Barbra's taste and a bit more formal than I anticipated. After the tour, during which I watched myself carefully — when would we get to talk about the movie? — how many actresses was she considering? — finally she said, 'Let's go into the library and read a couple of scenes.' She said she just

891

wanted a sense of how our voices balanced with each other. I have never been at my best during a reading. She may not have thought of it as an audition — I, however, did. So, we read and I hadn't a clue how it sounded. I only knew, coming back into the living room, I was not in a social mode. I was talking to a director and a producer. I was in a business mode.

I knew auditions were not me at my best. Some actors thrive on them. I do not. Barbra asked me to wait a few minutes while she met with her partner and producer, Cis Corman. I was a nervous wreck, of course. I was finally called back to the living room. I'll never forget the setting. Barbra and Cis were seated on a small sofa, Barbra pointing out some of her beautiful and valuable antiques. She said, 'You were very good. We'll be in touch.' It was time for me to leave. I said something on leaving, 'Thank you. Good to see you again.' As I headed for the door, Barbra said, 'So, you think you could play my mother?' I replied, 'Yes, I can play your mother.' (Though come to think of it, I would have had to be a teenage mother to qualify.) And out the door I went, able to take my first big breath in the elevators taking me to the lobby and air. Did I think I was too young to be her mother? Or did she think I was too young to be her mother? Had I read the scene as an older woman? These questions are perfect ways to torture yourself. I found myself shaking and wondering yet again why, at this point in my life, with my years of acting successfully in movies and the theatre, why was I still so low on self-confidence? Childhood anxieties, childhood fears never disappear entirely. They fade, but not away.

After a week or so of biting my nails, bugging my agent, I finally got the word. I had got the part. What a joyous moment that was. I was truly happy, thrilled at the prospect. A really good part, a funny character, the best I'd had in years. I had seen movies that Barbra had directed and knew how good she was. The movie was to be shot in New York, which was ideal for me as I could be at home and sleep in my own bed. Jeff Bridges was the leading man in the movie, my first time working with him — a really wonderful actor and lovely guy. Everyone in *Mirror* was hand chosen by Barbra, as the custom is with directors. It was a good company.

When we started shooting, I saw firsthand how Barbra functioned. It was very odd for us at the beginning because she would be directing the scene behind the camera, then come around in front of the camera and act in the scene. How she did it, I'll never know, but she did and she does and she can. She is meticulous in her direction — both visually and in the playing of the scenes. Every detail is as important to her as the words. I remember her telling me that she woke up at four o'clock in the morning and sketched exactly what the cape I wore should look like. Then she couldn't go back to sleep.

She is so concentrated that many days were many hours long. She had the drive that a good director needs, she knew what she wanted in a scene and she wouldn't quit until she got it. Many days we worked fourteen and sixteen hours — fatigue entered the picture from time to time, but never took over. Barbra was so focused, so concentrated, she lost track of time. She controlled every aspect of the film — wardrobe — colors — every detail. Yet no matter how many hours she had worked the day before, she was on set early every morning. Amazing stamina. I marveled at her ability and though I had some frustrating moments, it was my feeling that it was her movie and she was entitled to every bit of it being the way she wanted it.

Her attention to detail was sometimes frustrating but, again, it was her movie, it's her way, she's the boss. As I've said, movies are a director's medium, not an actor's. We got along well. She is not a schmoozer on set. All professional. I like that — I am a professional. Between takes, I tend to loosen up with a laugh or two. Between takes, Barbra's thinking of what shot comes after and what came before, how many shots she needs for each scene. And, with all of that, she takes her time when her close-ups are shot. She knows every light, where it should be and what it should do. I've never been able to know all that. I've left it to the cameraman and to the director, often to my detriment. Her best side is her left side. That happens to be my best side as well. Guess who won? Those are the breaks. Without her, there would have been no movie and that's a fact.

Barbra is many faceted. To take on the job of directing a movie is not an easy task. It takes full commitment, total concentration, the willingness to have no other life until the movie is completed. Barbra enjoys all that and does it. I admire all of the above and I respect her choices even when I don't agree with them. I love her talent, God-given and amazing. I love her looks and she makes me laugh. I recognize her frailties and the self-involvement which has enabled her to have the incredible career she has had. I have heard the gossip about her, mostly negative, mostly untrue. She's been called difficult, tough, etc. So have I. All she wants is for whatever she is working on to be better than it is on the page. My sentiments exactly. What you hear normally comes from people who don't know her, plus that old time emotion — jealousy! Barbra has a good heart and is very, very smart. In other words, I think she's terrific. She impresses me and I'm filled with admiration and affection for her. Long may she wave! Finally we went a few weeks over schedule. And, finally, we were finished.

I was very happy with my character in *The Mirror Has Two Faces*, had some truly funny lines, some really good scenes. I felt good about my work. Barbra was satisfied and so was the studio. They kept talking about my being nominated for an Academy Award. As I'd never been nominated, much less received any acting award in all my years of work in motion pictures, I put no stock in the talk. There are some actresses who are always nominated and some who always win. I have never been in either category. So, imagine my shock when I was nominated for the Screen Actors Guild Award, the Golden Globe, the Broadcasters' Award and the Academy Award for Supporting Actress. I couldn't believe it, but I still had no illusions about winning.

Award season in Hollywood gets crazy — all P.R. people working overtime, taking ads in all the trades, pushing, pushing — it's nerve-racking and much too competitive. The heat was on and I was in the middle of it. I had no — nor have ever had — a concentrated P.R. team working for me. I tried it once for a short time and found it uncomfortable. Also one must attend every event, every lunch, one must talk to the press endlessly and answer idiotic questions like, 'How does it feel to be nominated?' 'Where were you when you heard the news?' 'How did you like working with and being directed by Barbra Streisand?' and on and on, getting sillier and sillier. The word was that I was the favorite to win all four. All my friends were convinced I was a shoo-in. I did win the SAG Award and the Golden Globe Award and the Broadcasters' Award. It was an exciting time. I was getting more and more jittery. I had to accept these awards and say a few words — that always makes me nervous. Except for various Lifetime Achievement awards, which I found very flattering and nerve-racking in their way, and my two Tony Awards in the theatre, it was new territory for me — and the movie scene was different. After all, I began my career on the screen. But the Academy Awards were much more public, with much more stress attached to them. Also, it was the year of *The English Patient*, a Miramax release, and Harvey Weinstein was known for being a master at pushing his movies.

There was a dinner the night before the awards. I attended, of course, with all of my children and in-laws. Steve and his wife Barbara had flown to California for the big event, Sam and his wife Sidsel, and Leslie and her husband Erich Schiffman, they were all my escorts. Kevin Spacey sat with us for the dinner. He was sure that I would win. My old crush and special friend Kirk Douglas and his wife Anne were there. Kirk delivered a most flattering and sweet toast to me. They all said I was a shoo-in. I said, 'Beware of shoo-ins. They often are the losers.' But they would have none of it. 'You deserve it — it's about time.' All those words were repeated by many. 'You can't lose.' My New York friends, city and country, gathered, also certain I would win.

The following day, you have to start getting ready for the Big Event at three o'clock in the afternoon. You must be headed downtown by around five to do the red carpet walk before entering the Shrine auditorium. My children arrived in my suite at the Bel Air Hotel along with my then agent, now manager, Johnnie Planco, and into the car we proceeded. It was hot — would my hair hold up? Make-up? They were all excited, sure we would be celebrating at the after Oscar party. On arrival, disembarking from the car, the long walk down the red carpet began. First my old friend Army Archerd, also sure I would win. He is always first with microphone and camera at the ready. He and I started in Hollywood at roughly the same time. All the while, and from the time you step out of your car, there are batteries of cameras from all over the world and hundreds of screaming fans. Your face cracks from smiling — waving. Every time another famous actor — star — appears, the roar goes up and you can hardly hear the questions being asked of you. Some of the interviewers are very busy while talking to you — looking past you to see who's coming up behind. If it's a big, huge star, you have the feeling you are being dismissed. Their attention span is not very long. The whole experience is torture and it is an endless day.

Being the front-runner in their eyes, I was stopped and had to speak to each member of the press — same questions, 'How does it feel?' 'How did you hear about the nomination?' etc., etc., and so forth. By this time, I was totally stressed, beyond nervous. We were finally led to our seats — all seven of us in a row — me on the outside — Steve sitting next to me holding my hand. The evening began with Master of Ceremonies Billy Crystal. I did my best — trying to look relaxed as though I was enjoying myself. I doubt that I was very convincing. The truth is, I wanted to win. No matter how you try to rationalize it, to be nominated is fine — chosen by your peers, etc. — but it's better to win. In any contest, that is the goal.

The first award — wouldn't you know — Best Supporting Actress. Kevin Spacey came out with the envelope in his hand, announced the nominees, looked at me and smiled, opened the envelope — 'And the winner is . . .' He was so sure — my heart was pounding so loud, I thought I would faint, Steve was squeezing my hand — his voice dropped. 'The winner is Juliette Binoche, *The English Patient.*' It was *The English Patient* down the line. Harvey Weinstein had done it again. I felt so badly for my children. They were so upset for me. Steve turned white. He couldn't believe it. Sam and Leslie were stunned.

We got through the rest of the program and headed for the great dinner — chocolate Oscars at every place. I felt very alone. No matter how you slice it, this was a ball for winners. Kevin Spacey was there. He came over and invited me on to the dance floor, thank heaven. It's not a good thing to be a shoo-in.

I did, however, receive a Cesar, the French equivalent of our Oscar, a beautiful sculpture by Cesar himself, the famous, ubiquitous and much loved French sculptor. It is large — in brass — easily identifiable as his creation. It is visible to me in my apartment and always gives me a lift at the memory of that occasion. It was not only in the same year as the Oscars, but also the second honor bestowed on me by the French. The first had been presented two years before — Commandeur des Arts et Lettres.

The Commandeur is a truly distinguished honor given by the Minister of Culture, Jacques Toubon. At the same ceremony, Dustin Hoffman was made Officer — the only time in my life or career I would be one notch above Dustin! The medal is on a blue and white ribbon — so lovely — and there is a tiny blue and white rosette to keep in your buttonhole. Dustin had found a poem by Francois Villon that he dedicated to me. I was so touched, it is one of the greatest perks in my life to know Dustin Hoffman, not well, but to have spent enough time together over the years to feel great affection for him. I have never worked with him and, though I'd love to, I guess I never will. But I really enjoy his company and am always happy to see him.

The Cesar was presented to me by Alain Delon. I accepted in French — speaking quite well, though nervously. The audience cheered me and I felt good, though I am never comfortable with that kind of reception. There was plenty of press but I do not recall a red carpet.

It's a funny thing about a red carpet, it has a place and life of its own. There is one at each of the award events in California — SAG, Golden Globe, etc. It is of varying length depending on the venue. Thinking of the many years I have walked that walk, I realize the more I walk it, the larger my hips — until one day they will pass the width of the carpet which tends to narrow anyway with the budget — and incidentally was quite short and turned to pink at the last Tribeca Film Festival. Yikes! What has happened to my world? Can we never preserve those special traditions?! It's the economy, stupid. I guess.

So the nomination came and went and I survived. Then, one day, later that year, I was opening my mail. I get an enormous amount of junk mail — announcements of openings — people from all over wanting time or donations. I don't expect too much when I'm opening the mail so I do it, letter opener in hand, quickly. I have been known on rare occasions to toss an envelope out leaving the letter in. Anyway, this morning I was about done with that day's offering — a few more envelopes left. Slit went the opener, out came the inside, I opened it to the following:

August 27, 1997
Dear Ms. Bacall:
This December we will celebrate the 20th annual Kennedy Center Honors.
On behalf of the Kennedy Center Trustees and our national Artists Committee, I am writing to invite you to receive the Kennedy Center Honors in recognition of your extraordinary contributions to the life of our country. The Honors are presented annually to individuals who have enriched American life by distinguished achievement in the performing arts. The primary criterion is excellence.

The letter continued with details of the weekend's events — December 6th and 7th. They requested confidentiality until George Stevens, Jr announced the honorees. The letter was signed, 'Jim Johnson, Chairman of the Kennedy Center for the Performing Arts.'
It took a while for the shock to wear off. I could not believe it. As for the flattery,

never in my wildest dreams could I ever envision such accolades being applied to me. It didn't sink in. I checked the envelope — Kennedy Center Washington — I reread the note. I still couldn't believe it. My God — that was completely unexpected. But so thrilling. I needed someone badly at that moment to share this with. My first three calls were of course to my children. My pal, Jean Kennedy Smith, who had known but had never said a word to me, was very happy when I called her. Now that was a very happy moment and a real surprise. And on the night you don't have to do a thing. Just sit there and be praised.

The state dinner on Saturday night is great fun. There is one person who delivers a toast for each honoree. My toastmaster was the wonderful Peter Stone, playwright and close friend of many years. He shone brightly that night. It was a marvelous weekend: a White House reception, a presentation of the medal by the President. It doesn't matter what side of the political spectrum you are on, entering the White House, seeing the portraits of the Presidents on the walls, climbing the staircase, the U.S. Marine Band Combo playing, meeting Senators you don't like much politically and finding them rather likeable — it's an absolutely unpolitical weekend —

and it is somewhat awe-making and truly exciting. And nervous-making.

Bob Dylan was also a nominee. He does not like crowds — feels very uneasy in the midst of ceremonies like this one. We had met in Sydney in 1986 when I was playing in *Sweet Bird of Youth* and he was giving a few concerts. He gave me tickets to his event and I gave him tickets for mine. I was totally thrilled to meet him, and Colin Friels, who was the leading man in *Sweet Bird*, was beyond excited. To attend a concert, much less sit with Dylan after a concert, was something he had only dreamed of — that, of course, made it even more fun for me. Dylan and I got along very well — supped after our shows and had fun. Apart from once at another of his concerts, we hadn't seen one another since that time. Of course I loved seeing him under these circumstances. I hugged him, introduced him to my children — all totally thrilled to meet him. And why not? It was a weekend to remember.

The Kennedy Center Honors must rank as the highest that it is possible to receive in the arts in the United States. The thrill for me was to be in the company of Bob Dylan, Edward Villela and Jessye Norman and, on the night of the gala itself, to be on the stage of the Kennedy Center Opera House, to see once more the incredible contribution each has made over a period of years and to share the honor with the Kennedy family who were present — Senator Edward Kennedy, who never fails to demonstrate his friendship for me on every special occasion in my professional life, my pal Jean Kennedy Smith, Eunice K, Sarge Shriver and Pat Lawford — I'm crazy about them all. They are all unique personalities and after friendships that began almost fifty years ago, our affection for one another remains the same whether we live in the same city or not, see each other very often or not. My face still lights up at the sight of them.

So with enormous gratitude, the work continued. I learned a few things during that year of 1996–1997 — that just like when I began in the theatre at age seventeen, it all was important to me, I needed to accomplish my goal, I needed to prove to myself that I was an actress, a good one. And I wanted the approval of my peers. The vulnerability of my being had never left me and clearly never would. As long as I continued to work and get better, good parts with good people would come my way again. I have taken some chances — acted in a French movie speaking French, no less. That was something — talk about nerves!

The French movie was titled *Le Jour et la Nuit* (Day and Night). Written and directed by Bernard Henri-Levy — a brilliant and highly respected writer, journalist, philosopher — everything. This was to be his first full-length feature film. He came to New York to convince me to be in it. I said that I could speak French well enough to get along socially but to act in France with Alain Delon, Bernard's wife, the lovely, lovely Arielle Dombasle, and others was quite a different thing. It would terrify me. I have spent enough time with my French friends to know that when they converse with one another the words flow so quickly that I am lost. So acting in French — I would miss all the nuances.

On the other hand, I'd always wanted to be in a French film, being such a Francophile. And to work in Paris — heaven. In addition, Bernard Henri-Levy convinced me he would have a coach who would help me with the dialogue, the scenes etc., and he himself would make sure I understood the scene before we shot it. He was very persuasive. So I said, 'Yes.' And guess what? The wardrobe was done in Paris — the movie was shot in Mexico. So not only did I have a problem acting French but also communicating in Spanish. A nightmare. The crew was adorable, though. I remembered the Mexican crew in *Treasure of the Sierra Madre* where Bogie and I spent eight weeks. They are the sweetest people on earth — smiling — happy — but not speedy. Alain, Arielle and the rest of the cast were charming. We each would have villas in Gueravaca and suites in Ziwataneyhu by the sea. Bernard Henri-Levy and his team were excellent but with its being B.H.L.'s first foray into the movie world, he didn't have as much time as he expected to focus on my French. We got through it miraculously. It was not the best nor far from the worst movie ever made. Again, it was the people, the experiences, but the glaring reality is that when it comes to acting, I'd better stick to English!

Having lived alone for more than twenty years, I think one of the more interesting parts of my life is the luck I have had in having a great collection of friends of all ages. It is the glorious parade of the variety of friendships made both here and in Europe that keeps me going. It is people who change you, who fill and enrich your life. I will do almost anything to keep a friendship alive and well. As of now my friendships of anywhere from twenty to fifty years ago are moving along quite well. There's an occasional slip or two but nothing major, and these last few years I have happily and luckily made a few new ones of the younger persuasion. I am counting on the combination doing me for as long as I am breathing.

As friendship has been the mainstay of my life — next to my children — the single most important factor in my own sense of well being, the loss of friends, particularly close friends, has been shattering. The most unexpected, heart-stopping loss was Roddy McDowall in 1998.

Roddy had the greatest gift for friendship of anyone I have ever known. He paid attention — more than attention — to his hundreds of friends he had made worldwide. And we each felt that we were the closest, and in a way I suppose we each were. Not a week went by when there wasn't some word either by phone, fax, postcard if traveling — or actual sight of, face to face. He was extraordinary. He forgot no one. He would call to see if I was headed to California, or heard that I was and then we'd make our dinner dates. Of course we'd speak before and meet before, one on one, but this dinner date had to be locked in. He wasn't a Virgo for nothing. He was the most organized man I've ever known, with filing systems for his extensive movie collection from silent days on, and keeping track of where we all were and what we were doing, plus his work as an actor (a fine one) in theatre, film, TV, book reading. Not a stone left unturned. And all the while laughter. He had so much to give and he gave it all.

Our friendship took hold when I moved back to New York in 1959. He was living here then — he in *Camelot* with Richard Burton and I in *Goodbye Charlie* with Sydney Chaplin. We shared many friends but mostly we shared our lives as actors, as singles living alone — on the constant search, in his words, 'of gainful employment.' When he moved to California the connection remained the same. He was someone I looked forward to — loved seeing — loved hearing from. He was always there when I was on Broadway and/or touring in a play, filling me with praise, telling all who would listen that they HAD to see me in this or that.

Then there were the dinners — ah, those dinners. The cast was always good, usually numbering twelve or more with place cards, silver candlesticks, votives, the dining room always alight with conversation and laughter. Food would arrive somehow — plates filled with meat and vegetables. He had one friend who purported to be a cook or wanted to be one. He never made it. But of course one always said how delicious the dinner was. Having gone to all that time and trouble, it was unthinkable that a negative word be said to Roddy. Anyway, an evening at Roddy's was not about food. I don't know who planned the menus but it wouldn't have changed anything. The meal was always food well bought — often overcooked — still edible — not an inch of space on the plate that was not covered. But we joked and laughed anyway and loved being there and with him.

Ringing his doorbell before entering his house for the usual unexpected but always interesting dinner group. The front door opening slowly with that sweet, mischievous face peering out to see who it was. Upon identifying — opening the door wide — accompanied by a giggle — 'Bagel' — his favorite name for me. Then ushering me into the living room where there, sitting around the coffee table, facing the roaring fire, would be Robert Wagner and Jill St John, the Axelrods, my first meeting with Emma Thompson and Kenneth Branagh, David Hockney — very, very special, Roddy always proud of his friends, of having brought people together. People who might otherwise not have met.

Another night Bette Davis came. That was a major event for me. I never really got to know her at Warner Bros. But I clearly remember the night at Roddy's: off in a corner of the living room, Bette holding forth about studio days with an aside to me — 'You remember what it was like.' Her first acknowledgement of me and my presence there. She having always been my major idol on the silver screen, me having grown up with her, adoring her, but never having a real relationship with her as I did with Katharine Hepburn.

Two more totally different women you will never find. Bette Davis's cool, unreachable self. Kate's direct but, though independent, warm, emotional self. It all boiled down to Roddy who admired so many, loved so many, was loyal to all. Though close to quite a few of us — closest of all to Sybil Burton Christopher, Kate Burton and Amy Christopher, and Elizabeth Taylor, of course. I just saw *The White Cliffs of Dover* on Turner Classic Movies the other night. Elizabeth and he had been friends since childhood working together at MGM — so amazing — with friendship growing into adulthood, only ending with Roddy's illness and death.

Loyalty was a supreme part of Roddy's character. Every meeting was a celebration. We'd all sit around the living room fireplace from the moment of entry into his house, with sofas and chairs and stools gathered around a coffee table that looked like a wagon wheel on which rested containers of M&Ms, assorted nuts, chocolates, all goodies. It was there we had our before-dinner, and sometimes after-dinner, drinks and coffee. After all that, if it wasn't too late, Roddy would run a movie, preferably an old one. All in all it was a special evening, special because Roddy made it so.

Our last date came five or six weeks before he died. It was going to be dinner, first at home, then in a restaurant (how unlike Roddy) then he rang me again to tell me his back was acting up — it had been a problem for him, starting years before when he was playing in *A Christmas Carol* and had to lift 'Tiny Tim' (who was not so tiny.) We finally decided on lunch at the Bel Air Hotel where I was staying and he preferred. He had been to the doctor, had some painkillers.

When I met him for lunch, he was walking with a cane, something he had not done before. He did not know what else could have put such a strain on his back. Anyway, we had our lunch. Roddy had to leave after a rather short meal because he was unable to sit for too long. I walked him to his red convertible car, gave him a big hug, many kisses and off he went. It never occurred to me it might be something serious. I called him before I left town to see how he was and his response to his medication. Always the same answer, 'Better. I'm fine.' I took him at his word.

After I'd been home for a couple of

weeks, he called, asked if I was planning to come to Los Angeles. He'd heard I was. I knew then that something was very wrong. I'd been in touch with my dear friend Joan Axelrod, who kept me informed. I had been planning to come out again for work reasons but realizing that Roddy, dear Roddy, was seriously ill, I decided to come sooner. I wanted to spend some quality or half-quality time with him, whatever he could give. Though he, God knows, had a multitude of close friends out there, I felt very isolated being in New York. Meantime one of his most cherished friends, and one of mine, as well, Sybil Christopher, went out to be with Roddy on a daily basis. Sybil and I became friends in 1951 on my first trip to England. She was Sybil Burton then — married to Richard. She was an instant plus in my life and remains so to this day. And she was major in Roddy's — she was probably the closest of all and dedicated to him. She would be with him — look after him — keep his spirits up. She loved him — they loved each other.

I had to see him. So I called him again to say I was on my way whereupon his assistant called to say he wanted to have a quiet dinner on the Saturday night after my arrival. Just Roddy, Elizabeth Taylor — his childhood friend — and me. Of course, no question, I'll be there. I couldn't believe that even with his illness he could still plan an evening. Nor had it ever occurred to me that, weeks before, when Roddy was told he was terminally ill, he had begun to make his lists.

He had hired (I think) a young acquaintance to help him get his affairs in order. And Roddy started to list which of his friends he wanted to leave what to. He was, as always, meticulous and specific. For example, he had a large collection of Hermès scarves. He put each one in an envelope and wrote our names on the outside — upper lefthand corners. So when we received the envelope there was no question that it was Roddy's choice for each of us and treasured as such. How many hundreds he had, I do not know, but for a man who had limited time left, that alone took up much of it. In addition, there was the dispersal of the rest of his worldly goods of which there was a plethora. He dealt with it all, one by one, in order of his priorities. That was Roddy. There was nobody like him.

When I arrived in Los Angeles, I received a phone call telling me the dinner was cancelled. Roddy wasn't up to it. I spoke to Sybil who told me to get over to Roddy's as soon as possible. She said she thought Elizabeth would be coming the fol-

lowing day. I quickly called Elizabeth —
asked her assistant if they could pick me
up at the hotel so that we could go together. Absolutely — it was arranged and
that's the way we went, both nervous at
what we might find and sad beyond words.

The following day Elizabeth and I, with
her assistant at the wheel, headed for
Roddy's house in the Valley. It was the beginning of the saddest of sad days. Entering the house was traumatic. No Roddy
to greet us. No lights on in the living
room. The house was dark — the only life
left in that house full of laughter and
friendship was Roddy upstairs in his room
gradually slipping away. The front door
was opened by his assistant who told us to
wait while he told Sybil we had arrived.
Elizabeth sat in a chair in the lifeless living
room filled with apprehensions at the prospect of meeting Sybil for the first time.
'She must hate me. I know she does.' I
said, 'Don't worry, Sybil will make it all
possible. This is about Roddy, nothing
else.' I went out to the entrance hall and
saw Sybil coming down the stairs. I told
her Liz was in the living room — very nervous. As I stood behind Sybil, I saw her
enter the living room, look at Elizabeth
with outstretched arms welcoming her to
the house. They gave each other a great,
big hug with their mutual love of Roddy

being their bond. After the years of pain sustained by Sybil, it was more than re-markable that she was able to do that. You see, the welcome was not about Elizabeth, it was about Roddy — a recognition of the importance to him of that bond between them, of their years as child actors, growing up together and sharing all of both their lives' happy and unhappy times. And, most importantly, it was about Roddy's dying. It was about each of us saying our goodbyes to a friend who meant so much to us. So one by one we went upstairs and had our private time with Roddy. There he was in his bed with his beloved opera music (Puccini, I think) sounding loud and clear. I went over and hugged him. We kissed each other and I sat by the bed holding his hand. He clearly had been given some drug to lessen the pain so he smiled at me. I told him how much I loved him, listened to the music with him — the glorious voice of Renata Tebaldi (who he adored). It was the music that transported him to a happy place. I had so many pic-tures in my mind that began in the days before *Camelot* in which he appeared with Richard Burton and during which his friendship with Sybil came to fruition. So many great evenings in his apartment on Central Park West over forty years ago. Suddenly Elizabeth came into the room. I was brought out of my reverie and I leaned over and kissed Roddy once more on his cheeks and on the hand that had been on mine. That was the last time that I saw that extraordinary man, friend, talent.

The following day he was gone and with him went that part of me that was connected only to him — his wit — his warmth — his total commitment to his friends — his loving generosity, never asking for himself. He was a truly unusual man whose life ended much too soon. We were Virgos together, we shared our aloneness together. For me, it was the first loss of one of my contemporaries. It was the beginning of my awareness of my own mortality and also of the gaping hole that was left with Roddy's leaving. It all happened so quickly — like a blink. There was no way to be prepared. He was young, too young. Always the good guys die young — the bad guys seem to go on forever. And it also brought home to me the luck I had in having such a friend and how careful I must be with those who are left that I value so highly.

I had worked with Kirk Douglas in the Fifties in *Young Man With a Horn* — he who had been my great infatuation at age sixteen while at the American Academy of Dramatic Arts together. Now, in 1998, I had an opportunity to work once more with this remarkable actor — who had become my friend over the last twenty years — in a movie called *Diamonds*. How lucky a woman am I! He has had some bad collisions with health but he has risen above it all. The movie we made together was his first after his stroke. He was amazing. To have always been this macho man — a wonderful actor — in control — then to have risen above his challenges in such an open, super-charged way — has been more than admirable. He continues, giving more of himself than ever before, learning more, accomplishing more. It was a marvellous and enlightening experience for me to work with him and get to know him again and his equally amazing wife.

After *Diamonds*, there were a couple of movies that did not set the world on fire. The people were wonderful, the places they were made were wonderful — Majorca (which was new to me and which I loved) and Venice (which I have always loved) — but the movies, for reasons beyond my control and understanding, have never been finished. Not because they were bad, but because they were seemingly taken over by money people who had no understanding of the stories, thereby making a confused I-don't-know-what of them.

Then, in 1999, after hoping for too

many years, a mini-series came my way. My first, and a terrific time I had. It took fifty years to finally be in a mini-series — never before and maybe never again as they seem to have stopped making them. The subject was the heiress Doris Duke, her life and death. She was always an interesting, fascinating woman. *Too Rich* was the title and was the basis of her demise. I had met her a couple of times and liked her.

What makes a mini-series so good to be a part of — what sets it apart from TV sitcoms — is that it is complete. It consists of two two-hour showings — that's four hours of whoever or whatever is the focus so there is, as in the theatre, a beginning, a middle and an end. And a mini-series, right or wrong, is treated publicly by both networks and producers as being an event. As for playing the part of Doris Duke, I was called upon to portray her many facets covering the last ten or fifteen years of her life.

Having been chosen to play her somehow made me feel very special. There was an aura around Doris Duke for obvious reasons. So much money. Money, which seems to be what everyone wants. We all need some, but is there ever enough? Money has brought destruction and misery more often than not. It may bring you comfort — it will certainly not bring you peace of mind. And in the case of Doris Duke, neither luck nor health nor personal satisfaction. She was used by so many. I always thought of her as being truly sad. When I met her, though briefly, she was friendly, waved to me, told me how she loved my mother. My mother was an exceptionally brilliant secretary — could do anything, including shorthand, typing — she had been working for Louis Bromfield who had known Doris Duke. Exactly when and where it all happened, I do not know. I only know that it did and for all I know my mother may have done and probably did do some work for Doris Duke. Whatever it was, the two women connected in a very positive way. Doris Duke always remembered my mother and always mentioned her with great affection so that automatically made her shine in my eyes. That made her a winner in every way.

Though her life ended tragically, as a victim of some of the people around her, she herself was a decent, generous woman. She did some good things with her fortune. Her downfall was her desperate need for love, thereby trusting all the wrong people. As an actress playing her, I not only learned more about her — the light and dark sides — but it made me wish I had known her then. Perhaps I might even have been able to help her.

The locations included many weeks in Montreal, two weeks in the glory of Hawaii and time in Los Angeles. I got to work with Richard Chamberlain again whom I had scarcely seen since his days as *Dr Kildare* when I guested on one of his shows. And I worked for the first time with John Erman, a class A+ director and my new friend. We had a great time — the series was well received. It was such a good story, such an interesting and sad, sometimes freaky life. In the end she was used and abused.

That summer an old producer friend, Alexander Cohen, sent me a script for the theatre, a little known play by Noel Coward, now to be produced in celebration of his one-hundredth birthday. The play had been put on once, years ago in England, but never got anywhere. I was not sure it was something I wanted to do. Noel was a much-adored good friend and I was very sentimental about him. Alex was a great salesman — relentless — giving me all the whys and wherefores, telling me how great it would be for me and I for it. He prevailed. He had chosen the director, Michael Langham, a man I didn't know. Alex could sell you anything, convince you of anything. He had Rosemary Harris for the other leading role, which was very fine with me as I'd admired her for years. So come fall, into rehearsal we went.

I was still uncertain, no apparent reason except that my last appearance on stage (though it was Chichester) had been the disappointment of *The Visit* in 1995. It had been such a contrast to the special experience for me — such a happy one, and such a hard act to follow — of Tennessee Williams's *Sweet Bird of Youth* some years earlier. In the case of *Waiting in the Wings*, I knew no one. I weighed the pros and cons — the pros far outweighed the cons — they included the cast. Everyone in the play was of the theatre, all first rate actors. It was an ensemble piece, which is a form that has always attracted me. The major con was that the director was completely unknown to me. My approach to all my work, be it movies, theatre or television, has always been to work in tandem with the director. I have never entered a rehearsal room with a 'star' attitude. Actually, rehearsal time has always been my favorite time. Feeling your way in a play, getting to know your fellow actors, loving the work and having fun. Unhappily my problem in this instance was the director — the last person I would like to have difficulty with. He had some kind of preconception of me — something to do with stardom — my name being recognized — all sorts of ideas that I could never figure out. So from the beginning there was unspoken friction. He expected everyone to do everything his way. He was a very experienced director with many years spent in the British theatre and repertory in the U.S. He was not really interested in the opinion of actors.

Often when I have started work in a movie, or anything for that matter, some people have the preconceived notion that I am formidable, difficult and opinionated. I am opinionated, I confess — the other questionable attributes come I think from the lower register of my voice and from rumor — people's idea of my life with Humphrey Bogart, thereby making me tough. From my own self-analysis, which I seldom indulge in, I am what I am. I mostly aim to please. I am insecure. I love to be part of a group of actors I am working with. I cannot work under tension, certainly will not fight unless backed against a wall. Even then, it is not why I became an actress in the first place. It is not supposed to be a competitive atmosphere or profession. Despite the difficulty with the director and the fact that I was slaughtered personally and professionally by the *New York Times* critic, the play had a successful run and I had a lovely time with my fellow thesps and count many of them — Barney Hughes and Helen Stenborg, Dana Ivey, Trish Connolly, Simon Jones — as my friends. We really did have and do have ongoing relationships that I value very highly. I wish my friend Noel Coward had been around. He would have added spice and put up with no nonsense from anyone.

Then, too, I had to sing a song ('I'm Old Fashioned' by Harold Arlen) in a scene in the second act where we (all women except for Barney Hughes and Simon Jones) were celebrating being alive. Anyway, I had to sing it more or less alone with my only guiding light being Trish Connolly at the piano (lovely, funny, one of the perks of the challenge). She had to learn the song in my key and play it on the slightly tinny piano on the set. Had it not been for John Kander, who came to the theatre several times to coach me and to give Trish my key which was somewhere between B minus sharp and outer space, I could never have gotten through it. Not being a singer, I, of course, needed a full orchestra behind me, which I couldn't have. Talk about living dangerously. Every performance was an adventure. Trish would try to give me the first note, I would try to hear it and then hit it, and, as if that wasn't enough, then I had to sing the song. All the while, everyone on stage knew what was going on — all of us hoping I'd get through it and not entirely embarrass myself or break up laughing. That's what I love about the theatre — we own our own space on stage — we know what to expect and we hope for perfection. We were not about to have either the expected or perfection in this musical interval but we did have fun. Through all this the audience sits wrapped up in the play (we hope) and the characters (please God), and we do so want to please them. I choose to think that we succeeded, at least most of the time. It's the little things that stand out, the little things that make being an actor such a wonder — when it works.

And the play was so worth doing. It was Noel Coward, for heaven's sake, and though not so well known, nor the most successful of his plays, it was still his idea — his writing — which is not only good enough for me but better than many a play. Anything of his is worth doing — being a part of. And Noel was very much a part of the Anglophile in me. As was John Gielgud — they were all connected — all the other actors who became friends.

Suddenly it was the millennium. And just as suddenly that millennium brought with it the start of a series of losses that made England a sadder place for me — the first being John Gielgud. John and I met in London before Bogie's and my African trip. We had several mutual friends so we met on each London visit and I saw him in every one of his theatre roles. After Bogie died, I came to London before leaving for India to film *Flame Over India*. After two months there, we returned to London for final scenes at Pinewood Studio. It was then that I began to see more of John, and our paths also crossed when he came to New York. I was in awe of him and his great talent and recalled to him my childhood experience of seeing him on Broadway in *Hamlet* and how I was so mesmerized by his performance, so affected that I kept walking into doors and pillars on leaving the theatre. That performance I believe left no doubt in my mind that I was determined to become an actress in the theatre. You must understand that John Gielgud's theatre history is unparalleled. If I am correct, he actually gave Alec Guinness his first break in the theatre when Alec was seventeen or eighteen years old. Gielgud's aunt was Ellen Terry, considered to be the great actress of her time. So theatre was the most natural venture for him — in his blood — where he belonged.

John Gielgud was quite an extraordinary man. An avid reader — saw every play he could in theatres large and small — witty — a staunch friend. Very easy to adore. As the years went on, I got to know him better, became closer to him. In 1962, he directed Jason in a play called *Big Fish, Little Fish* with Hume Cronyn co-starring. I'll never forget the sight of John sitting up front watching a run through of the play — his great head and profile, his hand to his chin in a Shakespearean pose, totally engrossed in what was happening onstage. He would often say to the actors, 'Oh *do* go on yourselves — you know so much more than I do.' Not bloody likely.

He brought his one man show *Ages of Man* to New York, playing Shakespeare's men from Hamlet to Othello to Macbeth to Lear, segueing into a sonnet or two — a performance of complete brilliance. And for once every coveted award went to the right person. Him. Then, during my two years living in London doing *Applause* onstage for a year in 1972–3, and filming *Murder on the Orient Express* in 1974, we saw each other more and more. Every day on the set of *Orient Express*, with the director's chairs, with our names printed clearly, lined up next to each other — John Gielgud, Albert Finney, Ingrid Bergman, Wendy Hiller, Sean Connery, Rachel Roberts, Richard Widmark, Vanessa Redgrave, Jacqueline Bisset, Michael York and me

— quite a gathering — all of us sat enraptured while John told us endless marvelous stories, anecdotes of theatre experiences and theatre greats. It was a once in a lifetime experience. And it was John who took me with him on a very special tour of the National Theatre before it was completed and officially opened. When we were taken to the backstage dressing-room area, John remarked, 'Tiny dressing rooms, as usual, for the actors.'

Every time I was in a play or a musical, he came to see me. When he came to *Applause*, he came back and asked me how long I would be playing. I said one year in London after a year and a half on Broadway and a year's national tour. He said, 'Oh, you're one of those actresses who stays in a play a long time.' You see, in England they usually don't, they have repertory theatres there. Actors have the great privilege of playing two different plays in a week. There's much more variety, more basic training in the classics and Shakespeare in England than we do in America.

So many memorable lunches, dinners, hours spent together. Whenever I came to London, there were flowers with a handwritten note from John. There was laughter continually. He was a joy to be with. Always with a story or two. I remember we were in Israel making an Agatha Christie movie together. While waiting for the camera to be ready, John would be doing the *Times* crossword puzzle in ink no less. When we lapsed into conversation, he would look up, having remembered something, and I would hear a funny, bawdy limerick come from John. Limericks, memories, people, incidents just popped out. So much to draw from. He was unique. Theatre — work — was his life really. He always worried there weren't enough roles for him to play. He told me once that someone, who was writing a book about favorite rooms, had asked him what his favorite was. John said, 'I wanted to say my bedroom but then changed my mind because I realized that one day I'd wake up dead in it.' He was the complete, perfect English gentleman — impeccably groomed, gold crested ring on pinky finger, cigarette case at the ready. When in the city, he could be seen walking down Piccadilly toward Fortnum and Mason with certainly two or three books in his hand having just left Hatchard's, the best bookstore anywhere, that was just up the street. Never an idle moment — ever curious — ever interested — ever active — the brain never slept. That was John.

He had a partner, Martin — a very attractive man — who was devoted to John, made the garden beautiful, had painted the gold leaf molding in the living room of their home. He would never attend an opening or a party, always stayed in the background. I loved his company. He was extremely well read (had to be with John overflowing with knowledge), and fun. Quite a bit younger than John. Imagine the shock when he suddenly became ill and died. That was completely devastating to John. He was so dependent on him — so many years together — somewhere in the neighborhood of fifty, I would guess. That left John, at ninety-four years old, bereft, rattling around that large, beautiful house alone. A housekeeper and gardener/chauffeur were there, yes, but that was hardly of comfort to him. I would call him from New York, first to chat, see how he was, give him some local gossip. I've forgotten how much time had elapsed before John really began to sound frail, when talking on the phone became more and more difficult for him, until one day I informed him that I was coming to London to appear on a TV show and would descend on him almost on arrival. He sounded pleased — he was too polite to deny me the privilege of seeing him. I took my friend John Erman with me and down we went.

It was to be my last time. I found him moving more slowly, speaking with less gusto, but there was tea and there was cake. I regaled him with every bit of information I could garner on happenings in the U.S.A. and mostly the theatre. He became more interested, more alert, was genuinely glad to see me. But he was alone in this house that had always had people and life in it. Now it was sad and I hated to leave him.

Not long after my visit, on May 21, he died. The same date as my wedding to Bogie. A few weeks later I received a call from his lawyer telling me John had left me a ring and asking when could he deliver it. I couldn't have been more surprised or more touched that John had done that and thought of me. The lovely jade ring arrived a few days later — oval jade set in simple gold. So lovely — so John — so treasured in friendship. I feel now as I felt when we first met, that I was lucky to have known him, lucky to be included in his life, lucky to have seen him so often on the stage. To think I actually heard him say to me about his friendship with Ralph Richardson as we left the Richardson home after an Easter Sunday lunch, 'He is such a great friend to me. I never thought anyone like Ralph would like me' — that alone tells you everything you need to know about that modest, lovely man, that great actor.

As if the loss of John were not enough,

less than three months later came the passing of Alec Guinness, another brilliant actor who happily became part of my life and allowed me to enter his. We hit it off that evening I first met him in London in 1959 at a Royal Command performance of his movie, *The Horse's Mouth*, but for some reason it was a long time before we really became friends. I always attended his theatre performances and went backstage after the show to see him and congratulate him. He was marvelous onstage — very rich and full of voice. When in New York I would see him, but it was in 1972, the beginning of my two years of living in England, that our friendship became more constant, more of a reality.

It's funny but in England actors like John or like Alec have lovely lunch dates with no more than four people including themselves. It is a habit I am very fond of when traveling. Europeans take time for such pleasures. I almost never do it except when truly special friends come to New York. And I do mean special. Both of these supreme beings fell into that category. They were very different men and actors who led very different lives. Both quite fascinating — supremely intelligent — fun and funny, with over-the-top talent.

Alec was very proper and meticulous when he hosted a lunch or dinner. When I was playing *Applause* at Her Majesty's Theatre in London, he invited me to dinner in a lovely restaurant on my day off. I always looked forward to his company. His wife Marella, a lovely, lovely woman, was present and I think Keith Baxter. He had ordered a special wine and when time came for the waiter to serve it — they didn't have it. Alec was furious. He said, 'I came down especially today to order our dinner and the particular wines to be served. I was told there was no problem. But now you say you don't have it. That is outrageous.' Of course the waiter and maitre d' were flustered and apologetic but Alec would have none of it. Nevertheless, he ordered two different wines and the rest of the dinner went off without a hitch. But I was amazed, amazed that he had gone to the trouble of visiting the restaurant beforehand to make certain that the dinner would be perfect, and having been assured that it would be, was beyond annoyed that it wasn't. He was right, of course. He didn't make a scene, that was not part of his character at all. He just made it clear that he was displeased.

In the more than twenty years that followed, our friendship solidified. As we got to know each other better, we became more open and I became more relaxed. The fact is I was always in awe of both

John Gielgud and Alec — also, in actuality, in awe of almost all British actors when I first met them. Laurence Olivier in particular, of course. That friendship having begun in the early fifties continued until his death. When 'How do you do' progressed to telephone numbers exchanged — flowers sent — lunches shared — friendships flowered. I am now, at this point in my own life, so grateful for those friendships, for the many of life's graces they unknowingly taught me — among which were that manners were not forever a thing of the past, that laughter was not always at the expense of somebody else, that intelligence — the reading of books in this computerized, robotic world — still counts, that quality and character can prevail and that status and acquisition are not and should not be a goal. Alec loved to wake up in his simple country house — to hear and watch the birds — to have a leisurely breakfast — a walk on a country road — a good book — a glass of wine and a good meal.

In 1993, I had the immense good luck to work with Alec for the BBC. Charles Sturridge, a fine young British director, came over to New York to give me details on *A Foreign Field*, a wonderful piece about revisiting Normandy and Omaha beach after World War II. Jeanne Moreau was also to star and Leo McKern. Can you imagine such a proposal? Working with Alec Guinness and Jeanne Moreau in a really interesting and first-rate bit of writing and an excellent part for me. I was more than thrilled to be included. It meant a month in Normandy — all living in a beautiful chateau, dining together nightly. Alec always waited for me before going into the dining room. Impeccably dressed — a blazer with waistcoat underneath, perfectly pressed trousers — the definitive English gentleman. And would I like a cocktail? We-ell . . . a light vodka on the rocks, perhaps. Even if I didn't want it, I didn't want to disappoint Alec. So we would have our 'cocktail' and then go into dinner. Alec was the kind of man who would stand when you entered the room, and pull your chair out (*not* from under you) so you could sit at your place for dinner.

My first day of shooting was with Alec. I was a nervous wreck. It was a short scene — a brief exchange between us at the door to his room: he on the inside, me on the out. When Charles Sturridge called action, I walked to Alec's door — knocked — he opened it and became the character he was playing so completely that the English Gentleman totally disappeared. And I began to tremble, like the kid I was when I started in pictures. I think it was because I suddenly realized I was in this movie for the BBC with the brilliant Alec Guinness and would I be good enough? That terrible insecurity from my beginnings reared its ugly head after all these years.

I guess a true sense of self-confidence is not in the cards for me. At least in certain special situations. It's a different kind of nervousness — not like opening night in the theatre. I think it's reverting subconsciously to my first dreams of becoming an actress — of being so star-struck. After watching for so many years Laurence Olivier, Ralph Richardson, Vivien Leigh, Gielgud, Guinness and more — to find myself meeting them — being accepted by them as one of them, no less — was quite unbelievable to me. And upon working with any of them — at the beginning I became eight years old.

Anyway — the working with Alec and Jeanne Moreau — everyone — turned out splendidly. The piece itself was high quality television and the entire experience was a marvel — a highlight for me. And, of course, it brought Alec and me closer together. From then on we were always in touch, mostly when I came to London, always at Christmas. I would call him when I was heading his way, and he always came to town so we could have a long lunch or dinner together. The last time I was in

London, I rang him and for the first time he said he didn't think he could come up; Marella had been ill and doctors were coming to see her. I was of course saddened, but understanding. About two days after our conversation, I was emerging from the elevator in the Connaught Hotel. I brought my room key to the concierge and as I glanced toward the hotel entry, I saw a man who looked like Alec rush into a taxi. I ran outside and asked the doorman if that had been Alec Guinness. Imagine my surprise when he told me indeed it was but he didn't seem like his usual self. I couldn't figure it out, couldn't call anyone without knowing where or who his close friends were. I guess I figured I would hear from him. I wasn't going to be in London very long, had to get back to New York. I left knowing nothing until less than a week later came the news of Alec's death.

It couldn't be. How could it happen so fast? Clearly that's why he came to London, why he had rushed into a taxi. No warning. Finally my friend Keith Baxter, who had been a close friend of Alec and Marella, came to New York and told me that yes, indeed, it had been quick. Clearly Alec's personal physician had found that he had cancer and must go up to London and hospital. It was obviously terminal as it was all over in less than a week. Keith said that with Marella at his bedside, Alec said what he hated most was leaving her. In Alec's worry about Marella, he had forgotten about himself. So, so sad — so touching. And she followed him about three months later.

To lose these two major men in such a short time was painful. My world was getting smaller. Shrinking too fast. And little did I think that the millennium would be the beginning of so many more endings. The chipping away of pieces of your life that had been there for so many years, threading their way through your work life and your personal life. Just as you think you can take a breath again, another jolt comes along. Then I get to thinking that my awareness of and learning to deal with losses started when I was eighteen and nineteen with the loss of my grandmother, followed by my Uncle Jack and my surrogate father Uncle Charlie. You never think of death at those ages — it seems so far away. Then as I moved into my twenties, when a friend became ill — seriously ill — other friends would remind me that I had been with people at least twenty-five years my senior as Bogie had been! I guess that was true then. It is not true now. But I also think how very lucky I have been to have had mostly good health in my life, with interruptions from time to time with physical injuries — nothing life-threatening, usually work related. And the real luck is in knowing and having the great friends I have had and the extraordinary people I have known who have graced my life, enhanced it and enriched it. I am so grateful for that.

So life went on, as it must. I had my children luckily and my work and still some friends that I treasured.

With my emotions at a low ebb, a most unexpected lift to my spirits appeared. A new relationship resulted in a roundabout way from my commitment to *Waiting in the Wings*. What has turned out to be my lifetime companion arrived in the form of a three-pound, four-legged tri-color beautiful Papillon. During rehearsals of the play, Alexander Cohen had told me he wanted to give me a dog for my birthday. In the mid-Nineties, I had begun a habit of going to the Westminster Dog Show in Madison Square Garden. Not to sit and watch the show as much as to walk behind the scenes where all the dogs are being prepared for the competition. After the loss of my Cavalier King Charles Spaniel in 1984, I was so upset that I couldn't think of having another dog. Clearly my decision to attend Westminster was the beginning of my need for another four-legged companion. Greg and Veronique Peck had been after me for years to get a Maltese. They had two and took them everywhere when they traveled. When I perused the different breeds at Westminster there were groups of Maltese, pink bows atop their little heads and hair in curlers getting ready for the big event. Show dogs are not the same as other dogs. They are trained to show, to prance around the ring, to stand perfectly still and in position for the judges' examination. These were so small. Anyway, I'd always had a sneaker for Pekinese.

Not long before starting *Waiting in the Wings*, I had gone to Westminster with Judy Green who had great seats down front. All the dogs were beautiful. If I lived on a farm heaven knows how many I would have. She knew some of the breeders who were down on the floor. It was soon to be time for the toy group to be judged. She introduced me to John Oulton who bred Papillons, a breed I had never seen before. They were all colors — black and white, brown and white, tri-color (black, brown and white). John was holding black and white Kirby who had won every Best in Show and Best in Breed in every important dog show anywhere. He was very appealing, but I just wasn't sure.

I'd never imagined myself with a small dog and yet, if I was going to have one, it made sense with all the traveling I do for work and pleasure — the dog I chose would have to travel with me on the plane, not in the hold. I took John's card and asked him to let me know when he was going to have another litter. Meanwhile the toy group was about to be called. Kirby won that one easily. When Best in Show came around, he pranced around the ring looking so happy, so sure of himself — he loved the event. He was a great dog, irresistible, and he won. It couldn't have gone any other way and, of course, I found myself thinking in terms of Papillons.

I wavered back and forth between Maltese and Papillons for ages, then came the call — the new litter had arrived. I had to choose. I wanted a girl but as I was about to go into rehearsal for the play, I couldn't think of training a puppy at that time. In any event, I had made up my mind not to have a dog under six months old. That was fine with John. I told Alexander Cohen I'd let him know when I could take the dog — it would have to be after we opened and after I'd settled in. Agreed! The day came a few months later and I called John Oulton saying I was ready, whereupon he told me he'd already given the dog I'd chosen months before to Alex. He thought naturally that as Alex had paid for the dog, he would give it to me. Wrong! There evidently was a young man visiting Alex at the time and Alex gave the dog to him. Knowing he was not in good health, I said nothing. I was mortified, hurt and angry. John, of course, did the right thing from his point of view. The dog had been paid for so he had no choice. The saga continued and I had to wait for the next litter. So we went for it — the same routine — John called me — the litter arrived — two tri-color Papillon girls — he would bring them down in a few months so I could choose. The time arrived, down they came. I defy anyone to make a choice between two adorable sisters. How do you know which is the right one for you? Of course, you don't. They played in the kitchen for a while, I picked each of them up, scrutinized them carefully hoping for a sign. There was none. Then fate stepped in — one of them licked my nose when I picked her up — I figured she liked me. So I chose her and after another few months and many phone calls for instructions — food, behavior, what she was used to, etc. etc. — delivery day arrived.

I was like a nervous mother, so anxious to do the right thing by this tiny, four-legged creature I had brought into my life. Well, it didn't take long before I was a goner. I took her to my old vet who pronounced her a beauty. I had lucked out. She had perfect markings, was by far the prettiest Papillon of those I had seen at Westminster — except for champion Kirby. She is a great traveler, a great companion, always happy to see me, never answers back. She is very independent, has a marvelous personality — it is all true and I am besotted. I had forgotten the unconditional love that a dog gives you. To top it off, she is a country dog. Now that I've sold my house I take her to friends where she goes wild. Runs around in circles — so happy to be free — chases squirrels, chipmunks. If I ever decide to buy another house, it will be for Sophie. That is her name, after my beloved grandmother.

Fantastic luck for Sophie and me comes in the form of my adorable dog walker Kerry Stevens — daughter of my building superintendent. She walks Sophie early morning and at night. Actually the entire Stevens family plays a life-saving role in Sophie's life. Whether I am home or away, she is always on familiar ground. What could be better?

My job is afternoon walking — our bonding time. I do most of the talking — a happy departure for me as I used to talk to myself or the walls exclusively — Sophie takes care of the sniffing and squirrel chasing. I even find myself talking to her when we are on the street or in the park. I can't imagine what people passing by must think. These days, if they've noticed, they probably think I'm just another nut, which of course I am and proud of it. Sophie is the high in highlights of my life. Even through rain, snow, ice and general laziness, she is the reason I smile when I wake up and a comfort to me continually. I could never have imagined that a now five-pound-six-ounce dog would take over my life. But it has happened and I am happy to have someone to look after and share my moods with.

After all the losses of the year 2000, a very large glimmer of light and laughter came to pass. This time it was sharing a stage with the irrepressible, unsurpassable, no-holds-barred funny Dame Edna Everage at a Dramatists Guild Awards gala. Years before this event I had appeared on television in the UK with Dame Edna on her own show. I remember reading the script with our scenes together spelled out. Barry Humphries called me at my London hotel to see if everything was all right with the hotel and with me. Everything was fine but, 'Tell me, Barry, this scene we have together when you are Dame Edna, could we change a few words?' His answer was, 'I don't know. I'll ask her.' After that I asked no more questions.

Going on the show was great fun. I talked to her before a live audience, mind you, as Dame Edna. She convinced me. Tom Jones appeared on the same show — the three of us did a song together. I had a great time and Dame Edna — Barry Humphries — both of them — are brilliant and very, very funny.

I seldom take part in awards presentation events but the Dramatists Guild is so important to the theatre, plus I love to laugh and Dame Edna makes me laugh non-stop. The recipients were particularly distinguished that year. Steve Sondheim, who I have known and loved for years, and Arthur Miller, who I have always been somewhat in awe of, were two irresistible reasons to appear. I guess I'm a bit of a snob. I love to be involved in even the smallest way with enormously talented people and have always, all my life, been impressed with them. A lot of 'awe' time.

I was asked to host a Leonard Bernstein tribute in Paris which Marlon Brando would co-host. Lenny, an old treasured friend, and Paris were reason enough to say yes, but to be on stage with Brando was like capturing the gold ring — even better. Of course, it never happened.

Brando cancelled. But I still had Paris. That trip was followed soon after by a television appearance in Milan during which I fulfilled my need to shop and eat Italian with new people and to have fun. From Milan, I went on to Stockholm where I had been invited to receive the Bronze Horse for Lifetime Achievement at their film festival. The great perk of movies rears its head once more — Lifetime Achievements seem to be recognized worldwide. That is how we visit new countries, meet new people and — being the center of attention for just a few days — have our failing egos (fed by unemployment) satisfied enough — just enough — to feel that perhaps our efforts have not been in vain after all.

At the end of the *Waiting in the Wings* run, I was in need of a break. I was weary. The theatre, while exhilarating, is also quite physically demanding — and emotionally as well — very much so. I needed to get away from New York and eight shows a week. Whenever I am in that state, it has been my instinct to head for Paris, the city that almost rejuvenates me. If for no other reason than the language change, I immediately feel lighter. It's fun, it's so much a part of my younger fantasies. The heart-stopping beauty of Paris is impossible to explain. It feeds my strong visual sense — for however long I am there, I become French. I attend concerts with my great friend Nicole Salinger. I hang out mostly in the same cafés, walk many of the same streets.

I am fortunate in that I was able to adapt not only to France, but to England and Italy too. Though by no means a linguist, I know roughly one hundred or more words in Italian and Spanish. French I am more fluent in, though far from fluent enough to satisfy me. Though basically I feel very much at home in France, let's face it, sooner or later it becomes clear that I am a foreigner. No matter how many friends (and I have quite a few in each country — which in turn add up to more than I have in America), or how much time spent, you cannot get away from the fact that you are not one of them. Perhaps in spirit, but not in reality. Nevertheless, I always return feeling refreshed, feeling better about myself and gung-ho to face the job market and the questionable mentality that decides my fate. For more than a year after *Waiting in the Wings* closed, I seemed to travel endlessly.

While travel is the great escape from the pressures — meaning stress — of my real world, I still always seem to be glad to come home. Home to my own things around me — the putting away of suitcases — thank God — the packing scene being the worst aspect of travel. So, home again, I lulled myself into my routine of watching the news non-stop — dinner on a tray, feet up and Sophie by my side. I like this routine I've settled into. I don't really remember how it came to pass but it's part of my days — after six or six-thirty when the house is empty of people, the telephone stops ringing and I move around my apartment, which has been home to me for over forty years, freely and quietly. With the noise of my city, silence is bliss.

Just as I was falling into a breathing-easy, pleasant cycle, came a mammoth emotional blow for me — the illness of Jason Robards — great actor, my husband for eight and a half years and father of our great son Sam. It's a funny thing: our marriage, though it didn't work, our caring for each other did. We shared our work and our humor and we were always glad to see one another and enjoyed our time together. I never thought of his being ill. He had a fairly rough childhood and young manhood; he beat up on himself during his early years in the theatre but he was never sick during our time together. And suddenly there he was with a malignant tumor.

He carried on for two years through some ups and major downs. Generally it was a bad two years for him and for those who loved him. Not long before he died, Sam was able to leave his own family in California and spend some real quality time with his father. As Jason had another life, I was not able to see him too often, but we did talk on the phone from time to time and that was a lot better than nothing. I count it a very special thing that he and I were able to connect with one another — and recognized, in spite of a divorce which was not altogether pleasant, that we did love each other and that a strong bond would last through our lifetimes.

In spite of knowing he was losing his fight against that miserable disease, his death came as a terrible shock. No more Jason. Thank God for memories of funny, crazy times together — even the not so funny times looked good. Jason, who had not always been around a great deal, saw what a talented actor and superior human being his son was — that was of great comfort to me. Jason is always in my thoughts and I happily remember the plays — his brilliance on the stage — those performances — always. Especially during our times together, though there were continuing attempts to keep us apart. Fortunately they were unsuccessful, and try though they might, no one could take those years away from us.

The following year I was in Los Angeles for a couple of weeks visiting my children — grandchildren — friends — taking care of some business. Sam and Sidsel had come by the hotel to have brunch and a swim with their boys, Calvin and Sebastian. I was leaving the following day. I stayed in that night, packing and room service being the order of the day. I left a wake-up call for 9:00 a.m. That would give me time for breakfast and a farewell swim before heading for the airport. I got into bed late as usual — packing does that to me. The phone rang, waking me from a deep sleep, which I seldom have. I asked the operator, 'What time is it?' She replied, 'Turn on your television.' Still groggy and thinking it was another hotel screw-up, I said, 'I left a nine a.m. call. What time is it?' She said, 'It's seven a.m. Turn on your television.' It was September 11 and the television came on as an airplane was flying into and hitting one of the twin towers. Enormous clouds of black smoke, flames — mayhem — voices of anchors. I woke up in a hurry, stunned as the rest of the country — indeed the world — was. Open mouthed, in shock and horror, I did not leave my television. (Nor did I leave California — not for five days after. I couldn't — security was major — airports closed. Even when I was finally able to leave five days later, I had to go in a special car, special driver — that part of it was very like a 'B' movie.) I was on the phone all day to those near and dear to me. I received calls from all over Europe and New York. In all the horror, I couldn't take my eyes off that screen. Who among us could ever forget the sights and sounds, that day of faces, people running through smoke trying to get away from it. And over and over came pictures of the planes — first one — then the second from another direction hitting another tower — pictures taken with a video camera by a man who happened to be there and who had the good sense to turn it on — though how he did it, I've never known.

It was the most horrifying yet surreal of days. Wives searching for husbands — husbands searching for wives — holding photos of them hoping someone had seen them — the wife talking to her husband who was on the plane that eventually crashed in the field in Pennsylvania. She kept telling him, 'Don't be brave, stay in the background.' He kept saying, 'We're going to crash anyway. The hijackers are here with guns. I've got to do something about it.' She said he was always doing things like that — trying to stop a fight. Save someone. He was that kind of person. His last words to her, as I remember them, were, 'I love you. Take care of yourself and the kids.' It was heartbreaking and the woman was amazing.

Then there was the interview with Howard Lutnick, C.E.O. of the financial firm Cantor Fitzgerald. They had lost more than sixty percent of their people having been on the top three floors of the first tower. Lutnick's brother was there when the plane hit and somehow Lutnick had been able to record, or the networks had, a conversation with his brother and his wife. The only reason Howard was not there as well was that he had taken his young child to school. It was an incredibly moving interview. The man broke down continually. He would try to speak, get a few words or a thought out and burst into tears. It wasn't an enormous company — he, of course, knew everyone in it and their families and continued to mention them with a cracking voice and tears spilling down his face. And his brother — his only brother. I heard after that he was criticized by some for trying to rebuild his company. What on earth was he supposed to do? Perhaps die with his remaining family members? Would that have satisfied those critics?

The shock, the actuality of it continued

for months. A friend of mine, Berry Berenson, was on the plane leaving from Boston going to L.A. — a young, vibrant, beautiful and talented woman who boarded the plane in Boston filled with anticipation at seeing the first concert of her younger son in Los Angeles. I kept on thinking — and still do — what must it have been like on that plane, sitting happily in your seat so excited to see your son perform and what was it like for the son to be waiting for his mother who he would never see again? All the while the television was showing you the faces of those still looking, not giving up hope of finding that most important and loved person in their lives.

The overpowering grief that came through that screen. The simplicity of the people who seemed so lost without their mates. The showing of that destruction. The reliving of the planes hitting the towers, the people madly running — the ones who made it out walking down thirty, forty, who knows how many flights of stairs being led by a fireman with one lone flashlight and a strong arm to save their lives — the people who were late for work that day, or in bed with a virus — who left some important papers at home and had to go back to get them thereby missing the attacks. Those twists of fate — those minutes or seconds that were the difference between life and death. And you think of the ifs and if onlys in your own life. There was no way, during that period of horror and loss, not to reflect on your own life. The brevity of it — some surprise endings — the value of time well spent. I myself think of one or all of those facts and possibilities often. I must live every day well — usefully — aware — encourage my sense of giving to the known and the unknown. I must consciously make my world, no matter how small, a better place for my loved ones — my friends — for my everyday acquaintances. That attitude, sense of promise, lasts for a while, then gradually fades. I care just as much, am just as admiring — it's the fervor that goes or seems to go.

About a month after 9/11, I took off for Paris. I needed to be in the midst of that most beautiful city of my heart's delight, to walk those streets, to see my friends, to sit at the Cafe Flore for as long as I wished with my life's partner, Sophie, by my side. The French were stricken by what had happened and totally compassionate. They all said they felt it was happening to them. When I had returned from California I had felt their reactions through their phone calls and faxes. It was surprising and wonderful. Their words — their worry — how was I? How was the city? How was the country? I wondered if we Americans would be equally as concerned if France had fallen victim to a similar event. Surely we would have cared and worried about our friends. Through the grimness of the event, it was comforting to sit in the midst of friends and even acquaintances at our usual Sunday brunch and to listen and to hear their worries and fears and complete awareness of every detail of that horrible day.

While in Paris, Berry Berenson's sister, Marisa, prepared a service for Berry in a small Left Bank church. Very sweet — very emotional. Very, very sad. I was so glad to have been in Paris at that time — to be able to attend that service which took place on a sunny day very much in keeping with Berry's personality. So that trip temporarily bumped up my spirits, made me more than ever grateful for my French friends — and made me glad to be alive. I was able to look around, and while still seeing the terrible sight of the Twin Towers in flame and smoke and collapse, the Arc de Triomphe could stand out clearly and in the foreground of my mind.

Later that year my high school pal, actually my oldest friend, Joan Axelrod, after some months of struggle lost her battle against cancer and died. She had played a large part in my life from the *Goodbye Charlie* days — my first starring role on Broadway — the play written and directed by her husband George. She was very wise — full of advice about my life and my 'take' on a few shared friends and happenings in the theatre and movie world. There was always a dinner. Their home, whether it be New York, California or London, was welcoming and available to me.

Joan had more information about more people. Heaven knows where she got the information, but she got it. She became a part, a large part, of each and every culture she found herself in. She was chameleon-like, changing as she needed to change, remaining totally supportive of George when he felt the need to move house. When I was going to appear onstage in *Applause* in London, it was Joan who found me a place to live, Joan who took me to the best antique dealers, the best markets for food and drink. In fact she was a remarkable woman, always in the service of her girlfriends. What was hard for her, living in California, was that her best girlfriends were somewhere else. Still she found a way — becoming a first-class interior decorator, something which she'd done before but not with such vigor. She was very successful, made more friends and thrived.

Joan had had two heart valve replacements that never slowed her down. I never considered her small complaints as being serious enough to be life threatening. Wrong again. Suddenly on my next to last visit to California, the seriousness of her illness became apparent. Walking became a problem. Still she was having massages and had someone come in to cook for her and George. We were about to go to her favorite restaurant when she called and asked if I minded dining at home — just herself, George and me. We'd done that often in the past and in fact I preferred it. I always enjoyed being there. This time she used a wheelchair to go from bedroom to kitchen to conserve her strength. I tried and I think succeeded in not showing my alarm. That apparatus and Joan did not go together. All the same, at the end of a cozy dinner Joan had to take to her bed. Of course said I, 'Not to worry. I'll sit with George for a while and pop in to see you before I leave.' George and I sat in the living room whose aura had already changed without Joan there and in charge. We talked as old friends can without discussing the obvious. Then I assured George I would not tire Joan and up I went to see her.

As we were so close and had seen each other through so many emotional crises in our lives, the talk came amazingly easily. Was there anything I could do? Then she said, 'I don't mind dying. I just don't want to be in pain.' I don't know what I said. I was so shocked. She must have been aware, her body must have told her something. I probably said something inadequate and not very convincing like 'But that's a long way away, nothing to think about now.' I was returning to New York a couple of days after that evening but I told Joan I'd probably be back soon for Cecilia Peck's wedding. I'd call her from New York and tell her exactly when.

I couldn't believe it. How had it happened so quickly? She was fine and then she wasn't. Back home, all of a sudden I decided I would have to return to California sooner rather than later — definitely go to the wedding. Could it be that I would come to California one day and not have Joan there to plan our girl days together? She was my one friend with a husband that I had real girl time with — catching up on our lives, our problems — having lunch in odd places — doing things together that were fun for us. Yes, it could be. And yes, it was. I called her as soon as my travel plans were made and heard something I never thought I would hear from her. She said, 'The hospice people were here. They were terrific. They really made me feel so much better, explained everything to me. Now I don't have to worry.

And they were so nice. Really made an enormous difference.' I knew what 'hospice' meant. That was reality. That meant it was going to happen. When I heard the sound of relief and pleasure in her voice I was happy for her. I told her that and how good it was to hear her sound so pleased at having found such really good people to visit her regularly and attend to her needs.

So upon boarding the plane a couple of weeks later I was filled with all kinds of emotions — joy for Cecilia and sadness for Joan. On arrival at the hotel, my first call was of course to Joan. How did she feel, how was she doing, when could I see her? The next day, of course. So off I went filled with apprehension.

George let me in, warning me not to tire her. Into the bedroom I went with a big (convincing, I hoped) smile on my face. I headed for the bed where she sat looking (except for the oxygen tubes in her nose) so much better than I had expected — in full make-up, perfectly groomed, in one of her favorite white cotton nightgowns. I pulled up a chair next to her side of the bed so we could have our time together. George discreetly left us alone. She brought me up to date with how she was — felt — never really going into the terrible world of cancer. Being a big boned woman, she never did look emaciated as so many victims of that disease do. She told me how fantastic the hospice people had been, how attentive. Then she took from her night table a bottle of medicine with an eyedropper lid, waved it and said, 'They left this for me — so if I am in pain, this will take care of that.' I was very shocked at the sight of that bottle, clearly morphine or some magic potion with morphine in it to alleviate pain for diseases such as this. The bottle from the hospice nurse signified the end of life to me. Joan was still able to talk about it, though whatever other medication they had given her did dull her mind to some degree. She was still determined to attend Cecilia Peck's wedding a few days later and Joan was the kind of woman who, once her mind was made up, would get enough adrenaline going to enable her to fulfill her wish. I begged her not to push herself, but I'd be there to hold her hand if she needed me. About then, George popped into the room saying it was time for me to go. She was getting tired. She said she was a bit and she clearly was. I hugged her, told her I loved her and would see her at the Pecks'. She handed me a small gift bag — told me to look inside — she wanted me to have it. It was a small double picture gold frame from *Goodbye Charlie*'s opening belonging to her and George in which I could place two photos of them or whoever I wished. That made me instantly teary so I blew her a kiss and said I'd see her at the wedding.

Come the wedding day and, by God, Joan came. She lasted through the ceremony, and for about a half hour more before she had to leave. I kissed her goodbye and said I'd call the next day. When I did, George picked up the phone and told me Joan was really too tired to speak. It's strange how a voice changes at such a time — it was clear that Joan was too weak — that I had said my last goodbye to her. It was a few days after that that George called to tell me she had gone. She had always been so innately strong, I never expected her to die so soon. But then even when someone is very ill, one does not expect it. There is no way to prepare yourself for disaster.

I had remembered her telling me she wanted friends to gather around her pool — raise a glass of wine, eat the snacks that she had listed in her will along with the above instructions, but I had to block it from my mind. Unhappily I couldn't be at the pool gathering as I had work in New York. However, we did share our thoughts and feelings for Joan in my apartment at roughly the same hour as the gathering in California. A fond farewell to a remarkable woman and a wonderful friend.

★ ★ ★

After all the sadness, suddenly, at the end of 2001, something surprising and positive happened: I was offered a part in Lars von Trier's movie, *Dogville*. The offer came from left field and I was thrilled. Lars had made a great movie, *Breaking the Wave*. He was an original, unpredictable director so, although my part in the movie was small, I said yes because of him.

Again it was an ensemble piece, though the star was Nicole Kidman. In addition to the appeal of working with Lars, I was attracted to it being an international cast headed by Nicole: Ben Gazzara and James Caan — both of whom I had known and liked before — Blair Brown — a great girl, lovely and so talented — Stellan Skaargard, that marvelous actor whose work I had seen in *Breaking the Waves* and who I got to know quite well and like enormously, and Siobhan Fallon — a funny, funny woman who was feeding a newborn baby and two of her other young children before the shooting day even started. How she did it, I'll never know. So good things came out of that small part. Nicole and I became fast friends. She is not only beautiful — which she is to the extreme — but she is very smart, very professional and a first-class actress of broad scope.

I was fascinated to see the way Lars von

Trier worked. I had envisioned him to be a very big man, tall and husky and somewhere in his late fifties. I couldn't have been more wrong. Blair Brown and I, having been on the same flight from New York, were met by the producer, Vibeke Windelov, upon our arrival in Sweden. She turned out to be a big plus from day one and all through the making of the film and after — a really terrific woman who I have tremendous affection for. She is smart, original and fun. Not many producers are fun. She is. We were taken to what was to be our home for the next six weeks or more in Trollhattan and on to the dining room for lunch. After a while, a man appeared in the room with a smile on his face and a small stuffed moose in his hand. He was of medium height and looked to be in his early forties. He was Lars von Trier. The direct opposite of my imaginings. He handed me the moose — named Oliver (I know not why) — and sat him on the television in my bedroom living quarters. He still sits on my bedroom television at home so in a way I see him every day and Lars remains in my mind.

Working with the unknown is amazement, amusement and angst. At least for me. And Lars's method involves an actor more or less forgetting what movies have taught him throughout his career. With

Lars, you don't have to worry about hitting the marks, you can change the dialogue and, in this case, the set was not a set but a floor with the town of Dogville drawn on it. We were shown where the doors and windows of our individual spaces were. That was so we didn't walk through a wall that wasn't there or jump out of a window, which I sometimes felt like doing in the confusion and frustration of forgetting it was a window. My character had this small shop where I sold potatoes and apples and some cleaning materials and I was famous for my gooseberry pies. Supposedly (although I never felt that way) I was the head of the town of Dogville, controlling all who lived there. That was the way it was presented to me. I was the only one with a door to leave and enter my shop. I had a collection of miniature figurines God knows from what country or how I came upon them. The Kidman character takes a fancy to them and those tiny creatures become one of the central parts of the story.

Lars had a humongous camera harness that weighed more than he did — and that he carried on his back and shoulders as he was photographing the scenes. He was in control — complete control — of all of us. From my point of view, as there were no walls, when the camera was photographing a scene at one end of the set, my shop, being in a direct line at the other end, might have been in camera range. That, in turn, meant there was a very good chance that I would be in the shot. Which, once again, meant that I had to be in character at all times just in case there was even a shadow of me in view.

As you might imagine, working that way took some getting used to. I'm not sure I ever really did get used to it, but I tried. I wanted adventure — a new experience — and I got it. I wanted to see how a super-talented director worked in this modern age — and I did. I'd worked with the one director I considered to be close to genius status, John Huston. The great thing about him was that he always listened to your doubts, ideas, anything, and you could always speak to him. Lars was a horse of an entirely different color. He spoke English fluently but he was not easy to communicate with during shooting hours. He was totally focused on his work and the technical problems he had to deal with while setting up the scene, all the while carrying this enormous harness and camera.

The time spent in Sweden was difficult for me as I was away from my little Sophie. I had become very attached to her, as is my wont with all the dogs I have had. With her it was even more so because, being so small, she snuggles. And I love that. She can snuggle in a way that a big dog can't. I called the trainer, who was keeping her while I was away, to see how she was — did she miss me? The trainer said she was very happy, whereupon my voice dropped. She continued with, 'You don't want her to be sad, do you?' My retort was, 'Yes, a little bit. Why should I be the only one who is sad?' Crazy, right? And yet . . .

Time passed and the cast all became closer — it was like boarding school, in a way. Meeting for dinner every night and sometimes for breakfast at 6:00 a.m. and for lunch on the stage next to our set. We were lucky to have such a compatible group. Movies on location have similar happenings. Come to think of it, most locations when isolated closely resemble one another. If the location is a city, you are lucky — there is other life present and available. People fall into groups — usually two to four. There is almost always one romance or two, or more depending on the obvious. Some relationships end with the last shot of the day or the closing night party. Amazingly some go further, even moving toward permanence. I was taught by Bogie (so much in my life goes back to him) never to mix business with pleasure. Let your status be known subtly from day one — not available. Unless, of course, you are. I've been involved with co-workers in the past and have found it is always a mistake. In any case, the question never arose. Different generations — different languages — different ways of expressing oneself — definitely different senses of humor (or lack thereof).

In the case of *Dogville*, living in the village of Trollhattan in Sweden, in the dead of winter with very little sun and short days, the atmosphere wasn't loaded with gaiety. Not to overlook the fact that the plot of the movie itself was very dark which did not encourage laughter.

With all the negatives, I would not have missed it. The result was a controversial — Lars is always controversial, a good thing and he's never dismissed, also a good thing — but very interesting and worthwhile movie. At the time, not having seen a foot of film, I was filled with anxiety at how the final cut would turn out.

More than one year later, *Dogville* was to be screened on the opening day of the New York Film Festival. I had to go through it with the same trepidation. I would finally see Lars's complete vision brought to life. And get a glimpse of myself as a character in that town. After the march down the red carpet with my faithful, constantly supportive manager, Johnnie Planco, by my side, we were led to our reserved seats in the theatre. Sitting there in the dark, I squirmed at first, not really knowing what to expect. Seeing our set, our town with the streets clearly drawn, I found myself relaxing a bit as I became caught up in the story, the characters — and except for an occasional twinge when I saw myself, I really liked it. But I mean really liked it, not having expected to. It's part of one of the most fascinating aspects of movie making. Even while watching the finished product, memories and flashes of moments during the shooting pop up in your mind. Pictures of moments shared with cast members, visions of Lars in his amazing camera contraption, awareness of the musical score, the narration, all parts of the movie, *not* jarring, all what Lars intended, all completing the picture.

When the lights went up, I felt quite fine. Always somewhat nervous at events like this but relieved to feel good about the whole. People congratulating me on my performance — incongruous considering my very small contribution. Nevertheless, I was glad to be in it. It was worth the seven weeks in Sweden and definitely worth my newly formed friendships. Also there was the wonder that I felt and the amazement that sixty years as an active participant in movie making has afforded me the privilege of not only viewing but actively working in a new, original approach to film making.

Confirming for me how right I was to know from the age of ten or twelve that I had to be an actress.

Not long ago, I went back to the same places in Sweden to be in the second film of von Trier's trilogy — *Manderlay*. The part was small but I was able to work with Lars once more and to see him on a different set — different theme — still ensemble acting, which I enjoy. Surprisingly there were the same trailers as in *Dogville* — same studio — same Trollhattan to live in, but a completely renovated suite this time, done in my favorite blue and white. Funnily enough, it made me want to stay there a little longer. An oddly nostalgic feeling.

Dogville was quite well received. Mixed reviews but attention and respect for Lars were always there. Unhappily it could not erase or stop the onslaught of friends dying that began in 2002. I'll start with Adolph Green, the man who jumped into my life on a musical (what else?) night at Ira Gershwin's home.

Adolph's energy. His incredible sense of the outrageous. His teeth, which always shone brightly and he had many of them. Our friendship began more than fifty years ago. He was a complete — a true — original, a genuine eccentric. He had a personality so strong, so infectious, so endearing that he demanded attention. When he invaded your life, and that's exactly what he did, you had to let him in. You wanted to — you knew a life force had entered your life and there was no getting away from it. He knew the title and cast of every movie ever made, from silent films to this day. He knew every note of classical music. He would sing it — dum-dic-a-dum, etc. He knew every note of show tunes and their lyrics. He knew books of all varieties and their authors. He was mind-boggling. I don't know how he knew all these things, and he was neither pompous nor condescending about his knowledge. He was the personification of laughter and, at times, infuriatingly stubborn while at the same time being the sweetest, most loving husband, father and friend. I knew about the first two from observation and from being very close to his wife, Phyllis Newman. I almost felt related and was known as Number Two Wife. A joke, don't you know? The last two years of Adolph's life were no fun for him — he'd lost much of his hearing and vision. But that didn't stop him from not only partaking of life but living it to the fullest. We attended an event on Long Island — many round tables full of friends and food. Adolph was sitting next to me. I was talking to someone on the other side of our table when I heard Adolph — loud and clear — say, 'Just because I am blind and deaf is no reason not to talk to me.' You see, the humor remained and that statement was as close to a complaint as I ever heard from this funny, adorable, life-enhancing visitor from another planet. All of us — friends, families, most especially children — think about him and talk about him very, very often. He had an uncanny connection with the young — why not? He was forever young himself. Steve and Leslie had known him from childhood — Sam, too, all through his growing up years. Adolph and Phyllis's son, Adam, and Sam grew up together. Sam always felt close to Adolph, understood and connected with him. Adolph will crop up on an almost daily basis in general conversation. Often when you needed early film information, anything connected to music, Adolph had the answer. And every scene brings laughter and the sight of Adolph who could never be mistaken for anyone else. I often have the sense that he'll come skipping around the corner and we'll pick up where we left off, there was so much life and unpredictability in him. Remembrance saves me where friends are concerned. In any case, there is no forgetting Adolph Green — not that I'd want to. I just couldn't. His imprint is permanent. I see him almost daily, as I do with all those I have loved and lost.

I was just beginning to be able to live without the presence of Adolph when along came the shock in 2003 of the death of playwright Peter Stone. Peter was robust, never sick, and seventy-three years old — not considered old by anyone's standards. Another friendship of more than forty years. We worked together twice — once with Robert Preston in a short story written by Peter for television and secondly on a larger scale, on *Woman of the Year* for Broadway. Both successful and happy experiences. He was far and away the best toastmaster in my world. Always funny, always the right words in the right place at the right time. He toasted me at every major honor I received in New York or Washington. I always felt safe with Peter. He never went for the jugular. If he cared about you, he was there totally. His opinions about plays and players were loud and clear. No pussyfooting around. I disagreed with him many times — we butted heads a bit — but that never put more than a momentary nick in our friendship and affection for one another.

I was in his and his wife Mary's country

home one weekend. Peter appeared in outdoor gear — cap, gloves, portable Sony with accompanying ear aides, walking shoes, etc. In all the years and all the weekends I'd spent in that house, I'd never seen Peter partake of anything athletic except tennis, which he loved. Upon my inquiry, 'What's going on?', he said his doctor had told him he had to walk an hour each day. He seemed slightly annoyed that this walk would take him away from his reading and phone calls — interrupt our regular lunch at Estins in Amagansett. He was, however, resigned, saying, 'I don't want to — but I have to. I'm fine walking downhill, it's uphill that's the toughie.' And that was that. I asked no more questions. He volunteered no more information, although the following morning reading the Sunday papers — me on the couch — Peter in his usual chair in this cozy, relaxed, ideal country living room — I suddenly became aware he was on the phone to his doctor. Most unusual. But I said nothing. Only the next morning, as I was leaving to return to New York, I said my goodbyes to Mary and on turning to Peter, I felt an air of vulnerability around him that led me to stroke his face and tell him, 'Take care of your sweet self.' 'I will,' and I left. I will never forget that picture of us standing by the screen door. And it is only now that I realize that was the last time I saw him.

I spoke to him a few times when he was in the hospital. Our final exchanges were: Peter, 'I think I've turned the corner.' Me, 'Great! Then I can come see you.' Peter, 'Yes, and thanks for calling. It means a lot to me.' So from having slight breathing problems — nothing serious — it turned out to be life threatening. In a month's time the breathing became more and more acute and the next thing I knew, he was gone. Gone? Not Peter. Not possible. So fast. So abrupt. So unfair.

I see him everywhere. I miss him. I miss the gleam in his eye — where can we find the laughter — the wit — the intelligence. Peter was so intelligent as to frighten me at times, but beneath his bluster he was super-sensitive, caring, insecure, politically wise, involved in all things environmental and anything favoring protecting birds, animals, endangered species, the world. So now he rests in a corner of the town of Amagansett that he loved, next to his friend Alan Pakula. I raise my glass — I have no toast — only to say, 'You were valuable. You made a difference.' And, as far as I'm concerned, 'You're still here, now and always.'

And so the epidemic of 2003 began and continued.

Less than two months later, my beloved friend Gregory Peck died. He was everything that Atticus Finch was and more. More because he was younger and living and working in a very visible profession, among actors who not only did not think as he did, but did not give voice as he did, and among some studio heads who preferred that he keep his beliefs to himself. There is not really a single word to describe Greg — not one word that might encompass all of him. Of course, our friendship began in 1956 when we made *Designing Woman,* one of my all-time favorite movies. It was the year of Bogie's surgery and subsequent fight against cancer. It was one of the worst years of my life. The movie was a romantic comedy, wonderful script and therapeutic for me. I was forced to keep my spirits up and light during daytime shooting of the movie. Greg would ask how Bogie was doing, I would tell him, but there was no dwelling on the subject. Greg was too much of a gent to pry and I was too much in denial to want to talk about it — trying to focus on the movie. *Designing Woman* and Greg were a blessing. They saved my sanity.

Greg and I worked wonderfully together — always in sync. It's such a pleasure to find yourself with an actor who is there all the time — no star stuff — just caring about the scene, looking for ways to make it better — that's the sum of acting, what makes it so rewarding as to make up for the lesser times. Working together, NOT competing. From *Designing Woman* on, our friendship grew and grew naturally with him and his great wife, Veronique. No matter where we were, always a postcard, always kept in touch. When I was on Broadway, they'd come to New York. Never missed. And every time I received any recognition, he'd be there to present me with an award or introduce me live or on television. Never a request made by me, mind you, always by others. I would never have put him on a spot where he might feel backed against a wall. When I received the Kennedy Center Honor, Greg was unable to attend — the only major one he missed. He sent me a fax (one of many over the years and always unexpected) that said:

Dear Honoree —
I am sending you bread, wine and music for Christmas.
What more do you want?
Don't answer that.
(Signed) Yours for all time,
G. P.

He recited a prayer once — Irish, I think — that I loved. I asked him for a copy and of course received it immediately. It goes like this:

> Dear Lord,
> I want to thank you, Lord, for being
>   with me so far this day.
> I haven't been impatient, lost my
>   temper, been grumpy, judgmental, or
>   envious of anyone.
> But I will be getting out of bed in a
>   minute, and I think I will
> Really need your help then.
> Amen.

I wish I knew where this originated, but I don't. Anyway, it doesn't matter — it came from Gregory Peck and that's good enough for me. That and the fax were two small samples of his wit. He had it in abundance and he shared it. For any one man to have all these gifts seems impossible, but with simplicity, humility, integrity, loyalty, honor, heart and soul, Greg had it all. He defied the gods, the naysayers, those who demeaned actors. You know, when a friend dies there is a natural tendency to sing his praises and perhaps endow him with more superlative qualities than he might have had. That is definitely not the case with Greg. On the contrary, there is no way to say enough. He was no saint, but he was a man of extraordinary gifts. Of course, he was tall, dark and handsome, but actually more than that — he was dazzling. With a brain — not afraid to show affection — and guess what? He had humor, he had wit, he had warmth. He may not have known it, but I needed his friendship. As an actress who has not been showered with attention in my movie career, knowing that Greg was glad to see me gave me more confidence than I would otherwise have had. When I knew I was going to see him and Veronique, my spirits lifted. The luck, the luck I have had to have a man like Greg Peck as a pal — a man I would trust under any circumstance. I was always and forever grateful to him and for him. And I hope his goodness has rubbed off on me and will make me better in all ways.

Thinking back to *Designing Woman*, it was the start of what was to become a friendship of almost fifty years. We never lost track of one another. Even through my rocky eight years with Jason. If we communicated less at times it was due to working on different coasts, often in different countries, and to living on different sides of the U.S. It seems that I always felt Greg and Veronique and I had unflagging affection for one another. It really didn't matter where or when, with Greg once it was fully and firmly established, it would not, could not change. We won awards together, solid gold Rudolph Valentino awards, recog-

979

nizing our contributions to movies. We remained sort of a team.

Then one day came the offer to play opposite Greg in *The Portrait* for Ted Turner's cable channel, me playing the wife of this magical professor with Greg's lovely daughter Cecilia playing our daughter in the piece. In the story, Greg and I were close as pages in a book, which led to the daughter feeling left out. So there we were in North Carolina, Veronique, Greg, Cecilia and me, living and behaving like one big, happy family — Cecilia calling me 'Mother' — Veronique and I going marketing together — all this proof positive that we loved each other. I never for a moment felt like an outsider. I was always welcomed with open arms into the tightly knit Peck family. Veronique made even locations feel like home. Though Greg was ten years my senior, we seemed, and we were, totally in tune with one another. We always had fun working together. On screen, we were a pair — the scenes and the action flowed. We were comfortable together, I felt safe with him.

There was an occasion during *The Portrait*, I think it was either Greg's birthday or Veronique's or their anniversary — there, I've covered all bases — anyway, it was a celebration and Veronique had arranged, in her incredibly thoughtful and thorough way, to have her great cook Carmen make a great Mexican dinner. And how she did all this I'll never know, but it was cooked, packed and shipped to North Carolina. A feast, one of my favorite cuisines. There was great wine, and simple and loving toasts. It was a family celebration and I was included. Perfect Peck. We continued to meet through all those years past and to the end of his life. Aside from seeing my children, no trip to California was complete without at least one dinner at the Pecks'. A highlight for me.

I give lectures from time to time and the venues have altered through the years. I always like to change the talks a bit depending on the audience and the location. Greg had started to do his 'Evenings with Gregory Peck' so I asked him what his format was. He gave me a rough idea and asked if I'd like to see one of his. Yes please, Greg. I would love to. On my return home, there it was, a video of Greg's evening. It was filled with anecdotes — Irish stories — his movie life — all warmth and laughter. What struck me particularly was the way he answered one question. Someone asked him how he would like to be remembered. His response, after a pause, was that mostly he wanted to be remembered as a good husband, a good father and a good grandfather. Extraordinary — pure Peck!

He of course was all those things but it clearly demonstrated how family oriented he was, how much he valued his wife, his children and grandchildren, his home, how much pride he took in all of it. And I think of what I have missed. Having lived alone for so many, many years, I never had a complete family life. My children and grandchildren are my family but we don't live in the same cities so we don't spend that much time together. And I work so much of the time that the work itself is temporary family for me. I love and adore my children and grandchildren but of course one learns very quickly that they have different interests and priorities, so we must do what we can when we can.

Less than two weeks after Greg's death, George Axelrod, another friend of fifty years, died. Of course, it was his play, *Goodbye Charlie*, that brought me back to Broadway and the beginning of making my childhood dream come true. He was a classy man of original ideas and great intelligence. 'I'm in the hit business, baby,' he would say to me. And he had been — until *Goodbye Charlie* which unhappily did not receive favorable reviews. I did — the play didn't — though it ran to full houses for three months. George could not take the rejection. He felt he was no longer the whiz kid. So when Hollywood beckoned, he left New York and settled in Los Angeles. He worked with Billy Wilder, Josh Logan, and John Frankenheimer. *Seven Year Itch,* one of his biggest hit plays, was transferred to the big screen to be followed by many more. He was a lovely man, vulnerable followed by hypersensitive. After *The Manchurian Candidate,* a wildly successful — and finally cult — classic, which he wrote brilliantly, George continued to make contributions to the motion pictures, well received but not compared to *Manchurian.* He did not feel appreciated, as those of us have felt the same for years, many years. It is the way of the motion picture mind. You start off being the flavor of the month, dwindling down to not being thought of, certainly unappreciated. If you're over twenty-five years old and not bringing in the big bucks, you are ignored. Not a pretty picture, but an accurate one. It happened to George as it has happened to me and countless others.

Anyway, when he and Joan moved to London they were welcomed with open arms. His talent was respected. He was. Life was good for many years there. Finally, however, what happens in many countries is you feel more like a foreigner, less like you belong, and work is scarce.

George was a writer, a good one. He needed to write. So as Joan had a magic touch when it came to living, back to California they went and finally settled happily there. And there they stayed until the end. George had everything to do with my reason to move back to America. And over a period of fifty years, we remained super friends. So once again a piece of my life had been chipped away. Getting older, though necessary, leaves a great deal to be desired.

Katharine Hepburn died eight days later — the final blow of 2003. It was not unexpected — she was ninety-six years old and the quality of her life had not been what she would have wished. But she was there. She was there and I could not conceive of there being a time without her. She was Miss Hepburn — Aunt Kat — Katie — Kate — Kathy (to Spencer Tracy). She was all of those depending upon your relationship. And she was also Katharine. With an 'A'.

She was loyal — demanding — pure and purely demanding — open — reserved — formally informal — proud — intimidating — exasperating — funny — touching. She was a worker — a riser above everything — passionate in her likes and dislikes — saying what she thought but keeping herself to herself — loving — sentimental — a lover of beauty — of nature. She was there for all who needed her — really needed her and were in need. She was especially, wonderfully, uniquely, one of a kind. For all she was — has been — has given on all levels — publicly or privately — she enhanced this life.

There was more public attention paid her than anyone in memory. Tribute upon tribute on television, newspapers, magazines devoting whole issues to her. It continued for months after her passing. As a woman, she had made a powerful impact on all who didn't know her. She was independent. She chose her way of life — hurting no one — and never vying for approval. She leaves me with so many pictures of her in so many different places at so many different times. She unknowingly made me aware of ways to live and to behave that were new to me. So although there is a large, empty space in my life without her, there is all that past to remember. She could do so many things. She applied herself. How many surprising, great meals that she cooked when I had evenings with her and Spence.

She painted — she drew a character portrait for Bogie and me. She watercolored a self-portrait for me — delivered the day after I won the Tony for my performance in *Applause* over hers in *Coco*. As I read her praise of me written more than thirty years ago, I am filled with nostalgia, great love for this amazing woman and am stunned by her flattery. For better or worse, here it is in her own words:

My own dear friend
DESERVED — WARRANTED
All that pure simplicity,
unguarded modesty and
Boyish courage
poured into a frame of leonine splendor
You ROSE — you CONQUERED
And none could be more pleased than
 I —
Your smeared* friend, [*referring to the
 edge of the printing]
Auntie Kate
ON THE OCCASION OF THE
 TONY AWARDS
April 19th 1970

I blushed when I first read it. I blush as I write it now. So flattering — so sweet — that she thought so highly of me. She could never say it, anymore than I could, but she could write it — as I could. Remembering the fifteen-year-old me in the third balcony watching her on stage in *The Philadelphia Story* — in complete awe — to the meeting of her, getting to know her, during the filming of *The African Queen* in the wilds of the Belgian Congo and the Victoria Falls, seeing the side of her few would have seen — to being accepted as a true friend despite the difference in our ages — with our bond growing stronger through Bogie's illness and death — then the following years of closeness as we traveled for work and life in general until Spencer's death, and being able to talk about our lives on a personal level — to her arriving at my apartment with a small bouquet of flowers in her hand a few hours after I brought my newborn son, Sam, home from the hospital — the first of my friends to set eyes on him — his godmother. Typical Kate — is it any wonder I adored her and felt and told her that ten minutes of her would be worth twenty-four hours of anyone else. Sentimental in spite of herself. When I was very rundown in the Bel-Air Hotel with two-year-old Sam, and Jason living the part of Eugene O'Neill's Hughie, disappearing — it was Kate who shook me up, telling me, 'You've got to get out of this. You've forgotten what a tree looks like — the sky. You have to come down to a beach house I rent in Trancas and breathe the ocean air.' I did that then and so loved it and the house that I rented it for several years after that, both with and without Jason.

Years of dinners on trays in Turtle Bay, cooked by devoted Nora. Katie never would go out — always meals at home — whether she was in a play or not — dinner was at 6:00 p.m. and you'd better not be late. I didn't dare. She was an early morning day person — I was a late morning night person. Except when making a movie, of course — waking at 6:00 a.m. and trying to sleep by 10:30 or 11:00 at night always took me the first week of shooting to get in the groove. I always adjusted my time to Kate's — if you wanted to spend time with her, those were the rules. By 8:30 you were out of there and she was mounting the stairs to her bedroom. She was a character all right, a fascinating one. I keep remembering seeing her in Paris with Spencer and the Garson Kanins. She was wearing a dress. Spencer refused to take her out unless she wore a dress. She wore one of the probably two dresses that she owned and she was glowing, brimming over with joy. As the years wore on, through good times and bad, right to the end, Kate always had a glow.

She was spoiled, I suppose. Spoiled in the sense that the rules she lived by had to be respected and agreed to by any and all who entered her domain. When it came to dinner invitations, Kate did the menu. Having a marvelous cook like Nora helped. I never worried about the food. I knew that

Katie was more a meat and potatoes person than a fish person. That was just dandy with me. Nora always climbed the stairs carrying the trays adorned with perfectly cooked lamb, roast potatoes, parsnips (which Kate loved and, as it turned out, I never had except from her kitchen). String beans were often on the menu, as were beets, lima beans, a green salad and Katie's favorite dessert of ice cream — chocolate and coffee topped off with her favorite brownies and Nora's lace cookies. I still have the brownie recipe. And I will NOT share it.

These dinners were very reminiscent of the dinners Katie cooked for Spence. She might always have been, but she certainly became, a first rate and inventive cook for Spence. And when I had a meal with them, it was always meticulously and carefully served by herself. Her sole aim was to please him, which she unfailingly did. The main difference in evenings with Kate after Spence died was that we always had a drink before dinner. Katie had her scotch whisky, I had either vodka or Jack Daniel's. I had hardly ever seen Katie take any alcohol before that time, only very occasionally in Africa during *African Queen* and then only rarely. She knew that both Bogie and John Huston enjoyed their drinks. She didn't want to encourage them but she did like to join in from time to time.

There was always an element of unpredictability and surprise about Kate. Looking back at those times — all of them — I realize that. I was privy to the sight of Kate, the woman. Not strident, still opinionated, but always willing to listen to John and Bogie. Knowing, of course, that they both adored her. Watching her sitting on the floor pouring coffee for Spencer, listening — no, hanging on — to his every word, looking up at him with total adoration. She was a woman in love, blindingly, unquestionably in love. Spence, on his part, was always sweet with her, affectionate, though not overly demonstrative. But there was no doubt in my mind, or anyone else's who saw them together, that they were totally committed to one another and that they were totally balanced and belonged together. I spent a great deal of time with them after Bogie died. Somehow, don't ask me how, I always felt Bogie was the invisible fourth. The vision of him always came up in conversation. Katie and Spence were that rarity — two actors who genuinely felt so close to one another — respect and love — plus non-stop laughter.

Until the day she died, I never thought of Kate without thinking of Spence and Bogie. After all, our friendship really began and solidified during the making of *African*

Queen in 1951. To think that Kate's and my friendship endured for more than fifty years is some kind of record. And it created a special bond between us — me without Bogie, followed by her without Spence. Those years of memories of four of us — then three of us — then two of us. Now only one.

After my first meeting with Katie when I was filled with fear — when I saw the many facets of her character, she was only once unkind to me. And even that once was not really her fault. A few years before she died, she said one day, 'I'm not spending any more money.' And on another occasion, 'Don't ask me any questions. I can't remember anything.' I suppose that was a slight indication of how her life would alter. The unkindness came one night as we were having dinner in her house on Turtle Bay. As usual, the two of us. Norah had cooked her customary delicious meal. Conversation was not exactly flowing. I was telling her of my activities, of Sam's — it was pretty much a one sided conversation. Some silence followed then she looked at me and said, 'What do you want?' I was stunned by that, not understanding until she said again, 'What do you want?' — then once more followed by an impatient letting out of breath. That made me so nervous, I was at a loss. After saying, 'I don't want anything, Kate' — which did not sit well with her, as she was still staring at me — I felt so uncomfortable. I finally said, 'I must be going. Thanks for dinner. I'll see you soon.' I then made for the kitchen where Nora was cleaning up. I told her what had transpired and how I never wanted to go through that again. Nora said, 'You know she doesn't mean that, Miss Bacall.' I said I hoped not but I was at a loss and very upset. That clearly indicated the major change that had come over Kate.

Not long after, she went to her house in Connecticut and that was where she would spend the last years of her life. I never went back to Turtle Bay. I continued to visit her in Connecticut. The visits were obviously not as often as in New York. It was a good two and a half hours to get to the Connecticut house so after allowing a solid two hours to spend with Kate and another two and a half hours back, it was a day gone. I called frequently and visited when I could. By then Katie's ability to recognize had visibly altered. I would enter the living room. She would be seated in her favorite chair. At the beginning, she would give me a blank look that would change to a flicker of an eye as she realized she knew me. As I talked on about Bogie and Africa — about Spence — our trip to

Paris — mutual friends — Olivier — Vivien Leigh — George Cukor — Ethel Barrymore — she seemed to connect me, them and her. She did not verbalize it. Nora said she knew, the young woman tending her would know. I'd ask, 'Do you want to go outside?' She'd say an emphatic, 'No.' She would sit in her chair, lost in her own thoughts. I would sit with her. Finally when it was time for me to leave, I would give her a hug. She would either say, 'Stay' or give some indication, couldn't I stay longer? For dinner? — I would say, 'Next time.' It was always sad to see her like that — though she did not seem unhappy — and it was always sad to leave her. She was ninety-three or -four then and had had a full life, a life of her choice. Even so, I had hoped she would live forever.

The very last time I saw her, I walked right over to her in her chair in the living room, sat next to her, kissed her. She seemed to know me a little. There were two large picture books — one with a shot of Bogie from *The African Queen* — one of Spence. As I showed each to her and spoke to her of these two men who meant so much to her, she miraculously seemed to brighten and understand. Television journalist Cynthia McFadden, who had driven me over, said she was sure Katie had connected and understood. Cynthia and Katie had become friends some years before. I think Katie almost thought of her as a daughter. Anyway, they were close and Cynthia had seen enough of Kate to know when she responded and when she didn't. That day when I was about to leave, she said, 'Please stay.' After I had stayed for a half hour longer, I leaned over and kissed her cheeks many times after which she looked at me and whispered, 'Thank you.' So touching — so sweet. I wondered how much she knew. It mattered not. She knew something.

There have been far too many in the losses column in 2004, but there is one that meant a great deal to me personally by the name of Alistair Cooke. Our friendship began in 1952 with Adlai Stevenson. Alistair was reporting on him, Bogie and I were appearing at various rallies and whistle stops with him. All very exciting, all great fun. Bogie and I and Alistair and Jane Cooke hit it off immediately. Alistair was a man who seemed to know a great deal about everything, wrote pieces for the *Manchester Guardian*, and delivered a *Letter from America* on radio. There was not an American or a Brit who did not tune in every Sunday morning to hear Alistair's resumé of the past week in the

United States. He had become a U.S. citizen and traveled the country filming and writing a book on *Alistair Cooke's America*. He was very visible on TV, in book form, endlessly interesting and inventive, with charm, good looks, wit and mind-boggling braininess. He also hosted two brilliant shows — *Omnibus* and *Masterpiece Theatre*. The four of us had great times together on both East and West Coasts. He and Jane contributed so much to my life after Bogie's death. Excellent at spirit lifting — both of them — and clarifying for me things I might feel cloudy or fuzzy about. And we would turn up at different locations with many of the same friends: me in London when he was there, him in San Francisco when I was touring in *Woman of the Year* and he was touring with *Alistair Cooke's America*, him in California when Bogie was surrounded by people telling him how to write his will, an eerie experience for all with me in complete denial. So many memories throughout those many years, they give you such a solid base — built in connections — conversations witty and informative with the extra perk of his piano playing of show tunes. At least there is so much to draw upon with all my losses — those friends who enriched my life — gave me pause — gave me thought — enlightened me.

In a way, friendship was my family. It

was my good luck to have such an array of friends — all different — all talented — all intelligent — all complicated — all witty. And lucky I am that there are more still who are laughing on along with me — not by a thread, but hanging on nevertheless. So there is reason to be grateful and to be able to laugh and even enjoy one's quirks, qualms and quackiness.

My need to work remained my focus and necessity. Without warning, a script arrived with an offer for a movie called *Birth* to be made completely in New York. Hooray! I get to sleep in my own bed! No suitcases adorning the room to pack and unpack, no goodbyes to Sophie. How lucky can you get? The director was to be Jonathan Glazer, whose first effort was a marvelous movie called *Sexy Beast* and, as if that weren't enough, which it most certainly was, Nicole Kidman was the star and I would most happily be her mother. I was thrilled beyond words. Not only because I love Nicole and admire her talent and mind but also because being her mother was such a good part in a terrific, original script written by Jonathan. So here it was — another adventure — this British director's second movie and at a time when there is little work for women of any age, how lucky for me to be wanted by this very talented young man.

The part was really first rate. I thought, my God at this time in my life and career to be in a movie like this, with this major director — an independent movie — little money of course — but that's the way it is in the movie business these days. If it's not a studio movie, salaries are small — and that is a gross understatement. However, I'd still rather work with talented, new people any day, than do some of the big, high-paying mediocre movies that are too often made in Los Angeles. I have nothing against high paying, mind you. I would love to be the recipient of high pay in a good studio movie. It's always a plus to be able to pay the rent. Unfortunately, I have not been chosen by either Steven Spielberg or Martin Scorsese or Woody Allen to appear in one of their films. I have tried to convince Martin Scorsese that I would be a perfect Mafia member. Why does it always have to be a man? He smiles sweetly, 'Yeah, great idea.' He's such a terrific director but I know it will never happen.

I didn't know what Jonathan would be like. He called me from London to make a date for dinner on his arrival. One must never have preconceptions — they are almost never right. First of all he's young — early forties — second, he's attractive, third, he's smart — knows exactly what he wants. No airs. Our dinner was great, at one of my favorite restaurants. Having just arrived from London, he kept apologizing for his clothes — jeans and shirt. (The jeans, by the way, were seen regularly during the shoot.) He openly talked about his life. Save for his exhaustion — plane ride and it being five hours later for him — he got through it. We talked of the movie, he explained his concept clearly and told me who he'd cast — the major one being John Huston's son, Danny, who had directed me in a movie called *Mr North* in 1988. Since then, he had turned actor and is absolutely terrific. Talk of 'six degrees of separation'. Proof positive once again that our lives go full circle and we are all connected, just as John Guare stated so clearly in his play of the same name. Danny was to play opposite Nicole. Zoe Caldwell was to play my best friend — what could be better? Thrilling to have Zoe with me, and Danny who was like family — so great to spend time with him, grown up and with a baby. I was really excited about the entire set-up, couldn't wait to start.

The *Birth* experience was in some ways diametrically opposed to *Dogville*. No location, for instance. I could stay home for the entire movie. That does not often happen. Being picked up every morning at

6:00 or 6:30 a.m. or thereabouts and driven to the studio in Queens, home of Silvercup, the popular white bread found in all the markets of my childhood. Upon arrival, being greeted by an assistant director and by Michael O'Connor, an assistant assigned to me who turned out to be great. Then being led to my dressing room which was next to the sound stage that all closely resembled the studio system of my young years. As a result, the day started off being much cozier — all working actors each day in the same building, walking on to the same sound stage, having the same Kraft Service coffee in paper cups and then on to the set where director, crew and cameraman were ready to get going. Somehow that system creates a more intimate feeling — though in the case of *Birth*, most of the cast were part of a family so familiarity was almost built in.

The role in *Birth* gave me more room to move emotionally and mentally than had *Dogville*. Nicole and I, having developed a friendship of great mutual affection, had a built-in feeling for one another that brought an extra dimension to our scenes together. Mind you, not knowing how Jonathan has cut the movie, what scenes are in, what are out, plus my not having seen the dailies, I can't guarantee the result on screen. Anyway, the feeling was there and I hope it shows. It's the doing of it that counts. It's the doing of it that I truly love. I do not go to the dailies during the shooting of the film. I learned very early on in my career that I do not like watching myself on screen. I am hypercritical and see only negative moves, awkwardness, wrong attitudes. That being said, I do not consciously think of how I look in a scene, vanity not being in the forefront of my self-perceptions. I have never spent extra time looking in the mirror, as I have never been enamoured of my face, which of course is magnified umpteen times on screen. Truly, it is the work that must come first; it is the work that gives the personal rewards, the sense of exercising all that I have learned from the beginning. The years of study, observation, practicing my craft, remembering Bogie's first teaching of the necessities of thought, awareness, concentration and focus. Of preparing. As his acting career began in the theatre, his own learning as an actor totally became an automatic part of him with each character he played, be it stage or screen. The basic necessities are the same even though the presentation and final rendition in performance may not be.

Working with Nicole, as opposed to just being in the same movie with her as in *Dogville*, was really very special. She is a wonderful actress — always concentrated and focused on the work and giving to me in our scenes together. Our friendship was cemented during this period to a degree that we felt almost related. The movie is complicated but fascinating and I was very grateful to have been a part of it. It's hard to describe but having been in this business for sixty years (unbelievable as it seems, especially to me) and to find that there are members (one or two perhaps) who still might want me in their films is more than gratifying. As work is what drives me — gives me a life and a continued goal despite my advancing years — the excitement goes on and the fact that there are still possibilities gives me that extra push to get up in the morning.

On *Birth* there was not a morning that I did not look forward to the day's work. Jonathan's head was so filled with ideas that arriving on set I knew there would be a surprise or two in the offing. Though I didn't always agree with some of his changes, I knew he was a man of vision who knew what he wanted in a scene. Yet he never failed to answer my questions and listen to my (what I thought were reasonable) doubts. I was never bored — he was non-stop interesting and intelligent. His process was new territory for me to explore as an actress so I had to be on my toes —

always alert. That, plus an often fourteen-to sixteen-hour day, made a nap at lunch almost a necessity. Amazing what a twenty-minute snooze will do for you in the energy department. Though I didn't do it on a daily basis, I highly recommend it.

No matter what the outcome, it was a happy experience for me and for Sophie, who loved every aspect of the shooting, from early morning pick up to arrival at the Silvercup studios. She trotted down the hall, stopping to say hello to wardrobe and make-up before stopping completely at the door of my dressing room. She owned the place and everyone in it. I have never had a dog who so completely left her mark wherever she might be. I continually marvel at her behavior and continually wonder what goes on in the brain of that tiny head.

Through the years I have become aware that aimlessness does not suit me. Having a purpose does, be it going to the bank, the market, the gym, wherever — it's a goal. In my subconscious from the beginning. Living in a city filled with activity does that. It's one of New York's main attractions. As I sit here confronting myself after roughly sixty years of New York living, this seems to be it. As they say, 'I'll never get out of here alive.' I always loved this city. You might say it was in my blood through my entire family, we belonged here. Even during the fifteen years I lived with and loved Bogie in California, I always wanted a small pied à terre here where we had many friends, I had family and there was life — theatres to go to, restaurants, nightclubs, coffee shops, endless variety. Then it was a city to walk in, day or night.

In my early teens, the fun I had window shopping, looking sometimes longingly into shops filled with lovely clothes I could never afford. And years later, I was still window shopping on Madison Avenue, Broadway, many streets East side and West side, only this time I could walk into these shops and I could buy what I yearned for sometimes. Before and after, New York remained a city of excitement filled with dreams that might be fulfilled. So much was possible whether you were rich, poor or medium. I was medium. But it never stopped me from dreaming. Even though the city has changed so much, I hope there are still those who have hope for the future, who feel the beat of the city. In a way it's still there, but you have to seek it out.

In 2003 — the first year in the last fifteen that I did not see Paris but once at the end of the year — I walked the streets of New York with my Sophie and I came to realize how this city of my childhood and my childhood dreams had changed. Dramatically and drastically. It was and still is a great city in what it has to offer educationally, historically, entertainment-wise and varied-neighborhood-wise, but it has become a city whose streets have been taken over by enormous trucks and buses (mostly empty) traveling two and three abreast. Dodging bicycles that you mostly cannot see or hear on sidewalks (against an unenforced law) — crosswalks marked for pedestrians and instead overrun by cars and taxis and vans extending their front halves into them — all in all it is hell trying to walk in this city now. It seems almost impossible to cross the street without being run into or being sideswiped by a car or taxi.

Yet I remain. Were I ten or more years younger, I would probably move. But I've lived in the same place for more than forty years — it is my home — my roots are here — many friends are here — theatre is here — even when I sit in my kitchen and look at only my endless cups and saucers, I know I can never move. I decry the fact that there are no manners anymore — is it the times? Cell phones — deafening noise on the streets, in the cars — blasting boom boxes — people walking towards you, not seeing you, never giving way so you can pass — not allowing you to get out of the elevator before they push themselves in — I began to notice this quite a few years ago and each year it all has grown and grown. Until it is almost bursting at the seams. Is it anger and if so, why to such a degree? There are not too many smiling faces. Where has all the humor gone, or was it never there? Did I just wish it?

Thank God some of my childhood haunts still exist. There is still nothing that can beat Zabar's, the New York delicatessen of my childhood that I shop in now. I love going there and choosing my own cream cheese with scallions, my own smoked salmon. There is an endless assortment of fresh food — coleslaw, egg salad, herring, chopped chicken liver, cold cuts and more. I am never disappointed with their offerings. And another thing that exists in New York that one does not readily find in Los Angeles and other cities is fresh and delicious takeout. As I live alone, I don't often cook for myself. What saves me are the specialty shops, William Poll, for example, with freshly cooked meals daily with different items every day, plus an assortment of fantastic soups, dips, chips — all homemade. And they deliver. And there are great markets — large and small. So I'm grateful for all that and miss it when I'm away from it for too long. So finally, I guess I'm stuck. The tough side, the noise, the bad traffic, the other obstacles will not go away. But when I am safely in my glorious apartment overlooking Central Park with all my things, my life of sixty years around me, I am quite content. Nothing's perfect, but I have my friends, my Papillon, my books, my music — so I'm lucky. Children a phone call away, work still there for me.

As I look outside my window on Central Park West in the afternoon sun, I see trees, all sizes, full and green (I never realized how many shades of green there are) being backed up by tall buildings — too tall — cement shutting out light. And I think how lucky I am to live where I do so that just by looking out the window I can almost feel I am in the country and how lucky to live where I live instead of being completely closed in by cement.

In the United States the focus has always been on success, on making it, which of course is followed by making money which in turn will buy you the biggest house on the block — the most expensive car — entrance to the corporate America club — the good old boys' club — the golf dates — the private planes and on and on. Unhappily quality does not count as number one, because with the accent on things, tables, chairs, tangibles — creativity, imagination and standards fall to the bottom of the ladder or off it. I really hate to see that this country — that once was about ideals, about people, about the land, about enriching the spirit, about accomplishment because you love what you do — has more and more become about corporate America — money, buying power, greed. It's all so cold, so humorless, so dead.

I know what you're thinking. Yes, money bought me my apartment, but it was money that came from years of work, hard work — doing what I love to do, not to acquire. I like money as much as most people — more because it gives me independence and as long as I keep working enables me to live here and go where I wish to go. I loved the America of Franklin Roosevelt, of John and Robert Kennedy — I grew up on that, had pride in it — but I do not love the administration of now. Now is not about people or ideals, ideas — it's about C.E.O.s — Bush buddies — Texas — oil secrecy — gun lobbying — anti-immigration corporations — all wrapped up in the American flag making this a pure Aryan (sound familiar?) country — a Christian country. Why don't people realize this country was built by immigrants? One of the great basics and selling points of the United States was that anyone from anywhere in the world could come here, make a life and prosper in freedom. We're all immigrants. I am an immigrant — my mother was born in Rumania. The glory has gone and, most devastatingly, the humor — the laughter has gone.

While I'm on the subject of non-functioning situations, here's one more example. While I was actually writing this passage — with a low bow to Joe Heller, Something Happened. The lights went out. At first I thought it was a fuse — until I discovered that all the lights in my apartment were out, then that all lights everywhere were out. I picked up the phone to see if it was something in my building that had gone awry. My phone was dead. I tried to reach my children on my cell phone — could not get through to anyone. All of New York City was doing the same thing. It was the total blackout. It was eerie to look out across Central Park and see only black buildings of different heights with nary a light in sight. On Central Park West there was not a streetlight, traffic light, even flashlight to be seen. Once in a while a police car showed up with headlights on full blast and the red and blue lights atop the cars twirling around. There were only people, stranded for the most part, hoping a bus would appear. One finally did in the wee small hours with all lights shining inside and out — a stark picture against the pitch darkness. Luckily, I had flashlights and many candles, this time not for the romantic setting candles usually convey.

What I found to be the most distressing factor was the complete inability to communicate with anyone, in my case my children, mostly, and friends. I couldn't get through to any city or state. I thought what would happen if someone had a health emergency under these conditions — just too bad! The radio station, which I was finally able to get on CBS and ABC, kept saying call 911 if you really need help. But the phones were dead, stupid! What were they thinking? There was the mayor giving advice — 'stay home' — not quite possible if you were stuck on a subway. The mindless radio voices reported that it was not a terrorist act — did anyone really think it was? — that people were walking across the Brooklyn Bridge — that the lights were out in Times Square — all theatres dark. They continued to repeat the same information over and over again. And then the President, from either Crawford, Texas, or California fund raising, gave a stilted speech about the safety of the country, how he was going to get to the bottom of the grid problem, etc. etc. Not exactly soothing and not a grain of humor or humanity to be heard. I repeat, where has all the humor gone?

When riding in a car, I'll note the endless traffic — almost bumper to bumper. Somewhere in the distance a siren sounds. As it gets louder, more persistent, I see that it is an ambulance. I also see that with the traffic the ambulance is now unable to move. So what's to be done? And if you happen to be the unlucky one needing an ambulance — forget it — you'll just have to die. That's life in the big city, as my son Sam says.

Forgive me if I'm sounding too grim. Maybe it's just one of those days. I hold the thought until I hit the street. It's a beautiful fall day — foliage still on the trees — no sign of Isabel (very feminine hurricane) as yet, though 'they' (the media) say she's on her way. It's nature that keeps us aware and awake — wet or dry. And it's nature finally that makes it possible to deal with the rest of it, the bad stuff. I hate to knock the city of most of my life but being exposed to it day in and day out makes the negatives hard to ignore. If I could wish it back to the way it was, I would in a minute. Garbage on the streets cannot possibly connote progress. The occasional quiet times — early morning —

dusk — are still appreciated and relished. I think for me, in addition to the obvious work reasons, friend reasons, it's memories that keep me here. Not that I'm one to dwell on the past — I'm not — or wallow in the negatives — I don't — but pictures of my growing up years crop up and my mother is always with me — on a certain street that I pass or is mentioned by someone. I either know that street, used to live on that street or wish I had. So it seems that I will stay where I am.

I still love traveling in Europe. Although, with the combination of airport security and the intense dislike of Americans, travel has become more difficult. Whereas for most of my life an American passport was more desirable worldwide than even the most desirable Tiffany diamond, now it is the Euro that has taken over and moved to number one on the popularity charts. So it is more than distressing to find the tables turned on the country of my birth. Here we are near the end of 2004 with the world in a mess, in my view due in large part to the Bush administration. Americans have become the most hated people on earth, we have run out of countries to visit. How we could declare war on Iraq — on any country — which did not attack us, I will never understand. As I write, November and the elections are looming. So there is hope that the present administration will disappear. (Please, God.) A new one will give a sense of openness, honesty and, at least, a fresh approach to the rest of the world. Experts have said that America has never been at such a low ebb. With our bombs destroying half of Iraq and its men, women and children, and our young men and women losing their lives as shown on every news program every day and night, there seems to be nothing but killing. And to what end? It is too horrible and not the same country I or my children grew up in. Having been brought up to be aware of my government and its elected officials and public figures, it's a shock to have to now explain or apologize for the existing powers. Before, I always took such pride in our leaders — even if I disagreed with and fiercely disliked several over the years, there always was that small ray of hope one could find and hang onto. Now there is futility — I don't know how it happened so fast — but happen it has. So I continue to cling to the great leaders of the past, hoping to instill in myself the pride of yore that was so much a part of me for so many years.

In my growing up years my idol was Franklin D. Roosevelt. He represented to me everything that was good — care for those in need, intelligence, quality, great wit, courage. Even as a child I remember being in awe of him, recognizing his courage in spite of his paralysis. Listening to his fireside chats he was the grandfather I never knew, the father who was never there, the friend, the teacher — he was warmth and comfort even when I was age eight, nine, ten and upwards — granted, I was needy and I romanticized every aspect of the man. He was worth it. He was a great man and he was a great leader. To this day I still feel the same about him. And his wife, Eleanor, who I was lucky to meet on several occasions in my twenties and thirties — she was the first woman in public life who made me aware or at least opened my eyes to the tremendous influence a woman could have, the contributions a woman could make and ultimately the power a woman could have in making her world and *the* world — then the man's world — a better place. There are no seconds — only one Roosevelt, one Truman, one John Kennedy and one Robert Kennedy — one Adlai Stevenson. It is that level that I personally yearn for. I'll keep searching for a glimmer of any one of those men and that woman.

So much in life seems to be compromise. Why can't we have the best? Why can't we be better than we are? Why can't we enrich our lives with appreciation of the arts, with books? Why can't that all be at least as important as making money, having a bigger house, a newer car? Why do we have to be submerged in commercialism? Why is tearing down a sign of progress instead of preserving? And there are many more whys. The big why to me in America is why don't we take the time to see what is around us — the earth, the sea, the sky? Are people so busy chasing the hours, hurrying them along so they can get to that first martini? I myself have been guilty of losing time — wasting it. However, the last few years I have become too aware of the passing of time — the losing of it.

As I sit here writing about the most vivid and affecting events and happenings of the last twenty-five years, I think of the lives I have led. The remarkable number of remarkable people I have known. The varied locations when memorable and lasting friendships have been formed — where work opportunities have allowed me to spread my wings in new directions. I can hardly believe that from the age of eighteen — riding on the Super Chief, alone, heading for the unknown in California — that from that moment on my life would change forever. New sights and sounds, new faces and experiences that even in my fantasy I never envisioned would happen at once and so quickly. Leaving the protective arms of my mother, my grandmother, my Uncle Charlie and the rest of my New York family, I was then on my own.

From my first meeting with Howard Hawks, who would own me, and Charlie Feldman, who would represent and also own me, the new world began to unfold. From the first movie came my first and most electrifying love. The wheels of publicity from Warner Bros. and Hawks turned me from an unknown to a completely new identity and spun me around so quickly I hardly had time to know what was happening . . . then to be married, to live in a house for the first time — with a swimming pool, a cook, a butler — to drive a car — to own a car — to have dogs and flowers and trees — to meet Robert Benchley, Nunnally Johnson, John Huston, Richard Brooks, Ira Gershwin, Dorothy Parker, Harold Arlen, Johnny Mercer, Hoagy Carmichael, John O'Hara, Cole Porter, David Niven, Clifton Webb, Cary Grant, Oscar Levant and more and more. To absorb it all is dizzy-making to me now. And to have a child — at twenty-four. All this in less than five years! Mind-boggling. I do not really understand how I was able to accept it all so readily. It's hard to believe I was a theatre usher living in Greenwich

Village and sharing a bed with my mother in the entry hall of our small apartment at the time I was offered the screen test by Howard Hawks that would send me to California and the opening chapter of my fairy tale life.

The pictures I have in my head from those early years are very clear to me: running down Beverly Drive in Beverly Hills, arms held wide, green three-quarters coat flying, toward Bogie waiting for me on the corner with James Gleason at four in the morning; Bogie walking up Highway 101 in espadrilles, huge sunflower in jacket lapel at six in the morning as I found him in my 1940 Plymouth — the headiest romance imaginable. The varied photos taken on the set of *To Have and Have Not* and *The Big Sleep* on the Warner Bros. lot — I know it's me — so young — but I can hardly believe it. The twenty-five-year difference between us is never visible. We just looked right together — always. Maybe I looked older and he looked younger. Whatever it was, it was most definitely the match made in heaven.

The chapters in my life unfolded with the birth of Steve first and, two and a half years later, Leslie — moving into new houses with each child. High times on a first trip to Europe and Africa — Academy Awards — the great friends — the beginning of my relationship with Katharine Hepburn and Spencer Tracy — the sailing life so foreign to me, so necessary for Bogie — my mother's wedding to the loveliest of men, Lee Goldberg, who was her prince on the white horse from the day she laid eyes on him a few years before — a bachelor until then, whisking her away to the life she always wanted.

I think of the steadiness of friendships that grew stronger with each year, even as the studio life changed and television became a serious factor in all our lives, and some friends had to move to Europe for work and this forced distance between us. My movie career had a few highs — quite a few lows — all saved by a happy house, the children, dogs and travel to Bogie's locations. Noel Coward, an old friend of Bogie's, entered our lives when he came to California and cast me in *Blithe Spirit* for live TV. Of course, Noel had invited Hedda Hopper, Louella Parsons and every star in town to sit on the sound stage in full view of us, the nerve-racked actors. That experience was a great high for me and Noel continued to be a factor in my life until his death. A most extraordinary man of extraordinary talents — those of a Renaissance man. And there appeared, whenever we were in the same city or country, the likes of Robert Sherwood — a brilliant, funny, marvelous man and writer who had been major in Bogie's theatre days with *Petrified Forest* — a turning point for Bogie's career. And there was the arrival in Los Angeles of Laurence Olivier and Vivien Leigh, who immediately became our best friends while there and after. Because we spent time in London before and after *The African Queen* location, our British friends became very important to us — and to me later on when those in the theatre world of England made my life richer and might I say happier at a time that I needed it. Once those special people were friends, they were friends for life. So it was that David Niven, Larry and Vivien, Noel, John Gielgud, Richard and Sybil Burton, Jack and Doreen Hawkins remained a permanent part of our, and finally my, life.

The days and nights at Ira Gershwin's home — the music, the assortment of composers, actors, writers jump out at me often — our musical years. Frank Sinatra, Jimmy van Heusen, Roger Eden, Judy Garland were constants — often daily visitors in Mapleton Drive, the location of our final home together. Those memories, the figure of our fantastic cook, and even more a fantastic woman, May Smith, carrying breakfast trays upstairs with her special style — a red rose over her right ear and an open, loving smile on her lovely face — did I actually live that way — did I actually know and hug all of those people — did I become part of their lives and they part of mine? It is so hard to believe.

All this was interspersed with the highlights of our trips to New York where our theatre friends became our focus. The theatre itself became a nightly event and Moss and Kitty Hart, George Kaufman, Leland and Slim Hayward, George and Joan Axelrod, Comden and Green and Leonard and Felicia Bernstein filled each visit with laughter and song. I can never forget how I loved sitting next to Lenny as he played his early, middle and latest songs — always aware that I should have lived in the speakeasy days when I could have sat on the piano and sung show tunes. I knew every lyric of most of Gershwin, Harold Arlen, Rodgers and Hammerstein and Hart, Jule Styne, Van Heusen, Kern. Little did I ever even dream then that this was preparing me — paving my way — to star in a musical on Broadway.

This may all be nostalgia to you. I do not usually dwell on the past, but every now and then these moments — and more than moments — that have had an impact on me pop up. They resonate with me clearly and loudly. All of the events big and small — all of the people close or not so — have shaped me. Every time I attended a play in New York it had a lasting effect on me — *Streetcar Named Desire*, my first sight of Marlon Brando — *The Glass Menagerie* starring the great Laurette Taylor — *Long Day's Journey Into Night* where Jason Robards showed how great an actor he was — so great it gave you chills. Yet who, on our first meeting backstage — a handshake, a how-do-you-do — ever thought for a second that I might meet him again, much less marry him. Each of those performances became a permanent part of my being: Geraldine Page in *Sweet Bird of Youth*, Maureen Stapleton and Eli Wallach in *Rose Tattoo*, Margot Fonteyn in *Ondine*, *Sleeping Beauty*, *Giselle* — everything. I never missed a performance of hers, starting in London where we met often at Larry and Vivien's, John Gielgud's and others, before Nureyev. Every experience — Zero Mostel in *Fiddler on the Roof*, Ethel Merman in *Gypsy* and every other show she was in during my time in the Big Apple, *South Pacific* with Pinza, *My Fair Lady* — Rex Harrison's perfect performance — Richard Burton and Julie Andrews in *Camelot*. Every one thrilled me, taught me something, and confirmed again and again why I wanted to be an actress from childhood on. But would I ever be as good as any of them — could I be?

Then, too, there was my political awakening with the appearance of Adlai Stevenson and my devotion to him. Since Roosevelt I had not heard anyone in public life speak like that. Though I was a staunch admirer of Harry Truman and brought up in a Democratic family, I was never so active as I was with Adlai Stevenson, during which time my friendship with Arthur Schlesinger, Jr and Alistair Cooke began and flourished. Stevenson opened sections of my brain that I had been unaware I had, with his straightforward honesty, brilliance of mind and, my favorite trait, unending wit even in bad times. I think he made me more of an activist since then than I might have been.

Then there was Bogie's illness and prolonged fight against cancer. I remember every moment from the first diagnosis, through the surgery, to every up and down instance during that yearlong climb — one step forward, three steps back. I never really faced the fact of his illness being terminal. I just went day by day going along running the house, playing with my children, welcoming friends — as if that was the way it would continue forever. That's the way he wanted it. Those days, that year, will be with me for the rest of my life. Though I most definitely do not dwell on them, I lived them and they are very much a part of me.

I learned to deal with death (if that were ever possible) at the age of nineteen with the death of my grandmother — and the deaths that followed of my beloved Uncle Charlie, my Aunt Rosalie and Uncle Jack, all in the course of a ten- or twelve-year period, and all too young. The shrinking of my family. The shock of my friends dying came later. All of these pictures appear before me. The pain of the loss of my beloved mother is with me every single day. I will carry that with me until the end. When you're young you never think of death — I didn't. Then you get a little jab here, another one there. Suddenly a friend is in the hospital with a heart attack. That would be Mark Hellinger, an old and great friend to both Bogie and me. We went to see him, of course. Suddenly he was gone and we, together with John Huston, were in a car going to his funeral. He was forty-four.

Those losses insidiously work their way into your head — a way of preparing you for what's to come, I guess. Up to then I was not one to anticipate disaster. The losses did that for me. I was lucky to have my two small children when I was young. They had my focus, they held my interest. They were my raison d'être. They helped me to laugh. But they were in their beds by eight o'clock. It was the nights that were brutal. That's when you need your strength. Those quiet, dark, empty nights when you are stuck with yourself, when the nightmares become routine. I am not and was not morbid. It's just that my sinking time was always at night or in the early morning. Though that is the norm for anyone, I think, who goes through those distressing times. You do not travel this life scot-free.

I find that through the sad times, work is what made my continuing, not breaking down, possible. In work, I was always someone else and I subconsciously reveled in that. I literally could not be me — I was back reading those fairy tales with a blanket over my head. Holding a flashlight on the book so my mother would think I was asleep. The fairy tales were my reality, especially during Bogie's last few months — from rising at 6:00 a.m. to heading home after 6:00 p.m. I thought I was dealing intelligently with everything — conversations made sense, being with my children made sense — yet I was out of it. We were playing a game with the grim reaper ever present.

People always ask, 'Are you happy?' or, if I'm working, 'You must be happy.' I wish I knew what 'happy' means. I was happy when I was nineteen, and when my life began at twenty. I was happy then, though something always shook me up in the middle of my joyous time. So my life has been very much a seesaw.

It's funny how things go. Hal and Judy Prince — people I had known for years yet never spent a great deal of time with, for no reason except work taking us in different directions at different times — invited me on a cruise they were taking in the late summer of 1999. They had always over the years been there for me, from the gypsy run through of *Applause* in late 1969, but it is only now, after those seven or eight or ten days of constant togetherness, that I feel we are forever bound. Anyway, I love them and can never see enough of them. So there you have it. Proof positive joy can enter one's life at later stages.

Living on my own as I have for the last twenty-five years can be lonely at times, but I am a loner, generally speaking, though I can't explain why. I suppose it has something to do with being brought up by a divorced mother working to support me. I did not think in terms of sharing my life with a man. I felt I would rather travel alone to reach my goal and never plan on permanence. That's the way my life has turned out. The one relationship, that with Bogie, which I thought would last forever was cut short by disease and death. I was alone once more but with two small children to care for. My second relationship of major importance, with Jason, I hoped would last, but unfortunately was cut short by bad luck and alcohol. Some lives go that way and I must say that now I am not lonely. I have Sophie to look after — to come home to. You may laugh — but if you're in my position, just try it and see if I'm right. I'm sure you'll agree there is nothing like having a companion who never questions you, who gives you unconditional love and is always glad to see you. Of course, there are times she wants to play and I don't, but then nobody's perfect. Not even Sophie.

The fact that I can still, and do, continue to work keeps me in high spirits and keeps my motor running — though not quite as fast as it used to. I still want to go to India once more. I've never been to Greece or Turkey or Russia and want to go badly, and I've never been to South America, to Rio where they dance in the streets. Twenty-five years ago I would have joined them — even now, if I have the opportunity to go, I would still join them. That is not because I think I could move at full tilt but rather because as long as I can walk and talk I'll try almost anything. I say 'almost' because the high wire is definitely out. So my curiosity is still alive. So I'm lucky — the work is still on the horizon. My goal is to stay healthy. So far — I'm hanging in. As I wander through the last twenty-five years and more, I realize that I've lived a long time, but still not long enough to suit me. I've made many a mistake and though I've learned from them, it's still not enough for me to stop making them. Also, I see clearly how trusting I have been — believing that some of the movie agents I had years ago were really going to work hard for me, not challenging advice which was iffy at the time and plain bad on reflection. But listen, if you're the kind of person I was — I still am — what really matters is that I matter to myself. My self-confidence, though still a bit shaky, is a lot stronger than it was. Progress has been made on many fronts. I am finally facing my age — the fact of it — though I still find it hard to believe. How has it happened so quickly? How have my children reached the ages I once — I think — was?

I clearly will never be offered the kind of parts I wanted, yearned for when I was younger, nor from time to time a part I would have liked to have been offered lately. The climb has been tough but mostly upward, and I'm still climbing. The life has been lucky and unlucky — happy sometimes. We all, if we're worth our salt, have monkeys on our backs.

But my life has had meaning, with the friendships full and valuable and essential to me. My children, Steve, Leslie and Sam, are all different — all first rate human beings with high standards — whom I completely and unequivocally adore — don't always agree with — but always admire and respect. They all have wit and a sense of humor and, thank God, I have hung on to mine.

The employees of Thorndike Press hope you have enjoyed this Large Print book. All our Thorndike and Wheeler Large Print titles are designed for easy reading, and all our books are made to last. Other Thorndike Press Large Print books are available at your library, through selected bookstores, or directly from us.

For information about titles, please call:

(800) 223-1244

or visit our Web site at:

www.gale.com/thorndike
www.gale.com/wheeler

To share your comments, please write:

Publisher
Thorndike Press
295 Kennedy Memorial Drive
Waterville, ME   04901

2005

DATE DUE

7-11			
8-03-05			
8-12.05			

By Myself and then Some
    Bacall, Lauren   L.P.
                      '05

DEMCO